Dictionary of Literary Biography

Dictionary of Literary Biography Documentary Series

Dictionary of Literary Biography Yearbooks

1980 edited by Karen L. Rood, Jean W. Ross, and Richard Ziegfeld (1981)

1981 edited by Karen L. Rood, Jean W. Ross, and Richard Ziegfeld (1982)

1982 edited by Richard Ziegfeld; associate editors: Jean W. Ross and Lynne C. Zeigler (1983)

1983 edited by Mary Bruccoli and Jean W. Ross; associate editor Richard Ziegfeld (1984)

1984 edited by Jean W. Ross (1985)

1985 edited by Jean W. Ross (1986)

1986 edited by J. M. Brook (1987)

1987 edited by J. M. Brook (1988)

1988 edited by J. M. Brook (1989)

1989 edited by J. M. Brook (1990)

1990 edited by James W. Hipp (1991)

1991 edited by James W. Hipp (1992)

1992 edited by James W. Hipp (1993)

1993 edited by James W. Hipp, contributing editor George Garrett (1994)

1994 edited by James W. Hipp, contributing editor George Garrett (1995)

1995 edited by James W. Hipp, contributing editor George Garrett (1996)

1996 edited by Samuel W. Bruce and L. Kay Webster, contributing editor George Garrett (1997)

1997 edited by Matthew J. Bruccoli and George Garrett, with the assistance of L. Kay Webster (1998)

1998 edited by Matthew J. Bruccoli, contributing editor George Garrett, with the assistance of D. W. Thomas (1999)

1999 edited by Matthew J. Bruccoli, contributing editor George Garrett, with the assistance of D. W. Thomas (2000)

2000 edited by Matthew J. Bruccoli, contributing editor George Garrett, with the assistance of George Parker Anderson (2001)

2001 edited by Matthew J. Bruccoli, contributing editor George Garrett, with the assistance of George Parker Anderson (2002)

2002 edited by Matthew J. Bruccoli and George Garrett; George Parker Anderson, Assistant Editor (2003)

Concise Series

Concise Dictionary of American Literary Biography, 7 volumes (1988–1999): *The New Consciousness, 1941–1968; Colonization to the American Renaissance, 1640–1865; Realism, Naturalism, and Local Color, 1865–1917; The Twenties, 1917–1929; The Age of Maturity, 1929–1941; Broadening Views, 1968–1988; Supplement: Modern Writers, 1900–1998.*

Concise Dictionary of British Literary Biography, 8 volumes (1991–1992): *Writers of the Middle Ages and Renaissance Before 1660; Writers of the Restoration and Eighteenth Century, 1660–1789; Writers of the Romantic Period, 1789–1832; Victorian Writers, 1832–1890; Late-Victorian and Edwardian Writers, 1890–1914; Modern Writers, 1914–1945; Writers After World War II, 1945–1960; Contemporary Writers, 1960 to Present.*

Concise Dictionary of World Literary Biography, 4 volumes (1999–2000): *Ancient Greek and Roman Writers; German Writers; African, Caribbean, and Latin American Writers; South Slavic and Eastern European Writers.*

Robert Penn Warren:
A Documentary Volume

Dictionary of Literary Biography® • Volume Three Hundred Twenty

Robert Penn Warren:
A Documentary Volume

James A. Grimshaw Jr.
Texas A&M University–Commerce

A Bruccoli Clark Layman Book

THOMSON

GALE

Detroit • New York • San Francisco • San Diego • New Haven, Conn. • Waterville, Maine • London • Munich

THOMSON

GALE

Dictionary of Literary Biography
Volume 320: Robert Penn Warren:
A Documentary Volume
James A. Grimshaw Jr.

Editorial Directors
Matthew J. Bruccoli and Richard Layman

LIBRARY OF CONGRESS CATALOGING-IN-PUBLICATION DATA

Robert Penn Warren : a documentary volume / edited by James A. Grimshaw, Jr.
    p. cm. — (Dictionary of literary biography ; v. 320)
    "A Bruccoli Clark Layman book."
    Includes bibliographical references and index.
    ISBN 0–7876–8138–5 (alk. paper)
    1. Warren, Robert Penn, 1905– 2. Authors, American—20th century—Biography. 3.
English teachers—United States—Biography. 4. Critics—United States—Biography.   I.
Grimshaw, James A. II. Series.
    PS3545.A748Z8624 2005
    813'.52—dc22

                                       2005020361

To Darlene

Contents

Facsimile: Pages from the Warren family Bible

An Old-Time Childhood–from Warren's poem "Old-Time Childhood in Kentucky"

The Author and the Ballplayer–from Will Fridy, "The Author and the Ballplayer:
    An Imprint of Memory in the Writings of Robert Penn Warren"

Early Reading–from Ralph Ellison and Eugene Walter, "The Art of Fiction XVIII:
    Robert Penn Warren"

Facsimile: Warren's essay on his first day at Clarksville High School

Facsimile: First page of "Munk" in *The Purple and Gold,* February 1921

Facsimile: "Senior Creed" in *The Purple and Gold,* April 1921

Writing for *The Purple and Gold*–from Tom Wibking, "Star's Work Seasoned by Country Living"

"Incidental and Essential": Warren's Vanderbilt Experience–from "Robert Penn Warren:
    A Reminiscence"

A First Published Poem–"Prophecy," *The Mess Kit (Food for Thought)* and Warren letter
    to Donald M. Kington, 6 March 1975

The Importance of *The Fugitive*–from Louise Cowan, *The Fugitive Group: A Literary History*

Brooks and Warren at Vanderbilt–from Cleanth Brooks, "Brooks on Warren"

A Fugitive Anthology–Warren letter to Donald Davidson, 19 September 1926

Katherine Anne Porter Remembers Warren–from Joan Givner, *Katherine Ann Porter: A Life*

A Literary Bird Nest–from Brooks, "A Summing Up"

The Fugitives as a Group–from Ellison and Walter, "The Art of Fiction XVIII:
    Robert Penn Warren"

Facsimile: Page from a draft of *John Brown*

Letters from Home: Filial Guilt in Robert Penn Warren–from an essay
    by William Bedford Clark

Plan of the Series

The advisory board, the editors, and the publisher of the *Dictionary of Literary Biography* are joined in endorsing Mark Twain's declaration. The literature of a nation provides an inexhaustible resource of permanent worth. Our purpose is to make literature and its creators better understood and more accessible to students and the reading public, while satisfying the needs of teachers and researchers.

To meet these requirements, *literary biography* has been construed in terms of the author's achievement. The most important thing about a writer is his writing. Accordingly, the entries in *DLB* are career biographies, tracing the development of the author's canon and the evolution of his reputation.

The purpose of *DLB* is not only to provide reliable information in a usable format but also to place the figures in the larger perspective of literary history and to offer appraisals of their accomplishments by qualified scholars.

The publication plan for *DLB* resulted from two years of preparation. The project was proposed to Bruccoli Clark by Frederick G. Ruffner, president of the Gale Research Company, in November 1975. After specimen entries were prepared and typeset, an advisory board was formed to refine the entry format and develop the series rationale. In meetings held during 1976, the publisher, series editors, and advisory board approved the scheme for a comprehensive biographical dictionary of persons who contributed to literature. Editorial work on the first volume began in January 1977, and it was published in 1978. In order to make *DLB* more than a dictionary and to compile volumes that individually have claim to status as literary history, it was decided to organize volumes by topic, period, or

genre. Each of these freestanding volumes provides a biographical-bibliographical guide and overview for a particular area of literature. We are convinced that this organization—as opposed to a single alphabet method—constitutes a valuable innovation in the presentation of reference material. The volume plan necessarily requires many decisions for the placement and treatment of authors. Certain figures will be included in separate volumes, but with different entries emphasizing the aspect of his career appropriate to each volume. Ernest Hemingway, for example, is represented in *American Writers in Paris, 1920–1939* by an entry focusing on his expatriate apprenticeship; he is also in *American Novelists, 1910–1945* with an entry surveying his entire career, as well as in *American Short-Story Writers, 1910–1945, Second Series* with an entry concentrating on his short fiction. Each volume includes a cumulative index of the subject authors and articles.

Between 1981 and 2002 the series was augmented and updated by the *DLB Yearbooks*. There have also been nineteen *DLB Documentary Series* volumes, which provide illustrations, facsimiles, and biographical and critical source materials for figures, works, or groups judged to have particular interest for students. In 1999 the *Documentary Series* was incorporated into the *DLB* volume numbering system beginning with *DLB 210: Ernest Hemingway.*

We define literature as the *intellectual commerce of a nation:* not merely as belles lettres but as that ample and complex process by which ideas are generated, shaped, and transmitted. *DLB* entries are not limited to "creative writers" but extend to other figures who in their time and in their way influenced the mind of a people. Thus the series encompasses historians, journalists, publishers, book collectors, and screenwriters. By this means readers of *DLB* may be aided to perceive literature not as cult scripture in the keeping of intellectual high priests but firmly positioned at the center of a nation's life.

DLB includes the major writers appropriate to each volume and those standing in the ranks behind them. Scholarly and critical counsel has been sought in deciding which minor figures to include and how full their entries should be. Wherever possible, useful references are made to figures who do not warrant separate entries.

Each *DLB* volume has an expert volume editor responsible for planning the volume, selecting the figures for inclusion, and assigning the entries. Volume editors are also responsible for preparing, where appropriate, appendices surveying the major periodicals and literary and intellectual movements for their volumes, as well as lists of further readings. Work on the series as a whole is coordinated at the Bruccoli Clark Layman editorial center in Columbia, South Carolina, where the editorial staff is responsible for accuracy and utility of the published volumes.

One feature that distinguishes *DLB* is the illustration policy—its concern with the iconography of literature. Just as an author is influenced by his surroundings, so is the reader's understanding of the author enhanced by a knowledge of his environment. Therefore *DLB*

volumes include not only drawings, paintings, and photographs of authors, often depicting them at various stages in their careers, but also illustrations of their families and places where they lived. Title pages are regularly reproduced in facsimile along with dust jackets for modern authors. The dust jackets are a special feature of *DLB* because they often document better than anything else the way in which an author's work was perceived in its own time. Specimens of the writers' manuscripts and letters are included when feasible.

Samuel Johnson rightly decreed that "The chief glory of every people arises from its authors." The purpose of the *Dictionary of Literary Biography* is to compile literary history in the surest way available to us—by accurate and comprehensive treatment of the lives and work of those who contributed to it.

The *DLB* Advisory Board

Introduction

Robert Penn Warren, identified as "the most complete man of letters in our time" by his colleague R. W. B. Lewis, published in every major literary genre, was awarded the Pulitzer Prize twice in poetry and once in fiction, and was a distinguished teacher, both in and out of the classroom. His contributions to American letters include ten novels, sixteen short stories, fifteen volumes of poetry, seven dramas, five textbooks, eight books of nonfiction, two children's books, and more than one hundred essays. His writings document his immense energy, intellectual stature, and artistic integrity.

Warren's active participation in a literary life began in high school in Clarksville, Tennessee, in 1921 with a story, a play, and a short vignette in *The Purple and Gold,* a monthly publication of student writing. His interest in storytelling, however, was whetted years earlier by his grandfather Gabriel Thomas Penn, who sat under a cedar tree on his farm in Cerulean Springs, Kentucky, and told his grandson stories about the Civil War. A turning point in Warren's life occurred in early summer 1921, when he was on his back in his family's yard in Guthrie, Kentucky, surveying the sky and contemplating his future education at the United States Naval Academy. On the other side of a hedge in the yard, his younger brother, William Thomas Warren, was hurling chunks of coal into the air—one of which landed in Warren's left eye. Permanently blinded in that eye, he was no longer physically qualified for an appointment to the Naval Academy. Consequently, he matriculated at Vanderbilt University and found unexpectedly a new life's calling in John Crowe Ransom's freshman English class.

The following year, 1923, Warren became an elected member of the Fugitives, a literary group composed of Nashville residents who shared an interest in poetry. The original Fugitive group members included Ransom, Donald Davidson, Allen Tate, Alec Stevenson, Stanley Johnson, Walter Clyde Curry, and Sidney Hirsch. Later others joined, expanding the group to include Merrill Moore, James M. Frank, William Yandell Elliott, Jesse and Ridley Wills, William Frierson, Robert Penn Warren, Andrew Lytle, Alfred Starr, and Laura Riding. Among the original members, Warren was closest to Ransom and Tate. Their meetings were often held in the home of James Frank, but in-between meetings in Ransom's or Curry's office or elsewhere were not uncommon. Not sponsored by Vanderbilt University and thus unfettered by institutional restrictions, the group provided for the undergraduate Warren a safe haven for independent thought and unencumbered creativity. The little magazine *The Fugitive* published twenty-three of Warren's poems in its three and one-half years of existence.

During his formal education, which included a master's degree from the University of California at Berkeley, doctoral study at Yale University, and a Rhodes Scholarship at Oxford University, Warren's literary productivity increased. His poetry appeared in *Poetry, New Republic,* and *Saturday Review of Literature;* he published a biography, *John Brown: The Making of a Martyr* (1929); he wrote an essay, "The Briar Patch," in which he endorsed the separate-but-equal status of the South for a collection of essays by Twelve Southerners, *I'll Take My Stand: The South and the Agrarian Tradition* (1930); and his novella, "Prime Leaf," was included in the anthology *American Caravan IV.* By age twenty-five Robert Penn Warren was a published author in poetry, fiction, biography, and sociology.

After returning from England, Warren taught one year at Southwestern College (now Rhodes College) in Memphis. In 1931 he returned to Nashville as an assistant professor of English, a position he retained for three years. Then in 1934 Warren joined the Louisiana State University faculty and began an important association with his friend Cleanth Brooks, whom he first met at Vanderbilt a decade earlier. Their work as editors of the *Southern Review* (1935–1942) and as authors of *An Approach to Literature* (1936), *Understanding Poetry* (1938), *Understanding Fiction* (1943), and *Modern Rhetoric* (1949) identified new writers and contributed to a redefinition of the way literature was taught in classrooms. They were branded "New Critics," a label Warren always resisted because he believed it was used too broadly and indiscriminately. The New Criticism, nevertheless, was understood as literary analysis that concentrated on elements of the isolated literary work, usually a poem, and how they combine—or fail to work together—to form a whole. The focus on the close reading of an individual work—as opposed to relating the work to its time and culture, or a tradition, or the author's body of writings—became the dominant teaching methodology in literature courses. By the late 1970s, New Criticism was challenged when deconstructionism and the other "isms" took hold in literary theory, but for three decades, the names Brooks and Warren remained ensconced in academic classrooms.

For their last textbook, *American Literature: The Makers and the Making* (1973), Brooks and Warren collaborated with R. W. B. Lewis as a third editor. The product of a decade of work, the volume was highly praised for its summaries of each literary period and its introductions to the authors whose works were included. Warren's part in the project led him to write acclaimed critical essays on Nathaniel Hawthorne, Herman Melville, John Greenleaf Whittier, and Theodore Dreiser. He also extended his critical writing to other fields. His 1956 book *Segregation: The Inner Conflict in the South,* a report of his conversations with people in Kentucky, Tennessee, Arkansas, Mississippi, and Louisiana, was the first of two books to address and alter the racial views he had expressed in "The Briar Patch." Warren wrote the last section in a question-and-answer format that he states was "an interview with myself." The second book, *Who Speaks for the Negro?* (1965), was based on interviews that Warren conducted with Civil Rights leaders, writers, and educators. Among his later works of nonfiction, three stand out. In *The Legacy of the Civil War: Meditations on the Centennial* (1961), Warren addresses the consequences of the struggle, asserting that "the War gave the South the Great Alibi and gave the North the Treasury of Virtue." *Democracy and Poetry* (1975) is the published version of his 1974 Thomas Jefferson Lecture in the Humanities, in which he discusses democracy, poetry, and selfhood, arguing that "a society with no sense of the past, with no sense of the human role as significant not merely in experiencing history but in creating it can have no sense of destiny." A third nonfiction book, *Portrait of a Father* (1988), is Warren's most directly autobiographical work.

Warren's talent as a poet was evident from the beginning of his literary career. In 1923 five of his poems were included in the Nashville Poetry Guild anthology *Driftwood Flames;* and the poem "Evening: The Motors" was included in *Best Poems of 1926.* His first three volumes of poetry—*Thirty-Six Poems* (1935), *Eleven Poems on the Same Theme* (1942), and *Selected Poems: 1923–1943* (1944)—show the influence of the seventeenth-century Metaphysical poets. His poems deal with the emotions of love and, to a lesser extent, with religion, with life's complexities, and with death. Warren's early poetry was intellectual and analytical; sometimes deliberately rough; written in conventional poetic forms, such as the sonnet, with measured meter and rhyme; and drawn from common experiences. In "The Ballad of Billie Potts," a poem included in *Selected Poems* that indicated a new direction in his poetry, Warren drew on Kentucky folklore and combined his abilities as a storyteller and a poet.

In 1944 Warren was named the Consultant in Poetry at the Library of Congress. More than forty years later, Warren was named as the first Poet Laureate Consultant in Poetry to the Library of Congress, when that position was established in 1986. Between 1944 and 1953, Warren remained busy with critical work and fiction. In 1945 he gave one of the Bergen Foundation Lectures at Yale University. It was a trial run for his essay "A Poem of Pure Imagination," which appeared in the 1946 edition of Samuel Taylor Coleridge's *The Rime of the Ancient Mariner.*

Warren began what may be considered his middle period in poetry, 1953–1966, with the book-length verse drama *Brother to Dragons: A Tale in Verse and Voices* (1953). During this period he made greater use of poetic sequences and freer verse forms; his individual poems became parts of larger wholes. Warren, who has admitted the autobiographical essence of much of his writing and in particular his poetry, returned to many of the themes he had explored in his early period, examining them more deeply and more personally. His next volume of poetry, *Promises: Poems, 1954–1956* (1957), earned Warren his first Pulitzer Prize in poetry; it was followed by *You, Emperor, and Others, 1957–1960* (1960) and *Selected Poems: New and Old, 1923–1966* (1966).

Readers of Warren's poems in his late period, 1966–1985, recognize his willingness to experiment and his continued development. The nine volumes published in these years include *Now and Then: Poems, 1976–1978* (1978), for which Warren won his second Pulitzer Prize in poetry, and two book-length poems: *Audubon: A Vision* (1969), based on the life of the ornithologist Jean Jacques Audubon, and *Chief Joseph of the Nez Perce* (1982), a rendering of the events surrounding the forced move of the Nez Perce to a reservation. In his last phase, Warren's verse is more loosely structured than in his earlier work; his imagery is graphic; and his diction is sometimes notably erudite. A dedicated artist, Warren pursued his own way, continuing his intense investigation of the human condition to his last poem.

In his first published novel, *Night Rider* (1939), Warren drew his inspiration from history—as he did for much of his fiction—and set his story during the tobacco wars in western Kentucky and Tennessee at the beginning of the twentieth century. Like *Night Rider,* Warren's second novel, *At Heaven's Gate* (1943)—in which the schemes of the unethical banker-businessman Bogan Murdock despoil the land and corrupt society in the 1920s—earned high praise from many reviewers, but the attention these novels received, either from contemporary reviewers or subsequent critics, pales in comparison to that afforded Warren's third novel, *All the King's Men* (1946), for which he received a Pulitzer Prize in fiction.

Warren began working with the material that became his most famous novel nearly a decade before it was published. In summer 1937, Warren began working on a play about a corrupt Southern politician—an idea suggested in part by the career of Louisiana governor and senator Huey P. Long. Warren completed the play, *Proud Flesh,* in 1939; three years later he decided to rework his material as a novel, adding a new dimension—the story of Jack Burden—and brought *All the King's Men* to publication. After his novel was made into an Oscar-winning movie in 1949, Warren continued to work on dramatic treatments of his story: a revised stage version, *Willie Stark: His Rise and Fall,* was produced in 1955; *Listen to the Mockingbird,* based on chapter 4 of the novel, was written in 1959; and an Off-Broadway production titled *All the King's Men* was produced in 1959.

Warren's only collection of short stories, *The Circus in the Attic and Other Stories* (1947), was followed by his fourth novel, *World Enough and Time* (1950), based on the 1825 murder of Colonel Solomon Sharp by Jereboam O. Beauchamp in Frankfort, Kentucky. It was Warren's first book published by Random House and was edited by one of their new editors, Albert Russell Erskine Jr., his longtime friend. Erskine and Warren had met in 1930 at Southwestern College in Memphis, Tennessee, where Warren taught for a year and Erskine was an undergraduate (but not one of Warren's students). At L.S.U. Erskine was a graduate student and was appointed managing editor of the *Southern Review*

under the supervision of Brooks, Warren, and Charles W. Pipkin, the editors of the new magazine. Erskine was Warren's editor for his subsequent six novels, all published by Random House. Warren and Erskine also edited two anthologies, *Short Story Masterpieces* (1954) and *Six Centuries of Great Poetry* (1955).

Historical events serve as starting points for Warren's next four novels: the Civil War and the issue of slavery in *Band of Angels* (1955); the exploitation of Floyd Collins, who made headline news when he was trapped in a Kentucky cave in 1925, in *The Cave* (1959); the Civil War again in *Wilderness* (1961); and the Tennessee Valley Authority project that flooded Johnstown, Tennessee, in *Flood* (1964). In his last two novels, Warren is more interested in psychology. *Meet Me in the Green Glen* (1971), which includes an element of mystery about the death of Sunderland Spottwood, explores the concept of justice in a small Southern community. In his last novel, *A Place to Come To* (1977), Warren focuses on the life and academic career of the protagonist, Jed Tewksbury, and offers a skeptical view of human ability to perceive and understand reality.

DLB 320: Robert Penn Warren: A Documentary Volume covers Warren's literary life in chronological order, thereby allowing readers to appreciate Warren's varied creative career as he moved from poetry to criticism to fiction and back. Each chapter includes representative insights by reviewers and critics, photographs, facsimile pages of manuscripts, and other documents that complement the text. Warren's own words about his works, his theories, and his critical perception of the realm of letters contribute to the understanding of what Cleanth Brooks wrote in *The Hidden God* in 1963: "The poetry, the fiction, and even the critical essays of Robert Penn Warren form a highly unified and consistent body of work."

James A. Grimshaw Jr.

Acknowledgments

This book was produced by Bruccoli Clark Layman, Inc. George Parker Anderson was the in-house editor.

Production manager is Philip B. Dematteis.

Administrative support was provided by Carol A. Cheschi.

Accountant is Ann-Marie Holland.

Copyediting supervisor is Sally R. Evans. The copyediting staff includes Phyllis A. Avant, Caryl Brown, Melissa D. Hinton, Philip I. Jones, Rebecca Mayo, and Nancy E. Smith.

Pipeline manager is James F. Tidd Jr.

Editorial associates are Elizabeth Leverton, Dickson Monk, and Timothy C. Simmons.

In-house vetter is Catherine M. Polit.

Permissions editor is Amber L. Coker. Permissions assistant is Crystal A. Gleim.

Layout and graphics supervisor is Janet E. Hill. The graphics staff includes Zoe R. Cook and Sydney E. Hammock.

Office manager is Kathy Lawler Merlette.

Photography editor is Mark J. McEwan.

Digital photographic copy work was performed by Joseph M. Bruccoli.

Systems manager is Donald Kevin Starling.

Typesetting supervisor is Kathleen M. Flanagan. The typesetting staff includes Patricia Marie Flanagan and Pamela D. Norton.

Library research was facilitated by the following librarians at the Thomas Cooper Library of the University of South Carolina: Elizabeth Suddeth and the rare-book department; Jo Cottingham, interlibrary loan department; circulation department head Tucker Taylor; reference department head Virginia W. Weathers; reference department staff Laurel Baker, Marilee Birchfield, Kate Boyd, Paul Cammarata, Joshua Garris, Gary Geer, Tom Marcil, Rose Marshall, and Sharon Verba; interlibrary loan department head Marna Hostetler; and interlibrary loan staff Bill Fetty and Nelson Rivera.

Clearly, without the support of the Estates of Robert Penn Warren and Eleanor Clark, this project could not have been produced. The editor's gratitude goes to Rosanna Warren Scully and Gabriel Penn Warren and to John Burt, Warren's literary executor, for their continued encouragement over the years.

Many individuals associated with a variety of organizations and institutions have helped along the way and deserve recognition for their professional service: Amon Carter Museum (Jane J. Posey), Beinecke Rare Book and Manuscript Library (Patricia Willis, Stephen C. Jones, and Laurie Klein), Columbia Pictures (Margaret Harder), Connecticut College Library (Lori Derideta), Harry Ransom Humanities Research Center (Tara Wenger), Louisiana State University Hill Memorial Library (Faye Phillips, Judy Bolton, Mary Hebert, and Emily B. Robison), Peabody Essex Museum (Christine Michelini), Robert Penn Warren Birthplace Museum (Jeane Moore, Dean Moore, Mark Moore, and Ann Alexander), Texas A&M University–Commerce Library (James Conrad, Latresa Wynn, Kelly Hughes, and Andrew Judd), University of Delaware Library (L. Rebecca Johnson Melvin), University of Maryland Libraries (Ruth M. Alvarez), University of North Carolina at Chapel Hill Southern Folklife Collection (Laura Clark Brown, Kelly Kress, and Jane Daley Witten), Vanderbilt University (Juanita G. Murray and Barbara S. Luck), Warner Brothers Studio (Judy Nowak), Western Kentucky University Museum Special Collections (Connie Mills, Jonathan Jeffrey, Nancy Baird, and Sandy Staebell), and William Morris Agency (Owen Laster and Kenyon Harbison).

So many other people have offered assistance or have in other ways enabled me to complete this work. I thank them all and apologize if I have inadvertently omitted the name of someone who should have been included here: Donna Anstey, Joseph Blotner, Stacey Bone, Carroll Brentano, Robert Buckman, Hugh and Mary Burns, John Callahan, George Carey, Deborah Carter, Leonard Casper, Kenneth Cherry, Carol Christiansen, D. Clark, William Bedford Clark, George Core, Amy Coughenour, Jo and Kay Coughenour, Robert W. Cowley, Nancy Crampton, John K. Crane, Jonathan S. Cullick, Dr. Eugene W. Dahl, Lloyd Davies, Barbara Thompson Davis, Carolyn Davis, David A. Davis, Joy and Howard Davis, Peter Davison, Gerald Duchovnay, Taji Duncombe, John Duvall, Steven Ealy, Charles East, Florence B. Eichin, Jon and Debi Eller, Charles Embry,

Joseph Epstein, Marisa Erskine, Chatham Ewing, Harvey Fergusson II, William Ferris, Agnes Fisher, Dr. and Mrs. John Fitts, Deborah Foley, Courtney and Cody Fowler, Aaron Frankel, Bob and Tommie Lou Frye, Thomas Frye, Tim Gabor, Laura E. Gentile, Janna Olson Gies, Norton Girault, Jim and Heather Grimshaw, Adrian Hall, John D. Hall, Bill Hammons, Margarita Harder, Richard Harteis, Scott Harvey, Chuck and Louise Hebert, Jennifer Hedden, Champlin B. Heilman, Ted Hovet, Lori Howard, Scarlett R. Huffman, Sidney F. Huttner, Russell James, Robert E. Jones, Marilyn Josephson, James H. Justus, David Kaufer, Brenda Keen, Sandra and Frank Kilpatrick, Judi Kincaid, Donald M. Kington, Helen Lothrop Klaviter, Paul Knoke, Irina Korotkova, Jill Krementz, Iris Lancaster, John Lane, David Lee, Nancy L. Lewis, Toby Lichtig, Sheryl Mackey, Brenda Macon, David Madden, Bill and Adele McCarron, J. D. McClatchy, Mack McCormick, Keith McFarland, Boynton Merrill Jr., Ferris Van Meter, Bud and Linda Kay Miller, Mary Ellen Miller, Victoria Thorpe Miller, Bill Moyers, Mrs. Honora F. Neuman, Helena Niedenthal, Judy Nowak, Sarkis V. Oganian, James Olney, John Ellis Palmer, Cathy Paré, William Parrill, Justin Pelegano, James A. Perkins, Paul Piazza, Stanley Plumly, Noel Polk, Christopher Pottle, Lucie Prinz, Jerome Rankine, Bess Reed, Cindy Reeves, Mrs. Henry Ring, Thomas A. Robinson, Randolph Paul Runyon, Hugh Ruppersburg, Judy Sall, Marcy A. Sanders, James B. M. Schick, Dr. Ben Schnitzer, Sister Monique Schwirtz, Barbara Shapiro, Allen Shepherd, Wilma Shires, Lewis P. Simpson, Dr. Norman Slusher, Charlotte Ann Smith, Dr. Perry Smith, Don D. Stanford, Peter Stitt, Bill and Jan Stone, Victor Strandberg, Anthony Szczesiul, Helen H. Tate, John J. Virtes, Marshall Walker, John M. Walsh, Norman Wells, Vicky Wells, Dr. Lawrence S. Weprin, Robert West, Earl Wilcox, Mary Frances Willock, Patricia Winn, Amy Woods, and Amy Zeisz.

To my wife, who has been of inestimable help for more than forty years, I say once again, thank you.

Permissions

University of Alabama Press. Warren, "The Uses of the Past" from *A Time to Hear and Answer,* © 1977. Permission granted by the University of Alabama Press.

John Aldridge. Aldridge, "The Enormous Spider Web of Warren's World," *Saturday Review,* 9 October 1971. Reprinted by permission of the author.

America Labor Conference on International Affairs. Phoebe Pettingell, review of *Rumor Verified, The New Leader,* 14 December 1981. Reprinted with permission of *The New Leader,* Copyright © the American Labor Conference on International Affairs, Inc.

AP / Wide World Photo. Illustration on page 75, © AP Photo (APA4664600).

Atlantic Monthly. Irvin Ehrenpreis, "Continuity and Change," *Atlantic Monthly,* December 1981. Reprinted with permission of *The Atlantic Monthly.*

Carlos Baker. Baker, "Souls Lost in a Blind Lobby," *Saturday Review,* 20 August 1955. Reprinted by permission of the author.

Joseph Warren Beach Estate. Illustration on page 111. Used by permission of The Joseph Warren Beach Estate, c/o Dr. Michael Hancher, Chairman, Department of English, University of Minnesota.

Joseph Blotner. Confirmation of dates and an excerpt from *Robert Penn Warren: A Biography,* © 1997. Used with the kind permission of Joseph Blotner.

Estate of Cleanth Brooks. Letters from Brooks to Robert Penn Warren; "Brooks on Warren," *Four Quarters,* May 1972; excerpt from "Forty Years of *Understanding Poetry,*" in *Confronting Crisis: Teachers in America* (Arlington: University of Texas at Arlington Press, 1979); and "The Origin of the *Southern Review,*" *Southern Review,* Winter 1986. Used by permission of the Estate of Cleanth Brooks.

Matthew J. Bruccoli Collection. Illustrations on pages 170, 171, 172, and 305. Used by permission of Matthew J. Bruccoli.

John Burt. Burt, "Idealism and Rage in *Proud Flesh,*" *RWP: An Annual of Robert Penn Warren Studies,* 2001, is used by permission of John Burt, the Center for Robert Penn Warren Studies, and Western Kentucky University.

University of California, Berkeley. L. A. Harper, "A Vivid Story," *University of California Chronicle,* July 1930. Used by permission of the University of California, Berkeley.

Chicago Tribune. Seymour Epstein, "Robert Penn Warren's Latest Celebration of the Years," *Chicago Tribune,* 6 March 1977. Copyright © *Chicago Tribune.* Reprinted with permission.

William Bedford Clark. Excerpts from *Selected Letters of Robert Penn Warren, Volume 1* (Baton Rouge: Louisiana State University Press, 2000) and *Selected Letters of Robert Penn Warren, Volume 2* (Baton Rouge: Louisiana State University Press, 2001). Copyright © 2000 & 2001 by William Bedford Clark. Reprinted by permission of the copyright holder. See also Duke University Press and *Sewanee Review* for additional permissions granted by William Bedford Clark.

Clarksville High School. Illustrations on pages 36 and 37, provided by Robert Penn Warren Center. Permission granted by Clarksville High School, Tennessee.

Columbia Pictures. Illustrations on pages 158 and 353. Copyright © Columbia Pictures Industries, Inc.

Peter Davison. Davison, "Questions of Swimming," *The Poems of Peter Davison 1957–1995* (New York: Knopf, 1995). "Deep in the Blackness of Woods: A Farewell to Robert Penn Warren," *New England Monthly,* March 1990. Reprinted by permission of the author.

Babette Deutsch. Deutsch, "Robert Penn Warren's Savage Poem: Old Murder, Modern Overtones," *New York Herald Tribune Book Review,* 23 August 1953. Reprinted by permission of the author.

Estate of James Dickey. Dickey, "Robert Penn Warren's Courage," *Saturday Review,* August 1980. Reprinted by permission of the Estate of James Dickey.

Duke University Press. William Bedford Clark, "A Meditation on Folk-History: The Dramatic Structure of Robert Penn Warren's 'The Ballad of Billie Potts,'" *American Literature,* 1978. Copyright, 1978, Duke University Press. All rights reserved. Used by permission of the publisher and of the author.

Charles East. Illustration on page 81 and "Memories of Baton Rouge." Used by kind permission of Charles East.

Educational Broadcasting Corporation. "A Conversation with Robert Penn Warren," *Bill Moyers' Journal,* transcript of the 4 April 1976 program. Copyright 1976, by Educational Broadcasting Corporation. Permission granted by Bill Moyers, Editor-in-Chief.

Estate of Albert R. Erskine, Jr. Illustrations on pages 83 and 273. Used by permission of the Albert R. Erskine, Jr., Estate. Permission to reproduce part of a letter from Albert Erskine to Robert Penn Warren is courtesy of the Albert R. Erskine, Jr., Estate.

Mark Ethridge, Jr. Ethridge, "Turmoil in the South," *Saturday Review,* 1 September 1956. Reprinted by permission of the author.

Estate of William Faulkner. Illustration on page 137. Reprinted with permission of The Estate of William Faulkner.

Francis Fergusson. Illustration on page 102, provided by Yale Collection of American Literature, Beinecke Rare Book Library. Permission to reproduce granted by The Estate of Francis Fergusson.

William Ferris. Illustrations on pages 324 and 325 are from the William Ferris Collection, Southern Folklife Collection, Wilson Library, University of North Carolina at Chapel Hill. Permission is granted by William Ferris.

Aaron Frankel. Frankel, "Working in the Theater with Robert Penn Warren," *RWP: An Annual of Robert Penn Warren Studies,* 2002; illustrations on pages 204 and 212.

Used by permission of Aaron Frankel, the Center for Robert Penn Warren Studies, and Western Kentucky University.

Mrs. Robert D. Frey. Illustrations on pages 21, 22, 23, 27, 29, 57, 90, 154, 176, 207, 335, 338, 339, and 340. Permission for reproduction is granted courtesy of Mrs. Robert D. Frey.

Genre. Neil Nakadate, "Robert Penn Warren and the Confessional Novel," *Genre,* 1969. Reprinted with permission.

University of Georgia Press. Excerpt from Hugh Ruppersburgh, *Robert Penn Warren and the American Imagination.* Copyright 1990 by the University of Georgia Press. Excerpt from Randy Hendricks, *Lonelier than God: Robert Penn Warren and the Southern Exile.* Copyright 2000 by the University of Georgia Press. Reprinted by permission of the University of Georgia Press.

Georgia Review. Malcolm Cowley, "Robert Penn Warren, *aet.* 75," *Georgia Review,* 1981. Copyright © 1981 by the Literary Estate of Malcolm Cowley. Permission to reprint is granted by the Estate of Malcolm Cowley and *Georgia Review.* Peter Stitt, "The Grandeur of Certain Utterances," *Georgia Review,* 1979. Reprinted by permission of *Georgia Review.*

Norton Girault. Girault, "Recollections of Robert Penn Warren as Teacher in the 1930s," *Texas Writers Newsletter* (1982) is reprinted by kind permission of the author.

Greenwood Press. John Lewis Longley, Jr. "When All Is Said and Done: Warren's Flood" in *Robert Penn Warren: A Collection of Critical Essays* (New York: New York University Press, 1965). Reprinted by permission of Greenwood Press.

James A. Grimshaw, Jr. Illustration on page 329. Used by permission of James A. Grimshaw, Jr.

Harcourt, Inc. Illustration on page 145. Copyright © 1946 and renewed 1947 by Robert Penn Warren. Reprinted by permission of Harcourt, Inc.

Harry Ransom Humanities Research Center. Warren letter to Katherine Anne Porter, 22 December 1934. Reprinted by permission of the Harry Ransom Humanities Research Center, the University of Texas at Austin.

Harvard University Press. Calvin Bedient, *In the Heart's Last Kingdom: Robert Penn Warren's Major Poetry.*

Copyright © 1984 by the President and Fellows of Harvard College. Reprinted by permission of the publisher.

Granville Hicks Estate. Hicks, "Some American Novelists," *American Mercury,* October 1946. Hicks letter to Warren, 9 February 1947, from Yale Collection of American Literature. Used by permission of the author's estate.

Richard Howard. Howard, "A Technician's Romance," *Saturday Review,* 19 March 1977. Reprinted by permission of the author.

Samuel Hynes. Sam Hynes letter to Warren, 25 March 1988; Hynes, "A Tale of Men Trapped in Their Own Darkness," *Commonweal,* 4 September 1959. Reprinted by permission of the author.

Johns Hopkins University Press. Alvan S. Ryan, "Robert Penn Warren's *Night Rider:* The Nihilism of the Isolated Temperament," *Modern Fiction Studies,* Winter 1961–1962. Copyright © 1962. Used by permission of the Purdue Research Center, Johns Hopkins University Press.

Kentucky New Era. Illustration on page 154. Reprinted by permission of the (Hopkinsville) *Kentucky New Era* and Mrs. Robert D. Frey.

University Press of Kentucky. Permission to reprint excerpts from the following publications is granted by the copyright holder, the University Press of Kentucky: Warren, *Portrait of a Father,* copyright © 1983; William Bedford Clark, *The American Vision of Robert Penn Warren,* copyright © 1991; and Floyd C. Watkins, *Then & Now: The Personal Past in the Poetry of Robert Penn Warren,* copyright © 1982.

Kenyon Review. James Wright, "The Stiff Smile of Mr. Warren," Autumn 1958; Leslie Fielder, "The Fate of the Novel," *Kenyon Review,* Summer 1948; Herbert J. Muller, "Violence upon the Roads," *Kenyon Review,* Summer 1939. Copyright by *The Kenyon Review.*

Donald M. Kington. Permission to reprint the 1975 letter from Warren to Donald M. Kington, 6 March 1975. Permission to reprint is granted by Donald M. Kington. Permission is also granted by the estate of Robert Penn Warren.

Richard G. Law. Law, "Warren's *World Enough and Time:* 'Et in Arcadia Ego,'" in *Time's Glory: Original Essays on Robert Penn Warren* (Conway: University of Central Arkansas Press, 1986). Reprinted by permission of the author.

Leaf Chronicle. Excerpt from Tom Wibking, "Star's Work Seasoned by Country Living," *The Leaf-Chronicle,* 21 February 1982. Copyright © 1982 by *The Leaf Chronicle,* Clarksville, Tennessee. Reprinted with permission.

Louisiana State University Libraries. Illustrations on pages 20 (RG#A5000.0020) and 76 (RG#A5000) are from the LSU Photograph Collection, Louisiana State University Archives, LSU Libraries, Baton Rouge. Illustrations on pages 73, 78, and 90 (photograph by Jerry Tompkins), 327, and 328 are from the Charles East Papers, Mss. 3471, Louisiana and Lower Mississippi Valley Collections, LSU Libraries, Baton Rouge. Illustration on page 110 is from Special Collections, Hill Memorial Library, LSU Libraries, Baton Rouge. Illustration on page 251 is from the Donald E. Stanford Papers, MS4715, Louisiana and Lower Mississippi Valley Collections, LSU Libraries, Baton Rouge. Images from the collections in the Louisiana State University Libraries are used by permission.

Louisiana State University Press. Excerpts from the following material are reprinted by permission of the copyright holder, Louisiana State University Press: James H. Justus, "Warren as Mentor: Pure and Impure Wisdom" (permission also granted by author), and R. W. B. Lewis, "Robert Penn Warren: Geography as Fate," in *The Legacy of Robert Penn Warren,* © 2000; Harold Bloom, "Sunset Hawk: Warren's Poetry and Tradition," and James Dickey, "Warren's Poetry: A Reading and Commentary," in *A Southern Renascence Man: Views of Robert Penn Warren,* © 1984; Lewis P. Simpson, "The Concept of the Historical Self in *Brother to Dragons,*" *Robert Penn Warren's Brother to Dragons: A Discussion,* © 1983; Jonathan S. Cullick, *Making History: The Biographical Narratives of Robert Penn Warren,* © 2000.

William Meredith. Meredith letter to Warren, 2 July 1979. Permission to reprint is granted by its author, William Meredith.

Victoria Thorpe Miller. Miller, "Shared Lives and Separate Studies: The Literary Marriage of Eleanor Clark and Robert Penn Warren," *RWP: An Annual of Robert Penn Warren Studies,* 2003. Reprinted by permission of Victoria Thorpe Miller, the Center for Robert Penn Warren Studies, and Western Kentucky University.

Mississippi Quarterly. Will Friday, "The Author and the Ballplayer: An Imprint of Memory in the Writings of Robert Penn Warren," *Mississippi Quarterly,* Spring 1991. Permission is granted by *Mississippi Quarterly.*

University of Missouri Press. Excerpts from James A. Grimshaw, Jr., *Cleanth Brooks and Robert Penn Warren: A Literary Correspondence,* reprinted by permission of the University of Missouri Press. Copyright © 1998 by the Curators of the University of Missouri.

Mouton de Gruyter. Excerpt from L. Hugh Moore, Jr., *Robert Penn Warren and History,* copyright © 1970. Permission granted by Mouton de Gruyter, A Division of Walter de Gruyter GmbH & Co.

J. D. McClatchy. McClatchy, "Rare Prosperities," *Poetry,* 1977. Used by permission of J. D. McClatchy and *Poetry.*

Nashville Tennessean. William Parrill, "Acute, Critical Eye Trained in 'Wild Man' of American Letters," *Nashville Tennessean,* 5 September 1971. Used by permission of William Parrill, Professor of Communication and English at Southeastern Louisiana University.

The Nation. Diana Trilling, "Fiction in Review," *Nation,* 24 August 1946, and Anthony West, "New Novels," *The New Statesman and Nation,* 20 January 1940. Reprinted by permission of *The Nation.*

National Observer. William Kennedy, "How a Poet Works," *National Observer,* 6 February 1967. Copyright © 1967 by *The National Observer.*

National Review. Richard M. Weaver, "An Altered Stand," *National Review,* 17 June 1971, © 1961 by National Review, Inc., 215 Lexington Avenue, New York, NY 10016. Reprinted by permission.

New Republic. C. Vann Woodward, "Warren's Challenge to Race Dogma," *New Republic,* 22 May 1965, © 1965 by *New Republic.* Reprinted by permission.

New York Historical Society. Illustration on page 178, copyright © The New York Historical Society.

New York Times, Co. Warren, "In the Time of *All the King's Men,*" *New York Times Book Review,* 31 May 1981. Copyright © 1981 by The New York Times Co. Reprinted by permission.

University of North Carolina Press. Excerpt from John M. Bradbury, *The Fugitives: A Critical Account.* Copyright © 1958 by the University of North Carolina

Press, renewed 1986 by Mrs. John Mason Bradbury. Used by permission of the publisher.

University of North Texas. Richard B. Sale, "An Interview in New Haven with Robert Penn Warren," *Studies in the Novel,* Fall 1970. Reprinted by permission of University of North Texas.

James Olney. Olney, "On the Death and Life of Robert Penn Warren," in *The Southern Review,* Winter 1990. Permission to reprint is granted by James Olney.

John Ellis Palmer. Excerpt from Warren letter to John Palmer, 24 December 1942. Permission is granted by John Ellis Palmer and The Estate of Robert Penn Warren.

Paris Review. Excerpts from Ralph Ellison and Eugene Walter, "The Art of Fiction XVIII: Robert Penn Warren," *The Paris Review,* Spring–Summer 1957. Reprinted by permission of Regal Literary, Inc. as agent for *The Paris Review.* Copyright © 1957 by *The Paris Review.*

Partisan Review. Alfred Kazin, "The Seriousness of Robert Penn Warren," *Partisan Review,* Spring 1959. Reprinted by permission of the *Partisan Review.*

Peabody Essex Museum. Illustration on page 306, Chief Joseph portrait, 1903, by Edward S. Curtis. Used courtesy of Peabody Essex Museum.

James A. Perkins. Perkins, "Robert Penn Warren and James Farmer: Notes on the Creation of New Journalism," *RWP: An Annual of Robert Penn Warren Studies,* 2001. Used by permission of James A. Perkins, the Center for Robert Penn Warren Studies, and Western Kentucky University.

C. G. Paulding. Paulding, "Mighty Like Despair: Review of *At Heaven's Gate,*" *Commonweal,* 6 August 1943. Reprinted with permission of the author.

Paul Piazza. Piazza, "Intimations of Immortality," *The Chronicle Review,* 30 October 1978. Permission granted by Paul Piazza.

Stanley Plumly. Plumly, "Robert Penn Warren's Vision," *The Southern Review,* Autumn 1970. Permission granted by Stanley Plumly.

Poetry. The Following articles first appeared in *Poetry*: J. D. McClatchy, "Rare Prosperities," December 1977, copyright 1977; John Frederick Nims, "Two Intellectual Poets," December 1942, copyright 1942; Morton

Dauwen Zabel, "Problems of Knowledge," April 1936, copyright 1936; Kenneth Burke, "Towards Objective Criticism," April 1947, copyright 1947. Copyright by The Poetry Foundation. Reprinted by permission of the editor of *Poetry*.

Katherine Anne Porter Estate. Katherine Anne Porter, note dated 6 October 1975, quoted in *Katherine Anne Porter: A Life* by Joan Givner (Simon & Schuster, 1982). Reprinted by permission of the Trust for the Estate of Katherine Anne Porter.

Estate of Frederick A. Pottle. Illustration on page 125, and Frederick A. Pottle letter to Warren, 19 June 1945. Reprinted by permission of Christopher Pottle as executor for the Estate of Frederick A. Pottle.

Princeton University Press. Excerpt from John L. Stewart, *The Burden of Time*. Copyright © 1965 Princeton University Press, 1993 renewed Princeton University Press. Reprinted by permission of Princeton University Press.

Progress Publishers. Illustration on page 316. Copyright © 1982 by Progress Publishers, Moscow. Reprinted by permission.

Sister Bernetta Quinn. Quinn, "A Kind of Unconscious Autobiography," *Southern Review,* Spring 1986. Reprinted by permission of Sisters of St. Francis, Rochester, Minnesota.

Random House. Warren, introduction to the Modern Library Edition of *All the King's Men.* Copyright © 1953, by Random House, Inc. Reprinted with permission.

Shirley B. Ring. Illustrations on pages 31–34. Courtesy of Mrs. Shirley B. Ring.

RWP: An Annual of Robert Penn Warren Studies. Materials from *RWP: An Annual of Robert Penn Warren Studies* are used by permission of the Center for Robert Penn Warren Studies, Western Kentucky University, and the respective authors, who are listed separately.

Robert Penn Warren Birthplace Museum. Illustrations on pages 24, 25, 28, 30, 38, 55, 92, 157, 187, 343, and 344. Used courtesy of the Robert Penn Warren Birthplace Museum, Guthrie, Kentucky.

Robert Penn Warren Center. Illustrations on pages 36 and 37. Used by permission of the Robert Penn Warren Center, Clarksville, Tennessee and Clarksville High School.

Louis D. Rubin, Jr. Excerpt from Rubin, *The Wary Fugitives: Four Poets and the South* (Baton Rouge: Louisiana State University Press, 1978). Reprinted by permission of the author.

Randolph Paul Runyon. Runyon, "Father, Son, and Taciturn Text," in *"To Love So Well the World": A Festschrift in Honor of Robert Penn Warren* (Peter Lang, 1992). Reprinted by permission of Randolph Paul Runyon.

Sewanee Review. The following material first appeared in the *Sewanee Review* and is reprinted by permission of the editor: William Bedford Clark, "Letters from Home: Filial Guilt in Robert Penn Warren," Summer 2002, copyright 2002 by William Bedford Clark; Robert B. Heilman, "Baton Rouge and LSU Forty Years Later," Winter 1980, copyright 1980 by Robert B. Heilman; Monroe K. Spears, "The Critics Who Made Us: Robert Penn Warren," Winter 1986, copyright 1986 by Monroe K. Spears.

Lewis P. Simpson. Simpson, "Robert Penn Warren and the South," *Southern Review,* Winter 1990. Permission is granted by Lewis P. Simpson and *Southern Review.*

Southern Literary Journal. Robert W. Hamblin, "Robert Penn Warren at the 1965 Southern Literary Festival: A Personal Recollection," *Southern Literary Journal,* Spring 1990. Permission to reprint is granted by the *Southern Literary Journal.*

Southern Review. Tributes to Warren by Donald E. Stanford, Cleanth Brooks, Lewis Simpson, and James Olney, from *Southern Review,* Winter 1990. Permission granted by the editor of *Southern Review* and the respective authors.

Donald E. Stanford. Stanford, "Robert Penn Warren and the *Southern Review*," *The Southern Review,* Winter 1990. Permission to reprint is granted by Donald E. Stanford.

Star Tribune, **Minneapolis.** James Shannon, "Overdue Tribute to a Teacher Who Made a Lifelong Difference," *Minneapolis Star and Tribune,* 7 September 1986. Reprinted by permission of *Star Tribune,* Minneapolis.

Syracuse University Library. Warren letter to Granville Hicks, 18 February 1947. Permission is granted by Syracuse University Library and the Estate of Robert Penn Warren.

Tamazunchale Press. Illustration on page 330. Permission is granted by Charlotte A. Smith for Tamazunchale Press and Western Kentucky University Library.

Helen H. Tate. Illustration on page 59, provided by Yale Collection of American Literature, Beinecke Rare Book and Manuscript Library. Permission is granted by Helen H. Tate.

University of Texas Press and Allen Shepherd. Shepherd, "The Poles of Fiction: Warren's *At Heaven's Gate*," *Texas Studies in Literature and Language,* Winter 1971. Copyright © 1971 by The University of Texas Press. All rights reserved. Permission also granted by Allen Shepherd.

Time. Paul Gray, "All the Nation's Poet," *Time,* 10 March 1986, p. 48. © 1986 TIME Inc. Reprinted by permission.

Times Literary Supplement. Henry Nash Smith, "State of the Nation," *Times Literary Supplement,* 20 February 1976; Julian Symons, "In the Southern Style," *Times Literary Supplement,* 29 April 1977; and Jay Parini, "The Vatic Mantle,"*Times Literary Supplement,* 29 January 1982. Reprinted by permission of *Times Literary Supplement.*

Carll Tucker. Tucker, "Creators on Creating: Robert Penn Warren," *Saturday Review,* July 1981. Reprinted by permission of the author.

U.S. News & World Report. Excerpt from "What Kind of Future for America?" *U.S. News & World Report,* 7 July 1975, copyright 1975 U.S. News & World Report, L.P.; and Alvin P. Sanoff, "A Conversation with America's First Poet Laureate," *U.S. News & World Report,* 23 June 1986, copyright 1986 U.S. News & World Report, L.P. Reprinted with permission.

Vanderbilt University Libraries. Permission to reprint the following material is granted by Special Collections, Jean and Alexander Heard Library, Vanderbilt University: Excerpts from letters from Robert Penn Warren to Andrew Lytle, 8 August 1925; Donald Davidson, 28 February 1935 and 9 October 1946; Frank Owsley, 25 December 1942; Arthur Mizener, 8 November 1966; and Brainard "Lon" Cheney, 22 January 1957, 19 May 1961, and 14 January 1966. Excerpts from *Fugitives Reunion,* 1959; "An Interview with Flannery O'Connor and Robert Penn Warren" in *Vagabond,* 1960; and Warren, "Introduction," *Nashville: The Faces of Two Centuries,* John Egerton, 1979. Permission granted by Vanderbilt University to use illustrations on pages 40, 41, 44, 49, 71, 191, and 209 from Photographic Archives, Special Collections, Vanderbilt University and page 35 from Stuart Wright Collection, Special Collections, Vanderbilt University.

Virginia Quarterly Review. Carlos Baker, "Through the Iron Gates," *Virginia Quarterly Review,* Autumn 1950. Permission granted by Janna Olson Gies of the *Virginia Quarterly Review.*

Eda Lou Walton. Walton, "Schoolroom Anthology: Review of Understanding Poetry," *New York Herald Tribune,* 28 August 1938. Reprinted by permission of the author.

Gabriel Warren. Excerpts from the 8 November 1966 letter from Robert Penn Warren to Arthur Mizener (see also Vanderbilt University) and "Travel in Service to Work," *RWP: An Annual of Robert Penn Warren Studies,* 2005. Illustrations on pages 173, 174, 304, and 319. Permission to reprint is granted by Gabriel Warren.

Estate of Robert Penn Warren. Materials from Robert Penn Warren's unpublished letters and an essay, and for illustrations on pages 51, 69, 100, 106, 115, 123, 129, 131, 151, 163, 165, 168, 171, 180, 182, 185, 205, 216, 223, 228, 238, 239, 246, 249, 251, 254, 260, 270, 271, 275, 288, 292, 307, 308, 312, 313, 314, 320, 323, 323, and 334. Permission is granted by the Estate of Robert Penn Warren.

Washington Post. Elizabeth Kastor, "Robert Penn Warren: A Voyage to the Heart," *Washington Post,* 16 September 1989. Copyright © 1989, *The Washington Post.* Reprinted with permission.

University of Washington Press and Leonard R. Casper. Excerpts from Leonard R. Casper, *Robert Penn Warren: The Dark and Bloody Ground,* © 1960. Reprinted by permission of Leonard R. Casper, Professor Emeritus, Boston College and University of Washington Press.

Washington State University. James E. Ruoff, "Robert Penn Warren's Pursuit of Justice," *Research Studies of the State College of Washington,* March 1959. Copyright © 1959 by Washington State University. Reprinted with permission.

Western Kentucky University. Permission to reprint material from *RWP: An Annual of Robert Penn Warren Studies* is granted by the Center for Robert Penn Warren Studies and Western Kentucky University and is acknowledged separately by specific authors.

Western Kentucky University Library. Illustrations on pages 92, 107, 128, 146, 194, 221, 226, 242–243, 259, 276, 297, 298, 299, 301, 303, 311, 316, 321, 325, 326, and 330 are from the Robert Penn Warren Collection. Permission is granted courtesy of Western Kentucky University.

Earl Wilcox. Wilcox, "Right On! *All the King's Men* in the Classroom," *Four Quarters,* May 1972. Permission to reprint is granted by Earl Wilcox.

William Morris Agency. Permission to reprint the following material is granted by the Estate of Robert Penn Warren and the William Morris Agency: selected lines of "Old-Time Childhood in Kentucky," "American Portrait: Old Style," and "A Vision, Circa 1880" from *The Collected Poems of Robert Penn Warren* edited by John Burt, copyright © 1998; Robert Penn Warren "Intro-duction" to *Nashville: The Faces of Two Centuries,* copyright © 1979; Robert Penn Warren "Introduction" to *All the King's Men,* Modern Library Edition, copyright © 1953; excerpt from *Who Speaks for the Negro?,* copyright © 1965; and "John Crowe Ransom (1888–1974)" in *The Southern Review,* copyright © 1975.

C. Vann Woodward. Excerpt from Woodward, "Exile at Yale," in *The Legacy of Robert Penn Warren,* edited by David Madden, © 2000 by C. Vann Woodward. Reprinted with permission of C. Vann Woodward.

Yale University Libraries. Permission to use images from the Robert Penn Warren Collection, Beinecke Rare Book and Manuscript Library, Yale University, is granted by the respective copyright holders noted elsewhere in these acknowledgments.

Robert Penn Warren:
A Documentary Volume

Dictionary of Literary Biography

Works by Robert Penn Warren

See also the Warren entries in *DLB 2: American Novelists Since World War II; DLB 48: American Poets, 1880–1945, Second Series; DLB 152: American Novelists Since World War II, Fourth Series; DLB Yearbook: 1980;* and *DLB Yearbook: 1989.*

BOOKS: *John Brown: The Making of a Martyr* (New York: Payson & Clarke, 1929);

Thirty-Six Poems (New York: Alcestis Press, 1935);

Night Rider (Boston: Houghton Mifflin, 1939; London: Eyre & Spottiswoode, 1940);

Eleven Poems on the Same Theme (Norfolk, Conn.: New Directions, 1942);

At Heaven's Gate (New York: Harcourt, Brace, 1943; London: Eyre & Spottiswoode, 1946);

Selected Poems, 1923–1943 (New York: Harcourt, Brace, 1944; London: Fortune Press, 1952);

All the King's Men (New York: Harcourt, Brace, 1946; London: Eyre & Spottiswoode, 1948);

Blackberry Winter (Cummington, Mass.: Cummington Press, 1946);

The Circus in the Attic and Other Stories (New York: Harcourt, Brace, 1947; London: Eyre & Spottiswoode, 1952);

World Enough and Time (New York: Random House, 1950; London: Eyre & Spottiswoode, 1951);

Brother to Dragons: A Tale in Verse and Voices (New York: Random House, 1953; London: Eyre & Spottiswoode, 1954);

Band of Angels (New York: Random House, 1955; London: Eyre & Spottiswoode, 1956);

Segregation: The Inner Conflict in the South (New York: Random House, 1956; London: Eyre & Spottiswoode, 1957);

To a Little Girl, One Year Old, in a Ruined Fortress (New Haven: Designed, illustrated, and printed by Jane Doggett in the Department of Graphic Arts, School of Design, Yale University, 1956);

Promises: Poems, 1954–1956 (New York: Random House, 1957; London: Eyre & Spottiswoode, 1959);

Selected Essays (New York: Random House, 1958; London: Eyre & Spottiswoode, 1964);

Remember the Alamo! (New York: Random House, 1958);

How Texas Won Her Freedom (San Jacinto Monument, Tex.: San Jacinto Museum of History, 1959);

The Cave (New York: Random House, 1959; London: Eyre & Spottiswoode, 1959);

The Gods of Mount Olympus (New York: Random House, 1959; London: Muller, 1962);

All the King's Men: A Play (New York: Random House, 1960);

You, Emperors, and Others: Poems, 1957–1960 (New York: Random House, 1960);

The Legacy of the Civil War: Meditations on the Centennial (New York: Random House, 1961);

Wilderness: A Tale of the Civil War (New York: Random House, 1961; London: Eyre & Spottiswoode, 1962);

Flood: A Romance of Our Time (New York: Random House, 1964; London: Collins, 1964);

Who Speaks for the Negro? (New York: Random House, 1965);

A Plea in Mitigation: Modern Poetry and the End of an Era (Macon, Ga.: Wesleyan College, 1966);

Selected Poems: New and Old, 1923–1966 (New York: Random House, 1966);

Incarnations: Poems, 1966–1968 (New York: Random House, 1968; London: W. H. Allen, 1970);

Audubon: A Vision (New York: Random House, 1969);

Homage to Theodore Dreiser, August 27, 1871–December 28, 1945, on the Centennial of His Birth (New York: Random House, 1971);

Meet Me in the Green Glen (New York: Random House, 1971; London: Secker & Warburg, 1972);

Or Else–Poem/Poems, 1968–1974 (New York: Random House, 1974);

Democracy and Poetry (Cambridge, Mass. & London: Harvard University Press, 1975);

Selected Poems, 1923–1975 (New York: Random House, 1976; London: Secker & Warburg, 1976);

A Place to Come To (New York: Random House, 1977; London: Secker & Warburg, 1977);

Now and Then: Poems, 1976–1978 (New York: Random House, 1978);

Two Poems (Winston-Salem, N.C.: Palaemon Press, 1979);

Brother to Dragons: A Tale in Verse and Voices (A New Version) (New York: Random House, 1979);

Ballad of a Sweet Dream of Peace: A Charade for Easter (Dallas, Tex.: Pressworks, 1980);

Being Here: Poetry, 1977–1980 (New York: Random House, 1980; London: Secker & Warburg, 1980);

Jefferson Davis Gets His Citizenship Back (Lexington: University Press of Kentucky, 1980);

Rumor Verified: Poems, 1979–1980 (New York: Random House, 1981; London: Secker & Warburg, 1982);

Love: Four Versions (Winston-Salem, N.C.: Palaemon Press, 1981);

Chief Joseph of the Nez Perce (Winston-Salem, N.C.: Palaemon Press, 1982; New York: Random House, 1983);

New and Selected Poems: 1923–1985 (New York: Random House, 1985; revised edition, Helsinki: Eurographica, 1986);

Portrait of a Father (Lexington: University Press of Kentucky, 1988);

New and Selected Essays (New York: Random House, 1989);

The Collected Poems of Robert Penn Warren, edited by John Burt (Baton Rouge: Louisiana State University Press, 1998);

Robert Penn Warren's All the King's Men: *Three Stage Versions,* edited by James A. Grimshaw Jr. and James A. Perkins (Athens: University of Georgia Press, 2000);

All the King's Men (Restored Edition), edited by Noel Polk (New York: Harcourt Brace, 2001);

The Cass Mastern Material: The Core of Robert Penn Warren's All the King's Men, edited by Perkins (Baton Rouge: Louisiana State University Press, 2005).

Editions and Collections: *Robert Penn Warren: 15 Poems* (Winston-Salem, N.C.: Palaemon Press, 1985);

Six Poems (Newton, Iowa: Tamazunchale Press, 1987);

A Robert Penn Warren Reader (New York: Random House, 1987);

Selected Poems of Robert Penn Warren, edited by John Burt (Baton Rouge: Louisiana State University Press, 2001).

PLAY PRODUCTIONS: *Proud Flesh,* Minneapolis, University Theater, 28 April 1947;

All the King's Men, Minneapolis, University Theater, 28 April 1947;

Willie Stark: His Rise and Fall, Dallas, Tex., Margo Jones Theater, 25 November 1958;

All the King's Men, New York, East 74th Street Theatre, 16 October 1959;

Brother to Dragons, Chicago, School of Speech, Northwestern University, 11 March 1960; revised, Providence, R.I., Trinity Square Repertory Company, 1974;

Ballad of a Sweet Dream of Peace, Cambridge, Mass., Loeb Drama Center Experimental Theatre, 27 April 1961;

Listen to the Mockingbird, Commerce, Tex., Texas A&M University-Commerce Performing Arts Theater, 7 October 1998.

WORKS EDITED: *The Southern Review,* by Warren, Charles W. Pipkin, and Cleanth Brooks (Baton Rouge: Louisiana State University Press, 1935–1942);

An Approach to Literature, by Warren, Brooks, and John Thibaut Purser (Baton Rouge: Department of English, Louisiana State University, 1936; revised edition, New York: F. S. Crofts, 1939; revised edition, New York: Appleton-Century-Crofts, 1952; revised again, 1964; revised edition, Englewood Cliffs, N.J.: Prentice-Hall, 1975);

A Southern Harvest: Short Stories by Southern Writers (Boston: Houghton Mifflin, 1937);

Understanding Poetry: An Anthology for College Students, by Warren and Brooks (New York: Holt, 1938; revised, 1950; revised edition, New York: Holt, Rinehart & Winston, 1960; revised again, 1976);

Understanding Fiction, by Warren and Brooks (New York: F. S. Crofts, 1943; revised edition, New York: Appleton-Century-Crofts, 1959; revised edition, Englewood Cliffs, N.J.: Prentice-Hall, 1979);

Modern Rhetoric, by Warren and Brooks (New York: Harcourt, Brace, 1949; revised, 1958; revised edition, New York: Harcourt, Brace & World, 1970; revised edition, New York: Harcourt Brace Jovanovich, 1979);

Fundamentals of Good Writing: A Handbook of Modern Rhetoric, by Warren and Brooks (New York: Harcourt, Brace, 1950; London: Dennis Dobson, 1952);

An Anthology of Stories from the Southern Review, by Warren and Brooks (Baton Rouge: Louisiana State University Press, 1953);

Short Story Masterpieces, by Warren and Albert Erskine (New York: Dell, 1954);

Six Centuries of Great Poetry: From Chaucer to Yeats, by Warren and Erskine (New York: Dell, 1955);

A New Southern Harvest, by Warren and Erskine (New York: Bantam, 1957);

The Scope of Fiction, by Warren and Brooks (New York: Appleton-Century-Crofts, 1960);

Selected Poems by Denis Devlin, by Warren and Allen Tate (New York: Holt, Rinehart & Winston, 1963);

Faulkner: A Collection of Critical Essays (Englewood Cliffs, N.J.: Prentice-Hall, 1966);

Randall Jarrell, 1914–1965, by Warren, Robert Lowell, and Peter Taylor (New York: Farrar, Straus & Giroux, 1967);

Selected Poems of Herman Melville: A Reader's Edition (New York: Random House, 1970);

John Greenleaf Whittier's Poetry (Minneapolis: University of Minnesota Press, 1971);

American Literature: The Makers and the Making, 2 volumes, by Warren, Brooks, and R. W. B. Lewis (New York: St. Martin's Press, 1973);

Katherine Anne Porter: A Collection of Critical Essays (Englewood Cliffs, N.J.: Prentice-Hall, 1979);

The Essential Melville (New York: Ecco Press, 1987).

SELECTED ESSAYS: "The Briar Patch," in *I'll Take My Stand: The South and the Agrarian Tradition by Twelve Southerners* (New York & London: Harper, 1930), pp. 246–264;

"A Poem of Pure Imagination: An Experiment in Reading," in Samuel Taylor Coleridge; *The Rime of the Ancient Mariner* (New York: Reynal & Hitchcock, 1946), pp. 59–117.

"Introduction," in *All the King's Men* (New York: Random House, 1953);

"The Way It Was Written," *New York Times Book Review,* 23 August 1953, pp. 6, 25;

"Knowledge and the Image of Man," *Sewanee Review,* 62 (Spring 1955): 182–192;

"A Lesson Read in American Books," *New York Times Book Review,* 11 December 1955, pp. 1, 33;

"Writer at Work: How a Story Was Born and How, Bit by Bit, It Grew," *New York Times Book Review,* 1 March 1959, pp. 4–5, 36;

"John Crowe Ransom (1988–1974)," *Southern Review,* 11 (Spring 1975): 243–244;

"A Reminiscence," in John Egerton, *Nashville: The Faces of Two Centuries, 1780–1980* (Nashville: Plus Media, 1979), pp. 205–213;

"In the Time of 'All the King's Men,'" *New York Times Book Review,* 31 May 1981, pp. 39–42;

"Poetry Is a Kind of Unconscious Autobiography," *New York Times Book Review,* 12 May 1985, pp. 9–10;

"The Origin of the *Southern Review,*" by Warren and Cleanth Brooks, *Southern Review,* 22 (Winter 1986): 214–217;

"The Episode in the Dime Store," *Southern Review,* 30 (Autumn 1994): 650–657;

"The Dramatic Version of Ballad of a Sweet Dream of Peace: A Charade for Easter," in *The Grotesque in Art and Literature: Theological Reflections,* edited by James Luther Adams and Wilson Yates (Grand Rapids, Mich.: William B. Eerdmans, 1997), pp. 243–274.

LETTERS: *Cleanth Brooks and Robert Penn Warren: A Literary Correspondence,* edited by James A. Grimshaw Jr. (Columbia & London: University of Missouri Press, 1998);

Selected Letters of Robert Penn Warren, Volume 1, The Apprentice Years, 1924–1934, edited by William Bedford Clark (Baton Rouge: Louisiana State University Press, 2000);

Selected Letters of Robert Penn Warren, Volume 2, The "Southern Review" Years, 1935–1942, edited by Clark (Baton Rouge: Louisiana State University Press, 2001);

Selected Letters of Robert Penn Warren, Volume 3, Triumph and Transition, 1943–1952, edited by Randy Hendricks and James A. Perkins (Baton Rouge: Louisiana State University Press, 2005).

PAPERS: The major collections of Robert Penn Warren's papers are in the Beinecke Rare Book and Manuscript Library at Yale University; the Western Kentucky University Library in Bowling Green; and the King Library at the University of Kentucky, Lexington. Other significant collections of Warren and related materials are in the Robert Penn Warren Birthplace Museum, Guthrie, Kentucky; the Hill Memorial Library at Louisiana State University; and the Jean and Alexander Heard Library at Vanderbilt University.

Chronology

1905
24 April   Robert Penn Warren is born in Guthrie, Todd County, Kentucky, to store proprietor Robert Franklin and Anna Ruth Penn Warren. He is the first of three children: his sister, Mary Cecilia, is born in 1908, and his brother, William Thomas, is born in 1911.

1911
Fall   Enters Guthrie School.

1920
September   Enters Clarksville High School; he awaits his sixteenth birthday and an appointment to the United States Naval Academy.

1921
Spring   Suffers an injury to his left eye; Warren's loss of vision in that eye disqualifies him from attending the United States Naval Academy.

Fall   Enters Vanderbilt University as a chemical-engineering major.

1922
Summer   Attends the Citizens' Military Training Camp (CMTC), Fifth Corps Area, Camp Knox, Kentucky, where he publishes his first poem, "Prophecy," in *The Mess Kit*.

1923
January   Rooms with Allen Tate, Ridley Wills, and William Cobb, all of whom become and remain his friends. Tate influences Warren's development as a poet.

Spring   Five poems are published in the Nashville Poetry Guild anthology *Driftwood Flames*.

June   "Crusade," Warren's first publication in *The Fugitive: A Journal of Poetry,* appears in the June–July issue.

1924
February   Elected to membership in The Fugitives, a literary group of some sixteen members made up of university students and faculty as well as Nashville townspeople who share an interest in poetry. Warren is listed on the masthead of *The Fugitive*.

20 May   Attempts to commit suicide by inhaling chloroform. Warren is hospitalized after he is discovered unconscious. His father takes him home to Guthrie.

Fall   Returns to Vanderbilt, where he meets Cleanth Brooks, who becomes a friend and his collaborator on textbooks.

November	Warren's first review, of John Crowe Ransom's *Chills and Fever*, is published in *Voices*. Ransom's English class at Vanderbilt convinced Warren that his true interests were in writing and literature rather than in chemical engineering. Warren wrote more than sixty reviews of literary and scholarly books, including F. Scott Fitzgerald's *The Great Gatsby*, Gilbert Chinard's *Thomas Jefferson: The Apostle of Americanism,* William Faulkner's *The Hamlet,* and Ralph Ellison's *Shadow and Act.*

1925

June	Graduates summa cum laude with a B.A. from Vanderbilt University.
August	Enters the University of California–Berkeley on a fellowship. Warren meets Emma "Cinina" Brescia, who becomes his first wife in 1929.

1927

Spring	"Evening: The Motors" is included in *Best Poems of 1926.*
June	Graduates with an M.A. in English from the University of California–Berkeley.
Summer	Meets Katherine Anne Porter, who becomes a lifelong friend, at the New York apartment of Allen Tate and his wife, Caroline Gordon Tate. Warren meets other literary notables, including Malcolm Cowley and Dorothy Day.
September	Enters the doctoral program in English at Yale University.
Fall	Publication of the poem "At the Hour of the Breaking of the Rocks" in the first volume of *American Caravan,* a literary yearbook edited by Paul Rosenfeld, Alfred Kreymborg, and Lewis Mumford.

1928

11 October	Enters New College, Oxford University, on a Rhodes Scholarship. This trip to England is Warren's first time abroad. European trips, usually with family and often with friends, will become customary for Warren.

1929

Summer	Returns to Guthrie because of experiencing continuing difficulties with his left eye. Because the Rhodes Scholarship specified single status, he secretly marries Cinina in Sacramento, California, before returning in the fall to Oxford.
2 November	Publication of *John Brown: The Making of a Martyr,* his first book.

1930

May	Receives B.Litt. from Oxford University; his thesis is on the satires of dramatist John Marston (circa 1575–1634).
12 September	Warren and Cinina are wed by a justice of the peace in Marion, Arkansas, to formalize their marriage publicly.
September	Teaches English as an assistant professor at Southwestern College (now Rhodes College) for one year in Memphis, Tennessee. Warren meets an undergraduate student, Albert Russell Erskine Jr., who becomes a friend and his editor.
12 November	Publication of *I'll Take My Stand,* by Twelve Southerners; it includes "The Briar Patch," a controversial essay in which Warren argues for the fair treatment of blacks but accepts the status quo of segregation in the South. Warren later takes an integrationist position.

1931

September   Begins a three-year appointment as assistant professor at Vanderbilt University. Randall
                  Jarrell and Jesse Stuart are among his students.

5 October   Death of Ruth Penn Warren, with whom he had a conflicted relationship.

Fall   Publication of "Prime Leaf" in *American Caravan IV*. This story, which deals with the
                  tobacco wars that occurred in western Kentucky and Tennessee in the early twentieth
                  century, is a precursor to Warren's first published novel, *Night Rider*.

1934

7 February   Warren's left eye is removed at Vanderbilt University Hospital.

September   Begins an eight-year stint at Louisiana State University (LSU) in Baton Rouge as an
                  assistant professor. Warren joins his friend Cleanth Brooks on the faculty.

Fall   Serves with Brooks as associate editor for the *Southwest Review*.

1935

March   Begins organizing a literary quarterly at the suggestion of LSU president James Monroe
                  Smith. Warren collaborates with Brooks and Charles W. Pipkin in the creation of the
                  respected journal *The Southern Review*.

July   Publication of the first issue of *The Southern Review*, with Warren and Brooks as manag-
                  ing editors. Charles W. Pipkin is the editor in chief, and Erskine is the business
                  manager. Warren speaks at the Rocky Mountain Writers' Conference in Boulder, Col-
                  orado, where he meets Robert Frost and Thomas Wolfe. The Warrens also travel to
                  Montana en route to their annual visit with Cinina Warren's family in Oakland, Cali-
                  fornia.

9 September   Senator Huey P. Long, the model for Willie Stark in *All the King's Men* (1946), is assassi-
                  nated in Baton Rouge.

1936

15 February   Publication of *Thirty-Six Poems*, his first volume of poetry.

21 April   Promoted to the rank of associate professor.

September   *An Approach to Literature: A Collection of Prose and Verse with Analyses and Discussion*, a text-
                  book prepared by Warren, Brooks, and John Thibaut Purser, is published by the
                  LSU English department. This book, which began as a mimeographed pamphlet
                  that Warren and Brooks prepared for sophomores who had difficulty reading
                  poetry, marks the beginning of Warren and Brooks's collaboration on textbooks
                  that spans six decades.

December   Warren and Brooks deliver a joint paper on "The Reading of Modern Poetry" at the
                  Modern Language Association (MLA) meeting in Richmond, Virginia. Warren
                  often participates in the annual MLA conferences.

1937

Summer   Begins work on the play *Proud Flesh*, which evolves into *All the King's Men*. In this first
                  version of what becomes several versions of the story, the main character is named
                  Willie Strong.

1938

6 June   Publication of *Understanding Poetry: An Anthology for College Students,* which becomes a standard text in classrooms for more than four decades.

Late June   Departs from Savannah, Georgia, aboard a freighter for Italy. The Warrens spend time in Perugia, Rome, Sirmione, and Venice before returning to the United States in late August.

July   Writes Allen Tate that he is working out plans for his next novel, *At Heaven's Gate.*

December   Delivers an essay titled "Tradition and Environment" at the MLA conference in New York.

1939

14 March   Publication of *Night Rider,* his first novel, about the conflict between tobacco growers and manufacturers in turn-of-the-century Kentucky.

22 March   Receives word that he has been awarded a Guggenheim Fellowship to work on a new novel.

20 July   Departs for Italy aboard a freighter. The Warrens spend nearly ten months in France and Italy, while Warren returns to work on *Proud Flesh.*

1940

January   Publication of the English edition of *Night Rider,* his first book to be published outside of the United States. Until the late 1970s, most of his major volumes of poetry and fiction are published in England after first appearing in the United States.

June   Works on *Proud Flesh* with Francis Fergusson in North Bennington, Vermont.

August   Visits John Crowe Ransom in Gambier, Ohio—a trip Warren and his wife often make during the next decade.

1941

Spring   Visiting lecturer in fiction at the Iowa School of Letters, Iowa City.

17 July   Travels to Chapala, Jalisco, Mexico, where he continues to work on his second novel, *At Heaven's Gate,* as well as his poetry and studies Spanish.

1942

4 April   Publication of *Eleven Poems on the Same Theme* in the New Directions Poet of the Month series.

Spring   *The Southern Review* stops publication because of lack of funds. Warren resigns from LSU after the school fails to meet an offer from the University of Minnesota.

5 August   Begins an eight-year stint at the University of Minnesota as a professor of English.

11 November   Writes Brooks that he has completed *At Heaven's Gate.*

1943

January   Publication of *Understanding Fiction,* another collaboration by Warren and Brooks that becomes a standard classroom text.

     Receives the Shelley Memorial Award for *Eleven Poems.*

19 August	Publication of *At Heaven's Gate,* a novel about an unethical entrepreneur who is destroying the land out of greed for money and power.

1944

6 April	Publication of *Selected Poems, 1923–1943;* nine years pass before Warren's next work of poetry is published.
July	Named the third Consultant in Poetry to the Library of Congress. Warren edits the *U.S. Library of Congress Quarterly Journal of Current Acquisitions* for one year.

1945

May	Delivers a Bergen Foundation Lecture at Yale University; portions of this talk are included in the essay "A Poem of Pure Imagination: An Experiment in Reading," which is published in a new edition of Samuel Taylor Coleridge's *The Rime of the Ancient Mariner* (1946).

1946

17 August	Publication of *All the King's Men,* a novel that in part was inspired by the career of Louisiana governor and senator Huey P. Long.
1 November	Publication of a limited, signed edition of the short story "Blackberry Winter."

1947

8 April	Awarded a second Guggenheim Fellowship.
28 April	*Proud Flesh* premieres at University Theater, University of Minnesota, and runs for seven days.
5 May	Awarded the Pulitzer Prize in fiction for *All the King's Men.*

1948

22 January	Publication of *The Circus in the Attic and Other Stories,* his only collection of short fiction. He writes only one more story, "Invitation to a Dance" (published in *Today's Woman,* February 1949), before giving up short fiction to concentrate on poetry and novels.
27 January	Departs aboard the MS *Sobieski* for Italy. The Warrens spend time in Taormina, Sicily, and Rome before returning to Minnesota for the fall term. Warren corresponds with Brooks about their new text *Modern Rhetoric* and works on *World Enough and Time.*
May	Publication of *All the King's Men* in England; the edition omits the Cass Mastern story, chapter 4 in the U.S. edition, because it is deemed irrelevant to the main story.

1949

23 March	Travels to Santa Monica, California, following the spring quarter at the University of Minnesota. The Warrens stay until the fall when they return to Minnesota for Warren's last two quarters at the university.
28 April	Publication of *Modern Rhetoric.* Warren and Brooks prepare a shorter version, *Fundamentals of Good Writing,* which is published the following year.
14 May	Cinina is admitted to a hospital in New York, presumably for psychological analysis.

June	Awarded an honorary D.Litt. from the University of Louisville, the first of more than twenty honorary degrees, from institutions such as the University of Kentucky, Yale University, Harvard University, and Johns Hopkins University.
November	Attends the premiere of *All the King's Men* in New York. The movie wins an Oscar the following year for best picture. Warren, who collaborated with director Robert Rossen, receives the Robert Meltzer Award of the Screen Writers' Guild.

1950

May	Receives a Distinguished Alumnus Award from Vanderbilt University.
20 June	Publication of *World Enough and Time,* his fourth novel. Random House becomes Warren's publisher with this novel, a decision influenced by Albert Erskine, who has joined the Random House staff.
21 July	Begins several-month stay at the summer house of Albert and Peggy Erskine in Saugatuck, Connecticut, while Cinina undergoes treatment for a psychiatric disorder in White Plains, New York.
September	Joins the Yale University faculty as a visiting professor.

1951

10 May	Elected to the American Academy of Arts and Sciences.
28 June	Divorces Cinina in Verdi, Nevada, after more than twenty years of marriage. The decision to divorce was initiated by Cinina on the recommendation of her doctors.
24 July	Finishes "The Wedding Ring," an unproduced, unpublished play based on the Cass Mastern story in *All the King's Men* that Warren originally wrote with Robert Rossen. Warren revises the play in 1959 as *Listen to the Mockingbird: A Drama of the American Civil War.* This latter version of the play was first performed on 7 October 1998 at the Performing Arts Theatre at Texas A&M University–Commerce.
Late July	Departs for England for a two-month vacation. He spends August on the Riviera, near Nice.
September	Appointed professor of playwriting in the Yale School of Drama, a position he holds for five years.
4 October	Writes Brooks from London that he is "deep in the middle" of his long poem *Brother to Dragons.*

1952

7 December	Marries the writer Eleanor Clark, a friend whom Warren had begun dating early in the year.

1953

Spring	Reconstruction on house at 2495 Redding Road, Fairfield, Connecticut, gets under way. At Christmas the Warrens move into the house, their main residence for the next thirty-six years.
27 July	Birth of Rosanna Phelps Warren, the first of two children born to the Warrens. Warren writes to Brooks that she arrived "without much warning, and very melodramatically, in the middle of the living room floor."

21 August	Publication of *Brother to Dragons: A Tale in Verse and Voices,* a tale of a murder committed by two of Thomas Jefferson's nephews.
23 November	Publication of *An Anthology of Stories from the Southern Review,* co-edited by Warren and Brooks.

1954

22 April	Publication of *Short Story Masterpieces,* the first of three paperback anthologies co-edited by Warren and Erskine. This collection and *Six Centuries of Great Poetry,* published the following year, have been in print for more than fifty years.
Summer	Travels to Italy. They spend about two months in La Rocca, a sixteenth-century fortress near the Village of Porto Ercole, where Warren begins what becomes a Pulitzer Prize–winning volume, *Promises: Poems 1954–1956.*

1955

17 January	Death of father from prostate cancer.
19 July	Birth of Gabriel Penn Warren.
22 August	Publication of *Band of Angels,* his fifth novel, about a mulatto searching for her identity prior to the end of the Civil War. The novel is a Literary Guild Selection.
December	Leaves Yale University to spend more time writing.

1956

3–5 May	Participates in the Fugitives' reunion at Vanderbilt University.
May	Travels to Italy, staying for several months, mainly in La Rocca and Rome. Warren works on poems and a children's book, *Remember the Alamo!*
31 August	Publication of *Segregation: The Inner Conflict in the South,* a self-interview about the race issue in which he repudiates the segregationist stance he took in "The Briar Patch" twenty-six years before.

1957

3 August	The film production of *Band of Angels* is released.
15 August	Publication of *Promises: Poems 1954–1956,* which includes poems dedicated to his daughter and son.
Fall	Publication of *All the King's Men: A Symposium.* This collection of the proceedings of a conference at the Carnegie Institute of Technology is the first book-length critical work about Warren's novel.

1958

11 March	*Promises* receives the National Book Award for poetry.
5 May	Awarded the Pulitzer Prize in poetry for *Promises.* Warren is the first author to receive a Pulitzer Prize in both fiction and poetry.
7 May	Departs for France and Italy on board the French liner *Flaudre.* The Warrens spend a few days in Paris before driving to La Rocca, where he works on poems and on his sixth novel, *The Cave.* They depart for home in October.

25 June	Publication of *Selected Essays,* a collection that includes essays on the work of Joseph Conrad, William Faulkner, Ernest Hemingway, Robert Frost, Katherine Anne Porter, Eudora Welty, Thomas Wolfe, and Herman Melville.
Early August	Travels to Italy.
28 August	Publication of *Remember the Alamo!,* the first of two children's books Warren writes for the Random House Landmark Books series.
Fall	Becomes a member in The Century Association, a New York City artistic club, limited to one hundred members, founded in 1846 by William Cullen Bryant and others.
25 November	*Willie Stark: His Rise and Fall,* the second play based on *All the King's Men,* premieres at the Margo Jones Theater in Dallas, Texas.

1959

February	Publication of *How Texas Won Her Freedom,* a pamphlet published by the San Jacinto Museum of History about Sam Houston and the Battle of San Jacinto. Warren's research for *Remember the Alamo!* provided the basis for this spin-off.
24 August	Publication of *The Cave,* a novel inspired by the death of spelunker Floyd Collins in 1925 that explores the values of a community in time of tragedy. Warren settled on the title of his sixth novel at the last minute in Erskine's office at Random House.
28 September	Publication of *The Gods of Mount Olympus,* his second book for children.
October	Purchases a summerhouse in West Wardsboro, Vermont.
16 October	*All the King's Men* is produced Off-Broadway at the East 74th Street Theatre.
4 December	Inducted into the American Academy of Arts and Letters.

1960

25 April	Publication of *All the King's Men: A Play.* Warren said it was the version with which he was most pleased, although he continued to tinker with the Willie Stark story.
May	Publication of *The Scope of Fiction,* a shorter version of *Understanding Fiction.*
31 August	Publication of *You, Emperors, and Others: Poems, 1957–1960,* his fifth volume of poetry.

1961

27 February	Publication of *The Legacy of the Civil War: Meditations on the Centennial,* of which Warren signed one thousand copies of the trade edition.
Spring	Makes a recording of his poetry for the Yale Series of Recorded Poets.
27–29 April	*Ballad of a Sweet Dream of Peace* is performed at the Loeb Drama Center Experimental Theatre, Harvard University.
May	Travels to France. The Warrens stay in Brittany, where Warren works on poems and on his next novel, *Flood.* They return home in September.
September	Agrees to rejoin the Yale University faculty as professor of English, a position he holds until his retirement thirteen years later on a one-term-per-year arrangement.
15 November	Publication of *Wilderness: A Tale of the Civil War,* his seventh novel, in conjunction with the centennial of the beginning of the war.

1962

May — Travels to France for the summer. The Warrens stay in northern France, where he continues work on *Flood* and Eleanor works on her book, *The Oysters of Locmariaquer.*

20 October — Publication of "Why Do We Read Fiction?" in *The Saturday Evening Post.*

1963

April — Speaks on the history of the notion of alienated writers at a world affairs symposium at Princeton University; other participants include Allen Ginsberg, Bernard Malamud, and Edward Albee.

1964

May — Publication of *Flood: A Romance of Our Time,* his eighth novel, which is based on the Johnstown Flood.

29 November — Brooks writes from London, England, referring to their work, along with R. W. B. Lewis, on *American Literature: The Makers and the Making* (working title at the time was "Understanding American Literature"), an American literature anthology published by St. Martin's Press ten years later.

1965

27 May — Publication of *Who Speaks for the Negro?,* based on Warren's interviews with civil rights leaders and his travel through the South.

1966

June — Travels to France. The Warrens spend the summer in Ile de Port-Cros and move to Magagnosc in the fall. Warren works on his next novel, *Meet Me in the Green Glen,* and on poems collected in *Incarnations: Poems, 1966–1968.* They remain abroad into the following year.

7 October — Publication of *Selected Poems: New and Old, 1923–1966,* his sixth volume of poetry, simultaneously in a trade edition and in a limited, signed edition of 250 boxed copies. Random House publishes limited, signed editions of Warren's fiction and poetry until the early 1980s. The new poems are grouped under the title "Tale of Time."

1967

February — Receives the Bollingen Prize for poetry for *Selected Poems, New and Old, 1923–1966.*

March — Travels to Egypt after a brief sojourn in Italy. After about two weeks in Egypt, they return to Ile de Port-Cros where they remain until their departure for home at the end of August.

29 August — Publication of *Randall Jarrell, 1914–1965,* co-edited by Warren, Robert Lowell, and Peter Taylor.

1968

16 October — Publication of *Incarnations: Poems, 1966–1968,* his seventh volume of poetry.

1969

20 November — Publication of *Audubon: A Vision,* his eighth volume of poetry.

1970

21 July   Announced as the winner of the National Medal of Literature for 1970; the presentation of the award occurs in December.

24 November   Publication of *Selected Poems of Herman Melville.*

1971

2 June   Publication of *John Greenleaf Whittier's Poetry.*

August   Travels to France, staying mainly in Grenoble in May 1972.

27 August   Publication of *Homage to Theodore Dreiser, August 27, 1871–December 18, 1945, on the Centennial of His Birth,* which includes a three-sequence poem, "Portrait," by Warren.

4 October   Publication of *Meet Me in the Green Glen,* Warren's ninth novel, which has elements of a murder mystery.

1972

Fall   Chosen by Yale University students for the Ten Best Teachers Award.

1973

May   Publication of *American Literature: The Makers and the Making,* co-edited by Warren, Brooks, and R. W. B. Lewis.

June   Retires from Yale University and is named professor emeritus.

1974

May   Warren delivers the Third Annual Jefferson Lecture in the Humanities, sponsored by the National Endowment for the Humanities.

3 July   Death of John Crowe Ransom; Warren gives a eulogy in December.

Fall   Teaches as a distinguished professor at Hunter College.

7 October   Publication of *Or Else–Poem/Poems, 1968–1974,* his ninth volume of poetry.

1975

19 February   Broadcast of *Brother to Dragons* on public television. Warren plays a cameo role as the writer's father in this adaptation by Adrian Hall and Ken Campbell.

July   *Democracy and Poetry,* Warren's 1974 Jefferson Lecture in the Humanities, is published by Harvard University Press.

August   Travels to Italy. The Warrens stay near Florence, where he works on poetry and his tenth novel, *A Place to Come To.* They return home in January 1976.

1976

May   *Or Else–Poem/Poems, 1968–1974* receives the Copernicus Award of the Academy of American Poets.

1977

January   Publication of *Selected Poems, 1923–1975,* his tenth volume of poetry; the section of new poems is titled "Can I See Arcturus from Where I Stand?"

March   Publication of *A Place to Come To,* his tenth, and last, novel.

17 May	Travels to Greece with the Vann Woodwards for what Warren calls "a little knockabout sailing tour of the islands."

1978

September	Publication of *Now and Then: Poems 1976–1978,* his eleventh volume of poetry.

1979

23 January	Publication of *Katherine Anne Porter: A Collection of Critical Essays.*
9 February	Death of Allen Tate, to whom Warren dedicates the poem "Eagle Descending," in *Being Here: Poems 1977–1980.*
17 April	Awarded second Pulitzer Prize in poetry for *Now and Then.*
September	Publication of *Brother to Dragons: A New Version.* Warren describes how he revised his original 1953 work in his foreword.
December	Publication of *Two Poems* by the Palaemon Press, a small Winston-Salem, North Carolina, publisher that subsequently brings out several broadsides and folios of Warren's poetry.

1980

25 February	Publication of "Jefferson Davis Gets His Citizenship Back" in *The New Yorker;* it is published in December by the University Press of Kentucky. Warren was inspired to write the essay after his attending ceremonies in 1979 to honor the former president of the Confederacy, a Kentuckian. He not only reflects on Davis's tragic career but also on history and the modern South.
17 March	Writes Brooks that the contracts have been signed and the opera *Willie Stark* is completed; it premieres the next year, composed by Carlisle Floyd.
July	Publication of *Being Here: Poetry 1977–1980,* his twelfth volume of poetry.
29–30 October	Celebration of Warren's seventy-fifth birthday at the University of Kentucky; presentations are published in the *Kentucky Review* the following spring.
31 October	Reunites with Brooks, Lyle Lanier, Andrew Lytle, and other remaining Fugitives and Agrarians in Nashville; their discussion is edited by William C. Havard and Walter Sullivan in *A Band of Prophets* two years later.

1981

24 April	*Willie Stark,* the opera, premieres in Houston on Warren's seventy-sixth birthday; it opens at the Kennedy Center in Washington, D.C., on 4 May. The Warrens attend both performances.
15 May	Warren receives a MacArthur Foundation Prize Fellowship.
August	Publication of *Rumor Verified: Poems, 1979–1980,* his thirteenth book of poems; Eleanor Clark did not like the working title "Have You Ever Eaten Stars?"
October	Travels to Montana to visit Bear Paw battlefield before finishing his poem about Chief Joseph.
November	Travels to North Africa. The Warrens ride camels in the central Sahara desert in southern Algeria with Gabriel and his wife, Ana. The experience inspires Warren to write poems and his wife to publish the book *Thirteen Days in the Sahara.*

1982

Spring   Publication of *Chief Joseph of the Nez Perce, Who Called Themselves the Nimpau–"The Real People,"* Warren's fourteenth volume of poetry, in a limited, signed edition. The first trade edition is published the following March.

1984

March   Travels to Oxford for the eightieth-anniversary celebration of Rhodes Scholarships.

1985

March   Publication of *New and Selected Poems, 1923–1985,* his fifteenth book of poetry. The new poems are collected in a section titled "Altitudes and Extensions."

16 May   Awarded the American Academy and Institute of Arts and Letters Gold Medal for poetry.

8 August   Undergoes surgery for cancer in Boston.

1986

26 February   Appointed the first U.S. poet laureate. The term of the initial appointment is two years; however, for health reasons, Warren serves only one year.

June   Travels to the Orkney Islands.

9 June   Yale University buys the Robert Penn Warren Papers, which have been on deposit in the Beinecke Rare Book and Manuscript Library.

1987

Spring   Publication of *The Essential Melville.*

July   Publication of *A Robert Penn Warren Reader,* edited by Erskine, who consulted with Warren.

1988

24 April   The Center for Robert Penn Warren Studies is dedicated at Western Kentucky University, Bowling Green; Rosanna delivers the keynote address.

18 June   Publication of *Portrait of a Father,* a memoir about his father, family lineage, and the mystery of the past. The volume includes his sequence of poems "Mortmain."

1989

March   Publication of *New and Selected Essays.* Erskine selects the essays and makes only minor changes.

June   Official opening of The Robert Penn Warren Birthplace Museum, at the corner of Third and Cherry Streets, Guthrie, Kentucky; it is formally dedicated 21 April 1990.

15 September   Death of Robert Penn Warren in West Wardsboro, Vermont. A private funeral for family and a few friends is held in Stratton, Vermont, on 8 October.

Launching a Career: 1905–1933

While traveling to Berkeley to start his M.A. program at the University of California, twenty-year-old Robert Penn Warren described his approach to poetry in an 8 August 1925 letter to his friend Andrew Lytle:

I think that my philosophy of poetry is right, at least for me, who am a relativist and who consequently would not erect it into a reified criterion. I feel that it is right, but I also know this, that my method demands discipline; it is too romantic in essence with too much sarcasm. I have never achieved a real irony which is the true alloy. If I may pursue a metallurgical metaphor, sarcasm is a sort of plating that flakes off and is not integral, while a true irony alloys the softer ore of romanticism and makes it usable. I speak for myself alone, but sarcasm, which has passed for irony with me, has usually meant a rejection of the poem in which it appears. It is a confession that you are ashamed of what you have said, and the sort of self mockery which this means is creatively suicide. I have felt the trouble vaguely but have not been able to phrase it for lack of self honesty.

—Selected Letters of Robert Penn Warren, volume 1, edited by William Bedford Clark (Baton Rouge: Louisiana State University Press, 2000), pp. 70–71

As a young man Warren sought to define himself through his writing, especially his poetry. In a 1977 interview with Benjamin De Mott, Warren recalled that his consuming interest in writing began early:

Both fiction and poetry became—poetry very early—for me a way of life. I had to live into them, had to have them. But there is a difference. Poetry is a more direct way of trying to know the self, to make sense of experience—freer from *place,* so though all my novels have Southern settings, I have poems involving Crete, Italy, France and even Vermont—or rather involving me and a relation to my life there.

—Benjamin De Mott, "Talk with Robert Penn Warren," New York Times Book Review, 9 January 1977, p. 22

His creative interests were quickened early in his hometown of Guthrie, Kentucky.

Robert Penn Warren in 1934, after he had joined the faculty at Louisiana State University (Louisiana State University Photograph Collection, LSU Archives, LSU Libraries, Baton Rouge)

Kentucky Beginnings

Born 24 April 1905 to Robert Franklin Warren and Anna Ruth Penn Warren, Robert Penn Warren grew up in a cultured home. The house the Warrens rented in Guthrie, Kentucky, a town at a railroad junction, was on the corner of Third and Cherry Streets. It survives today as the Robert Penn Warren Birthplace Museum. In 1904 Anna Ruth Warren taught school in her home; and from the titles Warren mentions in his interviews and his writing, the house must have been filled with books.

Warren was the oldest of three siblings. His sister, Mary Cecilia, born about twenty-two months after him, followed in her mother's footsteps as a teacher, and his brother, William Thomas, about six years his junior, became a grain dealer. Warren's father

Warren's parents, Anna Ruth Penn and Robert Franklin Warren (courtesy of Mrs. Robert D. Frey)

held a variety of jobs—clerk in a dry-goods store, bank clerk and cashier, investor—but his unfulfilled passions were poetry and the law. A well-read man who had studied Greek on his own, Warren's father on at least one occasion had seen some of his poems in print, a fact his son discovered when he "was about eleven or twelve":

> . . . I was idly prowling in a bookcase and happened to find, flat against the wall behind other books in proper places, a thick black volume. The title was *The Poets of America.* I certainly had no particular interest in poetry, but I idly happened to open the book. By accident—or was there a reason why the book came open there?—it had opened to a page with the name of my father in print across the top. Below, at the head of the left column on that page there was a photograph of my father as a young man. He must then have been about twenty-two or perhaps twenty-three. There were several poems on the page. His poems. The discovery was, in itself, a profound and complex surprise. Of what nature I cannot remember.
>
> I could not wait for my father to come home. When he did get there I showed him the book. He took it, examined it, and wordlessly walked away with it. That was the last time I was ever to see it.
>
> Many years later, long after his death, I happened to mention the episode to a friend. Later the friend sent me a photostat of the title page of the book and of the page of

The Warrens with their children, circa 1910: left to right, Mary Cecilia, Robert Penn, and William Thomas (courtesy of Mrs. Robert D. Frey)

FAMILY RECORD

Name.	Place of Birth.
Robt Penn Warren	Guthrie, Todd Co. Ky.
Mary Cecilia Warren	" " " "
Wm S Thomas Warren	" " " "
Vivian Ruth Warren daughter of Wm Thos Warren + Alice Proctor Warren	
Tommie Louise Warren daughter Wm Thos + Alice B. Warren, at Clarksville Hospital, Tenn	
Sandra Alice Warren	" " " "
Shirley Ann Barber. daughter of Mary C Warren Barber & H E Barber.	

The family Bible with birth dates and wedding dates of Warren as well as his sister, brother, and four of his nieces (courtesy of Mrs. Robert D. Frey)

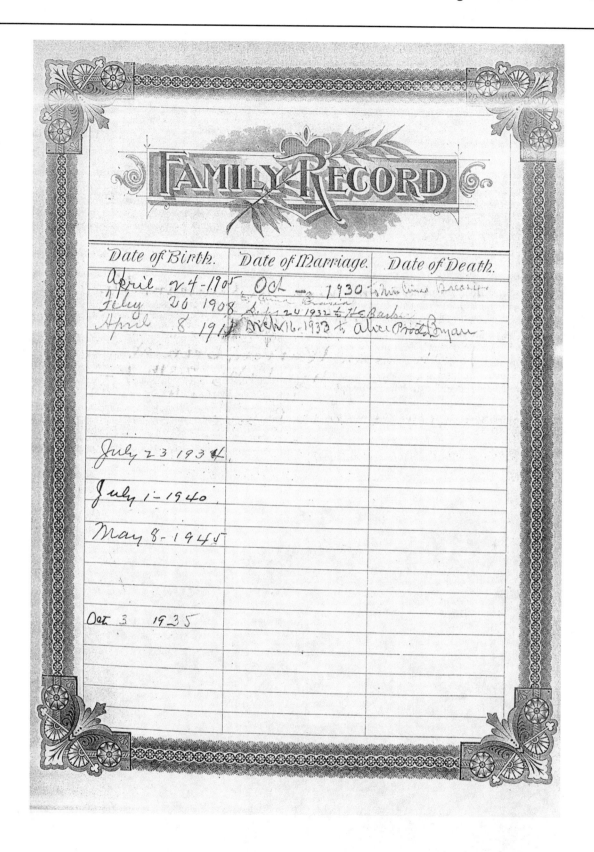

FAMILY RECORD

Date of Birth.	Date of Marriage.	Date of Death.
April 24-1905	Oct — 1930	to Marlínez Brown
Feby 20 1908	Sept 24 1932	to H.E Bash
April 8 1911	Nov 16 1933	to Alice Brooks Bryan
July 23 1938		
July 1-1940		
May 8-1945		
Oct 3 1935		

the photograph and the poems. He had advertised for the book and bought a copy of what must have been that old "vanity publication." I was later to learn that my sister, a little younger than I, had finally encountered the book again hidden by our father, and had simply, as she said, "stolen" it. He had not managed to destroy it, after all.

—*Portrait of a Father* (Lexington: University Press of Kentucky, 1988), pp. 40–41

Warren's maternal grandfather, Gabriel Thomas Penn, lived near Cerulean, Kentucky, about thirty-five to forty miles northwest of Guthrie. Warren spent his summers on his grandfather's farm:

Grandpa's house gave me my impression of a "home place"—the vital center of life. But I soon began to realize that it was a home place only for me, and in a very special way. Nobody ever came there except on business, and business was always cut brief. Only one family ever came to dinner: a widow named Rawls with a son I played with, and a grown (or growing) daughter who studied elocution. I finally understood why that family came to dinner on Sunday. The gifted daughter was supposed to recite my grandfather's favorite poems by the hour, with appropriate gestures and stances. And this too often meant that her brother and I had to squirm for hours before we could break for the woods.

—*Portrait of a Father*, pp. 46–47

An Old-Time Childhood

In Warren's last volume of poetry, New and Selected Poems *(1985), one of the new poems, "Old-Time Childhood in Kentucky," suggests the importance of his childhood and his grandfather Gabriel Thomas Penn on Warren's life. In the first stanza, the speaker recalls a world that remains vivid in memory:*

When I was a boy I saw the world I was in.
I saw it for what it was. Canebrakes with
Track beaten down by bear paw. Tobacco,
In endless rows, the pink inner flesh of black fingers
Crushing to green juice tobacco worms plucked
From a leaf. The great trout,
Motionless, poised in the shadow of his
Enormous creek-boulder.
But the past and the future broke on me, as I got older.

The speaker later refers to the Civil War cavalry battle at Bryce's Crossroads in which his grandfather probably participated and recalls reading to his grandfather the "books he wanted," including James Henry Breasted's History of Egypt, *a book Warren also mentions reading to his grandfather in* Portrait of a Father. *In the penultimate stanza of the poem the speaker remembers the advice of "Grandpa": "Love / Your wife, love your get, keep your word, and / If need arises die for what men die for. There aren't / Many choices. / And remember that truth doesn't always live in the number of voices."*

Guthrie School, where Warren entered first grade in 1911. Grades 1–12 were taught in this building (Robert Penn Warren Birthplace Museum, Guthrie, Kentucky).

His summers at the farm gave Warren a rich background for his writing, for his grandfather told stories about the region and about battles he had experienced in the Civil War and passed on his keen interest in history.

* * *

One of the Warrens' neighbors in Guthrie was the Green- field family. Warren became good friends with Kent Greenfield, a boy about seven years older than he who became a major- league pitcher. In an 11 August 1987 videotaped interview with William Ferris, Warren recalled the early years of a friend who had a short baseball career and eventually "drank himself to death." Warren began talking of Greenfield when he was asked, "what are the memories of your childhood in Kentucky that you see most clearly?":

. . . And the son of that family, the youngest son, was a man named Kent Greenfield. He pitched for the New York Giants later on and had a very fine record, I've been told. You can look in the books about that.

Well, he and I were friends; he was a few years older than I. He was a natural-born woodsman and even had been training bird dogs when he was seven or eight. And there was always a crowd of dogs around him. He was a fine woodsman, and he was one of my two friends—my old boyhood friends, and later too. And we spent a lot of time in the woods. First BB guns; then, twenty-twos. I would use his twenty-two because my father wouldn't let me have a firearm. . . .

Kent was pitching a sandlot baseball game near the railroad station in Guthrie, and a man walked down the railway station, the train had stopped for water or something, and he watched the baseball game Kent was pitching. He was number 18–19, maybe. He was a drifter then. Couldn't finish high school, didn't want to. In school he had a slate and would draw a bird on a piece of paper and pass it around with the bird saying, "Shit!" That's what the bird was saying. That was in high school. Then he quit. . . .

He was seen pitching in a baseball game, and the stranger walked out and said, "Son, come here a minute." Kent had been pitching. "You're going to come to New York to this address," and he wrote out the address for him. "Now, you'll receive in about ten days or two weeks a contract from the New York Giants. They'll be putting you on a farm team first in Connecticut. You'll pitch there first. I'm recommending you. They'll keep an eye on you. You carry the letter to a lawyer to check and have the lawyer answer it." Kent thought he was kidding. It came. The next thing he was pitching—Allentown [?] first, then the Giants very quickly. . . .

–James A. Grimshaw Jr., "Robert Penn Warren: A Reminiscence," *The Gettysburg Review,* 3 (Winter 1990): 210

Kent Greenfield, Warren's boyhood friend who pitched for the New York Giants, in the mid 1920s (Robert Penn Warren Birthplace Museum, Guthrie, Kentucky)

Warren based a short story, "Goodwood Comes Back," and a poem, "American Portrait: Old Style," on his friend's life.

In this excerpted essay, Will Fridy examines Warren's relationship with Greenfield and how Warren made use of the friendship in his literary works. Fridy first interviewed Green- field in 1977 when he was working for the Kentucky Bicenten- nial Oral History Project; his essay includes parenthetical references to the tape and typescript page numbers made for the project. The text of "Goodwood Comes Back" cited here is from its appearance in the 1962 edition of The Circus in the Attic and Other Stories.

The Author and the Ballplayer

Warren's uses of Kent Greenfield in "Goodwood Comes Back" and in "American Portrait: Old Style" demonstrate how Warren shapes the products of his memory and imagination into fiction and poetry.

After the boyhood days were over, Kent Green- field left Guthrie, Kentucky, to become a pitcher for the New York Giants teams of 1924–1927, then for the Bos-

---

Early Reading

Warren discussed his memories of childhood reading in a Paris Review *interview.*

INTERVIEWERS: What were the works that were especially meaningful for you? What books were—well, doors opening?

WARREN: Well, several things come right away to mind. First of all when I was six years old, *Horatius at the Bridge,* I thought was pretty grand—when they read it to me, to be more exact.

INTERVIEWERS: And others?

WARREN: Yes, *How They Brought the Good News from Aix to Ghent* (at about age nine). I thought it was pretty nearly the height of human achievement. I didn't know whether I was impressed by riding a horse that fast or writing the poem. I couldn't distinguish between the two, but I knew there was something pretty fine going on . . . Then *Lycidas.*

INTERVIEWERS: At what age were you then?

WARREN: Oh, thirteen, something like that. By that time I knew it wasn't what was happening in the poem that was important—it was the poem. I had crossed the line.

INTERVIEWERS: An important frontier, that. What about prose works?

WARREN: Then I discovered Buckle's *History of Civilization.* Did you ever read Buckle?

INTERVIEWERS: Of course, and Motley's *Rise of the Dutch Republic.* Most Southern bookshelves contain that.

WARREN: . . . And Prescott . . . and *The Oregon Trail* is always hovering around there somewhere. Thing that interested me about Buckle was that he had the one big answer to everything: *geography.* History is all explained by geography. I read Buckle and then I could explain everything. It gave me quite a hold over the other kids, they hadn't read Buckle. I had the answer to everything. Buckle was my Marx. That is, he gave you one answer to everything, and the same dead-sure certainty. After I had had my session with Buckle and the one-answer system at the age of 13, or whatever it was, I was somewhat inoculated against Marx and his one-answer system when he and the depression hit me when I was about twenty-five. I am not being frivolous about Marx. I know how much we and the world we live in are conditioned by him and how deep some of his insights are. But when I began to hear some of my friends talk about him in 1930, I thought, "Here we go again, boys." I had previously got hold of one key to the universe. Buckle. And somewhere along the way I had lost the notion that there was ever going to be just one key.

–Ralph Ellison and Eugene Walter, "The Art of Fiction XVIII: Robert Penn Warren," *Paris Review,* 4 (Spring–Summer 1957): 114–116

---

ton Braves teams of 1927–1929; he ended his major-league career with the Brooklyn Dodgers in 1929.[1] The *New York Times* said of him: "Greenfield broke into the limelight last season with several winning games and is counted upon as one of the star pitchers of the staff for the coming campaign" (9 February 1926, p. 19, Col. 5). Greenfield was very successful until he succumbed to his nemesis–"booze." Later, the same newspaper states:

Neither [Hugh] McQuillan nor Kent Greenfield has been very successful this season. . . . Greenfield has been a complete loss. McGraw gave him every opportunity to make good by putting him in to finish up close games, often in the face of criticism. Kent just couldn't stem the tide, however, and invariably was rapped for a run or two more, which in most cases cost the Giants the game. (12 June 1927, p. 4, Col. 4)[2]

So Greenfield returned to Guthrie, his proper place. As he put it: "I always came home 'cause I loved it down here. . . . No, I couldn't get out of New York quick enough" (#7620, 29). He came home–*literally*–to drink whisky and to raise his bird dogs.

Robert Penn Warren, on the other hand, was only able to "return" home *literarily.* He explains in a 1977 interview with Benjamin DeMott:

I began to look for a place down there, but suddenly I saw it was a different world. The people aren't the same . . . not the kind I had known–with a civic sense you might say, and a certain personal worth. So we are stuck with a new world. . . . If I had a farm there now I'd have to go get in my car and go somewhere to find somebody to talk to. Nobody to just sit on the corner of the fence and pass the time of day with. . . . I suddenly realized I would be a stranger forever.[3]

. . . .

Warren's literary reconstruction of his childhood friend Kent Greenfield is a special part of that "return." Whenever he came home to Guthrie, Warren usually visited Greenfield. Greenfield recalled such visits:

Like I said, up until he was thirteen or fourteen, we played together, and after that he was just gone. And the only time I would ever see him is when he'd come

Warren's father, far right, in front of his store in Guthrie, circa 1914. The other men, left to right, are W. E. Rogers, J. A. Goodman, C. P. Allensworth, T. C. Rawlings, and Mr. Watkins (courtesy of Mrs. Robert D. Frey).

back ever' once in a great while. He'd always call me up or come see me. . . . But we always had a good relationship, you know, and talk old times. (#7630, 3)

Warren incorporates such casual visits into "Goodwood Comes Back" and into "American Portrait: Old Style." In "Goodwood" the two young men meet and talk, but seem rather remote. At the time "Goodwood" was published (1941), Warren and Greenfield had drifted apart. Greenfield had returned home a failure, or at least as Floyd C. Watkins put it, "a cheap imitation of the big league pitcher he might have become."[4] Thus, the image of Greenfield reflected in the character Goodwood is more harshly realistic, less sympathetic than the image of "K" in "American Portrait"; yet in both works, the representation is accurate and even compassionate in places. In "Goodwood" Warren focuses upon the ball player in his decline, but the details of their acquaintance are accurate.

Even Warren's description of the "Goodwood" house and family is consistent with the memories Mrs. Nanny B. Dorris (Greenfield's sister), and Greenfield himself, had of the Greenfield home (#7620, 53). In the short story, Warren wrote:

The Goodwood house was a man's house with six men sitting down to the table, counting the grandfather, and Mrs. Goodwood and her daughter going back and forth to the kitchen. . . . There would be men's coats on the chairs in the living room, sometimes hunting coats

with old blood caked on the khaki, balls of twine and a revolver on the mantel-piece, and shotguns and flyrods lying around. . . . And the bird dogs came in the house whenever they got good and ready. (pp. 108–109)

Mrs. Dorris concurred that it was a man's house, and that, although her mother was an excellent housekeeper, the hunting dogs were allowed into the house on occasions.[5]

Warren also described Luke Goodwood as being as "Good a shot as you ever hope to see" (p. 110). Tom Allensworth, a contemporary of Warren and Greenfield, also remembers Greenfield as an excellent shot: "Whenever he went to a shooting gallery, they would not let him shoot for a prize. He was too good."[6] Maxie Finn, another contemporary, said: "He could throw a rock to win a gun back"; and "Kent could get drunk and still hit a dime with a rifle."[7] Thus, when Luke Goodwood boasts "I still got control boys," after hitting a distant telephone pole with a rock to prove to some locals that he can control his "likker" (p. 114), Warren is being consistent with his memory of Greenfield if not consistent with reality. Warren uses that same memory in 1978 in "American Portrait" when he writes:

Like young David at brookside, he swooped down,
Snatched a stone, wound up, and let fly,
And on a high pole over yonder the big brown insulator
Simply exploded. "See—I still got control!" he said.[8]

The Warren home at Third and Cherry Streets in Guthrie, circa 1915 (Robert Penn Warren Birthplace Museum, Guthrie, Kentucky)

Watkins points to a possible glitch in Warren's memory of this incident: "Kent told me that he destroyed the insulator *before* he left Guthrie and played baseball in the major leagues" (p. 161). In this instance, Warren takes the episode out of the milieu of his memory and arranges it into the sequence of his plot to arrive at the truth of his specific story and poem. When the event actually occurred is secondary in importance to the meaning of the event in the story and poem.

Although there are numerous other parallels between the memories recorded on the tapes of my interviews and the details of the short story, these will suffice to illustrate how Warren's imagination transformed the facts of memory into art.

The conclusion of "Goodwood," however, goes beyond the record of Warren's memory and is purely imaginative. Greenfield, unlike Goodwood, did not marry a woman whose brother murdered him. He did, however, marry, and he did "die" in importance to many who thought they knew him. "Goodwood" would seem to indicate that he had also faltered in Warren's esteem.

In spite of Warren's somewhat negative image of Greenfield as Goodwood in "Goodwood Comes Back," the memories shared by these two old friends continued and deepened over the years. Greenfield reflected this closeness when he said: "I really, to tell you the truth, I like the kid. He was one of my best friends" (#7620, 21).

Greenfield also mentioned what he called a "valentine" Warren had sent him when they were boys. On it, he remembered, was inscribed "Kent is a good boy." Greenfield continued: "And after he got to be famous and moved up in Connecticut, I sent it to him with a request that he'd send it back, and he did. And he sent me a picture of his children" (#7620, 13–14). Warren's reaction to the "valentine" episode is expressed in the following excerpt from a letter he wrote to me:

> It wasn't a "valentine"–God No. It was a Christmas card. I remember it distinctly. I had printed cards for several friends and Kent's showed Santa Claus looking over his ledger–on the left page "Bad Boys," on the right page "Good Boys," where Kent headed the list. I was about 7 or 8 then. Some 40 years later, Kent sent the card back to me with a note saying simply: "Please return Kent." I returned it. Needless to say, I was deeply touched by the episode.[9]

This long-lasting and touchingly close friendship is echoed in another memory and response. Greenfield, recalling their childhood, mused: "I remember this–that 'Horatio at the Bridge' stuck in my craw, because he would recite it, you know, to me, and he'd make gestures, you know, those soldiers on the bridge holding that army back, you know . . . and that stuck with me" (#7620, 21). Warren responded to these remarks in a letter to me dated July 17, 1979:

> I had forgotten, too, about "Horatio at the Bridge"–my then favorite poem–from which I learned to read when, after about the 1000th time, my father refused to read it to me, saying I could read it anyway. And, having unconsciously memorized it, I found that I could. Odd Kent remembering that.

Of "American Portrait," with its more positive and accurate assessment of Kent Greenfield, the Reverend Frank Qualls Cayce, a long-time acquaintance of Warren's, said the following (May 28, 1978): "The great poem about Kent Greenfield . . . the baseball player . . . The warmth of Red's hero worship of this person . . . is so healthy" (#7660). In the poem, the nostalgia is thick as memories of youth spurt to life in nostalgia touching on elegy. As Wade Hall wrote in his review of *Now and Then,* "American Portrait: Old Style" depicts the poet back home visiting "a companion of his youth, now an old man."[10] Warren not only recalls some of his and Greenfield's childhood and life experiences but also ruminates upon their aging, their impending deaths, and the meaning of it all.

. . . .

Thus, Warren's imagination, when focused upon his memory of Greenfield and him as boys playing in the trench envisioning chickens in the roles of Indians and Bluebellies (or Yankees)–in what Watkins aptly termed their "post-frontier" days (p. 139)–provided what he calls in the poem "the lie we must learn to live by" or "what imagination is": memory with meaning.

Warren further expanded his memories of "the trench." Although Greenfield remembered this as simply "diggin' out tunnels" (#7620, 11), Warren transformed the trench into the image of the grave that is the focus of his reflections upon his own and "Ks'" mortality: "the trench, six feet long. / And wide enough for a man to lie down in." The tone becomes elegiac when Warren turns from his memories to thoughts of his own death:

Late, late, toward sunset, I wandered
Where old dreams had once been life's truth, and where
I saw the trench of our valor, now nothing
But a ditch full of late-season weed-growth
Beyond the rim of shade.

There was nobody there, hence no shame to be saved
    from, so I
Just lie in the trench on my back and see high,
Beyond the tall ironweed stalks, or oak leaves
If I happen to look that way,
How the late summer's thinned-out sky moves,
From *where* on to *where,* and I wonder
What it will be like to die,
Like the nameless old skull in the swamp, lost,
And know yourself dead under
The infinite motion of the sky.

But why should I lie here longer?
I am not dead yet, though in years,
And the world's way is yet long to go,
And I love the world even in my anger,
And love is a hard thing to outgrow. (VII–VIII)

Here Warren's memory, filtered through his naturalistic focus, is expanded and transformed by love. His naturalistic knowledge allowed him to see the Goodwood in Kent Greenfield; but his affirmation of love enables the poet to transcend the harsh reality of Goodwood and thereby see in Greenfield the qualities of "K." These two perspectives are two halves of a whole, and they provide the essential meaning of the man Kent Greenfield. Greenfield was in this world, but he was also somehow above it. Warren best conveys the transcendent qualities of the man when he writes:

Well, what I remember most
. . . .
Is how K, through lane-dust or meadow,
Seemed never to walk, but float
With a singular joy and silence,
In his cloud of bird dogs, like angels,
With their eyes on his like God,
And the sun on his uncut hair bright
. . . .
Polite in his smiling, but never much to say.

(IV, 1, 5–10, 13)

Watercolor by Warren, circa 1919. He showed an early interest in the arts, but he did not pursue painting and later said he did not have a musical ear (courtesy of Mrs. Robert D. Frey).

Robert Penn Warren's final unpublished statement on Kent Greenfield is contained in his letter to me dated July 17, 1979. It reads:

Poor old Kent–He didn't belong in the modern world. [John J.] McGraw wouldn't let him have a farm in Connecticut for the bird dogs he had brought up. Wouldn't let him go to a gym from 8:30–12 AM–"Wouldn't be fresh for the game." To which Kent replied: "I never get tired." But McGraw was adamant–and that, Kent said, started his morning drinking. "Night drinking," he said, "never hurt anybody." There were girls of course (he being extremely handsome), but he said, "You know a girl doesn't take forever, and a man can't spend all his time at that." So booze. The Army nearly cured him. And after his [discharge], he tried to take old likker pals out to his farm and reform them–some of my old high school classmates. Usually, no dice. So finally Kent began to drink again, and, when his wife got cancer and then became a terminal case, he took to it hard. He should have been with Lewis and Clark on their Pacific expedition–or something like that. A hero of an earlier age, [wasted] in ours.

–Will Fridy, "The Author and the Ballplayer:
    An Imprint of Memory in the Writings of
    Robert Penn Warren," *Mississippi Quarterly,*
    44 (Spring 1991): 159–166

—

1. For an account of Greenfield's baseball career, see Joseph L. Reicher, ed. *Baseball Encyclopedia* (New York: Macmillan, 1988).
2. The *Baseball Encyclopedia* lists Greenfield's win/loss record in the major leagues as follows: 1924, 0/1; 1925, 12/8; 1926, 13/12; 1927, 2/2 for the New York Giants and 11/14 for the Boston Braves; 1928, 3/11; 1929, 6/0 for Boston and 5/0 for the Brooklyn Dodgers. Greenfield's six-year win/loss record was 41/48.
3. Benjamin DeMott, "Talk with Robert Penn Warren," *The New York Times Book Review,* 9 January 1977, p. 24.
4. Floyd C. Watkins, *Then and Now* (Lexington: University Press of Kentucky, 1982), p. 140.
5. Telephone interview with Nanny B. Dorris, 22 January 1977.
6. Telephone interview with Tom Allensworth, 19 January 1979.
7. Telephone interview with Maxie Finn, 19 January 1979.
8. "American Portrait: Old Style," *Now and Then: Poems 1976–1978* (New York: Random House, 1978), VI, 25–28.
9. Letter to Will Fridy, 19 July 1979, in my personal collection.
10. Wade Hall, in *The Courier Journal,* 11 February 1979, D:5:1–3.

Clarksville High School

Warren skipped three grades during his years at Guthrie School, graduating in 1920 at the age of fifteen. He wanted to attend the United States Naval Academy, but he was then too young to be admitted. Based on the advice of one of his teachers, he and his parents decided he should enter Clarksville High School in Tennessee as a special student. Respected academically, "The School," as it was known, was a fortunate choice for Warren, who continued to excel in his studies and began to write stories for the student journal, The Purple and Gold.

Clarksville also had the advantage for Warren of being away from home and parental supervision, especially the control of his mother, which he had begun to resist. At the beginning of his year at the high school Warren rode the train from Guthrie to Clarksville and returned each evening, but his father later arranged for him to board in the town during the week. This excerpt from a newspaper article describes Warren's earliest published writings.

Depot in Guthrie where Warren boarded a train to commute to Clarksville High School in 1920
(Robert Penn Warren Birthplace Museum, Guthrie, Kentucky)

The First Day of School

It was on the unlucky thirteenth
of September that I boarded
the train at Guthrie to come
to Clarksville to enter the
C. H. S. It was with fear
and much trembling that
I entered Mr. Smith's office
to enroll. I was told to have
a seat and wait — and I
waited, and waited, and
waited. Nine o'clock, ten
o'clock, half-past ten and
eleven rolled by and still
I sat — and waited.
Meanwhile the opening
exercises had been concluded, —

Essay Warren wrote about his first day of classes at Clarksville High School (courtesy of Mrs. Robert D. Frey, used by permission of Shirley Ring)

pupils had come, received their assignments and gone; others came and departed but still I waited— "Patience on a monument." But at last patience was rewarded, and Miss Bailey summoned me to her desk to be classified. She asked me how many years I had had in high school and I replied, "Three."

"Have you your last grade card?" In my wild excitement, I produced, after much fumbling, a report, reading:—

"Robert Penn Warren
    8th Grade".
    Imagine my confusion;
frantically, I ran through
my pockets and finally
came upon the object of
my search.
    Before the task of class-
ification was half completed,
Mr. Moore suggested that
it was time for dinner.
On my return to the
school building after
lunch, there began a
series of consultations,
alternately with the

schedule and my desires.
At some time near two, my
admission card was handed
to me and I was a bona-
fide member of the
student body of the
Clarksville High School.

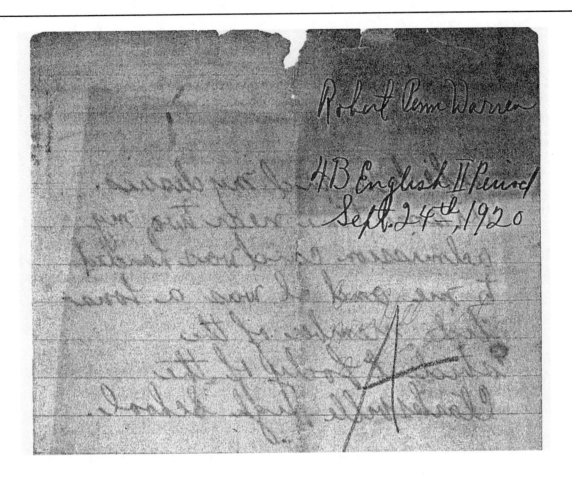

Warren's report card after the first term of his senior year (Stuart Wright Collection; Special Collections, Vanderbilt University)

The Purple and Gold

PUBLISHED MONTHLY BY THE STUDENTS OF THE HIGH SCHOOL
SUBSCRIPTION, 75c PER YEAR.

MUNK

Well ole Charlie Darwin may be right, I dunno, but sometimes it seems like 'e wuz. Once I knowed er man that mighter supported 'is idea pretty wal. I guess he must 'a been the missing link er what ever you call it. 'E claimed his name uz Gregor, James Gregor, sir 'e uster say. But his mates in the fo'cas'le called him Munk an so far as looks went 'e certainly deserved the name. 'E wuzent er tall man but broad across the chist with shoulders 'at aluz made me think uv an ape, an with long hairy arms 'anging almost ter his knees an er head covered with long black hair all tangled an matted. But it uz 'iz face that made me think most 'at he uz 'ardly er man. 'Is forehead uz low an 'is nose flat an broad lak er ape's an 'is chin stuck out pass the rest uv his face while 'is teeth uz long an yellow when 'e opened 'is mouth ter snarl at one uv his mates 'at happened ter speak ter him.

At that time I uz first mate on er brig tradin in rum, sugar, coffee er most any thing 'at could be got 'tween the Wes' Indies an London. I didn't like the fellow's face from the first an I never would 'ave shipped 'im if able seamen haden't been mighty scarce at the time. Anyway I did an I regretted it most all the voyage. Gregor uz wer mean sullen brute, disobedient an insiubordnate an al'uz quarrelin' an wranglin' with the rest uv the crew. By the time we had left the Canaries he 'ad beat half the men in the fo'cas'le an every bit uv the trouble with the crew might be traced ter Gregor. 'E simply had the spirit uv er beast in the body uv er man. 'E never used er knife—that wasn't in 'is line. 'E just bit an tore an clawed lak the big beast 'e wuz, an ape er a gorilla. A man he had 'ammered up at the first uv the voyage tr,ed ter

First page of what is believed to be Warren's earliest published short story, which appeared in the February 1921 issue of the monthly student publication at Clarksville High School (Robert Penn Warren Center, Clarksville, Tennessee, used by permission of Clarksville High School)

SENIOR CREED

I believe in the omnipotent Seniors, wearers of the cap and gown and in their power and prestige in C. H. S.; in the various trials and vicissitudes of their career, beginning in Howell and continuing into the High School under the leadership of Moore and the watchful eye of Miss Bailey; in the kindly guidance of Miss Foust, our sponsor, and in every member of the faculty who has had a hand in the shaping of our destiny. I believe in the tenacity and perseverence of the entire Class of '21; in the ability of Michael, our President; in the literary productions of Dorothy and Bessie, our editors; in the grace and beauty of Virginia, our queen; in the line-bucking propensities of John D. and Niles; in the flirtations of Harry, in the redness of Bill Penn's head, the antics of Bogus and the wit of Pick. I believe in the glories of our past; in the honors of our present; in the brilliancy of our future. I believe in ignoring the Freshmen; in teaching unto the "Sophs" better manners and in enduring the Juniors. Amen.

R. P. W., '21.

Warren's class creed for the graduating seniors of Clarksville High School was published in the April 1921 issue of
The Purple and Gold *(Robert Penn Warren Center, Clarksville, Tennessee).*

Writing for *The Purple and Gold*

Every school day started and ended with his riding the Pullman which passed through gently rolling, cultivated fields of corn and tobacco, by ponds ringed with groves of poplar and elm.

There were three stops on this "milk run" from Guthrie to Clarksville—Tate, Hampton, and St. Bethlehem stations—and the ride lasted 30 to 40 minutes.

. . . .

In the class of '21 history, recorded in the Purple and Gold, the monthly students' magazine, Dorothy Traughber wrote: "For Better Speech Week, during the first term, our Society presented a play entitled, 'Dr. Good English and His Patients.' This play was written by Robert Penn Warren, one of our most talented members."

The 1920–21 Purple and Golds contain several works by Warren. Short stories entitled "Munk" [February 1921] and "The Dream of a Driller" [April 1921] may be his earliest published works.

"Munk" is an uplifting narrative of a Russian Royal Guard turned seaman who is repulsive to the rest of the crew—and the reader—until he gives his life to save a child from a shark attack. Warren here experimented with a crusty sea accent.

In "Driller," he related the dream of an oilman as the derrick plunges into the earth. He traces the evolution of oil from prehistoric times to the moment the gusher appears.

Both stories are marked by keen description, smooth development, and a firm resolution. The tip of his talent was clearly emerging.

These early themes followed him in his writing. Munk was a grotesque character seemingly without a past but who accepted responsibility and identity in death. "Driller" dealt with technology and merging past with present.

In one issue of the student magazine, he wrote as secretary of the Senior Society, a literary group, and summarized a play he had written in two sentences.

Maybe he was modest. Maybe he didn't want credit.

In another issue, the society's minutes show he reported on "The Present Situation in Ireland." Finally, he wrote the senior creed and alluded to himself by writing, " . . . I believe in the redness of Bill Penn's head . . ."

Why Bill Penn? A Guthrie resident explained that it was a well-known fact that "his mother descended from William Penn, founder of Pennsylvania."

Robert Penn Warren's writing reflects his life in Guthrie. He was part of the changing South, his family had pride in the past, he was an inquisitive observer, he saw the passing of the Pullman, and he saw the land and knew that even it would never be the same.

–Tom Wibking, "Star's Work Seasoned
by Country Living," *Clarksville Leaf-Chronicle,*
21 February 1982, p. D-1

Warren (lower right corner) in his senior-class photograph for Clarksville High School
(Robert Penn Warren Birthplace Museum, Guthrie, Kentucky)

Becoming a Fugitive

During the spring before his graduation from Clarksville High School, an accident occurred that changed Warren's plans and forever affected his life. His young brother threw a chunk of coal into the air that hit Warren, who was lying on the other side of a hedge, in his left eye. Loss of vision in that eye cost him his appointment to the United States Naval Academy in Annapolis, as he could no longer pass the physical exam.

Warren entered Vanderbilt University and soon shifted his focus from chemical engineering to literature. He graduated from the university summa cum laude in 1925 and went on to earn an M.A. in English from the University of California–Berkeley in 1927 and a B.Litt. from Oxford University, which he attended on a Rhodes Scholarship, in 1930. As Warren relates in this excerpt from his reminiscence of Nashville, the most important part of his Vanderbilt experience was his extracurricular involvement with the group known as the Fugitives.

"Incidental and Essential":
Warren's Vanderbilt Experience

Nashville belongs to my earliest childhood memories. I was born in the little town of Guthrie, Kentucky, just over the Tennessee line some fifty miles north of the city, and I can remember going there with my father, first on the Kentucky and Edgefield Railroad and later by car.

A First Published Poem

In summer 1922 Warren attended the Citizens' Military Training Camp at Camp Knox, Kentucky, a half day's train ride from Guthrie. Warren's first published poem, "Prophecy," appeared in the CMTC annual.

Prophecy

You see no beauty in the parched parade,
The quivering, heat-glazed highways mile on mile,
The fields where beauty holds a debt unpaid,
The gray, drab barracks in monotonous, grim file.

You take no joy when dust wraiths dimly curl
Above the winding column crawling on far hills.
You see but short beyond the present whirl
Of circumstance, your little wrongs and petty ills.

But when it all has passed and you have lost
The swinging rhythmic cadence of the marching feet,
Then you will reck as paltry small the cost,
And memory will purge the bitter from the sweet.

–The Mess Kit (Food for Thought), edited by Edgar
Dow Gilman (Camp Knox, Ky.: Military
Training Camps Association,
1922), p. 41

In his 1995 history of the Citizens' Military Training Camps, Donald M. Kington relates his discovery of the poem. He includes a 6 March 1975 letter in which Warren confirmed his authorship:

Dear Colonel Kington,

Even if the poem is as awful as it is, I can't deny paternity. But I had, mercifully, forgotten all about it.

About the poem but not about the summer, which meant something to me.

As for the greetings to the reunion–by all means.

Even if I had never been the target of a shot fired in anger I do know what a Kentucky sun can do in July. So warmest regards to all, & I hope all shoulders could still bear the weight of a Springfield.

Warm regards to you too, sir.

Yours,

Robert Penn Warren

*–Donald M. Kington, Forgotten Summers: The Story
of the Citizens' Military Training Camps, 1921–1940*
(San Francisco: Two Decades Publishing,
1995), p. xiv

Of the train ride I can remember only the thrill of going through a tunnel, the sensation of being plunged into darkness and then being delivered from it. The trip by car was a different experience. It was practically a half-day's journey in those days, and you could always count on having at least one or two blowouts.

Of the city itself, I remember more. I lived in a small town and spent my summers on a farm, a very remote farm, with my grandfather–a Confederate veteran, a captain under Forrest, a lover of history and poetry–and in my country boy's eyes, Nashville seemed like a perfectly huge city to me. I was much impressed by its grandeur and size and scale, by its hurry and bustle. The most remarkable place to me was the Arcade, a strange and exotic structure. There was certainly nothing like that in Guthrie. And no football games there, either–my father took me every Thanksgiving to Nashville to see the Vanderbilt game.

But I didn't really see Nashville then, except in a superficial way, and even when I was a student at Vanderbilt in the 1920s, I had only surface impressions of the city. It no longer awed me. It was simply there, and I took it for granted, without giving it any thought. I had other things on my mind.

I finished high school in Guthrie when I was fifteen, and since I was a little too young for college, I spent another year at the high school in Clarksville, hoping for an appointment to Annapolis, for to be an admiral of the Pacific Fleet had been my romantic boyhood dream. I did receive the congressional appointment, but then I had an eye injury from an accident, and so I turned in disappointment to my second choice, which was Vanderbilt, and enrolled there in 1921, when I was sixteen.

My intention was to study chemical engineering, but that notion lasted only three weeks or so. Chemistry was taught primarily for pre-med students–it was very deductive, having nothing to do with the nature or philosophy of science–and that turned me away. The English classes were much more interesting. Edwin Mims taught literature one class a week–Tennyson the first term–and John Crowe Ransom taught grammar and composition two days, and they got me started. I enjoyed writing English themes and I began to dabble a little in poetry, and it didn't take me long to find out where my true interests lay.

I've always been grateful to Dr. Mims for demanding that every student memorize hundreds of lines of verse. His old-fashioned method was total immersion in poetry. It should be the new-fashioned method.

John Crowe Ransom, receiving a gift box from Kyushu Imperial University, Japan (Photographic Archives, Special Collections, Vanderbilt University)

But the two people who influenced me most at Vanderbilt were John Crowe Ransom and Donald Davidson. They were young men in their early thirties; they had been in World War I; they were writing poetry I could identify with and understand. With both men I would maintain a lifelong friendship.

Ransom's house later became almost a second home to me. He was a splendid teacher and a fascinating personality. He was a classical scholar, had been to Oxford, and he was the first real poet I had ever seen—his first book, *Poems About God,* had only been out a couple of years. When I read it, I saw Ransom making poetry out of the life and objects of my boyhood. He had grown up, as I had, in the rural upper South—his father was a very learned country parson—and Ransom had found in that familiar setting the stuff of poetry. It was strange and even disturbing to me, that discovery. In his poetry and in his performance as a teacher, I saw a first-rate mind at work. He could be distracted and uninspiring two days a week, but on the third day he might catch fire, like a man possessed, and pursue a thought into fascinating nooks and crannies, creat-ing fresh ideas before your very eyes. That's what education should be—seeing a first-rate mind catch fire. And with all that, Ransom could also be very witty and amusing.

Donald Davidson was different—a superlative teacher, very systematic, humorous only in his intensity and in his utter seriousness. He was a darkly handsome man with an intense gaze, passionate in his convictions but kindly and generous in human relations. Davidson was particularly fond of folk balladry. His father was, I think, a county school superintendent in Middle Tennessee, and Don had spent much time in the country, as I had, but he really woke me to the special beauty and poetry of the country tongue. And that's only one example of the broad impact of his teaching. Years later, I would realize how deeply he had made me feel a pleasure, a necessity, in writing, for he allowed me to write an "imitation" of an author being studied—say, a new episode of Beowulf—instead of the regular bi-weekly critique.

We had certain fundamental disagreements, Davidson and I—on poetry, on social questions. When, in later years, we would meet, there would be the first warm greeting, then I would get a stirring lec-

Donald Davidson, a member of the Fugitives (Photographic Archives, Special Collections, Vanderbilt University)

ture from him on the error of my ways. That done, old friendship and old discussions were revived, and I found again the kindliness, the warmth, the keen critical sensibility. Looking back, I see a man somewhat divided against himself—on one hand a remarkable and gifted prose writer, on the other a poet whose gift was often distorted by a literary theory and several passions. But I remember most the superlative teacher and warm-hearted friend who meant so much to me. I saw him last on a visit to his bedside at Vanderbilt Hospital, a day or two before his death. The visit was prearranged and purely personal, but brutally interrupted and taken over entirely by a stupid scholarly interviewer, notebook on knee, asking fool questions for some fool book he was writing. So the parting with Davidson was only an exchange of glances, and his grip still firm but dying.

In their quite different ways, Davidson and Ransom touched part of my experience and opened up my mind. I learned from others too—from Walter Clyde Curry, who taught Shakespeare with a real dramatic sense and a sense of scholarship. But I suppose my real university was not Vanderbilt as such—it was classmates and friends I had the good fortune to know, people whose intellectual and philosophical interests and literary tastes were sometimes far more sophisticated than my own. A peculiar feature about the little university that was the Vanderbilt of the 1920s was an active and spontaneous interest in literature and in writing among a great many students. There were two official writing clubs, "Blue Pencil" and "The Calumet," but even more unusual were the informal groups, one of which issued a book of poems, some of which actually resembled poems—though I doubt that mine did.

I recall Charles Moss and I were admitted to "Blue Pencil" at the same time. Charlie was a very handsome young man, a romantic, a humorous fellow, wonderful company, and he was also a very promising poet, but he turned instead to journalism and was for years editor of the *Nashville Banner*.

Another fellow who pops into mind was Ralph McGill, who had no interest in poetry whatsoever, not the slightest, but who was a marvelous companion. He lived on West Side Row, where a good many of the students were considered "offbeat." McGill worked as a sports writer at the *Banner*—he and Moss were both part-time reporters. The association is what I remember. We used to sit around telling tales, sharing a bottle, arguing. McGill could not have dreamed that he would become publisher of the *Atlanta Constitution*. Years after our time at Vanderbilt together, he helped me with the background material for a book I wrote on race relations in the South.

And there was William Bandy, a dashing young man, a great dancer, popular with the ladies—and mad for them. He had the air of a Frenchman, and though only an undergraduate, he was already a French scholar, especially of the poet Baudelaire. Bill Bandy ran a sort of informal French seminar in his living quarters, a kind of competing university in French. The sessions sometimes went on until four o'clock in the morning—lubricated, as often as not, with a jug of corn whiskey. He had already begun collecting the works of Baudelaire, the first step toward the famous collection he has since given to the university.

Bandy also had the only Stutz Bearcat on the campus. About three o'clock one morning, with several of us as passengers, he undertook to climb the great story-high stone flight of entrance steps to Wesley Hall in the Bearcat. He succeeded, and then made a hair-raising descent, bouncing back step by step in reverse as astonished theological heads popped out of the upper windows of the building. Bandy leveled off at the bottom and we sped away. The culprits were never identified.

Wesley Hall (now long since burned down) was an enormous brick building of Early Methodist architecture, you might say, dating back to the dark ages of the founding of the university. It was an imposing building, ugly as sin, but the theological school. However, non-theologians had crept in as rooms became vacant, for it was a wonderful place for privacy. I lived in Kissam Hall, but in my sophomore year I got into Wesley.

Ridley Wills lived there. He was a senior who had returned to finish his degree after fighting in France in World War I, and after we became acquainted, he invited me to move in with him. I was overwhelmed with pleasure and flattered beyond belief. He impressed me greatly, not just with his age and rich experience but with the fact that he was the only undergraduate who had actually published a book, a real novel in a real publishing house in far-off New York. Not only that, but he was marvelously amusing and full of anecdotes.

Soon Allen Tate, that genius of a poet, moved in with us. He was six years my senior, returning from a siege of illness to finish his degree. (For several years, Tate could not force himself to do freshman chemistry and math; finally, in spite of his aversions, he graduated *magna cum laude*.) A fourth young man, William Cobb (later to be an editor at Houghton Mifflin) came to occupy the last of our two double-decker beds. The room was a sty—dirty shirts in the corners, match stubs and cigarette butts over the floors, empty or half-empty bottles—but there was also the conversation and the poetry. Both Ridley Wills and Allen Tate were members of the Fugitives, a group of young philosophers and poets whose presence was already being felt around Vanderbilt (though the group, as such, had no relation to the university), and they were willing to look at my attempts at poetry and give me detailed criticism and long lectures on the subject.

Our room became an informal gathering place for others of like inclination, and all enjoyed the irony of a little Bohemia in the citadel of a divinity school. Merrill Moore, another member of the Fugitives,

Wesley Hall, where Warren roomed with Ridley Wills, Allen Tate, and William Cobb (Robert A. McGaw, The Vanderbilt Campus: A Pictorial History *[Nashville: Vanderbilt University Press, 1979]; Thomas Cooper Library, University of South Carolina)*

lived on the floor above us. Before the year was out, Ridley and Allen had taken me as a guest to a meeting of the group. Later, I published a poem in their magazine, *The Fugitive,* and I was invited to join. My cup truly ran over.

The first issue of *The Fugitive* had appeared in 1922, during my freshman year, with an introduction declaring whimsically that the Fugitives fled from various things but from nothing more speedily than the "magnolia and moonlight" type of Southern poetry. In fact, the magazine was primarily a manifestation of modernism, or rather a battleground for debating modernism and traditionalism. The group had been founded long before my time–before the war, in fact–but after the war there were new faces and new interests.

The original group had been more interested in philosophy than poetry. It brought together a few young professors (principally Ransom and Davidson), some local businessmen, a banker, and a Jewish sage–I have no other word for him–who presided at the meetings. The sage was Sidney Mttron Hirsch, who in younger wanderings was reputed to have been heavyweight boxing champion of the Pacific Fleet. He had lived in the Orient and in France. He was a mystic, a man of brilliant and undisciplined intellect. He was the catalyst, the magnet to whom the others were drawn. Those first meetings were held at his apartment on Twentieth Avenue South.

Hirsch and his brother, Nathaniel, and James M. Frank, who married their sister, and the Starr brothers, Alfred and Milton, were all young Jewish men in Nash-

Brooks and Warren at Vanderbilt

Cleanth Brooks and Warren, whose names later became almost inseparable in conversations about critical theory and pedagogy, first met at Vanderbilt in 1924. In this excerpt Brooks remembers his impressions of his future collaborator.

My first acquaintance with Robert Penn Warren began at Vanderbilt University in the fall of 1924. He was a senior, I, a freshman, but through a set of circumstances (of no consequence for what I have to say here) I happened to be rooming with a senior, Saville Clark, who was a good friend of Red Warren, of Andrew Lytle, and of several others who were about to launch themselves into literary careers. Warren had already done so, as a member of the Fugitive Group.

Warren was a tall, lanky, red-haired youth of nineteen, full of a wonderful energy and endowed with obvious genius. He appeared so at that time to my quite dazzled eyes and surely my youthful impression has long since been completely vindicated.

As a freshman I did not see a great deal of Warren except for the visits that he paid to the dormitory rooms that I shared with Bill Clark. But from the very beginning he was warm and kind to me, and even took an interest in my attempts to write English prose. I remember his looking over an early freshman theme–I had not asked him to do it–and giving it a commendation which I now value much more than I did at the time.

–Cleanth Brooks, "Brooks on Warren," *Four Quarters,* 21 (May 1972): 19

ville who would be identified with the Fugitive group for as long as it lasted. Sidney Hirsch and James Frank and Alfred Starr were the principal off-campus members–they and Alec B. Stevenson, a banker, whose father had taught Semitic languages at the university. From the faculty came Ransom, Davidson, Walter Clyde Curry and Stanley Johnson, and the students were Tate, Ridley Wills, Merrill Moore, Jesse Wills (Ridley's cousin), William Yandell Elliott, William Frierson and me. Laura Riding, the only woman, came late into the group from outside Nashville. There were sixteen of us in all, over the years, who were actually members and whose poems were published in the magazine.

I was an eighteen-year-old sophomore when I became acquainted with the Fugitive group in 1923, and it was an exhilarating experience to be suddenly involved in an intellectual exchange with men twice my age. It was anything but a college club. That's where I got my education, where I began to find my way in the world–and Vanderbilt was both incidental and essential to the experience.

For the remainder of my undergraduate years, *The Fugitive* was my main interest. The magazine prospered–

The Importance of *The Fugitive*

In her study of the Fugitives, Louise Cowan argues that the project of publishing their writings in a journal in large measure accounts for the coherence and influence of the group.

. . . Without *The Fugitive,* no doubt the group would have continued to meet and converse, and no doubt the most serious poets among them would have published their poetry in other journals. But the necessity of fulfilling an obligation to the outside world, of gathering material into shape so that the group would not be put to shame, of making editorial comments and conducting literary contests–these tasks precipitated quarrels, arguments, and experiments that caused a group of talented men to interact upon each other and, finally, to share in an experience of reality which has provided one of the major insights in modern literature.

–Louise Cowan, *The Fugitive Group: A Literary History* (Baton Rouge: Louisiana State University Press, 1959), p. xxiii

Front page of the 27 May 1923 special section of the Nashville newspaper (Thomas A. Underwood, Allen Tate: Orphan of the South *[Princeton & Oxford: Princeton University Press, 2000]; Richland County Public Library)*

THE FUGITIVE

VOLUME II.

No. 7

BOARD OF EDITORS

Walter Clyde Curry   Sidney Mttron Hirsch   John Crowe Ransom
Donald Davidson   Stanley Johnson   Alec. B. Stevenson
James M. Frank   Merrill Moore   Allen Tate
     Jesse Ely Wills   Ridley Wills

In Absentia: William Yandell Elliott, William Frierson.

CONTENTS

JUNE-JULY, 1923

Table of contents for the issue that included Warren's first contribution to the literary journal published by the Nashville group to which he belonged (Thomas Cooper Library, University of South Carolina)

that is, it attracted attention nationally, and even in England. It was poetry or death for me then, and some of the others shared that passion. We usually met at James Frank's home on Whitland Avenue, each of us in turn reading our poems and having them criticized by others. Among my contemporaries in the university, I became especially close to Tate and Ridley Wills, and also to Merrill Moore, who was a fascinating young man. His father was John Trotwood Moore, well-known in Nashville as a writer and a librarian. Merrill became a psychiatrist, but in those days, as ever after, he wrote sonnets.

Merrill was unique in the history of literature. Even during the Fugitive days he had settled on the sonnet form as his special concern. It became such a natural form of thought for him that even while waiting for a traffic light to change he could compose one in shorthand—or later, in the course of technological change, dictate one to a recorder. At his death in the 1950s he left several remarkable volumes in print and some 50,000 items in manuscript, shorthand or tape, in code of some kind, at the Library of Congress. He was unique as a psychological curiosity. He once joked to me, "I am my most interesting patient." Or was it a joke?

The remarkable thing is that Merrill was a highly gifted poet, not merely a peculiar prodigy. Naturally in such a massive work the percentage of really fine achievement would be relatively small, but a small percentage would constitute the life work of many a man of reputation. He had splendid flashes in his characteristic form, and the challenge to scholarship and criticism waits in those pages and tapes at the Library of Congress. He will be a discovery.

I made other friends at Vanderbilt outside the Fugitive group: Cleanth Brooks, with whom I later wrote several textbooks, and who is now generally recognized as one of the foremost literary critics of our age; and Andrew Lytle, with whom I later attended Yale; and Bill Bandy the French scholar, and Charlie Moss and Ralph McGill and others. I have often looked back on the 1920s in Nashville and at Vanderbilt and wondered how it hap-

A Fugitive Anthology

As he pursued his English studies in California, Warren continued to write poetry and fiction and to begin work on a biography of John Brown. The "projected volume" referred to in this letter to Davidson was published by Harcourt, Brace as Fugitives: An Anthology of Verse, *in 1928. The volume included six single poems and two poem sequences by Warren. "The Last Metaphor," listed below, was not chosen for the anthology: "Croesus in Autumn" and "Pro Sua Vita" were added to Warren's other suggestions.*

Warren to Donald Davidson, 19 September 1926

Dear Don:

By the sheerest accident I happened to go today to my old place in the city and the present occupants gave me your letters which they said had been there for several days. It seems that they had not the grace to forward them to me and in consequence I almost lost any opportunity of taking advantage of the possibility they offer. It may not be too late now, and so I am spending the evening preparing the manuscript.

The projected volume interests me tremendously, Don, and I devoutly hope that it materializes. I think the Fugitive group needs and is worthy of such a thing, which ought to be, as you say, important if the group fulfills its apparent promise. I can visualize a volume of some dignity with Allen's, John's, and your work and Jessie's sonnets in it.

In accordance with the scheme enclosed in your letter I am submitting a group of poems arranged in order of preference. The number is perhaps somewhat larger than my just quota but I am sending them in order to give you as editor a greater range of choice. They are as follows:

(1) Letter of a Mother

(2) Kentucky Mountain Farm

(3) To a Face in the Crowd

(4) Images on the Tomb

(5) The Last Metaphor

(6) The Wrestling Match

(7) Admonition to the Dead

I feel that within the limits of its intention the Letter of a Mother is easily my most finished poem. Kentucky Mountain Farm is second because it presents a more specialized and perhaps more subtle if weaker treatment of the same attitude as that of the first poem named. The next four poems are about on the same level I suppose with little to choose among them, while Admonition to the Dead is technically well done, I feel, even if trivial and derivative to a certain degree. There are two or three other poems that might be considered as options for the last three of those listed. These are Easter Morning: Crosby Junction, Iron Beach, and perhaps Alf Burt; accurate versions of these are in the Fugitive files, but I shall make copies and send tomorrow. All of the poems named with the exception of (7) are unpublished or appeared in the Fugitive, which makes the matter of acknowledgment in my case rather simple. Number seven was published in the Double Dealer, I believe. After Teacups and Midnight are not possible for the volume, because of their obvious and wavering experimental quality. Don't hesitate to work any violent readjustment in the list if you think best, Don, for I am probably a rather bad critic of my own work. The only poem that I ultimately regard with any degree of confidence is the first. I am including none of the summer's work, for I am tremendously unsatisfied with it; I'll be sending it however for your personal inspection in a day or so.

Did I tell you in my last letter that L. A. G. Strong asked for the Image on the Tomb poem for his anthology? With extreme reluctance, of course, I agreed to the arrangment.

Will you please send me John's address. I understand by rather roundabout channels that he is not in Nashville, and I am extremely anxious to get in touch with him if he will hearken to me after a long silence. Remember me to Jessie and the others when you all meet again and know how regretful I am that I cannot have a comfortable chair at the session.

Write soon and don't forget to send the promised poems of yours.

Affectionately,

Red

—Special Collections, Vanderbilt University

pened, how this land-locked and then small and provincial university assembled the students and faculty who, with the off-campus Fugitives, so profoundly shaped my life. Why should a small university like Vanderbilt, drawing primarily from young people of the region, become a center of such creative ferment? (The ferment, by the way, was so insidiously widespread that even an all-Southern football player wrote, as I later learned, little poems like A. E. Housman's—but never read them aloud in the locker room. A kinsman of his betrayed him to me in 1932, and showed examples.)

Maybe the best answer is the most obvious: Ransom and Davidson. They were such extraordinary teachers—two particular accidents in a certain place and time, with no explanation for the fact. They drew talented people to them, and drew out talent in many who didn't know it was there. They were bright and literary and accomplished; they had fought in the war, yet they were still young, still in their thirties. I in my teens felt no great separation in age from them (only in experience and wisdom and achievement), and between us in age were Tate and Wills and others. When we sat down together to discuss poetry, we sat as equals. It was one long seminar, and I was getting a priceless education writing boyish poems. I *was* a boy. Ransom and Elliott had been Rhodes Scholars, Frierson had studied at the Sorbonne, Hirsch had been around the world—and I had been to Nashville, and almost nowhere else. We were all Southerners, coming together around a common interest—poetry—but it was Ransom and Davidson who gave us purpose and direction.

I had another friend at Vanderbilt in those days, Saville Clark, who was far ahead of most people—a generation or two ahead—on a subject that was to become the dominant issue of our time: race. For a time I shared an apartment with Saville and his brother, Cannon Clark, on Grand Avenue. Saville had gone over to Fisk University and become acquainted with a good many students, and he brought one or two of them—to the horror of the landlady—to our apartment for conversations. This was in 1925, I believe, during a big student-administration clash at Fisk. I remember what an eye-opener it was for me, that small beginning in conversation across racial lines. I would think of it often in the 1950s and 1960s, and wish there had been more Saville Clarks.

Social issues didn't interest me then. Still, other things besides literature were happening at Vanderbilt. Football, for instance. Vanderbilt was a football power in those days. As I remember it, there were two all-Americans in my class—Hek Wakefield and Lynn Bomar—not to mention Gil Reese and Alf Sharp, who were all-Southern. I think Reese starred in the first game ever played at Dudley Field, in about 1922.

And of course, there were girls. Female enrollment at Vanderbilt was limited, I think, to ten percent, and in chapel each Wednesday morning the segregation was maintained, with the girls sitting in a balcony at the rear of the assembly hall, surveying the goings-on among their betters below. Once or twice a year when we (the males) entered the hall and saw the balcony empty, we were prepared to give more attention than usual to the business of the day, for an empty balcony meant it was time for what we called "the clap talk." On this occasion, some member of the medical faculty described in technical detail, sparing no horror, the ravages of venereal disease, and always added that beneath the finest, fairest flower—my metaphor—"the viper might lurk." The doctor would tell us that even that smiling and smartly dressed secretary or telephone operator might have loved not only too well but too widely, and we should be wary of them. I do not

recall that the speaker ever touched on morality, or gave instructions for preventive measures. Perhaps he was forbidden to do so, or perhaps he trusted common sense and a mother's prayer in such matters. In any case, the clap talk was welcome and titillating and even provocative. I can't be sure that the female ten percent were given any equivalent admonition; at that time, there wasn't even a dean of women in that purlieu of purity.

Occasionally, greater drama broke routine. A classmate of mine became convinced that he was in the wrong pew—his real passions were not a B.A. and a respectable position, but girls and motorcycles. In those old days before any hint of progress had changed the campus, it was in spring a bosky place full of the chancellor's iris and magnolia blossoms in profusion, and toward late afternoon, ladies from the city would flock there in their black electric automobiles to breathe the clean air and admire the beauties of nature.

One afternoon my nameless friend must have reached the breaking point. His great Harley Davidson, or whatever it was, exploded into action and, as reported to me, began to twine in and out among the automobiles from West End and Belle Meade. That was bad enough to bring well-bred shrieks from the ladies—but worse, according to report, my friend was wearing scarcely a stitch—if even that. He may have been the first streaker. On he wove among the screams of fear and outrage to his doom and destiny. Back then, Vanderbilt University had only a single cause for expulsion: "conduct unbecoming a gentleman." It must have been applied in this case. (A footnote about expulsion in those days before the worldwide exfoliation of professional administrators: Our dean was a classical scholar noted for sweetness of nature and a

---

Katherine Anne Porter Remembers Warren

In summer 1927, Warren met Katherine Anne Porter at the New York apartment of Allen Tate and his wife, Caroline Gordon Tate. The two writers became lifelong friends. Porter, who was thirty-seven at the time, remembered her impression of Warren, who was then actually twenty-two, in her notes.

I saw him first when he was 21, a poet born who was growing from one form to another, those of his friends knew even then that he was taking off on a long journey—at that time I happened to see a portrait drawing of John Keats when he was about 20, 21—a fine thin black line profile, spare and perfect—It could easily have been a portrait of Robert Penn Warren. He had brilliant flaming gold-red hair, and a skin fire-white, like a lighted frosted lantern—a most beautiful head of a young man.

—Joan Givner, *Katherine Anne Porter: A Life* (New York: Simon & Schuster, 1982), p. 179

halo of white hair. It was generally understood that if he even called you in and, affectionately but sadly, laid his arm across your shoulders, your goose was cooked. And he suffered far more than you.)

How long ago it seems since a freshman with a hat cocked on one side of his head and a cigar in his mouth entered a poolroom with a friend and began to chalk his cue, and how long ago the sophomore's first transaction with a bootlegger. I have one vivid memory of a summer job as an American Express truck driver, and briefly as a money guard with a sawed-off shotgun and a gray felt hat with the brim pulled low and sinister. Candor forces me to say that the boss who appointed me to that post drew me aside and said, "Warren, I'm giving you this job because you're expendable—you're the worst driver I've got. All you have to do is close your eyes and pull both triggers if anybody sticks his head in the back of the truck." To my eternal disappointment, nobody did.

By the time I graduated from Vanderbilt in 1925, *The Fugitive* had almost run its course. Its final issue was published in December of that year. The members of the group were beginning to scatter in all directions, and though the effort was made, there was no hope of holding us together. The university had given no recognition or encouragement to the magazine—Chancellor Kirkland had ignored it as best he could—yet the reputation of the journal was substantial. It was called "the most distinguished poetry magazine in America." In retrospect, I think it is fair to say that it was a modest historical document in American literature—not so much for what it contained as for the school of poets and writers it spawned. The creative ferment around Vanderbilt at that time made it a rare place, the only place of its kind.

–"Robert Penn Warren: A Reminiscence," in *Nashville: The Faces of Two Centuries, 1780–1980,* edited by John Egerton (Nashville: Plus Media, 1979), pp. 205–213

* * *

Some of the names associated with the Fugitives were not official members of the group but were "adopted" later as friends. One such friend was Cleanth Brooks, who participated in the Fugitives' reunion in 1956 and in this excerpt recalled the collective experience of some thirty years earlier.

A Literary Bird Nest

And now I have a few words to say, and though I speak from an excited mind and out of a full heart, I will try to be modest in scope. As a matter of fact, if there were a different kind of audience for whom I were summing up, there would be some point in a detailed summary. But I

shall discard any notions that I had of that kind. That very fine though limited poet, and good provincial, and representative man of the eighteenth century, Dr. Samuel Johnson, used to be very proud of his college at Oxford—Pembroke College—because he said, it was a "nest of singing birds." There had been lots of poets there. He was able to count up three or four. As a matter of fact, Johnson's phrase describes exactly the present occasion, which has been so pleasant to all of us. We have been looking at a last year's bird nest—a rather glorious bird's nest. [*laughter*] A bird's nest of considerable more splendor than the rather modest little nest—it was no more than that, I'm afraid when all is said and done—that Dr. Johnson, with a fine sanity and proper piety, rejoiced in.

What does one examine a bird's nest for, particularly when a good many of the birds have flown? And even the birds that remain in this habitat are no longer fledglings—I am looking at that fine poet, Donald Davidson, who spreads his own wings and beats the air powerfully. But many have flown, migratory birds. I suppose in one sense the study of bird-nest building could be regarded as an art—as the study of the kind of community out of which literature grows. Dr. Samuel Johnson would have called—in fact, did call it—the art of nidification, bird-nest building. I suppose we have learned a great deal about the context out of which this brilliant group came. I, certainly, have learned a great deal; because the campfires were still glowing when I was here as a freshman, and one went on from one to the other, and the embers were not yet quite cold. The Fugitives were getting ready to suspend, but by a series of lucky accidents I ran into Red [Warren], and then through him met Andrew [Lytle]; as a matter of fact, those meetings changed very quickly my notion of the glamorous life—which was originally that of being a really shifty half-back—to authorship. Here were people who actually wrote poems and stories and got them printed. That redirection of interest came for me earlier than the meeting with Donald [Davidson] and with John [Crowe Ransom] in classes a little later.

I have learned—I'm sure all of us have learned—a great deal about this community. I hadn't realized, for example—and it's been exhilarating to realize—how powerful some of the tensions were in the group, and how useful they must have been—the pull back and forth. I won't call them "divisions"; I'll call them tensions. I hadn't realized—I couldn't realize—the role that Sidney Hirsch must have played, for example. Or all sorts of other things. But all that is, let's hope, in the tape. And I'm not going to try to summarize that part or talk about it. As far as history—literary history—is concerned, it's there embalmed in a manner of speaking; and somebody, the scholar of the future, can work at it. I don't think it'll last any seven centuries; with the

Warren (middle row, right) with others who attended the 1956 Fugitives reunion at Vanderbilt: top row, William Y. Elliott, Merrill Moore, Jesse Wills, and Sidney M. Hirsch; middle row, Milton Starr and Alec Stevenson; bottom row, Allen Tate, Ransom, and Donald Davidson (Photographic Archives, Special Collections, Vanderbilt University)

way in which the American graduate schools are going into super-production, I am sure that that tape will be worn out in ten years. [*laughter*] What I am really concerned in is this matter: what is the use—aside from history and preserving the past—what's the use of the study of literary bird-nest building? Does anyone have the foolishness to think that thereby he can learn how to build such a nest? I don't think so. I would use an analogy: I am very much interested in talking about poems and trying to see, in so far as one can see, how they are put together, how they are built. But if you do that, very frequently somebody says, "You are trying to find out the secret so you can write a poem by a formula." That's not the point at all. One doesn't study these things in any hope that they can be reproduced in that fashion.

Yet I think that there is an application to the present and even a pointing toward the future in such study and not merely reference to an antiquarian's past. Because one can learn, I believe, some of the conditions which have to be propitious for the development of a literary community. I think here that that really remarkable book—little read and misunderstood—by T. S. Eliot, called *Notes Toward a Definition of Culture*—is very important. His theme, as you will remember, is that you can't fabricate a civilization as you can a house or a wall; you grow one, or you find it growing. You water it, you nurture it, you cultivate it, you are careful about it; you can do something to promote its growth but you can't create it *ex nihilo*. The burden of what has been said, through the very interesting sessions, seems to me all to bear on that point.

The Fugitives as a Group

INTERVIEWERS: When you started writing, what pre-occupations, technically and thematically, had you in common with your crowd?

WARREN: I suppose you mean the poets called the Fugitive Group, in Nashville–Allen Tate, John Crowe Ransom, Donald Davidson, Merrill Moore, etc.?

INTERVIEWERS: Yes.

WARREN: Well, in one sense, I don't know what the group had in common. I think there is a great fallacy in assuming that there was a systematic program behind the Fugitive Group. There was no such thing, and among the members there were deep differences in temperament and aesthetic theory. They were held together by geography and poetry. They all lived in Nashville, and they were all interested in poetry. Some were professors, some businessmen, one was a banker, several were students. They met informally to argue philosophy and read each other the poems they wrote. For some of them these interests were incidental to their main concerns. For a couple of others, like Tate, it was poetry or death. Their activity wasn't any "school" or "program." Mutual respect and common interests–that was what held them together–that and the provincial isolation, I guess.

INTERVIEWERS: But did you share with them any technical or thematic preoccupations?

WARREN: The answer can't, you see, apply to the group. But in a very important way, that group was my education. I knew individual writers, poems and books through them. I was exposed to the liveliness and range of the talk and the wrangle of argument. I heard the talk about techniques but techniques regarded as means of expression. But most of all I got the feeling that poetry was a vital activity, that it related to ideas and to life. I came into the group rather late. I was timid and reverential I guess. And I damned well should have been.

–Ellison and Walter, "The Art of Fiction XVIII: Robert Penn Warren," *Paris Review,* 4 (Spring–Summer 1957): 121–122

I've been interested in how much classics came into the development of the Fugitives, the study of Latin and Greek; a sense of a community in some very real sense, even with family ties back and forth; the sense of concrete exchange of ideas; the sense of common principles so deep and so common that you didn't even have to talk about them, but they were there underneath you all the time, and you could unconsciously rest upon them; and, therefore, put your attention on the other things. All of those matters I think are terribly important. For me they are much more important now than they would have been for me eight years ago; because I have spent the last eight years at a big Eastern university. And I have learned a great deal to admire in that university. On the other hand, what I have learned there makes me regard this experience as all the more remarkable and precious. Now I am not going to do what I would consider the snide trick of deprecating the university where I now teach in order to glorify this occasion. I think that Yale has some very precious things. It has qualities which Vanderbilt might well aspire to. It has certain other things–resources in books, manuscripts, men, and money–to which Vanderbilt probably cannot aspire. But it lacks, at least unless I am completely prejudiced, this very precious thing which Vanderbilt once had. Does Vanderbilt itself still maintain the cultural conditions which made the emergence of the Fugitive Group possible? I certainly do not know. But the disintegration that is going on all over the country makes me fear that the conditions necessary for the nurture of a literary community such as the Fugitives' was may have disappeared. But the situation of the young writer in all of our more distinguished universities makes me fearful. The young writer has plenty of talent. But his environment in its sophistication is aridifying. The young writers know too much. (Of course, they really don't know too much; you can't know too much if you really know it.) But they do run into the difficulty of knowing all the techniques as abstract techniques, knowing the full bag of tricks as a special bag of tricks; knowing what the newest fad is going to be before the new bandwagon actually rumbles around the corner. I think such knowledge can be a crippling thing. I think that a certain kind of provincialism, a certain kind of innocence–though I think that probably is a wrong term–is indispensable.

In saying these things, I am probably speaking to the converted here. I don't know, of course, how many of you have any real influence over Vanderbilt's destinies. But what I would like to say, in summing up, is this: there is probably nothing that any of us can do to insure the emergence of another group like the Fugitives. Inspection of last year's bird's nest will not tell us how to make Vanderbilt once again a nest of singing birds. The fortunate circumstance of the concurrence of so many talented men is unpredictable and rarely repeated. But there are other important matters about which we might do something. Granted the need for talent, granted a great many other things, unless you have the proper seed bed, the proper nurturing circumstances, the seed of a literary movement perishes. It perishes from adverse conditions, but it can also actually be killed by the wrong sort of kindness, or even by too much kindness–by a "programizing" of the whole thing. Now, this is all that I have to say. . . .

–Cleanth Brooks, "A Summing Up," in *Fugitives' Reunion: Conversations at Vanderbilt, May 3–5, 1956,* edited by Rob Roy Purdy (Nashville: Vanderbilt University Press, 1959), pp. 219–222

24. (insert)

The brother-in-law, Milton Lusk, also got into trouble. The colonization societies that wanted to dispose of the negroes by shipping them off to Africa, were in full flower at this time. The free negroes we e generally
                        there were stringent "black laws", and a negro had few
unpopular in Ohio; xxxxxxxxxxxxxxxxxxxxxxxxxxxxxxxxxxxxxxxxxxxxxxxxxxxxxxx
rights of citizenship.
xxxxxxxxxxxxxxxxxxxxxxxxxxxxxxxxxxxxxxxxxxxxxxxxxxxxxxxxxxxxxxxxxxxxxxxxxxx

xxxxxxxxxxxxxxxxxxxxxxxxxxxxxxxxxxxxxxxxxxxxxxxxxxxxxxxxxxxxxxxxxxxxxxxxxxx
                                                    xxxxxxxxxxxxxxx
xxxxxxxxxxxxxxxxxxxxxxxxxxxxxxxxxxxxxxxxxxxxxxxxxxxxxxxxxxxxxxxxxxxxxxxx. x
When Mr. Randolph of Virgina died he set all his slaves free on condition that they should be settled in Ohio; the free negroes got their land only to be
              white farmers, who   those
mobbed by xxxxxxxxxxxxxx didn't like the new neighbors. The colonization idea was popular; it gave an opportunity to do a benevolent deed and remedy a social nuisance at the same time. Furthermore it appealed to the few radicals, for some of the promoters claimed that it was a blow to slavery
        The church took up the crusade and raised moeny to deport black brethren.
itself. Ladies' Colonization Societies and Children's Colonization Societies
                                                                and
flourished side by side with missionary societies, xxx sewing circles, xxxx revival meetings. Only the negroes seemed to object to the project; they would hold meetings, xxx pass violent resolutions and condemn colonization as unChristian. Black laws or no black laws, Ohio was a better home to them than the jungle.

One day Milton Lusk saw a statement by Chief-Justice Marshall to the effect that colonization would help the slave-holders of Virginia by disposing of the trouble-making free negroes. A paradox began to dawn in Milton Lusk's mind; in Ohio the ministers said that colonization was a step toward abolition and in Virginia they got money by saying it would bolster up their peculiar institution. He threw the paper down and stamped on it. "What ails you, Milton, " asked his sister. "I'm through raising money for colonizing the negroes," was his answer. That night the pastor called on Brother Lusk to pass the plate for the colonizing collection, and Brother Lusk flatly refused. "If our money goes into the same fund with the Virginia money, I'll never help raise another dollars," he explained.

Page from a draft for Warren's John Brown, *which he wrote while he was a graduate student at Oxford University* (*Yale Collection of American Literature, Beinecke Rare Book and Manuscript Library*)

A Glimpse into the Warren Family

While he was studying in Berkeley and working summers in Oakland, Warren became romantically involved with Emma Cinina Brescia, who was also a student at the University of California. Because Warren's Rhodes Scholarship to Oxford depended on his being single, the couple married secretly in 1929. In 1930 Warren began his teaching career at Southwestern College in Memphis, Tennessee, and the following year he was hired at Vanderbilt, where he taught for three years.

During these years and later, Warren and his wife received letters from his parents, some of which were preserved. In this excerpted essay, William Bedford Clark uses these letters from home to discuss the influence of familial relationships upon Warren's poetry and fiction.

Letters from Home:
Filial Guilt in Robert Penn Warren

My subject is Robert Penn Warren, particularly the love and anguish that typify his work whenever he turned to the question of his parents, Anna Ruth Penn and Robert Franklin Warren; but I will begin with a look at a once popular, now forgotten poem by a sentimental lyricist of the second half of the nineteenth century: Elizabeth Akers Allen (1832–1911). However sincere, her "Rock Me to Sleep" exemplifies the kind of "pure poetry" Warren and his fellow New Critics distrusted, dealing as it does with a "soft subject" without discernible irony. Mrs. Allen lost her mother in childhood, and the speaker in her poem, a mature woman who has clearly lived an emotionally exhausting life and now craves sleep and peace, longs to return to that Edenic time when her mother comforted her and set all things right:

> Backward, turn backward, O Time, in your flight,
> Make me a child again just for to-night!
> Mother, come back from the echoless shore,
> Take me again to your heart as of yore.

Readers of Warren's "The Return: An Elegy," the first of the *Thirty-Six Poems* (1935), have heard these lines before, but with an "impure" twist:

> turn backward turn backward O time in your flight
> and make me a child again just for tonight
> good lord he's wet the bed come bring a light

It is possible, of course, to set aside autobiographical concerns for a moment and admire on a purely technical level the mordant intertextuality Warren brings to bear on the Victorians' saccharine cult of motherhood. While the voice in Mrs. Allen's poem is univocal in its yearning for maternal care, Warren gives us a speaker who reveals just how often grief and relief are inter-

twined. Despite himself Warren's persona exults in his new independence ("the old bitch is dead"), only to convict himself of a shameful breach of social and filial decorum ("what have I said!"). Given the demands of conventional piety on the one hand and barely suppressed resentment on the other, the son teeters on the edge of full-blown hysteria, which in turn endows him with a reluctant, unintended honesty that compels the reader to accept the son's ultimate description of his sorrow as a "dark and swollen orchid"–an image that might otherwise seem "soft and spurious"–as Cleanth Brooks pointed out long ago.

Were "The Return: An Elegy" an isolated instance, we might be justified in leaving things there. The poem is, after all, wholly fictive in terms of situation and setting, and, if we take Warren at his word (he was a man of remarkable probity), its initial composition antedates the death of the poet's mother in the fall of 1931. Yet the theme of "The Return"–a wandering and errant child is called home–reasserts itself throughout the Warren canon, and the autobiographical significance of that motif becomes explicit by the 1950s. Even a cursory reading of John Burt's magisterial edition of the collected poems reveals how Warren revisited, reenvisioned, and rewrote this poem with compulsive frequency during his career. At times the child is delinquent at the most trivial level, hiding in the darkness or absenting himself from home out of vaguely articulated motives, only to be called back by the worried parent's distant voice (in "The Leaf" and "Code Book Lost" for example). Then we recall those large-scale and unmistakably autobiographical poems in which the son, a citizen of the great world, busy with an agenda of his own, is suddenly called to the bedside of the dying parent, most notably in the sequences "Mortmain" and "Tale of Time," two of Warren's undisputed masterpieces. The insistent tug of the parent's solicitous love is somehow threatening, posing as it does potential restrictions on the child's quest for the fullest possible individuation, and is therefore to be resisted. But the call of the parent will not be denied and cannot be evaded. Indeed, in the final analysis, the questing self wanders in the broad world in search of glory (a poor surrogate for love) only to arrive once more at home, bearing a goodly measure of prodigal guilt.

. . . .

Clark goes on to discuss All the King's Men *and three poems from his collection* Being Here (1980)–*"October Picnic Long Ago," "The Only Poem," and "Grackles, Goodbye"–before discussing the letters that were preserved by Warren's wife.*

Ruth Warren died at the beginning of October 1931. Her husband and all three of their children are dead, and her grandchildren never knew her. Only a tiny remnant of the living, like Granville (Doc) Frey, a childhood friend of Thomas Warren now in his nineties, can remember her and recall her voice—the apparently lilting voice that haunted Robert Penn Warren's memory and that we hear, however tentatively, in many of his finest poems. But some of Mrs. Warren's letters have recently come to light, and in them she "speaks" again for herself and in her own distinctive cadences. These letters span an important period in the relationship between Robert Penn Warren and his family—roughly the last two years of Ruth Warren's life. The file includes two letters from late 1929 addressed to Warren at Oxford, where he was concluding his appointment as a Rhodes scholar; Ruth Warren subsequently began writing Emma (Cinina) Brescia in the

spring of 1930 in anticipation of her son's return to the States and the couple's pending marriage. (It is unclear if she knew they had already married secretly.) Most of the correspondence dates from the fall of 1930, a time of storm and stress on many levels. Warren was just entering into married life with Cinina, who almost immediately grew homesick for her native California, and the couple found themselves in a cramped apartment in Memphis, where Warren faced a further challenge—adjusting to his first full-time job as an assistant professor at Southwestern (now Rhodes College), a position he would find increasingly frustrating. Even under the best of circumstances it was hardly an auspicious time to begin a new marriage and inaugurate an academic career. The Great Depression had hit, and back home in Guthrie, Kentucky, the senior Warrens

---

Warren and Brooks at Oxford

In this excerpt, Brooks recalls that after his first year at Vanderbilt, he did not see Warren again until they were both Rhodes Scholars at Oxford.

. . . More than four years elapsed before we met again in the fall of 1929, at Oxford. I remember that I arrived about dusk on an October evening, spent my first night in Exeter College, and perhaps the very next afternoon I found, when I returned to my room, a note from Warren, saying that he had called and inviting me to come to see him. As I knew, he had been elected a Rhodes Scholar from Kentucky two years earlier, and I was gratified that he had noticed my name in the new list and with his usual kindness had got in touch immediately.

At Oxford Warren was working for a B. Litt. degree on some topic in Elizabethan literature. I decided that I would not do a graduate degree but the Honors B.A. in English language and literature, believing that at Oxford I should attempt to do the traditional Oxford degree. Thus Warren was again in a somewhat different world from mine—one composed of graduate students doing research and writing theses, whereas I was going to see my tutor once a week and ranging through English literature. Nevertheless, we saw a good deal of each other during that year, and since Warren had several friends in Exeter College besides myself, I saw him there as well as at his digs in Wellington Square. (He was a member of New College but did not have a room in the college during that year.)

After some forty-odd years one's memory brings up flotsam and jetsam rather than an ordered array of significant incidents. Yet, since nothing particularly momentous that involved us both occurred during our year together at Oxford, it is perhaps just as well to set down here the first couple of such fragments that rise to the surface of my mind. They will at least suggest the Warren that I remember from this period of my life.

One evening at Exeter College a number of us had got onto the subject of the Civil War. It was a matter of intense interest to Red and he promised to lay out before us then and there precisely what had gone on at the Battle of Gettysburg and particularly what had gone awry for the Confederate side. His account was engrossing, not only to this Confederate, but also to our Yankee and British friends who were seated about the table. Unfortunately, just before the batteries opened up on Cemetery Ridge in preparation for Pickett's Charge, the college bell began its hideous racket, warning that one had to be in his rooms before 12:15. So Pickett's Charge was over before it began, Red was out of the room in a trice, his scholar's gown fluttering behind him as he fled.

One of the more memorable occasions at Red's place on Wellington Square was the dinner party that he gave for a friend who was going down from Oxford. The feast was to be served in Red's rooms and his landlord had assured him that he was up to not only serving the meal but preparing the particular dishes that Red wanted. Consequently, he was startled to see the landlord bearing to the table a punch-bowl filled with what proved to be rather sweet martini in which a dozen raw oysters floated. Red asked what in the world it was. The landlord's reply was "The gentleman asked for oyster cocktail, didn't he?" I was not present on that occasion, alas, but I soon heard of it, and I know exactly what the expression on Red's face was—controlled rage. I saw that expression years later when, having stopped in a roadside restaurant for breakfast while on a motor trip, Red ordered an egg, thoroughly well done. As his fork cut into it and the lovely yellow yolk ran out, there was a moment when I believe the fork came close to being plunged into the waitress's innards.

—Cleanth Brooks, "Brooks on Warren,"
Four Quarters, 21 (May 1972): 19–20

were having a bleak time. Ready money was scarce; both Ruth and Robert Warren were beset with bad health; and the future of their youngest child, Thomas, was a source of constant concern. The letters of Ruth Warren to Robert Penn and his bride offer us a unique window on the world of the Warren family, a glimpse into its quotidian details and tensions, and they reveal something about why the motif of filial guilt came to exert such a shaping power over Robert Penn Warren's poetic imagination.

. . . .

In his superb biography Joseph Blotner tells us that as a Vanderbilt undergraduate Robert Penn Warren allowed letters from his mother to accumulate unopened on his desk, and students of Warren's poetry may recall an ambiguous and ambivalent early poem, "Letter of a Mother," published in the *New Republic* in 1928. Surely no one who had read it can forget the sequence "I Am Dreaming of a White Christmas" (1973), one of the most macabre and disturbing poems Warren ever wrote. With this in mind I want to present in its entirety a letter of Ruth Warren addressed to her son at New College, Oxford, and written sometime in early December 1929 (the postmark is illegible):

Dear Son—
    The snow is fast disappearing today & it is much warmer & clear. I do hope we will have some better weather. This country has seldom ever had such a spell of zero weather this time of year. I could do without any more snow forever.
    I am getting rather impatient to hear from you but I know you are busy & have not looked for a letter till the exams are over, but don't wait long then, please.
    It looks now that I am not going to be able to send you anything for Xmas—just love I guess.— We find it very hard to make out these days.—Like Micawber I am hoping something will "*turn up*"—
    We had a nice letter from Sister today written Tues. She said her cold was better. I am glad. In about 2½ weeks she said Tommie will be coming home. I wish we could have you one more Christmas. You have missed so many now that I feel sad when I think of it.— It is the normal thing but it is sad to see our children grow up & leave us.—
    I hope you are well, dear. Let me know how you are. Take care of yourself—Do *rest* & get lots of sleep during your vacation. I believe you said you were going to stay in Oxford—Always write us where to find you, Son. Never go off till you have notified us.
    Have you heard about J. B. [*John Brown*] from the Publishers & to whom did you send your 13 copies?
    Be a good boy, Son. God bless you & help you make your decisions.
    Our best love & prayers.
                    Devotedly,
                    Mother

However spontaneous and straightforward, this letter is nonetheless a rhetorical triumph, but we need not unpack its many nuances here. Let the record show that Warren spent the Christmas holidays that year not at school in Oxford, but in Paris in the company of the Tates, and that he was probably not a good boy in quite the way his mother had hoped. It is unlikely that he got much rest and sleep. Floyd Watkins was right. Like many bright and ambitious young persons (and he was exceedingly bright and ambitious), Robert Penn Warren inhabited "two countries." There was the glittering world of distant places, intellectual (and physical) stimulation, and seemingly limitless possibilities. Then there was home, with its narrow horizons and the shackles born of duty and love. He understandably preferred the charms of Oxford and Paris, but in the long run it would be Guthrie that fed his art.

However proprietary her interest in her son, Ruth Warren did not appear to resent the role Cinina Brescia had come to play in his life. By the spring of 1930, the women had been in regular correspondence for some time. One bond they shared was an eagerness to hear from Robert Penn and disappointment and worry when they didn't. In the earliest surviving letter to her future daughter-in-law (April 8, 1930), Mrs. Warren addresses her as "Dear Little Girl" (in subsequent letters she will be "Darling Cinina" or "Dear Daughter"), and she signs off with "Dad joins me in lots of love[–] Hastily and Devotedly[,] *Mother*." She urges Cinina to convince Robert Penn to accept whatever job might be available upon his return from Oxford, at least until he finds something more to his liking, and she has wisdom to impart: "You children are young & can stand most any place the first year [just] so you are together. It will no doubt be your hardest year—for you will have to get adjusted to each other & to many things—'Keep two *bears* in the house—bear and forebear.'" As Cinina prepared to leave California at summer's end to join Warren in Memphis and set up housekeeping, Mrs. Warren welcomed her to the family with a combination of warmth and realism: "I am glad to hear you say you want to feel one of us—not just *kin*[,] for we want you to be 'one of us' and while we do not always agree we never let anything overshadow our love & respect for each other." In this same letter (August 10, 1930), Ruth Warren again reveals herself as womanly-wise: "Even if Son can not always come you can run up to see us when you get tired or want to see us.—You will be blue & lonely . . . often & the first year is always the hardest—adjustments[,] disillusionment[,] etc." Mutual understanding and a woman's guiding hand will prove essential:

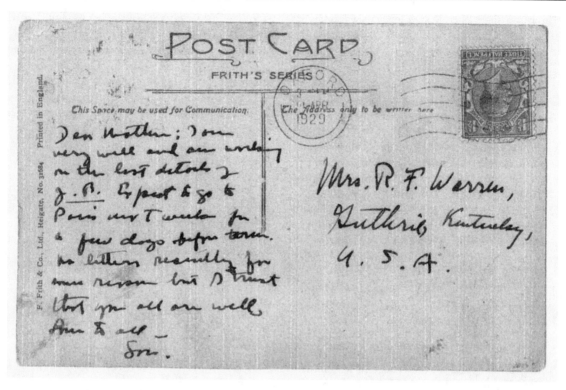

*Postcard Warren sent to his mother in April 1929 in which he reports progress on his biography of John Brown
(Robert Penn Warren Birthplace Museum, Guthrie, Kentucky)*

You must take into consideration differences in people & environment but if I judge you rightly you can do whatever you try to do little lady & . . . you will be fair not only to *yourself* but to *Red*. He is fine, I know, but of course in the many years away from home he has changed & developed—more for the better I hope but in some ways I perhaps will deplore. It [rests] greatly in your hands now, dear, the man he will be—a wife can inspire & help a man to climb or drag him down. I feel I am going to be so *proud* of you both.

The nag of motherly worry is never absent for long: "I just hope he is well and strong this fall & that he likes his work. . . . Rest will be good for you & him too. He has had to work hard to do three years in two." Then there is a slight but telling note of recrimination: "If you had not been waiting for him I am sure he would have taken the three years."

When Cinina did in fact grow "blue & lonely" later that fall, she did not visit her in-laws in Guthrie half a day away, but instead returned to the San Francisco area and her father's house. Her departure seems to have been an impulsive response to homesickness and in no way a trial separation, but Cinina's need for a change of scene may have been exacerbated by an early test of her husband's family loyalty. In spite of Ruth Warren's awareness of the pressure the newlyweds might expect in the ordinary course of things, she and Mr. Warren sent their son Thomas to visit with Red and Cinina in hopes he would take a job in Memphis and enter school at Southwestern. On September 22, in a letter to her older son, Mrs. Warren made her motives clear: "If I thought you could really afford it I would say insist on him staying for I do not know what on earth we can do for him or with him here. Granville [Frey] left yesterday . . . & there is not a really decent boy left—only the wild loafing class and T— will naturally fall into that gang for he loves a crowd & it will be his ruination. If he could only get a job there & stay even without school I would be glad—anywhere in preference to here."

One cause of concern was the presence in Guthrie of Robert Penn's old friend Kent Greenfield (subject of several important later poems), whose career as a major league pitcher had been cut short by drink: "Kent has been begging him to go to San Antonio with him & *drive an oil wagon* . . . & you know what that means for our boy—absolute ruin for K— is in the gutter and will soon be penniless even if he did draw over $13,000 a year." Ruth Warren acknowledges that "we are putting a lot on you and Cinina but we are at our wits' end it seems & times are perfectly awful. . . . We are not making expenses by any means. . . . Oh for more *filthy lucre*." In closing she writes:

Drop us a short letter at once for we are frankly worried about our little son. I hope he has been nice but I am sure he has. I think he likes his new sister very much–I know we shall all love her very much–in fact we do now–and we love our big son *very dearly.*

Son, we appreciate your kindness, & that of Cinina very much–this seems to be our *extremity*–and we need encouragement to go on–

In an earlier undated mailing, Ruth Warren had enclosed a long note to Thomas that bears attention: "We miss you very much–going and coming–but hope you have had a pleasant Sun. and that you feel better and went to church. . . . I am unhappy because I know you are unhappy–. . . I want you to be the best, finest man possible." She then sought to offer a measure of motherly encouragement: "That job you so much want may come soon. I pray it will."

Predictably the experiment ended in failure, and Mrs. Warren expressed her disappointment to Robert Penn in a letter postmarked September 29, 1930: "Your letter came today & we were quite glad to have *a letter* from you but sorry its contents had to be so unpleasant." Young Thomas had misbehaved, and his mother was "grieved" and apprehensive: "I am so unhappy that he acted so boorish & fear Cinina will take it as a reflection on Father & me." Robert Franklin Warren was "heartbroken about the school part of it" and felt guilty: "You know how he feels about education & how he has striven for you all & now that he is so poor he can not get T– through [it] is killing him." (Readers familiar with the memoir *Portrait of a Father* [1988], which deals with the youthful R. F. Warren's own frustrated pursuit of knowledge under inauspicious circumstances, will find this last remark particularly poignant.) Ruth Warren cannily surmises that Thomas's return to Guthrie may have its roots in romance: "I suspect Alice [Bryan] has something to do with it–I could shake her too. Girls are all right–but I do wish they could let boys grow up!" Later letters not only chronicle the evolving courtship of Tommie and Alice, who would marry in 1933, but testify to Thomas Warren's extraordinary business sense as he begins to make his own way in the world.

. . . .

Ruth Warren's letters from fall 1930 communicate a range of motherly concerns. From Cinina she wants an account of wedding gifts as they arrive and assurance that they have been properly acknowledged. She repeatedly pleads with the newlyweds to attend church and urges Warren not to cut the compulsory chapel at Southwestern. She commiserates with her son's onerous workload, especially paper grading, advising him to put Cinina and their guest Andrew

Lytle (clearly a favorite of the entire family) to work at that purgatorial chore, and she reports on visits to and from the Tates–in residence at Benfolly, their recently acquired farmhouse outside Clarksville, just over the Tennessee line. Fleeting remarks suggest that Mrs. Warren found fault with Caroline Gordon's housekeeping and regarded her as a dowdy dresser. She kept a close watch on her son's writerly career, eagerly awaiting forthcoming publications and notices of his work and speculating on his dealings with Joseph Brewer, his publisher, and she is curious about the pending visit of a certain Malcolm Cowley. Dismal weather and the deepening inroads of the depression are recurring motifs, and the letters are laced with local news and gossip. Funerals, club meetings, automobile accidents, fires, radio broadcasts, and everyday family matters (meals, day trips) are duly noted, and taken together the letters–given their very frequency–amount to something like a pastiche of small-town life and hold considerable human interest of a general sort. Ruth Warren was not without a literary flair of her own. A rare letter from Robert Penn is an occasion for celebration, though Cinina seems to have been a fairly faithful correspondent. Running throughout is a preoccupation with health. Ruth cautions Red and Cinina to stay warm and dry and worries when they are run down or have colds; she warns Cinina to keep fresh pork off her table (Robert Penn was allergic to it); and she reports regularly on the health of Warren's sister, Mary Cecilia (away teaching in another town), Thomas, and her husband–"Daddy Bob" (who suffered ailments his son would later describe in *Portrait of a Father,* though Mr. Warren's reluctance to see a physician or dentist is confirmed in these letters). More ominous, at least in retrospect, are Mrs. Warren's own increasing complaints of fatigue and pain. In less than a year she would be dead.

No synopsis can do justice to the steady stream of letters Ruth Warren wrote to her son and his wife during the last year of her life. They deserve publication in full and with proper annotation. But a few milestones are worth marking. From a letter postmarked October 10, 1930, it appears that the couple did not make their first real visit to Guthrie until that weekend, which may hold some significance in and of itself. Mrs. Warren remarks: "Cinina, we were *so very* glad to know you better and Son, you would be delighted to hear the nice things said about her here. Your Daddy is especially pleased with her & who wouldn't be?" This seems strange coming from a woman who had addressed Cinina as "daughter" or "our big girl" for months, but the praise Warren's mother lavished on her daughter-in-law here and elsewhere gives every indication of being sincere. Ruth Warren even took pains to encourage Cinina's own (ultimately thwarted) literary ambitions, and when she prepared to depart from Memphis in early November to visit her father on the West Coast, Mrs. Warren urged her in an undated letter to return by Christmas so as not to "leave Red [alone] at that season" and admonished her not to "tax" or "overdo" herself once she was in Oakland—hardly a gratuitous concern given Cinina's history of serious pulmonary complaints. In a subsequent letter to Cinina in California (December 1, 1930), Ruth Warren indicates her willingness to forego a Christmas visit from the couple if it seems likely that the drafty Warren house in Guthrie might prove injurious to Cinina's health, but she also suggests that economy is a consideration: "I realize how deeply in debt you are and that you must pay part of it at once." However much she might want their company, she wonders if travel might be an unnecessary expense and suggests that gift-giving might well be curtailed.

. . . .

Throughout the spring of 1931 Ruth Penn Warren wrote and hastily posted letters (so as to get them out on the next train) even when she admitted she had nothing substantive to say. The act of writing, in itself, was a way of reaching across the miles from Guthrie to Memphis and making herself somehow present. To one for whom each letter is a profession of love, the absence of a response is no trivial matter. It is a willful act of neglect: "I feel it is time to hear from you all. Cinina has spoiled me quite a bit about hearing regularly. For a number of years Red had been so careless about writing regularly, daughter, and I suffered in consequence[.] We have felt you were a Godsend. These gray hairs were made partly by worrying because he did not write, or mail the letters when he did write. I daresay there are letters among his effects now addressed to me" (March 10, 1931).

Yet for all the stock she put in letters, it was the literal presence of her son that she craved. His hasty stopovers in Guthrie—on the way to Nashville or combined with a stay at the Tates' outside Clarksville—were occasions of joy, but Mrs. Warren longed to visit the young couple in Memphis, and the correspondence attests to her careful planning and keen anticipation. Though she would eventually make her visit, it was postponed twice at the last minute owing to illness: first Cinina's and then her own. The Vanderbilt appointment came through, and not long afterward Red and Cinina departed for a summer in California before moving to Nashville. They enjoyed a particularly pleasant and productive summer, including several weeks at a scenic lake in the mountains. At home in Guthrie, Ruth Warren declined toward death.

Thomas Warren, who stayed with his older brother and his new wife during the year Warren spent as an assistant professor at Southwestern College in Memphis (courtesy of Mrs. Robert D. Frey)

Toward summer's end, Red and Cinina received what may well be the last letter Mrs. Warren ever wrote, in an envelope postmarked August 24, 1931, with the twice-repeated inscription *Air Mail:*

                                        Sunday

Darlings—

Your joint letter came today and it did cheer me—thank you dears—I am setting up some today for the first time since last Fri. a week ago—9 days of bed—such a thing has not been since Tommie was born. I feel pretty bad & look worse but of course am better—perhaps only temporarily for Dr. F— [Emmett Frey, the family physician] says I am likely to have another spell any time. . . . I do not think he will have an operation unless I do have another attack. If I get strong enough I want to get gowns etc ready for fear I do need them. . . . It seems these attacks I have had all year have been gall stone trouble & each one got a little worse—I just thought I was run down and *lazy*.

Warren's mother soon moved on to what she called "the important thing"—news that her son's first attempts at a novel had received favorable attention from the publisher Macaulay and a contract might be in the offing. Characteristically she advises him to "take some time" with it and not let his new duties at Vanderbilt suffer, and she then moves on to say that she has had so many visitors during her illness that she could not see them all—"nor could they still the pain": "I have never dreamed there was such suffering on earth . . . no *dope* put me to sleep & I could not move or let anyone move me. You must not worry for we will wire if I get very sick again & I hope the worst is over. . . . Let us know when to expect you, please. We want to see you so much." She urges her son to begin house hunting in Nashville as soon as possible and concludes by congratulating him again on the "auspicious" prospects for his novel: "I feel C— needs more praise than Red for she has inspired you & made it possible for you to work." A hasty postscript scrawled in the right margin ends with these valedictory words: "Sorry I have not written before. Regards to Mr. B— [Domenico Brescia, Cinina's father]."

Much happened in a month's time. Robert Penn and Cinina returned from California and looked for housing near Vanderbilt, and then they received this letter from Warren's father:

Sept 23–9:30 p.m.

Dear Son and Daughter

I went to see mother this afternoon [in the hospital at Hopkinsville, where she was operated on]. . . . I left her at 5:30. She has had a very bad day. The Drs say she will have her worst days today and tomorrow. Miss Kathleen went over this a.m. and stayed with her until some time after I came. Mrs. Miller went with Miss K. I fear mother is not doing so well. I will let you know at once if she gets worse—We hope and pray she will make a speedy recovery. She was so run down it is hard for her to gain strength very fast.

I hope you got located to your satisfaction and that your room is pleasant. Tommie will come for you Sat aft[ernoon]—

God bless and keep you both.

Devotedly, Father Bob

[P.S.] Had a letter from Sister this a.m.

We know the rest. Things went steadily downhill, and Warren was summoned to the hospital in Hopkinsville. Here is one account of what happened—as shocking as anything we might find in Lowell, Sexton, or Berryman:

> They have taken out her false teeth, which are now in a
>   tumbler on the bedside table, and you know that only
>   the undertaker will ever put them back in.

You stand there and wonder if you will ever have to wear
    false teeth.

She is lying on her back, and God, is she ugly, and
With gum-flabby lips and each word a special problem,
    she is asking if it is a new suit that you are wearing.

You say yes and hate her uremic guts, for she has no right
    to make you hurt the way that question hurts.
You do not know why that question makes your heart
    hurt like a kick in the scrotum,

For you do not yet know that the question, in its murderous
    triviality, is the last thing she will ever say to you. . . .

—"There's a Grandfather Clock in the Hall" (1974)

After surveying her letters, we have a pretty good hunch why Ruth Warren's question hurt so much and why Warren, as was frequently the case, sought to deflect his pain through a recourse to anger and callousness—rather like his most memorable character, that hypersensitive cynic Jack Burden. In a later poem, "What is the Voice That Speaks?" (1979), anger at his mother's question (and its many implications, intended or otherwise) will give way to tender regret, and, later still, in *Portrait of a Father,* Warren dispenses with her final words altogether and describes Ruth Warren's last moments like this: "Her eyes were open, the face upward and smiling, momentarily bathed in a lost youthfulness." (Something of a breakthrough? Perhaps, but in Warren's life and art such moments are hard won indeed and tenuous by their very nature.)

In the wake of Ruth Warren's death, her husband assumed the duties of correspondent, and the collection at Emory contains some two dozen letters from him to Robert Penn and Cinina, spanning the years 1932–1938. Like the letters of Warren's mother, those of Robert Franklin Warren should eventually be printed in their entirety; but a few observations are in order here. This correspondence attests to the suffering and courage that would ultimately define the father in his son's eyes. We see a man of proud dignity whose material aspirations have turned to naught, largely through forces beyond his control. He emerges at times as a quixotic (almost comic) figure who nevertheless manages to achieve and maintain a quiet, stoic heroism, and his letters offer a moving gloss on those memorable passages in the first version of *Brother to Dragons* (1953) that deal with the failures (and residual virtue) of fathers and the seemingly disproportionate remorse of sons. We know from Joseph Blotner and from the poet's own reminiscences that his relationship with his father was by all conventional measures a good

Allen Tate and Ruth Penn Warren, circa 1930 (Yale Collection of American Literature,
Beinecke Rare Book and Manuscript Library, used by permission of Helen H. Tate)

one. But much of the poetry suggests that it was somehow not good enough. Little delinquencies matter in the logic of the heart. Compared to his wife, Robert Franklin was not a prolific letter writer, but he understood the emotional transactions involved in the process. In a letter to Red and Cinina dated June 12, 1937, he allowed himself an uncharacteristic complaint: "I am looking for the letter you were to write me. I might get a few words from you at least twice a year." Did his son remember these lines or something like them immediately after his father's death in 1955, when he investigated the old man's sitting room and made a discovery he would incorporate into section three of the late sequence "Paradox of Time" (1980)?

> I saw the end. Later,
> I found the letter, the first
> Paragraph unfinished. I saw
> The ink-slash from that point
> Where the unconscious hand had dragged
> The pen as he fell. I saw
> The salutation. It was:
> "Dear Son."

Resurrecting and publicly analyzing family letters, by their very nature personal and private, is a risky business. There are temptations attached, largely stemming from the "therapeutic" mindset that afflicts our time. One must avoid the search for "pathologies"—often quite negligible—for their own sake (a form of high-toned gossip) and resist the impulse to derive a cautionary tale from the human drama such correspondence inevitably entails (a form of moralistic self-congratulation). Yet, in the end, the scholar *is* called upon to make some sense of the data, and in this case the philosopher Gabriel Marcel may provide us with the best means of fulfilling that obligation. We are accustomed to speaking of parent/child relationships in problematic terms, as if they admitted of definite answers, whereas Marcel implies that talk of "problem" parents and "problem" children is reductive and quite often pernicious. Instead he insists upon what he calls the "mystery of the family." A "mystery" partakes of the sacral dimension and thus invites us into a deepened sense of what it means to be human. Central to Marcel's view is a clear distinction between *having* and *being*. We are mistaken if we think of ourselves as *having* children rather than *being* parents. By the same token we do not *have* parents; we *are* sons and daughters. The mysterious intersubjectivity inherent in family life is crucial to establishing and maintaining an authentic selfhood (one of Robert Penn Warren's obsessive concerns), and, as the young Mexican philosopher Pedro Pallares notes, this presupposes the giving of the self to the Other, though in a "broken world" (the only world we inhabit according to Warren and Marcel) we of necessity give and receive selves that are fraught with imperfection.

This is, I would argue, the dynamic that drives much of Robert Penn Warren's finest poetry. The giving and taking was a continuous process that–by virtue of its authenticity–precluded a safe and comfortable resolution, and so it was reenacted over and over again. It is almost as if Warren were addressing Ruth and Robert in these terms: *I accept your damned meddling and fecklessness along with your unremitting love, and I give you my unworthy love–tainted as it is with resentment, embarrassment, shame, and guilt–in return.* In *Homo Viator* (1944) Gabriel Marcel gives us the image of a little boy who wanders far afield to pick wildflowers as a gift to his mother. In presenting them to her, he is in effect presenting himself. The image is perhaps too sentimental, but the principle holds true. Warren's gift to his parents, like that of the speaker in "The Return: An Elegy," is more disturbing, a body of poems resembling a "dark and swollen orchid." We, his readers, share in this legacy of anguish and love.

–William Bedford Clark, "Letters from Home: Filial Guilt in Robert Penn Warren," *Sewanee Review,* 110 (Summer 2002): 385–405

A First Book

Published by Payson and Clarke on 2 November 1929, Warren's first book, John Brown: The Making of a Martyr, *combined poetry, history, and fiction. Reviews were mixed.*

Allan Nevins begins his review, excerpted below, by discussing John Brown's stature. "To admirers of the Abolitionists," he writes, "John Brown will always be a hero," but he contends that his "real historical importance was small." He compares Warren's treatment of this "intensely interesting figure" to Hill Peebles Wilson's John Brown, Soldier of Fortune. A Critique *(1913) and Oswald Garrison Villard's* John Brown: 1800–1859. A Biography after Fifty Years *(1910).*

Martyr and Fanatic
Review of *John Brown*

. . . Mr. Warren's capable volume drives a path almost midway between the hostile treatment by Mr. H. P. Wilson and the laudatory treatment by Mr. O. G. Villard. Mr. Wilson pictured John Brown as a crafty, unscrupulous soldier of fortune, an adventurer who gambled with the money and lives of other men merely to gain riches and fame, and did not halt at the meanest crimes. In Mr. Villard's far abler and more careful book, he is pictured as an enthusiast whose motives were wholly unselfish, who aimed always at the freeing of a race; who committed murder at Pottawatomie and other crimes elsewhere, but who atoned at Harper's Ferry by the nobility of his philosophy and by his sublime readiness to give his life for his principles. Mr. Wilson oversimplified John Brown's character and motives; Mr. Villard seemed to many to take too much the position of Brown's pleader. To weigh the evidence on both sides and attempt to render impartial judgment was a useful enterprise.

Mr. Warren is severe on John Brown. He is much harsher than Mr. Villard, harsher even than Rhodes, in dealing with Brown's misdeeds–his embezzlements or at least reckless carelessness with his employer's money, his chicanery, his cruelty, his bloody violence. Yet his final verdict is not very different from that of such cool writers as Rhodes. The crux of the matter is the question of Brown's sincerity. Many of the acts which he committed were atrociously wrong– there is no doubt of that. The chief aim he kept in view, the freeing of the slaves, had moral grandeur– there is equally little doubt of that. Was he sincere in holding that his noble end justified his ignoble means? Mr. Warren answers this by saying that he was no hypocrite, but a man of enormous and criminal egotism. He was convinced that he was an instrument of Providence, that his will was God's will, that God had said to him, as to Joshua and Gideon, "Go forth and slay." He stole money, but not for himself, for he lived like an anchorite–it was for his cause. He killed innocent men, again for his cause. Mr. Warren, almost in spite of himself, admits that he always had an inner conviction that he was right. It did not fail him when he sat in his Virginia cell reading for the last time his cheap Bible.

> From the time when inflamed eyes stopped his ambition of becoming a minister–the usual career of the more intellight and ambitious frontier youth–until the time when he rode a murdered man's horse out of the Pottawatomie valley, every effort had ended in some unpredictable failure. Superb energy, honesty, and fraud, chicanery, charity, thrift, endurance, cruelty, conviction, murder and prayer–they all had failed, only to leave him surer than before that he was right and that his plans were "right in themselves."

In short, he was a fanatic. Mr. Warren is no doubt right in saying that he was not insane, and was as responsible

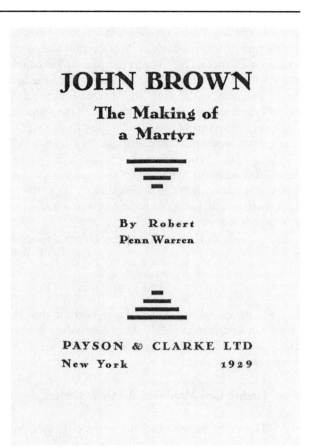

JOHN BROWN

The Making of a Martyr

By Robert
Penn Warren

PAYSON & CLARKE LTD
New York   1929

Frontispiece and title page for Warren's first book, published 2 November 1929
(Special Collections, Western Kentucky University Libraries)

for his deeds as are the general run of those we call criminals. But what other men regarded as crimes he regarded as the execution of a divine mandate.

Apart from this reading of Brown's character, and its brisk and dependably accurate recital of Brown's career, Mr. Warren's book is notable for its interpretation of the last act in the grim fanatic's life. His raid at Harper's Ferry is interpreted by Mr. Villard as primarily a foray for the liberation of slaves, without intention of causing a general slave insurrection. Mr. Warren believes that it was a good deal more than a foray. He concludes that Brown hoped and expected not merely to bring about a servile revolt, but to hasten the imminent conflict between North and South. His raid was to be the spark which should cause the whole border to blaze up as Kansas had blazed in 1856, and should lead to a general war. Necessarily he could not make any elaborate plans. But his scheme was not to take a few slaves and retreat to the Maryland hills; it was to seize the arsenal, arm hundreds of Negroes, march southward organizing the blacks, and wait for the aroused North to follow him. This theory is hard to reconcile with some of Brown's own statements, but Mr. Warren believes he made these statements in order to lead on his men till they could not turn back. If so, this was an insanely impracticable scheme, but also one of striking grandiosity. Mr. Warren's theory gives to the last great coup of John Brown a breadth and daring that lift it to a new dignity.

–Allan Nevins, "Martyr and Fanatic," *The New Republic,*
62 (19 March 1930): 134–135

* * *

This reviewer complained of "a lack of balance and of perspective" throughout Warren's biography but still had praise for him as a writer in this excerpt.

"A Vivid Story": Review of *John Brown*

John Brown, The Making of a Martyr can thus summarily be disposed of; but a reviewer who wishes to be fair cannot so dispose of the author. When not destroying the saint Mr. Warren can tell a vivid story. His simple narrative of the massacre at Pottawatomie and of the events at Harper's Ferry brings the past to life before the reader's eyes. Although he has not attained the balanced judgment of the poet, Mr. Warren is clever and has a neat habit of expressing himself. "Only once in these confused years of business did John Brown see, as many more honest men have seen, the very unattractive inside of a jail." When relieved of prejudice his cleverness often leads to sympathetic understanding: "Big talk was a Kansas habit; in a new country men have a tacit agreement to bluster in order to assure themselves that man is important after all."

–L. A. Harper, *University of California Chronicle*
(July 1930): 390

* * *

In this excerpt from Robert Penn Warren and the American Imagination *(1990), Hugh Ruppersburg discusses the themes in Warren's biography of John Brown that he returned to in later works.*

The "Higher-Law Man" and the Civic Order

The early novels, and the early biography of John Brown, explore the acquisition and exercise of power on both a personal and political level. Power in these works is linked directly to Warren's conception of the state as *polis.* In a 1981 introduction to *All the King's Men,* he explained: "The issue is between legitimacy and *de facto* power; and here to bring matters up to date, we substitute for the old meaning of legitimacy as heredity and God's will the new meaning of constitutionality." That is, the issue is whether power is wielded in a Constitutional manner, whether it is used to uphold democratic principles, to strengthen and sustain the Union, or to endanger it. The ultimate use to which power can be committed is for the protection of the state and the individuals it shelters. For this reason Warren remained a stalwart Unionist throughout his career: a believer in the mystic concept of unity among the American states, in the ideals and values on which that unity is based.

Had he expressed it in no other form, Warren's belief in the principle of civil order would be sufficiently evident through his portrayals of the emblematic figures who endanger it. The first such individual in his writing is the visionary, self-styled prophet-abolitionist John Brown, the subject of his first book, *John Brown: The Making of a Martyr,* published in 1929. The biography presents Brown as a man so obsessed with a Cause that he loses all sense of humanity and perspective, turns against his govern-

ment, and murders other human beings in the name of a Higher Good: the abolition of slavery. The evil he desires to purge exists for him in no real context–no relation to history, morality, or humanity. Warren's dislike grows not out of Brown's abolitionism but from his utter indifference to human life and social order, his willingness to foment anarchy if necessary in his battle against slavery. To Warren, Brown was the most dangerous among men. Thirty-four years later, in *The Legacy of the Civil War,* he explained why: "The conviction . . . that 'one with God is always a majority,' does not lend encouragement to the ordinary democratic process. With every man his own majority as well as his own law, there is, in the logical end, only anarchy, and anarchy of a peculiarly tedious and bloodthirsty sort, for every drop is to be spilled in God's name and by his explicit directive" (33). And Warren apparently suspects that Brown consciously exploited Higher Law absolutism to justify his actions.

Brown is the first in a series of social misanthropes in Warren's fiction who sever all ties with humanity in the service of a personal or political cause. Warren portrays Brown as a master of deceit who fools everyone around him, perhaps even himself. An expert in duplicity, he is especially adept at beguiling the leading transcendentalists of the day, those men who made virtue and morality the genuine basis of their professional lives. With more-than-apparent satisfaction, Warren describes Brown's visits to Thoreau and Emerson in Concord, Massachusetts, and cites Emerson's glowing accolade that Brown "is so transparent that all men see him through. He is a man to make friends wherever on earth courage and integrity are esteemed,–the rarest of heroes, a pure idealist, with no by-ends of his own. . . . He believes in two articles . . . the Golden Rule and the Declaration of Independence." Warren observes, "And it is only natural, that Emerson, in his extraordinary innocence, should have understood nothing, nothing in the world, about a man like John Brown to whom vocabulary was simply a very valuable instrument" (*John Brown,* 245–46).

Warren's attitude in the biography towards known figures of American history is the characteristic stance of his career. He rarely stands in awe of them. His recording eye is dispassionate and analytical. Accordingly, we can discern here a theme prominent in the later works, a theme which might seem paradoxical for a writer who so venerates the Great Men of History: the idea that the so-called Great Men of History often had at best only a tenuous link to those people and issues and events which were history's substance. They were, perhaps, spokesmen, commentators, symbols, even, like Brown, exploitative opportunists, relatively isolated from the elements of which history is made. Warren illustrates this notion in a discussion of the Kansas Free Soil disputes:

> "They killed one of the pro-slavery men, and the pro-slavery men killed one of the others, and I thought it was about mutual," an eye-witness told the politicians who, six months later, came to investigate the Kansas affairs. What did Calhoun sitting in his last Senate, or Garrison burning the Constitution, or Webster speaking at Syracuse know of this sort of thing? That generation-long debate between two orders of living, two sets of ideas, two philosophies, was finding strange and brutal repercussions along the frontier country, where men needed peace and all their energies to dig in and live before the harshness of nature. The issues and ideals which to Calhoun, to Garrison, to Webster, were so passionately clear, were very vague here, but what they lacked in clarity was made up for by violence and savagery. Perhaps it is the Gibsons, the R. P. Browns, the Collins', and the Sheriff Jones' [participants in the disputes] who, after all, must settle such issues. It is not a happy thought. (136)

It is not a happy thought because Warren worries that Great Men, and men in general, might in fact exert little force at all over history. They merely reflect it. History itself might churn on unaffected by those who pretend they can affect it, who themselves are its hapless victims. Such pessimism is a major theme of *Night Rider* (1939) and the other early novels, though later in his career Warren evinced muted optimism: *The Legacy of the Civil War* (1961) at least raises the possibility that individuals can influence history. Warren's pessimism in *John Brown* anticipates a valuation consistently expressed in his writings: the importance of the individual's private self over whatever public persona he might assume. *Jefferson Davis Gets His Citizenship Back* (1980) evinces a clear concern with Davis, Lincoln, Sherman, and other figures of the Civil War as *human beings,* not as shapers of history or wasters of cities. They are identifiable human personalities, with virtues and weaknesses, products of their era and environment. They become great because their society comes to see them as such, or because they come to view themselves as such, not because of innate ability or vision. Such qualities are always acquired in Warren's world.

John Brown is only one of many individuals in American history whom Warren faults for a "private, subjective moral idealism." In *The Legacy of the Civil War,* the transcendentalists, who helped provide a justifying logic to the most extreme among the abolitionists, receive his special blame: arguing that the individual owed allegiance to a Higher Law before any other, they provided reason for ignoring the laws

of the land. To be fair, Warren's real concern is with only a particular and small segment of the abolitionists, the extremists, those caught up in blood lust, hatred, and treason. "The cause for which the Aboli-

---

Stumbling into "Prime Leaf"

INTERVIEWERS: At least you could say that as a Southerner you were more conscious of what some of the issues were. You couldn't, I assume, forget the complexity of American social reality, no matter what your aesthetic concerns, or other concerns.

WARREN: It never crossed my mind when I began writing fiction that I could write about anything except life in the South. It never crossed my mind that I knew about anything else; knew, that is, well enough to write about. Nothing else ever nagged you enough to stir the imagination. But I stumbled into fiction, rather late. I've got to be autobiographical about this. For years I didn't have much interest in fiction, that is, in college. I was reading my head off in poetry, Elizabethan and the moderns, Yeats, Hardy, Eliot, Hart Crane. I wasn't seeing the world around me—that is, in any way that might be thought of as directly related to fiction. Be it to my everlasting shame that when the Scopes trial was going on a few miles from me I didn't even bother to go. My head was too full of John Ford and John Webster and William Blake and T. S. Eliot. If I had been thinking about writing novels about the South I would have been camping in Dayton, Tennessee— and would have gone about it like journalism. At least the Elizabethans saved me from that. As for starting fiction, I simply stumbled on it. In the spring of 1930 I was in Oxford, doing graduate work. I guess I was homesick, and not knowing it. Paul Rosenfeld, who with Van Wyck Brooks and Lewis Mumford, was then editing the old *American Caravan,* wrote and asked me why I didn't try a long story for them. He had had the patience one evening to listen to me blowing off about night-rider stories from boyhood. So Oxford and homesickness, or at least back-homeward-looking, and Paul Rosenfeld made me write *Prime Leaf,* a novelette, which appeared in the *Caravan* and was later the germ of *Night Rider.* I remember playing hookey from academic work to write the thing, and the discovery that you could really enjoy trying to write fiction. It was a new way of looking at things, and my head was full of recollections of the way objects looked in Kentucky and Tennessee. It was like going back to the age of twelve, going fishing and all that. It was a sense of freedom and excitement.

–Ellison and Walter, "The Art of Fiction XVIII: Robert Penn Warren," *Paris Review,* 4 (Spring–Summer 1957): 120–121

tionists labored was just," Warren explained in *Legacy*. "Who can deny that, or deny that they often labored nobly? But who can fail to be disturbed and chastened by the picture of the joyful mustering of the darker forces of our nature in that just cause?" (23). He adds that the national atmosphere which prevailed in the decades before the Civil War "did not, to say the least, cement the bonds of society. The exponent of the 'higher law' was, furthermore, quite prepared to dissolve the society in which he lived and say, with [William Lloyd Garrison], 'Accursed be that American Union.'" In the biography itself he observes that "the higher-law man, in any time and place, must always be ready to burn any constitution, for he must, ultimately, deny the very concept of society [and] repudiate all the institutions in which power is manifested–church, state, family, law, business" (26–27). These social institutions insure the order which Warren regards as important.

–Hugh Ruppersburg, *Robert Penn Warren and the American Imagination* (Athens & London: University of Georgia Press, 1990), pp. 24–27

Warren's "Briar Patch"

Warren's most controversial early writing was "The Briar Patch," one of a dozen essays included in I'll Take My Stand, *a collection "by Twelve Southerners," published in November 1930. The authors were associated with two groups, the Fugitives and the Agrarians. Although some of the Fugitives were also associated with the Agrarians, the groups were distinct in their approaches to the South and its history. As Louise Cowan points out, the Fugitives were literary and the Agrarians were mostly social and religious in their stances. Or, as Louis D. Rubin Jr. states in* The Wary Fugitives: Four Poets and the South *(1978), "An Agrarian . . . was a farmer with a philosophy."*

Contemporary reviewer Sterling Brown in Opportunity *excoriated Warren for his paternalistic endorsement of the separate-but-equal doctrine–a position Warren later repudiated. Later critics have viewed "The Briar Patch" as a product of Warren's thinking at the time and as an early example of his more general concern with the issue of justice. In* Racial Politics and Robert Penn Warren's Poetry *(2002), Anthony Szczesiul argues that critics have given "short shrift" to Warren's early racial views and have "tended to read 'The Briar Patch' by superimposing over the text Warren's later, more liberal ideas. In other words, they read forward in anticipation of his conversion to an integrationist position."*

In this excerpt from his essay "Robert Penn Warren's Pursuit of Justice: From Briar Patch to Cosmos"–one of the earliest critical essays to explore connections between Warren's fiction and

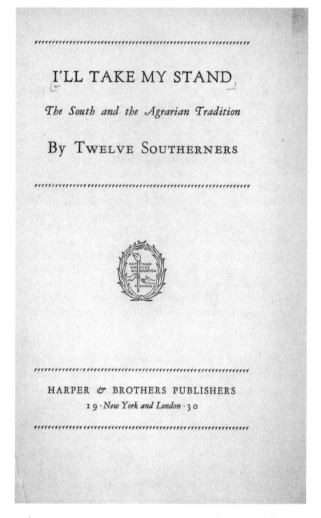

Title and contents pages for the collection intended as a defense of rural culture against those who argued for the benefits of industrialization. Donald Davidson, who gave Warren the assignment "to prove that Negroes are country folk . . . 'born and bred in a briar patch,'" was alarmed by the "progressive implications" of his essay (Richland County Public Library).

nonfiction– James E. Ruoff *examines what he sees as Warren's limited perspective on justice not only in "The Briar Patch" but also in* John Brown: The Making of a Martyr *and the novella "Prime Leaf," which Warren published in* American Caravan IV *in 1931. He goes on to argue that all of Warren's work through his 1943 novel* At Heaven's Gate *was similarly limited:*

in dealing with the problem of justice, the one theme of significance in his early fiction, Warren was hamstrung by an evident inability to achieve a synthesis of philosophy and art, a union of mind and heart, so that his "images"–and especially his characters–could rise to some dialectical configuration and yet exist independent of, but related to, the philosophical generalizations they were created to express. (25)

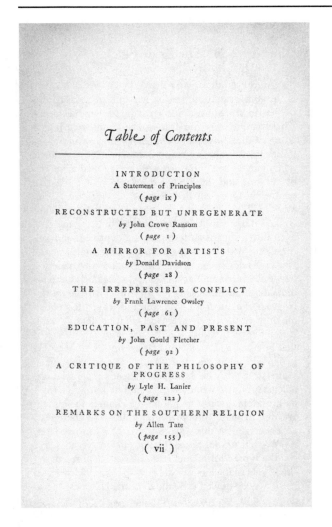

Table of Contents

For Ruoff, Warren's All the King's Men *"marks the end of his experience as an agrarian regionalist and the beginning of his work as a mature philosophical novelist."*

A Hamstrung View of Justice

In his essay on Joseph Conrad's *Nostromo,* Robert Penn Warren defines the philosophical novelist as ". . . one for whom the documentation of the world is constantly striving to rise to the level of generalization about values, for whom the image strives to rise to symbol, for whom images always fall into a dialectical configuration . . . ."[1] This definition describes not only Conrad's method but Warren's own development from a parochial writer largely preoccupied with regional "images" to a mature philosophical novelist concerned with universal themes. In fact, the whole range of his work from 1929 to 1956 shows that, in his quest for a rationale of justice, he has moved from a comparatively simple and empirical

"documentation" of the South toward increasingly complex generalizations about values. Formerly a regionalist justifying the traditions of the South, he has become a philosophical novelist justifying the ways of God to man.

Nothing could better demonstrate this movement from documentation to generalization than the contrast between his early essay "The Briar Patch" (1930) and his recent book *Segregation: The Inner Conflict in the South* (1956), both dealing with the problem of justice for the southern Negro. Although in "The Briar Patch" Warren defended segregation and in his recent book he opposes it, the significant difference between the two works lies not so much in this change of conviction as in a remarkable transmutation of elemental values. "The Briar Patch" was "documentation": it was sociological, empirical, and objective. Optimistically, it viewed injustice to the Negro as a regional problem soluble within the context of an irrevocable tradition of Southern apart-

What Might Be Done: The Argument for the Negro in "The Briar Patch"

John L. Stewart summarizes Warren's essay in this excerpt from his book on the Fugitives and the Agrarians. He notes that the essay, written while Warren was still at Oxford, "was notably restrained and patiently logical and specific in surveying the position of the Negro and what might be done for him."

His thesis was simple: the welfare of Southern white man was inextricably bound up with that of the Negro, and to have any chance of success a program aimed at preserving the good life of the past for the white must aim as well at a secure, stable, and dignified life for the Negro. Moreover, Warren reiterated, any person who would obstruct the Negro's self-fulfillment did not respect himself as a man: to deny the dignity and humanity of the Negro was to confess his sense of his own inferiority. But industrialism would bring no help to the Negro. Under it he would be exploited as cheap labor and, because he competed with the poor whites for jobs and forced them to work for almost as little as he did, he would become the target of their hatred and violence—as he was already wherever an industrial economy, in the form of the crop lien system, had been established in an agrarian area. The Negro, Warren believed, could live best on a subsistence farm. "In the past the Southern negro has always been a creature of the small town and farm. That is where he still chiefly belongs, by temperament and capacity; there he has less the character of a 'problem' and more the status of a human being who is likely to find in agriculture and domestic pursuits the happiness that his good nature and easy ways incline him to as an ordinary function of his being." For this he required vocational training: education of the Negroes should aim not "to create a small band of intellectual aristocrats . . . [but] to make the ordinary negro into a competent workman or artisan and a decent citizen." Once the Negroes had more economic freedom, as a result of vocational training, they could support Negro doctors, lawyers, and other professional men. As for those Negroes who went into industry, they should be permitted to organize and should receive pay equal to the whites', for otherwise the Negroes dragged all labor down.

As for segregation, "Equal but separate" appears to be as far as Warren was then prepared to go. One must be careful to avoid underestimating just how far Warren *had* gone when he insisted on respect for the rights and dignity of the Negro as an individual, and one must recognize that the essay is everywhere suffused with a quiet humanity and decency. Yet reference to the Negro's "good nature" and "easy ways" and the almost casual assumption that the farm was

his natural setting suggest that Warren, for all his generous spirit, saw both the Negro and the satisfactions of life on the subsistence farm in too simple terms. There is, one feels, too little realization of what humiliation of the individual even such kindly proposals as these might involve—proposals eminently realistic when judged solely in terms of the regional economy of the time and the limited sums available for Negro education. One feels this because in *Segregation* (1956) Warren himself told us exactly what the Negro wanted most: simply to be treated like everyone else, even if that means suffering, being deprived, and failing along with the rest. Anything that comes to the Negro under a system that makes a distinction between white and black, even if it appears to be to his immediate advantage, is an affront. Two thoughtful Negroes explained it to Warren this way: "'It's not so much what the Negro wants as what he doesn't want. The main point is not that he has poor facilities. It is that he must endure a constant assault on his ego. He is denied human dignity.'" And: "'It's different when your fate is on your face. Just that. It's the unchangeableness. Now a white man, even if he knows he can't be President, even if he knows the chances for his son are one in many millions—long odds—still there's an idea there.'" But this was a quarter of a century later. As Warren wrote, he could not talk to Negroes. He could not read John Dollard's *Caste and Class in a Southern Town*, that clumsy, startling book, published in 1937, which showed how much of the Negroes' "good nature" and "easy ways" were a protective manner, so habitual as to be quite unconscious, but readily dropped when the Negroes were among their own people and hurt pride, hostility, and even contempt could be revealed without fear. But, for all the limitation of his perspective, Warren wrote with that eye for naturalistic detail which already distinguished his poetry and gave his brief excursion into sociology and economics authority and concreteness not found in most of the other essays. Moreover, he had his vision, here so rudimentary when compared to what it would become in his long poems and the novels, of a man's compelling need to fulfill himself. Otherwise, the essay had little connection with or significance for his development as a writer. It was not in the least philosophical, and it was the philosophical bases of Agrarianism which counted most with him.

–John L. Stewart, *The Burden of Time: The Fugitives and Agrarians* (Princeton: Princeton University Press, 1965), pp. 164–166

A Pastoral Rebuke

In his book The Wary Fugitives: Four Poets and the South, *Rubin asserts that Warren believed he and his friends wrote* I'll Take My Stand *as "a kind of pastoral rebuke." The "lasting qualities" of the book, Rubin writes, "have to do not with its supposed 'alternative' to an industrial society, but with its assertion of permanent, ongoing humane values, as a protest against the dehumanizing possibilities of that society."*

Robert Penn Warren, I think, has given perhaps the most cogent explanation of the ultimate worth of *I'll Take My Stand* and why he and his fellow Fugitive poets became involved in it. At the Fugitives' Reunion in Nashville a quarter-century afterward, in 1956, Warren talked about his own involvement. It came, he said, after he had lived away from the South and the kind of life he had been accustomed to living. He had been talking and thinking about the disintegration of the idea of the individual in modern society and how this problem related to democracy. "It's the machine of power in this so-called democratic state; the machines disintegrate individuals, so you have no individual sense of responsibility and no awareness that the individual has a past and a place." Along with this notion about the present, there were the pieties and loyalties and sentiments of his southern background, including the Confederate heritage—"a pious element, or a great story—a heroic story—a parade of personalities who are also images for their individual values." Thus his involvement in agrarianism was a protest "against certain things: against a kind of de-humanizing and disintegrative effect on your notion of what an individual person could be in the sense of a loss of your role in society."

Rubin later speculates as to Warren's motive for writing his essay.

. . . It seems to me that he saw his role in the enterprise as a method of *action*. It was a vehicle for protest, and not merely a general, metaphorical rebuke to dehumanization and the society of scientism and mass culture, but a specific, tangible strategy for assailing what seemed so vast and unassailable—not industrialism alone, but all that must have appeared, to a young southern poet in the late 1920s, to go along with it: finance capitalism, the cultural dominance of New York City and the commercialism of the literary marketplace, the debasement of language as practiced in advertising and social science, the defeat and impoverishment of the South, the glib parlor Marxism of the period that was already being mouthed in advanced metropolitan intellectual circles, the self-serving Babbittry of American business, the sense of dislocation, the breakdown in manners and forms, the threat that naked, unchecked economic power posed to democratic society. Here was a way of hitting back. Whether it was practically feasible didn't really matter as much as the opportunity to have an impact. Poets, scholars—the alienated, the cut-off—were together acting *in* the realm of economics and political power.

—Louis D. Rubin, *The Wary Fugitives: Four Poets and the South* (Baton Rouge & London: Louisiana State University Press, 1978), pp. 243–244, 339–340

heid. The recent *Segregation,* however, is on the level of "dialectical configuration": it is philosophical, psychological, and profoundly subjective. Pessimistically, it sees injustice to the Negro as a universal problem perhaps insoluble because symptomatic of "a thousand unsolved problems of justice."[2] Whereas "The Briar Patch" glossed over complexities with projects for quick and easy reforms, *Segregation* is skeptical of the inevitability of progress and grimly dubious of human nature.

For the most part, "The Briar Patch" is unimaginative in its social conceptions. In 1930 the deleterious psychological effects of segregation seemed of little importance to Warren. The Negro who wanted to sleep in the white man's hotel, eat in the white man's restaurant, or send his children to the white man's school was simply betraying a "defect in self-respect" or adhering to a spurious concept of justice.[3] To Warren the problem was chiefly economic: the Negro must equip himself with agrarian skills in order to make his services of "indispensable value" to the Southern community. At the same time he must be

chary of the new industrialism that was transforming the economic and social structure of the Old South and had reduced his Northern brethren to wage slaves. In short, what little there was in "The Briar Patch" that rose to generalization—hostility to industrialism and mystic faith in agrarianism—was derivative of Fugitive attitudes expounded in *I'll Take My Stand* by John Crowe Ransom, Allen Tate, Andrew Nelson Lytle, and other Southern conservatives.[4]

Ruoff goes on to argue that from the very beginning of Warren's career "the patent injustice of the Negro's situation in the South turned his pen toward a consideration of related problems of justice."

In fact, his first publication, *John Brown: The Making of a Martyr* (1929), was about slavery. Written, like "The Briar Patch," with the regional bias of the Southern Fugitive, it was an elaborate attempt to exonerate the South by exposing the North's hypocritical attitude toward slavery in the person of its "martyr," who in Warren's ironic portrait was shown to be a thief, a windbag, and a slaveholder. Like the zealots he inspired, he was, in Warren's view, the frenzied, wild-eyed prophet of John Steuart Curry's painting. This conception of Brown is important as archetype for the character who recurs throughout Warren's later fiction—the man fanatically devoted to a private vision of perfect justice. According to Warren, Brown was a lunatic and a fraud deified during the North's intellectual carpetbagging after the Civil War; having won the victory the North canonized the saints of abolition and exorcised the devils of the Southern cause. Hence *John Brown* is a cynical book in its suggestion that justice is what those who survive choose to call it.

Warren's first attempt at fiction a year later, the novelette "Prime Leaf,"[5] was equally limited in philosophical range. When, during the Kentucky Tobacco War of 1904, the growers' association coerces farmers into boycotting the monopoly, Mr. Hardin and his son are on opposite sides until young Hardin joins his father against the association and is shot down in resisting a raid. For the most part "Prime Leaf" restricts its impact to this simple irony of young Hardin's being killed when he decides to follow the cause of justice, a thematic simplicity paralleled by the psychological one that all the main characters are arbitrarily presented as good or evil: it is a simple matter of Hardin and his son, independent and virtuous landowners in the best tradition of the Old South, pitted against the cowardly terrorists of the tobacco association. For the most part, too, "Prime Leaf" confines itself to a realistic presentation of regional images—the agrarian Southern family at work and play, whimsical descriptions of rural Kentucky—without any rising to the level of generalization about values.

It was "Prime Leaf" that gave birth, nine years later, to Warren's first novel *Night Rider,* which employs the same scene and conflict, namely Bardsville, Kentucky, during the tobacco war; and yet the novel has so much more psychological and thematic content that there is little apparent relationship between the two stories except in germ of locale and history. Actually, *Night Rider* bears more direct affinity to *John Brown* than to "Prime Leaf," for it was obviously Warren's concept of the martyr of Harper's Ferry which inspired the character of Percy Munn in *Night Rider.* Like Brown, Percy Munn is what Warren in his later fiction was to call "the man of idea" who becomes so passionately absorbed in an abstract concept of justice that he destroys himself and other people in compulsive pursuit of it.

–James E. Ruoff, "Robert Penn Warren's Pursuit of Justice: From Briar Patch to Cosmos," *Research Studies of the State College of Washington,* 27 (March 1959): 19–23

1. "Nostromo," *Sewanee Review,* LIX (Summer, 1951), 391.

2. See *Segregation: The Inner Conflict in the South* (Modern Library, 1956), p. 113.

3. "The Briar Patch," in *I'll Take My Stand: The South and the Agrarian Tradition,* by Twelve Southerners (New York, 1930), pp. 252–53.

4. For the social and political views of this group, see John Bradbury, *The Fugitives: A Critical Account* (Chapel Hill, 1958), pp. 3–28.

5. First published in the magazine *American Caravan* in 1930 and reprinted in Warren's *Circus in the Attic and Other Stories* (New York, 1947).

A Return to Nashville

In this excerpt Warren reminisces about the years he spent teaching at Vanderbilt and living in Nashville during the early 1930s.

Happy Years

I taught at Vanderbilt for three years, beginning in 1931. Edwin Mims was still chairman of the English department; he and I were never close, to put it mildly, and after the second year, when Davidson had returned, Mims fired me. Then, just before Christmas, John Donald Wade, who didn't get along with Mims either, made a visit to my house to say that he had just resigned with the stipulation that I be returned to my old post. But I was "let out" the following year. I had come back deliberately, and I didn't want to leave, never wanted to leave, but there was no way I could stay. I hated to give up Nashville and Middle Tennessee, hated to part with the friends—we seemed to have so much to say to one another—but the next fall I left for Louisiana State University, where I had found a job and where my close friend Cleanth Brooks, with whom I had overlapped at Oxford, already was teaching.

Tom Zerfoss had wanted to buy a farm where I could live, a place where he could keep his horses and I could keep a garden and write, hoping the combination would be enough to put something on the table. I made a search and did find such a place, a perfect little farm in Williamson County, and he subsequently bought it, but by then I had been fired and my dream of Middle Tennessee country was gone. Before all that had happened, an old black carpenter named Carpenter and I had fixed up the little house at Riverwood, the Burch place, and I had whitewashed it, and my wife and I had lived there

2 Taumalpais Rd

<u>THE APPLE TREE</u>

beyond it,

~~Some forty feet away~~

It was an old tree. On one side, the stone chimney stood awkward-

ly like a disgraced relic in the April sunshine. On the other side

each April

were the peach trees, which still put forth ~~their~~ bloom, ~~painful and~~

rich on the black bark of age. ~~But the~~ apple tree was much older than

the peach trees, nobody knew how old. It had been an old tree twenty

years before when the cabin burned, and then the peach trees had

been scarcely in their prime.

"It was # pretty old ~~tree~~ then," Miss Kate would say, " and I

recollect exactly how long ago that was. It was the spring John was

born."

that time

Since ~~that~~ the apple tree had never shown its sparse white

blossoms on the side toward the chimney; for there the boughs were

the

more gnarled and abrupt, as if on ~~that~~ spring night twenty years ~~before~~

they had lifted their buds

before, ~~their branches just as they had lifted~~ toward the unnatural

then

brilliance, ~~and~~ jerked back, like crooked fingers, withered beyond ~~the~~

whirled

repair of ~~the~~ seasons. The flame had ~~spun~~ up like a rocket from

just dry from the damp of winter

the ~~dry~~ shingles, and Ben and Rosemary and old Jake, ~~scattering~~ and ~~all~~ the little

the door like   burning trashpile

niggers had scattered from ~~like like~~ cockroaches from a ~~trashpile~~ at

springcleaning, ~~time.~~ The children, and even the grown ~~ones,~~ had

~~scattering~~

stood as near ~~to~~ the fire as they could, ~~with~~ their faces showing a

peculiar

~~strange~~ mingling of the ~~devout~~ excitement of barbecue picnic and

a

the awe of Judgement Day, while ~~every~~thing they owned in the world

burned up. The only thing they ~~had~~ saved was a 10 gauge shotgun,

which Jake, for all his seventy years, had enough wit to seize

before he hobbled out after the others. He didn't know ~~that~~ it

~~was hell~~

Page from a draft of Warren's first attempt at writing a novel, circa 1930–1932. Revised and retitled as "God's Own Time,"
the novel was rejected by Harcourt, Brace and Bobbs-Merrill and was never published (Yale Collection of American
Literature, Beinecke Rare Book and Manuscript Library).

for two years. It was perfectly situated and had its own cranky charm, and leaving it was not easy.

One of my most vivid memories from that house is of the tornado that struck in East Nashville in 1933. A good many people were killed by that storm, as I recall, and the devastating effect of it was everywhere to be seen. I was propped up in bed reading papers when it hit. I heard a noise like a freight train passing over my head, and then a crash. The tornado had picked up part of a brick barn not far off and hurled it through the air. The next morning I walked through the village outside the gate of the farm. It looked like a bombed-out town.

A week later, another storm came. I was in the car when suddenly it got very dark, like turning off a light switch. A tree fell in front of me, and I got stuck trying to get around it. When there was a lull I got out of the car, but the wind returned and literally pinned me against the door. That was one of the most frightening experiences in my memory.

The little whitewashed house was several miles from the university, and I drove back and forth first in a Baby Austin and then in a big old Studebaker we bought from Harriet and Frank Owsley for fifty dollars.

The Owsleys were special friends. Frank was an Alabamian, a tall, sandy-haired, high-spirited man with a warm sense of humor and a great natural dignity. He was a historian who also had a passion for William Faulkner in the early days when the Mississippian was a young and little-known writer, and one of our constant topics of conversation was Faulkner and his work. Frank and Harriet had a camp on a bluff overlooking the Cumberland River, and I remember well the square dances, the summer swimming, the whiskey breakfasts on frosty mornings, all interlaced with ferocious but good-natured arguments about politics, history, and literature. Once when I had a sudden and unexpected operation, it was the Owsleys who took me in for recuperation, and did it with such matter-of-factness and grace. Generosity was the hallmark of that household.

The other home I knew best was Ransom's. He was no longer my freshman English teacher but a close friend, and at the same time a kind of model of human worth. John and his quite beautiful wife, Robb, had two growing children (and later a baby, whom they affectionately called Alibi), and theirs was a place of enormous energy—for work and play and study, for poetry and talk, for writing, even for

watching sunsets. They were full of games. My wife and I often disastrously played bridge with the Ransoms on Saturday night. I remember one marathon performance that began early one Saturday afternoon and continued until Sunday night, with only short breaks for necessary food and drink and a little sleep. It seemed scarcely less than natural that the Ransoms rented a bankrupt country club for a year before they settled in the country and invited friends to share their tennis courts and billiard tables.

Many of the people I have been talking about—Ransom and Davidson, Lytle and Lanier, Wade and Owsley and Tate and others—were members of the Agrarian group, a spinoff of sorts from the Fugitives (a few of us had belonged to both), but a different group in many ways, more concerned with economic and social questions than with poetry. The Agrarian movement was an umbrella, a tent, with a big menagerie of arguing animals under it. It was not a cohesive group at all. We were Southerners asking old questions as if they were new, questions about the nature of modernism and technology as they related to the South's economy. We had begun to see that modernism meant a shift in the sense of man's relationship to nature and to his fellow man. There were questions about race for some of us, and others mourned the demise of the Confederacy and wanted to raise again the dream of Southern nationalism, and in many of those matters we disagreed sharply among ourselves. But I think all of us were concerned about the consequences of mindless and uncontrolled change—what most people call progress.

To my mind, the questions were fundamental ones. They had to do with the destruction of the family, the isolation of the old, the loss of a sense of continuity and fellowship, the absorption of the individual in mass society. Today, in all the public debate about oil and gas and energy, about nuclear power, about ecology and environmental quality, the questions are still the same—only the vocabulary is changed. Will man run technology, or will technology run man? Now, as then, there are no ready answers.

When I came back to Nashville in 1931, *I'll Take My Stand* had just appeared to as many jeers as cheers, and some of the cheers depressed me as much as the jeers. In the anthology, I had written an essay on race, a piece called "The Briar Patch." I learned later that some of the brethren didn't want the piece in the book—they thought it was too liberal. It certainly couldn't be considered liberal now. It was a plea to make the separate societies of whites and blacks truly equal. I couldn't see then, as I do now, that the very separateness of the societies was at the heart of the inequality.

The race issue continued to be a preoccupation in my fiction and poetry, and in two other books I wrote–*Segregation: The Inner Conflict in the South* and *Who Speaks for the Negro?* But back then, in 1930, I saw it as merely one aspect of a larger question. How long ago that old book seems, that Agrarian anthology. Race has been the most serious domestic issue of this century in the United States, and it's not settled, not yet. If it is ever resolved, the South may do it first, and best. I've heard many blacks and whites say that, and I believe it too.

For all the difficulties of those three years I spent at Vanderbilt in the 1930s–the Depression, the temporary status of my job, the Agrarian controversies–I think of them as very happy years for me. So many of the friendships have been lifelong friendships. And so many of the writers who were there went on to have distinguished careers. I wrote one novel in Nashville (fortunately, it was rejected), but years later, my second published novel, *At Heaven's Gate,* was suggested by the Nashville of the period of Rogers Caldwell and Luke Lea. I hadn't known that I was living in the midst of suggestions there, but my life during those years was full of suggestions, full of melodrama. Nashville appears quite often in my work, and I can't write fiction at all except about the South. Not specific facts–imagination doesn't work that way–but suggestions out of what I know and what I am.

With Ransom and Davidson still there to work their magic, the very active literary life around Vanderbilt continued. But there were some students who brought their own magic with them. One, now dead, was a brilliant poet, a Nashville boy from Hume-Fogg High School named Randall Jarrell. My first year there I taught a small section of sophomores who had been selected as the brightest and best prepared, and Randall was among them, though he was only a freshman, because it was already quite clear that no freshman class could hold him. He was so gifted that he terrorized my bright group of sophomores, not out of malice but with the cruel innocence of a baby. Finally I told him that he was scaring them to death.

Edwin Mims, the chairman of the English department at Vanderbilt who decided not to renew Warren's contract. At the time Warren was not seen as having adequate scholarly credentials (Paul K. Conkin, Gone with the Ivy: A Biography of Vanderbilt University *[Knoxville: University of Tennessee Press, 1985]; Thomas Cooper Library, University of South Carolina).*

"What am I doing?" he demanded in sincere innocence.

I suggested that he put his mind to helping them, that being more productive than withering criticism. He did. He was already writing extraordinarily beautiful poems. He was in fact a genius.

Randall and I became very good friends. He would come out to my little whitewashed house and talk poetry and philosophy and brutally criticize my poems. I listened carefully. He was often right and more often amusing, so amusing that it didn't matter much that it was at my expense.

Later, he followed Ransom to Kenyon College. Then, I believe, he washed out as a flyer in World War II, but remained in that branch of service, and the experience gave him some of his finest poems, some of the finest poems ever written on the subject of war by an American. I treasure a letter he wrote to me a few weeks before his tragic death.

To the same period at Vanderbilt belongs Jesse Stuart, a man remarkable in his way and in a very opposite way from Jarrell's. He was a product of Eastern Kentucky mountain schools, and he had absorbed the life and speech and folk sense of his region and had a fanatical drive to write about them. In one of his courses (not mine), he handed in a term paper that became a 350-[page]autobiography, later to be published as a book, to a very good reception. After the autobiography, story followed story and poem followed poem into print. As the volume of his work increased, one reviewer said of him that he had something of the value of a national park. Flannery O'Connor once remarked that Jesse's ego was like the light on the front of a train.

He came often to my house, and I liked nothing better than to catch him in an anecdotal mood and listen to him discuss the world he came from and the raw material of his poems. He was often better in conversation than on the printed page. His poems and stories were simple, sometimes too simple, but many of them contained flashes of true poetic perception, and they always revealed his flawless ear for language, for the poetic terms of folk speech and the characteristic detail of his native region.

Other outstanding students came to Vanderbilt after my time there, and went on to become fine writers. One was Peter Taylor, who was descended from Bob and Alf Taylor, brothers who had run against each other for governor of Tennessee. I knew Peter at Louisiana State, where he went after leaving Vanderbilt. He has become one of the finest writers of short stories in the country in our time. Another notable example is James Dickey, a poet of tremendous power and of promise even beyond the power he has exhibited. There is no doubt that some of his work will be permanent, and he will be one of Vanderbilt's most valuable advertisements.

And it was not at Vanderbilt alone that creativity flourished in the Nashville of the 1920s and 1930s. Among the writers who led the literary renaissance of black America in that period were James Weldon Johnson and Arna Bontemps, both of whom were to teach at Fisk University. Nashville has always been a good book town, too, with its church publishing houses and especially its bookstores. Mills and Zibart's have been there for decades, and there was Stokes and Stockell, and early in the nineteenth century there was a famous bookshop, Berry's, and others before that.

Nashville was to me an interesting place full of interesting people in the 1930s, and I didn't want to leave it. I haven't suffered from being forced out, but I haven't forgotten how special those years were. I have gone back often for visits, but there are fewer and fewer old friends left. Early in 1979 I went for the funeral of Allen Tate, my greatly admired friend who had been really a combination of older brother and tutor to me. Some years ago I remember Tate saying he wondered what would have been the result if the poets and writers around the Vanderbilt campus had been scattered among the great Eastern universities of that period. He would have made his way anywhere, of course, and maybe some of the rest of us would have too—but Tate called Nashville a happy accident for us all, and it was.

The little Nashville of fifty years ago was my first big city. I don't even know my way around the new Nashville, not even around the Vanderbilt campus, but I carry the old Nashville in my head, grateful for the friends it gave me and for so much else. How remarkably lucky I was to have been there. I have often thought that for me and my purposes and aspirations, it was the best place in the world. I couldn't want it to have been any different from what it was.

–"Robert Penn Warren: A Reminiscence," in *Nashville: The Faces of Two Centuries, 1780–1980,* edited by John Egerton (Nashville: Plus Media, 1979), pp. 215–220

Poet, Teacher, Novelist: 1934–1950

Twenty-nine years old when he left Vanderbilt University for Baton Rouge and a teaching position at Louisiana State University (LSU), Warren had completed what William Bedford Clark calls his "apprentice years." In the next sixteen years—eight spent at LSU and eight at the University of Minnesota—he became a major figure in American letters, respected for his work as an editor of The Southern Review *and for his collaborations with Cleanth Brooks on influential textbooks such as* Understanding Poetry *(1938), and acclaimed for his poetry and fiction, beginning with his first collection,* Thirty-Six Poems *(1935), and his first novel,* Night Rider *(1939). Warren's years in Baton Rouge were particularly important because there he became an interested observer of the career of Huey P. Long, the populist Louisiana politician whose presidential ambitions ended in assassination. Warren explored the literary possibilities of a Long-like figure, first in drama, and then in his most celebrated work, the Pulitzer Prize–winning novel* All the King's Men *(1946).*

"A Marvelous Arrangement"

This excerpt is from a letter in which Warren asked Porter for a story to publish in the Southwest Review, *the journal on which he worked as an associate editor when he first came to LSU.*

**Warren to Katherine Anne Porter,
22 December 1934**

. . . As you see from the heading of this note I am at Louisiana State University. I am delighted with the place, and especially with my job, which seems designed for my demands. I teach three days a week, and the courses I want. It is really a marvelous arrangement for a person who is trying to do something else at the same time.

—*Selected Letters of Robert Penn Warren, Volume One, The Apprentice Years, 1924–1934,* edited by William Bedford Clark (Baton Rouge: Louisiana State University Press, 2000), p. 259

The Baton Rouge home the Warrens rented for three or four years beginning in 1934 (Charles East Papers, Louisiana and Lower Mississippi Valley Collections, Louisiana State University Libraries, Baton Rouge)

Baton Rouge in the 1930s

This undated essay, titled "Memories of Baton Rouge," was written by Charles East, former editor in chief of the LSU Press and longtime resident of the city. The new state capitol East mentions— a project championed by Louisiana governor and U.S. senator Huey P. Long—was completed in March 1932; Long was assassinated there on 8 September 1935.

My earliest memories of Baton Rouge are of a small cottage on Spain Street–a house that is still standing, by the way–where my aunt had a room with Missy and Lindsey McKee and where I would sometimes venture one block over to Government to watch the streetcars pass. Later I would ride them myself–out Government to North 19th (or Dufrocq, as it was known then), then north past the cemeteries to Main, and west on Main to Lafayette. At Lafayette the cars turned south to the Old State Capitol and made their way to St. Louis Street by way of North Boulevard. Eventually you came back to where you started, and the ride–which in those depression days cost a nickel–was known as riding the Belt.

About 1936 the streetcars were replaced by buses. Baton Rouge was then a small city of perhaps 30,000 people, nothing like the city it would become. The city ran east as far as the airport on Government, and south to the university by way of Highland Road (Nicholson Drive was about to be built, and I remember riding the dirt right-of-way on the back of a bicycle). To the north of course, above Choctaw Road and across Scenic Highway from a section known as Dixie, was the refinery–Standard Oil then, later Esso, and still later Exxon.

The city's main street was Third Street, a busy thoroughfare where crowds thronged to Dalton's and Rosenfield's to shop, or to the Paramount Theatre, one of the few cool spots in the city in the hot summers before the arrival of air conditioning. For those willing to brave the heat for the Saturday serials, there was the Louisiana Theatre in the next block.

On my visits to Baton Rouge those summers there never seemed to be a lack of something to do. There was, for instance, the new State Capitol, a source of pleasure and discovery even before bullets nicked the marble in the hallway outside the office of the governor one night in 1935. In the basement under the Senate and House chambers were, not legislators, but exhibits of the agricultural and mineral products of the state– and huge glass tanks in which the saltwater and freshwater fishes of Louisiana swam.

Beginning in 1935 there was the swimming pool in City Park, which even had a concrete island you could swim out to, and nearby there was a merry-go-round house with its menagerie of carved animals that rode around and around into the afternoons. Down the hill and under the railroad overpass was the city's zoo, a not very spectacular collection of real animals that I remember included a wolf and several cages of monkeys as well as an alligator or two. On a hill beyond the zoo the Redsticks, those sunburnt boys of summer, played their hearts out.

Summer meant ice cream, and the best ice cream this side of a hand-turned freezer was at the Blue Bird Ice Cream place on Plank Road across from the Louisiana Creamery. Better still, the Blue Bird offered curb service. You could also, by the mid-thirties, drive up in front of Stroube's Drug Store at the head of Third Street, where carhops were at the ready with metal trays that they attached to the car windows. These were forerunners of the enormously popular drive-ins that flourished in the forties–places like Alessi's on Florida Boulevard and Hopper's on Scenic Highway.

If you were of a mind to watch the trains, you could visit the Y&MV depot at the foot of North Boulevard or the less impressive L&A station out Government Street, where the first streamliner I ever saw, the *Southern Belle,* came in. I think some of my happiest afternoons were spent on North Boulevard in front of the old Stanocola Medical where my aunt, Annie Linstrom (later Holcombe), worked–flying one of the rubber-band driven planes that I had bought at Kress's or Woolworth's on Third Street.

Actually there were four dime stores on Third, the other two being W. T. Grant and McLellan's, all of them filled with toys for a boy's asking and tanks of exotic goldfish. Kress's had a lunch counter that offered the most delicious bacon, lettuce, and tomato sandwiches anywhere, and by the mid-thirties the Piccadilly Cafeteria in the second block of Third was drawing crowds that sometimes waited in a line stretching to the corner and east on Convention Street.

Sometimes the afternoons were spent simply watching from the upstairs gallery of my Aunt Belle East's on Convention across from the old red-brick First Baptist Church. There the world–or at any rate the Baton Rouge world–eventually passed my great-aunt's doorstep: the drummers who boarded next door at Mrs. Scott's, children on their way home from Vacation Bible School, the vegetable man calling up to ask if we wanted a mess of greens or some freshly picked corn or a nice sweet watermelon.

Alas, those summers passed. Dalton's became D. H. Holmes and in time, a part of it at least, another parking lot. The dime stories closed or moved. The trains ceased to run. A wrecking ball sent the Paramount to its doom. Yet I have never quite forgotten the sound the streetcars made and the ding-ding-ding of the bell the motorman rang when he welcomed you aboard.

–Charles East Collection, Hill Memorial Library,
Louisiana State University

The Old War Skule

After Huey P. Long's inauguration as governor in 1928, Louisiana State University—known as the "Old War Skule" for its graduation of many military cadets—was one of his highest priorities. Long increased expenditures on the university and, with the approval of the LSU Board of Supervisors, hired James Monroe Smith as president. While critics questioned Long's motives, his efforts to make LSU a first-class institution helped to create a vibrant intellectual climate that afforded Warren opportunities to distinguish himself.

In Parnassus on the Mississippi: The *Southern Review* and the Baton Rouge Literary Community 1935–1942 *(1984), Thomas W. Cutrer describes how Warren had no sooner "arrived on campus than he found his name on the editorial board of the* Southwest Review," *which at the time was being published jointly by Southern Methodist University and LSU. This collaborative effort, which Cutrer maintains was marked by tensions between the liberal Dallas editors and the more conservative Baton Rouge contingent, ended when LSU decided to publish a literary journal on its own. In this*

essay Brooks and Warren give their version of the experience with the Southwest Review *and the start of the* Southern Review.

The Origin of the *Southern Review*

Man is the king of the beasts because he is the master maker. Birds make nests, bees make honeycombs, but man makes paintings, constitutions, and nuclear bombs. He also makes fictions, some pieces of which are called history—history being concerned not only with established facts, but with attitudes and interpretations. The truth is not in man, except sometimes on oath and only if objectively established facts are at stake. In general, man cannot report a fact without reworking it a bit, if only unconsciously, as something of a creative artist.

The "history" of the *Southern Review* is a case in point, though *history* is not quite the right word here. We would do better to speak of *histories,* because in the folk imagination, as embalmed even in accounts

Senator Huey P. Long addressing LSU students, November 1934 (AP Wide World)

The Louisiana State University campus in the early 1930s (Louisiana State University Photograph Collection,
LSU Archives, LSU Libraries, Baton Rouge)

in print, there are various contradictory tales. But the account to follow, though possibly containing some minor slips, would be given on oath if such were required.

Soon after R. P. Warren came to the Louisiana State University in the fall of 1934, Charles W. Pipkin (who held a D. Phil. from Oxford University, was professor of Government and dean of the Graduate School), Cleanth Brooks and R. P. Warren (Brooks and Warren being assistant professors in the English department) went to Shreveport, Louisiana, to meet John McGinnis and Henry Nash Smith, editors of the *Southwest Review,* published by the Southern Methodist University of Dallas, Texas. The meeting had been arranged to discuss the possibility of LSU's joining with SMU in editing the *Southwest Review* and in financing it. Undoubtedly, Pipkin had earlier been discussing the matter with the president of LSU, James Monroe Smith, but neither Brooks nor Warren had had any conversation with the president or any other official, and had had no word from Pipkin except the bare outline of the mission. In any case, after the meeting in Shreveport, Brooks and Warren had no special inclination in favor of such an arrangement, even though their names were later to appear on the masthead as "contributing editors." With regard to the views held by the editors of the *Southwest Review,* it has only recently been reported by a contributor to the *Southern Review* that an alliance with LSU was hardly pleasing "to the more liberal McGinnis and Smith." As far as Brooks and Warren can recall, such a question was never discussed. Their attitude toward large editorial boards may be summed up in the old saying that a camel is a "horse designed by a committee." In any case, the matter was never brought to the attention of Brooks and Warren by anyone. Not many months later, with LSU's funding of its own publication, the *Southwest Review* reverted to its former status.

The first official conversation, or any conversation with either Brooks or Warren about the founding of a review at LSU, occurred in the late winter or early spring of 1935, when one Sunday afternoon the limousine of President Smith—*mirabile dictu*—drew up in front of the house rented by Warren on the outskirts of Baton Rouge. The mission of President and Mrs. Smith was ostensibly to show the newcomers something of the countryside. At this time Albert Erskine, an old friend of Warren and then a graduate student at LSU, was living in the Warren house, and so was asked to join the party.

After some idle conversation, perhaps about the Louisiana landscape, the real mission of the president was disclosed. He asked if a quarterly review published by LSU could get "good" contributors. Warren's answer was "yes." After more landscape, the president said that Warren might get in touch with Brooks and Pipkin to draw up a prospectus of such a quarterly review. He added that he would be ready to sign the authorization the next day.

Brooks and Warren called on Pipkin the next morning. The prospectus was drawn up and offered to President Smith, who signed it. Pipkin was to be editor, Brooks and Warren, associate editors, and Albert Erskine, business manager. There was not much business for him to manage as far as subscriptions went. Local enthusiasm was not great; typically there were fewer subscribers in New Orleans than in Tokyo. Erskine was in fact one of the editors along with Brooks and Warren, reading manuscripts and participating in decisions.

This is definitely the whole matter of the *Review*'s origin as far as Brooks and Warren can reconstruct the past. It has been reported that President Smith had earlier discussed the creation of the *Review* with Pipkin. Such discussion may well have taken place, but if so, Pipkin never reported the matter to Brooks and Warren, not even by any glancing reference to it. Whatever dealings Pipkin may have had, or probably did have, with the administration or any official person concerning the *Southern Review* were never disclosed, or even hinted at, to the associate editors.

The funding of the *Southern Review* by LSU was set at ten thousand dollars a year. This funding was clearly one aspect of the general expansion of the university, and money available for this expansion was the result of the state legislature's voting additional funds for LSU as well as for various other state activities. (LSU's funding is still the responsibility of the state legislature.)

It is clear that this new and unprecedented generosity of the legislature was due to pressure exerted by Huey Long and a function of his political power in the state. He meant to provide the citizenry with paved roads, hospitals, better schools and universities; and LSU, in all sorts of its activities, including the football team, profited from the flow of funds. But there is no evidence that Brooks and Warren know of to suggest that Long ever planned the creation of, or even knew of the existence of, the *Southern Review*. Long was preoccupied with his own national career and his hope to win the 1936 Democratic nomination for President of the United States.

In any case, for the associate editors there was no direct *financial* reward. The new assignment provided neither promotion in rank nor rise in pay. It did cut the teaching load of each from four courses to three, but the reading matter brought in by each day's post far outweighed the student papers one freshman class could provide. The rewards offered by the new post were certainly not monetary.

There is one expression of the creative imagination that has appeared in several slightly variant forms. It attributes to Huey Long's direct hand the creation of the *Southern Review*. Maybe so, but not a crumb of such evidence has ever come to Brooks's and Warren's attention. William Faulkner, in his long story "Knight's Gambit" provides another account, this one avowedly the product of Faulkner's imagination. Faulkner has his character Chick Mallison quote his uncle, Gavin Stevens, on

---

Writing, Teaching, Editing

In this excerpt from a letter to his former teacher at Vanderbilt, Warren refers to an unpublished novel and to the poems "Resolution" and "History," which were published in the July 1935 issue of Virginia Quarterly Review. *The mimeographed analytical anthology mentioned was the forerunner of his and Cleanth Brooks's first textbook,* An Approach to Literature *(1936).*

Warren to Donald Davidson, 28 February 1935

. . . I only lack two chapters of the new novel now, and hope to finish that within a month. I've managed to do seven poems, three of them longish, two reviews, and a short story of some 6000 words in the last few months. Two of the new poems will be in the *V.Q.* anniversary number; and a story, too, but not a very new one. I am sticking some of the shorter poems in this letter. What do you think of them? I've been occupied recently in making up a syllabus and analytical anthology of a modest order to be mimeographed for use in the sophomore poetry term here. For the most part the thing is a chore, but it offers moments of interest. I'll send you a copy when the entire thing is run off; only a part has been mimeographed yet. I've got a good deal of material together for the spring issue of the *Southwest Review*. . . .

—Selected Letters of Robert Penn Warren, Volume Two, The "Southern Review" Years, 1935–1942, edited by William Bedford Clark (Baton Rouge: Louisiana State University Press, 2001), p. 19

University photograph of Warren's wife, Cinina, who taught Italian at LSU (Charles East Papers, Louisiana and Lower Mississippi Valley Collections, Louisiana State University Libraries, Baton Rouge)

the subject of Long and the *Southern Review* as follows:

> Huey Long in Louisiana had made himself founder owner and supporter of what . . . was one of the best literary magazines anywhere, without ever once looking inside it probably nor even caring what the people who wrote and edited it thought of him.

Brooks and Warren are grateful to Faulkner for putting this generous comment in the mouth of the resident intellectual of Yoknapatawpha County. But what is more important is that Stevens' surmise seems to them to have the ring of truth.

The one opportunity to test whether Long really didn't care "what the people who edited [the *Review*] thought of him" was cut short by Long's death. About the time of Long's death there appeared in the second issue of the *Review* an article written by Norman Thomas, who at the time was sharply critical of Long. Had this article been called to Long's attention Pipkin, Brooks, and Warren might have learned how brave (or foolhardy?) they were in their editorial policy. They shall, of course, never know.

–Brooks and Warren, "The Origin of the *Southern Review*," *Southern Review*, 22 (Winter 1986): 214–217

* * *

In this excerpt Robert B. Heilman, a colleague of Warren and Brooks at LSU, remembers the varied professional activities of his friends. In the first part of his essay Heilman describes the intellectual atmosphere of the school where the faculty and students "enjoyed a remarkably free air and lived with an unquarrelsome diversity of preferences."

LSU in the 1930s: Remembering the Boys Next Door

This hanging loose instead of going rigid paralleled a certain living with differences encouraged by the demographic makeup of Louisiana. Baton Rouge lies roughly between the Baptist north (often called "hardshell") and the Catholic south, between the hill country from which sprang the Long revolution and the delta country rich in the plantation houses of the ancien régime. Besides, there were the rural Catholicism of the Cajun (Acadian) regions, and the urban Catholicism of New Orleans: the puritanical and the worldly versions of the church. These divergent communities evolved a modus vivendi, and the university made some adjustments instead of proclaiming its own infallibility. In our day there was some sort of local Index, and at times it included titles on the reading lists of English courses. So we had alternative titles ready, and readings could always be found which seemed neither sinful to the readers nor shameful to the instructors (though the stronger in mind could get a bit exclamatory about it). The Index had more influence with rural than with urban students, who tended to smile at the alternate-readings people but of whom few would have been up to the observation made to me by an English major from New Orleans: "The safety of the Church does not depend on what I read." My impression is that departmental accommodatingness allowed more persuasive maneuvers than high-toned combat would have. "Oh, you can't read that? Too bad. I think you would have enjoyed it." But if there was a fair amount of urbanity in the air, I must not claim a cosmopolitanism beyond the over-all university talents. I remember some students coming in bug-eyed over the heroics of an intellectual desperado in geology who kept pounding his lectern in a fury over the cosmological shortcomings of Genesis. We took him to be a recent fugitive from the upstate hardshells or the Cajun Catholics; either neoworldling was likely to get the shakes from the new-thought alcoholism of graduate school. The unchainer of mankind was not an LSU special, though; to this day virtually every faculty endures a local Prometheus, who brings fiery thought to local mankind as he boldly discloses falsities in elders, powers, and traditions and thus becomes a darling of the youngsters and the press.

The Swimming Man

Throughout his life, Warren tried to find residences that were located near a "swimming hole." Swimming was as much a part of his routine as was writing. As the first issue of The Southern Review *was being published, Warren had embarked on a trip to the West to visit his wife's family in California and along the way to teach at the University of Montana and to participate in the University of Colorado's writing conference. At that conference, directed by Edward "Ted" Davison, Warren befriended Davison's son, Peter, the future poet and poetry editor at* The Atlantic Monthly, *then seven years old. Peter Davison always remembered the experience of accompanying Warren to Baseline Lake on the outskirts of Boulder for his swim.*

Questions of Swimming, 1935

What was the nub of wonder? Was it
the man, giant to my child-eyes, strapping
a shiny black rubber bathing cap over the cap
of his red hair, plugging his nostrils and ears,
and lowering his lean body into the yellow
lake in Colorado, down into the frightening
water, to begin the steady trudge
that took him, as long as my skipping patience
could endure, steadily farther from sight
as far as the far shore, a mile, and without
pause, brought him back to me, bobbing
far out in the water, then thrashing,
then finally splashing, and gasping and rising,
and then, again, human and near me, dripping and walking?

Wonder at the man, or at the task?
What sort of way was it to spend
an hour in thrashing straight across a lake
and, turning, swimming straight back to the start?
Where was he setting out for when he began, fresh?
Where had be been to when he returned, winded?

Or take the style: laboring akimbo,
a steady crawl across the sheet of water
without a pause to whoop or whistle or blow,
a style as awkward as inexorable,
in which the completion of the task seemed to count
more to the swimmer than not drowning.

The lake? A captive body
the dry climate had permitted
to rest between the knees
Boulder had bulldozed to keep
the water from evaporating: a reservoir.
The man swam back and forth between its walls.

What of the rhythm of the exercise?
Not like a dog or deer that simply walks
on water, but a dactyl, a quantitative
excursus, a distribution of forces between
the limbs, these legs working like scissors,
these arms working like flails, these lungs
working like bellows, this mind working,
working on lessened oxygen, this body
moving against every interference to imitate
its forgotten grandfather, the fish.

To the destructive element submit yourself,
and with the exertions of your hands and feet
make the deep, deep sea keep you up.
Once kept up, where do we go from there?
To the headwaters, the spawning ground?
To the floating pyre, the fire ship?
To the other shore? Which is the other shore?
Could it be the place where a boy could watch
a man pull on the helmet of a bathing cap
and set out, swimming, for a farther shore?

—*The Poems of Peter Davison, 1957–1995* (New York:
Knopf, 1995), pp. 222–223

After the death of Huey Long in 1935, the Long movement fell into the hands of henchmen not gifted enough to let private perquisite be decorously shaded by public profit, and by 1939 they were heading colorfully into various state and federal jails. Among them was the president of the university, who was using state funds in a grandiose stock-market venture that didn't quite come off. Such doings seemed—if my impressions after four decades are reliable—less like appalling vice and crime that demanded an all-out fight by everybody than like some kind of Gilbert and Sullivan picturesque and picaresque rascality. If the principals had all been as wittily jesting as they were cynical, they might have been Falstaffs. Their doings hardly stirred us into a cru-

sade; on the contrary the ironic probability is that the nonpuritanical air of state politics contributed indirectly to the sense of freedom and ease on the campus. Be that as it may, the university could enjoy an increasing academic stature traceable ultimately, if not directly, to Huey's almost paternal concern. If his primary interest was in the football team and the band, nevertheless it was in his day that some strong general impetus to new life sprang up in LSU. The results on our side of the campus were a first-rate music school, a superior fine arts department, a flock of good appointments in various departments, and at least four new journals (among the ones with scholarly specialties I remember those in history, sociology, and political science), of which the outstanding one was the *Southern Review*. Its life spanned the seven years from the death of Huey (1935) to the final winding up of the post-Huey scandals in a shift of political power in the state (1942). The *Review* grew famous; the English department picked up luster from it and attracted some very good graduate students; and through it the university as a whole gained respect in quarters that had hardly known of it before. Indeed it won some honor among a laity of whom such reading might not be expected. Once a Baton Rouge printer showed me with pride his own seven bound volumes of the *Review*. His sense of it as a regional achievement of national repute was surely not unique.

Whatever the trick-and-treat musical-comedy shenanigans at the north edge of downtown Baton Rouge, where the state capitol shot up forty floors above the endless flatness, there was great professional activity some miles to the south where the campus spread over many acres. Some of us worked a little for internal changes, that is for the introduction of academic and administrative patterns that we had known elsewhere and thought salubrious. I don't know whether we had any impact; perhaps some on the filling of headships and deanships, which may have gone a little less readily to good old local boys of dependable innocuousness.

Cleanth Brooks and Robert Penn Warren were interested in these strivings, thus differing from literary people who have since become fixtures in universities and who rarely care about university well-being. Brooks and Warren did not use the combined demands of their own writing, their editing of the *Review,* and their teaching to justify an indifference to institutional welfare. Brooks in particular was active on the university front, and many a caucus took place at his house. Our activities involved collaboration among instructors of different social and political views. This finding of common grounds, or of accommodation among diverse ones, appeared in such English department activities as planning curricula and setting up degree requirements. We new PhDs, of course, drew on the practices of our own graduate schools, which now looked more nearly ideal than in predoctoral days, and these had to be reconciled. Yet in all of them the basic expectation was a wide knowledge of English literature as a historical sequence of events. Brooks and Warren, on the other hand, wanted to have candidates know critical methods and be able to apply them in specific judgments—quite a jump from the loose critical impressionism practiced by the older order of PhDs and assumed to be reliable because the individual had such vast historical knowledge. I do not recall the details, but doubtless we worked out some con-

---

Warren and Brooks at LSU

Cleanth Brooks remembers the excitement of working at LSU in the 1930s and early 1940s.

In the summer of 1932 I came home from Oxford for good and started job-hunting. The depression had set in and university posts were hard to come by. At the very last moment I had the luck to get a place at the Louisiana State University at Baton Rouge. In the spring of 1934 Warren was invited to come down to give us a lecture. Shortly after that he was offered a post at LSU and our real work as associates began.

It was a highly interesting time. LSU was one of the few universities in the United States that was then actively recruiting faculty. Its net was thrown wide, and swept in all sorts of people: those who could only be regarded as so-so; those who were undistinguished but solid and useful citizens of academia; and those—they were considerable in number—who were intelligent, imaginative, and intellectually vigorous. By the middle of the 1930's there were at least 35 or 40 young family people on the campus whose talk I still remember as the most stimulating that I have ever heard. Besides Warren and a good many interesting people in my own department, there were painters, sculptors, a geologist, several political scientists, historians, linguists—the range was broad. We saw each other not only rather constantly on the campus but perhaps twice a week, some eight or ten of us would find our selves together at a dinner party or at some other evening gathering. During the late '30's and early '40's the University had attracted an unusual group of students, especially in the humanities: notable among them were such people as Robert Lowell, Peter Taylor, and the late Alan Swallow.

—"Brooks on Warren," *Four Quarters,* 21 (May 1972): 21–22

flation of disparate aims and methods. What I do remember is an absence of that furious and disruptive factionalism that theoretical differences can breed in English departments. Brooks and Warren combined conviction and urbanity; theirs was not the all-or-nothing stance of people newly come into Truth. Besides, Brooks had an especially beguiling way of buttonholing colleagues and explaining, gently and reassuringly, that their positions and his were really not far apart. Our faculty decisions (this was before the day when graduate students clamor via committees for degree requirements catering to their desires and what they take to be their needs) must have been at least workable, for we had a number of crops of very talented students.

. . . .

Warren and T. S. Stribling, the Tennessee-born author of a controversial epic trilogy about the South, standing on the steps of the building that housed the Southern Review *offices on the LSU campus. Warren published an essay on the writer, "T.S. Stribling: A Paragraph in the History of Critical Realism," in the February 1939 issue of* American Review *(courtesy of Mr. Charles East).*

Heilman lists outstanding students and faculty as well as contributors to the Southern Review*—"a striking element in the life of LSU and of the larger community in which the university was not only a many-sided force but an object of devotion."*

. . . The *Review* brought not only a larger, but a very large, world into the local scene; and at the same time it took the local world out into the larger scene. The shapers of the ideas that shaped political and literary action were not merely untouchable exercisers of power or debaters on inaccessible platforms. They now came to display their wares in the local market; there they had to compete with one another and with regional voices; and this under the management of colleagues who were themselves persistently and independently influencing the way things were to go. Fashionable clichés about politics and society were all open to challenge; the going traditions in literature were surprisingly not sacred any more; and on a front closer to home, neither the sentimentalizers of the old honeysuckle South nor the get-with-it modernizers were going to get away with it. These were heady experiences. Yet they fell rarely, if at all, into a too easily gratifying "us" and "them" melodrama; anyone might find his own preferences and habits of mind tripped up at any time. One could often hear grumbling about the general directions or specific turns that the magazine was taking. Inevitable. But few could have failed to experience excitement over these notable, and widely noted, doings of the boys in the office next door. Behind that, in both university and its larger public, lay a new participation in both the current events of the mind and the nonhistorical issues agitated by the reflective in every age.

. . . .

Working on *The Southern Review*

Cleanth Brooks remembers Warren's skills as an editor.

With the decision to found *The Southern Review* early in 1935 Warren and I came to share an office and to work at some of the same basic problems: soliciting articles, reading manuscripts, scribbling notes on rejection slips, making plans for future numbers. At about this time we also began our collaboration on our first textbook.

These activities gave me at first hand a glimpse of Warren's great gifts as an editor, a practical critic, a teacher, and an executive. Since his remarkable abilities in these fields have been overshadowed by his creative genius as a novelist and poet, I call special attention to them here. One thing that impressed me from the beginning, perhaps even more than his keen intelligence and original ideas, was the enormous energy that he possessed. The energy required to edit a quarterly review or to put together a textbook is obviously not of the same order of importance as that that goes into writing a poem or working out a novel. But there is a relationship. In fact, one can say that to know Warren in the *Review* office was to gain a further insight into his resources of power, of which the more precious creativity was simply the finest manifestation.

Another trait in Warren that I speedily came to recognize and admire was his carefulness and zeal for accuracy. At this period of my life I still retained some lingering traces of the romantic notion of a poet. A poet worked by inspiration, flashes, insights. He was therefore privileged to be a little cavalier with facts and figures and could be forgiven if he brushed aside tiresome particularities as ultimately of not much account. In Warren the flashes of insight were clearly visible and one was conscious of his creative surge. (During just these years he was continuing to write poetry and was hard at work on his first two novels, *Night Rider* and *At Heaven's Gate*.) But for him facts were important too. If one was to edit a magazine or write a textbook or engage in any other enterprise, there were mundane obligations that had to be honored.

This little parcel of reminiscences may well conclude with an illustration of another obligation that Warren believed had to be honored—a concern for other young writers and a concern for the good estate of the republic of letters. In the 1930's we were both teaching three courses in addition to our editorial work, and we were hard pressed for time. We once calculated that we were reading something like ninety fiction manuscripts in order to get one usable story. I remember suggesting that perhaps we ought to give up publishing short stories altogether except when one came in from a writer whose quality we already knew. The selection of articles and reviews consumed far less editorial time. Some we could commission—and many of our best ones were commissioned—and those that were unsolicited presented no very great problem; one could fairly easily sort out those that had real quality. Poetry, of course, we would continue to publish, but there was not such a flood of it nor did the poems take quite so much time to sort out as the stories did. But Warren's answer was emphatic: a great part of our job as editors of a literary quarterly was precisely that of providing a publication channel for the young fiction writer, who, most of all, needed to see his work in print. We simply couldn't take the short cut, hard-pressed for time though we were. The decision was characteristic and is a measure of the quality of the man.

—"Brooks on Warren," *Four Quarters*,
21 (May 1972): 21–22

Warren remembers "a glorious and challenging time in the literary office" working on the journal with Brooks and Albert Erskine, who he writes "was as much an editor in fact as anybody else."

What I remember most vividly is the comradeship in that office, the arguments, the banging together of opinions and temperaments, arguments that, in general, ended with an agreement. It was, I should say, one of the most educational experiences of my life. I learned as much there about literature as ever in any graduate seminar I had ever taken—Cleanth with his learning and scrupulously considered judgments and critical sensibility, and Albert with his darting, astute, penetrating, and ironical intelligence and wide reading.

But there was another aspect to the goings-on in that office. Now and then, among contributions by such people as Katherine Anne Porter, F. O. Matheissen, Eudora Welty, Richmond Lattimore, Delmore Schwartz, Randall Jarrell—even the sainted T. S. Eliot—most of them then young or youngish but destined for eminence, we published work by students. If it was good enough, or could be made good enough. There was a peculiar excitement in sitting by a student's side to work with him, or her, to lick a story into shape. I remember one Cajun boy, a sophomore, I seem to remember, who came into the office only to stand tongue-tied in shyness and embarrassment before managing to fling a wad of papers on my desk. Then he fled. It was an extraordinary story. We published it, and it was (like some others) later anthologized. But, for better or worse, he lost interest in writing by the time he was a senior and entered medical school. In any case, the thick, bound volumes of the *Southern Review*, now in the dark on the library shelves, must speak for themselves.

—*The Southern Review, Original Series, 1935–1942*,
edited by Lewis P. Simpson (Baton Rouge:
Louisiana State University, 1983),
pp. 16–18

Albert Erskine at LSU in the 1930s. Warren was teaching at Southwestern College in Memphis, Tennessee, in 1930 when he first met Erskine, who was an undergraduate. The two men became close friends as they worked together on The Southern Review, and Erskine later became Warren's editor at Random House (courtesy of Marisa Erskine).

The Brooks-Warren impact may have been most pervasive in informal and personal ways. The literary materials in their magazine were ignored by some and contested by others, but what the contributors said was in the air and could not be unfelt. Few teachers might move from literary-history-as-all to literary-structure-as-all, but it took a hardy soul to remain wholly closed to the concept of formal nontemporal characteristics as qualitative determinants of the work. Brooks, of course, could easily manage dialogue with the historical lads, since as the author of a linguistic work and an editor of Percy's letters he was exhibiting an established form of scholarly reliability. So he could not be completely mad as he brought out essays that, tracing the revolutions in English poetry, undermined the romantics revered in, and exalted some sixteenth- and seventeenth-century poets undervalued in, the schools. It seems odd now, in the days of a different radicalism, that the upgrading of Wyatt and the metaphysicals, the new look at Shakespeare as something of a modern (including Ransom's denigration of the sonnets), and the deolympianizing of Wordsworth and Shelley should have stirred up so much of a kerfuffle. Brooks was a bit of a corridor missionary: the gospel was "Read Empson," "Read Richards; he's no longer just a mechanical psychologist,"

"Read Eliot." Brooks was busy with Yeats's *Vision* but probably did not try to push it as a public park for literary exercises by everyone. (I recall an occasional invitation to try *I'll Take My Stand,* and the expending of some energy pro and con on the Agrarian front.) "The Waste Land"–later to be called by Eliot an "insignificant grouse" and "rhythmical grumbling"–became an index of one's literary progress. One faculty wife said that "Shantih shantih shantih" made the tears come. Graduate students, with their receptive ears for new voices, could easily turn "The Waste Land" into a separator of human cream from human skimmed milk. Nathaniel Caffee, master of an easy geniality with students, once walked into an office where a half-dozen graduate students were in sober discourse. "What is the text?" said he. "'The Waste Land,'" said they. Caffee said, "I do not understand it." One of them, later a well-known professor, said, "We do." Caffee chuckled as he reported it to me.

Understanding Poetry appeared in 1938. But it had a departmental preview in a mimeographed edition which was the text in a multiple-section basic course. (This may have happened for *Approach to Literature,* 1936.) For most of us it was a baptismal experience in the detailed objective analysis of poetic method and quality. Once we had just announced ex cathedra what was worthy; now we had to make a case for it, as well as come to terms with the asserted unworthiness of some poems heretofore assumed to be worthy. Doubtless our responses ranged from conversion to intransigence; others must have shared my own attitude, which was instinctive hospitality to the method, but difficulty with some of the new tools and with some judgments that were not congenial. We were, of course, in on an educational revolution, though we had no way of knowing this then. It is now gratifying to look back and say: "Great things were happening, and we were there." Perhaps it is just as well that what was to become quite an event in the history of academic humanism did not seem, to us who worked near the birthplace, much more than procedural innovations introduced by amiable and talented colleagues who did not look or sound like revolutionaries. Had we been able to say "We are at a historical crisis," the passions of collaboration and resistance might have been greater; the latter might have led to such declarations as "My sentence is for open war" rather than stopped at that unprogrammatic grousing with which the profession usually greets proposed alternatives. Besides, oppositionist zeal tended to be defused by a genuinely experimental air. Brooks and Warren had strong convictions, but my impression is that they were quite open to all kinds of responses, did listen to arguments, and were willing to make adjustments, certainly in approach, perhaps occasionally in conclusions reached. Unlike most revolutions this one did not exclude a sense of humor. Brooks told me that Warren had said that applying their method to Wordsworth was like "manicuring an elephant."

There was excitement, then, on the teaching front. There was also the excitement of internal efforts to alter the university, and, more peripherally, of the statewide political goings-on. The denouement was the "scandals" of 1939, when facts caught up with the adventurers, and prosecuting attorneys had better headline and campaign materials than usual. It was also in 1939 that Brooks's first, and enormously influential, book appeared–*Modern Poetry and the Tradition.* And in 1939 that Warren's first novel appeared–*Night Rider.* Then in 1940 appeared Kirby and Caffee's *Studies for W. A. Read,* a festschrift (before festschrifts had become monthly events) for the distinguished linguist who had been department head since 1902 (a charming gentleman, as well as a scholar, of the old school: a Virginian, he had taken his PhD at Heidelberg and had studied at Göttingen, Grenoble, and Oxford); it had local, national, and European contributors. I mention these three books together, with their dates, for two reasons. One is that neither external events in a spectacular style, nor a diverse schedule of activities by department members, interfered with the major professional activity that led to books. The other is that the three volumes represent all the kinds of activity that are expected of a department of literature–the critical, the creative, and the scholarly (and two of them not yet expected). *Night Rider* must have been almost the first novel by a full-time professor of English, and in its extraordinary fusion of physical violence, moral sensitivity, and philosophic inquiry–these would be the characteristic Warren triad–it had a preenlightenment fullness infrequent in the latter flood of faculty fiction.

This touching of all bases was symptomatic not only of a productive surge but also of a nurturing background in which there was much to modify the provincial. Long before international travel had become a cliché of American mobility, southerners had an affinity for things European. There was a small symbol of this in the presence of six Rhodes scholars on the faculty in my time (Brooks, Warren, Palmer in English; Pipkin, Daspit, Kendall in Government). The LSU faculty were drawn from all sections of the country. The Esso installation at Baton Rouge included the experimental laboratories; scientists there had both intellectual and artistic interests. They added a citizen-of-the-world flavoring, especially when the war meant evacuation of Americans from European fields.

. . . .

In his conclusion Heilman considers the causes and influences that led to "a literary and intellectual florescence of more than local visibility" at "a seventy-five-year-old school with a dominant military tradition."

. . . one can recognize, in retrospect, a kind of laissez faire which, while it may have disadvantages for the ill-organized and self-indulgent, is admirable for those with talent and direction. The underlying puzzle, of course, is that laissez faire, and with it a literary and intellectual flowering of a distinctly highbrow sort, should accompany a populist revolution at the heart of Huey Long's rise to power. One rummages around in the historical armoire for psychological and cultural materials which could beget a seeming paradox. The urban worldliness of New Orleans (since then a refurbisher of its has-beens into one of the country's great tourist traps), a brake on the tendency of revolutionary energy to roar into narrow channels and gain destructive force? The ironic and imaginative sides of Huey, too gamesome ever to become a Robespierre? An ambitious expansiveness through which he inadvertently set up kinds of achievement hardly embraced in the formal programs? More generally a subterranean kinship between the freedom conducive to art and thought, and a sociopolitical relaxation with a built-in risk of messes and rackets? One playful speculation of the time suggested analogies with the Italian Renaissance, when the masters of commercial and political banditry were also the patrons of a great art. But if Baton Rouge could not quite be taken for Florence (as Arno, the Mississippi is a bit grandiose), the scene was still marked by a coexistence of apparently contradictory elements. Such unlikely juxtapositions, in their resistance to logical clarity, are always a little troublesome to observers from other sections, who expect the distant to have a unitary identity. When Warren's *All the King's Men* appeared in 1946, everyone knew that any good man and true who glanced at Huey in any way–never mind how fictional art employs raw materials–had to scarify him; since Warren's mode was in no way polemic (it was tragic, much less easy on writer and readers), the knowing understood that Warren was committing an apologia for a monster, and for all who had lived in Louisiana and had failed in their civic duty–a duty defined from far away in time and place–of becoming tyrannicides. Surely no other work has ever been the victim of such dreadful nonsense.

The *Southern Review,* a natural centerpiece in the past I am recalling, was killed under a "reform" administration in the state in 1942. (A faculty wit remarked that in post-Huey elections we had a choice between stupid do-gooders and bright crooks.) The rationale was budgetary constraints brought on by the war. The war took various good people away from LSU, some into other lifetime careers. Continuing productivity brought others into professional visibility, and offers from other universities kept coming in. Some good people moved. Many good ones stayed—more than enough to contradict the supposition, heard occasionally, that at LSU some sort of bubble had burst. If the state's old mingled tonalities, tantalizing in their antinomian picturesqueness, were more muted than before, still it was not that a stolid ordinariness superseded imaginative venturesomeness. The Longs survived their henchmen and returned, never a dull company. The *Southern Review* spiritually survived a budgetary crunch. Its genuine life-after-death was followed by a formal resurrection and a new life that is still flourishing.

–Robert B. Heilman, "Baton Rouge and LSU
Forty Years After," Sewanee Review,
88 (Winter 1980): 126–143

Reviews of *Thirty-Six Poems*

In 1935 Ronald Lane Latimer, director of the Alcestis Press and editor of the quarterly poetry magazine Alcestis, *invited Warren to contribute a volume of poetry for the series of limited-edition volumes he was publishing. Wallace Stevens and William Carlos Williams were also published in the series.* Thirty-Six Poems, *Warren's second book, was published in November 1935.*

Although Thirty-Six Poems *was Warren's first book of poems, he had already established a reputation through the appearance of his work in respected journals. This excerpt is from a review article titled "Five American Poets," in which Warren's poetry is considered along with works by Edwin Arlington Robinson, Allen Tate, John Peale Bishop, and Wallace Stevens.*

"The Uncertain Violence of Transition"

In "Thirty-Six Poems," Robert Penn Warren mixes some native moments with a good many intellectualized efforts, and the latter are remote and impersonal in effect. We have in this volume seven parts of his "Kentucky Mountain Farm," the strong and unforgettable picture of the fleeing Negro in "Pondy Woods," and the no less familiar if somewhat surprising "Letter of a Mother." Others will be familiar to readers of the Southern quarterlies, and of the fine poetry supplement of the American Review last year. There is a poem in this book called "To a Friend Who Thinks Himself Urbane" which is direct, and deftly cutting, satire; one would wince at being the subject. But it is direct. The feeling of most of the other poetry is of savagery for its own sake, not for satire's. The poet's

vocabulary seems deliberately edged, flinty, and roughened; designed not to please; designed to strike somewhat cruelly the mind and ear. Robert Penn Warren was the youngest of the Fugitives, and his poetry was at first closer to his native region in sympathy and subject than it is now. But even then it was pulling away, or it touched on a sort of inner conflict unknown to the others of the group. Just now he seems to be passing through a phase of his growth during which he looks in many directions at once for poetic manners. His best poetry, in spite of this search, is that in which he is at home with himself and simple. The last three poems in the volume become suddenly calmer, in movement at least; "To One Awake" comes as a relief to the ear. But outer influences are at work on him, and the uncertain violence of transition marks this book.

–John Holmes, "Five American Poets,"
Virginia Quarterly Review,
12 (April 1936): 292

* * *

THIRTY-SIX POEMS

BY

ROBERT PENN WARREN

NEW YORK
THE ALCESTIS PRESS
551 Fifth Avenue
1 9 3 5

Title page for Warren's first volume of poetry, published in a limited edition of 165 copies (Special Collections, Western Kentucky University Libraries)

Dust jacket for a 1937 anthology that includes twenty-two stories by as many authors. In his introduction Warren writes, "There is no rough-and-ready answer to the general question: What is a Southern writer? But the particular question about a particular writer rarely causes confusion, for we can leap to our conclusion without bothering about definition" (Special Collections, Western Kentucky University Libraries).

In Robert Penn Warren: The Dark and Bloody Ground *(1960), Leonard Casper argues that for Warren there was "a handicap as well as a blessing in having been a Fugitive and a Southerner. . . . One consequence has been the constant need for critics to rediscover Warren after each cycle of being satisfied with a stereotype or substitute." In this excerpt, reviewer Morton Dauwen Zabel, the editor of* Poetry, *begins by considering Warren's Fugitive roots.*

Problems of Knowledge

The scruples of Mr. Warren's talent are first announced in the fact that his first book of thirty-six poems is the work of ten years. They are next apparent in the exacting craftsmanship he has spent on all its entries; nothing unconsidered or unfelt has been given a place here, and nothing untested by severely examined personal values and decisions. But the most compelling sign of his worth as a poet appears in the independence he has shown in growing beyond his studious youthful efforts at style and the

formidable influences that supervised them. To belong to the Fugitives was one of the best fortunes that could befall, in America at that moment, any young poet interested in craft and its uses. But schools of style offer as much risk as benefit; a premature forcing of the intellectual manner, while essentially more profitable than the flaccid impressionism encouraged among most beginners, can breed as deluding and pretentious an ambition in a poet as the visionary arrogance or lyric softness which it aims to correct. It has been the misfortune of several Fugitive followers (perhaps all but the two who have survived as remarkable poets) that in becoming disciples they did not resist being stultified by their models, their ambitious critical and historical ideas, and particularly by the mannerisms of literary irony and erudition which—whether studied in Eliot, Yeats, Ransom, or the classic models of these men—seldom admit of safe transmission to other hands.

. . . .

Zabel goes on to argue that it is "in recognizing two sources of poetic sincerity that Mr. Warren shows unmistakable strength."

. . . The first of these sources is a really critical sense of a local ideal–the culture of the South stated neither as sentiment nor as argument, but in terms of a tragic vision that defines a faith without dictating it and presents it with so intense a feeling that local images and symbols become the natural medium of the sense. The best evidence of this lies in Mr. Warren's detail and metaphor; they manage to convey their shock and brilliance without becoming exotic or forced, and they build up a strong and authentic atmospheric pathos in the volume. Even in those poems most obviously plotted in thought, visual contact and penetration supply a sharpness of detail so invariably tempered by the right sense of situation and tone that extravagance and mere decorative cleverness are avoided. This might be illustrated by isolated images: "the faithless yellow flame" of wheat, "the sunshine of consent's good season," and "the blue tense altitudes" of the buzzards over Pondy Woods; but obviously a fuller presentation of context than is possible here would be necessary to make their quality apparent.

The second source is Mr. Warren's emphasis on his own conflict of spirit, writing it down without making it vulgarly personal, but insisting that it rescue him from the elaborate subterfuges and disguises of his literary education. Many of these poems are on directly personal themes; that alone would not give them personal authority, and in fact several are too obviously intimate or hortatory to be convincing. But the persistence in them of an increasing lyric clarity, and of a tonal richness that includes serious mental habits without overwriting them, is evidence of how soundly instructed the personal discipline has been. The poems in free-verse best describe the course of this discipline, but its real fruits appear in *The Last Metaphor, To a Face in the Crowd, The Garden,* and two fine examples of the right kind of austere craftsmanship, *Pacific Gazer* and *Calendar.* These are the work of a poet who honors his school by requiring no comparison with it, and of a writer who more and more shows himself, in both his verse and prose, one of the most serious and gifted intelligences of his generation.

–Morton Dauwen Zabel, "Problems of Knowledge," *Poetry,* 48 (April 1936): 37–41

Understanding Literature

Warren collaborated with Brooks on two textbooks in the 1930s, An Approach to Literature *(1936) and* Understanding Poetry *(1938). In this excerpt Brooks writes about the impetus that led the two men to begin to think about ways to teach their students to appreciate literature.*

Confronting a "Practical Problem"

. . . Among other things, each of us was teaching a section of the department's course in literary forms and types. Granted that Warren and I were young men excited by the new trends in literature–Warren was already a published poet–and granted that our heads were full of literary theory–drawn from the poetry and critical essays of T. S. Eliot and from the then sensational books on theory and practical criticism written by I. A. Richards–nevertheless, our dominant motive was not to implant newfangled ideas in the innocent Louisiana sophomores we faced three times a week. Our motive was to try to solve a serious practical problem.

Our students, many of them bright enough and certainly amiable and charming enough, had no notion of how to read a literary text. Many of them approached a Shakespeare sonnet or Keats's "Ode to a Nightingale" or Pope's *Rape of the Lock* much as they would approach an ad in a Sears-Roebuck catalogue or an editorial in their local newspaper. For example, one of Warren's students, to whom he was teaching *King Lear,* would mournfully shake her head and mutter: "I just don't like to read about bad people."

Our students were not stupid. They were simply, if I may use a theological term, almost "invincibly ignorant." Nobody had ever tried to take them *inside* a poem or a story, or tried to explain how a poem *worked,* or, if I may borrow a phrase from Emily Dickinson, no one had shown them how a poem, in telling the truth, has to tell it *slant.* For all our students' previous reading and instruction had stressed one virtue only. The purpose of all discourse was to convey information and to deliver it straight. All must be rendered as plain as a pikestaff. Alas, the prose that our students themselves wrote was scarcely a model of lucidity and concision. In fact, the pressures toward direct statement had succeeded in killing their aptitude for poetry without teaching them how to write decent expository prose.

–Cleanth Brooks, "Forty Years of 'Understanding Poetry,'" in *Confronting Crisis: Teachers in America,* edited by Ernestine P. Sewell and Billi M. Rogers (Arlington: University of Texas at Arlington Press, 1979), pp. 167–168

* * *

Warren as a Teacher in the 1930s

This excerpt is from a 1982 essay by Norton R. Girault, a retired captain in the United States Navy who was a student in Warren's classes in 1938.

Warren's teaching style is hard to describe. He was straightforward and serious, but taught with humor and wit. Two things stood out: one that he enjoyed what he was doing, the other that he was a fireball. "I like to keep in touch with the young," he told John Baker in an interview in 1977. "If I weren't paid to teach, I would pay for the privilege–as Jarrell once said." I always marveled at how he could find time to get long discussion papers back to us, and with comments, the class immediately following the one in which we'd written them. And I'll never forget walking across campus with a former teammate, a two-miler, when Warren and Brooks passed us, Warren with long, resolute strides, the shorter Brooks really hoofing it to keep up. "Where the hell they going–to a fire?" my friend exclaimed. "No," I smiled, "they're just going to look something up in the library."

My first perception of Warren was the first time I saw him come into his two-semester Shakespeare class. Here came this intense man in his early thirties with red hair and rugged good looks charging in right on the bell, smiling, saying "Good morning," then, with the vigor of a finely honed boxer going a series of very fast rounds, launching into a brilliant discussion of what tragedy was. Between brilliant bursts, he would pause, head high, chin slightly elevated, giving the effect of a bird dog on the point, maybe call for questions, then resume. He kept that up until the bell, then gave us the assignment and name of text and went barreling off leaving us in euphoric daze. And yet, with all his intensity, Warren somehow managed always to communicate a genuine gentlemanliness, warmth and concern, not only to students, but to everyone he came in contact with, on and off campus.

His method was basically explication of the text, and, as we got into the course, it was clear that he was searching, probing, re-experiencing the plays–learning them all over again and seeing new things; the process was infectious. He managed to give us the "scholarship" stuff too–dates, folio dope, sources–often by mimeographed handouts, but he concentrated on the good stuff: analysis of the plays, which included a good deal of close looks at the poetry. His insights and scholarship were, to me, awesome. Flicking through the big stack of notes I kept, I see random things that remind me of the course: his discussion of Shakespeare's playing off of the Latinate against the Anglo-Saxon (as in "To lie in cold obstruction and to rot"); his marvelous analysis of metaphor and prosody; his ideas on "the thematic tie, which provides a more fundamental unity than plot connections"; and his character analyses (always brilliant, but particularly so of Falstaff, Antony, and Cleopatra, Brutus, Lear, Hamlet). This list in no way approximates the depth and variety of the course, but may give some idea of the kinds of things he covered.

In Creative Writing, his approach was different. In this course he was, if you'll pardon the modern expression, laid back. He read our manuscripts–sitting down!–and we critiqued them. Standard writing workshop procedure. He was no less brilliant, no less helpful and stimulating in the writing course, but Shakespeare was his masterpiece for my money.

–Norton R. Girault, "Recollections of Robert Penn Warren as Teacher in the 1930's," *Texas Writers Newsletter,* no. 31 (April 1983): 5–6

Reviews of textbooks in major newspapers are rare. This review by Eda Lou Walton–a poet, professor of English at New York University, and a critic who wrote for periodicals such as The Saturday Review of Literature–*appeared in the* New York Herald Tribune, *the preeminent New York newspaper in the 1930s.*

Schoolroom Anthology
Review of *Understanding Poetry*

Today some very intelligent books for the use of teachers and students are being published. Recently we have had Louise Robsenblatt's "Literature as Exploration," and now we have a book on poetry from which, clearly, both students and teachers can learn much. Mr. Brooks and Mr. Warren have compiled an anthology of poetry which, in its juxtaposition of older and modern poetry, is, as is too seldom believed, proof that poets are still about their business, even as were the older masters of verse.

But this text is much more than anthology. The poems are arranged in a scale of increasing difficulty of poetic communication and are, furthermore, arranged to emphasize a certain aspect of poetic method in writing. The editors hold that emphasis must be kept on a poem as a poem and that the treatment of any poem should be concrete and inductive and that a poem should be treated as an organic system of relationships and the poetic quality never understood as inhering in one or more factors taken in isolation. They point to a fact that most good teachers of poetry are aware that poetry is usually studied only as a starting point for paraphrase of content, or for biographical and historical materials, or for such inspiration and didactic interpre-

Practical Criticism and Understanding Poetry

In his 1986 essay on Warren for a Sewanee Review *series titled "The Critics Who Made Us," Monroe K. Spears discusses the origins of Brooks and Warren's approach in* Understanding Poetry.

When it was published in 1938, *Understanding Poetry* was not a manifesto nor a profession of critical theory but a practical textbook designed to answer a specific need. It was the first, but by no means the only, alternative to the historical-biographical approach, which was widely felt to be inadequate because it did not teach students to read. I. A. Richards's *Practical Criticism* (1929) had shown that students in the Cambridge Honours School, presumably the flower of the existing system, were helpless when confronted by new poems of whatever period. Brooks, in an essay published in the *Sewanee Review* in 1981, says that Warren introduced him to *Practical Criticism* at Oxford in 1929–30 and they discussed it and Richards's other work. As Brooks suggests, many of the characteristic doctrines implied in *Understanding Poetry* derive, at least in part, from *Practical Criticism:* the dangers of stock responses, message-hunting, sentimentality, preferring smooth and regular meters; the importance of context and tone; the values of tension, irony, inclusion as against exclusion. But the motive of Brooks and Warren was not to inculcate any doctrine: instead they wished to remedy the reading deficiencies they had observed in their students at Louisiana State University and elsewhere.

—Monroe K. Spears, "The Critics Who Made Us," *Sewanee Review*, 94 (January–March 1986): 100

The editor's interpretations of the modern poems by Eliot, Crane, Tate, Cummings, Yeats are sound and should confute those critics who believe modern poetry obscure. The choice of modern poems is, of course, somewhat determined by the personal tastes of the editors.

—Eda Lou Walton, "Schoolroom Anthology," *New York Herald Tribune Books*, 28 August 1938, p. 17

* * *

John M. Bradbury was one of the first scholars to examine the legacy of Brooks and Warren's critical approach in Understanding Poetry.

The Value of *Understanding Poetry*

Warren's insistence on the centrality of irony, an insistence which we must feel that Brooks already shared, dominates *Understanding Poetry*. However, the emphases of all the leading aesthetic formalist critics are represented in

UNDERSTANDING POETRY

AN ANTHOLOGY FOR COLLEGE STUDENTS

BY

CLEANTH BROOKS, JR.

AND

ROBERT PENN WARREN

THE LOUISIANA STATE UNIVERSITY

NEW YORK

HENRY HOLT AND COMPANY

Title page for the 1938 textbook that sold more than 250,000 copies in the 1950s and 1960s. It was credited with changing the way poetry was taught in American colleges (Special Collections, Western Kentucky University Libraries).

tation as may or may not have been the poet's intention. The truth, in general, is that many teachers of poetry do not themselves understand poetry.

This book begins with narrative poems because they communicate their meaning most easily and because, in these, one can point out the difference between poetry and prose. Poems of objective description are then taken up, classical and modern, and ways of obtaining reactions to description are studied. Each difficult poem is analyzed. When one poem has been carefully studied another group of poems affording the same general problems for study is introduced. Metrics is studied incidentally to the poem itself. The latter chapters deal with "Tone and Attitude" in poetry and with "Imagery." Theme is analyzed last—not, as so often in text books, first—because theme in poetry is properly introduced through choice of treatment in tone, imagery, etc.

Warren in the late 1930s (courtesy of Mrs. Robert D. Frey)

There are no "beauties" which are not aspects of the total effects of the poems analyzed, no ideas apart from their dramatization in terms of all other factors present (unless, indeed, the poem is being overtly or covertly condemned). The individual exegeses of poems, however, though many of them are brilliant and all provocative, do not constitute the permanent value of the book; the vital contribution is one of focus and of techniques for analysis and appreciation. For the first time in textbook history, a valid objective method for introducing poetry to the common reader was offered in this book, and its effect on teaching faculties and on subsequent writers of poetry texts was immense. The poems were not destroyed, as some critics claimed, by the attention given to minute detail, nor were they converted into substitutes for actual living by the stress placed on their revelations or insights. Furthermore, the book was not theory-ridden at the expense of the poems themselves. The authors distinguished clearly between poetry and scientific statement on the one hand, and between poetry and life on the other, without setting up dogmatic definitions about the essence or function of poetry in general. Its examples were varied, illustrative, and often definitive; finally, it did not evade the problem of judgment among bad, mediocre, and good poetry.

–John M. Bradbury, *The Fugitives: A Critical Account* (Chapel Hill: University of North Carolina Press, 1958), p. 233

this volume. If any one influence can be said to be preferred, it would have to be that of Allen Tate. The consistent focus for the authors is the whole poem, seen as a self-sufficient entity—not as a combination of elements, but as an organic thing in which every element is integral.

House that Warren built with the aid of an out-of-work carpenter. He and Cinina lived in it from 1938 to 1941 (photograph by Jerry Tompkins; Charles East Papers, Louisiana and Lower Mississippi Valley Collections, Louisiana State University Libraries, Baton Rouge).

Dust jacket for Warren's first novel, which was set during the tobacco wars in Kentucky and Tennessee around the turn of the century
(Special Collections, Thomas Cooper Library, University of South Carolina)

Night Rider

Warren's first novel, Night Rider, *was published on 14 March 1939 and received favorable reviews. This review was by Christopher Isherwood, an English novelist, whose fourth novel,* Goodbye to Berlin, *was also published that spring.*

Tragic Liberal
Review of *Night Rider*

The action of this novel passes in Kentucky, around the beginning of the present century. It opens with the return of Perse Munn, a young lawyer, to his native town. Perse, seen on the threshold of his career, seems to have everything in his favor. He is happily married to May, a charming and devoted wife. He wins his first case, a murder charge against a young farmer named Bunk Trevelyan, by a flash of brilliant intuition. Bunk's life is saved, and Perse Munn's reputation securely established.

But already the future is piling up its stormclouds. For Munn has become one of the leaders of the Association of Growers of Dark Fired Tobacco, a local coöperative organization which has recently been founded to fight the prices and demands of the foreign buyers. From the first, the Association has a hard struggle. The farmers are obstinate or timid; many of them refuse to join. The coöperative fails to impose its terms; the buyers buy elsewhere; funds run low. Step by step, Munn and his friends are driven towards acts of violence. Step by step, they find themselves compelled to establish an illegal, terroristic organization. At first, the Night Riders confine themselves to small punitive raids on non-coöperating farmers—the victims are compelled to destroy their own crops. But inevitably, violence breeds greater violence; murder is committed; petty sabotage is followed by big armed raids on the enemy warehouses. Munn's own life begins to follow the pattern of his public acts. His wife leaves him; he is drawn into a passionate, unhappy love affair with the daughter of his principal associate, Mr. Christian. The story ends, as it had to end, with Munn's death: he is shot while trying to escape from the troops whom Big Business has called in to protect its threatened interests.

Disclaimer

Warren included the following note in the front matter of Night Rider.

Although this book was suggested by certain events which took place in Kentucky in the early years of this century, it is not, in any strict sense, a historical novel. And more particularly, the characters in this book are not to be identified with any actual persons, living or dead, who participated in those events.

The Robertson County News.

DER SERIES: VOL. IV.—NO. 48.   SPRINGFIELD, TENNESSEE, FRIDAY, SEPT. 28, 1906.   NEWS SERIES: VOL. VIII—NO. 10

GREAT DAY AT GUTHRIE.

Twenty-five Thousand Members of the Planters' Protective Association Assembled There Last Saturday to Celebrate Second Anniversary of the Organization.—Old Officers Re-Elected and Rousing Speeches Made By Famous Orators.

Headline indicating the importance of the Planters' Protective Association in Tennessee in the early twentieth century (Special Collections, Western Kentucky University Libraries)

A parade in Guthrie, Kentucky, held to celebrate the "Dark Tobacco Association" meeting in 1904 (Robert Penn Warren Birthplace Museum, Guthrie, Kentucky)

History and *Night Rider*

INTERVIEWERS: It's very interesting that you were influenced by historical writing so early in life. It has always caught one's eye how history is used in your work, for instance *Night Rider*.

WARREN: Well, that isn't a historical novel. The events belonged to my early childhood. I remember the troops coming in when martial law was declared in that part of Kentucky. When I wrote the novel I wasn't thinking of it as history. For one thing, the world it treated still, in a way, survived. You could still talk to the old men who had been involved. In the 1930's I remember going to see a judge down in Kentucky—he was an elderly man then—a man of the highest integrity and reputation—who had lived through that period and who by common repute had been mixed up in it—his father had been a tobacco grower. He got to talking about that period in Kentucky. He said, "Well, I won't say who was and who wasn't mixed up in some of those things, but I will make one observation: I have noticed that the sons of those who were opposed to getting a fair price for tobacco ended up as either bootleggers or brokers." But he was an old-fashioned kind of guy, for whom bootlegging and brokerage looked very much alike. Such a man didn't look "historical" thirty years ago. Now he looks like the thigh bone of a mastodon.

–Ralph Ellison and Eugene Walter, "The Art of Fiction XVIII: Robert Penn Warren," *Paris Review*, 4 (Spring–Summer 1957): 116–117

Both in design and execution, this is a large-scale novel: it must be judged by large-scale standards. The publishers, and Mr. Allen Tate, are certainly of my opinion—they even go so far as to invoke Tolstoy's name on the cover. Very well, let us seriously ask ourselves the question: Is this a masterpiece? I believe not. Why? Because, I feel, Mr. Warren has failed in his presentation of the chief character. Perse Munn is conceived as a figure of tremendous significance: he is the noble liberal gone astray in a world of power politics. Maneuvered by the logic of events from his democratic platform, he tries to use Force, and Force uses him. Such a man must be very vividly and subtly described by his creator—from the inside as well as from the out. He must be an individual, not a mere type. Perse Munn, as I see him, is the weakest character in this book.

In fact, he embodies the only weakness in a very brilliant, powerful and profound novel. All the minor characters in "Night Rider" are well done. Mr. Christian fairly bulges out of the page; Bunk Trevelyan is an original and convincing Judas. And Mr. Warren has, to

a high degree, the conspicuous American literary virtue of being able to make people talk. Not only the big dramatic scenes—the trial, the murder of Trevelyan, the burning of the warehouse—but equally the little moments of everyday life are vividly evoked. From the very first sentences you begin to hear and see and smell the Kentucky of forty years ago. Mr. Warren reconstructs an entire world. That he has reconstructed it for myself, a foreigner, without previous knowledge of the social background, is a measure of his great success. Indeed, so important is the theme of this novel and so considerable its achievement, that I almost wish he would rewrite it—as George Moore used to—ten years from now, when the powers already apparent in this first attempt have come to full maturity.

–Christopher Isherwood, "Tragic Liberal," *New Republic*, 99 (31 May 1939): 108

* * *

This excerpt is from a review article for Partisan Review *in which Philip Rahv commented on seven European and American novels. Rahv was one of the founders of the* Partisan Review, *a leftist literary journal that had become independent of the Communist Party in 1938.*

"Vivid, Sensuous Writing"
Review of *Night Rider*

At long last we come to Mr. Robert Penn Warren's *Night Rider*, patently the most distinguished work on my list. Known as a poet and literary critic, Mr. Warren has achieved the seemingly impossible: his first novel shows none of the strains and shifts that ordinarily mar such prose narratives as poets and critics have been able to produce. *Night Rider*, manifesting an almost classic normality of form and rare qualities of a dramatic and pictorial order, is told with so much ease and power that its author can be said to have attained in one bound a leading position among American novelists.

Mr. Warren has designed his narrative on more than one plane. Its exterior reality is that of the strife in Kentucky, some thirty-five years ago, between the tobacco farmers and the tobacco trust, while within or behind it there exists the interior reality of the moral process and of the hazards and mutations of personality. And the inner and outer themes are unified by a constant exchange of meaning, by a never-interrupted dialogue between the visible act and its psychic shadow.

The problem of identity is deeply implanted in the novel. Percy Munn, whose life is overpowered by the passions and cruelty of the tobacco war, feels that if he only knew who he is he would surely know how to resolve his bewilderment. In a numb, awkward fashion he attempts to arrest the loss of inner continuity. He tries to fathom the ambiguous connections between things done and things remembered, between the present self and the vanishing and perhaps contrary selves of the past. But since "the future was dead and rotten in his breast, the past, too, which once had seemed to him to have its patterns, began to fall apart, act by act, incident by incident, thought by thought, each item into brutish separateness. . . ." His sense of identity cannot withstand the shock of his experience and, finally, he wills his own destruction. And in some obscure way one perceives that the disintegration of Munn, though the reasons for it in the story are immediate and specific, may have its larger implications. Possibly its meaning relates to that compulsive element in the history of the South whose objective equivalent in its literature is the obsessive theme of violence and death.

But aside from its value as a psychological fable, *Night Rider* is exceptional for its vivid, sensuous writing, and for its realistic picture of sectional life. It has, however, its opaque side. Given the desperate economic struggle in which Munn acts as a leader, we are never certain whether his fate is being determined by forces in the main social and impersonal, or whether the objective events serve merely to provoke his own intrinsic temper. The author, of course, draws both curves of determination, but the way in which they interact is not quite clear. Still, despite this uncertainty, Munn is wholly convincing, and Bill Christian, Lucille, Senator Tolliver, Doctor MacDonald, and Willie Proudfit are equally real. Willie Proudfit's tale of the frontier days forms an heroic chapter recalling the lost innocence of the continent as well as the terror of its subjugation. There are at least half a dozen superb scenes of action, such as the search of the Negro cabins by deputies and the burning of the warehouses in Bardsville by the night riders; and from the less resounding parts I would single out for comment that wonderful passage, rendered through the memory of Munn, which tells about a Miss Ianthe Sprague of Philadelphia. Resembling a species of marine life, this ageing and nondescript spinster is unforgettable.

–Philip Rahv, "A Variety of Fiction," *Partisan Review*, 6 (Spring 1939): 112–113

* * *

A Story Within a Story

At the suggestion of his Houghton Mifflin editor Robert N. Linscott, Warren had spent time in December cutting his novel by some eighteen thousand words. Both Allen Tate and Linscott had suggested he cut, or perhaps even eliminate, the story Willie Proudfit tells of killing buffaloes and Indians in the West. In this excerpt he explains why he decided to keep his story within a story, a device he often employed in his novels.

Warren to Allen Tate, January 1939

. . . All in all, I feel that the cuts improved the novel. I used something over half of Linscott's suggested cuts and then made some cuts of my own. You, you recall, suggested a cut, or drastic reduction, of the Proudfit story; so did Linscott. With grave misgivings, I finally left the thing in, although I reduced it some. I had hoped that the thing would have some organic reference to the total meaning of the novel and would, really, make a contribution to the effect of the last chapter. I'll try to say what I had hoped would come across. First, the thing you mentioned, the exhausting, on psychological grounds, of the possibility of going West, etc. Second, the reference, almost as in terms of oblique fable, of the "ghost dance" to the night-riding, a kind of dancing of the buffalo back by the ritual—outmoded, too—of personal violence. Third, the reference to Munn's private situation in general. This may be stated along these lines: Proudfit is a man who has been able to pass beyond his period of "slaughter" into a state of self knowledge. If he is not at home in the world, practically (losing his place, etc.), he is at least at home with himself, has had his vision. It is an incommunicable vision, and is no solution for anyone but himself. He is, in a way, a foil for Munn, who has tried to embrace his vision by violence (discovery of humanity leading him into the act, murder, which is the cancellation of humanity, the act which defines isolation). But more specifically, as the tale relates to Munn's decision: Munn feels, as it were, that though he cannot achieve the vision, he can, perhaps, by a last act of violence, inject some rationality into his experience, he can round it out in terms that on mechanical grounds at least would be comprehensible—that is, by committing his murder, he can in a way justify his present situation, for he is on the run for a murder he did not commit and the murder of the Senator would be the first completely personal and private murder for him. Fourth, the Indian business, obliquely again, implies the tribal loyalties, the conflict within the tribe (Lone Wolf and Mamanti against the idea of Kicking Bird, who would grasp the white man's hand and not beat his head on a stone, etc.); all of this has some extensions into the situation among the people involved in the tobacco troubles. This stuff—all of these points—may be mistakenly developed in the novel, but this may indicate some of the reasons why I felt I had to keep the section. But I did write in, in the last chapter when Munn goes up to the bluff for the last day, a clue for his own basic relation to Proudfit's narrative. I hope it will do something to tie the thing together.

–*Selected Letters of Robert Penn Warren, Volume Two*, pp. 178–179

This excerpt is from a generally favorable review that appeared in the Kenyon Review, *which was edited by Warren's mentor and friend John Crowe Ransom.*

"A Notable Achievement"
Review of *Night Rider*

All this is not to say that *Night Rider* is an epic. It does not have the reach or glow of the masterpiece, and it does have some definite faults. The leading women are forgettable; in recent fiction there have been too many fragile little ladies like Perse Munn's wife, bravely supporting masses of coiled hair that appear too heavy for their smallness. Perse Munn himself is at times too blurred as an individual, too cloudy as a reflector. And most seriously disappointing, it seems to me, are the overlong concluding chapters; here the tragedy loses force through an excess of symbol and contrivance. At the end there is an unhappy compromise between the alternatives of intense drama and a sombre, brooding close. After seventy pages of twilight, the story suddenly flares up, somewhat luridly; Mr. Warren calls in the army and has Perse Munn shot.

Nevertheless *Night Rider* remains a notable achievement. I should remark, finally, that it makes an excellent text for the regionalists. Kentucky and its people are vividly recreated but do not become merely picturesque or quaint; although Mr. Warren is perhaps a little too fond of his local color, he does not lay it on with a trowel. In general, he takes full advantage of his rich materials without exploiting the region or being taken in by it.

–Herbert J. Muller, "Violence upon the Roads,"
Kenyon Review, 1 (Summer 1939): 324

* * *

The first English edition of Night Rider *was published in January 1940. The English reviews, such as this excerpt from a column in* The New Statesman and Nation, *were positive.*

"The Power to Evoke"
Review of *Night Rider*

It is pleasant to begin the new year with a notice of two such novels as *Night Rider* and *Capricornia,* for both are first novels which would be outstanding even if they were the work of experienced writers of established reputation. *Night Rider* is the story of a lawyer from an up-country parish of Kentucky whose popularity with the local tobacco-growers draws him rather against his will into an Association of Farmers who are attempting to break a buyers' ring by pooling their crop and selling co-operatively at an agreed price. Legal and law-abiding as the Association is at the beginning, the corrupt methods of coercion and intimidation practised by its opponents drive its members to desperation. The crisis comes when the President of the Association sells out to the buyers and resigns after advising the acceptance of a price lower than the agreed price for the tobacco crop; the price offered by the buyers is high enough to be tempting, the resigning President carries weight in the community, and the Association begins to break up. Loyal members begin to burn the crops of waverers, seedbeds are hoed up, and acts of violence increase until the lawyer finds that he has been swept up into one of those agrarian rebellions which are a recurrent feature in American history. The lawyer is an unimpressive, rather weak character, and he is swept along with the Association; his descent from a law-abiding

Advertisement for the first English edition, which was published by Eyre and Spottiswoode in January 1940
(Thomas Cooper Library, University of South Carolina)

citizen to a hunted man seeking a private enemy to do murder is brilliantly described. The breakup of his marriage as he becomes increasingly secretive and increasingly strained by his familiarity with brutality in itself would justify the book as a psychological study, but there are added to that descriptive passages—the night search of negro cabins for the missing weapon in a murder, a raid to burn tobacco warehouses in a country town, the arrival of the National Guard after a night of riot—and a richness of characterisation which gives the book the power to evoke the complete picture of a society and its situation. Satisfactory as a work of art in that it successfully re-creates a man's experience for the reader, it is also worth reading as an explanatory note to all those curious anarchist outbreaks from Shay's Rebellion down to the Harlan County Riots. And even if it had none of these things in its favour, this would still be a good exciting story.

—Anthony West, "New Novels," *New Statesman and Nation,* new series 19 (20 January 1940): 77

* * *

Critics have read Night Rider *as an important forerunner to Warren's later fiction. In this excerpt from his 1961 article "Robert Penn Warren's* Night Rider: *The Nihilism of the Isolated Temperament," Alvan S. Ryan compares Warren's aims to those of Joseph Conrad and argues that "*Night Rider *can be said to define the central motives of Warren's art." For Ryan, Percy Munn's "nihilistic attitude is of central importance" but it "is not at all to be equated with the novelist's vision."*

Munn's Search for Self-knowledge in *Night Rider*

The theme of the novel is the search of the hero for self-definition and self-knowledge. This is Warren's first treatment of a theme that has frequently been pointed out as central to all of his fiction. The hero's discovery, under the pressure of moral choice and action, of what kind of man he is, of the terms within which he can act, and of what fulfills or destroys his search for meaning and significance, is the burden of the novel. From the outset Mr. Percy Munn is set apart from the other characters; he is always an isolated man. The theme is embodied in the action of the novel in a powerfully ironic way, for the action traces Munn's progressive discovery that in allying himself with a political and economic association calling itself a "Brotherhood" he discovers only his own emptiness in his relations with his mistress, Lucille Christian, and finally the very basis of his sense of selfhood, the relation between his present actions, his past, and a possible future, disintegrates completely.

What kind of man is Mr. Munn? The essential thing is that he is a divided man who does not know himself and the terms within which he can act. Yet he struggles toward this knowledge and broods over his acts after they are committed. It is, in fact, Munn's relentless self-scrutiny that makes him a character of essential dignity, and gives to the novel much of its impact.

. . . .

In concluding his essay, Ryan compares the ending of Night Rider, *in which he argues that Munn fails to break through his isolation, to the ending of Conrad's* The Nigger of the "Narcissus," *in which the narrator expresses a sense of solidarity with his shipmates: "Haven't we, together and upon the immortal sea, wrung out a meaning from our sinful lives?"*

. . . This is exactly what Munn has been unable to do. Nor does Munn, night rider that he is, ever win from his journey into the heart of darkness, or from his confrontation of his alter ego, the recognition and self-knowledge that [Conrad's] Marlow returns with. It is rather the Jack Burden of *All the King's Men* who finally emerges from nihilism and isolation, to see the spider web image of Cass Mastern's diary as a symbol of what Conrad calls "the solidarity in mysterious origin, in toil, in joy, in hope, in uncertain fate, which binds men to each other and all mankind to the visible world." Yet *Night Rider* is a powerful dramatization of the efforts of a man deficient in self-knowledge to emerge from isolation into solidarity. His failure is that the solidarity he embraces is at its roots immoral and absolutist, a travesty of the true solidarity that begins with "the deep, inner certainty of self."

—Alvan S. Ryan, "Robert Penn Warren's *Night Rider:* The Nihilism of the Isolated Temperament," *Modern Fiction Studies,* 7 (Winter 1961–1962): 339, 346

* * *

In this excerpt from an essay written in Warren's honor, Randolph Paul Runyon discusses the beginning of Night Rider, *which he claims is the first instance of a fictional pattern that runs throughout Warren's career.*

The Father-Son Motif in *Night Rider*

Percy Munn, who for most of *Night Rider* seems powerless and inarticulate, caught up in events beyond his control and for which he cannot give a clear account, did display a surprisingly effective eloquence when he addressed the crowd at the Bardsville rally in the first chapter of Warren's first published novel. Even then, however, he was the victim of someone else's design, manipulated into giving a speech he had neither the desire nor the preparation to give. Senator Tolliver, "a real orator" whose "flowing, full, compelling voice" commanded the attention of his audience, was indeed a hard act to follow. Tolliver's speech is described as a fullness that overcomes a void: "The Senator was speaking, his full, rich voice . . . dominating the hot emptiness of the afternoon air" (21). When Munn, after the shock of having been introduced as the next speaker, stood to face the crowd and tried to speak, at first no sound would come. He looked up to the sky and felt that emptiness all the more intensely when he noticed that even the single buzzard that had "at a great height . . . hung motionless" when the Senator was speaking was gone now, "leaving nothing but the empty and intense blue of the sky." That "nothing but . . ." would become the theme of Munn's impromptu oration, as he makes the emptiness of his own speechlessness the subject itself of his speech: "My friends," he began, addressing the farmers oppressed by the tobacco corporations who would not give them a fair price for their crop, "you came here . . . because you thought you could get something here to help you. . . . But there is *nothing* here to help you . . . *nothing* here in Bardsville for you" (24–25; emphasis added). At that point the Senator and his Association colleagues must have begun to realize how much of a gamble it had been to lure Munn into speaking to the crowd. Munn could hear the anxious shuffling of feet on the platform behind him, and a nervous cough. "There is *nothing* here," he continued, "*except* what you have brought with you . . . no hope except the hope you bring" (emphasis added). He played his rhetorical trick—with the result that his speech in the end turned out, despite the emptiness he had felt before he started and despite the theme of emptiness and despair with which he began it, to be a rousing success. He seized his listeners' attention by appearing to say the unspeakable and then twisting it into invigorating eloquence. This rhetorical solution finally became for Munn what had seemed so inimitable in the senator's oratory, a kind of fullness: "He could not tell whether they were listening to him, and found that he did not care, for his own voice *filled* him and he was completely himself" (emphasis added).

The predicament in which Munn had felt trapped, first enraptured by the Senator's "full and powerful discourse," and then enveloped by a "wave of nausea" as he heard his own name spoken and began to realize that he would have to follow that discourse with one of his own—that predicament is one that will return with remarkable regularity in Warren's fiction. It is, essentially, the situation of a son who finds that he has been preceded by his father, and specifically by his father's *text,* and that

Title page for a 1941 edition. On 24 December 1942, Warren wrote to his friend John Palmer: "By the way, I discovered in the most pleasant way possible—by opening the envelope and finding a check for an advance fall out—that Night Rider has been bought by an English Book Club, for a very nice figure" (Special Collections, Western Kentucky University Libraries).

now he must in his turn speak, act, or interpret that paternal text. The reading of Warren I undertake in *The Taciturn Text: The Fiction of Robert Penn Warren* and *The Braided Dream: Robert Penn Warren's Late Poetry* is grounded in this recurring scene.

That Senator Tolliver played a fatherly role in the protagonist's life, and that Munn responded as a dutiful son, is clear. . . .
> —Randolph Paul Runyon, "Father, Son, and Taciturn Text," in *"To Love So Well the World": A Festschrift in Honor of Robert Penn Warren,* edited by Dennis L. Weeks (New York: Peter Lang, 1992), pp. 113–121

Proud Flesh

Warren first began working on the material that evolved into All the King's Men *in summer 1937, originally envisioning a play. He continued working on the play—among other projects—the following summer, when he and Cinina traveled to Italy. In 1939 Warren was awarded a Guggenheim Fellowship and the couple again traveled to Europe, where Warren completed the first draft of a five-act play, titled* Proud Flesh, *in December. After the Warrens returned to the United States in June 1940, he started to revise the play, accepting the offered aid of Francis Fergusson, a professor of literature and drama at Bennington College in Vermont. He later decided to reconceive his material as a novel.*

In 1947 the revised, three-act version of Proud Flesh *was performed at the University Theatre at the University of Minnesota, but the play was not published until it was included in* Robert Penn Warren's "All the King's Men": Three Stage Versions *(2000). In this essay, John Burt, the editor of* The Complete Poems of Robert Penn Warren *(1998), analyzes the play and compares it to* All the King's Men.

Idealism and Rage in *Proud Flesh*

Proud Flesh is the verse tragedy from which *All the King's Men* emerged. The first version, recently edited by James A. Grimshaw, Jr., and James A. Perkins, occupied Warren from 1937 to 1940. It has the shape of a five-act Shakespearean tragedy but also employs many of the stylistic devices of expressionist drama, and is written in the densely coiled, bristlingly intense verse Warren employed in his roughly contemporary, *Eleven Poems on the Same Theme* (1942). As poetry, *Proud Flesh* is a work of a high order. As drama, however, it proved unplayable, and after considerable reworking (rearranging the play into a more modern three acts, adding a scene, even changing the name of the protagonist from Willie Strong to Willie Talos) Warren ultimately abandoned the attempt to bring this project into final form as a play, choosing to reconceive it as a novel, although the play did have a brief run, arranged by Eric Bentley and directed by Frank Whiting, in Minneapolis in the late spring of 1947, during Warren's time at the University of Minnesota.

Proud Flesh is not merely a rough draft of *All the King's Men* but an independent work, which shares many characters and situations with the novel, but which sees the action in a different way and develops some possibilities which Warren's later treatments of this story (both in the novel and in the later stage versions) foreclose. The principal difference, of course, is that we do not see the action in *Proud Flesh* through the sensibility and judgment of Jack Burden.

(Indeed, all we see of the character who will develop into Jack Burden is a brief moment of childhood reminiscence he shares with Keith Amos, the play's equivalent of Adam Stanton, as the latter lurks in the lobby of the State Capitol preparing to assassinate Governor Strong.) The play lacks Jack's irony, his moral insight, and the perspective his own developing moral drama gives on the political drama at the novel's center. But it also is not confined by Jack's blinders, and sees some of the main figures—particularly the play's equivalents of Anne Stanton and Lucy Stark—very differently from how the novel sees them.

The plot turns on the Hospital construction project which also structures the last third of *All the King's Men*. Governor Strong prevails upon the surgeon Keith Amos to head the medical staff of his hospital, and almost simultaneously begins an affair with Keith's sister Anne. For purely pragmatic reasons he agrees to allow his corrupt protegé Tiny Harper (the novel's Tiny Duffy) to give the hospital construction contract to Gummy Satterfield, a sleazy builder rather like the novel's Gummy Larson. Willie no sooner makes this deal than his son Tom is injured at a college football game (Willie has made the deal in the stands). When Tom dies, Willie, stung with remorse, backs out of the deal, breaks with Anne and with Sue Parsons, the novel's Sadie Burke, in an only partly successful attempt to reconcile with his estranged wife, and is betrayed by Harper and Sue, who, in ways familiar from the novel, spur Keith Amos to murder Willie Strong.

We see Willie Strong in *Proud Flesh* only at the height of his power and in the full blaze of his cynicism; and although there is a hint of an earlier and more virtuous career in some comments by Sue Parsons, we are not given accounts of the things in the novel like the Mason City schoolhouse construction incident or the first campaign for Governor that make Willie Stark's turn to a more hard-edged style of politics more palatable. Nor is Willie driven into the hospital construction project in the play, as he is in the novel, by the desire to prove to himself that all of his corrupt exercises of power have really been aimed at serving the public good, although the play leaves open the possibility that Willie's motives in building the hospital (and in other things) are not entirely cynical ones. Indeed, the motives for actions in the play are simpler all around than they are in the novel. It is not, for instance, the dark story about Judge Irwin (who does not appear in the play anyway), but merely Anne's persuasiveness, that convinces Dr. Amos to accept the hospital position. It is not the blackmail attempt against Willie's son, but pure pragmatism, that moves Willie to enter the bargain with Satterfield. And the characters are quite differently conceived. Clara Strong, for instance, is a much sterner and less forgiving character than Lucy Stark, her counterpart in the novel. And Anne Amos is a harder, more opportunistic, more bluntly sexual character than Anne Stanton is in the novel.

The key difference, however, is in the prominent role given to Keith Amos. Adam Stanton, despite being the ultimate killer of Willie Stark, is scarcely even a fully rounded character in the novel, and although he is always wired a bit too tightly and is stern in rather scary ways, he never quite crosses the line that separates the merely scary from the frankly sinister. But Keith Amos is sinister indeed in ways that only a hero-villain can be.

Consider the brilliant opening scene, in which Keith is stopped by a motorcycle policeman as he rushes to his first meeting with Governor Strong, who will ask him to head up the grand new hospital he is planning. When the trooper realizes who they are (and that, as Keith's snide and oily passenger Dr. Skipworth, reminds him, ticketing them will lose the trooper his job), his swagger evaporates, and he is reduced to begging to be allowed to do the two doctors favors—fixing their nearly flat tire—to save his neck. Keith will have none of it: He never lets the trooper off the hook, demanding that the trooper do his duty and give him the ticket, and he promises the trooper nothing. Perhaps Keith sees this as playing by the rules. But he also takes a bit too much pleasure in making the trooper writhe, who is finally described not as a thuggish Myrmidon of the police state but as "a big clumsy boy confused almost to tears." Nothing in the novel shows so clearly that close kinship in Keith's nature between rigid devotion to principle and naked sadism that makes him ultimately such a frightening alternative to Willie.

Keith is already in a rage when he is stopped, and it is only partly a rage against having to meet with the Governor, whose corruption (alleged corruption—we never see him doing anything that is corrupt in the sense Keith means) offends his nostrils. Keith thinks he is enraged about political corruption. But what he is really enraged about is having a human body, subject to desire and to decay, a porous bag of foul-smelling fluids:

A stink, and on a man's fingers,
Whatever he lays hand to, it's there,
And the stink climbs the multitudinous sweetness of air,
Lovingly lingers, a kiss upon the tongue,
And fouls the nostril's secret stair—
Smell it, it's there
On your fingers, and mine—

Whatever you touch,
The cup lifted familiarly, morningly, to the lips,
The friend's hand—that delicate
Film of moisture slick upon the palm
There, there it will live, proliferate,
Swelling like algae spored upon a pond—
The flower you pluck, and the door-knob
Kind to your fingers, accustomed, the door
Which opens to the innermost room where love lies.

This is not just priggishness; there is something sexually charged, even positively kinky, about Keith's disgust here. These are not the accents of a rejecter of sexual life but of a sexual sadist, whose rejection of sexuality is a kind of erotic cruelty. He has a natural cousin in the Thomas Jefferson of Warren's *Brother to Dragons* (1953), whose speeches likewise often drip with sexually charged disgust; and he has a natural ancestor in Angelo of *Measure for Measure,* perhaps the original of all of those characters who link Puritanism and sadism. His later tirade in which he compares the male genitalia to "a sly purse of pleasure" sounds like Angelo at his most revolted and mesmerized. It is not for nothing that it is Keith's sister Anne's sexual involvement with Willie, rather than anything political, that drives him over the edge. Something of this view of Adam is plausible even in the novel, but we do not focus on it there in the way we do here, because there it is obscured by Jack's own moral drama and by his inability, so strange in a narrator proud of his toughness, to see his friends with perfect clarity.

Keith's disgust is not merely disgust with the political machine. Skipworth offers the suggestion that however rough Strong's methods are, the medical center he offers is unquestionably a good thing. Keith's response starts out in the cynical mode of Jack Burden:

All right, we get the medical center. All right. We patch
up a few more bodies. A healthier people. Better
babies. Apple week. Jesus Christ.

But Keith's argument takes a different turn—a turn never taken by Adam Stanton—when he wonders whether fixing up broken bodies really is on the whole a good thing. Pain he argues is "an evil," which is to say a disagreeable but ethically neutral thing, rather than "evil," which is to say something ethically bad the abatement of which would be ethically good. Now Adam Stanton makes this same distinction between "evil" and "an evil" in *All the King's Men,* but there it seems to be something of a debater's trick. Keith develops the distinction in an altogether darker direction, arguing that nothing that affects bodies,

Chorus:

What hand flings the white road before us?
Over the hills and the swamplands,
Over the damplands and ~~hxyx~~ highlands,
~~Over the~~ Gully and bayou? and flings us,
Fast as the lead from the gun-mouth
And hard as the words from his own mouth,
And us nameless and yet he has ~~ffxxeduX~~ named us,
And aimless and yet he has aimed us
And flung us, and flings us

This was the first fragment written for Proud Flesh, which later became All the King's Men. This is the opening chorus of Highway Patrolmen.

RPW

Page from Warren's first draft of Proud Flesh, *identified by the author (Robert Penn Warren Papers, Beinecke Library, Yale University)*

their pain, their mortality, their misery, is actually finally of any moral account. Although this view rather makes mincemeat of Keith's own vocation as a surgeon, it does set him further from Willie's views than Adam Stanton ever is, since after all tending to human disease and pain is in the same category as tending to poverty and misery. For Keith, tending to disease, like tending to poverty, is merely attending to the order of nature, and to do that estranges one from the order of meaning and right. He demands of Skipworth, "[D]id you ever ask yourself when you put your hand on some poor bastard's belly and sewed him back together—did you ever ask yourself what was in him?" "I'll tell you," he says, breaking into verse,

> The stink.
> If the stink's all, why bother?
> Think?
> But we don't, you and I,
> Blind fingers, rag-pickers,
> Mumblers and patchers of remnants.
> For what?
> To get the wind out of a worn-out gut?
> We don't know.
> Know!
> The caterpillar knows its leaf, the mole
> Its hummock, the fox the fetid hole,
> The cat the cushion, the hog the sty
> And the swill-trough, who
> Has known his heart?
> Who? Not I,
> And Bill, not you.

Indeed, in Keith's description of Willie as a tumor, which follows immediately upon this, the body and its diseases are not merely the vehicle for the political tenor of the metaphor (in which Willie is a tumor in the body politic). The vehicle overwhelms its tenor: the body is the real subject, and Willie is disgusting chiefly because he leads Keith to the thought of the body.

> We touch only the surface, and our fingers
> Stink. Whiff only the breath breathed out,
> *(He shifts his attention more and more from his friend, as the light*
> *begins to fade, except on him.)*
> And it stinks.
> But he lies inside.
> He is deep inside.
> He is growing,
> A cancerous growth which now grows proud in the dark,
> Iridescent in darkness, the flesh's final pride
> Thriving on flesh; and the sluggish blood now sways
> And swags to his mass, like sway of the sea's tide.
> He burns, is peacocked in flame, but utters no light.
> *(The light fades rapidly now.)*
> Eastern and mogul, his mass savagely drowses,

> His coils stir. Our name in him is essential,
> O nomenclature swollen now! O splendid
> And inward that apple, that fat fruit which gleams
> *(By this time, the light is entirely gone, and there is only the voice in*
> *the darkness.)*
> On the bough of our darkness, till dark itself is rescinded,
> Till the night is ended
> Till the dark
> He is in the dark.

It is Anne's persuasion that moves Keith to change his mind about accepting the hospital position, and she does it not exactly by outlining the nobility of the healer's position but by pointing out that Keith's profession arises from an animal urgency, like lust or hunger, that cannot be gainsaid, a lust towards becoming that never fully transcends natural process but cannot be reduced to it either. Keith points out, in his most vivid lines, the magnetic emptiness of the body:

> I have held a heart, alive, in my own hand,
> *(He leans as though to confide a secret.)*
> Beating , a tremulous blood-blob—it did
> Not speak, it did not say a word, it said
> Nothing.

Anne remembers evocative and lyrical scenes from their childhood—waiting for a fox among ferns and moss, lying on warm sand, drifting in warm sea water—some of them lyrical memories given to Jack Burden in the novel, and one a lyrical scene Warren would himself return to much later in his poetic career, in "Debate: Question, Quarry, Dream." But unlike Jack, for whom these memories remain a somewhat sentimental refuge from acknowledging his later self, Anne repudiates the memories, remarking that

> No matter what Strong is, the good
> Is fact, no matter what
> The world is, even if it's not the world
> We thought—no lying on beaches now, and the light,
> Wings lost in that light, I remember, I
> Remember, it was once—but still it's a world
> To do what you can in.

Anne notes that Keith's revulsion against what he calls Governor Strong's vanity is another and darker form of vanity, for Strong's vanity (in Anne's view) is merely the vanity of the body, Keith's the vanity of a fierce spirit that spurns the body but cannot be free of it. Her argument here is very like the argument that Lucy Jefferson uses when she seeks to persuade Thomas Jefferson to take the hand of the murderer Lilburne Lewis in *Brother to Dragons*. (Taking the hand of a repellent person is a repeated figure in *Proud Flesh* as well.) Her final, and successful move, however, is to

May 9, '41.

Dear Red,

I'm returning at long last four scenes which I have worked
over and annotated and generally cut up. They are I think all much improved, but I have shortenedx them still more, and xxxx marked some
passages which I think should be rewritten for clarity. The main principle in my cutting has been to eliminate the multiplication of meta-
phors, and I am rather pleased (as I hope you will be) with the result.
The one metaphor which I leave in each case seems to me to gain vastly
in dramatic emphasis from having to stand alone. In general, I have the
sensation of disengaging a very fine drama from too many words---the
too many words being perhaps a sign of uncertainty in the medium, perhaps a bad habit left over from novel- or lyric-writing. Do let me know
how it looks to you in its new nudity!

Act I, scene 2 may be a bit abrupt now, but that depends partl
on the subsequent developments of Anne, and I should like to think it
over again when we have the whole play.

The sequence in Act II---scenes 2, 3, and 4 seems to me vastly
improved in speed and intelligibility , and also in your grasp pf
Clara's character. I have marked the spots which I think unclear or
underdeveloped. I like the general construction of this act now---the
alternation between large public scnes and the small intimate scenes wit
Clara. The football scenes I think is very successful, amd I have done
nothing to it. The ball scene , which is in some ways built rather like
the football scene, is less successful. I don't know why, yet---perhaps
I shall find out later, and if so I'll write to you. It will do, but I
think it could be a lot better....Scene 4 I like very much. For the fina
chorus I suggest something which sums up the entire act---the medicos
remind us that he has been slipping , now comes this collapse; the progn
nosis is very bad.

As I think over the move ment of the whole play, I like the
plot, the arrangement of scenes, the main drive of the story. I think
some of the proportions may be wrong, and I propose to work on that poin
as soon as we have a complete version again. Most of the characters now
are good; I am dubious only about Anne, Amos and the chorus. I do not ha
a late version of Act I scene 3, where Anne falls for Strong, not of
Act III scene 2, where Amos and Anne meet again for the peripeteia.
Are those available yet? What I should like to do now is to study the
role of these two in the story as a whole, and also their characters
in themselves.

As for the chorus, I think its story needs to be simplified.
It is all for Strong in the begin ing, gradually comes to doubt him,
and t last reads him out of the party. My criti cism of it at present
is that its irony (conscious and unconscious) tends to grow too elaborat
so that we lose our sense of the chorus as a force, an entity, a dramati
persona. Also, I think the convention of the chorus would be still clea
if you made a sharper distinction between the times when it participates
in or punrently interject comments on the dialogue, and the times
when it bursts into more extended song. I have shortened what it says,
for instance, in Act I scene 2, when it nters the dialogue.

I am keeping the scenes I didn't mark up. What I should like,
as soon as you have time, are these these scenes back with your comments,
and Act I scene 3 and the last two scenes of Act III.

Believe it or not, we're still stewing about the summer school
The enrollment has picked up; but we la ck any reserve, and none of us
can afford to put up a thousand bucks. My guess is, we'll have it. WeRe

Letter in which Francis Fergusson, a Bennington College professor whom Warren chose as a collaborator, critiques the five-act version of Proud Flesh.
Fergusson wrote the 1949 book The Idea of Theatre *(Yale Collection of American Literature,*
Beinecke Rare Book and Manuscript Library).

su.posed to make the absolute final positively ulʸimate decision this
week-end; and then I'll plan my summer.
                My apologies for all these delays in work on the play. Believ
me, it's not lack ᵒ interest, but a series of very ᵘnwelcome worries
and distractions.

turn Keith's key word, "nothing," the nothing that the "tremulous blood-blob of the heart" says, against him. For this nothing is an urgency beyond words, an urgency which works through Keith's hands but is ultimately an urgency of the body, not of the spirit. Of Keith's hands she says,

> They are not yours, I'll tell you what they belong to:
> The swollen abdomen and the gray lips,
> The mouth which shapes like an O but utters no breath
> When the pain strikes, the running sore and the sore
> With the tentacled fingers which beckon, and beckon you,
> The eyes which turn slow in the head and find
> Nothing, have demanded nothing.
> AMOS: (Slowly.) Nothing.
> ANNE: Nothing.
> And in the eyes there's nothing, and the nothingness
> Devours, devours you, gray gullet, enormous, void—
> And effortless that ingurgitation, and you
> Defenseless. The fact. The act. You've seen it.

Anne sees Keith's vocation as an urgency of the body, as electric but as blind and silent as the sexual drive, driven by an almost preternatural insistence it cannot explain, evade, or understand the meaning of, driven towards an end it cannot conceive. Keith's attempts to describe this urgency have a desperate ring, and Anne interrupts Keith's speech only to ridicule its intention:

> AMOS: Yourself,
> What man can name it, what he is, can name
> The flame which at center does not bend, the essence
>   unending?
> Who has named it?
> ANNE: (Almost scornfully.) Only children try.
> AMOS: O Anne,
> There's a tooth which gnaws, and gnaws our definitions,
> A current in things, we look and their shapes alter
> And falter, we falter, doors bang, bang open
> On dark and the wet: cold gust at the ankle, the flame
> Jerks from the wick, the wick stinks in the darkness.

This vision of an inarticulate imperative which seeks, beneath the intelligence and perhaps without its will or awareness, to instantiate itself in acts even as it cannot be rendered in concepts, is shared by all of the play's various choruses (each act opens with an ode by a chorus of masked people–motorcycle policemen, masked ladies, surgeons, and so on), and by Willie himself. The opening chorus captures the spirit of unfathomable drivenness:

> What hand flings the white road before us?
> What hand over hills and the damplands,
> Over the highlands and swamplands,
> Gulley and bayou? And flings us
> Fast as the slug from the gun-mouth–
> Us nameless, and yet he has named us,
> And aimless, and yet he has aimed us
> And flung us, and flings us, a handful
> Of knives hurled, edged errand–O errand
> Blind with the glittering blindness of light!

Clara Strong, arguing with Willie over the fate of their son, describes this insatiable but inscrutable driving force as the sign of a kind of emptiness, as the irresistible pull of a vacuum:

> It is the last delusion, the gut-gnaw
> Of those born empty, of the insatiate
> Hollowness of heart, who have no inward answer,
> Who would devour the world, drowse listening
> In what aridity of the deep dark
> To their own gut's rumble, rapt and lulled, alone
> In darkness, the shudder in solitude.

Clara might well be giving here the author's view of Willie, who hungers for power because of the essential emptiness of his character. But I think this might be to underread what Willie is about, to see him and those who follow him as suffering under a merely psychological debility. For the fact is that to labor under an insatiable and inscrutable urgency which can neither be fathomed nor mastered is the fate of all of the characters in the play, no matter what their views. Since whatever might fulfill this kind of spiritual craving is unknown to Warren early and late, it is a mistake to think of this kind of craving as a symptom of a weakness; it is in fact finally the source of the bleak sublimity of Warren's late poetry, which, too, is driven by a dark insistence upon serving a more than human but also inhuman meaning that escapes poetry's comprehension and demands its life.

The alternative to bleak sublimity is a mute and animal life. Willie makes this clear in his reply to Clara:

Listen:
It was a house set on the bare ground,
House bare, bony, set on the chunks of stone.
Shutterless, night's blind eye pressed to the pane.
The boy lay, tick-straw harsh to the bare side, heard
The oaks utter under the wind's long drag.
Under the unremitting percussion the timber,
Cold-taut, groaned, and I saw how across the Dakotas,
The icy and pearl-blind plain, the Ozarks, the wind
Came, and did not stop, and I did not know
The name of what was big in me, but knew
It. And once, sun hot on neck, I lay
On the broom grass, and felt beneath my palm
The enormous curvature of earth; and wept.
It has no name but the act, no being in the bland
Intermission of blood, between the stroke and stroke,
But its heat fuses all the mind to clarity,
As the whistling-white blast of the furnace, sand to glass,
For the world fulfills itself, for the perched stone
Throbs for the depth, and the dynamite atoms strain,
In their structures creak like a ship's metals in travail,
Groan; and I knew it. Who knows it and would deny it
Turns the knife on himself, the cut boar grunting for slop,
Fat dog in the sun. Which you, no doubt, admire
As exemplifying some superior principle
Lacking to me, and to, thank God, my son.

Willie's language here is strangely like Adam's. They are not opposites after all, for they share the same kind of Gnostic insistence, the same kind of fascinated and obsessed revulsion from the physical and from the body. And both can deal only in and with the body, although in revulsion.

At least as startling as Adam Amos in *Proud Flesh,* particularly if we come to the play from *All the King's Men,* is Anne Amos, the play's equivalent of Anne Stanton. Perhaps the chief reason she seems so strange to us is that we see Anne Amos, as we never see Anne Stanton, outside of the veil of Jack Burden's idealization of her; we see Anne Amos as someone with motives of her own rather than merely as the person who suffers the consequences

of Jack's moral and sexual failures of nerve. Lucy Ferriss, in *Sleeping with the Boss,* her study of Warren's female characters, argues that the novelist has a grittier vision of Anne Stanton than the *narrator* does, because Jack Burden sees Anne only in terms of his story, not in terms of her own. Ferriss's views are richly borne out by Anne Amos, who is a firmer and more frankly sexual character.

When we first see her—Keith Amos, leaving his first meeting with Willie, bumps into her on her own way in to see him—she is a woman of the world who knows what you have to do to get something done and is not shy about doing it. In *All the King's Men* as well, Anne has her brisk side, but when Anne Stanton is brisk in the novel we see it not as an indication of her worldliness but as a sign that, like her brother, she is rather tightly wound: there is something slightly frenetic about everything she does, and that frenetic quality extends even to her somewhat overdone imitation of a woman of the world. Indeed, rather like her brother, Anne Stanton always bristles with the electricity of sexual feelings that are not only unacknowledged but actively disowned. She also, rather like her brother, does everything she does with a kind of urgency that betrays an unacknowledged or evaded crisis of vocation as well. Just as Adam does his doctoring a little too hard, and plays the piano a little too intensely, so Anne throws herself into good works a little too passionately, as if to persuade herself that she is doing what she is really intended to do. (An unacknowledged crisis of vocation and a disowned or disordered sexual life seem in the novel to be versions of the same thing, perhaps because Jack Burden himself sees them in his own case to be versions of the same thing. But Anne Stanton sees things the same way: she keeps disguising her erotic disillusionment with Jack as impatience with his inability to settle upon a career.) Anne Amos's briskness is quite different from Anne Stanton's, having nothing trembly or vulnerable or evasive about it. Anne Stanton never seems to know herself very well; Anne Amos is never in any doubt about herself, and there is something frank about her, both politically and sexually, that we never see in Anne Stanton, whose sexual attractiveness, indeed, has something to do with her inability to see herself in a sexual way.

This is not to say that Anne Stanton is an asexual creature, only that her sexual feelings are, relative to what we see in Anne Amos, indirect ones. Even in *All the King's Men* Anne Stanton sees Willie as someone who is able to cut through illusion and inhibition in the service of justice; his roughness, relative to the priggish and self-serving Good Government types who complain about Willie back in Burden's Landing, is a sign to her of his deeper knowledge of the world and his more intense commitment to do good in it, and a sign also of a stern and morally heroic manliness. She is visibly struggling with sexual attraction for Willie as early as the impeachment rally scene, when she asks Jack whether Willie really means what he says at the rally. We see in this scene that the charisma of a prophetic if transgressive political calling is also a sexual charisma, although Jack doesn't seem to understand it at that moment and Anne herself does not seem clear about the meaning of her own feelings. Anne's moral and political passion in *All the King's Men* has an unmistakable sexual edge, sharpened both by the sexual thrill of Willie's dark power and by the sexual thrill of her own class transgression: we know that in some sense to Anne Willie is the demon outlaw lover from the wrong side of town, but we do not know whether Anne knows this herself. Even Jack is obliquely willing to concede that Anne somehow, if not with full self-consciousness, sees Willie as more of a man than Jack is, and that the origin of Willie's erotic magnetism is not only his prophetic willingness to break the rules in order to serve justice, and not only his power, but also the self-assurance with which he sets himself up as a transgressor, his lack of inhibitions, second thoughts, and qualms.

That is why Jack portrays his own moral qualms as sexual cowardice: making love to the gangly, sister-like, but suddenly naked and all too grown up Anne, once she undresses for him when they are alone in his room in his mother's house, really would have had a more than vaguely incestuous flavor for him, and his inability to get past that— he is indeed relieved when his mother's car inconveniently pulls into the driveway—is not merely a sign of simple sexual cowardice but also a sign that Jack lacks the sexual charisma of the unhesitant bad boy. If he had had that charisma and owned up to it, he would also have had to own up to things about Anne that even Anne will not own. He is of course right to have qualms about making love to Anne since Anne always seemed to Jack more of a sister than a lover (when she is not bathing him with motherly baby-talk), and her chief erotic relationship early and late is a repressed one with her brother Adam. And Jack knows that that self-doubt marks him ever after as not quite a man in her book. But however unmistakable all this may seem to us, Jack never acknowledges it directly himself, nor allows Anne the insight to discover it on her own. We are never given a sense that Anne knows any of

these things about herself, that she sees her own motivations or even her own feelings with much clarity, whether in relation to Willie or in relation to Jack. The sexual and moral world of Anne Stanton is if anything a more complex one than the sexual and moral world of Anne Amos, but we are allowed only the most indirect glimpses into the former, because we are only allowed to see it through Jack's eyes, who cannot face what he sees.

Indeed, Jack never really allows us to look very deeply into Anne, perhaps because he wants to lay the responsibility for everything Anne does at his own door. When Jack argues in all seriousness that his failure to make love to Anne as a young man somehow made her later affair with Willie inevitable, he seems to imagine that Anne never had any motives, acknowledged or unacknowledged, of her own. Jack is so eager to disown the darkly sexual side of Anne and of his own relationship with her, that there is something disingenuous about his avowal of sexual cowardice. Jack had at the time thought of his failure to make love to Anne as a kind of noble refusal to see the young Anne in a sexual fashion, as a refusal to exploit her vulnerability. Jack jeers at this idea by novel's end. But at the novel's end as much as at its beginning Jack sees all sexual feeling as exploitative, which is why all of his own sexual talk is so shamefaced and why his description of his sexual adventures with his first wife are so unpersuasive—it is not for nothing that Sadie Burke, turning down a jocular and completely unserious proposition by Jack, tells him she "prefers mine with vitamins" and compares him to a spilled box of spaghetti. It is not that Jack does not obliquely know that there is a dark side to Anne and to his own relationship with her, never mind Willie's relationship to her (or Adam's); it is that Jack cannot acknowledge what he knows, and he will not allow Anne to do so either. Jack's view of Anne is always a foreshortened one, stunted by his inability to bear the thought that she has sexually ambiguous feelings and a morally ambiguous life. Whatever his bedroom failure with her was, it was not merely his inability to make love to her as any normal adolescent would; it was his inability to let her be a moral adult, with all the ugliness that moral adults have to face up to.

In *All the King's Men* we never see Anne and Willie together; we do not have a sense of the quality of their relationship. But in *Proud Flesh* we see them dancing together, and we see the sexual hunger and desperate need on both sides. The scene occurs at a vulnerable moment for Willie. He has just, in the scene before, made his corrupt bargain

I-1-1

(A blue, concentrated light, blue like the light of an
operating room, reveals the Chorus, which is composed of
surgeons with white robes, rubber gloves, caps, and some
of the incidental paraphenalia of their profession.
Except the Chorus Leader, who is free to move about,
they are inside of a little raised, and railed-in,
enclosure, with seats--somewhat like the cross section
of the benches in an operating theatre. The surgeons
are always present during the play, interested spectators
of all events, commenting, conferring together, agitated
or complacent as the occasion dictates. The box of the
Chorus is situated at the right of the stage, and forward,
the position retained throughout the play. It is placed
at an angle that permits the members of the Chorus to
watch the events of the play and to turn toward the
audience at will.

Now the members of the Chorus have their attention fixed
on a man who is facing the audience, on a little circular
platform, stage right. The man wears the natty uniform
of a highway patrolman, black leather boots, goggles
over eyes, cap set jauntily back, revolver at hip. He
has his hands on the control-grips of a motorcycle. His
position is rigid, while the Chorus Leader moves about
him inspecting him, like a specimen, occasionally
referring to a card in his hand.)

CHORUS LEADER: (Turning to the Chorus) Yes, gentlemen, a very fine
                  specimen. A very fine specimen of that delicate and
                  beautiful mechanism, the human being. Our only concern
                  is, of course, with how this marvelous mechanism works,
                  but sometimes we are all human enough to wonder why
                  this mechanism works and to wonder -

PATROLMAN: (Speaking with body unmoving, eyes fixed out over audience.)
                  What hand flings the white road before me?
                  What hand over hills and the swamplands,
                  Over the highlands and damplands,
                  Gulley and bayou? And flings me
                  Fast as the slug from the gun-mouth,
                  Hard as the word from his own mouth --
                  I was nameless, but he has now named me.
                  And aimless, but he has now aimed me,
                  And flung me, and flings me -- Oh, errand
                  Blind with the glittering blindness of light!

CHORUS LEADER: (Continuing his examination of the specimen, referring to
                  his filing card.)
                  Yes, yes, homo sapiens. But for non-scientific purposes
                  known as -- as -- (Consulting card) -- as Al Suggs; sex,
                  male; race, white --

First page for the typescript of Proud Flesh *(Robert Penn Warren Papers, Beinecke Library, Yale University)*

with Satterfield, in which he will gain control of the Fourth and Fifth districts in exchange for the hospital construction contract. He makes this bargain not, as in the novel, to evade political pressure put on him by his son Tom's carryings on, and not, as in the 1955 play *Willie Stark: His Rise and Fall,* to outflank a threatened impeachment, but simply because it gives him an advantage over his entrenched opposition in those districts. At the very moment he closed the deal–Tiny Harper had sprung Satterfield on him as he was watching his son's heroics at a football game–Tom was injured on the field. So in the dancing scene with Anne that follows he has both political and familial problems in mind. Willie is uneasy about the deal he has just made, but when he explains the deal to Anne she not only is persuaded to accept it, she is even a little turned on by its Machiavellian realism:

ANNE: I know, I know–but isn't there some other way? Does it have to be like this? And the medical center contract.

STRONG: Buck up! It's no news. You know how things are.

ANNE: No. No news.–*(She faces him directly.)*–I know how things are. I'm not a child. What has to be done, has to be done. Oh, Willie–*(She hesitates, then reaches out to touch him on the lapel.)*–I love you.

STRONG: *(Apparently paying no attention to her declaration.)* I wanted you to know. Before I told you what I have to tell you. I want you to marry me.

This proposal turns out to be a very bad move on Willie's part: Anne seems instantly to become chilly. It is not Willie's realism here that bothers Anne–she announces, rather formidably, that she is "not biddy hearted to brood / And fluff on opportunities like eggs,"–but his self-doubt. Willie has been pondering a remark by his estranged wife Clara that he has become fragmentary and unstrung, that he has lost his way. When he wonders aloud whether Clara had it right, Anne not only gives him no help but begins to wonder whether he is man enough for her, or whether he is instead fool enough to think that love will somehow give him back his sense of a transforming moral purpose. From the novel one imagines Anne's feelings for Willie as clingy and dependent, and one thinks of her as not fully aware that her romantic feelings for Willie are sexual feelings; it is a surprise to see Anne in *Proud Flesh* as having the emotional upper hand, and as being the more forthrightly sexual of the two. Certainly Tiny Harper understands this, for when Willie is called off to the hospital, Tom having taken a surprising

turn for the worst, he too presses himself upon Anne, with the air of one who knows what kind of woman she is.

Anne's turn against Willie, indeed, is startlingly cruel:

> What do you expect of me? Be honest
> Who have been honest with honesty of water or wind
> Moving, guilelessness of glacier. Do you think love
> Is a fix-it, a household cement, to patch pieces,
> The putter and piddle of cupboards, will polarize
> At a word the fragments, the fractures, the filings of all
> The invidious iron disorder of the enormous world?

That may be a trifle over-written. But it could not be further from Anne Stanton of *All the King's Men.* Anne Amos, too, is a kind of dark gnostic. She puts it as bluntly as possible in her speech in the Choral Ode that opens Act III:

> Life pays a price for life, and I know it.
> For vitality, violence, for good, evil–our doom,
> and only the butter-hearted deny it,
> Whose praise would retch at the dunged rose's bloom.

This commonality of motivation makes one point clear that the novel might obscure. In *All the King's Men* it is tempting to describe the workings of the characters in psychological language: that Adam runs idealism and sadism together is a fact about him, not about idealism; that Willie runs the terror of emptiness together with a taste for tyranny is a fact about him, and about those who are attracted to men like him, but not a fact about all politics or all men. But the similarity of motivation in all of the characters in *Proud Flesh* argues that what we are in the presence of here are metaphysical rather than psychological facts, kinships among concepts rather than accidental predicaments of men and women. All of the characters are in the grip of a world in which they are desperate for a purpose, but no purpose declares itself, a world in which the hunger for meaning keeps exact pace with that world's perfect meaninglessness. It is a world in which characters do evil chiefly because they are driven to make an affirmation, but, as Keith remarks, "affirmation has a fist."

–John Burt, "Idealism and Rage in *Proud Flesh,*" *RPW: An Annual of Robert Penn Warren Studies,* 1 (2001): 45–61

UNIVERSITY OF MINNESOTA
COLLEGE OF SCIENCE, LITERATURE, AND THE ARTS
MINNEAPOLIS

DEPARTMENT OF ENGLISH
OFFICE OF THE CHAIRMAN

February 5, 1942.

Professor Robert Penn Warren
Department of English
State University of Louisiana
Baton Rouge, Louisiana

My dear Mr. Warren:

The retirement of one of our professors at the end of the
present academic year leaves us with a vacancy to fill in the
English Department, and I have every reason to think that we
shall be able to fill this place with another man of full pro-
fessorial rank. The man who is retiring is a critic and writer
of great distinction, and we are very hopeful of appointing for
his successor someone of similar quality. It is the hope of
many of us in the department to offer this place to you if you
are available. The matter has not been passed upon formally,
and for all appointments we have to secure the approval of the
Dean of the Arts College and the President of the University.
In any case, it would be much more convenient to discuss the
various details of our situation and the possibilities in the
way of curriculum, etc., in personal conversation than by letter.
It has been suggested by President Coffey that if you are free to
consider a possible offer - that is, free from commitments which
would prevent you from considering an offer - you might be willing
to make us a visit in Minneapolis in the near future at our expense, and we should like to suggest that in that case you might
give a public lecture while here. We should, of course, wish to
avoid any suggestion of your being a candidate for a post here -
a situation in which I should be very unwilling to place a person
of your quality. Since it is so late in the year, it is important
that we should act without delay in this matter. Will you please
let me know at your early convenience whether you would consider
meeting this suggestion, and if so, when you could come? The
sooner the better.

Sincerely yours,

Joseph Warren Beach

Joseph Warren Beach.

JWB:DS

*P.S. If for any reason you should prefer not to lecture,
or if your visit should fall on a week end when no
lecture could be arranged, we should be most*
come anyway!
                                                        JWB.

Letter in which Joseph Warren Beach, the chairman of the University of Minnesota English Department, encourages Warren to consider teaching at the school. After Warren's visit he was offered a full professorship at a salary of $4,000 a year. LSU offered $3,800. Warren later said, "I left out of pride" (Yale Collection of American Literature, Beinecke Rare Book and Manuscript Library).

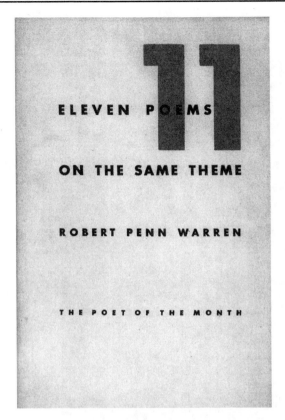

Cover for Warren's second book of poetry, published in April 1942 by New Directions, where Warren's friend Albert Erskine was an editor (Special Collections, Western Kentucky University Libraries)

A Time of Transition

In the 1940s Warren began to become dissatisfied with LSU. The state government was cutting support for the school, and a new president was reorganizing the administration. Warren was also disappointed by promises of higher pay that were not realized. The last issue of The Southern Review, *cancelled by LSU because of the expense, was published in spring 1942. Despite the turmoil Warren continued writing.* Eleven Poems on the Same Theme *was published in April 1942 before Warren left LSU.*

Warren was hired as a full professor at the University of Minnesota, largely through the efforts of Joseph Warren Beach, the chairman of the English department. After teaching that summer at the University of Iowa, Warren and Cinina traveled to Minneapolis and rented an apartment on West Calhoun Boulevard. That fall Warren wrote reviews for the Chicago Sunday Tribune of Books *for pocket money. His classes were full and the demands on his time remained high. Crofts published* Understanding Fiction *in January 1943, the third Brooks and Warren textbook, and Warren received the Shelley Memorial Award for* Eleven Poems.

This excerpt from John Frederick Nims's review of works by Warren and R. P. Blackmur, "Two Intellectual Poets," provides a critical but generally positive assessment of his new poems. Nims became a distinguished poet and was well known as the author of a

widely used textbook, Western Wind: An Introduction to Poetry *(1983).*

"Notable Virtues"
Review of *Eleven Poems on the Same Theme*

The distinction that Robert Penn Warren's *Eleven Poems* attains is due to a number of causes. First of all, they do not have the limitation of poems based on a mere perception or feeling. They are solid because based on thought, controlled by intellect and not vagary. An intellectual principle does not merely suggest each theme, but organizes and directs it to the close. Each poem is a study of some aspect of reality or of reaction to reality–a study that aims at realization through aggregation and analysis. The subjects are immediate; not remote, not striven for:

> Season by season from the skein
> Unwound, of earth and of our pleasure;
> And always at the side, like guilt,
> Our shadows over the grasses moved.

In addition to intellectual vigor, Mr. Warren's work has another merit, indicated by the nature of his subjects: the intellectual framework that might otherwise be dry and pallid is vitalized by an emotion that is of the very substance of the poem–an emotion that flows within the poem and is not merely troweled around it, an emotion that is blood to the bone of thought.

This blood-and-bone relationship is a key to the excellence of form that is found in these poems. It is not the kind of form whose determining principles are stanzaic structure and rime-scheme. These are utilized by the poet for the fulfillment of a higher unity whose principles are emotional and logical. The poems show a unity that is fundamentally (to use a cliché of criticism) organic.

The conventional modernism of the meter, without originality but not without distinction, is easy and imperious, often overriding the expected rule. Rime is used often so mutedly that it gives the effect of being not rime but the echo of rime. One device which Warren uses, I think functionally, is to hide in surprising ambush an unrimed word where rime is expected. In a poem in which the second and fourth lines generally rime, for example, we find this stanza:

> So, waiting, we in the grass now lie
> Beneath the langorous tread of light:
> The grasses, kelp-like, satisfy
> The nameless motions of the air.

The nature of the diction differs in different poems. Two kinds are chiefly used: a terse, perhaps overbrilliant idiom with inversion and turns of speech that recall Donne:

Poet of the Month . . .

ROBERT PENN WARREN, distinguished author and critic, member of the University English faculty and editor with Cleanth Brooks, Jr., of *The Southern Review*, was cited as "poet of the month" by New Directions publishing house last month, a collection of his poems appearing under the impress of the company in its "poet of the month" series. The poems represent Mr. Warren's choice of his work since the publication of an earlier collection of his poems, "Thirty-Six Poems," in 1935. Mr. Warren is the author of a biography, "John Brown: The Making of a Martyr," a number of articles, and a widely-acclaimed first novel, "Night Rider." He is the author of a second novel, "At Heaven's Gate," written under a Guggenheim fellowship, which is to be published later this year. He is also at work on a first play.

Feature in the 3 May 1942 issue of the Baton Rouge Morning Advocate *on Warren's award and other literary activities (Special Collections, Hill Memorial Library, Louisiana State University Libraries)*

That all the world proportionate
And joyful seemed, did but consent
That all unto our garden state
Of innocence was innocent;
And all on easy axle roved
That now, ungeared, perturbedly turns,
For joy sought joy then when we loved,
As iron to the magnet yearns.

Warren also uses, in his longer lines, a more ample, more orotund diction, as in *Terror:*

Not picnics or pageants or the improbable
Powers of air whose tongues exclaim dominion
And gull the great man to follow his terrible
Star, suffice . . .

A colloquial tone is used (not often enough, I think) in several poems. On the whole, the imagery, through symbolism and association, is closely integrated with meaning. Some "metaphysical" figures are brilliant but perhaps distracting in the context:

The match flame sudden in the gloom
Is lensed within each watching eye
Less intricate, less small, than in
One heart the other's image is.

Distinguished as *Eleven Poems* is, occasionally I found myself reading with some uneasiness. For each excellence it seemed there was a corresponding defect. Thought is at the heart of these poems, but

ELEVEN POEMS ON THE SAME THEME

The theme is guilt and innocence, or innocence and experience; but it has many facets, as there are many angles from which to regard it, or associated themes. At times it appears as time and eternity, at times as the sub-moral and the positively moral. At times the feeling of guilt is subconscious or unrelated to the consciously organized life; and does not count in the calculations (even the moral calculations) of the superliminal or practical life.

Thus in Original Sin. (Why a short-story? or is this merely an apologetic or deprecatory sub-title, intended to give an ironical lightness to an attitude that might seem too earnest?) Here the guilt is a sort of subliminal hant,--a ghost, perhaps partly hereditary (connected with "your" grandpa), or born with one, or of childhood origination (Revelation). It is unimportant except as a hant is important. For it has nothing to do with "your" public experience or private reformation, i.e., with your social-political conduct or your conscious private moral life. Nor is it involved in your sentimental and passional life (are the orchard anguish and ovoid horror sex-symbols?) It is not even at the root of your exclamation of desire for a new innocence, after the betrayal of hopes by disastrous glory of sea-capes, sun-torment of whitecaps. These latter are images for the human adventure in which personal ambition has scope, but which betrays hopes and produces disillusionment. But the hant is a sense of guilt that persist in the twilight zone, and becomes so familiar that it is almost welcome in places where one is sick for home. For it is associated with early childhood, having first taken the form of childish temptation, the bribe of chocolate or the toy you used to treasure. (Or is it simply a reminder of guilty pleasures taken in early childhood and since denied, or no longer forbidden, and so making appeal to the nostalgia of the adult for childhood?)

In Pursuit the man is seeking after some secret of well-being which he has lost or the lack of which makes him sick. The secret is perhaps possessed by the hunchback on the corner, but the general in the greatcoat, perhaps by the girl whom the other guests shun or by the old lady who blinks and croaks like a toad or Norn, but whose crutch may blossom like the pilgrim's staff--all of these persons who have had the initiation of suffering, and have thus arrived at the lost secret-- perhaps also the feverish old Jew who stares at you in the clinic with such stern authority--the same abstract Jew as in Original Sin) That the secret of all these is connected with the thought of innocence is suggested by the reference to the imperious innocence of the general staring from the thicket of his familiar pain; also by the fact that the seeker goes to the seashore, and that the seashore is associated in End of Season with lustral rites.

In End of Season the man has been on his seasonal holiday, bemused and pure, washing away guilt like the Hebrew prophet, Ponce de Leon, and Dante cleansing Virgil cleansing Dante, plunging down into the pure depths where no voice can penetrate. Voice, speech is associated with impurity; for purity was wordless, and all our conversation is index to our common crime. (It is true that there may be a language for purity, but that is not the language you know. You will have to learn a new language to say what is to say,/ But it will never be useful in school-

First page of Joseph Warren Beach's detailed critique of Warren's second collection of poery, which he offered after the chapbook was published. Warren often solicited comments on early drafts of his work from friends. Beach later read and commented on All the King's Men *as a work-in-progress (Yale Collection of American Literature, Beinecke Rare Book and Manuscript Library).*

Christmas in Minnesota

Warren gave good reports of his new situation during his first Christmas in Minnesota. John Palmer had been a student of Warren's at LSU and later had been on the staff of The Southern Review. *In this excerpt Warren mentions Professor Huntington Brown; his upcoming novel,* At Heaven's Gate; *and his editor at Harcourt Brace, Lambert Davis.*

Warren to John Palmer, 24 December 1942

Minneapolis has turned out to be a very pleasant place. I really do like the town, and find a good deal of pleasant and stimulating companionship. It's better than I had anticipated in that respect, and if the wit and rage here is not quite at the temperature to which I had grown accustomed in the SR office, I still survive agreeably enough. Brown is always good for a Shakespeare argument, and knows a hell of a lot, and Beach is a fine fellow. I have had a sort of burst of poetry, too. I can't say that I've pushed anything quite over the line yet, but I've got drafts of seven or eight poems, which only need the last tinkering. And I've got starts on others. The novel is in the hands of Harcourt, and I've just heard that it is in their spring catalogue, or will be–for they have written me for material, etc. They claim they like it, but they always claim that. But I know that Davis was damned nervous about sales possibilities. And God knows I am. By the way, I discovered in the most pleasant way possible–by opening the envelope and finding a check for an advance fall out–that Night Rider has been bought by an English Book Club, for a very nice figure.

–Selected Letters of Robert Penn Warren,
Volume Two, p. 395

Warren dedicated At Heaven's Gate *to Frank and Harriet Owsley, friends from his Vanderbilt days. Frank Owsley was one of the "Twelve Southerners" who contributed an essay to* I'll Take My Stand *(1930).*

Warren to Frank Owsley, 25 December 1942

My classes are the ones I want–and the schedule is arranged so that I have to go to the University only three days a week. This past term I've had Literary Criticism, Twentieth Century Literature, and one Freshman course. Next term I have Criticism, Twentieth Century, and Graduate Writing. I was slated for Sixteenth Century instead of the second term of Twentieth Century, but the decline in graduate enrollment has knocked that course out, it seems. I'm just as happy about that, for it means I have more time of my own. A graduate course is bound to take up more time than an undergraduate one (and I have a very able and experienced assistant in the Twentieth Century, anyway). And I already have the Literary Criticism, which is a graduate course, with one precocious undergraduate in it. Sinclair Lewis had the Graduate Writing this term, but he only teaches the one term.

The good schedule has meant that I've had some time of my own. I finished the revision of the new novel–At Heaven's Gate–and it is now in the hands of Harcourt. It is slated for spring publication, they tell me. As I asked you before informally, I now ask you more formally, for permission to dedicate the book to you. I hope that it won't disgrace you.

–Selected Letters of Robert Penn Warren,
Volume Two, pp. 398–399

---

objections might be made to the nature and employment of thought. At times it becomes unruly: the result is intellection or rationalization. It is rationalization of the most subtle and elegant kind, but it does sometimes result in a loss of immediacy–the debating toward the end of *Picnic Remembered* is an example. Again, the means employed are sometimes more intellectual than the end attained, as in *Monologue at Midnight,* in which the statements of the poem arouse not thought but only mood. It might be objected too that although the thought is not obscure, it does sometimes lack clarity, in the sense of incandescence. Sometimes the idea is so smothered by conceit or rhetoric that it does not detonate; it only fizzles. And the bones of thought sometimes stick through pretty leanly in the flat statements at the end of some poems:

We live in time so little time
And we learn all so painfully,
That we may spare this hour's term
To practice for eternity.

The individual line is generally concise and sharp, but it seems to me that in some of the poems there are too many. His vocabulary too is inclined to be somewhat bookish and traditional; he is fond of words of four syllables or more: luminescence, convolution, unformulable, immitigable. And the freedom of the rhythm and the use of half-rimes are not unfailingly deft. These defects however are far from fatal or even serious, and the book's notable virtues combine to make it a distinguished one.

–John Frederick Nims, "Two Intellectual Poets,"
Poetry, 61 (December 1942): 505–508

Understanding Fiction

By CLEANTH BROOKS, Jr.
LOUISIANA STATE UNIVERSITY

and ROBERT PENN WARREN
UNIVERSITY OF MINNESOTA

1943

F. S. CROFTS & Company NEW YORK

Title page for the third textbook by Brooks and Warren, published in January 1943 (Special Collections, Western Kentucky University Libraries)

At Heaven's Gate

At Heaven's Gate, *published in August 1943, received both harshly negative and admiring reviews. The novel focuses on the life of former-athlete-turned-businessman Gerald Calhoun and the corruption of land developer Bogan Murdock. This unsigned review was published in the Catholic journal* Commonweal.

Mighty like Despair
Review of At Heaven's Gate

Robert Penn Warren knows how to write. He has a few artifices of style which become tedious, especially an excessive peppering of his language with connectives, and occasionally he gets very close to the edge of being arty, but when he really does make something come off, it comes off terribly well. Hence such a novel as "At Heaven's Gate" seems to us all the more tragic, not merely because its plot is

formally tragic, but because it is tragic in a corrupt and brutal way. It is tragic for the author and for the reader. Once you have read the book, you will not recommend it to anyone, and it is not here recommended. It is frankly used as a springboard for a few reflections.

Irving Babbitt used to ring the changes on what he held to be an axiom of literary criticism and of morals: the astronomer who keeps his gaze fixed upon the stars is sure in time to fall into the well, the poet absorbed in his idolizing of the blue flower will stumble into the dung heap; naturalism of the tough variety is merely sentimentalism turned inside out. Of this axiom one suspects that Mr. Warren—and several of his fellow Southern writers—is a prime example.

We all remember the hollow gentility, the emotionalism, the romanticism which has characterized Southern sentiment. It has produced novels fairly reeking with idealism, it has produced that whole phony chivalry which political orators loved (and still love) to parade, it produced strange nostalgias and dream worlds. Nor is it a Southern monopoly; the same phenomenon has walked the streets and lanes of all the world. But in the South it became characteristic, a sort of protective coating to compensate for defeat and for frustration. Indeed it became a sort of easy substitute for religion among the well-to-do whites. Now given an intellectual climate of this sort—romantic to the core and unrestrained in its violence—what will happen when people awaken to man's occasional vileness? Instead of taking it in their stride, they revolt against humanity and take pleasure in elaborating with equal violence the worst evil in man's nature.

This seems to be what has happened to many of the present generation of young Southern writers. Mr. Warren, in this novel, is a peculiarly striking instance. For here it is dealing principally with the most "advantaged" classes in society—the comfortably off, the socially privileged, the educated. His story is laid, one might guess, in Tennessee, or better, in an imaginary state having about that latitude and topography. It contains mountains and mountaineers and it contains rich industrial centers and a university. Two separate narratives interweave—the story of a simple and hard-bitten hillbilly who is smitten by a genuine conversion to crude evangelical Christianity and the story of a group of city people, united by their connection with the daughter of the financial boss of the metropolis, Sue Murdoch. The second is the larger canvas. The first story—a sort of pointless Odyssey—is told by the hillbilly himself. It is not without dignity and feeling; in it one detects the only faint hint that Mr. Warren believes a man capable of acting a little better than an animal. The second story is unrelieved violence, brutality, arrogance, dissipation and cynicism.

The heroine is supposed to win our sympathy because she is trying to break away from the tyranny of her father; she scarcely succeeds, for she herself is a selfish tyrant. She makes her fiancé eat dirt; she throws him over because he won't change his whole life to suit her. She becomes the mistress successively of a pervert poet (who eventually strangles her to death, and lets the Murdoch Negro chauffeur "take the rap") and of a labor organizer who has "cleansed" himself of selfishness by years of deliberate steeping in slime in order to rid himself of all family tradition. The "hero" ("jeune premier" would be a better tag) hates his father because his father is clumsy, and has no principle except that he likes to be popular with his banking associates.

But why go on? This sort of fanciful garbage pile, crawling with every known breed of bug or maggot, is by now well known. It gives rise, however, to a question. Is not this the very picture on which is based the inner fascist or nazi conception of man and society—so degenerate it must have a fuehrer? Is not the Hitler idea a direct outgrowth, psychologically, of romantic *gemütlichkeit?* People who have cherry blossom festivals readily turn into homicidal maniacs. Perhaps there is a larger moral to this literary phenomenon. Let us hope America works it out in novels, not in political action.

–"Mighty like Despair," *Commonweal,*
38 (6 August 1943): 398

* * *

The wife of Allen Tate and a friend of Warren, Caroline Gordon was a Kentucky-born novelist and short-story writer whose early novels were set in Clarksville, Tennessee, where Warren attended high school.

Passionate Southern Eloquence
Review of *At Heaven's Gate*

In the last twenty-five years there have been a great many novels in which the authors have tried to portray and interpret the Southern scene. The results have been a spiritual geography that is confusing. One might almost say—if one were not tempted to cry out, as this reviewer, on occasion, has cried out: "Hold! Some of my best friends are Southerners!" There are as many Souths as there are writers. Erskine Caldwell portrays a South very different from that of Margaret Mitchell, and facets of Southern life that present themselves to William Faulkner go unremarked by Miss Mitchell and Mr. Caldwell.

Robert Penn Warren, author of "At Heaven's Gate," has more in common with Faulkner than with Caldwell and Miss Mitchell. He has at his command the technical devices that have enriched the serious fiction of the last fifty years, and he writes with Flaubertian exactness. Like Faulkner he is rhetorical but, as with Faulkner, the rhetoric is so aptly timed, so infused with meaning, that it becomes eloquence, and eloquence of a peculiarly Southern kind. He is passionately concerned with the South, its spiritual past, present and future. Unlike Faulkner, he seems to have found the inspiration for his novel in public events.

Twenty-five years ago a red-headed sergeant from the mountains of Tennessee lay behind scant cover in a wood in France and with a rifle picked off, one by one, thirty-seven Germans, then, single-handed, compelled the surrender of the rest of the regiment. He returned from the war to find himself a national hero. Ten years later a Southern financier, once famous as a colonel of artillery, built up a financial empire that covered half the South, saw it crash almost over night, was convicted of defrauding a bank and was sentenced to ten years in a North Carolina penitentiary. To the friends and neighbors who thronged the railway sta-

---

The Shadow of Fact and Fiction

INTERVIEWERS: From the first your work is very explicitly concerned with moral judgements, even during a period when much American fiction was concerned with moral questions only in the narrow way of the "proletarian" and "social realism" novels of the 1930s.

WARREN: I think I ought to say that behind *Night Rider* and my next novel, *At Heaven's Gate* there was a good deal of the shadow not only of the events of that period but of the fiction of that period. I am more aware of that fact now than I was then. Of course only an idiot could have not been aware that he was trying to write a novel about, in one sense, "social justice" in *Night Rider,* or for that matter, *At Heaven's Gate.* But in some kind of a fumbling way I was aware, I guess, of trying to find the dramatic rub of the story at some point a little different from and deeper than the point of dramatic rub in some of the then current novels. But what I want to emphasize is the fact that I was fumbling rather than working according to plan and convictions already arrived at. When you start any book you don't know what, ultimately, your issues are. You try to write to find them. You're fiddling with the stuff, hoping to make sense, whatever kind of sense you can make.

–Ralph Ellison and Eugene Walter, "The Art of Fiction XVIII: Robert Penn Warren," *Paris Review,* 4 (Spring–Summer 1957): 119–120

I-a.

I.

                                        windless   ~~Windless~~ The blue was paler
    It was the brilliant, high sky of early autumn, ~~the blue positive but~~
than the blue of summer, but
                                                                    drenched
~~seemingly washed~~   not leached out, still positive, and ~~fxkxxxfx~~ in
                    treated with
sunlight as though ~~washed~~   a wash ~~which~~ was transparent but full of

minute gold flecks. When you stared at the sky, if you stared very long, it

seemed to be pricked with those tiny flecks of gold,which winked and glittered.

    Sue Murdock stared at the sky, northward, and narrowed her eyes against the

light. She could see nothing in the sky.
                              folded
    She was leaning her ~~xxxxxx~~ arms on the white top-bar of the paddock, with

her chin braced on her forearms. On her left, her brother Hammond Murdock

lounged against the paddock, and on her right, Slim Wogan stood, not leaning ,
one of   hislong white hands laid
~~xgxinxtxthexpadxxxk~~   on the bar, not for support but as in a posture of
              as though it were a warrior's hand
control, ~~Hxxwxxxexxinx~~   laid on a sword hilt or a bearded
~~marimer's~~ hand laid, as in an old engraving, on a globe.
    Slim Wogan had just stated that he did not care for riding.

    "Have you ever been on a horse?" Sue demanded, not taking her eyes off

the bright sky.

    "No," Slim Wogan confessed quite candidly, and added that he did not

think that riding a horse would be very interesting.

    "Of course not, of course not," she murmured, "not at all interesting, oh,

no," and did not look at him.

    "For Christ sake," Ham Murdock said, amiably.

    "The cult of horsemanship is a very peculiar thing,"Slim Wogan continued

evenly. "It is probable that most people who devote themselves to it do so
despite the fact
~~for~~   that they do not enjoy it at all, or enjoy it very little.

They simply enjoy the idea of it. They enjoy the picture of themselves on a

horse. It is a symbol. It is a snob symbol derived from the Middle Ages. It -- "

    Which was exactly what ~~sxxx~~ he had said to her in her car on the way out
from the University
here to see Starlight, and now he was saying it over again, and there was

not a word of truth in it for she didn't enjoy the idea of being on a horse, she

First page of a typescript draft of At Heaven's Gate *(Robert Penn Warren Papers, Beinecke Library, Yale University)*

tion to greet him when he came home he made a terse speech. "I have been in Gethsemane," he said.

Mr. Warren's novel concerns the lives and fates of a group of people, all of whom are dominated in one way or another, by Bogan Murdock, a powerful, fearless and unscrupulous banker of the late '20s. His wife, his son, his daughter, the young poet and the young agitator who are in love with his daughter, the football star who might have been a geologist if he had not been taken into the firm of Meyer & Murdock immediately after graduation, all seem to be trying to escape from him in order that they may be–simply themselves.

Running counter to the story of these people is that of Ashby Wyndham, a six-foot mountaineer who leaves his farm to become a miner in the Murdock-controlled mines on Massey Mountain. In the midst of a roistering youth he has a religious experience and sets out to seek salvation. His search lands him in the county jail. His cousin, the famous "Private" Porsum, now a banker and one of Murdock's henchmen, comes to see him. He refuses to let the private use his influence to get him out of jail; he is concerned with problems graver than those of material welfare. The story flows through the book like a cold mountain stream, providing at first only refreshing emotional contrasts to the scenes from urban life. Later the stream widens, takes to itself tributaries and rushes to the sea. Sue Murdock, the financier's honest, wayward daughter, the four young men who are in love with her, the economist who tries to retain his intellectual independence while serving the firm of Meyer & Murdock, all are involved in the fortunes of Ashby Wyndam and all, finally, stand at the bar of his judgment.

All, that is, except Bogan Murdock. He defies analysis or judgment and remains inscrutable and apparently fearless. At the end, ruined, arraigned before a battery of news cameras, he smiles at the reporters and points to the portrait of George Washington over the mantel, "Courage," he says, "courage. It is the heritage of all of us."

Those characters in fiction who, while clearly and roundly portrayed, yet seem to retain some mystery for their creator, who are, so to speak, nuts too hard for him to crack–Bovary, Prince Andrey, Stavrogin–are those whom posterity has found most fascinating. Bogan Murdock is as proud as Ashby Wyndham, as brave as Private Porsum. But at bottom he is capable of an infinite amount of self-deception. It is this dualism in the Southern spirit which, I think, Mr. Warren as novelist is most concerned. He has provided in "At Heaven's Gate" not only a stirring novel–the account of Private Porsum's exploits will stand with the best writing of our times–but one of the most profound interpretations that has yet been made of Southern life.

–Caroline Gordon, "Passionate Southern Eloquence,"
New York Herald Tribune Weekly Book Review,
22 August 1943, p. 5

* * *

Dust jacket for Warren's second novel, for which the working title was "And Pastures New," the last words of John Milton's "Lycidas" (Special Collections, Western Kentucky University Libraries)

This review was written by Malcolm Cowley, the literary editor for The New Republic. *Cowley met Warren in New York in the 1920s and admired his poetry. As an editor for the Viking Press, Cowley wrote introductions for and edited works by Thornton Wilder, F. Scott Fitzgerald, and William Faulkner. His edition of* The Portable Faulkner *(1946), which Warren warmly praised in a review, contributed to the renewed interest in Faulkner's writings.*

Luke Lea's Empire
Review of *At Heaven's Gate*

This is one of the very few serious American novels I have read since we entered the war. That, I suppose, is pretty faint praise at a time when most novels have been careless or trivial or written with one eye on the headlines, but there is more to be said about *At Heaven's Gate*. It is full of interesting characters, some of them new to contemporary fiction. Its background, which is a Southern city at the end of boom years, is freshly observed and convincing. Its author is Robert Penn Warren, a talented poet and story writer who has worked for years over this second novel, with the result that it is full of surprises for the reader; some of the passages are better written than anything else in recent fiction. Because of all these virtues, the book has to be judged by extremely strict standards. Here is an injustice that reviewers ought to explain and serious writers have to accept. Fourth- and fifth-rate books get praised because they try to do so little that they could hardly fail. The almost first-rate books get severely blamed for trying to do much, even if they partially succeed.

I should say, for example, that Warren succeeds with his heroine. Sue Murdock is not one of his new characters; essentially she is the lost girl of the 1920's, the girl in the green hat, the heroine of "The Sun Also Rises" and "Butterfield 8." Warren's portrait of her is less moving than Hemingway's and less accurate in details than John O'Hara's, but he does one thing the others fail to do—that is, he gives a satisfactory explanation of how she came to be lost and what she has tried to escape. She is rebelling against her father; that is why she plunges into a series of love affairs and why two of them end abruptly when she finds that her lover is taking her father's place. There is Freud in the novel; there is also a good deal of high finance. Sue's father, Bogan Murdock, makes you think of Luke Lea, the banker and promoter whose empire used to extend over the Middle South. Her first lover, Jerry Calhoun, is a farm boy who becomes a football star and then a vice-president of a big Murdock bank. Her second lover is a self-centered esthete with no interest in financial affairs, but the third is a labor leader directing a strike against one of the Murdock industries. The most sympathetic portrait in the book is that of Ashby Wyndham, a mountain evangelist who, simply by being a sincere Christian, puts a sudden end to Murdock's reign.

Each of these portraits is convincing and some of them are brilliant, considered by themselves. The trouble with the novel as a whole is that it tells too many stories in too many styles. Here is a series of quotations that might easily have come from five different novels:

1. The river . . . came gleamingly out of the haze of distance to the south, and the tributaries converged toward it across the land. He knew the names, Big Duck, Little Duck, Holly Mill Creek, Still Deer, Pine-Away, and had heard, years back, or so it seemed, the ripple of their waters at dams, at fords, over stones, had felt it upon his wrists or about his ankles, and had called to friends across their easy widths.

2. Dust, it lays on the floor, under the goin forth and the comin in, and ain't nothin, and gits stirred up in the trompin, but a sunbeam come in the dark room and in that light it will dance and shine for heart joy.

3. "On this shoal water of morality, criticism, even when flying the Jolly Roger of estheticism, has foundered whenever it has undertaken to investigate the tragic theme."

4. He reckoned if you'd been around that baby much and had a dose of the hogwash he put out under the label of soothing syrup, it'd take you more than a pissing-spell to come to grips with reality and face the challenge and roll up your sleeves and spit in the palms of your hand.

5. . . . and they put me to bed at dark every night and it was the man with the eyes always wet and sad behind the glasses and he said, my dear, it won't hurt, it won't hurt a bit, it—

The first of these quotations is supposed to represent Jerry Calhoun's stream of consciousness, but actually it is Warren writing a poem, and a good one, about the land he loves. The second is part of Ashby Wyndham's long story, the best narrative writing in the novel. The third is Slim Sarrett, the esthete, composing an essay that might have been printed in The Southern Review. The fourth is a meditation by Sweetie Sweetwater, the labor leader, and seems to me completely false; the spit on his

---

Writing by Feeling

In a discussion in which he participated with Flannery O'Connor in 1959, Warren insisted that he wrote his novels without an established plan.

. . . I don't think it's knowing how the story comes out that's the point. As Flannery just said, you know what you want it to feel like. You envisage the feeling. You may or may not know how it is going to come out. You may have your big scenes in mind before you start. You may even be moving toward them all the time. You don't know whether they will jell out or not jell out. But it seems to me the important thing is to have enough feeling envisaged and pre-felt, as it were, about the way the book's going to go. If that feeling isn't there: unless it dominates your thinking somehow . . . you know, be the thing that is behind the muse, the thing that keeps it under control: if you ever lose that feeling, then you start floundering. But as long as that feeling as to how the book is going to end is there, something is guiding it. And then your mechanical problems have a sort of built-in correction for error. I mean, you have fifty ideas, but somehow you know they're wrong. If you keep this feeling firmly in you . . . I don't know how you will it . . . but as long as it is there, you have something to guide you in this automatic process of trial and error. You know what the book ought to feel like. Of course you're going to modify that feeling.

—"An Interview with Flannery O'Connor and Robert Penn Warren," *Vagabond*, 6 (February 1960): 10

palms smells dry and bookish. The fifth is Sue Murdock in a drunken stupor, just before her death; she has nightmares like those of Faulkner's novels. In presenting each of these five people, Warren asks us to look at him through a different pair of glasses. The book lacks a unifying medium; it might have been written by five authors in collaboration, but also in violent disagreement.

The one element that holds it together is not a character or an idea or a point of view. It is a city, one that anybody can recognize as Nashville, Tennessee, with a few traits borrowed from Memphis—let us simply call it a state capital in the Middle South during a period of economic revolution. Warren lets us see all sides of it. Here is the social crowd; here are the politicians; here are the dispossessed farmers and the underpaid workmen; here is the university, which might be Vanderbilt, and the intellectuals who might have belonged to the Fugitive group; and here, dominating the others, is the dishonest but far-sighted promoter working to transform the whole region—to carry it from an area of agriculture and small handicrafts straight into the age of finance capitalism. Almost everybody suffers morally from the change; nobody feels at home; but even after Luke Lea's empire is destroyed, the city cannot go back to its old ways. That is the real subject of Warren's book, though I doubt that he ever regarded himself as a social historian.

—Malcolm Cowley, "Luke Lea's Empire,"
New Republic, 109 (23 August 1943): 258

* * *

In this excerpt from his 1971 essay "The Poles of Fiction: Warren's At Heaven's Gate," *Allen Shepherd takes up a point raised by Cowley in his review.*

History and Idea in *At Heaven's Gate*

In his review of *At Heaven's Gate,* Malcolm Cowley concludes that "the trouble with the novel as a whole is that it tells too many stories in too many different styles," in proof of which he quotes five dissimilar passages. There is a sense in which one can agree with Cowley, for Warren readily turns aside from his narrative to fill us in—at unnecessary length—on the backgrounds of some of his characters, and these diversions often become stories in their own right. What Warren accomplishes with the novel's multiplicity of characters, however, is at least equally important, for by the use of a relatively large cast he achieves a more solid and extensive relation between "history" and "idea" than he could manage in *Night Rider.* Precisely because each of the characters is separate and distinct, because each is involved in and responds to the central situation, Warren is better able to resist that inclination toward the editorial commentary which weakens *Night Rider.*

Yet concerning the characters through whose actions ideas are made to live, there are two other observations to be made. The main characters, with the exception of Ashby Wyndham, are distinctly unsympathetic (although one might also exclude Sue Murdock), and a number of them are almost repulsive. It is of course not necessary that we like or admire the characters, but we must be able to believe in their integrity, that is, we must believe in the words Warren puts in their mouths. It is thus decidedly disconcerting to note, repeatedly, that Warren cannot convincingly attribute his insights to Jerry Calhoun, one of the principal characters. This is important not only because Calhoun is frequently on stage but because his regeneration (Ashby Wyndham is to a considerable extent *sui generis,* and Duckfoot Blake's enlightenment is very cryptically described) is central to the novel's conclusion and thesis. Calhoun is in the end left back at home in bed, aware at last of the extent, if not the meaning of, his rejection and betrayal of his father. Yet one is not prepared even for this limited perception. While the ambiguity of the novel's conclusion is inherent in Warren's thesis, one does have to believe—to accept the novel's conclusion—that Calhoun has made a start in his ascent from egocentricity. The problem is, it would seem, that our dissatisfaction with Calhoun, and hence with the conclusion of the novel, derives from our perception of its achieved rather than its intended meaning. And this split is directly attributable to Calhoun's insensitivity, to his inadequacy as a central intelligence.

Yet Warren is in *At Heaven's Gate* both the philosophical and the observant novelist, possessed of a rich store of recollection, of voices, of faces, of clothes, of tools, of the lay of the land, perhaps of an almost excessive appreciation of life. Thus the vividness and overall effectiveness of the novel's minor characters: Marie, who is Wyndham's wife; Calhoun's Uncle Lew and Aunt Ursula; Anse, who is Bogan Murdock's chauffeur; Private Porsum, Major Murdock, Duckfoot Blake. The problem with these characters—and it is an unusual though, I think, explicable one—is that they tend to overshadow the principal characters. Why this is so, is hard to say, but it may be that shortly after the introduction of each of the major characters one attaches to or associates with him an idea or thesis (one quickly sees through Bogan Murdock, for example: he is the man of power, the capitalist). Thus, although one does not know what is going to happen to him, one senses what he stands for and anticipates Warren's judgment of him.

Throughout *At Heaven's Gate* Warren pursues a rather uneasy and uneven course between the poles of history and idea. Warren's Dantesque construction of the principal characters is consistent, though ultimately, it would seem, self-defeating. The character best situated to make an investigation of Bogan Murdock's world, Jerry Calhoun, is patently inadequate to the task. Ashby Wyndham's narrative, on the other hand, achieves that success which Warren attributes to "the sense of one picture superimposed on another, different and yet somehow the same." Here history effortlessly implies idea. The noteworthy effectiveness of minor characters in the novel derives from their possessing in full measure "the vividness of the actual world," while not being thesis-bound.

In his Modern Library introduction to *All the King's Men,* Warren establishes a plausible relation between Bogan Murdock and Willie Stark (the two, despite their emptiness, vicariously fulfilling the needs of others) and recalls that "the effort of *At Heaven's Gate* had whetted my desire to compose a highly documented picture of the modern world." Despite its own considerable intrinsic merit, *At Heaven's Gate* will likely continue to be read as the immediate precursor of *All the King's Men,* in which Warren achieved that near perfect focus which unites documentation and depth, history and idea.

    –Allen Shepherd, "The Poles of Fiction: Warren's 'At Heaven's Gate'," *Texas Studies in Literature and Language,* 12 (Winter 1971): 709–718

SELECTED

POEMS

1923-1943

ROBERT

PENN

WARREN

HARCOURT, BRACE AND COMPANY, NEW YORK

Title page for Warren's third volume of poems, which included "The Ballad of Billie Potts" (Special Collections, Western Kentucky University Libraries)

Selected Poems, 1923–1943

Warren divided Selected Poems, 1923–1943, *published in April 1944, into two sections—"Late" and "Early"— and included an explanatory note after the contents:*

The *Late* poems in this collection have been drawn from among pieces composed during the last eight or nine years. Most of them, however, are relatively recent. The *Early* poems belong to the previous decade, some of them going back into student days.

                                    R.P.W.

Minneapolis, July 26, 1943

Reviews were generally favorable, with Willard Thorp, the reviewer in the 7 May 1944 issue of The New York Times Book Review, *labeling Warren as "one of the most important poets of our generation."*

In this review Warren's former teacher John Crowe Ransom refers to five poems in an American Review *supplement: "Letter to a Friend," "Aubade for Hope," "Eidolon," "Aged Man Surveys the Past Time," and "Toward Rationality."*

The Inklings of "Original Sin"
Review of *Selected Poems, 1923–1943*

Of more than seasonal magnitude is the literary event which gives to the public the whole staple of Robert Penn Warren's poetry. For ten years my head has rung with magnificent phrases out of the five poems which he contributed to a Special Poetic Supplement in *The American Review* of March, 1934. I felt they must have made a great commotion (as I knew they had not) and established him at once as a ranking poet; they were so distinctive, those poems of twenty lines each, with their peculiar strain of horror, and their clean-cut eloquence and technical accomplishments. But evidently the rating of the poet waits upon the trial of his big book. The five poems are in the present book, and serve very well as its center, though some later ones may define a little better the special object of this poet's tragic sense.

For a text I will try the easiest of the five, "Aubade for Hope." The speaker (or hero: sometimes he is in the third person) appears to be an adapted and adult man waking, in the company of his bride it would seem, in the Kentucky farmhouse on a winter morning:

Dawn: and foot on the cold stair treading or
Thump of wood on the unswept hearthstone is
Comment on the margin of consciousness,
A dirty thumb-smear by the printed page.

Thumb-smear: nay, other, for the blessed light
Acclaimed thus, as a ducal progress by
The scared cur, wakes them that wallowed in
The unaimed faceless appetite of dream.

All night, the ice sought out the rotten bough:
In sleep they heard. And now they stir, as east
Beyond the formal gleam of landscape sun
Has struck the senatorial hooded hill.

Light: the groaning stair; the match aflame;
The Negro woman's hand, horned gray with cold,
That lit the wood—oh, merciless great eyes
Blank as the sea—I name some things that shall

As voices speaking from a further room,
Muffled, bespeak us yet for time and hope:
For Hope that like a blockhead grandam ever
Above the ash and spittle croaks and leans.

The waking is out of a dream in which the speaker was faced with some nameless evil, and he is glad to be woken; and the dawn to which he wakes is a symbol of hope though sadly short of brilliant in its accessories and triumphant. The waking or rational world does not altogether displace the dark world of the unconscious. The "merciless great eyes" that are addressed in parenthesis bring a difficulty of identification; they are new in the present version, having displaced some less telling original item. But in the light of other poems I should hazard that they belong to an ancestor, or a ghostly mentor, and survive from the dream as a counterpoise to hope, and attend their victim much as the Furies would attend the Greek hero under a curse. We feel they will not be propitiated though the citizen start punctually on his round of moral daylight activities.

But what is his curse? "Aubade for Hope" is of the very type of the Warren poems, whose situations are always fundamentally the same. It is true that the poet is fertile, and I find quite a few titles to suggest his range of variation upon the one tragic theme; as, "Terror," "Pursuit," "Crime," "Letter from a Coward to a Hero," "History," "End of Season," "Ransom," "Aged Man Surveys Past Time," "Toward Rationality," "To a Friend Parting," "Eidolon," "Revelation," "Variation: Ode to Fear," "Monologue at Midnight," "Picnic Remembered," "Man Coming of Age," and the Marvellian "The Garden." It is the quality of a noble poetry that it can fixate powerful living images of the human crisis, and be received of us with every sense of the familiar, yet evade us badly if we would define its issue; and that is why poetry, intuitive in its form like religion, involves us in endless disputation when we try to phi-

losophize it. I proceed with peril, but I rely on a conviction that Warren's version of horror is not only consistent, but more elemental and purer than that of other poets. For there was Poe, for example, with whom it was almost vulgarly "literary" and supernatural; and Baudelaire, for whom it recorded his implication with the monstrous and obscene, and his detestation and disgust. The terror they felt was perhaps chiefly for crazy breaches of the common moral code, but ours here is stranger and yet far more universal than that.

The recent poem, "Original Sin: a Short Story," furnishes us with a philosophical term, or at least a theological one; which we should use provided we remember that the poet has not put all his secrets into one word.

Nodding, its great head rattling like a gourd,
And locks like seawood strung on the stinking stone,
The nightmare stumbles past, and you have heard
It fumble your door before it whimpers and is gone:
It acts like the old hound that used to snuffle your door
    and moan.

You thought you had lost it when you left Omaha,
For it seemed connected then with your grandpa, who
Had a wen on his forehead and sat on the verandah
To finger the precious protuberance, as was his habit to do,
Which glinted in sun like rough garnet or the rich old
    brain bulging through.

But this nightmare, the vague, inept, and not very presentable ancestral ghost, is not to be exorcised. It appears even in Harvard Yard, for the victim's handsome secular progress has led him so far, where the ghost is ill at ease indeed. But you must not think the illusion of the ghost is the form of the speaker's simple nostalgia, for that is painful, too, but goes away:

You were almost kindly then in your first homesickness,
As it tortured its stiff face to speak, but scarcely mewed;
Since then you have outlived all your homesickness,
But have met it in many another distempered latitude:
Oh, nothing is lost, ever lost! at last you understood.

This ghost will not be laid. Yet it is an ineffectual ghost, unlike that portentous apparition of Hamlet the Elder, which knew so much about "theatre," including how to time and how to make an entrance: our ghost does not interfere with the actions of the living.

But it never came in the quantum glare of sun
To shame you before your friends, and had nothing to do
With your public experience or private reformation:
But it thought no bed too narrow—it stood with lips askew
And shook its great head sadly like the abstract Jew.

Never met you in the lyric arsenical meadows
When children call and your heart goes stone in the
    bosom:

At the orchard anguish never, nor ovoid horror,
Which is furred like a peach or avid like the delicious
    plum.
It takes no part in your classic prudence or fondled axiom.

We must return to the title, and take its consequences: Original Sin. And here it may be of some moment that we ourselves have had dire personal inklings of Original Sin, hustled and busybody creatures as we are yet perhaps painfully sensible of our treachery to some earlier and more innocent plan of existence; or, on the other hand, that we know it by theology and literature. The poets and priests who dramatize it in Adam's Fall seem to have known it

---

Shorthand for Poetry Reviewers

In this excerpt from the introduction to the first book-length study of Warren's work, Leonard Casper offers a critique of many reviewers of Warren's poetry.

Another version of classification without differentiation is the habit of so many reviewers of attempting explication of a book by Warren not by reviewing the author's unique context first, the direction that his prior thoughts have taken, but by incomplete comparisons with some more removed and irrelevant portion of literary history. Because no adequate analysis is made of the "original" function of a method or persuasion, the question of *present* function in Warren is rarely permitted to arise. The critic is satisfied with name-dropping and often, by innuendo, a charge of imitation. Warren's work presumably derives from Eliot, MacLeish, MacNeice, Faulkner, Spender, Melville, St. Augustine, Santayana, Shakespeare, John Webster, Milton, Dostoevsky, De Maupassant, Yeats, Aeschylus, Graham Greene, Anatole France, D. H. Lawrence, Carlyle, Bernanos, Kenneth Burke, Duns Scotus, Emily Dickinson, Seneca. Not all readers have been as perceptive as Dudley Fitts, writing of Warren's *Selected Poems* in 1944: "even in responding to his influences Mr. Warren shows his strength. He does not 'write like' Marvell; he becomes Marvell in our time, as Yeats became Swift, as Eliot became Andrewes." Perhaps only Pound, for resorting to calligraphy, has ever been accused of greater learning. The most that is proved is what has never been denied: that Warren does not repudiate past knowledge but rather commemorates it by his contributions.

–Leonard Casper, *Robert Penn Warren: The Dark and Bloody Ground* (Seattle: University of Washington Press, 1960), p. xii

---

precisely in the same sense with Warren's protagonist; and historically it has proved too formidable an incubus to rate as an idle "metaphysical" entity, for it can infect the whole series of our human successes with shame and guilt. Briefly, Original Sin is the betrayal of our original nature that we commit in the interest of our rational evolution and progress. Anthropologists may well imagine–if they are imaginative–that the guilt-feeling of Original Sin, though it opposes no specific adaptation or "conditioning" of the pliant human spirit, might yet have some business on the premises as an unassimilated core of resistance and therefore stability; so precarious would seem the unique biological experiment of equipping an animal species with reason instead of the law of its own nature. Original Sin obtains a sort of poetic justification when we consider the peculiar horror to which the strict regimen of medieval monks exposed them; acedia; the paralysis of will. Or, for that matter, the horror which has most shaken the moderns in their accelerating progress: the sense of psychic disintegration, that is, of having a personality which has been casually acquired, and is still subject to alteration, therefore hollow and insincere.

By the present account Original Sin seems to be nearly related to the Origin of Species–of that species at least which is most self-determining of its behavior. It may be tempting to assume, and dogmatic theology at its nadir of unrealism is apt to assume, that the blame falls only on Adam, and we are answerable only in some formalistic sense to Adam's ghost. But here we should take into account the phenomenon of "recapitulation"; for it is understood that individually we re-enact the evolution of species. We do it physiologically, but there is a conscious side to it too. We have a nature, and proceed to "condition" it; and more and more, from age to age, are subjected to the rule of reason, first the public reason which "educates" us, and then, when we have lost our native spirits, our own reason which draws corollaries to the public reason. If we may venture now upon a critical impertinence, and commit the biographical fallacy, we will refer the nightmare of our poet's verse to the admirable public datum of his life, to see what edification it will bring. As follows. The South Kentucky country of his nativity is distinctive among landscapes, and the sense of it is intimate and constitutive in the consciousness of its inhabitants; and his breed, the population of that country, acknowledges more firmly than another the two bonds of blood and native scene, which individuate it. If then the ancestral ghost really haunts the mature poet, as the poetry professes, it might be said to have this excuse, that the circumstance of his origin is without visible consequence upon his social adaptiveness, which is supple and charming, or upon his capacity for such scholarship and industry as his professional occasions may demand, which is exemplary. The poetic torment of his sensibility is private, and yet here it is, published. But we need not think it something very special. The effect is universal as philosophers use that term: it is the way a fine native sensibility works, in those who have the sensibility and keep it.

Besides the poetry, Warren has a well-known body of fiction, including an important recent novel; the aforesaid nightmare of Original Sin showing in the fiction too. But the poetry, I think, is superior to the fiction, for a curious reason. Warren has fallen in increasingly with the vogue of the "naturalistic" novel; and this means that he likes to take low life, or at any rate life with a mediocre grade of vitality, for his material. His characters are mean, and inarticulate too, though their futilities and defeats furnish him faithfully with documents of the fateful Original Sin. But they do not know what tune they are playing, and the novelist has the embarrassment of having to speak for them. In the recent novel, *At Heaven's Gate,* he has to contrive a quaint though marvelously realized rural saint, to furnish a significant commentary; and it is not very organically connected with the action of the plot.

I mention this because Warren begins to import the naturalistic method into his verse; as in the Kentucky ballad of "Billie Potts," the most substantial poem in the present volume. With great skill he expands the primitive ballad form (in this case the loose and vernacular American form) without quite breaking it down, though he goes much farther than Coleridge did in his "Ancient Mariner." The story is of how Young Billie left Old Billie (and his old mother, too) behind in Kentucky, and went West to make his fortune on his own power (and his own reason) with scarcely a backward look. The Pottses, incidentally, are most unsympathetic characters; they are a nest of Kentucky rattlesnakes. But after ten years' success Young Billie has a sort of "conversion," and returns to the ancestral rooftree; where

his parents promptly kill him; for one cannot return. It is true that they do not recognize him, but the accident is at least the symbol of the intention. To interpret all this in terms of his thesis Warren uses long parentheses, filled with his own matter and language and that is a gloss far more implausible than that which Coleridge wrote upon his margins.

I suggest that this is not the best strategy of composition. And I would add something else, which for me is of paramount importance: I wish we had a way of holding this poet, whose verse is so beautiful when it is at his own height of expression, to a level no lower than this height.

–John Crowe Ransom, "The Inklings of 'Original Sin,'" *Saturday Review of Literature,* 27 (20 May 1944): 10–11

The Significance of "The Ballad of Billie Potts"

Selected Poems, 1923–1943 *included "The Ballad of Billie Potts," "one of Warren's most interesting and significant poems," according to William Bedford Clark in his 1978 essay on the poem. Clark argues that it is "an especially rich and elaborate presentation of the poet's characteristic view of man as engaged in a symbolic progression from sin to ultimate reconciliation." While conceding that Warren's alteration "between two levels of language, reflecting radically different levels of awareness, does seem at first to raise some serious questions as to its final unity," Clark asserts that "here, as elsewhere in Warren, theme and form are in the end inextricably related."*

. . . for all its structural peculiarities, *The Ballad of Billie Potts* is the kind of poem the reader might logically expect its author to write. Not only is its thematic thrust typical of some of Warren's best-known work, its structure, viewed in dramatic terms, may be seen to be an obvious outgrowth of one of his most characteristic preoccupations as a writer—an overwhelming need to come to terms with the significance of the past, whether it comes to us from the printed page, or, as in *The Ballad of Billie Potts,* through the oral history of the folk.

–William Bedford Clark, "A Meditation on Folk-History: The Dramatic Structure of Robert Penn Warren's *The Ballad of Billie Potts," American Literature,* 49 (1978): 645

September 21, 1959

Dear Larry:

It is interesting to know that you heard a version
of Billy Potts from a barber in Cadiz, Kentucky,
for, unless my memory fails, I first heard it in
that same county, at Cerulean Springs, from a great
aunt, some kind of limited version of it. I later
read an account of it in a book on The Cave-In-Rock
outlaws, written by a Louisville judge, whose name
escapes me. But he was a member of the Filson Society,
and the Society, I think, published his book. It was
reaing this that started me to think about the
tale .

It is pleasant to think that you may be around in
October. Why don't we try to have a lunch in NY.
Write ahead, please. If you are here after October
16, I'd like to see that you get tickets -- if you
want them -- for a play I shall have in the 74th
Streer Theater -- if it survives the openimg. The
new -- and last and final forever -- version of
AKM. I had to get it into shape for pubcication, at
last.

Yours,

Letter to Lawrence Thompson, director of the University of Kentucky Libraries, in which Warren discusses the origin of "The Ballad of
Billie Potts" (Special Collections, Western Kentucky University Libraries)

"A Poem of Pure Imagination: An Experiment in Reading"

In 1945 Warren lectured at Yale University in the Bergen Foundation series. His talk, "A Poem of Pure Imagination: An Experiment in Reading," became the basis of his essay published in the Reynal and Hitchcock edition of Samuel Taylor Coleridge's The Rime of the Ancient Mariner *in 1946, before the publication of* All the King's Men. *This review of Warren's essay by Kenneth Burke, a sophisticated literary critic whom Warren had known since the 1920s, appeared after the novel.*

Burke included a footnote at the end of this essay:

The proportions of this review are not quite satisfactory. There is no mention of the many incidental observations, which I liked greatly. The gloss on the "objective" significance of the "silly buckets" seemed to me exceptionally good.–K.B.

Towards Objective Criticism
Review of Warren's Essay on *The Rime of the Ancient Mariner*

Surely it is a rare writer, here or anywhere, now or at any time, who could have a critical work of exceptional merit appearing when an exceptional work of fiction by him was also new before the public. Yet here it is, in Warren's essay on *The Ancient Mariner,* published in book form, with notes, while we are still mulling over his recent novel.

Though it is not a very long study, it is a packed one, with many excellencies of detail which the reader should savor for himself. I shall here confine myself to only its more salient aspects, which are also its more problematic aspects.

Warren is among those who would treat of Coleridge's poem from the standpoint of Coleridge's own

"The Bird-Church Business"

Warren and Brooks's correspondence displays an unusual quality in their friendship, one of give and take, of sincerity, and of collegiality. This excerpt is from a letter Brooks sent in reply to Warren's request for comment on his essay on The Rime of the Ancient Mariner.

Brooks to Warren, 5 June 1945

I have gone over the A.M. paper several times and with a growing admiration. It is easily the finest thing that has ever been done on that poem–and probably the only essay on it that makes entire sense.

I have made a few quite trivial comments on the margins, but I have nothing of importance to say about it. The brevity of comment is a measure of the extent of my agreement with you. I regret a little that you did not bring in the Industrial Revolution as you did once in conversation with me; but I can see that that would be needless–you've cut beneath it, and it might bring the personal matter to too much focus again, or might put off the reader by making him think that your argument was to prove Coleridge an Agrarian. I think that something might be made of the sexual imagery–the penetration of a virgin world: "We were the first that ever burst / Into that silent sea." I noticed with interest your showing that the bird actually came to church because I thought that that was a discovery of mine; until I reflected that I had probably heard it from you in conversation in Washington, and then forgotten that I had. It's a pretty point, and, if I did come upon it independently, that fact ought to help confirm the interpretation.

–Cleanth Brooks and Robert Penn Warren: A Literary Correspondence, edited by James A. Grimshaw Jr. (Columbia & London: University of Missouri Press, 1998), p. 93

Warren's quick response to Brooks's remarks show he was eager to acknowledge the help of his friend.

Warren to Brooks, 8 June 1945

Well, you overwhelm me with your remarks on the Ancient Mariner paper. I have read the letter over several times, not because I had to do so to know what [is in it] but because it was a pleasure. It may very well be that the bird-church business was picked up from you in conversation. I just don't recall. I am going to make more of the sexual business in the re-write, I think, and shall acknowledge you[r] silent sea business. I want to get that in in so far as it is objective–not a mere index of Coleridge's disorders, etc. As you see, at the present I have left the personal stuff out entirely. I am glad that you have put some comments on the paper itself.

–Cleanth Brooks and Robert Penn Warren: A Literary Correspondence, p. 95

favorite word: Imagination. A poem may be viewed in many perspectives (that is, in many critical terminologies); and high among them, always, in criticism, is the insight got by viewing the poem in the perspective set by the poet's own favorite title for poetic method.

With "fancy," the junior partner of Coleridge's dialectical pair, Warren is not concerned. He focuses the attention on the other, and follows a line of reasoning designed to prove that the killing of the Albatross symbolizes a crime against the imagination. To do this, he distinguishes between a "primary" and "secondary" theme in the poem. Of the primary theme, which "may be defined as the issue of the fable," he writes:

> In *The Ancient Mariner* it receives only a kind of coy and dramatically naive understatement which serves merely as a clue–"He prayeth best, etc." But the theme thus hinted at is the outcome of the fable taken at its face value as a story of crime and punishment and reconciliation. I shall label the primary theme in this poem as the theme of sacramental vision, or the theme of the "One Life."

This "One Life" theme, as distinct from the "story of crime and punishment and reconciliation," is probably most joyously expressed in "The Aeolian Harp," where an aesthetic of impulsive unity is expanded to universal scope in the somewhat pantheistic lines:

> And what if all of animated nature
> Be but organic Harps diversely fram'd,
> That tremble into thought, as o'er them sweeps
> Plastic and vast, one intellectual breeze,
> At once the Soul of each, and God of all?

However, Warren is centering his attention upon *The Ancient Mariner,* where the oneness is most explicitly stated in the "moral" that arises out of the Mariner's sin and suffering. Hence, he distinguishes the "One Life" theme from the "secondary theme," which he calls "the theme of the imagination." Having thus taken the two themes apart, he later asks us to rejoice in their rejoining; though, once so unitary and unifying a principle as Coleridge's "imagination" is introduced, it is hard for one to avoid seeing the fusion everywhere.

Warren next takes several important critical steps hinging about a contrast between "personal" and "objective" motives. He wants to deal only with the "objective" ones. But if he were to be *wholly* "objective," I think that much of the material he introduces would be excluded by the rules of evidence. For a truly "objective" analysis of a poem (as Warren uses the term, in contrast with the "personal") would seem to require that one discuss that poem *without any reference whatsoever to its author.* In so far as one treats the poem in terms of other writings by that author,

1504 A Yale Station,
New Haven, Conn.
June 19, 1945.

Dear Mr. Warren,
                    I have been nearly a month getting around
to write something about your essay: the material is difficult,
the argument is subtle, and I have not had enough continuous
time to finish the reading before. I am now composing directly
on the typewriter, and shall be verbose and perhaps not very
clear, but I send you some comments for what they are worth:
first, comments on particular passages, and then some general
criticism. I have had a good time reading the essay, and am
much impressed by the thoroughness with which you have covered
all that has been said about the poem.

p.1. There are some crucial points about the crucial passage
      from the Table Talk that need to be frankly faced. In note
      80 you raise the question whether H.N.Coleridge may not
      have misunderstood what Coleridge said about the story from
      the Arabian Nights. Is it not possible that Coleridge actu-
      ally said "a work of such pure fantasy" instead of "a work
      of such pure imagination"? I agree that Coleridge at that
      date was not likely to use the word "imagination" loosely.
      I don't know whether H.N.Coleridge was sufficiently indoc-
      trinated to preserve S.T.C.'s nice distinctions. And I
      confess that that paragraph makes better sense to me in
      the circumstances if "fantasy" is substituted for "imagina-
      tion." I mean, taking it in isolation, as a prose paragraph
      making a statement. There is a clear implication that both
      The Ancient Mariner** and the tale from the Arabian Nights
      are somehow fantastic in their plots; so much so that to
      attribute a serious "moral sentiment" to either is bad;
      worse, to advance such a sentiment "as a principle or cause
      of action." Your defence, I suppose, would be to maintain
      that S.T.C. said "imagination" and meant it, but that H.N.C.
      didn't get the point at all, and, though he kept the word,
      wrote the paragraph under the impression that S.T.C. had
      meant "fantasy." Please don't misunderstand me. I can easily
      believe that S.T.C regarded The Ancient Mariner as a work
      of pure imagination in his own technical sense, but when
      I read that passage in Table Talk fairly and without pre-
      conceptions I have great difficulty in persuading myself
      that the man who wrote it meant what you think it means.
      I can't help feeling that there is in it an intended contrast
      between "imagination" and "meaning" as you use the term.

p.56, n.62. Wordsworth's criticism must be taken more seriously,
      I think, for the chances are high that Coleridge acquiesced
      in it. The MSS of the 1800 Lyrical Ballads show Wordsworth,
      Coleridge, and Dorothy working in closest partnership. S.T.C.
      made corrections in the MS of the Preface; the note giving
      the titles of his poems is in his hand, and it appears to be

First page of a seven-page critique Professor Frederick A. Pottle sent Warren after his lecture on Samuel Taylor Coleridge's poem The Rime
of the Ancient Mariner *at Yale University. Pottle became the chief editor of the Yale Edition of the Private Papers of James Boswell
(Yale Collection of American Literature, Beinecke Rare Book and Manuscript Library).*

one is relying upon facts involved in its *authorship*. Hence, these facts would be "personal" in so far as the knowledge of the author's identity figures in the interpretation of a symbol or image in the poem. A criticism that wholly avoided "personal" reference could say only such things about the poem as could be said even if its author, or personal source, were wholly unknown.

Warren's interpretation, in hinging about the proposition that the killing of the Albatross symbolizes a crime against the imagination, secondarily involves an interpretation of the sun image, which is

> the light of practical convenience, it is the light in which pride preens itself, it is, to adopt Coleridge's later terminology, the light of the "understanding," it is the light of that "mere reflective faculty" that "partook of Death." And within a few lines, its acceptance by the mariners has taken them to the sea of death, wherein the sun itself, which had risen so promisingly "like God's own head," is suddenly the "bloody sun," the sun of death.

If we on our own account turn to Coleridge's writings, however, we find such highly relevant passages as these:

> (From *The Friend;* Shedd edition, p. 100): The light of religion is not that of the moon, light without heat. . . . Religion is the sun, the warmth of which indeed swells, and stirs, and actuates the life of nature, but who at the same time beholds all the growth of life with a master-eye, makes all objects glorious on which he looks, and by that glory visible to all others.

> (On the next page, we find vice discussed in terms of moonlight, thus): This is indeed the dread punishment attached by nature to habitual vice, that its impulses wax as its motives wane. . . . Its own restlessness dogs it from behind as with the iron goad of destiny.

> (*Aids to Reflection,* 131): the sun of love, the perfect law of liberty
> (P. 167): the dawning of this inward sun, the perfect law of liberty.

Though there are very many passages in Coleridge where he speaks ill of the imagination, I know of no reference in Coleridge's conceptual writings where the sun has the content which Warren has attributed to it, and which is more like the content he "personally" gives to the "day self" (in contrast with the "night self") in his own excellent novel, *Night Rider.*

There is a crime indeed. And this crime involves the imagination. But it is not a crime *against* the imagination, as Warren would contend. It is a crime of *imagination against reason* (which in Coleridge's language is equated with religion). There was a morally suspect ingredient in the nature

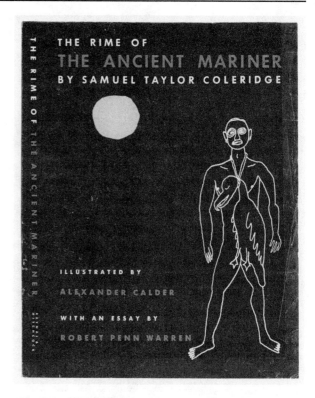

Dust jacket for the edition of Coleridge's poem that included Warren's essay "A Poem of Pure Imagination: An Experiment in Reading" (Yale Collection of American Literature, Beinecke Rare Book and Manuscript Library)

of Coleridge's aesthetic itself (his aesthetic of pure spontaneous "impulse" as contrasted with the ethics of a straining, striving will). Carried to its ultimate metaphysical or theological limits, his aesthetic was a pantheistic offense against God. And the sun became severe after the commission of the crime because its severity represented the conscience (*Friend,* 140: "The conscience bears the same relation to God as an accurate time-piece bears to the sun").

Warren finally introduces the subject of the *poète maudit* purely in terms of "ambivalence." But "ambivalence" is not an explanation, it is a gerundive, a to-be-explained. And he does not use the new interpretation to revise the whole. If one interprets the crime as a crime against religion, one can relevantly note that Coleridge's aesthetic of pantheistic coadunation is similarly but furtively described even in *The Aeolian Harp,* as I indicated in my *Philosophy of Literary Form.*

Of course, when one examines the letters and theological writings with this interpretation in mind, the symmetry of the pattern is complete. We know exactly wherein the "crime" of imagination consists "personally," with Coleridge, in the interweaving of his impulsive aesthetic with the euphoric stages of his drug. And there are also plenty of references that link his drug addiction with an offense against his marital duties (not the least of the "personal" things that were symbolically slain when the Albatross was shot was his "pensive Sara"), while these duties themselves are equated with both religion and the sun. But I am willing to go along with Warren in his feeling that Coleridge's drug problem and marital problem may, in their particulars, be exceptionally "personal," and so should fall outside even his modified rules for an objective criticism. I cite them merely because they help clinch the case. But it seems clear enough without them, once you make the one central correction that follows when one sees the sun as religion, bringing "the Terrors . . . that precede God's love." And as for the cure by moonlight: precisely because it is a cure by moonlight it is not completed. But the moralistic ending was prophetic indeed. Coleridge was henceforth to rely more and more upon such language, using religion to undue the damage which his imagination, as tainted by his weakness, had done to him.

Unfortunately, my engrossment in Warren's engrossing essay has prevented me from discussing the book as a whole. I should add that it contains a beautifully printed copy of the poem, along with several unforgettable line drawings by Alexander Calder, whose deft gestures of simplicity in many ways parallel the archaizing simplicity of the verse in what is perhaps the world's greatest *sophisticated* ballad.

–Kenneth Burke, "Towards Objective Criticism,"
Poetry: A Magazine of Verse,
70 (April 1947): 42–47

On Writing Criticism and the New Criticism

WARREN: On this matter of criticism, something that appals me is the idea going around now that the practice of criticism is opposed to the literary impulse. Is *necessarily* opposed to it, in an individual or period. Sure, it *may* be a trap, it may destroy the creative impulse, but so may drink or money or respectability. But criticism is a perfectly natural human activity and somehow the dullest, most technical criticism may be associated with full creativity. Elizabethan criticism is all, or nearly all, technical—meter, how to hang a line together—kitchen criticism, how to make the cake. People deeply interested in an art are interested in the "how." Now I don't mean to say that that is the only kind of valuable criticism. Any kind is good that gives a deeper insight into the nature of the thing—a Marxist analysis, a Freudian study, the relation to a literary or social tradition, the history of a theme. But we have to remember that there is no *one, single, correct* kind of criticism—no *complete* criticism. You only have different kinds of perspectives, giving, when successful, different kinds of insights. And at one historical moment one kind of insight may be more needed than another.

. . . .

INTERVIEWERS: Do you see some new ideas in criticism now emerging?

WARREN: No, I don't see them now. We've had Mr. Freud and Mr. Marx and—

INTERVIEWERS: Mr. Fraser and *The Golden Bough.*

WARREN: Yes, and Mr. Coleridge and Mr. Arnold and Mr. Eliot and Mr. Richards and Mr. Leavis and Mr. Aristotle, and so on. There have been, or are, many competing kinds of criticism with us—but I don't see a new one, or a new development of one of the old kind. It's an age groping for its issue.

INTERVIEWERS: What about the "New Criticism"?

WARREN: Let's name some of them—Richards, Eliot, Tate, Blackmur, Winters, Brooks, Leavis (I guess). How in God's name can you get that gang into the same bed? There's no bed big enough and no blanket would stay tucked. When Ransom wrote his book called the *New Criticism* he was pointing out the vindictive variety among the critics and saying that he didn't agree with any of them. The term is, in one sense, a term without any referent—or with too many referents. It is a term that belongs to the conspiracy theory of literary history. A lot of people—chiefly aging, conservative professors, scared of losing prestige or young instructors afraid of not getting promoted—middle-brow magazine editors—and the flotsam and jetsam of semi-Marxist social-significance criticism left stranded by history—they all have a communal nightmare called the New Criticism to explain their vague discomfort. I think it was something they ate.

INTERVIEWERS: What do you mean—conspiracy?

WARREN: Those folks all had the paranoidal nightmare that there was a conspiracy called the New Criticism, just to do them personal wrong. No, it's not quite that simple but there is some truth in this. One thing that a lot of so-called New Critics had in common was a willingness to look long and hard at the literary object. But the ways of looking might be very different. Eliot is a lot closer to Arnold and the Archbishop of Canterbury than he is to Yvor Winters, and Winters is a lot closer to Irving Babbitt than to Richards, and the exegeses of Brooks are a lot closer to Coleridge than to Ransom, and so on. There has been more nonsense talked about this subject than any I can think of.

–Ralph Ellison and Eugene Walter, "The Art of Fiction XVIII: Robert Penn Warren,"
Paris Review, 4 (Spring–Summer 1957): 130, 131–132

All the King's Men

All the King's Men, *published in August 1946, was widely reviewed and is the most written-on single work by Warren. It also earned him his first Pulitzer Prize. Much of the initial interest in the novel was the result of speculation about the connection between Warren's character Willie Stark and Louisiana's "Kingfish," Huey P. Long. At the same time that he was enjoying his greatest professional success, Warren was experiencing personal difficulties, as his wife's health was poor and their marriage was deteriorating.*

In this introduction for the 1953 Modern Library edition, Warren looks back to how he came to write his novel and responds to the Stark-Long controversy.

Introduction to *All the King's Men*

Some time in the winter of 1937–38, when I was teaching at the Louisiana State University, in Baton Rouge, I got the notion of doing a verse play about a Southern politician who achieved the power of a dictator, at least in his home state, and who was assassinated in the Capitol which had been the scene of his triumphs. As well as I can recall, the notion began to take on some shape when, sitting one afternoon on the porch of a friend's cottage, I began to describe my intentions.

Very often it is in conversation during the germinal stage of a project that I stumble on my meanings, or they stumble on me, and I recall this particular conversation rather vividly because it was then that I hit on the idea that the politician—then unnamed—would not simply be a man who by force or fraud rises to absolute power, offends the principles of decency and democracy, and then is struck down by a self-appointed Brutus. There would be no drama to such a story—no "insides," no inner tensions, no involvement of the spectator's own deep divisions. My politician would be—or at least I was groping toward some such formulation—a man who in many ways was to serve the cause of social betterment, but who was corrupted by power, even by power exercised against corruption. That is, his means defile his ends. But more than that, he was to be a man whose power was based on the fact that somehow he could vicariously fulfill some secret needs of the people about him. The choruses—and it was in talking about the place of the choruses in the proposed verse play that the notion came—were to develop this in a subsidiary way—a chorus of builders, a chorus of highway patrolmen, a chorus of surgeons, etc. And, naturally, each of the main characters should bear such a relation to the politician, even the Brutus assassin. But over against his power to fulfill, in some degree, a secret need of those about him, the politician was to

Warren, circa 1946–1947, when he was a professor at the University of Minnesota in Minneapolis (Special Collections, Western Kentucky University Libraries)

discover, more and more, his own emptiness and his own alienation. So much for that conversation in the unseasonable sunshine of a Louisiana winter day.

The play did get written. I wrote a couple of choruses in the next few months. In Italy, the next summer, the summer of 1938, I got a little more done, beginning the process, I recall, in the late afternoon, in a wheat field outside of Perugia. The thing dragged on all the next winter and spring, in Louisiana, with a bit done after classes and on week-ends, but the bulk of the play was written in Rome, in the fall and winter of 1939, with the news of the war filling the papers and the boot heels of Mussolini's legionaries clanging on the stones. During that time I was deep in Machiavelli and Dante. Later, in the novel *All the King's Men,* Machiavelli found a place in the musings of Jack Burden, and Dante provided the epigraph.

When the play was finished, it was somewhat different from the thing dreamed up in the conversation with my friend. For instance, another theme had crept in—the theme of the relation of science (or pseudo-science) and political power, the theme of the relation of the science-society and the power-state, the problem of naturalistic

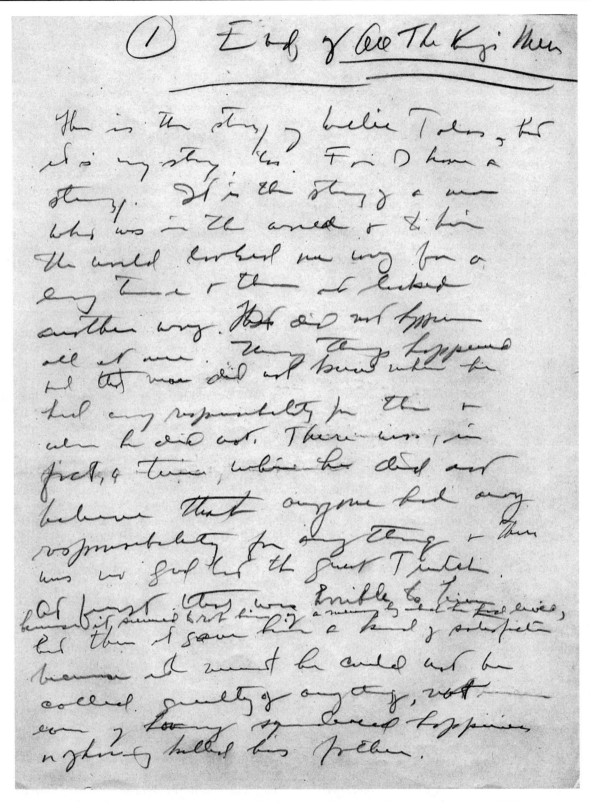

Page from an early draft for the ending of All the King's Men *before the name Willie Talos was changed to Willie Stark*
(Robert Penn Warren Papers, Beinecke Library, Yale University)

The First Chapter of *All the King's Men*

In the discussion in which he participated with O'Connor, Warren responded to the question, "In All the King's Men, did you write the first chapter first?"

No, it was the second chapter originally. There was a shift in material there which the editor did. The present opening chapter was the second chapter, or part of the second chapter. The original opening got off to a very poor start with the narrator talking about the first time he had seen Stark, the politician. He goes back into the scene which now appears later, in the second or third chapter, when he comes into town to get a political favor, make a political connection, in a restaurant or beer hall in New Orleans. There is this portrait of him coming in, the boy with the Christmas tie, you know, and his hat in his hand. Well, that was a very predictable kind of start. It had not urgency in it. So expository in the worst sense. I was trying to step that up by a kind of commentary on it, and the commentary was pretty crude, and that's the way the thing remained when it went to the publisher. And Lambert Davis said, "Look here, this is a very poor way to start a novel. You've got a natural start in the second chapter, and what's in the first chapter that's important, you can absorb very readily." And I think he was right. I know he was right about its being bad.

–"An Interview with Flannery O'Connor and Robert Penn Warren," *Vagabond*, 6 (February 1960): 10–11

determinism and responsibility, etc. At least, if such grand topics did not find explicit place in the play, and if I did not pretend to wisdom about them, they were casting a shade over the meditations of composition. The play, by the way, had the title *Proud Flesh*. I was rather pleased with the double significance of the phrase.

I mailed off the play to some friends back home. I knew that it was not finished, but I would postpone the rewriting for the benefit of the judgment of my first readers and my own more detached contemplation. Back in America, in the summer of 1940, I did do some rewriting, with the subtle criticism and inspiring instruction of Francis Fergusson. But still the play was not, to my mind or taste, finished. And besides, I had already begun a novel, to appear as *At Heaven's Gate*, which was drawing on some of the feelings and ideas involved in the play.

It was not until the spring of 1943 that I began again on the play. I had taken the manuscript out of its cupboard with the intention of revising it, but immediately I found myself thinking of the thing as a novel. That idea wasn't entirely new. Now and then I had entertained the possibility of making a novel of the story. But now, all at once, a novel seemed the natural and demanding form for it, and for me.

This new impulse was, I suppose, a continuation of the experience of writing *At Heaven's Gate*, just as that novel had been, in a way, a continuation of *Proud Flesh*. Despite important contrasts, there were some points of essential similarity between my businessman hero, Bogan Murdock, in *At Heaven's Gate*, and the politician hero of the play. And even some of the contrasts between them were contrasts in terms of the same thematic considerations. For example, if Bogan Murdock was supposed to embody, in one of his dimensions, the desiccating abstraction of power, to be a violator of nature, a usurer of Dante's Seventh Circle, and to try to fulfill vicariously his natural emptiness by exercising power over those around him, so the politician rises to power because of the faculty of fulfilling vicariously the secret needs of others, and in the process, as I have already said, discovers his own emptiness. But beyond such considerations, the effort of *At Heaven's Gate* had whetted my desire to compose a highly documented picture of the modern world–at least, as the modern world manifested itself in the only region I knew well enough to write about.

There was, however, another consideration, if one can use such a term of scruple and calculation to describe the coiling, interfused forces that go into such a "literary" decision. This consideration was a technical one–the necessity for a character of a higher degree of self-consciousness than my politician, a character to serve as a kind of commentator and *raisonneur* and chorus. But since in fiction one should never do a thing for merely a single reason (not if he hopes to achieve that feeling of a mysterious depth which is one of the chief beauties of the art), I wanted to give that character a dynamic relation to the general business, to make him the chief character among those who were to find their vicarious fulfillment in the dynamic and brutal, yet paradoxically idealistic, drive of the politician. There was, too, my desire to avoid writing a straight naturalistic novel, the kind of novel that the material so readily invited. The impingement of that material, I

Rejected first chapter, AKM

ALL THE KING'S MEN

I

The Boss was a son-of-a-bitch, and I will not deny it. He was a son-of-a-bitch of purest ray serene. I will not deny it, for I do not wish to rob his name of any of its lustre. Now, the real son-of-a-bitch is one of the rarest works of God. In the dreary grind of daily living your sensibilities get blunted and your values get warped and your metabolism gets out of gear and your ideals get tarnished and your nervous system gets shattered and you fall into the habit of bandying that term licentiously about without due regard for the eternal verities. Some pus-gutted public servant dips his finger into the till or some snot two-times his loving wife or some punk who happens to be a deacon in the Presbyterian Church forecloses a mortgage on the widow of his best pal, and you say, the son-of-a-bitch. Alas, it will never do. It is a deplorable practice. Are there no standards? You ought to save that sacred name. You ought to save it like a good, clean Christian girl saves her maidenhead until the customer who in the jargon of the trade is known as the "right man" comes along. Maybe he won't come along. But if he doesn't, then you just take that name to the grave with you and rest happy in the consolation that you did your little part to keep the world from falling into semantic confusion and relativistic pother. But if he does swim across your ken, praise God, and lift up your little patties in thanksgiving. For not to have seen a real son-of-a-bitch does grave discredit to your travels.

And did you once see Shelley plain? as the poet saith. No, but I shore-God saw the Boss, plain as a pikestaff, and he was the son-of-a-bitch nonpareil, par excellence, and his belly was a sheaf of wheat set round with lilies, and violets sprang up in his footsteps. I have seen him, and Lord, let thy servant depart in peace.

The first time I saw him, be it said to my shame, I didn't recognize what I

First page of the opening that Warren discarded on the advice of his editor, Lambert Davis
(Robert Penn Warren Papers, Beinecke Library, Yale University)

thought, upon a special temperament would allow another perspective than the reportorial one, and would give a basis for some range of style. So Jack Burden entered the scene.

But that is not quite a complete account of his origin. In *Proud Flesh,* at the time when Dr. Adam Stanton is waiting in the lobby of the Capitol to kill the Governor, and is meditating his act to come, an old friend, now a newspaperman, approaches him, and for one instant the assassin turns to him with a sense of elegiac nostalgia for the innocence and simplicity of the shared experiences of boyhood. This character, who appears so fleetingly in the last act of the play to evoke the last backward look of the dedicated assassin, gave me Jack Burden. And the story, in a sense, became the story of Jack Burden, the teller of the tale.

The composition of the novel moved slowly, in Minneapolis, in 1943 and through the spring of 1944, in Washington [D.C.] through the rest of the year and up till June of 1945, in Connecticut in the summer of 1945. The work was constantly interrupted, by teaching, by some traveling, by the duties of my post in Washington [Consultant in Poetry to the Library of Congress], by the study for and writing of a long essay on Coleridge. The interruptions were, in some way, welcome, for they meant that the pot had to be pushed to the back of the stove to simmer away at its own pace. The book was finished in the fall of 1945, back in Minneapolis, the last few paragraphs being written in a little room in the upper reaches of the Library of the University of Minnesota. The book, after a good deal of revision along the way, with the perceptive criticism of Lambert Davis of Harcourt, Brace and Company, was published in August, 1946.

One of the unfortunate characteristics of our time is that the reception of a novel may depend on its journalistic relevance. It is a little graceless of me to call this characteristic unfortunate, and to quarrel with it, for certainly the journalistic relevance of *All the King's Men* had a good deal to do with what interest it evoked. My politician hero, whose name, in the end, was Willie Stark, was quickly equated with the late Senator Huey P. Long, whose fame, even outside of Louisiana, was yet green in pious tears, anathema, and speculation.

This equation led, in different quarters, to quite contradictory interpretations of the novel. On one hand, there were those who took the thing to be a not-so-covert biography of, and apologia for, Senator Long, and the author to be not less than a base minion of the great man. There is really nothing to reply to this kind of innocent boneheadedness or gospel-bit hysteria. As Louis Armstrong is reported to have said, there's some folks that if they don't know, you can't tell 'em.

Creating Jack Burden

In the discussion in which he participated with O'Connor, Warren recalled how the transformation of the play Proud Flesh *into the novel* All the King's Men *was effected through the creation of his narrator.*

. . . But the tone of the play had not been the tone of the book. For better or for worse. And the tone of the book turned on the question of getting a lingo for this narrator. I remember that fact quite distinctly. It was a question just of this lingo, and fumbling around with how he's going to talk–he's got to talk some way. A straight journalistic prose would not do. That is the trap of all traps. There has to be an angularity to any piece of writing that claims to have a person behind it. The problem was to find a way for him to talk. It was really a backward process. The character wasn't set up–aside from the lingo, and trying to find a way for him to talk.

. . . .

His ambivalence about what he saw–as a road, as people, as things–was a start. His division of feeling was the way it came out of the start of the lingo. That was the germ. It didn't start with a plot, or conception. This guy gets power, and he gets shot. All the details of Burden's life were improvised. They were improvised in terms of some envisagement of his feelings about everything at the end. But I didn't know what the last chapter was going to be until I got there. I didn't know how I wanted it to feel. Just as Flannery was saying: you go back a little bit, and keep looking back. After you are along the way, keep looking back, and your backward looks along the way will help you go forward. You have to find a logic there that you pursue. If you can't find it, you're in trouble.

–"An Interview with Flannery O'Connor and Robert Penn Warren," *Vagabond,* 6 (February 1960): 12

But on the other hand, there were those who took the thing to be a rousing declaration of democratic principles and a tract for the assassination of dictators. This view, though somewhat more congenial to my personal political views, was almost as wide of the mark. For better or for worse, Willie Stark was not Huey Long. Willie was only himself, whatever that self turned out to be, a shadowy wraith or a blundering human being.

This disclaimer, whenever I was callow enough to make it, was almost invariably greeted by something like a sardonic smile or a conspiratorial wink, according to what the inimical smiler or the friendly winker took my motives to be–either I wanted to avoid being called a fascist or I wanted to avoid a lawsuit. Now in making the disclaimer again, I do not mean to imply that there was no connection between Governor Stark and Senator Long. Certainly, it was the career of Long and the atmosphere of Louisiana that suggested the play that was to become the novel. But suggestion does not mean identity, and even if I had wanted to make Stark a projection of Long, I should not have known how to go about it. For one reason, simply because I did not, and do not, know what Long was like, and what were the secret forces that drove him along his violent path to meet the bullet in the Capitol. And in any case, Long was but one of the figures that stood in the shadows of imagination behind Willie Stark. Another one of that company was the scholarly and benign figure of William James.

Though I did not profess to be privy to the secret of Long's soul, I did have some notions about the phenomenon of which Long was but one example, and I tried to put some of those notions into my book. Something about those notions, and something of what I felt to be the difference between the person Huey P. Long and the fiction Willie Stark, may be indicated by the fact that in the verse play the name of the politician was Talos–the name of the brutal, blank-eyed "iron groom" of Spenser's *Faerie Queene,* the pitiless servant of the knight of justice. My conception grew wider, but that element always remained, and Willie Stark remained, in one way, Willie Talos. In other words, Talos is the kind of doom that democracy may invite upon itself. The book, however, was never intended to be a book about politics. Politics merely provided the framework story in which the deeper concerns, whatever their final significance, might work themselves out.

–Warren, "Introduction to *All the King's Men*"
(New York: Random House, 1953)

* * *

The year 1981 marked the thirty-fifth anniversary of the publication of All the King's Men, *and Warren wrote a new introduction in which he discussed the influence of living in Huey Long's Louisiana on his conception of his novel.*

In the Time of *All the King's Men*

Thirty-five years ago, *All the King's Men* was published. With any event in your life, you know more after 35 years than after one. True, you may know less in some ways. Time does not necessarily improve memory. But in the course of time, strange odds and ends–or even fundamental facts not recognized in the noonday sun–may, out of blank idleness of a later mind, rise up, trailing God knows what, like a half-rotten log disturbed in a creek bed trailing algae, patched with

moss, clung to by some strange, snail-like creatures, with a rusty length of barbed wire still nailed to it. What rises so gratuitously out of the deep of time may be a set of relationships and connections of which you had been unaware when things were fresh. The unconscious thing may, years later, become startling conscious, seemingly by accident. That is why it is always hard to say precisely when and how a book–or anything else–"began."

I might, in a certain kind of accuracy, be arbitrary and say that *All the King's Men* began when, in September 1934, I moved to Baton Rouge, to teach at the Louisiana State University and thus entered the orbit of Huey P. Long, who had previously been for me only an occasional headline. But, in another sense, it is more accurate for me to begin by saying that for three years earlier, in the darkness of the early Depression, I had been at Vanderbilt University, in Nashville, Tenn., back in the days when Nashville was the scene of the purest melodrama, political, financial and personal. I had watched that melodrama with absorbed interest, and it was the germ of a novel of mine written after the first version of *All the King's Men,* a play, was in manuscript, and published before the final version of *All the King's Men* was finished. That is, when I entered Louisiana, my imagination was already trapped in speculation about the struggle for power in a world of politics–specifically in a Southern state.

Louisiana was to present something much more complex than the Tennessee situation, which was more old-fashioned, the perennial story of greed, ambition, vanity and deception behind a facade of Southern mythology. But Louisiana became a parable of a worldwide situation, with deeper historical reverberations.

No novel of any kind was in my mind as I drove a carful of suitcases, crates and gear down toward Baton Rouge and the job I so sorely needed and had been lucky enough to get. Huey Long's university was "hiring." All other universities were "firing," and I had just been fired. I had been assured that Huey would not mess with my classroom, that he wanted a "good" university almost as much as he wanted a winning football team.

In my first year there, in a large class of sophomores, a hulking brute of a young man turned rude and offensive on several occasions, and I finally ordered him to get up and leave the room and never come back. He left with insulting casualness. After class I was surrounded by a group of curious, horrified, astounded or sympathetic students. I had, they told me, just thrown out so-and-so, who was a star of the L.S.U. Tigers. That, however, was the last I heard of it. A man as smart as Huey, who was well aware that the American Association of University Professors would like

Dust jacket for Warren's third novel, which won the Pulitzer Prize in fiction in 1947 (Yale Collection of American Literature, Beinecke Rare Book and Manuscript Library)

nothing better than to blacklist his university, had no need to mess with classrooms.

But the classroom runs ahead of our real concern. I had, unwittingly, encountered the real concern on the roadside as I drove south. After I had crossed the northern Louisiana line, probably on the second day of the journey, fate gave me a passenger. He was a somewhat aging fellow, unshaven, missing a tooth or two, with tobacco juice oozing from the gap where a tooth had

been, not quite as ragged as a tramp, skin baked to leather, the kind of rural drifter born in some shack with a roof you could see stars through at night, living at the end of a road in which, come the fall rains, a wagon would mire to the axle, especially with the kind of half-starved mules that would be trying to pull it. He was a "wool hat." He was a "redneck." He was "poor white trash." He was a citizen of Louisiana, and he probably couldn't write his name. Or barely.

What SINCLAIR LEWIS Says About *All The King's Men*

"For his poetry and for his two earlier novels, Robert Penn Warren has had distinguished appreciation, but with *All the King's Men* he emerges as probably the most talented writer of the South and certainly as one of the most important writers in the whole country; as one of the ten or fifteen—maybe one of the five or six —at the top. His novel is massive, impressive, yet so full of light subtleties and surprising drama that it is never ponderous. This story of a Southern Governor who is a scoundrel and a saint, a booze-hoisting vulgarian, and a wise and incorruptible leader of the people, a very funny fellow and somehow wistful and lost, and of the seedy men and lively women who follow him, is one of our few national galleries of character. I wish Mr. Warren could have seen the Southerners who are called 'colored' as clearly as he d'd the poor whites, but even in Balzac you can't have everything."

(Continued from front flap)

for faith. Anne Stanton is drawn to Stark through her frustration in the genteel society in which she has been raised. Her brother Adam, the ascetic doctor, is persuaded that his desire to help mankind can be fulfilled if he becomes director of the great hospital that Stark has built to justify his power.

From the moment that Stark gives Jack Burden the job of digging up political dirt on a friend of the Burden and Stanton families, the story weaves into a single drama of ever mounting intensity. In Willie Stark, Mr. Warren has added a notable figure to our literature, a man of the people corrupted by success, caught between his dreams of service and his ruthless urge to power. In brilliant contrast are Adam Stanton, the man of ideas, Judge Irwin, the old-fashioned man of honor, and Jack Burden, the uprooted seeker for a faith.

When Mr. Warren's AT HEAVEN's GATE was published, Paul Engle wrote: "I believe that no other novel in 1943 will prove as abundant as this one, as full of insight into as many kinds of men and women, as idiomatic in speech or as opulent in narrative prose, as powerful in its acceptance of human motive, as warm in sympathy for poor human emotions." Mr. Engle's words apply even more forcefully to ALL THE KING'S MEN, which is clearly the mature work of a major American novelist.

HARCOURT, BRACE AND COMPANY
383 Madison Avenue, New York 17

He was also a portent and a sage, as I was to decide later and write in a comment on *All the King's Men* long after it was first published. He was what made Huey possible. He was what Huey had been smart enough to see would make him possible. He was what people in offices in the Capitol at Baton Rouge, or in drawing rooms in New Orleans, or in the shade of the live oaks of a plantation garden had never thought about at all.

He was also my introduction to the legendry of Huey. He told me how Huey would build you a road. How he would build you bridges with no toll. How he was going to fix your teeth free. He told me what Huey had said to a certain "son-a-bitch." Then he vengefully spat. "That Huey," he said, "he gits 'em tole, and tole straight."

Later on, I was to hear that phrase over and over, Huey was, indeed, a wit, a stand-up comic, a tale teller, a master of vituperation and high rhetoric, a master of many "lingos," a murderous debater. In 1935, the university (of which William Tecumseh Sherman had once been head) celebrated its 75th anni-

"The Hardest Kind of Audience"

Brooks, who had received an advance copy of All the King's Men, *realized that many readers would be tempted to read the novel as a commentary on Louisiana events.*

Brooks to Warren, 13 July 1946

I have been owing you a letter for some time, and I am the more ashamed because I have also been owing you a comment on your novel–which I stayed up most of the night to finish when it came in some three weeks ago. It is very fine–the best of the three; and, unless I miss my guess completely, as solid as a rock. I feel that the ending is particularly powerful, but I do not find it in any way forced–it is thoroughly inevitable.

It must have been a hard book to write–as it is for the Louisianian a hard book to read–in the sense that one is tempted to impose his own interpretation of events upon the pattern of events in the novel. That is why I am so confident of the book's goodness, for I think that I provide in a way the hardest kind of audience–at least the kind of audience which is subjected most to the temptation to wrest the book away from its own pattern and so misread it.

In particular, I am delighted with your handling of the mistresses–both of them, at the end of the book. You will remember that in the play [*Proud Flesh*] I was not quite satisfied with the motivation of some of the main characters. (I may very well have been wrong there.) But, in any case, for whatever it's worth, I feel completely convinced by your handling of them in *All the King's Men.*

The story of Cass Mastern was a stroke of genius. It furnishes you with a very powerful lever–which you use admirably. . . .

–Cleanth Brooks and Robert Penn Warren: A Literary Correspondence, p. 110

---

versary, the celebration including an enormous formal luncheon with many guests notable beyond the confines of the state: deans of famous institutions, journalists, writers, politicians.

At the high table were seats for the president of the university, ambassadors of countries that had influenced the history of Louisiana, various academics of stature, plus a few types I can't remember. Suddenly, when the hall was nearly full but the high table was still vacant, Huey appeared at one end. He strode along behind the table, apparently looking for place cards. When he reached a location near the middle of the table, he leaned slightly forward, swept some cutlery and such aside, giving the impression that he was just making a place for himself, wherever the hell his place card was, and sat down, all as

calmly as though coming into his own kitchen late at night for a snack.

A waiter or two straightened out things, the great figures appropriate for the high table arrived and rather lumberingly the invocation and the formal events proceeded. At some point the president, quite naturally, called on Huey for a few words. Huey was in top form, or near. About all I remember is this, my paraphrase: "People say I steal. Well, all politicians steal. I steal. But a lot of what I stole has spilled over in no-toll bridges, hospitals–and to build this university." There was more–and better–in various keys.

That was the only time I ever saw Huey (except perhaps once in a passing car). In one sense I wasn't really much interested in him as a man. My guess is that he was a remarkable set of contradictions, still baffling to biographers. But I had a great interest in what Huey did in his world, and a greater interest in Huey as a focus of myth. Without this gift for attracting myth he would not have been the power he was, for good and evil. And this gift was fused, indissolubly, with his dramatic sense, with his varying roles and perhaps, ultimately, with the atmosphere of violence which he generated.

Rumors of violence were constant. You heard that conspiracies for assassination had been formed, that the straws had been drawn. There was, for instance, an anti-Long group called the Square Dealers, organized (as we can now read on the sober pages of history) in squads and companies, armed, baying for blood. On one occasion, a man I assumed was a Square Dealer showed me his new sawed-off shotgun, loaded. How the young man–a filling-station operator–fondled the polished stock! Not long after, at legal hearings, a presumptive spy in the organization reported lurid plottings. The National Guard imposed martial law. Long announced a conspiracy of assassination and no doubt believed it. There does not seem to be any overwhelming reason for disbelief, even if such conspirators had no direct connection whatsoever with the eventual assassin, young Dr. Carl Weiss, an able and intelligent member of the medical profession.

Meanwhile, before the fatal shot, you heard the argument among true believers that Long, in that moribund and self-satisfied state of Louisiana, had chosen the only means to deliver his social goods. But this was, of course, the alibi of all grabbers of power everywhere. It was said all around Louisiana, and I, in certain moods, may well have said it myself. True, it was the alibi of Mussolini and Hitler, and every Communist and fellow traveler loved to mouth the cliché that you can't make an omelet without breaking eggs. (And that was to be their alibi for Stalin after the Moscow Trials a year or so later.) As for Huey's motives, good or bad,

Oxford, Miss.
25 July.

Dear Mr Davis:

I received Warren's book. Thank you for it.

The Cass Mastern story is a beautiful and moving piece. That was his novel. The rest of it I would throw away. The Starke thing is good solid sound writing but for my money Starke and the rest of them are second rate. The others couldn't be bigger than he, the hero, and he to me is second rate. I didn't mind neither loving him nor hating him, but I did object to not being moved to pity. As I read him, he wanted neither power for the sake of his pride nor revenge for the sake of his vanity; he wanted neither to purify the earth by obliterating some of the population from it nor did he aim to give every hillbilly and redneck a pair of shoes. He was neither big enough nor bad enough. But maybe the Cass story made the rest of it look thinner than it is. The Cass piece was beautiful and moving. '...couldn't bear the eyes watching me.' That's all right. It's fine the way Warren caught not only the pattern of their acts but the very terms they thought in of that time. There are times when I believe there has been little in this country since that time ---1860 - '70 etc. good enough to make good literature, that since then we have gradually become a nation of bragging sentimental not too courageous liars. We seem to be losing all confidence not only in our national character but in man's integrity too. The fact that we blow so hard so much about both of them is to me the symptom.

But this has got away from Warren's book. He should have taken the Cass story and made a novel. Though maybe no man 75 years from that time could have sustained that for novel length.

W Faulkner

William Faulkner

Letter from William Faulkner to Lambert Davis in which he comments on All the King's Men
(Beinecke Rare Book and Manuscript Library, Yale University)

the question was soon to become academic. The slug from the little Belgian revolver of Dr. Weiss relegated the question to history.

Meanwhile, if you were living in Louisiana, you know you were living in history defining itself before your eyes. And you knew that you were not seeing a half-drunk hick buffoon performing an old routine, but were witnessing a drama which was a version of the world's drama, and the drama of history, too, the old drama of power and ethics.

How many factors, and facts, flow strangely together as I look back on those days. One of my duties was to teach a senior Shakespeare class, and in Shakespeare that question of power and ethics—and the ques-

tion of determination in history—is frequent and vivid. I read Shakespeare, and many books about him, with a growing thought of Huey—who, behind his mask of idiotic or vulgar clowning, might suddenly be brilliant, inevitable, ruthless. And I was not alone. There were the students. I remember when we came to *Julius Caesar,* and the day I lectured, no doubt in a bumbling fashion, on the fall of the Roman Republic and the rise of Caesarism. For once in my life, had an audience spellbound and breathless. That was in early 1935, at the height of violent commotion in the state and with Huey very rambunctiously alive. And his daughter Rose discreetly in the back row in my class. (Rose, I may interpolate, was extremely intelligent. She never spoke, and

I never addressed a question to her, but her papers were always deservedly "A".)

The dullest dullard in my class, even before the current dictator, like Caesar, was to die in his capital, could see certain parallels with Shakespeare's play. But there was much more of Shakespeare than that in my mind as Rome gradually became a mirror to Louisiana. Certain questions began to gnaw at me. Shakespeare had dealt with the question of power, its various justifications, ethical and otherwise, and its dangers. His "history plays," in which the issue appears not in Rome but England, run chronologically (though not in terms of composition) from the reign and later deposition of Richard II, who has a perfectly "legitimate" claim to the throne, legitimacy meaning not only the hereditary line but also the "deputy elected by the Lord." Even when Richard's excesses and incompetencies approach their logical disaster, the Bishop of Carlisle comforts him with the words: ". . . that power that made you King/ Hath power to keep you King in spite of all." Richard may be "God's anointed," but Bolingbroke, with no legitimate claim, understands the logic of power, and seizes it to become Henry IV. Even so, Bolingbroke–who could openly rejoice in the death of the Bishop of Carlisle–recognizes the ambiguous nature of his position, and when one of his lords, hoping to curry favor, murders the imprisoned Richard, Bolingbroke banishes him, and for his own complicity vows a pilgrimage to the Holy Land "to wash the blood from off my guilty hand."

In other words, boiled down, the issue is between legitimacy and *de facto* power; and here to bring matters up to date, we substitute for the old meaning of legitimacy as heredity and God's will the new meaning of constitutionality.

But back to Huey: He was, in various ways, totally contemptuous of what many of his opponents would call legitimacy. He lived in terms of power, and for him ends seemed to justify means. He was, I suppose you might say, an extreme exponent of the "realistic view" of law, the "sociological view" that law is not sacrosanct revelation from on high, but grows out of the needs of a changing society. He might well have carried that attitude to the extent of treating the constitution with the respect usually reserved for Scott's Tissue.

And here I may add that in the decade of the 1930's I was reading William James, instinctively led, I suppose, to try to see the difference between philosophical pragmatism and that unphilosophical pragmatism represented by Bolingbroke–or Huey. Or by Mussolini, who, as I seem to remember, regarded himself as a kind of disciple of the gentle William. I was also reading such things as Machiavelli, Dante and Burckhardt on the Italian Renaissance, on tyranny and power–not prompted by a thought of Huey, except incidentally, but to provide background for a graduate seminar in nondramatic Elizabethan literature.

With the mention of that seminar, I am reminded of a relation that grew in my mind between Huey and Spenser's *Faerie Queene*. In Book V, concerned with the Virtue of Justice, the Knight of Justice, Artegall, is served by his "iron groom," Talus (whom Spenser had drawn from Greek mythology–from "Talos," a sort of robot of bronze forged by the god Hephaestus to guard Crete). The function of Spenser's "iron groom," who was without ordinary human consciousness and certainly without moral sense, is to administer the dire punishments decreed by his master. I remember the moment the name Talus came to me for the political dictator in the verse play that was to become *All the King's Men:* a summer morning in 1938, as I sat in the shade of an olive tree in Umbria, with grapevines running from my tree to others along the edge of a wheatfield, trying to organize the speculations provoked by Huey. The name must have been "Willie" Talos–but to be sure I'd have to rummage through stacks of old manuscript. Anyway, "Talos" sounded somehow like a Southern name to my ear.

All the King's Men

By

ROBERT PENN WARREN

Mentre che la speranza ha fior del verde.
LA DIVINA COMMEDIA, PURGATORIO, III

New York
HARCOURT, BRACE AND COMPANY

Title page with an epigraph from Dante's Divine Comedy: *"As long as hope still has its bit of green" (Special Collections, Western Kentucky University Libraries)*

Behind this flash that led to the christening lurked some shadow of the theory that the "great man" is merely created by historical forces, that he becomes "great" not from his own isolated strength but from the weakness of others, or from a whole society that has lost its mission. The "great man," then, is simply the "iron groom" of history. And I have speculated now and then that some sudden image of the brute stolidity of the Duce's face, the iron and ruthless mien he cultivated, may have been one of the elements that evoked the name from Spenser and my seminar.

I have run ahead of events. I sat under the olive tree almost three years after the death of Huey. Back in September 1935, driving across Nevada on my way back from California to Louisiana, I stopped at a desert filling station, and the operator, seeing the plates on my car, said: "They done shot that feller of yours, that Huey. Heard it on the radio." At filling station after station, the Louisiana plates drew attention. Especially after the death, a little group of idlers would gather to talk about "your fellow." Almost always the views were

favorable to Huey—that "feller that might do somethin'." These idlers of the Depression were unphilosophical pragmatists. What would that have meant in 1936, the election year, if Huey had been alive? But by then, there was only the "legitimate" Landon, powerless against an expert in power.

The death of Huey did not relieve the mind of only the incumbent F.D.R. It also relieved the "Long machine" of the burden of Huey. Long had not been a looter. He had been concerned with power, and had ways of raising money for his purposes. There was, for instance, the famous "deduct box," so named because much of the fortune it presumably contained came from forced deductions from salaries of state employees; and the box was always in Huey's personal possession. No doubt, there was some general "looting" in the machine. There is the story that Huey, sitting in the midst of his cronies and lickspittles, in an hour of ease, regarded them all, shook his head sadly and remarked: "You know, if I died, you'd all go to jail, you just couldn't keep your hands from grabbing anything loose." Time was to prove that he read them like a book.

As for the Kingfish himself, though he lived high, all the powers of Washington, including the I.R.S., with the President breathing hot down their necks, could never pin any charge on Huey. Only with the Kingfish dead did the holiday of big looting begin. Even the university was a center, with tales of cattle rustling from the Agricultural College for private estates, of a health official of the university charging $5,000 worth of Scotch whisky at a favored drugstore as "serum," of a university contractor putting gold fixtures in bathrooms of his own "little mansion." And it was reported that the president of L.S.U., with a Ph.D. from one of our most famous teachers' colleges, was idiotic enough to forge the name of a dead Governor on bonds dated after that Governor's death, these bonds to be used as collateral in the educator's financial speculations. No loose cash was safe, not even Federal money for student aid.

Ironically enough, it was the "little looting" at the university that touched off the final explosion. In the spring of 1939, somebody in the university inner circle got the idea that United States Attorney General Frank Murphy, whose hounds must have picked up a scent, might be lulled by an honorary degree and a invitation to give the commencement address. Mr. Murphy accepted the invitation, but on the way loitered a few days in New Orleans with J. Edgar Hoover (who was said never to go anywhere except on business) before coming to Baton Rouge for the great banquet in his honor at the Governor's mansion that was to precede the commencement under the floodlights of Huey's football stadium.

But something went awry. On the morning of the commencement the highway patrol was ordered to stop the cars of all the distinguished guests who were flocking to the Mansion (so the president's secretary, a very nice lady who loathed him, told me face to face that day). But some of the guests trickled through the net and rushed to the mansion, where they found little jollity. Murphy, according to later report, was not conversational. Nor would he enter the dining room to break bread with the mob. He sent out one of his assistants, it appears, to buy some ice cream from a drugstore. He ate it in the drawing room.

At commencement, where faculty, graduates and fond parents had been waiting a long, long time under the floodlights, I saw Murphy march across the sacred greensward, a thin, tense man with the gaunt aquiline look of a 16th-century Inquisitor, between the two hulking, beefy, begowned figures of the Governor of the state and the president of the university. The look on the face of each of the hefty flankers was that of a condemned man being led to the block. Or that of heretics being led to the stake.

The beefy pair had to sit through a ringing indictment of the spread of corruption in state governments. Not long after, both were in the penitentiary, along with a crew of their ilk. And the cold muzzles of revolvers had been put to more than one anguished temple.

By that time I had actually begun basic work on what was eventually to become *All the King's Men,* and as I sat through the commencement I had the odd impression that I was looking at an epilogue of my own project. That project had suddenly taken a first, cloudy shape in the spring of 1937, as I sat on the porch of a little house back of a sleazy tourist court and filling station, a house where lived Albert Erskine, one of my colleagues on the *Southern Review* and later my editor, and John Palmer, then a graduate student and an appointed Rhodes Scholar (later a naval officer in two wars and a dean at Yale).

What struck me that afternoon was that I might write a verse play out of my observations and speculations. So I tried to tell my friends what I had in mind, and even as I talked a new idea came. There would be choruses, with each chorus a special group drawn into the orbit of the "Boss." At that moment I could specify only two of the choruses: one of uniformed state constabularies, with their beloved motorcycles and revolvers, in love with violence; one of surgeons, clothed in white, in love equally with healing and with technology. The account did not seem to absorb the attention of my friends.

Nor did it absorb me, except at moments. I was teaching, writing a novel (having lately received an award from Houghton Mifflin)—to be my first published novel, *Night Rider.* And poems kept popping up, too. And I was involved in protracted conversation with Cleanth Brooks about poetry (and his scrupulous criticism of my own pieces as they came along), and deep in the actual collaboration with him on a text book, *Understanding Poetry.* Not to mention work with my friends on the *Southern Review.*

But *Night Rider* got finished, and in the summer of 1939, on a Guggenheim, I fled to Italy to gaze at real Fas-

cism in action, carrying notes and scribbled sections of my play. In Rome, in December of that year, with, on a couple of occasions, boot heels of Benito's Black Shirts clacking on the cobbles of Via Aurelia Safi outside my window, I finished the draft. I sent copies to several friends, including Allen Tate, Kenneth Burke (I think), and Francis Fergusson. Having fled Italy in May 1940, when I had inside information from an Italian friend that Mussolini would enter the war in early June, I went to Bennington, Vt., where every day Francis gave me a seminar on drama and I worked at revision. The name of the hero was, as I have said, Willie Talos, and the title was *Proud Flesh*—a philosophical pun with which, at the moment, I was well pleased.

I was not well pleased with the play. I dumped it into a drawer, went back to writing poems and a novel (a relic of Nashville, Tenn.), sold my house in the country some miles from Baton Rouge (with its beautiful grove of live oaks with Spanish moss, where I had contentedly thought of spending the rest of my days), moved to the University of Minnesota, and one Saturday morning, in the late winter or early spring of 1943, took *Proud Flesh* out of a drawer.

As soon as I read it, I knew what dissatisfied me. The idea that I'd had about the choruses back in the spring of 1937 had not been developed sufficiently, and it was the key I had overlooked. I now saw that my man of power,

---

"The Problem of Presenting Anne Stanton"

This excerpt is from a letter Warren began by thanking Davidson for sending him a copy of his book Tennessee River.

Warren to Donald Davidson, 9 October 1946

I owe you thanks, too, for your letter and your comments on AKM. You have put your hand on a real problem when you talk about the point-of-view business in regard to ethical reference. Almost always the personal, limited view will break down, either for mechanical or other reasons. It broke down badly for me in AKM in the problem of presenting Anne Stanton. I couldn't for the life of me figure out a way to give a proper rendering of her relation to the Boss in terms of the narrator. So I finally did what I did—simply threw that matter on the reader's mercy. I know the limitations of the treatment in general, but I couldn't find any other way into this particular book. The first-person narrative may be what Allen [Tate] once called it, the great alibi of the novelist. But I tend to find more and more that I write best when I write with a very formally defined sort of mask, another person's self. My next novel, I fear, will be of the same sort, but with a very different narrator....

—Special Collections, Vanderbilt University

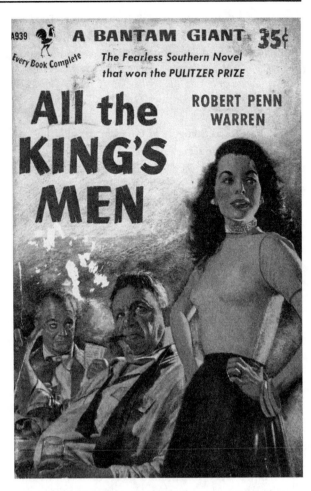

Covers for the first two paperback editions. The Armed Services edition was published in 1946, and the first commercial edition was published in 1951 (left, Matthew J. Bruccoli Collection, Thomas Cooper Library, University of South Carolina; right, Special Collections, Western Kentucky University Libraries).

Talos, had power because he could fulfill some need, some emptiness, of those around him–or far off. I saw that if this idea was part of the center of the action, a play would never serve. The thing had to be "told" in the "voice" of one of the characters whose emptiness Talos fulfilled, but a character intelligent enough to understand everything except himself. I kept looking at the play. I saw the man. He was an unnamed character, not appearing until near the end, a newspaperman, a boyhood friend of Adam Stanton, whom he now greets (with reference to the good times they had had in summers by the sea, in innocent boyhood)–this while Stanton, pistol in pocket, is waiting for Talos to come out of the legislative chamber. The boyhood friend–and his name I suddenly knew–was Jack Burden.

So I had my pattern for the world around Talos–who was to become Willie Stark. Burden was the most complex example, and the most simple was Sugar Boy, the stuttering little chauffeur and gunman for the Boss,

who, when Stark is dead, mourns him, saying: "He could t-t-t-talk so good." I worked at the thing in Minneapolis (distance from the scene and time giving me perspective); then in Washington, where, in the summer of 1944, I had gone to the Library of Congress to "the Chair of Poetry" (in which I wrote some fiction); then in New London, Conn., in the summer of 1945, where on a couple of nights great fleets of bombers, roaring, sky-filling constellations returning from Europe and victory, shook the house; then in an attic room of the library of the University of Minnesota.

The book appeared on August 19. The first major review took it to be an apologia for fascism.

Well.

Further the deponent saith not.

–Warren, "In the time of *All the King's Men,*" *New York Times Book Review*, 31 May 1981, pp. 9, 39–42

* * *

An intellectual who wrote for The Atlantic, Partisan Review, The Nation, The New Yorker, *and* The Saturday Review, *Diana Trilling in this review applied the historical conception of the German philosopher Friedrich Hegel to Warren's novel in this review. Trilling also wrote on Warren in her book* Reviewing the Forties *(1978).*

"The Dialectical Struggle of Good and Evil" Review of *All the King's Men*

Robert Penn Warren's "All the King's Men" (Harcourt, Brace, $3) is not the first novel to draw its inspiration from the career of Huey Long. Some years ago there was John Dos Passos's "Number One," which I have not read, and a few seasons ago there was Hamilton Basso's "Sun in Capricorn," which, as I remember it, dealt rather freely with the actual biography of the Louisiana Kingfish. Mr. Warren would seem to stay closer to his original: he gives us a complete life-story, from the days when his Willie Stark was just an earnest, urgent, back-country farm boy to his early years in law practice and his first venture into politics, through his flashing rise to political power and the governorship, to, finally, his assassination. I say "would seem" because, acquainted with only the broadest outlines of Long's life, I have no way of knowing how much of Mr. Warren's detail is a matter of record and how much supplied by the novelist's imagination. But since Mr. Warren offers his story wholly as fiction, the question of factual accuracy need not be raised.

And a very remarkable piece of novel-writing "All the King's Men" surely is. For sheer virtuosity, for the sustained drive of its prose, for the speed and evenness of its pacing, for its precision of language, its genius of colloquialism, I doubt indeed whether it can be matched in American fiction. Mr. Warren's method is the method of great photography, his poetry an overtone of photographic documentation. Perhaps one must imagine the camera of Walker Evans inching over mile after mile of the South, piling up its record of personal portraits and place portraits and portraits of things, catching fact after fact of the Southern heat and mystery, indolence and venality and despair, in order to begin to have a notion of what and how Mr. Warren sees.

Nor are its imposing gifts of composition the only recommendation of "All the King's Men." There is also its largeness of intention. Mr. Warren's study of a political leader is intended to investigate the moral relativism inherent in the historical process. One might describe it as a fictional demonstration of Hegel's philosophy of history. For what Mr. Warren seems to be saying, with Hegel, is that spirit or goodness arises only out of the ruck of living and the clash of self-seeking wills. He is questioning the absolutes of good and evil which are so much the assumption of a large part [of] our present-day political morality.

ROBERT PENN WARREN

ALL THE KING'S MEN

LONDON
EYRE & SPOTTISWOODE

Title page for the first English edition of Warren's novel, published in 1948, which omitted the Cass Mastern story in chapter 4 (Special Collections, Western Kentucky University Libraries)

But all relativistic positions are peculiarly liable to misinterpretation, and the Hegelian relativism especially must be read very purely not to be translatable into a justification of means by their end, or not to be understood as the belief that good always, even often, has its source in evil. Yet here precisely is the inadequacy of "All the King's Men," that it can give rise to just such misconceptions of what I am sure was its very much purer informing idea. It is in fact difficult *not* to infer from Mr. Warren's novel that a Willie Stark's absolute power is justified by such public benefactions as the fine hospital he builds, or that we are to welcome the Willie Stark type of political unpleasantness as a step in political progress.

In part, of course, this may be the inevitable result of translating the hero of history into a hero of fiction. For concerned with the world historical figure, Hegel was concerned only with his historical or force aspect, not with his ethical aspect; but fiction always deals primarily with individual human beings, and only by suggestion with philosophical abstractions, and when Mr. Warren personifies his abstractions, as the novelist must, he in effects alters a way of viewing history into a system of personal morality from which, then, we evolve a system of political morality. Thus,

---

A Teachable Novel

In this excerpt from a 1972 essay, a college teacher writes about All the King's Men *from the perspective of having taught it in his classes for ten years.*

. . . one sound reason for the continuing popularity and discussion of *All the King's Men* is that it is eminently teachable. *All the King's Men* has for more than twenty years been the subject of countless discussions in the college and university classrooms and corridors. And I assume that a salient reason for this appeal lies exactly in the complex nature of the novel itself. In particular the novel insists on literary, historical, psychological, sociological, philosophical relevance. Its tone is at once satiric and humorous; its mode is both realism and tragedy. Its style, themes, and characters continue to excite both students and teachers alike.

All the King's Men is most teachable as a piece of fiction primarily because it *is* fiction before it is a tract for dictators or a thinly-veiled biography of Huey Long. (But I do not mean that the novel does not accommodate itself well to all these and other approaches simultaneously: indeed I think that it does accommodate itself to a multiplicity of approaches.) No one has yet claimed that this novel is the mythical "great American novel" which every writer is said to be trying to write; but the novel does have literary excellence on several levels.

. . . .

. . . *All the King's Men* succeeds best in the classroom when one has time enough to explore more precisely how the characters, the plot, structure, tone, symbolism—indeed all of these and other elements blend into a pattern. When the multiple themes in the novel are unravelled and made pertinent to modern man, the dimensions of the novel as a work of art begin to unfold.

After all these analyses have been drawn between the novel and life itself, I detect that one important—even overriding—aspect of this book often goes unnoted. The novel is finally about the power of love in the universe to change a man. Warren hints at this in the Dantean epigraph, and he develops this theme in several ways throughout the novel. As a love story with far richer impact than the brand offered in Segal's best

seller, the novel makes an important comment. Jack Burden serves as the catalyst in the objective correlative: he sees, records, and though trying not to, he reacts to his impressions. All of the "love affairs" (Jack's, Willie's, Anne's, Jack's mother's, and others) eventually amount to far more than all the political affairs. Some critics have urged that the novel ends on a sentimental note, that the essential comic ending is too easy, even weak. Perhaps one should argue that it is difficult for calloused moderns to accept readily that the power of love in the universe does radically alter the lives of those who experience it. Jack Burden learns that he has instinctively loved Judge Irwin, though Burden does not know why until long after he discovers that the Judge is his real father. Burden learns to love his mother, whom he has thoroughly despised previously. Burden finally forgives and accepts Anne with all her blemishes, knowing that she too suffers from the deep hurt resulting from her life with Willie and the unmasking of her father's life. Even the Scholarly Attorney takes on a new attraction for Burden, who finally consoles the old man in the face of imminent death. This newest role for Jack is an entirely different one, a sympathetic, compassionate sensitivity brought about by his Damascus-like conversion foreshadowed throughout the book. Popular lyrics of today's songs suggest that what the world needs now is love, love, love. If the novel ends unfashionably tame, one must remember that the comedy envisioned by Dante was a *divine* comedy. Warren is not depicting a Christian medieval world view, but he is suggesting a thoroughly moral universe. A world devoid of love, Warren seems to say, is as chaotic, as purposeless, as irreconcilable as it was before man entered it. (Warren draws the same conclusion in his most recent novel, *Meet Me In the Green Glen.*) This is man's world, and man controls his destiny, and he can "put it back together again" if it seems to fall apart. The novel is not a program for reform nor an apology for an ethical system to discover precisely how man reassembles Humpty Dumpty. But the novel does assert that so long as Eternal Love exists man can be redeemed. Who could ask for anything more.

—Earl Wilcox, "Right On! *All the King's Men* in the Classroom," *Four Quarters,* 21 (May 1972): 69–70, 77–78

Willie Stark is not an evolutionary force, but first a person on whom his author exercises an ethical judgment; and if only because he is the hero of the novel, we must assume that this judgment is largely admiring or approving. The result is that it is the demagogue's usual dull ambivalence—half the obsession with power and half a soft generosity and idealism—that is made to stand for the dialectical struggle of good and evil in both individuals and society.

But it is not merely because he is the hero of the novel that we assume that Stark is approved by his author. We also have the word for it of Mr. Warren's narrator. "All the King's Men" is told through the point of view of a young newspaperman-researcher attached to Stark—one of those prefabricated figures out of the city room whom Mr. Warren endows with a wonderful eye but with no equivalent gift of inward vision. "Wise," cynical, tough but touchable, Jack Burden is better educated than his usual

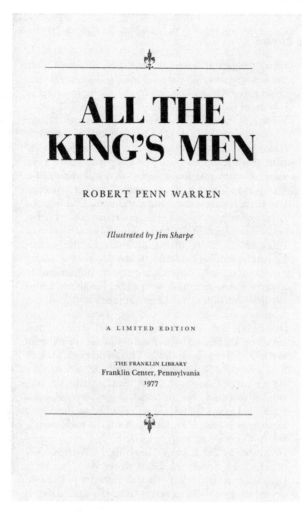

Title page for the second Franklin Library edition of All the King's Men, *which had a tipped-in leaf signed by Warren (Special Collections, Western Kentucky University Libraries)*

And if the low quality of Burden's moral awareness is responsible for most of the ethical and political confusion in "All the King's Men," so must it in some measure account, I think, for the failure of Mr. Warren's novel to achieve an artistic stature commensurate with the author's writing gifts. For one has the idea that were Mr. Warren's narrator to inhabit wider realms of thinking and feeling, he would not only alter our view of the book's central character but also give greater meaning to its subsidiary people, that he would raise all his associates out of the realm of the commonplace and raise their conflicts from melodrama to drama. Certainly the conception of almost all Mr. Warren's characters fails to match the energy of the prose in which they are delineated. While Mr. Warren's language draws upon every resource of actuality, his creation of people lacks all freshness of perception. It is the inner human mystery that Mr. Warren blinks as he pursues the mystery of the historical process.

–Diana Trilling, "Fiction in Review," *Nation*, 163 (24 August 1946): 220

* * *

On the Nature of Things
Review of *All the King's Men*

Robert Penn Warren's third novel is in the tradition of many classics; while it deals with themes and characters that are not confined to its given time, its action is composed of Sunday-supplement history and melodrama. *All the King's Men* is at least the fourth novel to make use of the Huey Long story–it was preceded by Hamilton Basso's *Sun in Capricorn,* John Dos Passos' *Number One* and Adria Locke Langley's best-selling *A Lion Is in the Streets*–but the idealization of Long in the fictional Willie Stark is so complete that Warren can hardly mean his novel to be taken as literal history. And when it is said that the action revolves around the adulterous love of an aristocratic Southern girl for the wool-hat boy who became Governor of a state that in many ways physically and politically resembles Louisiana–when that girl's honor is avenged by her brother and when even a mid-Victorian mysterious parenthood is used to provide a major climax, it must be remembered that the great classic writers from the Greeks to Hemingway worked with no more inventive fables.

To reduce Warren's "plot" to its elements and at the same time avoid a dry absurdity is comparable to an attempt to suggest what "Hamlet" is "about" through a brief paraphrase. In his youth Jack Burden of Burden's Landing had been the friend of Adam and Anne Stanton, the children of Governor Stanton. There had been one summer when Jack and Anne had taken it for granted that they would marry–why they didn't is one of the reasons you will have to read *All the King's Men* practically word for

counterparts in fiction and the movies, but his values are scarcely more fortifying. He is the kind of man, for instance, who, when he perceives that the only thing alive in the face of an Okie to whom he gives a lift on the road is the twitch near his eye, goes on to evolve from this observation an embarrassingly maudlin philosophy–a phantasy of the Great Twitch as a god of doom. Even more significant, he is the kind of man who feels virtually no emotion about his share in the blackmail of a friend, a blackmail that leads the friend to shoot himself, except the pleasure of recognition that a good–a truth–has come from it. But although Jack Burden is so essentially shabby a person that he vulgarizes any thought he entertains or acts out, it is to him that Mr. Warren entrusts an idea of history that requires the nicest discrimination. It is Burden's morally ambiguous evaluation of Stark that we are forced to accept as Mr. Warren's.

word to find out. Years later Jack, having passed through the corruptions of the university, fruitless marriage and newspaper reporting, is the confidential adviser of Willie Stark, who had come down out of the hills to become Governor and overthrow what was left of the world and traditions of the Burdens and the Stantons. The day came when Jack Burden walked into Anne Stanton's room to ask if she and Willie—"Then I looked into her face. She met my gaze quite steadily. I did not say anything. And I did not need to. For, looking at me she slowly nodded." And inevitably Adam was told, and in the corridors of the monstrous capitol that Willie had built, Adam shot him down to be killed immediately by Willie's gunman.

This, with an Elizabethan prodigality of subplotting and an even older use of *in medias res* and the flashback, is the story Jack Burden is given to tell. For in the first place *All the King's Men* is a story, though it is also an excellent political novel, and a genuinely philosophical novel, accomplishments which are rare enough in the history of our fiction. But it is primarily a superbly written narrative in which the surface of the writing is brilliantly integrated with the character of the narrator

and the nature of his experience. The touchstones of such writing in our literature are, of course, *Moby Dick* and *Huckleberry Finn,* and more recently *The Sun Also Rises* and *The Great Gatsby.* The single quality that encompasses these varied books is the use of the full resources of the American language to record with imagination and intelligence a significant aspect of our life. Warren's last novel, *At Heaven's Gate,* suggested that he was one of the few of our writers who knew enough, had thought enough and was blessed with the ability to express his knowledge and his thinking in a dramatic narrative, to produce the really big book *All the King's Men* has turned out to be.

There is one section of the novel that even a preliminary review—as distinguished from a considered criticism—of Warren's novel should attempt to explain. In the course of Jack Burden's work at the university he is given the diary and papers of an ancestor who had died in the Civil War. This Cass Mastern, who becomes the subject of Burden's unfinished doctoral dissertation, had drifted into a violent affair with the wife of a friend which ended with the suicide of the husband and the estrangement of the lovers. When, later,

ROBERT PENN WARREN

All the King's Men

With a New Introduction by the Author

and Illustrations by Warren Chappell

HARCOURT BRACE JOVANOVICH

New York and London

Frontispiece and title page for the thirty-fifth anniversary edition, published with the Book-of-the-Month Club in 1981
(Special Collections, Western Kentucky University Libraries)

the truth of Burden's parentage is uncovered by his own second "job of historical research," after Willie Stark has ordered him to get something on a political rival, the immediate reason for the lengthy (and brilliantly contrived) Cass Mastern story is clear. But it is only upon looking at the novel as a whole that the full meaning of this "journey into the enchantments of the past" begins to take shape. For Warren is not only writing a novel about a group of people at a given time, he is reflecting upon the history of the race and attempting to arrive at a judgment of human action:

> This has been the story of Willie Stark, but it is my story, too. For I have a story. It is the story of a man who lived in the world and to him the world looked one way for a long time and then it looked another and very different way. The change did not happen all at once. Many things happened, and that man did not know when he had any responsibility for them and when he did not. There was, in fact, a time when he came to believe that nobody had any responsibility for anything and there was no god but the Great Twitch. . . .
>
> But later, much later, he woke up one morning to discover that he did not believe in the Great Twitch any more. He did not believe in it because he had seen too many people live and die. He had seen Lucy Stark and Sugar-Boy and the Scholarly Attorney and Sadie Burke and Anne Stanton live and the ways of their living had nothing to do with the Great Twitch. He had seen his father die. He had seen his friend Adam Stanton die. He had seen his friend Willie Stark die, and had heard him say with his last breath, "It might have been all different, Jack. You got to believe that."
>
> He had seen his two friends, Willie Stark and Adam Stanton, live and die. Each had killed the other. Each had been the doom of the other. As a student of history Jack Burden could see that Adam Stanton, whom he came to call the man of idea, and Willie Stark, whom he came to call the man of fact, were doomed to destroy each other, just as each was doomed to try and use the other and to yearn toward and try to become the other, because each was incomplete with the terrible division of their age. But at the same time Jack Burden came to see that his friends had been doomed, he saw that though doomed they had nothing to do with any doom under the godhead of the Great Twitch. They were doomed, but they lived in the agony of will.

This then is a story of some definable people in a certain time and place, and an inquiry into good and evil and the nature of things. All together it is the finest American novel in more years than one would like to have to remember.

–George Mayberry, "On the Nature of Things," *New Republic,* 115 (2 September 1946): 265–266

* * *

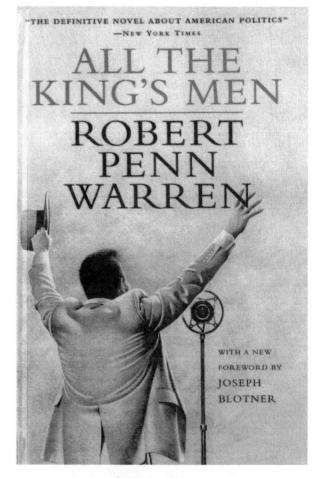

"THE DEFINITIVE NOVEL ABOUT AMERICAN POLITICS"
—NEW YORK TIMES

ALL THE KING'S MEN
ROBERT PENN WARREN

WITH A NEW FOREWORD BY JOSEPH BLOTNER

Cover for the fiftieth-anniversary paperback edition (Special Collections, Western Kentucky University Libraries)

A communist critic through the 1930s, Granville Hicks was the author of The Great Tradition *(1933), a Marxist interpretation of American literature after the Civil War. He resigned from the Communist Party in 1939. This excerpt is from a long review article in which he considered several American novelists.*

"High Craftsmanship"
Review of *All the King's Men*

Like John Dos Passos' *Number One,* Robert Penn Warren's *All the King's Men* was inspired by the character and career of Huey Long, although Warren takes plenty of liberties, just as Dos Passos did. Again like Dos Passos, Warren sees clearly the problem Fast dodged in *The American*—the problem of the leader-demagogue. Warren, however, does more with the problem than Dos Passos managed to do, and in that respect and in almost every other his is a better book than *Number One.*

Indeed, it is such a good book that it puts Warren in the very front rank of American novelists.

Number One is a study of betrayal, the betrayal of an intellectual by a practical politician who lets nothing stand in the way of his conquest of power. *All the King's Men* is a poet-novelist's inquiry into the meaning of history, the meaning of human life itself. Dos Passos' Chuck Crawford may, for all I know, be closer to the real Huey Long than Warren's Willie Stark, but as a character in a novel Willie is more complicated, more convincing, and vastly more interesting than Chuck.

Jack Burden, the narrator of *All the King's Men,* is also a more significant character than Tyler Spotswood, from whose point of view *Number One* is told. Both are déclassé intellectuals who have attached themselves to political bosses, partly because of disillusionment with the ineffectuality of the liberals and the hypocrisy of the respectables, partly because of a remnant of idealism. Tyler fits into the story well enough, but he is too corrupt and too superficial to render all the subtleties of the situation. Jack Burden, on the other hand, not only performs his appropriate rôle in the story of Willie Stark but makes the perfect spokesman for the author. His sensibilities are not dulled, and it is right that his quest for meaning should become the novel's dominant theme.

The first problem of *All the King's Men* is one to which Lincoln Steffens devoted his life, the problem of the political boss. Willie Stark is not a gentleman; his methods are immoral; his egotistic drive for power is boundless. But he gets things done. The second problem is that of Shaw's early plays: in a corrupt society there is no such thing as freedom from guilt. Shaw and Steffens found the same answer to their respective problems: change the system. Warren does not say anything about socialism, but the whole novel demonstrates that it is not enough to alter the rules of the game. Jack Burden's immediate response to his climactic disillusionment is an acceptance of blind materialism—"the dream that all life is but the dark heave of blood and the twitch of the nerve." In time he rejects this dream. He does not say—he cannot say explicitly—what he puts in its place, but he has come to terms with himself, and he can go on living.

It is a temptation to write at length about Warren's ideas, but to do so would be unfair to so rich a piece of fiction as *All the King's Men.* Warren has given his narrator a colloquial and yet sophisticated style that is wholly appropriate to Jack Burden and beautifully suited to the purposes of the novel. Warren keeps as close to common speech as Dos Passos in his best vein, but his prose rises when necessary into brilliant but unforced imagery, and it takes on dignity as Burden's character changes and the demands of the story grow

more intense. It is a prose that is never mannered and yet never lapses into stylelessness.

Although the novel is broad in its scope, the structure is skillfully fashioned, and there is a steady rise from climax to climax. One long interlude, the story of Cass Mastern, who died in the Civil War, seems irrelevant, albeit impressive, at the time one reads it, but its place in the novel is established before the end. As in his earlier novel, *At Heaven's Gate,* Warren shows a surprising knowledge of political and economic affairs—surprising, that is, for a poet and professor—but details of this order are never introduced for their own sake. In every paragraph of the book there is a sense of mastery, which can be given only by high craftsmanship.

In some parts of *At Heaven's Gate* a kind of murkiness suggested William Faulkner. In *All the King's Men* everything is clear, subtle but clear. This is not to say that Warren is a better writer than Faulkner but merely that he has found his own line. He has taken a field for himself, too, an important one. *All the King's Men,* like its predecessor, could be called a social novel, but Warren has discovered that the so-called social problem cannot stand by itself, and he has had the courage to tackle the social problem and the moral problem and the philosophical problem all together. What he makes of them each reader will have to decide for himself. At least the book demonstrates that values are not handed down from on high, nor dreamed up by ambitious social planners, but discovered by men of insight and integrity.

—Granville Hicks, "Some American Novelists," *American Mercury,* 63 (October 1946): 498–500

* * *

Francis Fergusson, who had worked with Warren on the initial stage version of the Willie Stark story, Proud Flesh, *waited until 1954 to write about Warren's novel.*

One of Three Novels

All the King's Men, by Robert Penn Warren, *Guard of Honor,* by James Gould Cozzens, and *The Middle of the Journey,* by Lionel Trilling, are three novels published since the War. They are examples of the best our American fiction can show. Each of them has high intelligence and art; they all have interesting and serious themes; and it would be possible and profitable to do a long study of any one of them.

. . . .

. . . I begin with *All the King's Men,* because it has more of the imaginative scope of poetry than the others. The central story of Mr. Warren's novel is that of the rise to power, the reforming zeal, the corruption and

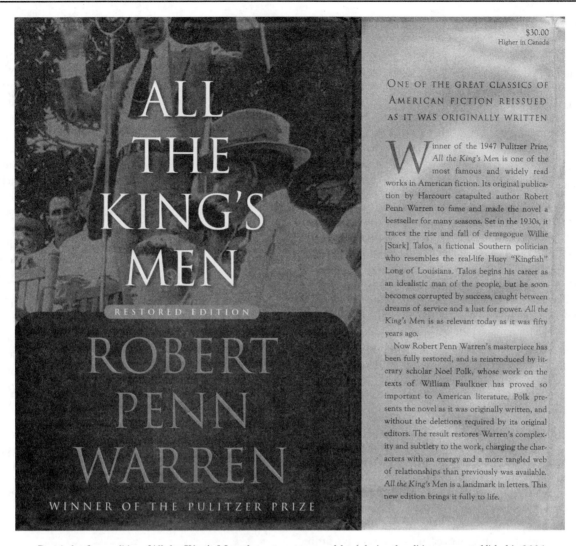

$30.00
Higher in Canada

ONE OF THE GREAT CLASSICS OF
AMERICAN FICTION REISSUED
AS IT WAS ORIGINALLY WRITTEN

Winner of the 1947 Pulitzer Prize, *All the King's Men* is one of the most famous and widely read works in American fiction. Its original publication by Harcourt catapulted author Robert Penn Warren to fame and made the novel a bestseller for many seasons. Set in the 1930s, it traces the rise and fall of demagogue Willie [Stark] Talos, a fictional Southern politician who resembles the real-life Huey "Kingfish" Long of Louisiana. Talos begins his career as an idealistic man of the people, but he soon becomes corrupted by success, caught between dreams of service and a lust for power. *All the King's Men* is as relevant today as it was fifty years ago.

Now Robert Penn Warren's masterpiece has been fully restored, and is reintroduced by literary scholar Noel Polk, whose work on the texts of William Faulkner has proved so important to American literature. Polk presents the novel as it was originally written, and without the deletions required by its original editors. The result restores Warren's complexity and subtlety to the work, charging the characters with an energy and a more tangled web of relationships than previously was available. *All the King's Men* is a landmark in letters. This new edition brings it fully to life.

Dust jacket for an edition of All the King's Men *that restores passages deleted during the editing process, published in 2001 by Harcourt Brace (Richland County Public Library)*

finally the murder of Willie Stark, a figure based upon the late Huey Long. Around the central story many subsidiary narrative strands are woven; and through them we see journalists and farmers, political racketeers and businessmen, bewildered survivors of the old well-to-do classes, in their struggles with each other, and in their attempts to master the industrial power of the new South. The figure of Stark, though very convincing and interesting in itself, is only the center of a panorama of a provincial society in rapid change.

Mr. Warren belongs with Faulkner, Tate, Ransom, Porter, Caldwell, and other distinguished Southerners of various literary persuasions, all of whom suffer and try to digest the changes, usually interpreted as dissolution, which the South has been undergoing since the Civil War. The South, more than any other part of the United States, has misfortunes, and also traditions, both humane and linguistic, which are common to the region, and give it a certain spiritual being. Hence the vitality of contemporary Southern writing. *All the King's Men* has this vitality: it is clear that Mr. Warren has something to say. The characters are objectively living, the language is firm and natural, and full of flashes of poetry. Mr. Warren seems to be talking about people and themes which he has known and instinctively understood for a long time. His prose sometimes touches deep roots, accumulations of meaning beyond the power of the individual merely to *invent*. In short, Mr. Warren speaks for more than himself in this novel: its poetry and authenticity come not only from his talent, but from the human, social, and linguistic forms of his native region.

But still, there is an important distinction between what might be called the materials, the basic inspiration of a work, and the ultimate form and meaning of the whole.

All the King's Men swarms with life; it seems to have the root of poetry in it; yet most readers have felt (and I among them) that it does not quite achieve imaginative coherence. And no wonder; for what Mr. Warren perhaps wanted to make, what the novel sometimes threatens to become, is a panorama of man-in-society in the grand manner, something comparable to one of Shakespeare's histories.

Mr. Warren first planned the Stark tale as a poetic drama, and wrote it as such. I saw an early version of this drama in 1940. The main plot—the story of Willie Stark—was about as we know it in the novel, but most of the sub-plots had not yet appeared. It was in verse, and the dialogue scenes alternated with choruses in lyric verse-forms. The effect of the choruses, if they had been completely successful, would have been to frame the action in a wider context of meaning; to place it, and to emphasize the poetic scope of the whole story. There is now another version of this play, and also a film which was made, not from the play, but from the novel. It would be interesting to study these transformations, to enquire what two different theater directors were able to make of the story which certainly has a not-quite realized, and very tempting, legendary quality. But instead of attempting that (it would lead us too far afield) I proceed to enquire what Mr. Warren did when he rewrote the original play as a novel.

When Mr. Warren turned from the theater to the novel, his native storytelling genius was released. The subplots, full of inherently fascinating characters, incidents, and scenes, clustered about the central theme. Mr. Warren made room for them all, in obedience to his inspiration. He seems to have an inexhaustible store of Southern lives, sights, sounds, and incidents—the immediately exploitable materials of naturalistic fiction. But with all this wealth, the problem of form remained. Mr. Warren endeavored to solve it by replacing the choruses of the play with the narrator of the novel, Jack Burden. That character took over the essential function of framing, defining, and placing the action of the novel as a whole.

Jack Burden is admirably fitted to be the "central intelligence" (as Henry James would have said) through whose eyes the reader gets the story, and learns to understand it. He comes of a good family, and so knows intimately the survivors of the upper class of the Old South. A former student of Southern history, he knows the quality of life before the Civil War. A newspaperman, passionately interested in social justice, he can follow Stark's early attempts at reform with knowledge, hope, and sympathy. And yet he does not quite succeed as chorus, or as Jamesian passionate spectator. He can tell us what happened, but not what to make of it. The typical Jamesian central intelligence, Fleda Vetch, for instance, in *The Spoils of Poynton,* learns and grows as her far simpler drama unfolds. The end of the story for her is very gloomy, but she

accepts it, and thereby gives the reader a sense that the action has some sort of general validity or symbolic value. Her growing, sad wisdom *is* the form and meaning of the novel. But Jack Burden does not really grow and learn in this sense. He is disillusioned rather than made sadder and wiser; thwarted rather than broken and remade. And the reader, looking in vain for the imaginative coherence of the rich scenes of the novel, shares Burden's undigested sense of failure.

But in making this observation I do not wish to be misunderstood. In comparing *All the King's Men* with masterpieces I am paying it a back-handed compliment. No one knows how its rich, diverse, and suggestive elements could be composed. No one knows the answer to the problems—historic, philosophic, or artistic—which it raises.

The South provided Mr. Warren with a great deal, nothing less than the authentic root, or source, of literature. But the Southern tradition does not seem to have offered him the means of composing the rich materials. When Shakespeare wrote his histories, he had the benefit of a myth of British history which had been developing in the work of many predecessors, historians, poets, and other playwrights, as Tillyard has shown. But there seems to be no way to understand the Southern story in Southern terms. *All the King's Men* is far more than local color, but it does not find a more-than-local awareness to appeal to. One feels that the forces at work in the story are not quite in focus; the uncontrolled dynamism of modern industry, for example: perhaps Stark is only its puppet. Or shall we say that like Hitler he is a symptom of the vast discontents of the rootless modern populations? We do not know; the picture grows vague around the edges; the real scene and the real drama (whatever it may be) is not quite grasped. Reading the novel in New York or Michigan, it looks like more than a study of Huey Long, and less than an image of our contemporary fate.

. . . .

. . . Together they [these three novelists] suggest the varied, complex, rich and shifting human life of the country in its instinctive search for form and meaning. They also show the high level which the art of fiction has reached. Thirty years ago one could not have found three novels as serious and as sophisticated as these. Perhaps they are signs of a general effort in this country for understanding and control; part of a pattern of cultural growth which we cannot yet make out.

—Francis Fergusson, "Three Novels," *Perspectives USA,*
no. 6 (Winter 1954): 30, 32–35, 44

Blackberry Winter
and *The Circus in the Attic*

Warren's story "Blackberry Winter," first published sepa-rately in November 1946, was included in his only collection of short fiction, The Circus in the Attic and Other Stories, *published in January 1948, which was composed of stories writ-ten over a span of sixteen years, from 1930 to 1946.*

Prompted by Brooks, Warren wrote this essay for the sec-ond edition of Understanding Fiction. *A version of the essay first appeared in* The New York Times Book Review, *1 March 1959, under the title "Writer at Work: How a Story Was Born and How, Bit by Bit, It Grew." The story is written as a man's recollection of his boyhood encounter with a tramp.*

"Blackberry Winter": A Recollection

I remember with peculiar distinctness the writing of this story, especially the balance, tension, interplay—or what you will—between a sense of compulsion, a sense that the story was writing itself, and the flashes of self-consciousness and self-criticism. I suppose that in all attempts at writing there is some such balance, or oscilla-tion, but here the distinction between the two aspects of the process was peculiarly marked, between the ease and the difficulty, between the elation and, I am tempted to say, the pain. But the pain, strangely enough, seemed to be attached to the compulsion, as though in some way I did not want to go into that remembered world, and the elation attached to the critical effort I had to make to ride herd on the wrangle of things that came milling into my head. Or perhaps the truth is that the process was more complicated than that and I shall never know the truth, even in the limited, provisional way the knowing of truth is possible in such matters.

It crosses my mind that the vividness with which I have always remembered the writing of this story may have something to do with the situation in which it was written. It was the fall or winter of 1945–46 just after the war, and even if one had had no hand in the blood-letting, there was the sense that the world, and one's own life, would never be the same again. I was then reading Herman Melville's poetry, and remember being profoundly impressed by "The Conflict of Convic-tions," a poem about the coming of the American Civil War. Whatever the rights and wrongs of the matter, the war, Melville said, would show "the slimed foundations" of the world. There was the sense in 1945, even with vic-tory, that we had seen the slimed foundations, and as I now write this, the image that comes into my mind is the homely one from my story—the trash washed by the storm from under Dellie's cabin to foul her pridefully clean yard. And I should not be surprised if the picture in

the story had its roots in the line from Melville as well as in such a fact, seen a hundred times in my rural boy-hood. So the mixed feelings I had in our moment of vic-tory in 1945, Melville's poem, and not only the image of Dellie's cabin, but something of the whole import of my little story, belong, it seems, in the same package.

For a less remote background, I had just finished two long pieces of work, a novel called *All the King's Men* and a critical study of Coleridge's poem *The Ancient Mari-ner,* both of which had been on my mind for years. Both those things were impersonal, about as impersonal as the work of any man's hand can be said to be. Even though much of my personal feeling had been drawn into both projects, they belonged to worlds very different from my own. At that time, too, I was living in a very cramped apartment over a garage, in a big, modern, blizzard-bit northern city, again a place very different from the world of my story.

In my daily life, I certainly was not thinking about and remembering that world. I suppose I was living in some anxiety about the fate of the two forthcoming pieces of work, on which I had staked much, and in the unspoken, even denied, conviction that some sort of watershed of life and experience was being approached. For one thing, the fortieth birthday, lately passed, and the sense of let-down after the long period of intense work, could account, in part at least, for that feeling.

Out of this situation the story began, but it began by a kind of accident. Some years earlier, I had written a story about a Tennessee sharecropper, a bad story that had never been published. Now I thought I saw a way to improve it. I don't know whether I actually sat down to rewrite the story that was to have the new avatar of "The Patented Gate and the Mean Hamburger," or whether I got sidetracked into "Blackberry Winter" first. In any case, I was going back into a primal world of recollection. I was fleeing, if you wish. Hunting old bearings and bench-marks, if you wish. Trying to make a fresh start, if you wish. Whatever people do in their doubleness of liv-ing in a present and a past.

I recollect the particular thread that led me back into that past: the feeling you have when, after vacation begins, you are allowed to go barefoot. Not that I ever liked to go barefoot, not with my bony feet. But the priv-ilege itself was important, a declaration of independence from the tyranny of winter and school and, even, your own family. It was like what the anthropologists call a rite of passage. But it had another meaning, too. It car-ried you back into a dream of nature, the woods not the house was now your natural habitat, the stream not the street. Looking out into the snow-banked alley of that iron latitude where I now lived, I had a vague, nostalgic feeling and wondered if spring would ever come. (It finally came—and then on May 5 there was again snow,

BLACKBERRY WINTER

getting on to
It was ~~near the middle of~~ June and past eight o'clock in the morning,
— even if it wasn't a big fire, just a fire of chunks —
but there was a fire, on the hearth of the big stone fireplace in the living
almost into the chimney,
room. I was ~~standing~~ on the hearth , hunched over the ~~fixxx~~ fire, working my
dark gray
bare ~~damp~~ toes slowly on the warm stone and watching the damp from my feet

fade to the pale gray of the stone as the moisture evaporated. I relished the
and creep
heat which made the skin of my bare legs warp and tingle, even as I called

to my mother, who was somewhere back in the dining room or kitchen ,and said:

" But it's June, I don't have to put them on."
     "You put them on if you are going out,"
     ~~Xxxxput×them×on×if×you×axexgxdxgxxx~~   her voice sailed.

     I tried to assess the degree of authority and conviction in the tone, but
I tried to analyze the tone, and then
at that distance it was hard to decide. ~~I×hadxbxbxbxb×x×xxxx×xxpxixtxx~~

I thought what a fool I had been to start out by the back door and let her see

that I was barefoot. If I had gone out the front door or the side door she would

never have known, not till dinner time anyway, and by then the day would have
                                                            from
been half gone and I would have been all over the ~~place~~ to see what the storm had

done and down to the creek to see the flood. But it had never crossed my mind that
they
~~xxykxdx~~ would try to stop you from going barefoot in June, no matter if there
                                                            fl
had been a ~~xixxxx~~ gully-washer and a cold spell. Nobody had ever stopped me in

June as long as I could remember, and when you are nine years old what you ~~can~~

remember seems forever for you remember everything and everything is important

and stands big and full and fills up Time and is so solid that you can walk

around and around it like a tree and look at it. You are aware that time passes,
that there
~~but~~   is a movement in time, but that is not what Time is. Time is not
     a flowing, a wind flow,
movement, but is, rather, a kind of climate in which things are, and when a thing

happens ~~its~~ it begins to live and keeps on living and stands solid in Time like

the tree which you can walk around. And if there is a movement, ~~ixxTixx~~ the

movement is not Time, ~~but~~ more than a breeze is climate, and all the breeze does
                              a little
is to shake the leaves on the ~~solid~~ trees which live and are solid. When you
                              ^

First page from a draft of what is probably Warren's most acclaimed story (Yale Collection of American Literature,
Beinecke Rare Book and Manuscript Library)

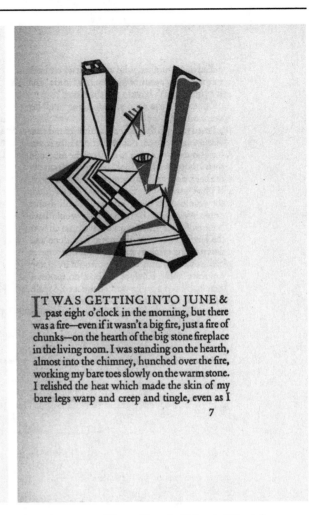

ROBERT PENN WARREN

Blackberry Winter

A STORY ILLUSTRATED BY
WIGHTMAN WILLIAMS

The Cummington Press: August 1946

IT WAS GETTING INTO JUNE &
past eight o'clock in the morning, but there
was a fire—even if it wasn't a big fire, just a fire of
chunks—on the hearth of the big stone fireplace
in the living room. I was standing on the hearth,
almost into the chimney, hunched over the fire,
working my bare toes slowly on the warm stone.
I relished the heat which made the skin of my
bare legs warp and creep and tingle, even as I

7

Title page and the first text page for an edition limited to 330 copies (Special Collections, Western Kentucky University Libraries)

and the heavy-headed blooms of lilac were beautiful with their hoods of snow and beards of ice.)

With the recollection of going barefoot came another, which had been recurrent over the years: the childhood feeling of betrayal when early summer gets turned upside-down, and all its promises are revoked by the cold-spell, the gully-washer. So by putting those two recollections together, the story got started. I had no idea where it was going, if anywhere. Sitting at the typewriter was merely a way of indulging nostalgia. But something has to happen in a story, if there is to be more than a dreary lyric poem posing as a story to promote the cause of universal boredom and deliquescent prose. Something had to happen, and the simplest thing ever to have happen is to say: *Enter, mysterious stranger*. And so he did.

The tramp who thus walked into the story had been waiting a long time in the wings of my imagination—an image drawn, no doubt, from a dozen unremembered episodes of childhood, the city bum turned country tramp, suspicious, resentful, contemptuous of hick dumbness, bringing his own brand of violence into a world where he half-expected to find another kind, enough unlike his own to make him look over his shoulder down the empty lane as dusk came on, a creature altogether lost and pitiful, a dim image of what, in one perspective, our human condition is. But then, at that moment, I was merely thinking of the impingement of his loose-footedness and lostness on a stable and love-defined world of childhood.

Before the tramp actually appeared, I had, however, known he was coming, and without planning I began to write the fourth paragraph of the story, about the difference between what time is when we have grown up and what it was when we stood on what, in my fancy phrase in the story, I called the glistening auroral beach of the world—a phrase which belonged, by the way, to an inland boy who had never seen a beach but whose dreams were all of the sea. Now the tramp came up, not merely out of the woods, but out of the darkening grown-up world of time.

The tramp had, literally, come up through the river woods, and so in the boy's literal speculations he sees the tramp coming through the woods. By now, however, the natural thematic distinction touched on in relation to time is moving into a pattern, the repetition in fiction of the established notion in a new guise. So when the boy sees the mental image of the tramp coming though the woods, there is the distinction set up between the way a man, particularly such a man as this, would go through woods, and the way a boy can stand in the woods in absolute quiet, almost taking root and growing moss on himself, trying to catch the rhythm, as it were, of that vegetative life, trying to breathe himself into that mode of being.

But what would this other, woodland, vegetative world of being carry with it in human terms—in terms, that is, of what a story must be about? I can promise that the passage was written on impulse, but an impulse conditioned by the idea that there had to be an expressed difference between boy-in-woods and tramp-in-woods, the tramp who doesn't know what a poult is and thinks the final degradation is to mess with a flower bed. And so here we are back to the contrast between the tramp's world and that of childhood innocence appearing in some sense of a rapport between the child and nature, his feeling that he himself might enter that very life of nature.

As soon as the passage was written I knew its import; I was following my nose, trusting, for what they were worth, my powers of association, hoping that those powers would work in relation to a pattern that had begun to emerge as a series of contrasts. And it was natural, therefore, after a few paragraphs about the strangeness and fish-out-of-waterness of the tramp, his not knowing about dogs for example, to have the mother's self-sufficiency set against the tramp's rude, resentful uncertainty, and then have her portrait at the time of the episode set against the time when she would be dead, and only a memory—though back then, of course, in the secure world of changelessness and timelessness, it had never crossed the boy's mind that "she would ever be dead."

The instant I wrote that clause I knew, not how the story would end, for I was still writing by guess and by God, but on what perspective of feeling it would end. I knew that it would end with a kind of detached summary of the work of time, some hint of the adult's grim orientation toward that fact. From now on, the items that came on the natural wash of recollection came not only with their, to me, nostalgic quality, but also with the freighting of the grimmer possibilities of change—the flood, which to the boy is only an exciting spectacle but which will mean hunger to others, the boy's unconscious contempt for poor white-trash like Milt Alley, the recollection of hunger by the old man who had ridden with Forrest, Dellie suffering in her "woman mizry." But before I had got to Del-

lie, I already had Old Jebb firmly in mind, with some faint sense of the irony of having his name remind one—or at least me—of the dashing Confederate cavalryman killed at Yellow Tavern.

Perhaps what I finally did with Dellie stemmed, in fact, from the name I gave Old Jebb. Even if the boy would see no irony in that echo of J. E. B. Stuart's fame, he would get a shock when Dellie slapped her beloved son, and would sense that that blow was, in some deep way, a blow at him. I knew this, for I knew the inside of that prideful cabin, and the shock of early recognition that beneath mutual kindliness and regard some dark, tragic, unresolved something lurked. And with that scene with Dellie, I felt I was forecasting the role of the tramp in the story. The story, to put it another way, was now shifting

---

The Stranger as Mentor in "Blackberry Winter"

Someone has attributed to Freud the observation that the world is what your neighbors, not your parents, say it is. In the case of the protagonist of "Blackberry Winter" and his avatars in the poems, the world is what both neighbors and a down-at-heels stranger say it is, and the stranger whom the boy follows "all the years" paradoxically becomes a mentor less remote and more ambivalently attractive than his biological father. Because they are loving, the parents are readily and predictably monitory figures; they order, they cajole, they reason with, they advise, they teach. The stranger emerges out of a world unshaped by love, whose lessons are pronounced in sparing croaks, taunts, threats. The stranger is untidy, old (even when the age is vague), grizzled, dispossessed, probably urban; he is enveloped by a private rage whose sources can never be known. The circumstances suggest that *existence* generates rage, explanations for which are hardly capable of being articulated except through weary exhalations, furious exclamations, and expletives that fall staccato-like on the ears of the boy.

The intrusive stranger is a mentor not because of what he says or does but because of what he is. If moral authority is invested, however reluctantly, in such a figure, we should not be surprised at the lack of consolatory wisdom in Robert Penn Warren's later writing. For with the rage to know, to understand, to interpret, what solace can be found in spiritual transience? deprivation and dispossession? restlessness as the moral equivalent of maturity? The stranger is, in a sense, the world's voice, the voice of actuality.

–James H. Justus, "Warren as Mentor: Pure and Impure Wisdom," in *The Legacy of Robert Penn Warren,* edited by David Madden (Baton Rouge: Louisiana State University Press, 2000), pp. 2–13

Fiedler on Warren's Long Stories

Iconoclastic critic Leslie A. Fiedler considered Warren's collection The Circus in the Attic *in a long review article in which he commented on eight books, including Truman Capote's* Other Voices, Other Rooms, *Ross Lockridge's* Raintree County, *and Lionel Trilling's* The Middle of the Journey.

The genius of prose fiction at the present moment seems to inhere in the long story, the novella, such forms as Robert Penn Warren achieves in "Prime Leaf," "Blackberry Winter" and the title story of his collection, pieces whose proposed unity is neither too tight for reflection, nor too loose for a single, anecdotal revelation; but such a form falls hopelessly between the demands of the magazine and book-length.

. . . .

Warren's successes are pre-eminently in the novel, especially in *All the King's Men,* into which has been absorbed what is perhaps the best short-story he has done. "Cass Mastern's Wedding Ring"–for in his basic understanding of fate and free-will there is justification for the full-blown plot of discovery and reversal, redeemed from technique to meaning. In the very short story his perceptions cannot find an adequate philosophical focus, but the Concept of Original Sin, the obsessive motif of his prose and verse, in longer things like the very early "Prime Leaf" or the quite recent "Blackberry Winter" is realized quite successfully in terms of political action and personal recognition: the revelation of choice and the limitation of evil. The 19th Century assertion of personal pessimism and social hope is here precisely reversed; freedom is inward, necessity outward; evil *real.*

–Leslie A. Fiedler, "The Fate of the Novel," *Kenyon Review,* 10 (Summer 1948): 519–527

Article in a Kentucky newspaper on the possible inspiration for the title story of Warren's The Circus in the Attic and Other Stories, *published in 1948 (courtesy of Mrs. Robert D. Frey)*

emphasis from the lyricism of nostalgia to a concern with the jags and injustices of human relationships. What had earlier come in unconsciously, reportorially, in regard to Milt Alley now got a conscious formulation.

I have said that the end was by now envisaged as a kind of summary of the work of time on the human relationships. But it could not afford to be a mere summary: I wanted some feeling for the boy's family and Jebb's family to shine through the flat surface. Now it struck me that I might build this summary with Jebb as a kind of pilot for the feeling I wanted to get; that is, by accepting, in implication at least, something of Jebb's feeling about his own life, we might become aware of our human communion. I wanted the story to give some notion that out of change and loss a human recognition may be redeemed, more precious for being no longer innocent. So I wrote the summary.

When I had finished the next to the last paragraph I still did not know what to do with my tramp. He had already snarled at the boy, and gone, but I sensed that in the pattern of things his meaning would have to coalesce with the meaning I hoped to convey in the summary about the characters. Then, for better or worse, there it was. In his last anger and frustration, the tramp had said to the boy: "You don't stop following me and I cut yore throat, you little son-of-a-bitch."

Had the boy then stopped or not? Yes, of course, literally, in the muddy lane. But at another level—no. In so far as later he had grown up, had really learned something of the meaning of life, he had been bound to follow the tramp all his life, in the imaginative recognition, with all the responsibility which such a recognition entails, of this lost, mean, defeated, cowardly, worthless, bitter being as somehow a man.

So what had started out for me as, perhaps, an act of escape, of fleeing back into the simplicities of childhood, had turned, as it always must if we accept the logic of our lives, into an attempt to bring something meaningfully out of that simple past into the complication of the present. And what had started out as a personal indulgence had tried to be, in the end, an impersonal generalization about experience, as a story must always try to be if it accepts the logic of fiction. And now, much later, I see that the story and the novel which I had then only lately finished, as well as the study of Coleridge, all bore on the same end.

I would give a false and foolish impression if I were to imply that I think this to be the only way a story should be written, or that this is the only way I myself have ever written stories. As a matter of fact, most of my stories and all of my novels (except two unpublished ones) have started very differently, from some objective situation or episode, observed or read about, something that caught my eye and imagination so that feeling and interpretation began to flow in. And I sometimes think it

strange that the last story I ever wrote and presumably the last I shall ever write (for poems are great devourers of stories) should have sprung so instinctively from the world of simple recollection—not a blackberry winter at all, but a kind of Indian summer.

I would give a false impression, too, if I were to imply that this story is autobiographical. It is not. I never knew these particular people, only that world and people like them. And no tramp ever leaned down at me and said for me to stop following him or he would cut my throat. But if one had, I hope that I might have been able to follow him anyway, in the way the boy in the story does.

—Warren, "'Blackberry Winter': A Recollection," in *Understanding Fiction,* second edition (New York: Appleton-Century-Crofts, 1959), pp. 638–643

Warren on Teaching

Despite his success as a writer, Warren remained dedicated to teaching, as is clear from his response to Granville Hicks, who wrote to Warren on 9 February 1947 in regard to an article he was planning to write on writers as teachers of writing:

I am writing to you because you have taught more consistently than any writer of comparable standing I know of. Would you be willing to tell me what conclusions you draw from your experience? I am interested, of course, both in the effect of your teaching on your writing and in the effect of your writing on your teaching. What, for instance, would you advise a young man who wanted to be a writer and was considering becoming a teacher? On the other side, if you were chairman of an English department, would you make a special effort to secure writers? If you do feel that writers should teach writing, can you suggest ways in which they could be helped to do the maximum of creative work? Should colleges, for instance, hire writers on a part-time basis or arrange for periodic leaves?

—Yale Collection of American Literature, Beinecke Rare Book and Manuscript Library

Hicks concluded his letter: "If you saw my review in the Mercury, you know how very much impressed I was by 'All the King's Men'—and I was a good deal irritated by some of the reviews."

Warren to Granville Hicks, 18 February 1947

Dear Mr. Hicks:

I'll do what I can—and gladly—to answer your questions about the business of mixing teaching and writing. But some of the answers will be rather fumbling efforts because on some of the questions my mind isn't too clear.

As for the effect of my teaching on my writing and my writing on my teaching, that is the most difficult question for me to have any answer for. For one thing, there are only twenty-four hours in the day, and either teaching or writing can be a full-time job. So, obviously, something is going to get robbed in such a situation and I don't see any use in trying to disguise that fact. Let's take the teaching: the amount of time one puts on writing and on doing stuff associated with the writing that doesn't have any connection with study for courses is undoubtedly to be discounted from the amount of time that would, ideally, be available for course preparation. So the writer-teacher has a strike against him right there. (He can draw some comfort from the fact that some of his colleagues who don't write don't devote much more time than he does to the business of study and teaching, but that point we shall let lie off to one side.) The question then arises, does the fact of writing give something to his teaching which wouldn't otherwise be there? I am inclined to think that, theoretically at least, there is some compensation here, that the effort to write does teach you something about the nature of literature. At least, I think I have learned some things, however small, by trying to write. But I must grant here that I am not one of those people who hold that only writers "understand" literature even in the close, technical way that a writer has to try to understand it. I know some people who have never written anything but straight expository prose in their ordinary line of academic business but who have, to my way of thinking, a wonderful sense of the things which writing is supposed to teach you. But by and large, I am inclined to believe that writers have a sense of the means-ends relationship in a piece of literature which is not had by a good many of their colleagues with a straight academic interest. How these things are to be weighed off against each other, I don't pretend to know. I suppose you would have to take each case on its merits.

Another matter: I am inclined to think, from my own experience, that teaching, or rather the academic environment, may help a writer in keeping him aware of some perspective on his own and on other contemporary writing. In some strictly "literary" associations I have been oppressed by the fact that everything seemed to hinge on what was written yesterday morning. I have encountered enough living examples in the academic profession to believe that it can produce people (not too many, but some) who can really assimilate their learning into a fine, humanistic attitude and who can keep, or gain, a discriminating literary sensibility. I know that I have profited greatly from my contact with such people in universities; and it [is] damned hard to find them outside of universities. They are, of course, not too easy to find in universities. I don't see any point in denying the fact that a certain number of teachers of

literature are academic plumbers and loathe any writing which doesn't come to them in the guaranteed, handy-pack, cellophane-wrapped carton of English 279 in such-and-such a graduate school. And they would loathe that piece of literature in the handy-pack carton, too, if they ever bothered to open the carton and see what they had really bought. But this kind of person isn't really much of a problem, unless, of course, he happens to have an administrative job just over your head. You can usually dodge them and get what benefit is available from your more admirable colleagues. The worst thing that such people do to you in a university is to distract you from the real good you can get from the good things in the academic world—make you feel like throwing out the baby with the bath.

All the way above I have been thinking of the teaching not being primarily the teaching of writing. In fact, I can't think of anything much worse than doing a full-time job of teaching writing. For me, at least. One of the advantages of teaching is that you are led to do some relatively systematic reading of things which you find valuable in themselves—that is, if you are teaching congenial courses. If you devote most of your time to teaching writing, then you don't get the reading done. You are reading student writing all the time. Now a certain amount of student writing is stimulating, even when it isn't good, because it raises a good many questions which are worth thinking about, usually technical questions. But to do nothing but teach writing would be pretty grim. I have always avoided giving more than one writing course, and sometimes I haven't given any. This line of objection would not hold, of course, if a man were, say, giving one writing course at a university on a part-time basis, or something like that. And it might not hold for anybody but me, anyway.

As for the way of teaching writing, I don't know any way but the attempt to teach reading, to show as well as you can how in standard pieces of literature means and ends are related, and how attitudes and ideas achieve some kind of form and are related to style. Then the students have something to go on, some basis for self-criticism. There are limited ways, of course, in which you can help with particular problems, but for one case where you can do some good in this direct way, there are dozens of cases where you can't. Or at least, I can't. So courses in writing boil down into courses in interpretation within some sort of historical framework.

You ask me what I would advise a young man who wanted to be a writer. I'm not long on advice. There are two factors here of great importance. One is, I suppose, the matter of the young man's temperament. If he doesn't have some kind of a taste for university life, it would be hell on earth to try to teach and write at the same time. The other factor is the kind of place where he is to teach.

Warren and Cinina in January 1948 en route to Sicily. The Warrens were experiencing serious tension in their marriage; each of them had seen psychiatrists about their relationship (Robert Penn Warren Birthplace Museum, Guthrie, Kentucky).

In the right kind of place, the relationship between the writer and his colleagues can be fruitful for all concerned. In the wrong kind of place, pretty bad. I've seen both situations, though I personally have always been pretty lucky on this count.

Yes, if I were a chairman of a department I would make an effort to hire a writer or two. But here there is a nice little problem. Just because a man is a writer, or even a good writer, doesn't mean that he would be worth a damned thing around a university. I've known one or two extremely good writers who couldn't communicate a thing except in their actual writing. And again there is no use having a writer around a university if the writer is contemptuous of the whole business and is cynically picking up some small change. It will almost certainly be small change. —Another point: I don't think that a man has to be a writer to be the best kind of teacher of writing. By and large, it is probably better to have a writer doing that work, but I know some men who are superb at it who are not writers themselves. And a course in Shakespeare taught right will teach a student a lot more about writing than most writing courses ever did. If the student is any good.

Should colleges try to hire writers on a part-time basis or arrange for periodic leaves of absence? God, yes. The question is getting the money, I suppose. The trouble with being both a writer and a teacher is that you are constantly scrambling for time. If an institution wants good writers it ought to realize that writing isn't something done late on Sunday afternoon or in the month of August. For a certain length of time you can keep on shifting gears back and forth, but in the end that becomes a considerable strain. Writing requires long periods of work with the feeling that you can afford to waste time if you have to. It is hard to do that in between classes.

Another thought: or rather, two thoughts: First, there is a sort of faddism that gets associated sometimes with writing courses in universities, the notion that you ought to try to teach a lot of people to write. I don't think we even ought to want to teach a lot of people to write. The best ones would probably become writers anyway, and the only thing that the university can do for them is to help them cut a few corners in the process. The long-range benefit educationally of writing courses is probably to make better readers, to give more people some sense of the way a piece of writing operates, to bring it closer home. Second, the terrible thing about teaching is that you have to say the same damned thing so often you begin to believe it yourself and forget that in the first place it was just a pretty good guess at the best. Robert E. Lee once said of war, that it was well that war was so terrible, otherwise you would come to like it too much; it is well that teaching is so terrible, otherwise you would come to like it too much and probably for the wrong reasons.

I look back over what I've written and it all sounds pretty flat and dull. Maybe it has to be. But in any case, it is the best I can do. If it is too dull, just throw it away.

Yes, I did see your review of AKM in the *Mercury,* and was greatly pleased with it. I couldn't have hoped for a more sympathetic reading, and I was grateful for it.

With sincere regards,
Robert Penn Warren

–Special Collections Research Center,
Syracuse University Library

The Movie of *All the King's Men*

These publicity notes for the movie version indicate some of the changes that director Robert Rossen made in Warren's novel. The movie, in which the focus is on Willie Stark rather than Jack Burden, won the Oscar for best picture in 1949.

Publicity Notes for *All the King's Men*

Not since the days of D.W. Griffith and the other early film makers has a picture been directed–and written and produced–as Robert Rossen has done all three for Columbia on "All the King's Men." One of the first pictures to be made in toto for the American market under curtailed European distribution, it is unlikely that the grass roots theme, grass roots aim, and grass roots production would even be understood by Europeans. This is a picture for Americans, about American state politics, made with and by Americans.

Almost the entire picture was made on location in the northern California towns of Suisun, Fairfield and

Scene from All the King's Men; *standing, left to right: Mercedes McCambridge as Sadie Burke, John Ireland as Jack Burden, Broderick Crawford as Willie Stark, and Walter Burke as Sugar Boy (courtesy of Columbia Pictures)*

Warren, 1...
1049

Columbia Pictures Corporation
Presents

ROBERT ROSSEN'S
Production
of

ALL THE KING'S MEN

Based upon the Pulitzer Prize novel,
"All The King's Men"
By ROBERT PENN WARREN

with

BRODERICK CRAWFORD
JOANNE DRU
JOHN IRELAND
JOHN DEREK

Mercedes McCambridge
Shepperd Strudwick
Ralph Dumke
Anne Seymour
Katharine Warren
Raymond Greenleaf
Walter Burke
Will Wright
Grandon Rhodes

Director of Photography........................BURNETT GUFFEY, A.S.C.
Art Director................................... STURGES CARNE
Film Editor................................... AL CLARK
Editorial Adviser............................. ROBERT PARRISH
Set Decorator................................. LOUIS DIAGE
Montages......................................DONALD W. STARLING
Gowns by...................................... JEAN LOUIS
Assistant Director............................SAM NELSON
Makeup by..................................... CLAY CAMPBELL
Hair Styles by................................ HELEN HUNT
Sound Engineer................................ FRANK GOODWIN
Musical Score by..............................LOUIS GRUENBERG
Musical Director..............................MORRIS STOLOFF

Assistant to the Producer..................... SHIRLEY MILLER

Written for the Screen and Directed by................ROBERT ROSSEN

CAST OF CHARACTERS

Willie Stark....................BRODERICK CRAWFORD
Anne Stanton....................JOANNE DRU
Jack Burden.................... JOHN IRELAND
Tom Stark......................JOHN DEREK
Sadie Burke....................MERCEDES McCAMBRIDGE
Adam Stanton...................SHEPPERD STRUDWICK
Tiny Duffy.....................RALPH DUMKE
Lucy Stark ....ANNE SEYMOUR
Mrs. Burden ....KATHARINE WARREN
Judge Stanton ....RAYMOND GREENLEAF
Sugar Boy ....WALTER BURKE
Dolph Pillsbury................WILL WRIGHT
Floyd McEvoy...................GRANDON RHODES
Pa Stark.......................H. C. MILLER
Hale...........................RICHARD HALE
Commissioner................... WILLIAM BRUCE
Sheriff........................A. C. TILLMAN
Madison........................HOUSELEY STEVENSON
Minister....................... TRUETT MYERS
Football Coach................. PHIL TULLY
Helene Hale....................HELENE STANLEY

* * * *

Credits for the movie version of Warren's novel (Robert Penn Warren Papers, Beinecke Rare Book and Manuscript Library)

*Poster for the movie that was released in 1949 and won an Oscar for best motion picture (courtesy of Columbia Pictures;
Robert Penn Warren Birthplace and Museum, Guthrie, Kentucky)*

Stockton, and in the countryside surrounding them. Unusual, too, is the fact that both interiors and exteriors were shot on the spot—courthouse and bar and house and hotel serving in lieu of sound stage.

But more than that, Rossen used literally thousands of the residents of the northern sections of the state, not only in background shots, although they were used extensively for this purpose, but in acting and speaking roles as well. Some of these northern Californians were even brought on to Hollywood later to complete their roles in the two weeks of work remaining on the sound stages after the company came back from location.

The book from which the picture was made is Robert Penn Warren's Pulitzer Prize-winning novel for 1946.

In transferring the novel to the screen, Rossen has departed in some measure from the story Warren wrote. His interpretation of the leading character, the venal Governor Willie Stark, is one of a man not black and white, both good and bad, as the writer made him, but a man with the seeds of his own and evil destruction already well sprouted when he begins his climb, ending in death and oblivion. This difference of interpretation does not affect the whole story, however, and is signalized by the absence of the memorial hospital which Warren had Stark build, and which Rossen leaves unbuilt in his story—since any such act would imply some good, however little, in the unsavory politician.

Broderick Crawford undoubtedly gets the best role of his career since the memorable Lennie he created on Broadway for John Steinbeck's "Of Mice and Men," as Willie Stark, the governor of an American state, who almost establishes an absolute government of his own before he is shot down by one of the three or four people he has befriended.

Joanne Dru is seen in the role of the patrician daughter of a former governor, in love with the young newspaperman played by John Ireland, but caught up, nevertheless, in the legend Willie Stark manages to weave about himself. It is Ireland who, when Stark is dead, remains on to destroy that legend—the legend that Stark was a great man. It's easily Ireland's biggest role up to now, too.

Mercedes McCambridge, brought on from the New York stage and radio, plays the hatchet woman, Sadie, who becomes the governor's secretary. Miss McCambridge is one of the most talented actresses in radio, and has been widely praised by the stars she has played with, among whom are Ronald Colman, Orson Welles, and others.

John Derek, Anne Seymour, Katharine Warren, Ralph Dumke, Walter Burke, Will Wright, and dozens of others, some of them from Hollywood and the screen, some of them from New York and the stage and radio and television, play supporting roles to Crawford, Dru, Ireland, and McCambridge.

But, aside from story and players, this is one picture that will be judged strictly on a production basis.

Rossen's method of procuring players was to advertise in the papers in towns surrounding San Francisco; and what he advertised for was people. "If they look like people who would live in these towns," he said, "they will look like the people in my picture."

How right he was was proved when scenes made later in Hollywood had to be retaken with northern California people brought down for the occasion, because worldly-wise looking Hollywood extras and bit players brought in for the scenes just didn't look like the rural Americans who had previously been used.

For more unusual parts, the director and his staff picked people they saw on the streets, rushed them before the cameras for a test, and put them in roles the following day.

As with people, so with the weather. The director took the weather as it came, and it came; this time, in one of the worst winters the west coast has seen in some time. Snow, sleet, hail, rain, mist and fog visited the company on alternate days during the month-long location, and Rossen shot in all of them.

"I suppose in almost any American state you can name," he said, "they have weather. This will be no Hollywood sunshine movie. Weather, and good strong weather, fits our plot. We'll take it as it comes." The cameras were handled by first cameraman Burnett Guffey and Ray Corey.

Shooting naturalistic scenes meant the use of thousands of people in this "unusual" weather, day and night, in the streets, in torchlight parades, at football games, before the governor's house, and before the other state buildings.

Wherever possible, people in actual jobs such as those needed in the picture were actually used. Thus state troopers were played by California highway police, and a state legislature was played in the Stockton County courthouse by Stockton jurists, lawyers, district attorneys and similar local figures.

It was very good fun for the native Californians who had a chance to play roles in this exciting picture; but it was very serious picture-making for Rossen, who used the same method to some extent in "Johnny O'Clock," when he brought real gamblers from Las Vegas to play the gamblers of the picture, and in "Body and Soul," when he used sporting district characters from all over Los Angeles to play themselves in the picture.

It is, he is convinced, the way to make a picture with body—with power—and to make it realistically, like a newsreel of the actual happening.

—Beinecke Rare Book and Manuscript Library

World Enough and Time

In the late 1940s Brooks and Warren were completing their fourth textbook, Modern Rhetoric *(1949), and Warren was working on his fourth novel,* World Enough and Time. *In 1948 Warren wrote Brooks that his three classes at the University of Minnesota had 190 students and that he was ready to leave Minnesota. Brooks had left LSU in 1947 to join the Yale faculty, and he did what he could to see that Warren be offered a position at the university.*

In 1949 and 1950 Cinina Warren was in and out of hospitals for inflammatory gastritis, back problems, and alcoholism. Finally, in spring 1950 she was admitted to a psychiatric hospital in New York after suffering a breakdown. Warren also experienced physical difficulties—a fall in 1948 had left him with a broken toe and pain in his ankle and knee; in 1950 he was treated for gallstones—but he was far more troubled by the stress he experienced because of his failing marriage. Through all of his personal difficulties, Warren remained dedicated to his writing.

Awards and recognitions continued to come his way. Vanderbilt University honored him with a Distinguished Alumnus Award, and he became a member of the National Institute of Arts and Letters as well as elected Chancellor of the American Academy of Poets. In fall 1950 he joined the Yale faculty, to which he was named professor of playwriting in the Yale School of Drama the following spring.

Random House published World Enough and Time *in June 1950 and became Warren's publisher for the rest of his career. His decision to change publishers was influenced by his friend Albert Erskine, who had joined Random House after he left Reynal and Hitchcock.*

World Enough and Time *received mixed reviews. This excerpt is from a review by Carlos Baker, who also commented on Ernest Hemingway's* Across the River and Into the Trees. *Baker is best known for his biography* Ernest Hemingway: A Life Story *(1969).*

Through the Iron Gates
Review of *World Enough and Time*

These two novels bear no superficial resemblances. Robert Penn Warren's *World Enough and Time* is a richly dense historical romance of the Kentucky frontier in the first thirty years of the nineteenth century. It is a work long meditated, painstakingly constructed, and written with that immense care and poetic attention which one has come to expect of the author of *At Heaven's Gate* and *All the King's Men*. Evidently Warren has crude and violent world enough, and above all time enough, for the pitiless and nearly exhaustive exploitation of his materials. In Ernest Hemingway's account of the last days of Colonel Cantwell, *Across the River and Into the Trees,* one finds on the other hand a sufficient world—the past thirty years of the present century in the half-bitter, half-loving

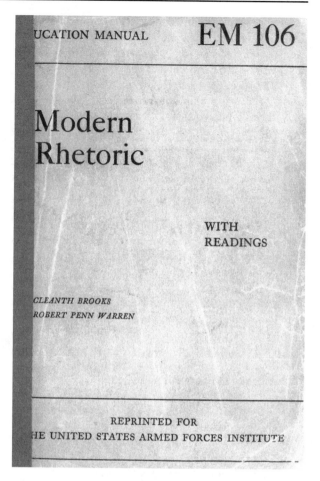

Cover for an edition of Brooks and Warren's fourth textbook (Special Collections, Western Kentucky University Libraries)

recollection of a professional soldier. But the intrinsic sense of urgency which arises from Cantwell's consciousness of imminent death-by-heart-failure is extrinsically reflected in the nervous conduct of the book, as if Hemingway (like his hero) could feel the horses of Time's winged chariot breathing uncomfortably down the back of his neck. For this novel is not, we are told, the long-awaited major successor to *For Whom the Bell Tolls,* the high-piled manuscript on which he has been at work sporadically since 1940. This is the short book he decided to write after he nearly died of a badly infected eye, the outcome of a shooting mishap last year in Italy. World enough, certainly. All the world that Hemingway has adventured in. But not time enough to wrap it up in.

Like Browning's story of Pompilia and Caponsacchi and Guido, Warren's novel grows out of the free imaginative reconstruction of one of the darkest old crimes in Kentucky's legal annals. Warren's "old yellow book," found in Frankfort rather than Florence, is the record of the trial of Jeroboam O. Beauchamp for the

CONFESSION

I am the second son of a most worthy and respectable farmer. My parents at an early period of my life became professors of the Christian religion, and ever after lived quite piously up to its dictates. The early part of my education, which generally has a lasting impression on the bent of the mind, was of a most pious and salutary kind. I was much of a favorite with my fond father, although of a most wild, eccentric and ungovernable temper of mind. But he was flattered by his friends that I early showed some indications of genius; wherefore, at their solicitation, he determined to give me an education much beyond his limited fortune; for he was not wealthy though his enterprise and industry had made him comfortably independent for the country life.

I was placed quite early in the best schools in his reach. I was naturally of a most volatile, idle and wild disposition. But the great ease with which I acquired whatever learning I turned my attention to, enabled me so far to gain the favor of my tutors as to interest my father's friends to advise him to put me somewhere under an able teacher, in order to acquire a thorough classical education, although his numerous, rising family seemed to render his ability to complete it hopeless. But fortune placed me under the care of a man of great abilities and learning, to whose paternal affection and attachment to me I cannot here withhld this last passing tribute of my gratitude. This was

First page from an early draft of World Enough and Time *that was titled "The Confessions of Jereboam Beauchamp"*
(Robert Penn Warren Papers, Beinecke Library, Yale University)

Erskine as Editor

Warren wrote to Brooks from Santa Monica, California, where he was meeting with director Robert Rossen.

Warren to Brooks, 12 September 1949

Albert was out here for two or three weeks. He and I worked hard at the revision of the novel. I had always known that Albert was about the perfect editor, but I really didn't understand how good he is until I was the subject being worked on. He did a truly remarkable job for yours truly. The best thing is that he can propose simple remedies for complicated diseases–remedies that really work. We had a little fun on the side, but we did get the job done in so far as he and I could do it together. Now it's a matter of my doing the private sweating.

–Cleanth Brooks and Robert Penn Warren:
A Literary Correspondence, p. 172

---

vengeance-murder (or political assassination, or both) of Colonel Solomon P. Sharp, one-time Attorney General of Kentucky. The trial stirred many Southern writers. For nearly two decades after Beauchamp's trial in 1826 men like William Gilmore Simms, Charles Fenno Hoffman, Thomas Holley Chivers, and even E. A. Poe exploited the case in fiction and drama. Among the back-country elaborations of the material were at least three folk-ballads on the bloody death of Colonel Sharp at the hands of his mortal enemy. But the recency of the event, together with the romantic tradition in Southern letters in the first half of the nineteenth century, placed limits on the hindsight and rose-colored blinders on the psychological insight of previous workers in the field. Mr. Warren has the advantage of a century of perspective on his materials. Even more important, the writing of *All the King's Men* gave Warren valuable experience in the evolution of fictional motives, both domestic and political, such as those which led to the assassination of Willie Stark. The Browning parallel is again instructive. For Browning's success with "The Ring and the Book" would certainly have been less marked without that careful attention to psychological complexes which distinguishes his earlier dramatic monologs, all of it standing solidly like a savings account behind a man in the act of acquiring new property.

But *World Enough and Time* is more than an investment of old funds in new real estate. To appreciate the size of Warren's achievement one must take into account the ironic relation between the manner of the novel and its thematic content. Mark Twain used to fulminate over the falsifying influence of Scott's romances in American fiction, and dramatized it through the contrast between Huck's moral realism and Tom's inveterate romanticizing in the closing pages of *Huckleberry Finn*. Twain's contrast,

of course, was humorous, where Warren's is at least ironic and at most tragic. Fortune never knew a nobler fool than Warren's Jeremiah Beaumont, nor did romantic chivalry and the people's rights ever entangle a more deluded fall guy. To build up his motivation takes an over-deliberate quarter of the story, but with the murder, the apprehension, the trial, the escape, and the final capture, the novel marches through Nemesis with a steady doomful tread. Beaumont's overpowering delusion enables Mr. Warren to hold his novel somewhere just short of the epic scale and the grand manner; it is when we glimpse, as through the iron gates of life, the crude actualities of his predicament, it is when we learn the extent of the gulf between his idea of the truth and the truth as it is, that the tragic irony implicit in the old yellow book begins to operate explicitly in Mr. Warren's admirable construction-transcending-reconstruction.

–Carlos Baker, "Through the Iron Gates," Virginia
Quarterly Review, 26 (Autumn 1950): 603–605

*   *   *

In this excerpt from his essay, written nearly forty years after the publication of World Enough and Time, *critic Richard G. Law argues that the novel marks a turning point in Warren's life and career.*

Warren's *World Enough and Time:* "Et in Arcadia Ego"

Charles Bohner's remark that in *World Enough and Time* we have "the weirdest tale Warren has given us" remains one of the best short descriptions of the novel. Accounting for the strangeness of the book is a difficult task. One senses greater psychological displacement in *World Enough and Time* than in any of Warren's other work, and greater disparity between the ostensible interests of the book and its submerged issues, which are elusive and well disguised. The novel's place in the writer's career has not yet been established–in fact, has hardly been addressed. Yet both chronologically and aesthetically, the novel marks decisively the end of Warren's early phase of development as an artist: after this performance, Warren emerges on a radically different track as a writer. Moreover, the blackness of the darkness of *World Enough and Time* is unprecedented; the novel represents quite the fullest look at the worst in Warren's entire canon. It is tempting to conjecture that the novel also records a personal crisis, a low-water mark of nihilism and despair in mid-life, and that it dramatizes (behind several layers of disguises) a violent leave-taking of earlier commitments. *World Enough and Time* resembles Warren's other work enough that the extent to which it parodies his earlier ideas and mannerisms

WORLD ENOUGH AND TIME

A Romantic Novel

by

Robert Penn Warren

I.

I can show you what is left. After the pride, passion, agony, and bemused aspiration, what is left is in our hands. Here are the scraps of newspaper, more than a century old, splotched and yellowed and huddled together in a library like November leaves abandoned by the wind, damp and leached out, back of the stables or in a fence corner of a vacant lot. Here are the letters, yellow too, bound in neat bundles with tape, so stiffened and tired that it parts unresisting at your touch. Here are the records of what happened in that court room, all the words taken down. Here is the manuscript he wrote, day after day, as he waited in his cell, telling his story. The letters of his script lean forward in their haste. Haste toward what? The bold stroke of the quill catches on the rough paper, fails, resumes, moves on in its race against time, to leave time behind, or in its rush to meet Time at last at the devoted and appointed place. To whom was he writing, rising from his mire or leaning from his flame to tell his story? The answer is easy. He was writing to us.

We have what is left, the lies and half-lies and the truths and half-truths. We do not know that we have the Truth. But we must have it. Puzzling over what is left, we are like the scientist fumbling with a tooth and thigh bone to reconstruct for a museum some great, stupid beast extinct with the ice age. Or we are like the louse-bit who finds, in a fold of land between his desert and the mountain of parapets and courts, and marvels what kind of men had h

Page from the setting copy for Warren's fourth novel (Yale Collection of American Literature, Beinecke Rare Book and Manuscript Library)

has been underestimated. On close inspection, however, the novel not only seems to represent a break with the writer's previous work, but to constitute an attack on and a mockery of previously held positions and assumptions, to mark not just his abandonment of agrarianism and his rejection of the Southern past as an image of a redemptive community, but an abjuring of some of his most fundamental aesthetic ideas as well. If the novel does indeed function as a busk, a ritual consignment of formerly valued goods to the flames, it represent Warren's most intriguing performance in any genre.

World Enough and Time is structured as a kind of philosophical detective story, with the narrator (a thin disguise for the writer) attempting to shape into coherent form what can be known or inferred about a series of bloody, melodramatic events from the past–the basic strategy employed again in Warren's next work, *Brother to Dragons*. The role of the narrator/detective/historian is to push the materials towards revelation–toward "Truth." Part of the evidence which the narrator assembles is itself a narrative–an effort by the nineteenth-century protagonist to make sense of his own actions: "exhibit A" is the journal of a condemned man who is similarly seeking the underlying truth of his experience–or, to use Warren's terms, "redemption" through self-definition and "knowledge." These parallel perspectives set in motion a highly self-conscious and self-referential dialectic. The reader is drawn into the same effort of puzzle-solving, and every major element in the novel is similarly aligned to illustrate (and to test) the form-making, meaning-generating activity of the mind. In lining up the consecutive imaginative acts of protagonist, narrator, and reader, all of which are focused on the same baffling questions, Warren implies, as elsewhere in his fiction and poetry, the identity of the artistic and moral imagination. But the most significant fact about this elaborate structure for dramatizing the self- and world-constructing power of the imagination is that it fails, and fails miserably. Neither nineteenth-century protagonist nor modern commentator uncovers the meaning of what Beaumont does; both end with the same unanswerable question: "Was all for naught?"

As a counterpoint to these quests for "truth," the plot of the novel seems designed expressly to frustrate any effort to obtain insight. The action illustrates (redundantly) the "doubleness" of Jeremiah Beaumont's experience, both in regard to his dualistic frame of reference and to a seemingly ingrained "duplicity" in events. Events are never what they appear; conclusions do not flow from intentions; and nothing has a single significance. Moreover, the narrative pursues (with an almost compulsive tenacity) every hopeful premise of the protagonist to its disastrous conclusion. Through the lenses provided by the impotent modern commentator, the

Dust jacket for Warren's novel that was based on the Beauchamp-Sharp episode in Kentucky in the 1820s (Special Collections, Western Kentucky University Libraries)

reader follows the erratic course of Jeremiah Beaumont as the action gradually cancels out possible resolution after possible resolution, until he arrives at an ultimate *reductum ad absurdum*. Such a plot is a kind of commentary in itself, especially as we recall Warren's artistic credo has always affirmed the identity of artistic form and meaning and implied that the form of the work and the perceptive gestalt of the mind are closely analogous, if not identical. The action of *World Enough and Time*, however, appears to take that notion and plunge it into an acid bath. As Robert B. Heilman has pointed out, the novel's total effect "is one of a manically exhaustive ripping apart of excuses, justifications, defenses, ruses, consolations; of a furious burrowing into ever-deeper layers of self-understanding until almost every clarity becomes a puzzle and every dependability a delusion."

. . . .

World Enough and Time is obviously Warren's most extreme–that is, his most skeptical–statement of the problem of knowledge, and at the same time, in a bizarre way, it is the most "pastoral" of Warren's early novels, if only in the strict sense of a work in which pastoral conventions are employed extensively. Pastoral images—especially as developed in relation to the New World—form a key part of the symbolic landscape of the last section. Moreover, the pervasive contrast of the two opposing worlds of experience which is the stock-in-trade of pastoral, is the main fact of the novel. The novel participates in the pastoral tradition in somewhat the same way that Marvell's "To His Coy Mistress" (from which Warren derived the title of the book) participates in the tradition of *carpe diem* arguments: it employs the main conventions of the genre but in a way which subverts their usual purposes. In *World Enough and Time,* traditional values associated with pastoral landscape are systematically inverted. In fact, it is hard to imagine a work more bleakly alien to the spirit of pastoral than *World Enough and Time.* Nature is not idealized as simple and uncorrupted; the natural world is Hobbesian rather than Edenic, treacherous as well as harsh, and the unspoiled wilderness of the western frontier is the abode of evil, a sinkhole into which the human disappears. The entire world of frontier Kentucky is a "dark and bloody ground," a breeding place of monsters and moral deformity, with more in common with the mere of *Beowulf* than with the vales or values of Arcady. The past world evoked both by the modern narrator and by Beaumont's "confession" is, in terms of its complexity and general unsatisfactoriness, a mirror image of the present, not an alternative world.

Warren took the epigraph for his novel from the prologue to the fifth book of the *Faerie Queene,* which contrasts (just as Beaumont habitually does) a corrupt present with an ideal "antique world,"

When good was only for it selfe desyred,
And all men sought their owne, and none no more;
When Justice was not for most meed outhyred,
But simple Truth did rayne, and was of all admyred.

The relationship of this epigraph to the novel is, of course, bitterly ironic. Warren projects the psychic divisions and uncertainties of the modern age backwards (convincingly for the most part) onto the early nineteenth-century South. Implicitly, there is no such thing as a Golden Age, no lost period of harmony and wholeness; or if there was, the South was far from having any portion in it.

One of Warren's strategies in employing conventions of the genre is to internalize the pastoral landscape within the mind of his protagonist. Pastoral images express not only Beaumont's system of values but his expectations of the world. These expectations, while

pervasive, are probably most obvious in the garden scenes where Beaumont courts Rachel by reading Plato's *Symposium* to her, in his reveries of dissolution in wild nature, or in his desires to escape his difficulties in the new land of the West. His deep urge to step outside ordinary life manifests itself during youthful hunts in the Western wilderness. There Jeremiah

. . . would lie awake and watch the stars and "wickedly" wish he had no family to go back to and that he could stay forever in the forest, "shedding blood and feasting on the wild flesh." All other things to come "seemed of no account and I made only for this life in the great silence and the dark shade of trees." He thought . . . that if a man could stay here he would never grow old and "know the burden of time and things." (16)

In that passage a typically American pastoral image functions as a disguise for unconscious impulses. Beaumont's desire to be exempt from the "burden of time and things," to transcend or escape from reality by sinking into "nature," is obviously a death wish which foreshadows his suicidal urges later in the book. Similarly, after he is convicted of murder and sentenced to death, the strange pleasure he takes in the absolute quiet and darkness of his cave-like underground cell is another expression of this tendency in him.

Pastoral images, then, have little reference in the novel to a real or realizable world; they exist as objects of fantasy rather than as a source of a corrective vision; they disguise things impossible to acknowledge. In Beaumont, the dream of recovered harmony with nature merges into an unconscious death wish. At the same time, his longing for a world partly defined by pastoral imagery illustrates his capacity for self-deception and a general human will to impose self-generated, solipsistic structures upon experience.

Significantly, most of the action of the novel illustrates the failure of the "exterior" world to match up with the "interior" image of it which Beaumont cherishes. The pastoral fantasy and the values they represent are resisted at every point by the world-as-it-is. Experience proves unmalleable to Beaumont's will and, by implication, inherently unaccommodating to human desires.

Pastoral conventions, then, operate in terms of a simple scheme: they represent an impossibly ideal version of an imagined world, rather than an actual past or a golden age of potentiality. The interplay of contrasting modes typical of pastoral is utilized to sharpen the reader's sense of the dichotomy between self and world, to polarize the sentient "I" and the universe outside the self. The pastoral "world" not only lies within, but in Beaumont's psychology, seems reducible to little more

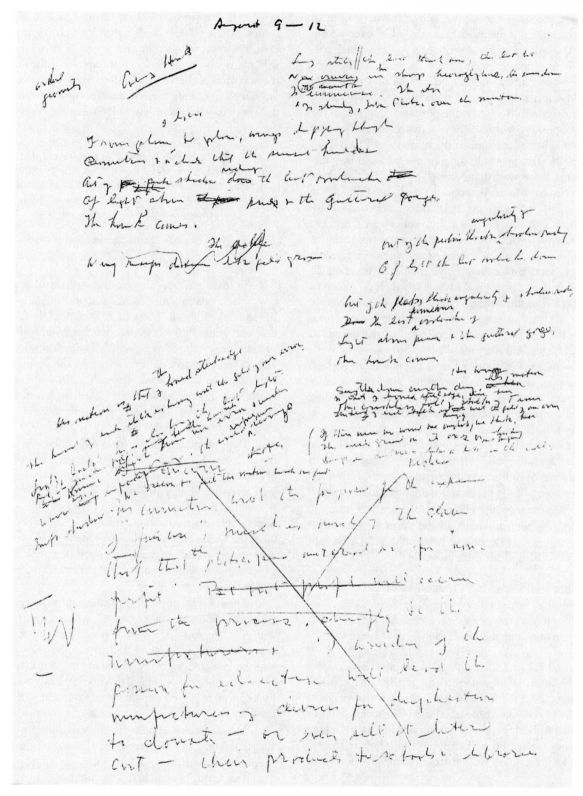

Page from Warren's notes for an unproduced television drama titled "Don't Bury Me at All," which he worked on with humorist Max Shulman in 1950 (Yale Collection of American Literature, Beinecke Rare Book and Manuscript Library)

than a reality-denying syndrome. The protagonist's interior world, his "idealism," is constantly undercut by the action of the novel and is ultimately dissolved by the corrosive irony of the narrator's point of view, which serves to validate or objectify the harsh actualities of the world in which Beaumont moves. In fact, one of the chief functions of the modern commentator, like the figure of Death in a painting by Poussin, is to deflate and devalue Beaumont's illusions without offering a positive alternative himself. The nature of the "actual" world is therefore largely defined for us by the absence in it of any genuine *locus amoenus;* there is no green retreat which is not delusional. There is neither world enough nor time.

. . . .

. . . Beaumont's sense of human nature and the larger nature of things form compatible sides of the same coin; man is a microcosm (or metonymy) of greater nature; nature's ultimate order and man's mind are harmonious and mutually intelligible because they form together a larger unity. The pain and terror of life derive, therefore, from ignorance and error and illusion. A solution to—or consolation for—all problems is therefore omnipresent in the discovery of Truth. One need but read nature correctly and interpret its "aspect and law" to return to "Truth" and "natural" harmony—a state long imaged in Western culture in the Myth of Eden and the pastoral idyll. Beaumont is faithful to these precepts till death. It might also be said that Beaumont dies of those precepts and that his disastrous life and decapitation constitute a savage rebuttal of them.

These are ancient and powerful ideas in Western cultures and represent, in various permutations, the *sine qua non* of pastoral tradition—pastoral representing one of the main vehicles for exploration of both our relationship to nature and our distance from an ideal existence. Without an ideal of the harmony or unity of man with nature, pastoral's ubiquitous play of contrasts between simple and complex, natural and artificial, good and evil, is without meaning, and the dichotomous models of life it portrays are incapable of generating either concrete moral judgments or a hierarchy of values. Without that fundamental premise, pastoral cannot organize the worlds of experience which it contains, either morally, intellectually, or aesthetically.

The conclusion of the novel seems to raise these apocalyptic issues; it depicts not just the unpleasant death of the protagonist but the inevitable defeat and destruction of the imagination—at its highest and deepest level of both fiction-making and interpretation. "In the beginning," Beaumont muses near the end of his life, "there was the Word and the Word was with God, but in the end there is the mud and the mud is with me" (481). There is no *Logos,* apparently, and no transcendent order in the cosmos; neither is there a "word," a fragment of text, left in his own life. *World Enough and Time* seems therefore to debunk the possibility of successful integration of self and world and to dismiss the very idea of harmony between man and nature. Finally, the "actual flux of things" in the novel not only appears unstructured and uninterpretable from any point of view available in the work, but inherently unstructurable.

–Richard G. Law, "Warren's *World Enough and Time:* 'Et in Arcadia Ego,'" in *"Time's Glory": Original Essays on Robert Penn Warren,* edited by James A. Grimshaw Jr. (Conway: University of Central Arkansas Press, 1986), pp. 13–41

The Yale Years: 1951–1973

Warren's life changed markedly in the first half of the 1950s, as his first marriage failed and a second marriage began. His troubled relationship with Cinina ended in divorce on 21 July 1951. His former wife continued treatments for a psychiatric disorder in White Plains, New York; she subsequently joined the faculty at Mitchell College in New London, Connecticut, and remarried. Warren left for England soon after the divorce. From London, he wrote Cleanth Brooks on 4 October 1951 that he was "deep in the middle of my long poem," a work that was published as Brother to Dragons: A Tale in Verse and Voices in 1953. Warren, who had been a visiting professor at Yale University in fall 1950, was appointed professor of playwriting in the Yale School of Drama the following year—a position he held until the end of 1955. The most significant change for Warren was the development of his relationship with writer Eleanor Clark, whom he married on 7 December 1952. In spring 1953 they began renovating an old dairy barn in Fairfield, Connecticut, that became their permanent home. The marriage lasted for the rest of Warren's life and produced two children, Rosanna Phelps Warren, who was born 27 July 1953, and Gabriel Penn Warren, born 19 July 1955.

Warren left Yale in December 1955 to concentrate on his writing, but he returned to the university in September 1961 as a professor in the English department, a post he held for thirteen years, teaching one term per year. In the period from 1951 through 1973 Warren published more than thirty books—novels, poetry, drama, nonfiction, textbook revisions, and edited works—and continued to receive recognition and awards, including his second Pulitzer Prize. The years were full, professionally and personally, and notable for travel. Warren was in demand as a speaker throughout the United States, and he and his family traveled to Europe, especially France and Italy, almost annually.

Warren and Cleanth Brooks, 1952 (Yale University 1953 Class Book [New Haven, 1953]; Collection of Matthew J. Bruccoli)

The First Peters Rushton Seminar in Contemporary Prose and Poetry
and the sixteenth in the series sponsored by the Schools of Engli...
13 March 1951   University of Virginia

WILLIAM FAULKNER AND HIS SOUTH

by
Robert Penn Warren

At the age of fifty-three William Faulkner has written nineteen books which for range of effect, philosophical weight, originality of style, variety of characterization, humor and tragic intensity are without equal in our time. I do not mean this in dis-
paragement of other writers. For instance, Hemingway or Katherine
Anne Porter. They have achieved absolute triumphs within their
range of operation, works of perfection and intensity which I imagine will be as permanent as the work of Faulkner. The person who
wrote Old Mortality and Noon Wine doesn't have to worry too much
about the future verdict. Nor does the person who wrote My Old Man
and A Farewell to Arms -- even if he has written more recently a
cruel parody of himself called Across the River and Into the Trees.
But their range is different from Faulkner's range, they do not have
his massive and fecund imagination.

William Faulkner is a Southerner, and I feel that we who are
Southerners can take a peculiar pride in that fact. When I say a
peculiar pride, I do not mean merely the pride in the fact that
Faulkner is gifted and world-famous, and that in some way his glory
is reflected upon us. I mean something different and somewhat
chastening, too. What I mean will in the end be -- I hope -- the
burden of this discourse.

But before I proceed I must remark that I have encountered no.
a few fellow-Southerners who regard Faulkner as somehow a family
scandal, a skeleton in the closet, a libeller who will never do much
good for the local Chamber of Commerce. This attitude usually
springs from the wrong kind of pride, the pride that must justify
itself despite fact and can thrive on self-deception. Keep things
dark, don't say the horrid word, and the facts don't matter, they
really aren't there. Sometimes, of course, the attitude toward
Faulkner springs merely from an inability to read -- and Faulkner is
a difficult writer. Sometimes the attitude toward Faulkner springs
from a sincere piety and local patriotism, the feeling that he has
spoken badly of beloved objects. With this piety itself I do find
some sympathy. It is a rich and valuable thing. But when it is
abstracted and uniformed and uncritical, when it becomes an end in
itself, then it ceases to be a virtue. I imagine that some members
of the UDC still prefer Thomas Nelson Page to William Faulkner.
I do not mean to say that liking the work of Faulkner is the test of
virtue. A lady might have every virtue and every grace and still
find Faulkner little better than Greek. But I would make the reasons for disliking Faulkner a test of virtue.

First page of a lecture Warren gave at the University of Virginia, mimeographed for distribution (Collection of Matthew J. Bruccoli)

Silliman College, Yale University, where Warren lived in a fellow's suite before his marriage (Yale University 1953 Class Book [New Haven, 1953]; Collection of Matthew J. Bruccoli)

Conrad and Divorce

Warren wrote to his friend and editor from Verdi, Nevada, where he was awaiting word of the divorce about a month before the papers were signed. The decision to end the marriage was initiated by Cinina, whose doctors believed that her relationship with Warren added to her stress. Warren's essay on Joseph Conrad appeared in the summer 1951 issue of the Sewanee Review *and later as the introduction to the 1951 Modern Library edition of Conrad's* Nostromo.

Warren to Albert Erskine, 27 May 1951

You ask me how things go. I have actually begun to write on the *Nostromo* piece. One trouble now is that I have accumulated so much material, and so many notions, good or bad, that the problem is one of scale and focus and continuity. I have assembled twenty-one topics for discussion, and five or six thousand words will scarcely accommodate the development of so much. I don't know why I've been so slow. The last week has been a trifle paralyzing. The lawyer has written me that nothing is settled, that the doctors have now raised new questions, that C[inina] is indecisive, and God knows what else. Furthermore he himself is sailing for Europe on May 30 or 31, and what it will all come to I can't well predict. He holds out some vague hope of getting things resolved before he leaves. Meanwhile I read a lot, take notes on Conrad, and clamber around the hills–which are magnificent. My arm improves, and my spirits. So I hope to have Conrad knocked off within a week. Finally the mountain may groan and bring forth the mouse.

–courtesy of Albert R. Erskine Jr. Estate

A New Life

Victoria Thorpe Miller, who is working on a biography of Eleanor Clark, describes the courtship, marriage, and family life of the Warrens in these excerpts from her 2003 article. The essay begins with Clark's sitting in midsummer 1994 "on the upper porch" of the Vermont cottage the couple bought in 1959 as a second home, remembering "her early days with Red Warren."

Shared Lives

"I made quite a play for him!" Eleanor Clark leaned back and laughed as she recalled events of almost half a century earlier. Her eyes were clear and comprehending, and she was amused by the memory of her "courtship," as she called it, with Robert Penn Warren.

. . . .

Both were living in New York City at the time–early 1952–but Warren, then teaching at Yale, sometimes stayed there during the week. Eleanor had planned a ski trip to Stowe, Vermont, and stopped at New Haven to see him. She went on to stay overnight at her mother's house in Roxbury, Connecticut, and the next morning on to Vermont. That day she mailed a postcard to him, one with a picture of the inn in which she was staying. As soon as he received the card, he phoned her and asked her to have dinner with him when she returned from skiing. That is, Eleanor said, he called the next evening "because he knew I'd be out skiing during the day." She was not one to sit by the telephone waiting for a call. Eleanor realized that was a milestone of sorts. As she said, "That was the first time he'd gone to that much trouble about me!" She laughed again, clearly enjoying the memory. Pausing, she added, "He was a very attractive fellow, you know–in all ways."

The Warrens had met much earlier than 1952, however. In fact, Eleanor Clark was an aspiring 24-year-old writer, when in 1938 she received a letter, very polite, from one of the managing editors of *The Southern Review,* rejecting a short story she had submitted. The editors liked her story so much that they worried that "on further reflection we'll decide that we have made a mistake in returning the story to you," and they hoped she would keep them in mind when she had something else to submit: "And soon, we hope." The author of the letter was Robert Penn Warren.

By coincidence, just a month earlier, in March of 1938, Clark had reviewed a new anthology of Southern literature for the *Partisan Review.* Titled *A Southern Harvest,* it had been edited by the 33-year-old Warren.

La Rocca, a fort above Porto Ercole on the Italian coast, where Warren and Eleanor Clark spent the summer before their marriage and often returned.
It is the setting for the sequence of poems Warren dedicated to his daughter, "To a Little Girl, One Year Old, in a Ruined Fortress,"
collected in Promises: Poems 1954–1956 *(Joseph Blotner,* Robert Penn Warren: A Biography*
[New York: Random House, 1997]; Richland County Public Library).*

While Clark praised a few of the stories in the collection, she was less gentle in her review of Warren's book than he had been in his rejection of her story. Never one to understate, she found that the qualities Warren applied to Southern literature in his introduction applied "equally to the best writing done recently not only in other sections of the United States but also in England, France, and perhaps China as well" and that "what does belong to them 'exclusively' is nothing but a hyper-sensitive resistance to Marxism." Fortunately perhaps for their future relationship, she did admit that the shortcomings in the volume were no reflection on Warren's editing: "He has made the *Southern Review* one of the few magazines in this country worth serious attention."

Clark's review of *A Southern Harvest*, of course, had no dampening effect on Warren's growing reputation; nor did the letter of rejection from the *Southern Review* convince Clark that writing was not in her future. Both events were fortuitous, for from this somewhat shaky beginning would grow an extraordinary marriage and literary friendship, one that would span

almost half a century. Much is known about Warren, but who was this woman of whom Warren would say, near the end of his life, that she was the best thing that had ever happened to him?

. . . .

. . . In Washington in 1944, Eleanor Clark and Robert Penn Warren first met, when he was negotiating for a position as Consultant in Poetry to the Library of Congress. After the war, in 1946, their paths briefly crossed again, when Clark and two male friends were driving to California. They stopped in Ohio to see John Crowe Ransom and spent one night there. Warren and his first wife, Cinina, were also staying at the Ransoms'.

. . . .

By the early fifties, both Eleanor Clark and Red Warren were living in New York City, he commuting to his new position at Yale and she having returned from Rome to continue working on her book about that city. It was during this time that Clark mailed her fateful postcard from the ski lodge in Stowe. After War-

Writing at 2495 Redding Road

After he and his wife moved into their converted dairy barn, Warren's home address did not change as it had in his earlier years. It remained 2495 Redding Road until the end of his life. The remodeling of the barn was imaginatively done with the help of a friend at the Yale School of Architecture. Their bedrooms were upstairs; a "great room," library/sitting room, and guest bedroom occupied the ground floor; and the dining room, kitchen, and another bedroom were downstairs in what had been the milking area of the dairy. With books in almost every room, stone fireplaces, and no television, the ambience was warm, cordial, and inviting.

In another building, formerly a stable, two tack rooms served as his and her studies for writing. When at home, their work hours were from 9:00 A.M. to 2:00 P.M., with no interruptions except for emergencies. Friends who had the Warrens' unlisted telephone number knew not to call until after two o'clock in the afternoon. Warren's study was cluttered with old letters, rejected drafts, and manuscripts from others sometimes strewn on the floor.

In 1959 the Warrens purchased a second house, in West Wardsboro, Vermont. It served as their "escape" or vacation home, especially in the summers when they were not traveling and after his retirement from Yale. Book-filled, with separate space for both to write, the Vermont house had the same ambience as their Fairfield home. For the Warrens, it was another place to come to.

this period that Warren began to produce some of his finest work. By his own account, Warren had been unable to finish "a single short poem" during the decade before 1954. After 1954, however, he began to compose poetry again. Warren recalled that "every time Eleanor and I went to Italy, it was poems, poems, poems. . . . It was magic. . . . From that time on, poetry never ceased again." This productivity continued. Ten of his sixteen volumes of poetry appeared when Warren was in his sixties and seventies, and this surge in creativity–in quantity and quality–in the latter half of his life is a phenomenon for which Clark seems to deserve at least some of the credit. As Warren said in a 1982 interview, he found life with Eleanor "just splendid"–and this just after she had told the interviewer that Warren had the habit of leaving his socks on the floor.

. . . .

Warren with his second wife, Eleanor Clark, and their first child, Rosanna, in July 1953 (Joseph Blotner, Robert Penn Warren: A Biography *[New York: Random House, 1997]; Richland County Public Library)*

ren's phone call to her, they began to see each other occasionally. According to her, not much happened at first. As she reported in 1994, "I began to think he was never going to kiss me goodnight; but he did, and from then on we were it!"

Indeed, they were "it" for the rest of their lives. Deciding on one Sunday to get married the next, they were married on December 7, 1952, when Eleanor was 39 and Red was 47. Cleanth Brooks was Red's best man, for, as Clark said, he wouldn't have dared have Albert Erskine there, as they had invited Katherine Anne Porter. Because there was a swimming pool available, the two rented a tiny place–a chicken coop, as Clark said–where Rosanna was born on the floor in 1953 in a now famous story. "We laugh about it now," Clark said in 1994, "but we weren't laughing then. Red kept shouting that a baby was being born on the floor, and the irritated operator kept telling Warren it wasn't *her* job to get them a doctor." Gabriel was born, in a hospital, in 1955.

The family unit that resulted was so strong that Rosanna would later write in a letter to her mother [9 December 1980] that it was like "a little cosmos poised defensively against . . . [the] universe." It was during

Eleanor Clark's Books

Although she was a devoted wife and mother, Clark managed to publish eight of her ten books after her marriage to Warren.

The Bitter Box (Garden City: Doubleday, 1946; London: Joseph, 1947).

Rome and a Villa (Garden City: Doubleday, 1952; London: Joseph, 1953; revised edition, New York: Pantheon, 1975).

The Song of Roland (New York: Legacy/Random House, 1960; London: Muller, 1963).

The Oysters of Locmariaquer (New York: Pantheon, 1964; London: Secker & Warburg, 1965).

Baldur's Gate (New York: Pantheon, 1970).

Dr. Heart: A Novella and Other Stories (New York: Pantheon, 1974).

Eyes, Etc.: A Memoir (New York: Pantheon, 1977).

Gloria Mundi (New York: Pantheon, 1979).

Tamrart: 13 Days in the Sahara (New York: S. Wright, 1984).

Camping Out (New York: Putnam, 1986).

Warren's letters to Clark, written during their rare separations, are full of affection, as are those written to his children over the years. Indeed, Helen Lockwood, a former teacher at Vassar, remarked on Clark's having written that their children had the best father in the world. To Rosanna after a family visit [in 1968], Warren wrote, "I'm selfish enough to say that maybe having you all to myself for our walk and talk was the loveliest part. No, I can't quite say that, for it was lovely to see how much joy your Ma and your Sib took in your presence, which rather compounded my own joy." Warren also took time to give Rosanna advice about her own poems, which she sent to her parents with regularity. To Gabe, struggling with some literary study at school in France [in 1972], he gave sympathy: he wished he could be "with you for the poems." He also gave advice: "Really try to locate what you have a feeling for, and ask yourself why. If a poem puzzles you, do give it a chance—and remember that you are not supposed to like every God-damned poem in the world. Just give a poem a chance for Gabe Warren, as of now." He closed with an appeal to "[b]e kind to your work-worn mother when she gets back to Claix."

Warren's solicitude was not without cause. One quality that makes a literary friend is that of seeing to it that a writer has the time to write. Clark knew this. When asked what it took to be a "decent writer," she replied that there are two requirements. The first is to have a "total

passion" backed by some "native talent"; the second, to spend your life "working like hell at it." Warren knew this, too. He believed that "[i]f anybody's going to be a writer, he's got to be able to say, 'This has got to come first, to write has to come first.'" Clark made it possible for him to work for long, uninterrupted hours. She seems never to have put her needs before those of her family, and it would not be stretching the truth to say that she put her career as a writer second to her husband's. She did not stop writing, however, and in fact there is scarcely a year between her time at Vassar in the early thirties to the appearance of her last novel in 1986 in which she didn't publish something.

. . . .

The Clark-Warren marriage *was* a kind of collaboration in the amassing of an extraordinary network of friends—his and hers. Regarding his marriage to Clark, Warren once said, "When I married I got, along with a wife, a remarkable bonus—a rich dowry—of friends." Clark, too, benefited in this way. For example, having known Red for years, Archibald MacLeish, upon meeting Eleanor, wrote her [in 1978], "Now I've seen you and talked to you and, somehow or other, whether you approve or not, you are an old and dear friend." The Warrens often invited friends to stay with them. In Vermont a steady stream of people would come for ski weekends, with activities carefully planned by Eleanor to suit each group. After such a weekend, one guest wrote Clark, "I hope you realize that you've given us another happy skiing memory. I will never cease to admire the way you plan for us all and make each day work from rousing at dawn to collapse at the end of the day!"

The holiday gatherings at the Warrens' were also famous for good food, music, and dancing, but what guests seemed to remember most was the spirited conversation. And Warren's best literary friend could hold her own in any of them. As one critic said, "With one vigorous thrust she [could] both impale and exalt." Among other topics, the guests reviewed, as [John Kenneth] Galbraith put it, "the adequacy—more often the inadequacy—of the writers of our generation, particularly those that were coming along." He said that Red was rather amiable as regards other writers, but not Eleanor: "She didn't . . . tolerate any form of inadequacy . . . or pretension. Moreover, Galbraith added, "You didn't argue with Eleanor. She didn't invite debate or . . . disagreement, and she did not allow any error to go uncorrected. One of the very few writers of whom she was really tolerant was Red."

Red, for his part, was usually tolerant of Eleanor's tempestuousness. "Angry joy," he called it in a poem called "Praise," seeing her as one who "whirls through life in a benign fury." "Birth of Love" presents her tender side, one that causes the narrator to "[cry] out that, if only / He had such strength, he would put his hand forth / And maintain it over her to guard, in all / Her out-goings and in-comings, from whatever / Inclemency of sky or slur of the world's weather / Might ever be." The tempestuousness was tempered by kindness to those she respected and cared for and an unfailing wit.

. . . .

Although Warren's personality was different from Clark's, both experienced great joy in life. They seem to have particularly enjoyed teasing one another, she calling him "You old Agrarian" and he calling her "You old Trotskyite." It's clear that Clark was sometimes on Warren's mind even when he was working, for his "old Trotskyite" played a prominent role in *Flood: A Romance for Our Time*. Although the gestation period for *Flood* was long, Warren completed the writing of it during the five months the family spent in Brittany in 1963, while Clark was at work on *The Oysters of Locmariaquer*.

Despite prevailing critical opinion, Warren always considered *Flood* to be one of his three best novels. In it, much of what he puts into the character Lettice Poindexter comes straight from Eleanor Clark. She is a Yankee[1] and an ex-Commie (25) who loved "tennis and French and riding and dancing" (359), and whose mother had lived in hotels in France and Italy, leaving her with strangers for extended periods (361). Brad remembers that

> Lettice had hated nicknames. "My name is Lettice, God damn it," she would say, and give a characteristic quick challenging little toss of her high head. She carried her height like a challenge, too. She was almost as tall as he [Brad] was. Five feet nine and a half. With naked heels– narrow, clean-tendoned heels set straight on the carpet– she could almost look him straight in the eye with a look that said: *"This is me."* (27)

We also learn that "[a]t calculated intervals she would lay aside the sneakers and old flannel and appear in clothes which, in their severity or flamboyance, it did not matter, indicated some deep self-confidence . . . " (59). She had "a sense of inner freedom. . . . She was, for instance, the first woman he [Brad] had ever heard use as an expletive the vulgar word for excrement, and the word came so naturally, so innocently, that his first shock was quickly absorbed into shame for having reacted with shock" (59–60). And Lettice was "dead game" for donning old clothes, grabbing some citronella and a shotgun, and heading out to the swamp with Brad and Frog-eye (106). This resembles Clark, tall, athletic, and elegant, refusing to be called anything but Eleanor, but happy to wear old blue jeans and flannel shirt and do without civilization entirely. In *Flood,* Brad's sister Maggie says of Lettice:

> I was awful timid in the beginning, she was so New York and grand and tall, and now and then she'd shuck off blue

Warren and Eleanor Clark on board a ship bound for France in the late 1950s (courtesy of Mrs. Robert D. Frey)

> jeans or old khaki shorts and appear with some wonderful dress and a great bangle or something that cost a million dollars, and she made sweeping gestures and sometimes talked in a bold, flashy way, like nothing I'd ever heard. There wasn't anything she wouldn't say, but it never seemed vulgar, just sort of gay and funny, sometimes even, you might say, delicate. She had such a gay innocent smile–it seemed to come right out of her, just because she loved you and everything around her. (179)

Similarly, Galbraith says that everyone who knew Clark "not only forgave, but rejoiced in her–not only independence–but her outspoken expression."

Maggie is struck by Lettice's naturalness regarding her own body–a naturalness Clark also possessed–when they lie naked tanning in the sun. In a remark that particularly echoes Clark's way of mixing the vulgar and the sublime, Lettice tells Maggie that she had to keep from "being boiled lobster, and she'd be damned if she wanted to be striped either, like the Cathedral of Siena'" (182).

While art was an enduring interest, Clark was also willing to work tirelessly with Warren on houses, barns, work cabins, or whatever came her way. Of Lettice, Maggie says,

Lettice would do all that primping and getting herself up fancy, and at the same time she could do the dirtiest work and not give a damn. She would break every fingernail. She would go to the woods and swamp with Brad and that Frog-Eye, and come back sweaty and muddy and grinning. It was a kind of split, a doubleness, right down her middle. She had to grab, it seemed, all kinds of life. She was boiling with energy. (182)

Warren has woven into *Flood* other connections to his wife, some of them recognizable only to those who know her past. For example, Yasha Jones refers to "the mysterious shudder of Einstein or Freud or Perse," a puzzling trilogy unless one is aware that Clark had met and had a relationship with the expatriate French poet Alexei Léger when she lived in Washington, D.C., and they remained good friends. Léger, or St.-John Perse as he was known in literary circles, had been France's Secretary for Foreign Affairs since 1932, and had left France in 1940 because he had opposed the appeasers.

Even more important than Warren's use of Clark in his writing were the couple's shared values. Each, of course, had brought his or her own set of values to the marriage; one of these was a strong sense of social justice, Clark's stemming at least in part from her early involvement with Trotskyism. Both of them recognized the importance of place and community, and they valued an awareness of time and history–cultural memory. The Warrens believed in the importance of meaningful work and the cultivation of personal strength, passion, and commitment.

Whether they were writing or, in their 70s, racing across the Sahara on camels (with Red tied to his camel like a package because he complained that his slippery socks made him slide off), Clark and Warren lived life to the fullest. Life, however, always ends. As Warren's health worsened, Clark, determined to fight the vicissitudes of life to the bitter end, used all the power she could muster to combat the inevitable, urging her husband to eat, to walk, to live, God damn it. As Rosanna said, "she took control with a vengeance." Joseph Blotner records a conversation between the Warrens shortly before his death in September of 1989: "One day in early August, sitting at the long table in the kitchen, he said, quite simply, 'I'm dying.' Around the corner at the sink Clark said, 'What did you say?' And he repeated the words very calmly. 'Don't be ridiculous,' she said. 'Of course you're not dying.' He replied, 'I am dying.' Clark said, 'Well, we're all dying,' and that was the end of the conversation." Despite Clark's tempestuousness and the occasional conflicts that resulted, Warren on more than one occasion said to Rosanna or Gabriel, "Eleanor is the best thing that ever happened to me." The year after Warren's death was, as the Warrens' niece Rebecca Jessup remembered it, "no doubt, the saddest year of her life."

. . . .

The marriage was an extraordinary one. Fortunately, the Clark-Warren legacy lives on: in the way their children live their lives and raise their children; in Gabe's sculpture; in Rosanna's poetry, particularly the poems she has written about her parents. Most of all, it lives on in the writings of this remarkable pair. The many instances of resonance among their respective works are testimony to the similarity of their values.

In *Flood,* Yasha Jones cautions Brad: "To be overwhelmed with the outward, moving multiplicity of the world–that means we can never see, really see, or love the single leaf falling" (113). Because of the sympathetic vibrations that must have passed between them, Warren knew that we must be able to see that single leaf, and Clark was able to describe it:

> Together we watched a yellow willow leaf that had just wriggled free from its twig, falling slow and erratic toward its last experience, at last touching down as though in unbelief on the water where its reflection had played all summer. There was something of a small child's totter and forgetfulness in its descent, and childish rapture in its sudden spinning dance as it was caught up by the wicked mirror, the only real leaf, for the moment, among so many dancing images of leaves. It was carried off and got stuck shortly in a mass of organic matter behind a log.[2]

Katherine Anne Porter, friend to both, gave testimony to the strength, the durability, of the Warrens' shared lives and separate studies. When writing to Clark requesting a copy of a photograph of the Warrens that had appeared in the *Saturday Review* [in 1971], Porter exclaimed, "the whole beautiful thing is so radiant with love and joy it lifts the heart to look at it. . . . What a life you two have made together. How splendidly you have done it in everything."

–Victoria Thorpe Miller, "Shared Lives and Separate
Studies: The Literary Marriage of Eleanor Clark
and Robert Penn Warren," RWP: An Annual of
Robert Penn Warren Studies, 3 (2003): 135–137,
145–151, 153–156, 158–159

1. Robert Penn Warren, *Flood: A Romance of Our Time* (1964; reprint, New York: Signet, 1965), 217. Hereafter, references to this edition are cited parenthetically in the text.
2. Eleanor Clark, *Baldur's Gate* (New York: Pantheon, 1970), 267.

Warren's "Exile" at Yale

Arkansas-born C. Vann Woodward was a colleague of Warren's at Yale from 1961 to 1971. While acknowledging that Warren's self-chosen exile from the South actually began in 1942 with his departure from LSU, Woodward argues for the particular importance of his Yale association in this excerpt from his tribute to his friend.

I will try to say what I could make of the effects of this long phase of his exile upon Warren's personal life and his writing. On the personal side I cannot help but think of the contrast between the happiness of Warren's experience and the miseries of two of the writers with whom I have compared him earlier–Ezra Pound, who carried his exile to the point of alienation and treason, and Faulkner, who rejected exile and stayed home to endure his pathological addiction to booze and the trials of a very troubled marriage.

Warren's life in exile was blessed by what he pronounced "a very happy marriage in process after a period of an unhappy one and the stopgaps in between." His second wife was the writer Eleanor Clark, "as Yankee as they come," declared Red. Asked if she would change anything in her career if she could, Eleanor replied, "I'd have married him earlier." She bore him two children, both born with gifts of their own–Rosanna, a poet, and Gabriel, a sculptor. Would their father's personal life have been any happier had he never become an exile? It is, of course, impossible to say, but I find it difficult to imagine.

Then there is the question of his new academic life. He no longer had to teach for a living. "But I discovered that I enjoy teaching," he said. "I quit teaching entirely three times but always drifted back in." He never taught more than one term a year and then only two days a week at Yale. But he needed "to keep in touch with the young," and, he added, "When I'm not teaching, I miss it very much." There were not only devoted and brilliant students, but in his words, "Also, you find in the academy certain people that you can't find outside. There are not too many, but there are some–the real humanists–brave men who love their learning and who love ideas." They were an essential part of his social as well as his intellectual life.

And finally, there is the creative life of the exile as poet, novelist, and I would add, literary and social critic. What bearing did exile have upon all that? Upon Warren the novelist I think of the relationship as somewhat paradoxical. He once said, "The farther I got away from the South, the more I thought about it." Walker Percy has commented on that question for writers of his time. "Indeed," he wrote, "more often than not, it is only possible to write about the South by leaving it." He then pointed to the writers of other regions: "Hemingway in Paris and Madrid. Sherwood Anderson in New Orleans, Malcolm Lowry in Mexico, Vidal in Italy, Tennessee Williams in Key West, James Jones on the Ile de St. Louis in Paris." As for Percy himself, he strongly preferred to live and to work in the South, and

C. Vann Woodward, Pulitzer Prize–winning historian of the South and race relations. He and his wife accompanied the Warrens on a sailing tour of the Greek Islands in 1977 (John Herbert Roper, C. Vann Woodward: A Southern Historian and His Critics *[Athens: University of Georgia Press, 1977]; Thomas Cooper Library, University of South Carolina).*

after some wanderings he settled in Covington across the lake and did his major work.

Certainly Warren's prolonged absence did not divert or distract him from the subject that remained to the end the central focus–concern, absorption of his fiction with his native region and its people. Any place, on the other hand, might inspire his poetry. As for his literary criticism, he said, "I'm just not a professional critic. That business is just something that happens. . . . But writing fiction, poetry, that's serious–that's for keeps." Yet he continued to be regarded as an important literary critic, and, I would add, as a social critic, a calling that took him back South and was expressed in his deeply felt books on racial segregation and the views and aspirations of black leaders of his time. He was a many-sided man.

We once stood on the shore of a Greek island in the Aegean. Without addressing anyone in particular he suddenly broke a long silence by saying, "I'm so happy, so happy." With that he stripped quickly and plunged into the sea. He swam out of sight and remained out of sight for quite a while. He was still in his prime then and a good swimmer, but I asked Eleanor if she was not worried. "Oh no," she said. "He loves to compose poems while he is swimming." I don't believe I ever knew a more completely fulfilled man.

–C. Vann Woodward, "Exile at Yale," in *The Legacy of Robert Penn Warren* (Baton Rouge: Louisiana State University, 2000), pp. 29–31

Writings in the 1950s

The first major work Warren wrote in the 1950s was Brother to Dragons: A Tale in Verse and Voices. *In "The Way It Was Written," an essay in the 25 August 1953 issue of* The New York Times Book Review, *Warren recalls that it was ten years before that he had first had the idea for writing about the historic crime of Thomas Jefferson's nephews brutally murdering a slave. He started to grasp his material more fully once he realized the reason the story captured his fancy: "It was that this was Jefferson's family. The philosopher of our liberties and the architect of our country and the prophet of human perfectibility had this in the family blood. Bit by bit, the thing began to take thematic shape."*

In a Paris Review *interview (Spring–Summer 1957) Warren answered a question about the use of history in his fiction by saying that he tried "to find stories that catch my eye, stories that seem to have issues in purer form than they come to one ordinarily." Warren maintained that most of his writing was contemporary to his life, but admitted a fascination with American history when the interviewer asked about* Brother to Dragons:

I have a romantic kind of interest in American history: saddles, shoes, figures of speech, rifles, and so on. They're worth a lot. Helps you focus. There *is* a kind of extraordinary romance about American history. That's the only word for it . . . a kind of self-sufficiency. You know, the grandpaws and the great grandpaws who carried the assumption that somehow their lives and their decisions were important, that as they went up, down, here and there, such a life was important and a man's responsibility to live it.

Brother to Dragons *received prominent, generally positive reviews. Poets Randall Jarrell in* The New York Times Book Review *(23 August 1953) and Robert Lowell in the* Kenyon Review *(Autumn 1953) called it his best book. This review is by poet and critic Babette Deutsch, the author of* Poetry in Our Time *(1952).*

Robert Penn Warren's Savage Poem
Review of *Brother to Dragons*

Every man who reads this page is brother to dragons. And the millions who will never read it, the living and the dead. But this is 1953. The stories of saints and of psychoanalysts, as of those archaic creatures, the poets, may be haunted by dragons. Such monsters are old hat to atomic physicists, to people working with supersonic weapons, to the children who play they are "space-men." With their dog tags swinging like scapulars. What can the phrase mean: "brother to dragons"? The meaning is, of course, the substance and significance of Robert

Cover for a paperback anthology, published in 1954, which has remained in print for more than fifty years. This book was the first of three paperback anthologies Warren edited with Albert Erskine; the others are Six Centuries of Great Poetry (1955), which also remains in print, and A New Southern Harvest (1957) (Special Collections, Western Kentucky University Libraries).

Penn Warren's poem. This savagely dramatic piece was originally planned as a novel, and at one time as a ballad, but the theme proved too intimate, too complex, to fit either form. Yet here is the novelist's gift for exhibiting character in action and in speech, and some times the sad mellifluousness, if not the simplification of balladry. The work also shows throughout the philosopher's concern with definition. If it were not a poem, it might be an exercise in moral semantics. Fortunately, it remains a poem, and a resonant one.

The search for definitions is plain from the start. The author, a native of Kentucky, was for years mulling over the meaning of a crime commit-

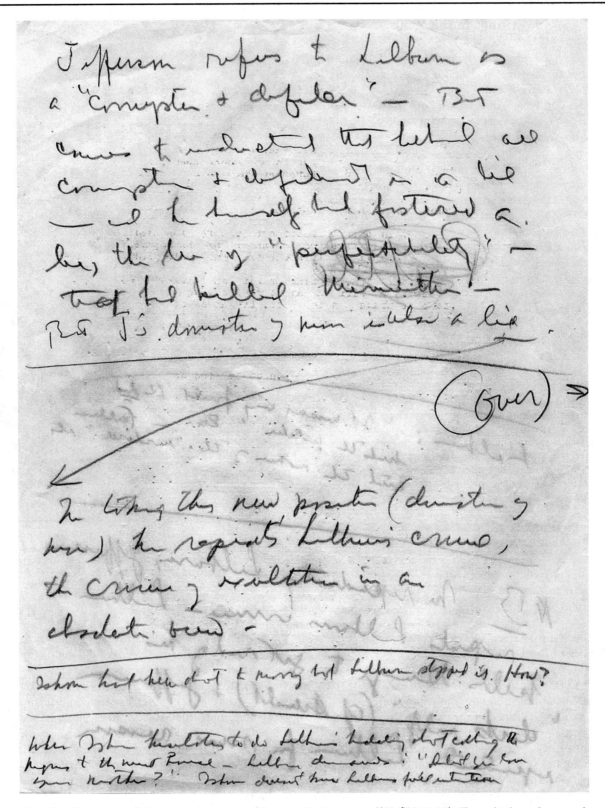

Page from Warren's notes for Brother to Dragons, *a title suggested by the despair of Job (Job 30:29): "I am a brother to dragons and a companion to owls" (Robert Penn Warren Papers, Beinecke Library, Yale University)*

Finding the Form of *Brother to Dragons*

In an interview session in which Warren and Flannery O'Connor met with faculty and students at the Vanderbilt Literary Symposium on 23 April 1959, Warren responded to the question, "how did you finally hit upon the form of Brother to Dragons?*"*

This is awfully like a dissecting room where the corpse is scarcely able to fight back. To answer your question: by fumbling. It started out to be a novel. It clearly couldn't be a novel because the circumstantiality would bog you down, would kill off the main line. And then it started off to be a play. I was doing it in collaboration with a dramatist and producer, and we couldn't quite make it, couldn't agree. I couldn't get a frame for it—the machinery got too much in the way for me. And I was thinking of the wrong kind of problems at the wrong time. But what I was concerned with were the characters, and the emotional sense of it; I didn't want to be bothered by the pacing of it, that technical side. In other words, I didn't naturally think in dramatic terms. The next step was to throw away the notion of the stage play, and keep what was to me the dramatic image, which was the collision of these persons under the unresolved urgency of their earthly experience. All the characters come out of their private purgatory and collide; everybody comes to find out or tell something, rehearse something; it becomes a rehearsal of their unresolved lives in terms of a perspective put on it. That is what the hope was. Then there was the need to tie this to a personal note, putting the writer character in so he could participate in this process, the notion being that we are all unresolved in a way, the dead and the living. This interpenetration, this face of a constant effort to resolve things, came back to the idea of a play again.

—"An Interview with Flannery O'Connor and Robert Penn Warren," *Vagabond*, 6 (February 1960): 13–14

ted by one of its earlier inhabitants: Lilburn Lewis, the elder son of Thomas Jefferson's sister Lucy. She died soon after her husband, Dr. Charles Lewis, had taken her away from Virginia, along with their two grown sons, Lilburn and Isham, and his slaves, to live near a frontier settlement overlooking the Ohio. "On the night of Dec. 15, 1811–the night when the New Madrid earthquake first struck the Mississippi Valley–Lilburn, with the assistance of Isham and in the presence of his Negroes, butchered a slave named George, whose offense had been to break a pitcher prized by the dead mother, Lucy Lewis." Thus the foreword, which relates further how, fol-

lowing the discovery of the murder, the brothers agreed to shoot each other across their mother's grave, but Lilburn alone fell. Isham fled and is reported to have been killed in the Battle of New Orleans. We are told that Jefferson appears never to have referred to "the tragic end of his family in Kentucky." But he is one of those who speaks here, as does another young kinsman who came to a tragic end: Meriwether Lewis, the leader of the Lewis and Clark expedition. The other speakers are the men and women, whites and Negroes, who were involved in the crime, physically or morally, directly or indirectly. Among them is the poet, the narrator. He tells how he first visited the scene, in the fierce blaze of a July day, directed up the mountain by a local farmer, who stared at him: "A fellow of forty, a stranger, and a fool, / Red-headed, freckled, lean, a little stooped, / Who yearned to be understood, to make communication, / To touch the ironic immensity of afternoon with meaning." The story of the murder is set between this confession and an account of his final effort, after a second and wintry visit to "the shrunken ruin," to arrive at an understanding of the condition of man. The poem as a whole is an attempt to define it.

But it must be emphasized that this is a poem, not an essay on morals. The dramatic interest is exploited fully. With one important exception, the speakers reveal themselves in dialogue as various as their natures. A remarkably different quality of tenderness and penetration is expressed by the white woman, Lucy Lewis, the mother of Lilburn, and the Negro Mammy who gave him suck, mother to the boy he hacked to death in the meat house, and again by that poor girl, Laetitia, whom he named in his will as his "beloved but cruel wife." A different sort of animal blindness finds utterance in the voice of Lilburn and his brother Isham, of Laetitia and of her brother, and of Lilburn's Negro body servant and victim.

Everywhere the poet shows his mastery of his craft in the physical actualizing of the mean detail and the superb prospect, the private intake of sensation, feeling and belief, the nonhuman landscape, lonely or inhabited, under the changes of weather and of season. There is a description of an encounter with a snake as actual as Lawrence's, and more symbolic than the poet admits. Whatever literary references occur, and they range from St. Augustine to Spender and beyond, they have been so thoroughly assimilated and are so integral to the text that they will delight the initiate and leave the uninstructed undisturbed.

FOREWORD
~~AFTERWORD~~

Early in the last century, Dr. Charles Lewis, a
planter and physician of Albermarle County, Virginia,
removed to West Kentucky and established himself on
a tract of land not far from the frontier settlements
of Smithland and Salem, in what is now Livingston County,
upriver from Paducah at the confluence of the Ohio and
Cumberland. He took with him his wife and two of his
children -- two grown sons named Lilburn and Isham --
and a number of slaves. On a bluff overlooking the
Ohio, he built a house, somewhat grand for the time and
place, and quarters for the "people". He called the
house Rocky Hill. His wife, Lucy Jefferson Lewis, the
sister of Thomas Jefferson, died soon after the removal
to Kentucky, and was buried on the bluff, some yards
from the house. Charles Lewis now spent little time
at Rocky Hill, making a trip to Virginia and leaving
Lilburn, with his wife and children, and Isham to
occupy the house and manage the estate.

On the night of December 15, 1811 -- the night
when the New Madrid earthquake first struck the
Mississippi Valley -- Lilburn, with the assistance of
Isham and in the presence of his Negroes, butchered
a slave named George, whose offense had been to break
a pitcher prized by the dead mother, Lucy Lewis.
After some months the crime was revealed, and Lilburn
and Isham were indicted for murder. They were released

Page from a late draft of Warren's introductory note for Brother to Dragons *(Robert Penn Warren Papers, Beinecke Library, Yale University)*

The form of the poem is an extremely flexible blank verse; except for two passages veined with song, the rhymes that the poet permits himself are rare and unobtrusive. It is the language, whether exalted or racily colloquial, delicate as Herrick's or harsh as one of Lear's diatribes, that makes for the poetry. Indeed, the interplay of vulgarity and nobility in the language is as it should be, the outward and audible sign of the poem's meaning.

The only failure of appropriateness is in some speeches given to Jefferson. He, not his nephew, the brutal, half-incestuous murderer, is the villain of the piece. He is the damned author of our failure, Warren insists, because he ignored the darkness of the heart of man, apparent both in the hideous act of his nephew Lilburn and in the moral desolation of his young cousin, Meriwether Lewis. When he moves onto the scene, the hands may be the hands of Jefferson but the voice is singularly like the voice of Robert Penn Warren. This is especially noticeable in the passages referring to some ugly incidents in more recent American history, such as the judicial murder of Sacco and Vanzetti.

It is not the absence of eighteenth-century locutions that one misses but the twentieth-century bluntness that sounds off key. Pondering the poem, one comes to believe that the poet's agonized rage is directed not at the hopeful Virginian who promulgated "the great lie that men are capable / Of the brotherhood of justice . . . that man at last is man's friend." To denounce that lie (is it a lie or only a half-truth?) with such ferocity, Warren must himself have cherished it. This notion is encouraged by his final pronouncement, couched in abstractions from which the body of the poem is relatively free:

> We have yearned in the heart for some identification
> With the glory of the human effort, and have yearned
> For an adequate definition of that glory.
> To make that definition would be, in itself,
> Of the nature of glory. This is not paradox.
> It is not paradox, but the best hope.

These words might have been spoken not by the poet but by Jefferson. As a man of the twentieth century Warren has an even deeper intimacy with "the wilderness of the human heart" than was possible to Lilburn's uncle. Nevertheless, he repeatedly attests to "the glory of the human effort." Sometimes he does so in one of the apothegms with which the work is studded. The sensitive, skillfully placed portraits of his father point toward a faith, not so different from Jefferson's, in human grace and dignity.

Early in the poem he declares that the single lesson worth learning "is that the only / Thing in life is glory." One might ask, as Alice asked Humpty Dumpty, what he means by it. He does not tell you, and of the yearning for identification with "the glory of the human effort" he does not speak until the very end. But first he must draw the

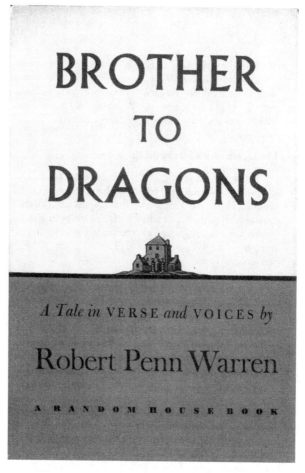

Dust jacket for the long poem that marked the end of Warren's ten-year hiatus from poetry. Warren did not publish a short poem until the sequence "To a Little Girl, One Year Old, in a Ruined Fortress" appeared in 1955 (Special Collections, Western Kentucky University Libraries).

motives of his characters from the stinking filth in which they tangle, make you hear the scream when Lilburn, "in affirming love lifts high the meat-axe" to bring it down on the Negro boy's bound, huddled body. First he must offer, speaking for himself or through the mouths of gentle Lucy Jefferson Lewis and of her brother Thomas, contradictory reflections on love.

When the tragedy has been recounted, Jefferson, assenting to his complicity, states his sorrowful conviction that "We shall be forged / Beneath the hammer of truth on the anvil of anguish," adding: "It would be terrible to think that truth is lost. / It would be worse to think that anguish is lost, ever." He puts his hope in knowledge, "It is bitter bread. / I have eaten that bitter bread," he says, finally, "In joy I would end." But the poet, for whom this work may represent an effort to redeem a small part of the anguish, answers: "We must consider those who could not end in joy." Let us indeed consider them. They are

Death of a Father

In January 1955 Robert Franklin Warren died in Clarksville, Tennessee. Warren wrote the poetic sequence "Mortmain" about his father; it was first published in 1960, and he included it at the end of his 1988 memoir, Portrait of a Father. *In it Warren recounted his memories of his father and the evening his father died.*

The Death of Robert Franklin Warren

He was approaching his eighty-sixth birthday. He had willed to die alone, and without any medical intervention. The doctor discovered that it was cancer of the prostate. My father . . . had never in his life seen a doctor or spent a day in bed except during a long illness when he was forty-two years old. This was simply independence of spirit.

—Portrait of a Father (Lexington: University Press of Kentucky, 1988), p. 79

In the last poem of the five-poem Mortmain sequence, the narrator has a vision of his father as a boy.

A Vision, Circa 1880

Out of the woods where pollen is a powder of gold
Shaken from pistil of oak minutely, and of maple,
And is falling, and the tulip tree lifts, not yet tarnished,
The last calyx, in which chartreuse coolness recessed,
    dew,
Only this morning, lingered till noon—look,
Out of the woods, barefoot, the boy comes. He stands,
Hieratic, complete, in patched britches and that idleness
    of boyhood
Which asks nothing and is its own fulfillment:
In his hand a wand of peeled willow, boy-idle and aimless.

Poised between woods and the pasture, sun-green
    and green shadow,
Hair sweat-dark, brow bearing a smudge of gold
    pollen, lips
Parted in some near-smile of boyhood bemusement,
Dangling the willow, he stands, and I–I stare
Down the tube and darkening corridor of Time
That breaks, like tears, upon that sunlit space,
And staring, I know who he is, and would cry out.
Out of my knowledge, I would cry out and say:
Listen! Say: *Listen! I know—oh, I know—let me tell you!*

That scene is in Trigg County, and I see it.
Trigg County is in Kentucky, and I have been there,
But never remember the spring there. I remember
A land of cedar-shade, blue, and the purl of limewater,
But the pasture parched, and the voice of the lost joree
Unrelenting as conscience, and sick, and the
    afternoon throbs,
And the sun's hot eye on the dry leaf shrivels the aphid,
And the sun's heel does violence in the corn-balk.
That is what I remember, and so the scene

I had seen just now in the mind's eye, vernal,
Is altered, and I strive to cry across the dry pasture,
But cannot, nor move, for my feet, like dry corn-
    roots, cleave
Into the hard earth, and my tongue makes only the dry,
Slight sound of wind on the autumn corn-blade. The boy,
With imperial calm, crosses a space, rejoins
The shadow of woods, but pauses, turns, grins once,
And is gone. And one high oak leaf stirs gray, and the air,
Stirring, freshens to the far favor of rain.

—Portrait of a Father, pp. [90–91]

beyond counting. But then let us ask why they are so many. Was Jefferson the architect of the meat-house where, on Dec. 15, 1811, the murder was committed? Was he the architect, as the poet implies, of the modern prison camps in Europe and Asia, and of this industrialized, mechanized, war-geared slum of a world? As much as he was able to foresee of it, he recognized it for what it was, and he warned his countrymen against letting it develop. Could he have implemented that warning? His mistake was to believe that because man is a reasoning animal, he is also a reasonable one. Paradoxically, judgment has joined with experience to teach us that reason is not enough. "What is any knowledge," asks the poet, "without the intrinsic mediation of the heart?" And yet how shall we adequately define "the glory of the human effort" unless the heart is guided by reason's uncertain light?

The poem raises these questions. It is an index to its contemporaneity that it should seem rather to raise than to answer them, in spite of the rather didactic pronouncements on virtue just before the end. The close is not didactic. Like the better part of the book—in both senses of that adjective—it is poetry: words that simply and precisely show a landscape with figures, words that give the particular atmosphere of the place and the quality of the persons who are passing through it, words that remind us of the sharp joy and the grief and the endurance that belong to those who, if they are brothers to dragons, are also men.

—Babette Deutsch, "Robert Penn Warren's Savage
Poem: Old Murder, Modern Overtones,"
New York Herald Tribune Book Review,
23 August 1953, p. 3

* * *

I-1. (Novel P)   R P Warren

I.

Oh, who am I? -- for so long that was, you might say, the cry of my heart. There were times when I would say to myself my own name -- my name is Amantha Starr -- over and over again, trying, somehow, to make myself come true, but then even the name might go away, and there would be just the little sound I made. The world is big, and you feel lost in it, as though the bigness recedes forever, in all direct-ions, like a desert of sand, and distance flees glimmering and empty from you, whatever way you turned your head. Or the world is big, and the bigness grows tall and close like walls coming together with a great weight, towering over you, and you will be crushed to nothingness. There are -- and suddenly these words fly into my head for the first time -- two kinds of nothingness. The nothing of being only yourself, alone in the sand with the distance withdrawing, and the nothing when the walls of the world come together to crush you. whatever you are.

Sometimes, as I now suppose, I used to fear one kind of nothingness, and sometimes the other, though in those young days I did not think to distinguish between them. I just knew the kind of unhappiness I had, even in the happiness I managed to extract from many situations, the faint, tight tingle in my fingers, and the sickness that would live in the middle of my stomach, so familiar that sometimes I didn't even know it was there, until, all at once, I knew again, and knew that, even in my happiness, it had never really been away. It had just been waiting.

I used to think that there must be some means of escape, and then I could be myself. I used to have a feeling that came to me in a picture, the picture of myself sitting in a place that was beautiful -- a grassy place, a place with sun, maybe water running and sparkling, or just still and bright. I can't recall too clearly, the way you can't recall a dream. When you try to tell somebody about a dream, you find in telling that you are just having another dream, and different. All you have left is the feeling of the old one. And that, you may suddenly realize, may have changed, too. But the feeling I had in this dream, if

Page from a draft of Band of Angels *(Robert Penn Warren Papers, Beinecke Library, Yale University)*

As he had for Brother to Dragons, *Warren found the germ for* Band of Angels, *his fifth novel, in American history. Warren left among his papers an untitled three-page typescript account of how this novel originated. From J. Winston Coleman, author of* Slavery Times in Kentucky *(1940), the author learned of a judge named George Kinkead, whom Coleman had interviewed. The judge's recollections went back to the years before 1861 around Lexington, Kentucky. He remembered the story of two little girls, "practically white," who were uncertain of their origin. When their father died and they returned from Oberlin for the funeral, they were seized, despite public indignation, and sold to a "discriminating" buyer from New Orleans to pay the father's debts. When Warren was writing the Cass Mastern story for* All the King's Men, *he recalled the judge's story. It stuck in his mind, he writes, because it raised questions that it did not answer. Why did the father not set them free legally while he was still alive? Why did the public indignation amount to nothing? What would their life be like after they were sold? What would happen to them after the fall of New Orleans? Would their past be eliminated by the "blue-clad deliverers" from the North?*

To answer the questions raised by the judge's story, Warren wrote Band of Angels *about Amantha Starr (whom he refers to as Manty) and her struggle for freedom even after her master sets her free. In his typescript account Warren asks, "Can anybody ever set you free?" Warren concludes his unpublished essay:*

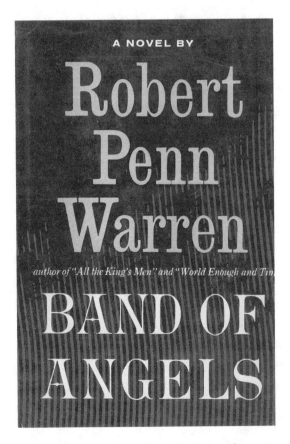

Dust jacket for Warren's fifth novel (Special Collections, Thomas Cooper Library, University of South Carolina)

A key idea is not, however, a book. It is merely the thing that makes a book possible, the atmosphere, the climate, in which the book may grow. It is not the people, the events. The people whose lives were to touch Little Manty's life . . . had to come out of the imagination, too—the dealer who took her downriver on a steamboat; the buyer in New Orleans . . . ; the Oberlin sweetheart who reappears in New Orleans in a Federal uniform; Miss Idell, the mistress of her dead father who also, reappears; Rau-Ru, the black child snatched from a jungle massacre on the Congo to become Lt. Oliver Cromwell Jones, hero; the Harvard graduate, an idealist to whom the butchery of war must be justified by "Truth."

Each one had to have his own story in relation to Manty's story, and since the book was about freedom, each one was groping out of his special kind of bondage toward whatever freedom might be possible for him.

—Robert Penn Warren Papers, King Library,
University of Kentucky

Band of Angels, *dedicated "To Eleanor," was published in August 1955; it was a Literary Guild selection that fall and became a movie starring Yvonne DeCarlo and Clark Gable in 1957. This review is by Carlos Baker, who had also reviewed* World Enough and Time.

Souls Lost in a Blind Lobby
Review of *Band of Angels*

With his sixth novel, "Band of Angels," it is clear that one central drive in Robert Penn Warren's career as a writer of fiction is the illumination, through people, of the dark backward and abysm of American time. In "John Brown: The Making of a Martyr," his nonfictional biography, he explored the fanatical darkness of a mind that glimpsed light but could not win it, and thus established a consuming interest that has since sustained him in the study of various other forms of fanaticism. There was, for example, the tobacco war between the fanatics and the compromisers in "Night Rider"; the case of Murdock and his rebellious daughter in "At Heaven's Gate"; the memorable portrait of Willie Stark in "All the King's Men"; the fanatical romanticism of Jeremiah Beaumont in "World Enough and Time"; and the story of the brothers Lewis, nephews of Thomas Jefferson, in "Brother to Dragons," Warren's novel in verse and voices of two years ago.

Each man, he said in the verse-novel, and each woman, too, is lost "in some blind lobby, hall, enclave, crank cul-de-sac, or corridor of Time. Of Time. Or Self. And in that dark no thread." The problem, sooner or later, for all his characters is the location of the thread, the following of that thread out towards whatever light there is. That a band of angels will come in thunder from the stars and carry people forth is unlikely in the extreme. The way out is step by step, with many backslidings.

Poster for the second Warren novel made into a movie. Gable and DeCarlo played Hamish Bond and Amantha Starr.
Warren sold options on World Enough and Time *and* A Place to Come To, *but the movies were*
not produced (Robert Penn Warren Birthplace Museum, Guthrie, Kentucky).

The blind lobby of self, the Cave of the Ultimate Spleen, is nowhere more apparent in Warren's work than in his latest novel, "Band of Angels," which in its deeper reaches is a parable of slavery and freedom, with a long dark road between the two poles. He tells the highly adventurous life story of Amantha Starr, an orphan of Kentucky, who flourished, if that is the word for it, between 1844 and 1888.

Little Manty spends her motherless childhood on a decaying estate called Starrwood in the country south of Lexington, and her adolescence at a Scripture-reading school in Oberlin, Ohio. Only when her father dies, on the eve of the Civil War, does she discover that her mother was a slave at Starrwood, and that she is therefore a chattel of the estate, to be sold, by her father's creditors, down the river to New Orleans. There she begins a life which spans the fall of that city to Farragut, the corrupt administration of "Beast" Butler, the great war to the north, the Emancipation Proclamation, and the passage of the Fourteenth Amendment, the piteous wandering of the displaced colored refugees, the New Orleans race riots of 1866, and twenty years of married life in St. Louis and sundry small towns in Kansas. What begins, one might say, at something like the level of Tara, the O'Hara plantation in "Gone With the Wind," turns into something like George Washington Cable's "The Grandissimes," and

concludes on a note that might be drawn from Hamlin Garland's "A Daughter of the Middle Border." For moods, that is. No "influence" is to be inferred.

As often happens in Warren, the life of the central character is defined by the people who environ it, governed by a dialectic of half-realized ideas, and dominated at times of crisis by a consuming desire to discriminate truth from error. Amantha will no doubt strike many readers as too much of a pawn, more sinned against than sinning, but a kind of waif-wife, with the waif's self-pity and half-clinging dependence. The shape of her life is drawn by the men who own her, in the various meanings of ownership—no band of angels, certainly, except in the most ironic sense, yet the means by which her waifism is stiffened and saved until she can discriminate her truth from her error and be born into life. Which is to say, into freedom: the good air at the mouth of the cavern.

Yet each of Amantha's "angels" is enslaved, too, awaiting the moment of egress, the mind-born conviction that one is at liberty to take action for good or ill, for ill or good, but in any case with free choice. Her father, Aaron Starr, to take the first example, conceived the child on the body of the slave Renie. He thinks that by raising Amantha as a lady he can deliver her from the bonds of her origin. But the solace he seeks with Miss Idell, whose name is almost a pun, is the very means by which his impoverishment becomes inevitable so that when he dies his daughter's bonds are riveted the more firmly. Or there is Seth Parton, Amantha's dour and pietistic Oberlin sweetheart, slave to the doctrine of self-sanctification, whose ultimate release, again through Miss Idell, comes in slashing cold-eyed financiering, the making of a fortune in the Chicago grain-market.

The forms human bondage may take are legion. The assumed name of Hamish Bond of New Orleans, Amantha's owner, protector, and lover, might also be a pun. His bondage to the past, which comes out in a horrific, bloody, nightmarish, half-cynical flashback to the days when he traded for slaves in the Congo, is only to be expiated now by a kindness so calmly powerful that it overruns him like a disease. Another disease, a form of social narcissism, besets Tobias Sears, the handsome young Union captain and idealistic disciple of Massachusetts transcendentalism, who marries Amantha Starr in a mixture of noble motives. His bondage is to his own sense of magnanimity. For if Bond had kindness like a disease, Sears had nobility like an epidemic.

If this is not Warren's best novel, a guerdon I would still reserve for "All the King's Men," it is a good book on a serious and important subject, giving another thematic emphasis to his perennial preoccupation: the perils of self-deception in the blind lobby of self. Freedom—from what? For what? These questions are as important as ever in the affairs of man. Warren offers a variety of applicable answers.

—Carlos Baker, "Souls Lost in a Blind Lobby,"
Saturday Review, 38 (20 August 1955): 9–10

* * *

Warren's Confessional Novels

Critic Neil Nakadate argues that Warren often writes novels that are "confessional." He begins his essay by placing Warren in the tradition of the American novel that is exemplified by Nathaniel Hawthorne's The Scarlet Letter *(1850) and Herman Melville's* Moby-Dick *(1851).*

There is a nineteenth-century cast to much of Robert Penn Warren's writing. This is not necessarily because his subject matter from his biography of John Brown (1929) to *The Legacy of the Civil War* (1961), has nineteenth-century American history as its common denominator. It is not because the unique historical period of *World Enough and Time, Wilderness,* and *Band of Angels* seems to have a tenacious hold on his creative imagination. Nor is it particularly because Warren has been traditional in political and economic beliefs that he recalls an earlier period in American experience. Robert Penn Warren evokes the nineteenth century largely because he writes fiction in the American tradition as it developed in the age of Hawthorne and Melville. This tradition has long been dominated by an artistic concern with what we have come to call "the power of blackness" and "the fortunate fall": it reflects an artistic concern with the alienated sensibility in a New World milieu. Terminology such as this reminds us that nineteenth-century American fiction was affected by some basically disheartening assumptions about the human condition, assumptions which informed and enforced the radical contradictions of American experience. The result of this has been a large body of writing concerned with a sense of darkness and guilt, an expression of the undertow which has always run beneath the high tide of American optimism and innocence. It is with this murky flux that Robert Penn Warren is concerned, and his concern typically follows the configurations of the confessional novel.

Nakadate defines the confessional novel as a subgenre in which the concern with personal guilt is central and "is revealed in the confessional imperative: that is, the frame of mind which perceives guilt, objective self-criticism, and confessional catharsis as stages in a moral continuum."

Warren's use of this sub-genre can perhaps be best understood in terms of one of his favorite literary devices, the inset narrative. Readers familiar with Warren's fiction will readily recognize the story within a story which functions in his novels as a paradigm, often an allegorical one, for the main story. The interpolated narrative usually appears as a confidential account of an individual's private history, a brief meditation on his past. Characteristically this past contains a sinful act or acts, which the individual feels compelled to "confess," either because of the manifest nature of the sin and the resulting feeling of guilt, or because of the confessor's unique relationship to his auditor (often the protagonist of the novel). The penultimate chapter of *Night Rider,* Warren's first novel, contains Willie Proudfit's account of an aimless life of buffalo slaughter and Indian killing in the West. Interpolated sections of the court confession of Ashby Wyndham are set in counterpoint to the central narrative of *At Heaven's Gate.* Chapter 4 of *All the King's Men* contains the journal of Cass Mastern, which acknowledges a tragic love affair and the betrayal of a close friend. In chapter 10 of *World Enough and Time,* Munn Short, the jailer (one of several sub-narrators in this novel), tells Jeremiah Beaumont of an early life when "I done all the meanness of man." In chapter 7 of *Band of Angels,* Hamish Bond tells Amantha Starr, his mulatto mistress, that he spent his early years as a slave trader on the African coast.

In all of these examples the confessional pattern is the same. The confession itself is an interpolated piece; by implication it is only part of a much larger statement made by the novel as a whole. . . .

—Neil E. Nakadate, "Robert Penn Warren
and the Confessional Novel,"
Genre, 2 (1969): 326, 327–328

At the end of 1955 Warren left Yale but returned to the university six years later. In the interim, his writing and traveling increased. His attention was turned for a time to cultural and social issues. In "A Lesson Read in American Books," an opinion piece for the 11 December 1955 issue of The New York Times Book Review, *Warren took on critics who had complained that American novels gave a negative impression of the country to foreign readers. He vigorously argued the paradoxical point that "the literature that is most truly and profoundly critical is always the most profoundly affirmative," concluding with an anecdote about an Italian officer in the Fascist Army who told him that reading American literature had led him to desert and fight against the Fascists. Warren asked how:*

"Well," he said, "the Fascists used to let us read American fiction because it gave, they thought, a picture of a decadent America. They thought it was good propaganda for fascism to let us read Dreiser, Faulkner, Sinclair Lewis. But you know, it suddenly occurred to me that if democracy could allow that kind of criticism of itself, it must be very strong and good. So I took to the mountains."

In 1956 Warren addressed his country's most sensitive social question directly in his sixty-six-page book Segregation: The Inner Conflict in the South. *In the first paragraph of this review, Mark Ethridge Jr., the editor of the* Raleigh Times, *refers to the* Brown v. *Board of Education* decision *of 17 May 1954 in which segregation by race in public schools was held to deny to black children the equal protection of the laws guaranteed by the Fourteenth Amendment.*

Turmoil in the South
Review of *Segregation*

Since the Supreme Court's decision twenty-seven months ago untold millions of words have been written about segregation in the South. Major magazines have acted as clearing houses of opinions. A plague of Northern journalists tours the South like Methodist circuit riders, pouring out copy by the column for home consumption.

Yet despite this torrent of words a major part of the picture has been largely overlooked. The facts of segregation and desegregation have been covered, but few if any writers have sought to explain to the rest of the nation the whys of this mid-century Southern turmoil. The depth of Southern convictions, the rationalizations and irrationalizations, the blind and bitter hatreds, and the profound helplessness of people caught in a web not of their own choosing and not entirely of their own making have been ignored in the attempt to categorize the South in terms of black and white.

It is just these whys that Robert Penn Warren examines in his short but sensitive and uncluttered

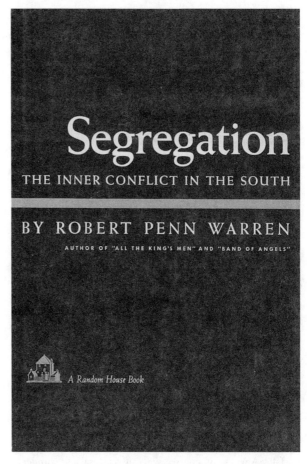

Dust jacket for Warren's 1956 book in which he repudiated his earlier acceptance of separate-but-equal treatment of blacks in the South (Special Collections, Thomas Cooper Library, University of South Carolina)

book *Segregation.* He has set down in interviews with Southerners of all colors and conceptions the first really comprehensive portrait of the racially torn South of 1956.

Warren is well qualified to write on this subject. He is a native Kentuckian and a raised Tenneseean. He went to school at Vanderbilt, taught at Southwestern, Vanderbilt, and Louisiana State. He has lived in the North long enough to view the South objectively but, as he has demonstrated in earlier books, the South has lived in him long enough for him to view it compassionately.

The book's title is a misnomer. The subject is really about prejudice, which knows no time and no locale. The conflict of the moment, as Warren points out in a unique interview with himself at the end of the book, is only a manifestation of the age-old failure of people to achieve perfect justice. The rigors of the South are typical of the reaction when society sets out to correct a long-standing flaw.

Working Without Teaching

These excerpts from letters, which give some indication of Warren's varied and active literary life after he left Yale, were written from Italy, where the Warrens stayed from late spring 1956 to early 1957. Despite the concern Warren expresses about the willingness of Random House to handle all of his work in this first excerpt, the publisher accommodated him by bringing out Promises: Poems, 1954–1957 *in 1957 and* Selected Essays *in 1958. An expansion of* Selected Poems, 1923–1943 *(1944) was not published until* Selected Poems: New and Old, 1923–1966 *(1966). Warren refers to "the Rocca poems"–his sequence of poems "To a Little Girl, One Year Old, in a Ruined Fortress," which first appeared in the* Partisan Review *in spring 1955 and were included in* Promises.

Warren to Erskine, 5 August 1956

. . . The poetic frenzy continues unabated. I have a batch more that you haven't seen, but which I'll be sending on to you before too long. What I now have, plus the Rocca poems of the *Partisan Review,* would not make a book, about twenty-eight poems, some of them quite long–about 1500 lines, I guess. I don't want these to be absorbed into a reissue of *Selected Poems* [1943]. They are quite different from anything in that book, and I think should appear separately. I should like to get them out in 1957, perhaps holding up *Selected Poems* until these, plus hoped-for new ones, could be absorbed into an enlarged volume. BUT–if poems come out in 1957, what about essays? Should essays be postponed another year? Or could we do essays in spring and poems in fall? Always, of course, we can let essays go under another imprint. Not that I want it that way, but if there's too much pressure on you all. I've just had another offer on the essays.

–courtesy of Albert R. Erskine Jr. Estate, Special Collections, Vanderbilt University

Brainard "Lon" Cheney was an old friend who had been in Warren's class at Vanderbilt. The book Warren refers to as coming out in June was Promises, *which was published in August.*

Warren to Lon Cheney, 22 January 1957

This December, or was it November, I suddenly got what I thought was the way of doing <u>BTD</u> as a play, and have lately finished it, or finished this draft. That's what has held up the start on the novel, that and poems, which keep coming, and to which I give precedence when the frenzy strikes. <u>Encounter</u> is doing a sizable batch in the spring, ditto the <u>Yale,</u> <u>Kenyon</u> has the theological series which failed, sad to say, to strike fire with you, <u>Botteghe Oscure</u> a little group. I am now into another little group, but don't know how it goes. In fact, I don't know what I've got in the whole thing. But it is fine to sit around with poetry hours everyday and hope for the best, as I have been doing for seven months or more. The book is due out in June–As for plays again,

<u>AKM</u> was translated into German in the spring and came out as a little book, Fischer Verlag doing it. Then Fischer got it put on in Frankfurt in the State Theater, then moved out to the main area of a chemical factory for one session. They got two stars for the leads, and Fischer reports a "success," whatever that means. My spies report a violently controversial reception, and the fact that the director rewrote the last act into almost unrecognizable form. Anyway, Fischer says they are going to do a lot of TV productions, live shows to start off, but we shall see. Meanwhile as a backwash the play is being reissued as a trade book there, with Lechte Verlag, and there seems to be a fair chance of it's going into a Stockholm production. <u>BTD</u> seems to have a fair chance of Berlin, at least the manager of the theater there has given a verbal commitment to my agent. But long since in that business I've learned to believe nothing until it is done. Words don't mean the same thing among theater producers as they do among either honest men or liars. Anyway, it is fun to be able to write–or not write, just sit–without worrying about when term starts. For a while in the fall I felt like a man with a leg just amputated, but more and more I am able to happily survive without the sound of my own voice going on without interruption for several hours a week in a classroom.

–Special Collections, Vanderbilt University

Rosanna Warren with her godmother, Katherine Anne Porter, at the Warrens' house in Fairfield, Connecticut (Special Collections, Western Kentucky University Libraries)

Allen Tate, Cleanth Brooks, and Warren at the Fugitive reunion, Vanderbilt University, May 1956
(Photographic Archives, Special Collections, Vanderbilt University)

Warren puts it this way:

We have to deal with the problem our historical moment proposes, the burden of our time. We all live with a thousand unsolved problems of justice all the time. We don't even recognize a lot of them. We have to deal only with those which the moment proposes to us. Anyway, we can't legislate for posterity. All we can do for posterity is to try to plug along in a way to make them think we–the old folks–did the best we could for justice, as we could understand it.

This book is not an apology for the South. Warren does not attempt to excuse Southern prejudice or Southern failures. But he does try to explain it through the words of people in the South. He has talked to a Southern Negro woman whose husband was killed by white men, to college students, to leaders of the NAACP and the Citizens' Council, to lawyers, plantation owners, preachers, and to the inevitable taxi drivers all interviewers talk to. He heard and reports their explanations for why integration is easier to say than to accomplish. "Pridefulness, money, level of intelligence, race, God's will, filth and disease, power, hate, contempt, legality" are words he quotes. And there's another one, which he calls piety and Hamilton Basso, in "The View from Pompey's Head," called Southern shintoism. This one is ancestor worship or respect for tradition, however you want to put it.

But this book is also more than an explanation of the whys. It is an insight into people themselves caught in a storm they can neither conquer nor fully comprehend. Warren shows the conflict among Southern people themselves is not just a division of man against man, but of man against himself. The inner conflict is one of respect for law fighting against tradition, of human decency against inborn prejudice, or long-view economics against personal profits by exploitation. In some areas of the South and in some people resolution came easy. Those who favored integration from the first resolved it quickly. So did Jimmy Byrnes and the South Carolina legislature. To those in the middle resolution comes harder, and the conflict is extremely personal. "I feel it's all happening inside of me, every bit of it," a girl from Mississippi told Warren.

Or, as a junk dealer put it:

Somebody ought to tell 'em not to blame no state, not even Alabam' or Mississippi, for what the bad folks do. Like stuff in New York or Chicago. Folks in Mississippi got good hearts as any place. They always been nice and goodhearted to me, for I go up to a man affable. The folks down here is just in trouble and can't claw out. Don't blame 'em, got good hearts but can't claw out of their trouble. It is hard to claw out from under the past and the past way.

It is indeed hard to claw out, and Warren does not pretend to know exactly how or when it will happen. It is a moral problem, but it must be solved concretely. It will take mutual education and mutual respect.

But Warren does offer hope. If the South, he says, can now face up to itself and its situation it may achieve moral identity. "Then in a country where moral identity is hard to come by, the South, because it has had to deal concretely with a moral problem, may offer some leadership." And because segregation is not really much different from Yankee Phariseeism, from smugness without justification, we as a nation need all the leadership we can get.

– Mark Ethridge Jr., "Turmoil in the South."
Saturday Review, 39 (1 September 1956): 14

* * *

Promises: Poems, 1954–1956, *which Warren dedicated to his children, included poems written about Rosanna and Gabriel. This review by James Wright, in part a response to other reviewers, was published after the collection was awarded the Pulitzer Prize in poetry, making Warren the first writer to win a Pulitzer in both fiction and poetry. Wright was at the beginning of his own career as a poet, having published his first collection,* The Green Wall, *in 1957.*

The Stiff Smile of Mr. Warren
Review of *Promises*

Although it is possible, generally speaking, to discover certain consistently developing themes in Mr. Warren's work—prose and verse alike—it is nevertheless impossible to know just what he will do next. In our own century he is perhaps the only American writer who, having already established his major importance, remains unpredictable. If anyone has noted any similarity between Mr. Warren and, say, Dickens, I should be surprised and delighted. But the two authors share the power—it is a very great power, and perhaps it is the heart of the poetic imagination—of unpredictability. A critic is right in being a little hesitant about such a writer. But how explain the neglect of Mr. Warren's poems when we compare it with the critical concern with his novels? I use the word "neglect" when I speak of the poems, simply because I have a hunch that they contain the best seedings and harvests of his imagination.

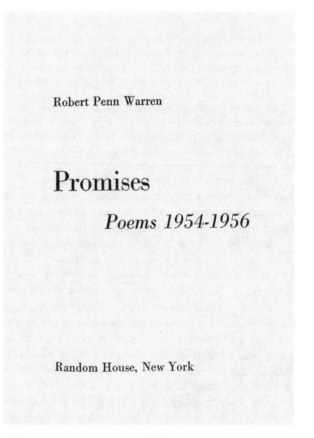

Dust jacket and title page for Warren's first book of poems since Selected Poems, 1923–1943 *in 1944.* Promises, *which included two sections for his children, the "Rosanna poems" and the "Gabriel poems," received the 1958 Pulitzer Prize in poetry (Special Collections, Western Kentucky University Libraries).*

2.

A good many reviewers of *Promises* have been taken aback by the violent distortions of language. But one reviewer is Mr. James Dickey, in the *Sewanee Review*, who describes and clarifies my own response to the book.

The first point concerns the distortions of language, and the critic felt that most of them were flaws: "Warren has his failings: his are a liking for the over-inflated, or 'bombast' as Longinus defines it; he indulges in examples of pathetic fallacy so outrageous that they should, certainly, become classic instances of the misuse of this device. Phrases like 'the irrelevant anguish of air,' and 'the malfeasance of nature or the filth of fate' come only as embarrassments to the reader already entirely committed to Warren's dark and toiling spell." I think this is a pretty fair description of the kinds of awkwardness that frequently appear in *Promises*. However, the really curious and exciting quality of the book is the way in which so many of the poems can almost drag the reader, by the scruff of the neck, into the experiences which they are trying to shape and understand.

But this very triumph of imaginative force over awkward language is Mr. Dickey's second point, and the critic states it eloquently: "Warren's verse is so deeply and compellingly linked to man's ageless, age-old drive toward self-discovery, self-determination, that it makes all discussion of line-endings, metrical variants, and the rest of poetry's paraphernalia appear hopelessly beside the point."

Yet, so very often in this new book, Mr. Warren simply will not allow the reader to consider the rhetorical devices of language "hopelessly beside the point." That he is capable of a smoothly formal versification in some poems, and of a delicate musical variation in others, he has shown many times in the past. We are not dealing with a raw, genuine, and untrained talent, but with a skilled and highly sophisticated student of traditional prosody. In effect, a major writer at the height of his fame has chosen, not to write his good poems over again, but to break his own rules, to shatter his words and try to recreate them, to fight through and beyond his own craftsmanship in order to revitalize his language at the sources of tenderness and horror. One of the innumerable ironies which hound writers, I suppose, is the fact that the very competence which a man may struggle for years to master can suddenly and treacherously stiffen into a mere *armor against experience* instead of an instrument for contending with that experience. No wonder so many poets quit while they're still behind. What makes Mr. Warren excitingly important is his refusal to quit even while he's ahead. In *Promises*, it seems to me, he had deliberately shed the armor of competence—a finely meshed and expensive armor, forged at heaven knows how many bitter intellectual fires—and has gone out to fight with the ungovernable tide. I mean no disrespect—on the contrary—when I say that few of the poems in this book can match several of his previous single poems. Yet I think there is every reason to believe that his willingness to do violence to one stage in the development of his craftsmanship is not the least of the promises which his book contains. I do not wish to argue about any of the poems in *Promises* which I consider at the moment to be failures, though I shall mention one of them. But I think that a book such as this—a book whose main importance, I believe, is the further evidence it provides for the unceasing and furious growth of a considerable artist—deserves an attention quite as close that that which we conventionally accord to the same author's more frequently accomplished poems of the past.

3.

The distortion of language in the new book is almost always demonstrably deliberate. When it is successful, it appears not as an accidental coarseness, but rather as an extreme exaggeration of a very formal style. The poetic function of the distortion is to mediate between the two distinct moods of tenderness and horror. This strategy—in which formality is driven, as it were, to distraction—does not always succeed. It is dishonest critical damnation, and not critical praise, to tell a gifted imaginative writer that he has already scaled Olympus when, as a matter of frequent fact, he has taken a nose-dive into the ditch. The truest praise, in my opinion, is in the critic's effort to keep his eye on the poet's imaginative strategy, especially if the poet is still alive and still growing. I think that the failure of Mr. Warren's strategy is most glaring when the material which he dares to explore will somehow not allow him to establish one of the two essentially dramatic moods—the tenderness and the horror of which I spoke above. An example of this failure is the poem "School Lesson Based on Word of Tragic Death of Entire Gillum Family." The horror is stated, and the reality of horror is a lesson which everyone must learn, as the poet implies in the last line. But there is no tenderness against which the horror can be dramatically drawn, and there is no dramatic reason that I can discern for presenting the ice-pick murder of the Gillum family. Now, I am sure the reader will allow me to claim a human concern for the Gillum family, wherever and whoever they were. All I am saying is that they are *not here:* that is, their death seems to me a capricious horror; and the distorted language, in spite of its magnificent attempt to achieve a folk-like barrenness and force, remains a capricious awkwardness.

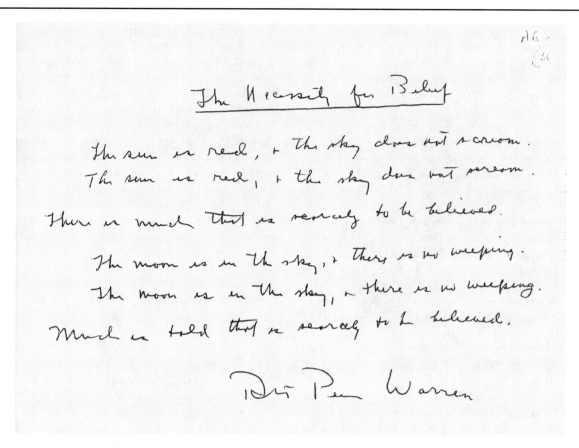

Warren's fair copy of the poem that appeared at the end of Promises *(Special Collections, Western Kentucky University Libraries)*

My speaking of "failure" in a poet of so much stature is of course tempered by my statement of a conviction which constantly grows on me: that a failure like the "School Lesson" is worth more than the ten thousand safe and competent versifyings produced by our current crop of punks in America. I am spared the usual but boring critical courtesy of mentioning names by the fact that we all know who we are. But I am not comparing Mr. Warren's performance in *Promises* with the performance of us safe boys. I am trying to compare it with his capacities. I want to look somewhat closely at a poem in *Promises* in which the poet's exploration past facility into violent distortion end in discovery. I suppose there are five or six fine poems of this sort in the book, but I will settle for a reading of one of them.

The poem is called "The Child Next Door." I hope that my reader will take time, at this point, to read aloud to himself the entire sequence of poems in *Promises* entitled "To a Little Girl, One Year Old, in a Ruined Fortress." Furthermore, since there can be no harm in our simply taking the poet at his word (and where else can we begin?) the reader had better read the dedication aloud also.

4.
There are two kinds of violent distortion in "The Child Next Door"—one of rhythm and one of syntax. I invite the reader to discover, if he can, some regularity of scansion in the following representative lines of the poem:

> Took a pill, or did something to herself she thought would not hurt. . . .
> Is it hate?—in my heart. Fool, doesn't she know that the process. . . .
> I think of your goldness, of joy, how empires grind, stars are hurled. . . .
> I smile stiff, saying *ciao,* saying *ciao,* and think: this is the world. . . .

I find no regularity of metrical stresses. Now, one reviewer has suggested an affinity between Mr. Warren's new verse and the verse of Hopkins. Suppose we were to read the above quoted lines according to Hopkins' system (I quote from one of the famous letters to R. W. Dixon): "It consists in scanning by accents or stresses alone, without any account of the number of syllables, so that a foot may be one strong syllable or it may be many light and one strong." (These are, of course, Hopkins' somewhat desperately oversimplifying words to a puzzled admirer.) The system seems promising, but even this way of reading Mr. Warren's lines does not reveal a regular pattern. Playing the above lines by ear, I can hear six strong stresses in the first line, six in the second, seven in the third, and seven in the fourth. Yet I am not sure; and my uncertainty, instead of being an annoyance, is haunting. Moreover, there are eighteen lines in the whole poem, and my feeling is that nearly all of the lines (mainly with the exception of the above) can be read aloud according to a system of five strong stresses. Here, for example, is the first line of the poem:

> The child next door is defective because the mother. . . .

I hesitate slightly over the word "next," but, with a little straining to get past it, I think I can find clearly strong stresses in "child," "door," the middle syllable of "defective," the second syllable of "because," and the first syllable of "mother." And so on. The regularity becomes clear only if the reader is willing to strain his senses a bit—to give his physical response to the rhythm, as it were, a kind of "body-English." We find the poet like the tennis player keeping his balance and not taking a fall, and feel some kind of relief which is at the same time a fulfillment. I get this kind of physical sensation in reading "The Child Next Door," a poem in which a skilled performer is always daring to expose his balance to chaos and always regaining the balance. In plain English, the rhythm of this poem may be described as a formality which is deliberately driven to test itself, and which seems imaginatively designed to disturb the reader into auditory exaggerations of his own. Perhaps what is occurring in the rhythm of this poem is a peculiar kind of counterpoint. We have "counterpoint," said Hopkins to Dixon, when "each line (or nearly so) has two different coexisting scansions." But these words explain only a part of Mr. Warren's counterpoint. I propose the hypothesis that one can hear in the poem two movements of language: a strong formal regularity, which can be identified with a little struggle, but which is driven so fiercely by the poet that one starts to hear beyond it the approach of an unpredictable and hence discomforting second movement, which can be identified as something chaotic, something very powerful but unorganized. It is the halting, stammering movement of an ordinarily articulate man who has been shocked. The order and the chaos move side by side; and, as the poem proceeds, I get the feeling that each movement becomes a little stronger, and together they help to produce an echoing violence in the syntax.

Some of the later lines do indeed sound something like Hopkins; but that is an accidental and, I think, essentially irrelevant echo. The lines have their own dramatic justification, which I shall try to show in a moment:

> Can it bind or loose, that beauty in that kind,
> Beauty of benediction? I trust our hope to prevail
> That heart-joy in beauty be wisdom before beauty fail.

The syntax in the earlier lines of the poem seems to be recognizably more regular:

> The child next door is defective because the mother,
> Seven brats already in that purlieu of dirt,
> Took a pill.

If the reader grants that the syntax of these earlier lines is fairly normal and regular as compared with the syntax of the passage beginning "Can it bind or loose," then I think he can identify the two kinds of distortion which I have mentioned: a distortion of rhythm, and a distortion of a syntax. But each distortion, however strong, is accompanied by an equally strong regularity. And in each case the violence of the distortion is identifiable as an exaggeration of the regularity itself.

What a neat stylistic formulation! And how dead, compared with the poem!

5.

Now, to say that the sound of a poem is not identical with its sense is different from saying that the two may not exist in rhetorical harmony with each other. I believe that the exaggerated formality of sound in Mr. Warren's poem is justified by the dramatic occasion of the poem itself. Let us consider the poem's dramatic occasion by limiting ourselves, at least temporarily, to the references which we can find within it, or in the title of the sequence of which it is a part.

First, the speaker is addressing a one-year-old child. He has told us so in the title of the sequence. Moreover, the fact that in this particular poem he is not merely brooding on things in general is made clear to us by his explicitly addressing the child in the next-to-last line: "I think of your goldness. . . ." In addressing the child he first points out something that exists in the external world; then he describes his own feelings about this thing; and finally he tries to convey the significance of what he sees in relation to the one-year-old child herself. It might be objected, either to the poem or to my reading of it, that a one-year-old child could not conceivably understand either the physical horror of what the speaker points out or the confused and confusing significance which he has to extract from it. She is defended against its horror by her youth. But the speaker is also incapable of grasping what he shows the child. And he has no defense. He is exposed

Dust jacket for the first English edition, published in 1959 by Eyre and Spottiswoode (Thomas Cooper Library, University of South Carolina)

to an almost unspeakably hideous reality which he can neither escape nor deny.

Indeed, what makes reality in nature seem hideous is that it is both alluring and uncontrollable. Once a man is committed to it in love, he is going to be made to suffer. "Children sweeten labours," said Bacon, "but they make misfortunes more bitter." The reason is that children tear away, if anything can, a man's final defense against the indifferent cruelty of the natural world into which he has somehow blundered and awakened. The speaker in Mr. Warren's poem speaks to his own appallingly precious child about another child who seems blindly and meaninglessly lamed and halted by something in nature itself for which it is absurd to assign anything so simple as mere blame. I would find it hard to imagine a dramatic situation in which the loving commitments of the speaker are subjected to more severe tensions than this one. And conceiving, as I do, that the speaker is an *actor* in this drama, and not merely a *spectator* of it, I would say that his "pathetic fallacy" of attributing "malfeasance" to nature and "filth" to fate is his dramatically justifiable

attempt to defend himself against something more horrible than malfeasance and filth–i.e., the indifference of nature and fate alike.

The speaker cannot escape the contemplation of this horror because of the very child whom he addresses. The tenderness with which he regards this child ("I think of your goldness, of joy") is the very emotion which exposes him to the living and physical evidence of the horror which man and child contemplate together, which neither can understand, but which the man is trapped by his tenderness into acknowledging.

For the horror (embodied in the defective child, the child next door) in its vast and terrible innocence of its own nature actually *greets* the speaker. He cannot ignore the greeting; for he, too, has a child–not defective, but nevertheless unknowingly exposed to all the possibilities, all the contingencies and promises (of course, Mr. Warren knows very well, and dramatizes in this poem with surpassing power, that not all promises are sentimental assurances of a return to Eden), the utterly mindless and brutal accidents of a fallen world. So every child, in a sense which is fundamental to the loving and moral agony of this poem, is defective–and the speaker himself is such a child. Perhaps the real "child next door" is the reader of the book.

The fallen world is chiefly characterized, in the poet's vision, by a tragic truth: that man's very capacity for tenderness is what exposes him to horrors which cannot be escaped without the assumption of an indifference which, to be sufficiently comforting, would also require the loss of tenderness itself, perhaps even the loss of *all* feeling–even the loss of hatred. The beautiful sister in the poem is not in agony, and her face is not stiff with anger, or contorted with tenderness. Her face is pure, calm. Her face is, in the most literal sense, unbearable. "She smiles her smile without taint." Without taint! To give my sense of the dramatic and human appropriateness of the poet's outburst against the maddening and untainted smile, I can only say that, if the speaker in the poem had not damned her for a fool, I would have written a letter to Mr. Warren and damned her on my own hook.

The speaker is trapped in his necessity of choice; and yet he cannot choose. Between the necessity and the incapacity the speaker is driven to a point where the outraged snarl of an animal would have been justified by the dramatic context. But this is where the imaginative courage of Mr. Warren's continuous explorations comes in. Instead of following the music of his lines and the intensity of his drama into chaos, he suddenly rides the pendulum back to formality–but this time the formality of the rhythm includes the formality of the drama, and I think that the strategy is superbly successful. Instead of snarling, the speaker acknowledges the horror's greeting. He faces the horror, and his acknowledgment is a perfect embodiment of what earlier I called a severe and exaggerated formality. Consider the emotions that the speaker must simultaneously bear in his consciousness: frightened and helpless tenderness toward his own child; horror at the idiot; rage at the calm face of the sister. His problem is like the lesson in Frost's poem: "how to be unhappy yet polite." And the speaker smiles–stiffly:

I smile stiff, saying *ciao,* saying *ciao.*

The stiffness of that smile, I think, is what we must attend to. It is the exaggerated formality with which a man faces and acknowledges the concrete and inescapable existence of an utterly innocent (and therefore utterly ruthless) reality which is quite capable not only of crushing him, but also of letting him linger contemplatively over the sound of his own bones breaking. And the exaggerated formality is, in the sound and syntax of the poem, that violence of language which I have described, and which many reviewers of the poems have found discomforting. I admit that the distortions, which swing on the living pendulum of the poet's imagination between the sound and the sense of the poem "The Child Next Door," are discomforting. All I suggest is that they dramatically illuminate each other, and that they are therefore rhetorically harmonious parts of a single created experience: a successful, though disturbing, poem.

–James Wright, "The Stiff Smile of Mr. Warren," *Kenyon Review,* 20 (Autumn 1958): 645–655

* * *

The first of two collections of Warren's essays, Selected Essays, *was published in June 1958. This review is by the literary critic Alfred Kazin, the author of* On Native Grounds *(1942), a study of American prose literature, and* The Inmost Leaf *(1955), a collection of critical essays on American and European literature.*

The Seriousness of Robert Penn Warren
Review of *Selected Essays*

Any critic who is really interested in himself, who is worth reading as an individual writer and thinker, is likely to be so much more various and subtle in practice than he is in theory that it is important to understand why his theory is important to the critic himself. Even if he is not an aesthetician or philosopher, but simply a sensitive intelligence responding directly to works of art, his general point of view, though he may often for-

Dust jacket for Warren's first collection of essays. In his preface he notes "the variety and internecine vindictiveness of voices" in literary criticism and calls for "intelligence, tact, discipline, honesty, sensitivity–those are the things we have to depend on, after all, to give us what we prize in criticism, the insight" (Special Collections, Thomas Cooper Library, University of South Carolina).

get it, serves as his formal code, his landmark–in actual practice, his way of defining his total experience to himself. This definition may not serve him in specific cases; the critic will often find himself in sympathy with writers he does not agree with. But his way of defining his life to himself can be so urgent as to become another presence in his work; what is important in his work is not only what he says, but what he would like to say.

This seems to me the case of Robert Penn Warren. The textbooks he had edited with Cleanth Brooks have more than any other single force helped to establish in our universities "critical" reading as a substitute for the old historical concerns; of course it was not Warren and Brooks who started this trend–they merely serviced it more effectively than others did. Yet

Criticism as Self-Definition

Critic Monroe Spears argues that Warren's Selected Essays *should be read in light of what he calls the writer's "central theme"—the belief "that poetry exists not in some purely aesthetic realm but in the everyday world of experience and change, which it interprets and which it can affect."*

In "Pure and Impure Poetry" Warren argues against the ideal of pure poetry, showing the value of impurity from the contribution of the ironic and irreverent figure of Mercutio to *Romeo and Juliet* to the fundamental importance of irony in the *Divine Comedy,* with its conflicts between human and divine conceptions of justice; and he elaborates the same thesis at much greater length in the long study of *The Rime of the Ancient Mariner.* He insists that poetry does have meaning and is related to the real world of history: there is the repeated image of the poet as earning his vision by submitting it to the fires of irony. In every essay Warren is exploring a writer who is like himself and is defining themes that are like those of his own novels and poems. This is criticism as self-definition, self-discovery. To put it another way, we might say that in each essay Warren explores certain possibilities of himself as writer, masks of the self, personae in Pound's definition. This is plain in the essay on Coleridge, a romantic-philosophical poet whose main theme is the sacramental One Life of man and nature, with the violation of this communion through Original Sin and its restoration through love and repentance; and whose secondary theme is the crime against the Imagination and the final restoration of unity. (In the most general terms the *Ancient Mariner* is "about the unity of mind and the final unity of values, and in particular about poetry itself.") "A Poem of Pure Imagination" is an essay in definition, all as relevant to Warren's work as to Coleridge's. As in "Pure and Impure Poetry" the critic argues for the unity of experience ("I cannot admit that our experience, even our aesthetic experience, is ineluctably and vindictively divided into the 'magical' and the rational, with an abyss between") and hence for a definition of art as impure, involved with history on the one hand and ideas, philosophical and religious, on the other.

The splendid essay on *Nostromo* defines the philosophical novelist, in terms that obviously apply as much to Warren as to Conrad, as not "schematic and deductive," but "willing to go naked into the pit, again and again, to make the same old struggle for his truth"; and as one for whom "the very act of composition was a way of knowing, a way of exploration." Conrad's central theme is the relation of man to the human communion, he says, and Faulkner's basic theme is similar—recognition of the common human bond, with the only villains those who deny that bond. Another variation of the theme is apparent in the title "Love and Separateness in Eudora Welty." Frost's theme of the relation between fact and the dream resembles Conrad's, and the title "Irony with a Center" suggests another dimension of irony, which may be purely destructive, the corrosive intellect when pure Idea; but, when held in balance, irony makes for inclusiveness and richness in art. The Wolfe and Hemingway essays define certain kinds of naturalism, together with a romantic antiintellectualism, that Warren seems to be exorcising in himself.

—Monroe Spears, "The Critics Who Made Us,"
Sewanee Review, 94 (January–March 1986):
103–104

the point here is that as a working critic Warren is not only far more elastic in his taste, shrewd in his judgment and generous in his interest than any other critic identified with the Southern "school," but that he remains all of these things without yielding in his allegiance to the same fundamental point of view that is shared by so many Southern poets and critics. This point of view I should describe as an attempt, through an ideal conception of poetry, to reclaim the Christian, sacramental vision of the world destroyed by scientific materialism. Although Warren, Brooks and Tate may disagree as to specific elements in poetry, it is clear enough that at least in the recent past (Tate is now a Catholic) they all believed that the poetic imagination gives us better access to supernatural knowledge than any other tool that man has developed since the rise of modern science deprived so many men of faith in such knowledge; for them poetry is not only knowledge, but it is in line with the kind of knowledge that men once claimed from religion.

Yet Warren is not only a steadier critic than Tate and an incomparably more generous and interested one than Cleanth Brooks; he is a particularly gratifying example of how utterly direct, objective and *concerned* a critic can be. There are many specific judgments one could disagree with in these ten essays. Warren attacks the idea of a "pure" poetry into which ideas do not enter. He writes about Conrad with an emphasis on stoical wisdom that overlooks the hallucinated, purely driven side of Conrad's work. He is marvelous on Faulkner and almost equally good on Hemingway, but as with Conrad, he gives too much stress to ethical themes in discussing Robert Frost—who has always been admired too complacently for this side of his work. One may admire Katherine Anne Porter without desiring to make the pedagogical inflation of her literary virtues that Warren tends to make, and in another way, one can admire Eudora Welty and yet admit about certain of her books, as Warren does not, the ineffectiveness of her charms. It is easy to agree with

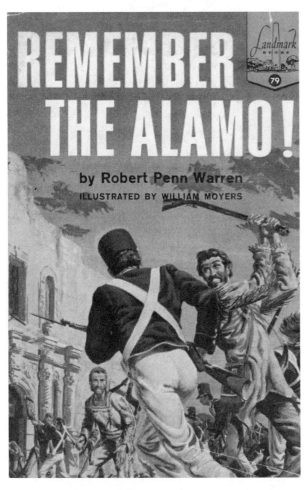

Dust jacket for the first of two books Warren wrote for children, published in 1958 (Special Collections, Thomas Cooper Library, University of South Carolina)

never learn—by the gift of speaking his own mind without being self-conscious. Probably only novelist-critics and poet-critics (Warren of course is both)—not critics who depend too much on criticism itself—ever attain this professional directness. Although he sometimes tends to inflate a particular text when he is really concerned with it only as illustration, it is even more to the point that Warren has learned from his long practice in the classroom to concentrate on the actual matter in hand in a way that emphasizes his own affection for a text rather than pride in the "method."

It is tempting to show in how many particular insights Warren has shown himself freer and more ranging than his school. Nevertheless, he does belong to a "school"—to a point of view, a doctrine, he shares with many Southerners and traditionalists. He sees the experience of modern man as one that cries out for the Christian vision of the world as sacramental, not accidental and meaningless. Warren states his own philosophy in a passage on Conrad: ". . . the last wisdom is for

ROBERT PENN WARREN

HOW TEXAS WON HER FREEDOM
The Story of Sam Houston & the Battle of San Jacinto

1959 San Jacinto Museum of History · San Jacinto Monument, Texas

Title page for a 1959 monograph Warren wrote after doing research for Remember the Alamo! *(Special Collections, Western Kentucky University Libraries)*

him on the hollowness of Thomas Wolfe and the extraordinary, self-won achievements in Melville's poetry; one can quarrel not so much with his claim that "The Ancient Mariner" is neo-Christian as with his failure to prove what, in his terms, is the artistic achievement of the poem. Yet whatever one's running response to them, the essential experience one gets from reading these essays is the close contact with a superb critical intelligence, with a mind that is deeply serious, in whom analytical power and real sensibility are constantly matched and mixed. Warren has learned the art of writing criticism from the teacher's need to point and to explain without yielding to the teacher's addiction to impersonal formula and condescending rules. Anyone who knows how unfelt the language of classroom critics can be finds himself exhilarated not only by Warren's freedom and robustness, but also—and this seems to me something that many good critics

man to realize that though his values are illusions, the illusion is necessary, is infinitely precious . . . in the end, his only truth." He says the motif in Conrad's fiction is the "true lie"—that which we believe because we must, not because we can.

In reading Warren's fiction and poetry I often have the sense that this theme of "the true lie," of the necessary contradiction between man's nature and man's values, offers an image of stoical struggle that is necessary to Warren. He refuses the sanctions of orthodox Christianity, which proclaim spiritual values as absolute truth, and the naturalistic interpretation of values as pragmatically necessary to man. For Warren values are something that man *insists* on heroically and arbitrarily in the face of everything. There is no *system* of values that he believes in; there is only the last-ditch faith in values themselves as they emerge through the activity of literature. At the heart of literature is the essential faculty of poetic imagination, which works through symbols that are recollections of our ancient connection with a spiritual world.

What Warren does in his work is actually to make the Christian sensibility, the awareness of "order" and "truth," an extension of the literary imagination. His struggle, the special struggle that goes on in all his creative work and divides it between introspective rhetoric and the nightmare of a totally corrupt society, is a peculiar one. Warren is really concerned only with literature (one reason why he is so strong a critic), but he seems to me beset by a need to keep alive the "sacramental vision" as a tragic discrepancy. Literature thus carries the burden of reminding man of his true values. It is as if Warren associated his "sacramental vision" with the classic power of literature itself—he writes like a man who has isolated this power in literature and given it a name. My complaint against this procedure is that it makes the great imaginative novelists he discusses, Conrad and Faulkner, sound much more noble, deliberate and coherent than the imagination itself can ever be, and that, as in the long essay on "The Ancient Mariner" with which his book ends, it makes him seem far more interested in making out a case for the would-be Christian in Coleridge than for what in the poem is—if not "pure"—abidingly mysterious. The opposite of Warren's "sacramental" vision is not, as he suggests in the essay on Conrad, the "sceptical" vision; it is the imagination working with what cannot be *entirely* construed as ideas and meanings; it is the imagination delighting in its own power.

—Alfred Kazin, "The Seriousness of Robert Penn Warren," *Partisan Review,*
26 (Spring 1959): 312–316

* * *

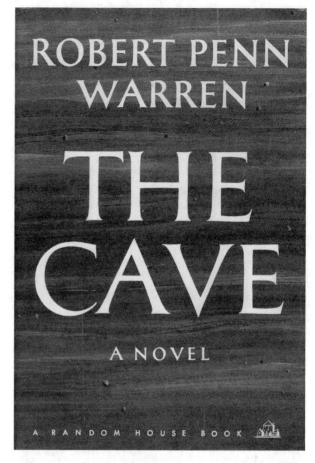

Dust jacket for Warren's sixth novel, which he had originally titled "The Man Below" (Special Collections, Thomas Cooper Library, University of South Carolina)

Warren wrote most of The Cave, *published in August 1958, while he was in Italy. The novel was inspired by the ordeal of Floyd Collins, a Kentucky spelunker who was trapped in Sand Cave for eighteen days, from 30 January to 16 February 1925. Despite dramatic rescue efforts—carried to the nation on the new medium of radio and through newspaper accounts—Collins died. The novel has an epigraph from the seventh book of* Plato's Republic:

You have shown me a strange image, and they are strange prisoners.

Like ourselves, I replied; and they see only their own shadows, or the shadows of one another, which the fire throws on the opposite wall of the cave?

True, he said; how could they see anything but the shadows if they were never allowed to move their heads?

A Tale of Men Trapped in Their Own Darkness
Review of *The Cave*

Although *The Cave* is Robert Penn Warren's sixth novel, he has been, for many people, a one-novel writer. This is true partly because the unquestionable greatness of *All the King's Men* has obscured Warren's other work; but also, I think, because his recent novels have been set in the past, and have therefore been regarded as "historical," and of a lower order of seriousness.

The joker in this is that *All the King's Men* is "historical" in exactly the same way that *World Enough and Time* and *Band of Angels* are historical; in all of his best work Warren has used a sequence of events that really occurred–a war, a crime, a political career–and out of those events has composed a significant pattern, a *myth*. If this is an historical technique, then Aeschylus was writing an historical drama when he wrote the *Oresteia,* and so was Shakespeare when he wrote *Macbeth* (which he cribbed from a history book, after all).

Warren uses history, but the thing he writes is not quite history; it lies half-way between actual event and folk tale, in that area where the popular mind has got hold of the facts, and rubbed the details off, and made them into a symbol of something that matters. It is always American history, and always Southern, but it is what the history of the American South might sound like if it were told us by poets. Warren's beautiful, and rather neglected first novel, *Night Riders,* is like that–a bare, urgent story of a man's brief destiny, historical (the occasion is the Kentucky tobacco wars of the early part of this century), but in the telling timeless. *Brother to Dragons,* his verse play, has the same quality of real events made formal, and in their formality significant; so has his fine long poem, *The Ballad of Billie Potts.*

On Trying to Be a Writer

At the 23 April 1959 Vanderbilt Literary Symposium, Warren was adamant that a writer should not use youth as an excuse for poor work. When he was asked what he called himself, Warren replied, "I say I am trying to be a writer."

Mr. Warren: I must say that I don't want to nag at a point here that has nothing to do with the one we're discussing, but thinking of oneself as a young writer: it's wrong. I mean, stop boasting. You see, you think you know everything, and you've got to put it down. Don't play yourself for a coward, play for keeps. I think you have to do it that way. Not that nice little exercise I am doing because I am young, and ought to be forgiven. Nothing will be forgiven. It will stink just as much if you did it as if Hemingway did it. It will be just as bad. "I am a young learning writer, and I mean well," is a terrible way to think of it. You're full of urgency and wisdom; you've got to spill it, and set the world aright. A young man I knew some time ago was such a talented young man, really, and so bright. He knew everything. He knew about Kafka and Aristotle; he had read everything. He was the most educated young man I had encountered in years. He was twenty-one years old, a senior at Yale, scholar of the house, prize product of an expensive educational system, and he was leaving his studies, he was so bright. "You just go write a novel or novelette for your project, no more classes for a year," and things like that. He wrote well; he knew all about how he should feel as a young writer of twenty-one. Like that cartoon I saw in *The New Yorker* some years ago of two little boys reading a book of child care, and one little boy saying, "Jesus, I'm going to be a stinker two years from now." This boy was writing just like that, that kind of self-consciousness, you know. He had dated himself, you see, along the way. He was writing a novel, a love story, and the boy got the girl after certain tribulations that were case book tribulations, it seemed to me, because I am sure he couldn't have gotten them out of real life. Nobody acts like that. They were all so right, intellectually. He knew what people should feel at the age of eighteen, nineteen, twenty, and twenty-one, and fifty-three, and fifty-nine, and seventy-six. He had it all worked out–the life pattern for the fruit fly there at his finger tips. He had a wonderful last paragraph. They got in a clinch and everything was fine, and then they were going to get married. Then this last paragraph: I found it sort of chilling. He said he knew of course this was not really love; he knew that love would come after years of shared experiences: you know, walking the baby with the colic, and the mortgages. Now just imagine a young man twenty-one years old who knows all about Kafka and Aristotle writing like that. The girl ought to run screaming into the brush. He's dated himself as a young writer, you see, a young human being, a post-public adult, some kind of thing like that. His life, everything, was all dated and scaled up. Romeo would never have thought of himself in that way: "This is not true love–that would be seventeen years from now, when we pay off the mortgage." I think it's a dangerous way to look at things. You've got to feel you know the truth, got to tell it–it's the gospel. Hate your elders.

–"An Interview with Flannery O'Connor and Robert Penn Warren," *Vagabond,* 6 (February 1960): 13

The Cave is an "historical myth" in the same way. The event, in this case, is the Floyd Collins story, of a hillbilly who got stuck in a cave, and caught a nation's anxious attention. Throughout the novel a man is caught underground; but the novel is not about him, and in fact we never see him at all. It is, rather, about the effect of this dark imprisonment upon the people of his town; upon his father, dying of cancer; his younger brother, in the first confusion of young love; upon the town banker and his family, the Greek restaurant owner, the Baptist minister, and his weak, ambitious son—each person caught in the cave of himself, panicky with the need to escape from the darkness and the loneliness there.

Toward the end of the novel, the banker thinks: "Thousands of people, he didn't know how many, had come here because a poor boy had got caught in the ground, and had lain there dying. They had wept, and prayed, and boozed, and sung and fought, and fornicated, and in all ways possible had striven to break through to the heart of the mystery which was themselves. No, . . . to break out of the dark mystery which was themselves."

But there is no breaking out of that dark mystery—one can only confront it, and try to understand it. The end of man, as Warren has repeatedly said in his books, is to know who he is, and to do that one must go into the darkness. Thus Jasper Harrick, the man in the cave, explains to his mother why he explores caves: "Well, in the ground at least a fellow has a chance of knowing who he is." By the end of the novel, some of the characters know who they are, and are free in that knowledge. But others are what they have always been, trapped and ignorant in their own darkness.

The man in the cave, then, is a myth—an old one (Warren uses Plato's myth of the cave as an epigraph to his novel) but still a viable one. But because Warren's version of the myth is also historical—because there *was* a man in a cave once, whose name and fate we remember, though we have forgotten the details—the novel is not limited to the bare symbolical bones of the myth, but can be rich and particular, even earthy, as well. As the story of a dramatic human predicament it is rapid and gripping; but the predicament is, if we ponder it, every man's predicament, and the cave is that darkness which every man must enter, to find himself.

—Sam Hynes, "A Tale of Men Trapped in Their Own Darkness," *Commonweal*, 70 (4 September 1959): 476–477

Working in the Theater

On 25 November 1958, a new dramatic version of the Willie Stark story, Willie Stark: His Rise and Fall, *premiered at the Margo Jones Theater in Dallas, Texas—the result of Warren's collaboration with director Aaron Frankel. In this essay Frankel describes working with Warren on that play as well as on a production of* Brother to Dragons *that was performed at the University of Washington in February 1968.*

Working with Robert Penn Warren

In November, 1958, as the new Artistic Director of the Margo Jones Theater in Dallas, Texas, I produced and directed a stage adaptation of Robert Penn Warren's *All the King's Men,* called *Willie Stark, His Rise and Fall.* I had started collaborating on it with Mr. Warren four years earlier.

This was the fourth version of the story. But let Robert Penn Warren himself provide the details of that, from the Playwright's Column he wrote for the 1958 Margo Jones Theater program:

> This play is new, and it is old. It is old in the sense that it is the last, and I trust the final, form of a piece of work I began twenty years ago [1938]. Then, as a teacher at the Louisiana State University, I was a fascinated observer of that instructive melodrama which was Louisiana politics; and very naturally I began to ponder a play about a back-country dictator.
>
> My dictator, I decided, could not be merely a man who by force or fraud had come to power. Such a story would have no "insides"—no inner drama. No, my man had to be, in one sense, an idealist caught in the corrupting process by his own gift for power.
>
> Into that notion flowed other notions, and the play got started—a verse play. It was finished in Rome, in the winter of 1939–40, while the boot heels of Mussolini's legionnaires clanged on the cobbles.
>
> That play, *Proud Flesh,* got finished but I laid it aside, showing it only to a few friends. I wanted to let it get cool before I did a final revision. Meanwhile I worked on something else.
>
> Then when I did get back to *Proud Flesh,* what I found myself doing was not revising the play but starting a novel out of the same material.
>
> Well, in the fullness of time, that novel, *All the King's Men,* got finished, too, and before too long there was the temptation to dramatize the novel. I succumbed to the temptation, but in trying to dramatize the novel I found myself, by the logic of the contrast between dramatic form and fictional form, re-interpreting, re-thinking, shifting emphases. This play, called *All the King's Men,* went out into the world. [It was produced, directed and designed by Erwin Piscator at his New School Dramatic Workshop in 1948.]
>
> Some years and several books later a young man named Aaron Frankel called on me. He wanted, he said,

to talk about directing a play–*All the King's Men.* So I got out the script and we talked. Talk led to more talk, and in the end what we had was not a revision of *All the King's Men,* but a new play, *Willie Stark: His Rise and Fall.*

There is a moral to this story. If you begin to alter, however casually, a form–which was what Aaron Frankel and I started out to do–you are bound in the end to alter meaning. For form is meaning. That is the moral to this story–an old moral, but one that I had been relearning in my long association with Willie Stark.

Yes, that is the question, the one of form. Robert Penn Warren left, of course, a huge mark on American literature. But I have always regretted that Warren did not work longer or more often in the American Theater. What a loss! For his insight into the theater was unique and original, a native American style a-borning. The only similar visions of the stage are Bertolt Brecht's in his "alienating" way and Thornton Wilder's in his didactic way. But Warren's I find is truer and fresher. He ignored the "fourth wall" in the most natural way.

His characters relate as directly to the audience as to each other–that is, the actors "narrate" as well as "play" their roles, much as we do when we tell a story to friends. On cues supplied by Warren, they will step outside the action of the story to observe, comment on and justify themselves to us. The illusion on the stage, while still sought after, counts only so long as the characters may argue about its meaning, making not merely the stage but audience and entire theater into a tribunal, a forum.

Ten years later in 1968, at the Glenn Hughes Playhouse at the University of Washington, I produced and directed another verse play by Robert Penn Warren, *Brother to Dragons,* about blood-drenched secrets in the family history of Thomas Jefferson. It moved back and forth in time. Warren was still wrestling with form. In his own words, from the program for that production:

> In one sense, the time is any time. That is, in our presence now, the living Writer and the long-dead Jefferson confront events in the distant past, re-enacted by members of Jefferson's own family.
>
> The events re-enacted occurred, historically, in Kentucky in 1810 to 1812.
>
> As, in one sense, the action is outside of time, so it is outside of place, and occurs only in the imagination. This is only a way of saying that the issue confronted seems to be a human constant.

Collaborating on *Willie Stark* with Warren produced its own double edge. He, the writer, searching out his vision of the play for the stage, suggested most of the directing ideas; I, the director, culling all the source material, suggested most of the writing ideas.

We began work in the second best way, by letters, four years before the Margo Jones opening. Then, sporadically, we began working in the best way, in person. That became more frequent, and by the last spring and summer prior to production, almost steady. We also became friends.

Red, as I got to know him, lived then in Fairfield, Connecticut, with his wife, Eleanor Clark, author of *Rome and a Villa* and other works, and their two young children, Rosanna and Gabriel. I would take the train up from New York and Red would pick me up at the station. We would stop off for grocery shopping on the way back to his house, then go out to work in the big backyard. The interchange was active but easy, searching but warm.

One time after lunch the afternoon also got warm, and Red dozed off. I, a city boy, got up and studied the backyard. I need to add here that Red had another and personal double edge. He had a machine gun Southern drawl that took some getting used to. Of course, when he awoke, the machine gun picked right up.

Once we had to work on very short notice in my apartment in New York. My wife had only franks and beans on hand for lunch. Red treated it as if it were the Waldorf Astoria.

I had seen that 1948 Piscator production and I remember being very taken by it. I wanted to direct it somewhere myself, with brash thoughts that I could also improve on it. Six years later I was guest directing at the Arena Stage in Washington, D.C., and thought after my first show there I had found a place to do *All the King's Men* at last. Well, that didn't work out, as such things go. But it got me in touch with Warren. Here are the first exchanges:

February 18, 1954

Dear Mr. Frankel,

I am glad that, as Helen Strauss [Warren's literary agent] has just informed me, you all are doing *All the King's Men.* But can you let me know which of the two versions you are using, the verse one (old title, *Proud Flesh*) or the prose one that Piscator did? My question is prompted by a little more than curiosity. This past fall, in preparing the manuscript for what now seems to be an assured London production (I say this with fingers crossed) I did a bit of revising on the verse version, and if that is your script I'd like to incorporate my new notions. Likewise, if you are doing the other I'd like to get some new notions in.... Anyway, the Piscator version was never finished. I had a sailing date and just went off and left it. And now I'd like to take another look. Can you let me have a copy of your text, whichever it is? I'd be very grateful.

Goodbye, and regards.

Robert Penn Warren

———

WILLIE STARK: HIS RISE AND FALL
                (Tentative Title)

A Play in Three Acts

Based on the Novel
"ALL THE KING'S MEN"

by

ROBERT PENN WARREN

Copyright

[July 1955]

William Morris Agency
1740 Broadway
New York 19, N. Y.

Title page and a revised page from Aaron Frankel's working script for Warren's second stage version of the Willie Stark story. Frankel directed Willie Stark: His Rise and Fall *at the Margo Jones Theatre in Dallas in 1958. The revisions were made by Warren (Yale Collection of American Literature, Beinecke Rare Book and Manuscript Library).*

STARK: (Cont.)   (toward distance)

          I was a man, and I lived in the world of men.

          ~~And if I did not know what a man might be --~~

          ~~even if I --~~

             (As STARK begins to speak, ANNE lifts
             her head from JUDGE IRWIN'S shoulder,
             stares at STARK, moves from IRWIN'S
             comforting, fatherly embrace, and
             raptly lifts her hands toward STARK.
             As she, and all the others on the
             forestage, look up toward STARK,
             SUGAR-BOY appears at extreme Stage
             Left -- an under-sized man of forty.)

SUGAR: (Stuttering)

          The B-B-Big Boss -- he k-k-kin talk so

          g-g-g-good!

SHIPWORTH: (Continuing)

          No, what is important is ~~that the~~ this hospital .

          ~~exists.~~ It does not matter how it came to

          exist, ~~it does not matter how it --~~

JACK: (Stepping forward, in excited protest,
             face toward SHIPWORTH)

          Oh, but it ~~does it, but does matter -- it~~

          ~~matters -- it always matters -- how everything~~

          ~~comes to be.~~

             (ADAM surges forward toward JACK, ready
             to burst into denunciation, but ANNE
             restrains him)

ADAM: It matters that foulness --

~~JACK:~~   ~~(Continuing, toward SHIPWORTH)~~

          ~~It matters -- it matters because everything~~

          ~~is part of everything else. The past -- all~~

          ~~the past -- it is always part of --~~

February 23, 1954

Dear Mr. Warren,

Thank you very much for your letter. Having just gotten your address from Miss Strauss, I was on the verge of writing you.

I'd like to say first how delighted and excited we are at the prospect of doing *All the King's Men,* and how getting your letter further encouraged us. I saw the Piscator production when it was done some years back, and I still remember the exciting potential that it held for me. It's gratifying to work on the play myself now. I'm . . . more than grateful for your interest in working further.

Now, the problem of the text is a poser. I found myself with four versions, when we finally got them all rounded up from the various sources. Two are verse versions (one incomplete), and two are prose. Going over them, and then going back to the novel, I found things I admired in all of them.

I therefore took upon myself the task of making a kind of adaptation which would incorporate into a new whole—virtues now scattered among all the originals—without presuming to write a single line of my own. This of course became a major enterprise. . . . It was at this point that I was going to write to appeal for your help and guidance.

. . . My intention at all points, however, is first to preserve and fulfill your purposes as I understand them, and second, to evolve a script which will have its own proper unity, form and effect.

. . . I hope that you will also understand that this "adaptation" represents only my own momentary, provisional and modestly submitted thoughts toward the play in its final working out, . . . and I defer at all points to your judgment and interest.

. . . I should like to propose . . . that I then visit you in Fairfield (my home is New York) at your convenience, if you feel that more could be accomplished by some old-fashioned sitting around to shoot the ducks on the pond than by mail. . . .

I hope we can meet . . . so that there will be good time . . . to get back into rehearsal down here and find out the things that only rehearsals and audiences can tell us. . . .

Going back to the novel was a wonderful experience all over again. . . . We feel honored and delighted to participate in bringing *All the King's Men* once more back to the stage. Our thanks again.

With high hopes and every good wish,

Sincerely,
Aaron Frankel

P.S. If you want a copy of the play in its present form anyway I shall be glad to send it along, verse or prose version. However, it was Robert Giroux at Harcourt, Brace in New York who sent them to us, and I assume he could also supply you copies.

——

March 1, 1954

Dear Mr. Frankel,

You certainly are doing it the hard way, but I shan't discourage you, for it will come out to my profit. That is, I don't feel that the thing is finished and your work will certainly turn up some valuable things for me. It will be fine to see you when you are ready. If we leave the country this spring, it will not be, I am sure, until the middle of April.

Best regards, and thanks.

Sincerely yours,
Robert Penn Warren

I took Warren at his word and plunged on. My next letter was an outline eleven single-spaced pages long! I have condensed the first quarter of it to indicate how in one way our collaboration proceeded.

——

March 16, 1954

Dear Mr. Warren,

Thank you for your gracious note. With every intention of answering it more promptly, I found I had to delay until the present moment.

. . . First of all, you were dead right when you said I was doing it the hard way. Second, I found myself rehearsing . . . on a continually changing schedule for the [next] show. . . .

I note, however, that you expect to leave for London about the middle of April. Not incidentally, good luck on the London production! On the possibility that a visit from me would not fit in with your plans that late at all, I thought it might be best to send along at least an <u>outline</u> of what I've done so far (half-way through Act II), and an <u>outline</u> of the remainder still to be done. . . .

As far as the outline goes, it's pretty much a matter of reorganizing the material. . . . I find I most admire the novel. Therefore within the play itself I find myself continually going back to the novel for the actual dramatization of scenes. The basic form that I'm following is that of the prose version. The basic material, the meat of the scenes, is from the novel. Then I'm incorporating a few elements, largely as counterpoint (though not exactly in the same way you used a Chorus), from the verse version.

I realize that using the novel can be misleading. But it seems to me that there are certain distinct advantages. For one thing I find that in the novel versions of the same scenes which appear in the play, there are immediate and tremendous <u>inner</u> impulses in the scenes which drive the story forward.

One of my objections to the Piscator version is that it seems to me the "bridges"—the stretches of discussion between Jack and the Professor—are used to move the story from point to point, ignoring or sometimes even cutting out the elements within the scenes themselves which lead them progressively from one to another.

Secondly, though not second at all, the wealth of characterization and revelation seems to me readily adaptable to the stage, at once dramatic and rich. Once again, the Piscator version skeletonized the story far too much, and against the play's best interest, which is exactly the complexity and the irony the novel captures. What I am saying, in a word, is that the novel seems to me remarkably and singularly adaptable to the stage in many of its scenes and that the main work in such instances is not "translation" but editing. . . .

One central problem in making a play of the novel I have found paramount, however. In the novel Jack Burden it seems to me is the central focus and this works because the novel form allows you to develop the story out of Jack's introspection. This, however, is not as easy to apply on the stage. Here one of my main suggestions occurs.

I think in the play Willie Stark should be the character in central focus, that the movement of the story from point to point has to come through his action. . . . In the book, part of the point is that all main characters in one way or another—Jack, Adam, Anne, Lucy, Sadie, Duffy, even the Judge—take their action and their definition from Willie. This seems to me to lend itself . . . admirably to the claim that Willie should be more clearly the focus of the play. I now find an ambiguity, a shift of focus between Jack and Willie which I think weakens the dramatic potential.

For all these reasons my impulse has been to cut down greatly on the scene "bridges," and their "labels." You shall have to judge whether I am right or wrong on this score, or missing more important considerations.

Similarly, I feel the Prologue could be more <u>organically</u> related to the story. I think its <u>situation</u> could be more integrated and more [theatrically] realized. . . . The central event of the <u>plot</u> [is] the building of the hospital—this I think provides an excellent hinge for the story to turn on, and we should have it clearly, constantly and centrally in focus before us. . . .

I should interject a brief discussion of the set for the play. . . . Whatever its general design elements, I suggest it include two platforms. One would be a bandstand platform . . . and the other a platform for the appearance of people <u>out of time</u> (e.g., those dead) . . . available all through.

Thus, we start [on the bandstand] at the hospital [dedication] . . . Jack challenges Shipworth from the audience. Adam appears on the out-of-time platform. Anne appears from the same part of the audience as Jack (being now his wife). Duffy, Sadie, Lucy, Larson, Sugar-Boy appear in turn from different parts of the audience. Judge Irwin and Willie, like Adam, appear separately on the out-of-time platform . . . leading to the introduction of "I'll tell you how that hospital came to be built!"

Now we come to Act I, Scene 1. Another new and wild suggestion. I think the first scene within the play ought to be the Byram B. White scene from the book, edited merely to fit the facts we will use in the play. . . . The scene leads quite naturally to two basic (and motivating) facts, Lucy's leaving Willie and Willie's resolve to build the hospital. . . .

Another and almost stronger reason for starting this way: Here, strong and true (as Hemingway would say) we start right out with Willie in action. . . . And we

Warren (right) with his younger brother, William Thomas, in front of Warren's home in Fairfield, Connecticut, circa 1957 (courtesy of Mrs. Robert D. Frey)

immediately begin to use one of the main questions the book raises, the creation of good out of evil. . . .

I then condense, in terms of organization, the next three scenes into one. . . . It still remains in three parts, first outside Judge Irwin's, then inside, then back outside again, but they all flow directly from one to another, which can also be managed set-wise. Here I also inserted several speeches . . . putting [more of] the meat of the novel back on the skeleton of the Piscator play-version. The third part of the scene would be the only one, obviously, that needs adjustment. . . . That's editing and easy: we keep the section where Stark tells Jack to dig on Irwin.

The rest of my outline of Act I went on in the same detailed vein, and it continued that way right through the half-way point I had reached in Act II; actually, it got even more detailed, suggesting even more reorganizing, while remaining contingent, provisional. Left were a couple of observations:

Perhaps I should make explicit that. . . . I think Piscator's intention, while off the track in execution, was right in general direction. There is a strong journalistic vein in *All the King's Men,* though of a high order, and I think the play would be best cast in the mold of a documentary. I myself see the form of the play coming out of such combined roots as the *Living Newspaper* style of the Federal Theater of the Thirties and the rapid-fire, audience-centered style of the Group Theater's *Waiting for Lefty.* And into a "new form, new form" of its own, in the words of Trepleff. . . . It must not mean at all that the scenes themselves in the play should be treated <u>only</u> as events and not also for character, relationships, atmosphere or spirit. Piscator's error, I feel, was to single out only the event. . . . A documentary can also be substantial.

I'd like . . . to make clear something [else]. . . . Actually, you don't deal in "flashbacks" [in the novel]. You stop time, if I may put it that way, and I'd love to find the theatrical equivalent for that [in the play].

. . . I must offer apologies for my typing and correcting along the way; I trust this has not been too difficult to read. . . . If I am on the wrong track . . . I shall not be afraid for you to tell me so . . .

Of course, the spirit more than the details of "having my long say" to Warren was what carried over to the final adaptation that became *Willie Stark: His Rise and Fall.*

Meanwhile, at the same time I was mailing my long account to him, he was mailing a short accounting to me.

March 17, 1954

Dear Aaron,

Here is the manuscript of the play. Hell broke loose here, including trouble about the typing, and just this morning it has been finished. I have made a few small revisions along the way and I'm sure we'll want to make others. For the moment all I now propose is attached herewith. POSSIBLE substitution for II-1-19 and II-1-20. I felt that this might set up Anne's situation a little more clearly. If you agree with this, will you draw out the old pages now in place and insert these? If you don't approve, hang on to them anyway. I have no copies.

Also, you had better run through the MS to see that all pages are in order. I did that this morning but with three children howling about my knees—one of my own children and two of the typist's.

We got a pretty good rate on the typing: $45. It is not wonderful and I had to correct about fifty pages, but it is as competent as most around here. The bill for the other version was $29.50. I'm just putting this down now to keep the record. If you will let me know what the cost of the photographing is, then I will send you the amount. Let me pay all now, and then we can work out proportionate costs at the end. That will save confusion, I think.

ALSO—over and above our six copies, I shall need an extra for other purposes, seven in all. Will you remember that, please sir?

Well, Lord love us!

Yours,

Red

Brother to Dragons went through a similar process of collaboration, sometimes perforce by letter, sometimes, praise be, in person, also over several years, and in several stages.

The story centers on an appalling crime committed by Lilburn Lewis, nephew to Thomas Jefferson: Lilburn's butcher murder of a young Negro plantation slave. In the known record, Jefferson never referred to the crime of his nephew—Warren's "convenient" seed for his theme. Jefferson, prophet of human perfectibility and American independence, is brought back to cry out in the twentieth century the words of Job (30:29): "I am a brother to dragons and a companion to owls." He of all men must discover that there is a terror, a primordial lurking, the minotaur in waiting, in all men. It is in the family, *in the blood,* even of Thomas Jefferson, American original of the Enlightenment, and he must acknowledge the terrible responsibility of it. It is the dark human condition.

It is also in the blood of the South. It fills *All the King's Men,* which also contains the beautiful long parable of the Mastern brothers. That is the same story, of good and evil. It seems at first irrelevant, until we realize that it is in allegory form the history of the South. The same may be said of the complete novel, *World Enough and Time*—Jeremiah Beaumont's high and fatal chivalry becomes an agony of emptiness.

Toward the end of *Brother to Dragons* the crowning story of Meriwether Lewis is introduced—Meriwether, first cousin to Lilburn Lewis, and in turn principal in a violent death (possibly, murder, more poetically, suicide). Yes, this is that Meriwether Lewis, once Jefferson's White House secretary, who was leader with William Clark of the Louisiana Purchase expedition, later Governor of the Louisiana Territory. He is not essential to the story of *Brother to Dragons* but is essential to its theme. Meriwether and Lilburn are both types of the Southern experience. Warren is telling the story of the South in every instance. And that story revolves around his primary subject, if not obsession. Confronted by evil, good must be created out of it. It is the definition of a man.

Robert Penn Warren represents an exemplar of the Southern apprehension that the light is small and the dark is wide and bloody, that our nature is violence and depravity and doom. I do not claim that only

Jesse Stuart, Randall Stewart, and Warren at the 1959 Vanderbilt University Literary Symposium (Photographic Archives, Special Collections, Vanderbilt University)

No Literature in Heaven

At the Vanderbilt University Literary Symposium in 1959, Warren insisted that it was flaws that made a character worth writing about.

You occasionally get a very complete man, and he has no story. Who cares about Robert E. Lee? Now there's a man who's smooth as an egg. Turn him around, this primordial perfection: you see, he has no story. You can't just say what a wonderful man he was, and that you know he had some chaotic something inside because he's human, but you can't get at it. You know he was probably spoiling with blood lust, otherwise he wouldn't have been in that trade, wouldn't have done so well at it. We can make little schemes like this, and try to jazz it up a bit, but really what you have is this enormous, this monumental self-control, and selflessness, and lots of things like that. You have to improvise a story for him. You don't know his story. It's only the guy who's angular, incomplete, and struggling who has a story. If a person comes out too well, there's not much story. Whoever wants to tell a story of a sainted grandmother, unless you can find some old love letters, and get a new grandfather? In heaven there's no marriage and giving in marriage, and there's no literature.

–"An Interview with Flannery O'Connor and Robert Penn Warren," *Vagabond*, 6 (February 1960): 15

Southern writers are possessed by this, nor that all of them are. But they seem to me its most eloquent exponents. A Hemingway may acknowledge the beast in us but retorts, "find an outlet for it so it won't devour you." Southern writers tend to cultivate the lust for violence, pain, and darkness as inborn, permanent, dominant, inescapable, from generation to generation. Sin is original with man (indeed). In Warren it is more than an idea, it is felt, a stench, an intuition made fact by belief. Goodness is only a hope. Evil is a conviction. It even becomes a principle, a cause.

The journey of *Brother to Dragons* to the University of Washington took twelve years and went through several stages, or better, straits. The very first should have been an omen. *Brother to Dragons* was originally conceived as a narrative poem, *A Tale in Verse and Voices*–not as a play. *Willie Stark* at least had the benefit of three rich prior sources, two of them in play form. Translating *Brother to Dragons* into a play took a prodigious effort.

Then there were early production prospects at Yale, where Red was still teaching but about to resign, and at newly opened Brandeis, where I had begun double duty, teaching and running the Theater Workshop. For various reasons, neither production got on. When I heard from Red again, he wrote, in passing, "I have resigned from Yale, and shall undertake to make an honest living. At least, I have dropped my academic alibi." Later he wrote from the American Academy at Rome, "commodiously put up" there with Eleanor and the children:

> . . . The script as it now stands needs, as you know, more work, particularly in the opening section. And the use of [Meriwether] Lewis has to be thought through again. I had hoped to talk this out with you, when I get back. . . . I feel that the thing is basically there and the revision should be done, for the most part, after a couple of stand-up readings, and in consultation. . . . Gosh, I hope it works out . . . for one reason because it would be a pleasure to work with you again. . . .

For the record, this is the first time doing rewrites out of script readings came up as a way of working. It is sometimes a useful way, but it never proved applicable in this case.

I next found New York co-producers, and sought others. Periodic revisions with Red never stopped. All of us knew *Brother to Dragons* was a long shot, "the sort of thing," Red wrote, "that is harder to get on." All of us were right.

So the final and climactic phase of putting *Brother to Dragons* on a stage arrived when I was able at last to take it to The Glenn Hughes Playhouse at the University of Washington, across the country in

Seattle. Resuming revisions for that production also reached a climactic stage.

There was one difference all along, however, from working on *Willie Stark*. This was not a writing collaboration but one between playwright and director, a more customary procedure. Otherwise, again separated by circumstances beyond our control, we fell back on exchanging letters and phone calls (sometimes hectically). One face-to-face meeting mid-way was all we managed.

November 22, 1967

Dear Red,

. . . Had the first reading yesterday. Wow! The power really comes through. I was very lifted, so was the cast. Hope we can live up to it.

I have to report one strange problem, so ironic, and a product of the inflammations of this year of I hope our Lord, 1967. Negroes don't want to play Negroes. I have been able to cast Aunt Cat, after dithering some, but that's now okay. Must still get to a John [the young plantation slave]. What happened in sum was that a choice came up: either cut the rest of the Negro ensemble or abandon the play. I couldn't take any more abandonments. I've worked out a way of doing the show with implicit effects [shadow-play] rather than explicit bodies, and I hope I can make them work. But I need a word or two from you. The scene most affected is the "dem bones" scene, which I'd like to find an appropriate way to keep.

Well, to answer your question, I will be home early for the recess, the week of December 11, in fact. May I call you then? . . .

———

ALL THE KING'S MEN

BY

Robert Penn Warren

A RANDOM HOUSE PLAY

$7.95

ALL
THE
KING'S
MEN

by

ROBERT PENN
WARREN

"As a portrait of politics, this is effective and provocative. . . . Willie in all his personal relationships is a fascinating man and often a winning man, too. . . . What is right and what is wrong? Mr. Warren makes a stimulating inquiry into that troublesome question."

Brooks Atkinson, New York *Times*

" 'All the King's Men' went off with a roof-shaking bang. . . . This is the most engrossing drama seen off Broadway in months."

**Frank Aston,
New York *World Telegram & Sun***

"This drama by Robert Penn Warren is a blockbuster. It is a major off-Broadway event. . . . A subtle and rich study of man in society." **Emory Lewis, *Cue***

"Strong merit. . . . 'All the King's Men' is thoughtfully and professionally presented."
**John McClain,
New York *Journal-American***

Dust jacket and front flap for the only dramatic version of All the King's Men *published during Warren's lifetime*
(Richland County Public Library)

January 14, 1968

Dear Red,

It was a deep pleasure to see you in New York. . . . In a few days or so, I hope to send off a script with the cuts I've so far made. . . .

I've otherwise followed our old *Willie Stark* method, meaning that I've avoided writing a single line of my own, and every word left is yours only. I've done this with transpositions, sometimes (not often) with whole speeches, or parts of a speech, or lines or parts of lines, and trying always to keep what I can sense is your metrical desire as well as the best acting answer. . . . Trouble is, I think I still need more cuts, because I fear [Act I] is still too long by ten minutes or more, and [also at the end], once Lilburn has been shot. . . .

The confrontation of the Writer and Jefferson bears the play's significance for me and I hope for the audience, and I guess that's what I'm trying to heighten in all the cuts I've made. One thing that's fun is getting Jefferson in close physical contact on stage with all the "family scenes"—to keep him, in other words, as much in the audience's eye at all times no matter what's happening. . . .

My other main problem has been working without the Negro ensemble, and in fact my first attempt to apply the solution we worked out in New York went astray. This was mainly because I didn't do it simply and directly enough, I think, and I hope yesterday's change in rehearsal solves that. If when you get the edited script you have any further suggestions for cuts, or any corrections of what I've done, please holler. . . .

———

January 28, 1968

Dear Red,

Well, here it is [the script]—not as soon as I'd liked, but still in time, I hope, for any corrections you want to make, or any advice I may still need to call you for, before the February 5th opening.

. . . I have in fact made a couple of further cuts . . . but I still find the first act running an hour and fifteen minutes, and the second act fifty minutes. . . . My feeling about the first act is not merely the 75 minutes themselves: the material is so loaded that I'm worried about exhausting the audience's emotional response too early, before we reach the first act curtain and, worse, before we get past the event [the butcher murder] to its Act II significance. I think the play's marvelous—but it's strenuous!

Gotta say, some of these cuts have hurt. . . . Lord knows I've wished you were on hand for this, and maybe another production can come out of this we could share hammer and anvil on. One interesting lesson, though: working this way sure teaches one to exhaust every acting and staging solution before going hollering to the playwright for rewrites. . . .

I do know a chunk I could take out of Act I. It occurred to me only this weekend. It would be the whole Big Court Day sequence, dance included (I–18 to I–22), and probably save 5 minutes worth. But I hesitate to do it for a couple of reasons. Even though all its information appears in some form elsewhere, it provides a welcome change of pace, even a needed one, and balances the act in a very helpful way. It would also mean depriving the five or six ensemble kids (who've worked hard) of their main appearance in the show, plus losing the musical and dance background that's been worked in, brief though it be. "Out of town" I'd be interested to see what would happen if it were cut—but not here.

As I look the script over one final time, I wonder how much I've done will justify itself to you, or seem right at all. Some line adjustments and cuts were for actor's benefit, certainly—but the proportion of these is small. How more than ever I wish you could see the show itself in its present form, to see for real if it's the way you want, on its feet. . . .

Meanwhile, I hope to heaven I've gotten it right. . . .

The show opened, to play its allotted two weeks. In the program was an insert:

Brother to Dragons is a new play. We are therefore making continuous adaptations in script and performance.

March 10, 1968

Dear Red,

The crazy press of things out here has delayed my writing you about the run of *Brother to Dragons* here. . . . I talked to [audience] kids: I think the play spoke to them most of all, and that pleases me greatly.

Which is to say in general that I was very happy to do the show and proud of the results. Yes, the play had mixed reactions, including extreme ones. The negatives disappointed me, of course, but did not surprise me. We kept working on the production, par for a new play, of course, and made acting and staging adjustments and continual script cuts right up to closing night.

The closing version was I think as tight as I could ever get the script without the benefit of your personal editing. I enclose the pages which contain all further cuts as a result of performances: everything in red pencil. I should add that the shape of the final ten pages or so came about experimentally in several stages, whereas I'm sending you only its final stage. (It assumed this shape only the final two nights, and played itself properly only the closing night.)

It represents . . . probably the most radical alteration of all. . . . The main impulse was that once Lilburn was shot the curtain kept pressing to come down. I therefore tried to get to all the wind-ups as completely and quickly as possible, and the action (and meaning) seemed to carry for the audience in natural dramatic terms and needed a minimum amount of words. . . .

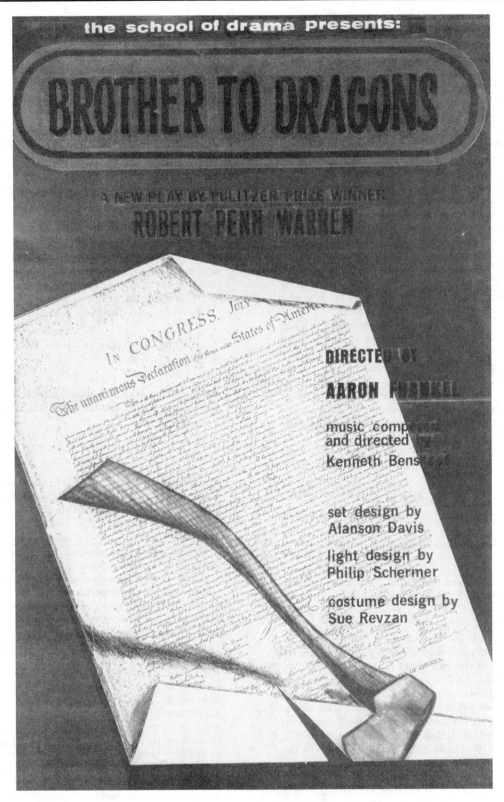

Poster for a production at the Glenn Hughes Playhouse, University of Washington,
in February 1968 (courtesy of Aaron Frankel)

You'll note, doubtless, that the main performance revisions involved further cuts for Jefferson and the Writer. That always remained the heart of the problem, for me, of making the play work. (Even one or two line cuts seemed to help, as well as "chunks.") It would also remain the heart of any future version of the play, were that ever in view. Thinking most radically, maybe the Writer could be cut after all. . . . Maybe the confrontation should be between Jefferson and Lilburn all through. . . . As you can see, I'm still fascinated by *Brother to Dragons*.

Thankfully, concerning the Writer versus Jefferson as framework for the play, I obviously got desperate but never that radical, and wrong. For I'd have gone conventional, and missed the boat completely. I'd have lost sight of what Robert Penn Warren brought uniquely to the American theater: a new form for the stage where actors "play" and "narrate" their roles at one and the same time, in elemental irony.

This double edge, this paradox of Robert Penn Warren, never ceased taking form, either: enlightened and haunted, courtly and driven, engaged and fragmented, cosmopolitan and Southern. It permeates his characters as well. Heightened knowledge meets deepened self-criticism. If struggle is the burden, self-awareness is the gain.

In Warren, time and place are re-invented, to reveal anew. Time is stopped, to fill it in. Place is framed, to make it moral more than physical. And they keep changing with every change that actor and beholder undergo. The meaning is in the form.

Full circle. What the American theater might have been, if only Red Warren had taken greater part in it!

—Aaron Frankel, "Working in the Theater with Robert Penn Warren," *RWP*, 2 (2002): 1–16

Title page for Warren's sixth volume of poetry, which includes his Civil War poem "Two Studies in Idealism: Short Survey of American, and Human, History" (Special Collections, Western Kentucky University Libraries)

Warren's Civil War

Four books by Warren were published in the first two years of the 1960s: All the King's Men: A Play *and* You, Emperors, and Others: Poems, 1957–1960 *in 1960 and his seventh novel,* Wilderness: A Tale of the Civil War, *along with the essay* The Legacy of the Civil War: Meditations on the Centennial *in 1961. R. W. B. Lewis, a colleague and friend of Warren's at Yale, in this excerpt comments on Warren's correspondence with Cleanth Brooks in the early years of the decade.*

Warren's Fascination with the Civil War

In 1956, Warren published the book-length essay *Segregation,* a work vitalized by a sort of intellectual and moral anguish. Its subtitle was *The Inner Conflict of the South;* but within a few years, Warren was meditating rather on the South and the North together, in conjunction and conflict. In the single year 1961 (the year of his reappointment at Yale), there appeared *The Legacy of the Civil War,* an eloquently ironic sketch of the ongoing posture of North and South toward the great collision; *Wilderness,* a novel about the war (from draft riot to battlefield), with characters of incompatible persuasion playing their parts; and the poem "Two Studies in Idealism," which pairs a plain-speaking southern countryman and a high-minded Harvard graduate of the class of 1861, the two meeting fatally at Shiloh. The subtitle of the twelve-stanza work is "Short Story of American, and Human, History"; for Warren the 1860s war virtually created American history, or the sense of history in the American mind, and as such was a paradigm of all history.

In their correspondence, meanwhile, Brooks and Warren repeatedly touched on matters southern. In the summer of 1960, both were pondering the question of Robert E. Lee's decision (to borrow Brooks's phrase in an August 2 letter) "to stay with Virginia." Brooks felt, and apparently Warren agreed, that as "against the more abstract claims of liberty, justice, etc.," there was for Lee "the concrete claim of the region, the community, the family." At other times, most notably in the fall of 1961, they speculated on what might have happened if the South had won the Civil War.

As to that, both were sure that a southern victory would have affected the pace but not the fact of southern industrialization. "My own view," Brooks wrote on October 15, 1971 (in a letter of considerable and diverse interest), "is that a Southern victory would have only slowed down the movement toward centralization, urbanization, and industrialization." It might also, Brooks added a bit wistfully, "have helped us preserve certain traditional views about life–at least have kept them alive longer." Warren put the matter more strongly. "If the South had won," he wrote on October 6, "they would have embarked socially and economically on much the same course. . . . They would never have settled for the plantation team–and many defenders of the Southern system were already aware of the industrial needs." Although to an obviously different degree, both had moved quite far away from the agrarian anti-industrial doctrine of the collective volume of 1930 (to which Warren had contributed), *I'll Take My Stand.*

This particular exchange bore on the treatment of the Civil War and southern society in the work then in progress, a textbook on American literature that Brooks, Warren, and I were coediting. The immediate concern of the other two was that the book should carry no hint of any editorial belief in a self-perpetuating old-style southern culture if the Confederacy had triumphed.

–R. W. B. Lewis, "Afterword," in *Cleanth Brooks and Robert Penn Warren: A Literary Correspondence,* edited by James A. Grimshaw Jr. (Columbia & London: University of Missouri Press, 1998) pp. 418–419

* * *

In this excerpt from his essay "Robert Penn Warren: Geography as Fate," Lewis argues that the tension inherent in Warren's "cultural geography"–"something that developed after the born-and-bred Southerner moved north and east and settled in New England"–is key to his development as a writer.

Warren's Southerner-Northerner Dialectic

. . . Warren and his second wife, Eleanor Clark, divided their family residence between a remodeled barn in Fairfield, Connecticut, and a ranging old house surrounded by woods and a lake in West Wardsboro, Vermont. The Vermont landscape elicited a number of poems, the most winning of them, perhaps, being "Vermont Ballad: Change of Season" in 1980. Autumn is giving way to winter in this sequence of ruminative tercets; "fitful rain" is making "new traceries" down the windowpane, and the outlook is gloomy:

> what do I see beyond
> That fluctuating gray
>
> Last leaf, rain soaked, from my high
> Birch falling, the spruce wrapped in thought. . . .

There is a certain unexpected Southern perspective in the image: only a Kentucky-born observer, one feels, would think that a New England tree, like a New England philosopher, was wrapped in thought. But then, at the poem's end, the Southern viewpoint becomes overt when the speaker sees a man outside

> trudging
> With stolid stride, his bundle on back, . . .
>
> A man with no name, in the gloom,
> On an errand I cannot guess.
> No sportsman–no! Just a man in his doom.
>
> In this section such a man is not an uncommon sight.
> In rain or snow, you pass, and he says: "Kinda rough tonight."

The Southerner-Northerner dialectic (Warren's stretch of cultural geography) had in fact become especially striking some twenty years earlier, in the wake of Warren's early-1950s transference to New England. It almost inevitably took the form of a greatly quickened interest in the 1860s war between the North and South, and it expressed itself most tellingly in two texts of 1960, the book-length essay *Legacy of the Civil War* and the novel *Wilderness,* along with the poem "Two Studies in Idealism" the year before.

Legacy opens with the thought-churning remark that "The Civil War is, for the American imagination, the great single event of our history. Without too much wrenching, it may, in fact, be said to *be* our history." And a little further on: "The Civil War is our only 'felt' history—history lived in the national imagination." It certainly lived in Warren's imagination in these years, and not least in the poems that evoked his grandfather Gabriel Penn, who had been a cavalry officer in the Confederate Army and had ridden with Nathan Bedford Forrest.

> Under the cedar tree,
> He would sit, all summer with me:
> . . . .
> Captain, cavalry, C.S.A.,
> An old man, now shrunken, gray,
> Pointed beard clipped the classic way,
> . . . .
> His pipe smoke lifts, serene.

So begins the poem "Court-martial" of 1957, with Warren, entering his fifties, looking back from his New England habitat to those summer afternoons more than forty years before, when Grandfather Penn would reminisce to his grandson about wartime episodes.

As its title indicates, *The Legacy of the Civil War* is primarily concerned with the abiding consequences of the struggle, about which, as the dialectic intensifies, Warren deposes: "To give things labels, we may say that the War gave the South the Great Alibi, and gave the North the Treasury of Virtue." "By the Great Alibi," he goes on, "the South explains, condones, and transmutes everything," everything from lynching to the whole problem of race, which, "according to the Great Alibi, is the doom defined by history—by New England slavers, Midwestern abolitionists," and so on. And then, turning north: "If the Southerner, with his Great Alibi, feels trapped by history, the Northerner, with his Treasury of Virtue, feels redeemed by history. . . . He has in his pocket . . . a plenary indulgence for all sins, past, present, and future, freely given by the hand of history."

Something of that merciless contrast shapes the poem "Two Studies in Idealism," a work that gives us, first, the voice of a Southern countryman killed at Shiloh, and next that of a young Harvard graduate, class of 1861, who apparently does the killing before he himself is shot. The poem's subtitle repeats the opening note of the *Legacy* essay: "A Short Survey of American, and Human, History." This Civil War incident, with the Southerner and the Northerner each having his say, *is* American his-

tory in essence, and even an image of all human conflict.

Rhetorically, "Two Studies" reverses the movement of "Folly on Royal Street," going from the most down-to-earth vernacular to the upper-class lofty. The Southerner is remembering the women he has enjoyed: "I reckon I taken my share, / Bed-ease or bush-whack," and his single regret as he dies is that he only managed to kill three Northerners:

> hell, three's all I got,
> And he promised me ten, Jeff Davis, the bastard. 'Taint fair.

The Harvard boy is already enveloping himself in the Treasury of Virtue and the well-stuffed language that goes with it:

> I didn't mind dying—it wasn't that at all.
> It behooves a man to prove manhood by dying for the Right,
> If you die for Right, that fact is your dearest requital.

It only annoys him that Southerners can die, like the man he has just killed, who are not fighting on the side of Virtue.

The novel *Wilderness* brings Adam Rosenzweig, a young Bavarian Jew, to America in 1863 to take part in what he regards as a war for freedom. He undergoes various adventures, both enlightening and disillusioning, is a witness to violence and commits violence, and at the end is perhaps ready to take his full part in the conflict. The work has some handsomely realized moments, such as an account of the New York City draft riots in July 1863, but it suffers from Warren's most dangerous rhetorical tendency—that of drifting toward abstract generalizations. The entire concluding section presents Adam lying on the ground after killing his first Southerner and thinking about the nature of human destiny. He says things to himself such as: *"What I have done I did for freedom. I would have died for freedom."*

—R. W. B. Lewis, "Robert Penn Warren: Geography as Fate," in *The Legacy of Robert Penn Warren,* edited by David Madden (Baton Rouge: Louisiana State University Press, 2000), pp. 17–20

* * *

In this excerpt from the introduction to his book Robert Penn Warren and History: "The Big Myth We Live" *(1970), L. Hugh Moore Jr. argues that* Wilderness, *a novel that received mixed reviews, is important to understanding Warren's use of history in his work.*

Tentative Title: BATTLE OF THE WILDERNESS (or The Wilderness)
                        Summary of a novelette by Robert Penn Warren

        The name of the hero is David, a Jew who is living, when
the story opens, in a village in South Germany. The story is
not told by him, but it follows his consciousness. It is his
story.

        When the story opens David is twenty-five years old, living
with an uncle and aunt in the village of, for the moment, X. His
father had been a student, an intellectual deeply imbued with the
new notions of freedom which had spread over Europe, and when the
street fighting broke out in Berlin in March, 1848, had been
involved. The father had been taken and sentenced to a long term
in prison. His wife, with the child, then 10, had fled to the
village where the uncle took them in. Even after the death of
the mother, the boy had been raised in almost superstitious
reverence for the father and the father's ideas. The father,
unannounced, arrives in the village, consumptive, having been
released from prison to die. The story opens just after the
death of the father, in a scene of mourning, with the recitation
of the Kaddish, the Hebrew prayer for the dead.

        The time is now 1862, and the American Civil War is in
progress -- an event of enormous importance to David, the war
that will, forever, confirm human freedom. As he learns of the
recruiting in Germany, he more and more feels that he must take
part -- escape from the prison house of Europe, fulfilment of

First page of a summary Warren prepared for his seventh novel (Robert Penn Warren Papers, Beinecke Library, Yale University)

Wilderness as an Historical Myth

Warren in his novels portrays three main groups of characters who have healthy attitudes toward tradition, who offer examples of a purposeful adaptation to life. The agrarians humbly follow the life of their fathers, hard labor growing crops. Associated with this life are the values of integrity, responsibility, submission to a harsh, Old Testament God, honesty, and respect and genuine concern for the rights and welfare of others. Secondly, there are the orthodox Christians, those who submit fully to the will of God and who love their fellow men. These two groups occur almost invariably in the exempla, and they are not completely involved in the main stream of the life depicted in the novel. The third group is made up of those who respect tradition but who realize that change is a necessary aspect of the historical process. These characters, the Hugh Millers and the Cassius Forts, use the traditions of the past creatively and imaginatively and modify them to suit changing times and needs. Completely ignoring the law and tradition as Jeremiah

---

"How a Jellyfish Eats an Oyster"

Warren wrote this letter from Locmariaquer, France, where his wife was doing research for her book The Oysters of Locmariaquer. *He was just beginning work on his next novel,* Flood: A Romance of Our Time, *which was published in 1964.*

Warren to Cheney, 19 May 1961

My new novel called *Wilderness* is out in August. A copy will find its way to you. I hope you like it. And the little Civil War [book] should be in your hands by now. I'm not really writing yet on the new one, just sort of prodding at the amorphous mass which lies on my table like an enormous jellyfish. By the way, do you know how a jellyfish eats an oyster? As follows: the jellyfish envelops the shell; it does not suffocate the oyster, as some believe and as one ignorant oysterman type told Eleanor in the presence of a biologist; rather it tires the oyster out with its attentions; finally the tired oyster, cloyed by it all, slightly opens the shell; the jellyfish lets some of its own gelatinous stomach join the oyster in its shell; the rest is silence. I find this rather a parable, disgusting though it be, of the relation of a writer to his novel. The prospective novel is the jellyfish, the novelist is the oyster. I leave you with this comforting thought. Everyday I learn something new about the oyster.

–Special Collections, Vanderbilt University

Beaumont does or modifying it at will to suit one's needs of the moment as Willie Stark does are always wrong and dangerous.

Because history is full of danger for man, he needs a myth. Since much of history has no meaning inherent in it, man must make sense of it. The sense he makes of it is part of the myth, and today the burden of our time is that with the old values and beliefs destroyed by science and the ideal of progress we must each construct our own myths. But myths are also needed to explain and justify traditions. Finally, we need them to help us bear the horror of historical reality, for man cannot bear too much brutal truth and maintain his sanity. Myths should go counter to the facts of history only to meet an urgent human need; myths are justified in ordering the facts to make them more bearable or in filtering out some of the horror of existence. Like Ibsen in *The Wild Duck,* Warren sees the value of illusions and the "true lie," true, that is, to human values even if false to the brute facts of the historical process. Myth is not superstition, but "a fiction, a construct which expresses a truth and affirms a value." It "defines the myth-maker's world, his position in it, his destiny, and his appropriate attitude."[1] Myth is also total communication appealing to the imaginative, emotional, and spiritual side, and not just to the intellectual; hence it is better able to make its values readily available and more capable of inspiring action than any other type of communication. The artist's greatest task and highest function, Warren believes, is the creation of a valid, usable historical myth for society as a repository of worthy, humane values. He has expended much effort upon the criticism and debunking of historical myths which he considers false to the complex facts of history or ones which he feels embody unworthy values; he has engaged himself especially with those myths that have grown up around the Civil War.

Warren sees the Civil War as the historical event that is most likely to yield a national historical myth. "It is," he has said, "an overwhelming and vital image of human and national experience. We instinctively feel that we can best understand ourselves and our country by it."[2] Most important for Warren's purpose, the Civil War is our only "felt" history[3] —the only history vitally alive in the minds and imaginations of the entire American society. The Civil War thus comes to the artist as a subject already partly mythologized, ready for the artist to shape it creatively and make it even more available.

Wilderness is Warren's attempt to make sense of the blind, coiling mass of complex event and overwhelming detail of the war, a function the novel shares with the historical analysis of *The Legacy of the Civil War*. But the novel goes further than the history: it attempts to embody worthy values, to dramatize them so that they appeal to the emotional, imaginative, and spiritual sides of man. *Wilderness* is thus in many respects similar to myth, sharing its main purpose and functions. Indicative of the novel's kinship with myth is the large number of mythic elements–superstition and mystery, legends, stylized details, the odyssey-like structure, and allusions to myths and mythical characters. At the Fugitives' reunion in Nashville in 1956 a recurring question was why, with all their promise, none of the group had attempted an epic, the creation of a myth for society, the task Homer performed for the Greeks. It cannot be maintained that Warren in *Wilderness* has created a full-fledged native historical myth, the most ambitious goal a writer can set for

himself. He does, however, seem to be preparing the way for such a myth by showing the kinship of the Civil War with the stuff from which myths are made, by mythologizing the historical material, that is, throwing over the subject an aura of myth, and by performing well the same task as myth–to dramatically embody worthy values in an appealing story in such a way as to make these values immediately available to the audience, so available that they carry over into the reader's own life.

There are other valid reasons for a close study of *Wilderness*. This novel represents the culmination of the trend in Warren away from the technique of proliferation of detail toward a more selective use of facts. It forms a striking contrast with his other novels such as *At Heaven's Gate* and *World Enough and Time,* which are approximately four times as long. Yet unlike the relatively short novel, *The Cave* (1959), *Wilderness* contains all of his major themes in effective and original dramatizations. *Wilderness* illustrates that throughout his career Warren has

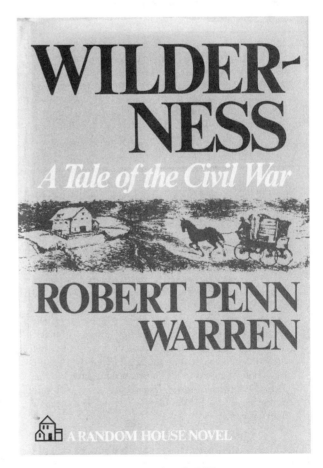

Dust jackets for the books Warren published in 1961, the centennial year of the beginning of the Civil War
(Special Collections, Western Kentucky University Libraries)

become more openly and seriously philosophical and concerned with meaning. Fortunately, this tendency toward a concentration on meaning beyond mere faithful reproduction of historical detail has not injured the literary worth of his novel as it well could have done, as a similar concentration has done to the works of Faulkner and Hemingway. Warren is far too concerned with physical presence to neglect factual development and verisimilitude. In fact, *Wilderness* is one of Warren's most artistically successful novels, particularly if we apply one of Warren's favorite critical dicta to it–the effective dramatization of themes in the work of art. Although Warren would allow the writer to deal with any theme whatsoever, even social protest or politics, he believes that the writer must wed his theme "with the concrete projection in experience, that is, his subject."[4] He must imaginatively assimilate his ideas. Theodore Dreiser in *An American Tragedy* was often able to absorb his theme imaginatively so that form and idea became one.[5]

A philosophical novelist such as Warren runs this risk of lack of assimilation of theme to a great extent; if he fails to avoid the risk he may become merely a propagandist. This has been one of Warren's knottiest problems, and he has not always solved it satisfactorily. In "The Ballad of Billie Potts," for example, the narrative and the commentary split apart. As Floyd C. Watkins states, the simple folk story is inadequate to bear the weight of philosophical commentary with which Warren loads it.[6] Confronting the same problem–the necessity to comment upon the action–in *Night Rider*, *All the King's Men,* and *Band of Angels* (1955), Warren has relied upon the device of an inserted exemplum, a story within a story. Although these exempla, which carry much of the philosophical burden of the novels, are adequate and even excellent as short stories–all were published separately–they are intrusions and represent an admission that the novelist was unable to dramatize his ideas in his main narrative. *The Cave* has no exemplum, but it also lacks much of the philosophical and historical richness characteristic of the other novels. *Wilderness* is the first novel in which Warren has been able to dispense with such intrusions, and it is also one of his most notable successes in the blending of theme and subject into an artistic whole. With *Flood* (1964) he continues this success.

Just as the philosophical novelist faces the danger of a split in narrative and commentary, the historical novelist, writing in one of the most abused genres, runs the risk of descending into melodrama. Again, Warren has not always avoided this pitfall. *Band of Angels* is as full of outrageous examples of stagey, unconvincing melodrama as a second-rate Victorian novel, Hollywood epic, or popular magazine short story. There is, for example, the slave auction scene, in which noble old Hamish Bond gracefully and easily intimidates and disarms the vulgar young dandy who tries to examine poor little Manty cowering on the block. Even technicolor, wide screen, and Clark Gable could not do full justice to such a scene. This is, of course, Warren at his worst. *Wilderness,* however, is almost completely lacking in such melodramatic scenes. He avoids melodrama first by originality, by avoiding triteness. Historical novels from those of Scott to those of Howard Fast almost invariably contain at least some sex; it is to be expected. Yet *Wilderness* is nearly sexless. We expect dramatic and often sentimental confrontations and partings such as the scene between Jack Burden and his mother or those in *War and Peace*. Yet Adam leaves the farm of Maran Meyerhof without even a goodbye. We expect also impressive scenes, but Warren keeps the large battles, the dramatic fighting and dying in the background. Despite the title, the Battle of the Wilderness never comes center stage. It is there, and the reader is always aware of it, but it comes to him as it comes to Adam, as a muffled roar. *Wilderness* also well illustrates that Warren's concern with and interest in the facts of the past and the meaning of history–the concerns of a historian–have not hindered him artistically; just the opposite is true, for his use of history and of the related subjects of tradition and myth is one of the best aspects of his novels and contributes significantly to the success of much of his poetry.

–L. Hugh Moore Jr., *Robert Penn Warren and History* (The Hague & Paris: Mouton, 1970), pp. 19–24

1. "John Crowe Ransom: A Study in Irony," in *Selected Essays* (New York, 1958), p. 96.
2. "The Second American Revolution," *Virginia Quarterly Review,* VII (April 31, 1931), p. 282.
3. *The Legacy of the Civil War* (New York, 1961), p. 4.
4. "Literature as a Symptom," in *Who Owns America: A New Declaration of Independence,* ed. by Herbert Agar and Allen Tate (Boston and New York, 1938), p. 279.
5. "An American Tragedy," *Yale Review,* LII (October, 1962), p. 5.
6. Floyd C. Watkins, "Billie Potts at the Fall of Time," *Mississippi Quarterly,* XI (Winter, 1958), pp. 26–27.

* * *

This review is by Richard M. Weaver, a politically conservative scholar who believed the agrarian South was the "last non-materialistic civilization in the Western world."

An Altered Stand
Review of *The Legacy of the Civil War*

The Legacy of the Civil War is a curious book to come from an author who began his career with *John Brown: The Making of a Martyr* and followed this with one of the most eloquent essays in the symposium *I'll Take My Stand*. A first impression could be that he had deserted what he knows (because no man, with the possible exception of Faulkner, has the South more in his bones than Robert Penn Warren) for the superficialities of modern Liberalism. This reviewer was amazed to find passages sounding almost like Mrs. Roosevelt: "Everyone agrees that the chronic poverty and social retardation of the South, have, in fact, been a national liability. . . ." Again, there is sarcastic reference to the "constitutional theorizing" of a Southern governor. These things we expect from the more imperceptive left-wing journals; we do not expect them from a writer who was able to create the complexity that is Willie Stark and present the tangle of motivation that appears in *Brother to Dragons*.

Not all of the book is thus suggestive of the current crusade against the South. The author explores the theme of common guilt as expressed in the facts occurring both before and after the great military collision. But when he sums up the South's sin as reliance upon the "Great Alibi" and the North's as belief in its "Treasury of Virtue," we are back in the language of journalistic formulation. Moreover, the fact is hardly unique; no defeated people can go on living without an explanation of that defeat; and without a theory that virtue was on its side, no victorious people can well avail itself of the fruits of the victory. The real nature of the legacy of the Civil War is therefore still to seek; but a fault of the book is that it may tend to freeze discussion at this level.

Like most students who have speculated seriously about the subject and who realize something of the thickness of it, Mr. Warren wonders why the South could have remained so attached to the memory of *ante bellum* society through a century of pressure to change. The true answer is that, although this culture was disfigured by an historical circumstance, it was based upon a paradigmatic ideal. And once a people have glimpsed that possibility, they are not easily beaten or bribed into giving it up. That is what the "nostalgia" is for. The cultural difference was deeper than the book allows, and belief in cultural pluralism is what keeps the contest going on, despite judicial ukases and decrees of a central government.

It is now conventional to refer to the Civil War as a tragedy, but we must keep in mind that in a tragedy something is lost. What was lost was a transcendent idea of community, and a kind of integrity of the personality. It was the latter which could lead Charles Francis Adams to say that if he had been in Lee's place, he would have done exactly as Lee did. Likewise it could cause Lee to say, with wry reference to his own nationalist sentiments (on an occasion when his forward brigades were being driven back), "I suppose it's up to us Union men to win this battle." Both felt somehow that their roles were laid upon them. Since then a more calculating type has come to predominate; and the book comes up with an odd verdict in favor of the pragmatic resolution, which is not very consistent with the apostrophe to tragedy in the closing pages.

Mr. Warren is right, and is in his usual felicitous vein, when he observes that the Civil War was the "mystic cloud from which emerged our modernity." But he shows a complacency toward some of the products of that modernity, material and human, which as a younger writer he would have spurned.

–Richard M. Weaver, "An Altered Stand,"
National Review, 10 (17 June 1961): 389–390

Last Years at Yale

Warren's eighth novel, Flood: A Romance of Our Time, *was published in May 1964. In an interview with Richard B. Sale, an editor for* Studies in the Novel, *Warren discussed how he came to write the novel.*

The Beginnings of *Flood*

SALE: I was thinking of the novel *Flood* and its central character. Much of his dilemma is the business of going back.

WARREN: Yes, that's a part of the novel. Clearly that novel has in it a kind of tangential, peripheral reference, an issue of coming back and trying to pick up a world arbitrarily. That was not the germ of the novel; that was something at the end of the novel, later on.

SALE: Or that entered it.

WARREN: Almost inevitably entered the novel. But I didn't start with that notion. As far as that theme is concerned, the novel begins to deal with the question "What is home?" Ultimately home is not a place, it's a state of spirit, it's a state of feeling, a state of mind, a proper relationship to a world. It represents a–I don't want to use a big

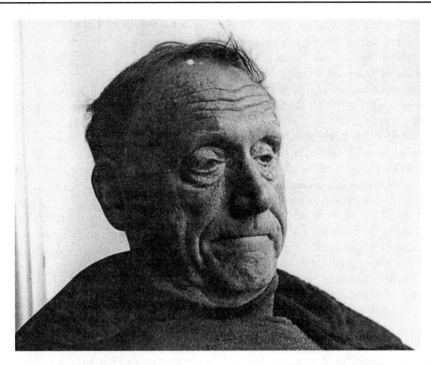

Warren, 1963 (photograph by Ellen Levine; Special Collections, Western Kentucky University Libraries)

word; it can sound too ambitious, too grand—but the world view is your home. Your world view in one sense is your home. At least that's what I was trying to say in that novel, one of the things I was trying to say. That you're no more at home; you go back to the place and the place may not be your home any more. It may stand for whatever you don't like, for instance, or that place where you're not at home. I would not interpret that as being my case if I went back to Tennessee or Kentucky; that certainly would not be the case. But there would be something artificial in doing it by an act of will. It would be an attempt to reenact sentimentally a piece of the past, which I think is always false.

SALE: Was your imagery of "washing it away," the flooding of the country, saying this same thing?

WARREN: That is a part, but it was not planned into it. That was just happen-so, as it were; it was a given. The novel itself started simply from—I can tell you how the novel started.

SALE: I'd like to hear it.

WARREN: If you think it might be of some psychological interest. In April 1931, the anniversary of the Battle of Shiloh, I passed through southwest Tennessee. I saw the old house, hanging over the bluff of the river, which I think was Grant's headquarters during the battle—the second day of the

battle, I think it was. Anyway, I forget the name of the house. I didn't go in; I just saw it, drove past it, and the village was the germ of Fiddlersburg and that house was the germ of the Fiddler house. I just caught a glimpse of it in passing, about a ninety-second glimpse. It stuck somehow. I couldn't describe the town now, only the impression I carried away from it. The—now, my God, what is it?—thirty or thirty-two years I've been writing that novel.

And another thing, I've seen one or two flooded-out places in the TVA system in Tennessee. For years and years I thought maybe somehow this was an image, this kind of doomsday to a community. Then, arbitrarily, *bang,* the community is gone. What happens to human relations in that context? This was something vaguely in the back of my mind, a speculation, no reference to fiction.

SALE: No reference to fiction in the original idea?

WARREN: No such idea then. As I began to move into the book the question arose of people who come back. I have friends who have arbitrarily attempted to come back and pick up a world by an act of will, and it's never worked for them, the ones I've seen—never worked for any of them. The sentimental reenactment without some practical justification—

SALE: –is somehow false?

WARREN: Those three things flowed in. Then the penitentiary, another germ from another place. I've seen a couple of prisons at different times. In fact, I started to write this novel, I toyed with it, twenty-odd years ago. And Elsa Morante, the wife of Alberto Moravia, wrote a novel which had to do with a very similar situation: the prison inside and out in a small place, an island prison. And this novel, in a way, was so close to the novel I was then meditating that it killed mine off. I put it aside. Her novel came out in the mid-fifties. I've forgotten the title, but it's a very powerful, very beautiful novel. So I laid my book aside for some years before I began again. I thought I'd better let that one cook, get the other one out of my mind. I wrote two novels in between before I finally came around to my *Flood* novel.

This is rather funny; critics are funny people. The name of the family of mine in *Flood* is Tolliver. And I was vaguely modeling the character who became Maggie on a woman I used to know, who I thought was a terribly nice woman, terribly attractive and bright–vaguely this woman was in the back of my mind in making that character. I was casting around for names. I called her a dozen different things. I'd always liked the name Maggie, and I'd known some nice people named Maggie; so, you know, it sort of seemed all right. And so I gave her the name Maggie. The next thing I knew I saw a review or an essay saying the book was clearly derived from *The Mill on the Floss,* a rewriting of *The Mill on the Floss,* because there's a Maggie T[u]lliver in there. I haven't read *The Mill on the Floss* since I was twelve years old, and I don't intend to, furthermore. A big construction of interpretation of some kind around Maggie Tolliver and other characters who have equivalents in *The Mill on the Floss.* Well, you better watch it, boys!

–Richard B. Sale, "An Interview in New Haven with Robert Penn Warren," *Studies in the Novel,* 2 (Fall 1970): 111–113

* * *

Flood received mostly negative reviews. Arthur Mizener, who argued that Warren's novel was misunderstood and undervalued in the Sewanee Review (October–December 1964), was one of the few reviewers who did not have serious reservations about the work. Frederic C. Crews's critical review in the 26 April 1964 issue of The New York Times Book Review brought a rebuttal from R. W. B. Lewis–and a reply from Crews.

An Exchange of Letters on *Flood*

'Flood'

To the Editor:

I am somewhat embarrassed for Frederick C. Crews and his review of Robert Penn Warren's novel, "Flood" (April 26). Mr. Crews may already be wincing at having allowed so slack commentary to get into print; I hesitate to add to his discomfort. But I would like to go on record as disagreeing in whole and in part with his reading, his interpretation and his judgment of "Flood." I disagree no less with Mr. Crews's appraisal of Warren's fictional career (which Mr. Crews seems to think has been going down hill since before it started), and with the manner in which it was expressed.

I have not been invited to offer a counter-review of "Flood." Let me say only that it is an uncommonly abundant novel–abundant in incident and character, in idea and rhetoric. With a sort of nerve-end sparseness much in favor, Warren's creative generosity is very welcome. It is also essential to his purpose. Here, as often in the past, Warren is bringing into play a great number of "mirrors" whereby the characters and situations give back distorted reflections of each other. As a result, the main elements in the novel–the death of a community; violence and guilt and justice; sex; the Negro north and south; the creative imagination, and so on–take on a growing complexity and significance. They become, quite simply, truer and more compelling. "Flood" is a far-ranging and handsomely designed exploration of contemporary life that enlarges and steadies our sense of that life.

One other point. Among other things, "Flood" exploits a good many of the going clichés of attitude and feeling toward the Negro, sex, personal identity, etc. Doing so, it has to sail pretty close to cliché at times itself, especially since Warren has never been afraid of the great simplicities, nor embarrassed by them. His novel takes a hundred risks, and, in my view, it triumphs every time. Warren is a genuinely mature artist, and what he so adventurously has to say makes much of the current cultural talk about these issues sound curiously shrill.

As to his career, every difference of opinion about this or that particular work should of course be honored. My only present thought is this: that any estimate of such large accomplishments (or, if you will, of such devoted literary ambition) requires a special stretch of mind and a special responsibility of utterance.

R. W. B. LEWIS
New Haven, Conn.

FLOOD   I-I 1-a

~~Flood~~

Setting Copy.

CHAPTER I

~~It was~~ *had* to be the place. There was the limestone
bluff jutting abruptly up, crowned by cedars. It ~~had to be~~ *was bound*
to be
the place.

/11 PRIMER
X23
D,S, FIGS,
REM A
INDENTS

[2] Long back, when he had passed this way, it had been that

sudden jut of gray stone above the trees that gave him warning

in time to avert, unconsciously, his face; and then, as he

whirled on, with eyes fixed down the road, he would know, in

conscious shame, that once more he had done it. He would

stare down the road and wait for the shame to thin out, to be

absorbed colorlessly, like a drop of ink in water, into the

general medium of his being.

In those years the road had been black top. Now it was

concrete. New concrete. Now he did not avert his face, Quite

consciously, he looked. Hell, it had been a long time ago.

He could look now.

2 fols

First page from the setting copy of Warren's eighth novel (Yale Collection of American Literature,
Beinecke Rare Book and Manuscript Library)

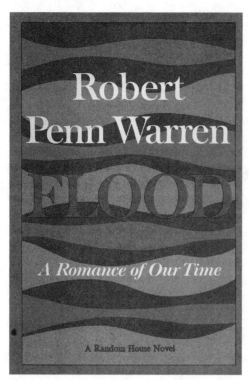

Dust jacket and title page for Warren's novel inspired by the Johnstown flood in Tennessee (Special Collections, Western Kentucky University Libraries)

Wincing

To the Editor:

Professor Lewis fails to communicate his embarrassment to me. None of the five or six reviews of "Flood" I have seen differs from my own judgment in any significant way, and none takes the awestruck tone that Professor Lewis considers Warren's due. Is this a conspiracy, or is it possible that Professor Lewis is the one who is guilty of "slack commentary"? His letter comes close to saying that we are obliged to like Warren's new book because it is the work of a "genuinely mature artist" (I agree that he is one) and because it is full of intensely topical themes. My review, in contrast, tried to deal with specific problems of execution arising from an overambitious thematic design.

Professor Lewis says that in my view, Warren's career "has been going down hill since before it started." What I said, however, was this: "Robert Penn Warren is a writer of major talent who has never produced the great novel everyone expects of him." Professor Lewis is entitled to misconstrue my words as he pleases, but not, I think, to lecture me about "a special responsibility of utterance." His letter amounts to a protest against critical frankness, and thus it does leave me "wincing"–but not on my own behalf. FREDERICK C. CREWS.

Berkeley, Calif.

–The New York Times Book Review,
31 May 1964, p. 18

* * *

In this opening excerpted from his long review essay, John Lewis Longley Jr. argues that reviewers mistake Warren's intention in Flood.

Warren's "Calculated Risk" Review of *Flood*

But I have done good things! is the agonized cry of one protagonist in *Flood* at the moment of final self-revelation. Mr. Warren's new novel is subtitled "A Romance of Our Time" and so deliberately runs the identical calculated risk which dogged the reception of *World Enough and Time.* It is certain to arouse the same obtuse misunderstanding in the bosoms of the popular reviewers which the earlier romance had to live down. On the surface, at the most obvious level, the novel is pastoral and lyrical. Mr. Warren has been many things in his time, but obvious is not one of them. Within the pastoral mode, and with a strict economy of means, he has constructed a powerful and moving Divine Comedy of art, Daedalian man, holy and profane love, damnation and redemption.

If the "romantic" intention of *World Enough and Time* was essentially to dramatize the failure of a personal, subjective ideal to become consonant with the realm of public life–the world as it is–then it seems probable that *Flood,* by a partial inversion of the coin, dramatizes the failure of a fragmented, subjective life activity to become a lasting, adequate equivalent for human fullness of being. The lonely passion of Jeremiah Beaumont was often testily dismissed as a mere riotous excursion into costume drama, and in some ways the era of Willie Stark seems even more remote, if that is possible. But *Flood* is explicitly a romance of our own time, and there can be no blinking of what it brings home to us. The metaphysical dimension is all there; it is only in the ease and flow of the pastoral mode that the common reader may be slow to detect it.

Fiddlersburg is a small crossroads in Middle Tennessee, dating back a century and a half. When the floodgates of the new TVA dam are closed, the water will eventually cover Fiddlersburg. The characters of the novel are persons who are present in the town during the last year of its life. Most of them have lived there always; they will be relocated a few miles away and be generously compensated by the federal government. Others have come from Hollywood to make a documentary about the flooding of the town. When the year is over, they have all gone their separate ways. This is the *donnée*. There is little in such data to engage the passionate attention of serious readers. Fiddlersburg, a handful of people, and their various responses to its passing is all there is. Time span covers only the present generation. Mr. Warren has chosen just such a limited arena in which to illuminate his vision of human significance. His method is to establish the tensions and polarities between true and false in art, in aspiration and desire, in human love in all its manifestations, and ultimately to show how all our choices or rejections flow from a basic theological awareness or lack of it. The novel is infused with a powerful and desolate sense of alienation, but in every case the aloneness is what the actor has earned by his choice between flesh and spirit, the self and the other, the self and God.

–John Lewis Longley Jr., "When All Is Said and Done: Warren's *Flood*," *Southern Review*, new series 1 (Autumn 1965): 968–969

* * *

Warren's last book in which he directly addressed the issue of race in the South and America, Who Speaks for the Negro?, *was published in late May 1965. A month before it appeared, Warren attended the 1965 Southern Literary Festival, hosted on the University of Mississippi campus 22–24 April. The last day of the festival was Warren's sixtieth birthday. Almost a quarter of a century later, Robert W. Hamblin reflected on the man and the occasion.*

Warren at the 1965 Southern Literary Festival: A Personal Recollection

In the spring of 1965 I was a third-year doctoral candidate in the English Department at the University of Mississippi in Oxford. Like many other students at the university, I eagerly awaited the convening of the annual meeting of the Southern Literary Festival, set for April 22–24 on the Ole Miss campus. The festival program had been planned as a tribute to William Faulkner; and Eudora Welty, Robert Penn Warren, Malcolm Cowley, Ruth Ford, and Martin Dain had been invited to lead the celebration. But I had a special reason for excitement which went beyond my interest in Faulkner and Southern literature: I had been asked by Gerald Walton, the supervisor of the graduate assistants in the English department and one of the festival coordinators, to serve as escort and chauffeur for Robert Penn Warren during his stay on the campus. Five years earlier, as a high school English teacher in Sparrows Point, Maryland, I had one day assigned an eleventh grade class busywork so that I could have the uninterrupted leisure to sit at my desk and read the final pages of *All the King's Men,* one of the most exciting and meaningful novels I had ever read. Now I was going to have the opportunity not only to meet its author but also spend some time with him, and perhaps even secure his autograph in that reading copy of *All the King's Men.* Little did I know that I was about to become a backstage observer of a mini-drama in which Warren would be caught on the horns of a dilemma created by the racial tensions that permeated the Ole Miss campus at that time.

In 1965 the University of Mississippi was still experiencing the aftershock of the violent confrontation that had accompanied the enrollment of the university's first black student, James Meredith, in September 1962. Meredith's admission to the university had come only after a protracted legal struggle between the U.S. Department of Justice and the governor of Mississippi, segregationist Ross Barnett; organized resistance by the White Citizens' Council, the Ku Klux Klan, and other anti-integration groups; and a campus riot on the night of September 30 that left two people dead, scores injured, numerous buildings and vehicles vandalized, and Ole Miss and Mississippi disgraced by the conscience of the nation. President Kennedy's response to the developing emergency was to assign federal marshals to accompany Meredith onto the campus, to federalize the Mississippi National Guard, and, following the riot, to send 30,000 troops (including several hundred of the Mississippi guardsmen) to restore order on the campus. There had been no more riots, and the troops had departed after a few weeks (though some

The Warren family in their Fairfield, Connecticut, home, circa 1964: Gabriel, Robert Penn, Rosanna, and Eleanor with dogs Joey and Aslan (Special Collections, Western Kentucky University Libraries)

federal marshals had remained until Meredith's graduation in 1963); but the legacy of discord and animosity would linger for several years. By 1965 only three additional black students had been enrolled at Ole Miss; and the university was still perceived by integrationists and segregationists alike as an essentially "all-white" school, one of the last bastions of segregation in the Deep South. Moreover, even some liberals and moderates (especially some in Mississippi) who defended Meredith's right to attend Ole Miss felt that President Kennedy's reaction to the crisis had involved an excessive use of force. Thus the old Southern question of states' rights versus federal intervention had once again been brought to the surface, as during the Civil War era, by the issue of race. These events and attitudes, as Warren well knew, had worked to create a tense and potentially explosive atmosphere on the Ole Miss campus by the time he walked onto it in April 1965.

Although I was not privy to the information at the time, Warren had expressed serious reservations about appearing on a program at a school which still had not altogether resolved the integration issue. In a detailed letter, dated August 29, 1964, to Evans Harrington, the Ole Miss English professor who was serving as the festival program chairman, Warren had expressed a keen desire to participate in the proposed tribute to Faulkner, having, as he noted, "a sort of old-time vested interest" in the subject. But he went on to explain that it would be impossible for him to speak about Faulkner without frankly addressing Faulkner's views on race relations, and any discussion of that matter, Warren continued, might prove unpopular with an administration and a campus community still smarting over federally-enforced integration. Just how volatile Faulkner's ideas might yet be Warren emphasized by observing, "If he had been alive at the time of the Oxford riots, the mob, had it been both logical and book-reading, would have burned him out."

In his letter to Harrington, undoubtedly intended not only to clarify his own position but also strategically to test the waters in advance, Warren made it quite clear that he identified with Faulkner's liberal views on race. "I am unequivocally opposed to segregation in any form," Warren stated; and he called attention to his forthcoming book "of interviews with Negro leaders in various parts of the country" (*Who Speaks for the Negro?*), the appearance of which might quite possibly make him "even less welcome" in Mississippi "than now." Still, Warren noted, despite the potential for controversy he would be willing to come to Ole Miss provided he could speak frankly and openly.

> It is not that I mind controversy–short of having my head punched by some patriot; and if I come I shan't be there to run in a popularity contest. Since there is, as you say, a deep division in your faculty and student body on this general question, any ventilation of the subject would, no doubt, be all to the good and I don't mind turning on my little electric fan for that purpose. But I shouldn't want to come with a desire to embarrass you or the administration, any more than I should want to come out of exhibitionism; but if I do come I'll have to turn on that particular electric fan. You can't help turning it on if you try to talk seriously about Faulkner.

Warren concluded by graciously offering Harrington "time to give the invitation a long second thought in the light of what I have had to say here." Then, in what surely would have been redundancies in any less ambivalent context, Warren added in a postscript that, "to keep the record clear," he was sending a copy of this letter to the Old Miss Chancellor and that, "again to keep the record clear," he had spoken the previous spring at Tougaloo, the predominantly-black college near Jackson, Mississippi.

As Warren's postscript makes clear, his letter of concern was directed as much to the Ole Miss administration as to Harrington. I do not know if Warren at this time was aware of Harrington's reputation at Ole Miss and in Oxford as a "liberal," a friend of such campus "radicals" as history professor James W. Silver and Episcopal minister and civil rights advocate Duncan Gray. Given Harrington's support of integration, one may logically wonder whether Warren may have been invited to the festival for the precise purpose of addressing the race issue and thereby promoting the cause of integration and civil rights. In any event, Harrington's invitation, and Warren's ambivalent response, set in motion a series of events that brought the question of race once again to the forefront on the already-troubled Ole Miss campus.

Chancellor J. D. Williams responded to Warren's expressed concerns on September 12. He thanked Warren for his frankness and added a clarifying point about race relations in Mississippi. "Since you have been most considerate of our situation," the Chancellor wrote, "I feel that it is incumbent upon me to let you know that the publicly supported universities and colleges in Mississippi have been since August 28, 1964, under direct order of the Board of Trustees to exclude Negroes from all public buildings on the campus except those Negroes who are enrolled as students. Unless this order is changed, we cannot admit Negro visitors to the campus to any program. I am sure that you will wish to take this policy into account as you consider what you should do just as we are thinking over what we should do in the light of your letter."

Warren replied to Chancellor Williams on September 19, stating that his principal concern was (as it had been all along) the freedom to speak his mind and not the makeup of the audience. "I do not mean to say that I would not accept your invitation if the audience is segregated. I mean to say that if I come (as I fully intend to do if you do wish to re-invite me) I shall feel free to discuss the question of race in Faulkner's work–with courtesy and detachment, I hope, but with an analysis of his position as I see it." Warren reiterated his keen desire to be a part of the program, "for I always like to come to the State which I regard as the literary capital of the English-speaking world."

On September 28, nearly two months after Harrington's initial invitation (dated July 31), Chancellor Williams wrote Warren again, this time "confirming the original invitation to speak on our campus next spring." Three days later Harrington also corresponded to reconfirm the invitation, and Warren communicated his acceptance to both men on October 12. None of the three, however, could have known that the biggest obstacle to Warren's appearance on the program–and, indeed, to the festival event itself–was yet to appear.

Despite the state trustees' ban on off-campus Negroes participating in university events, one of the groups attending the 1965 Southern Literary Festival was a biracial delegation of three black coeds, two white male students, and a white male professor from Tougaloo College. Although this group had earlier in the day registered for the conference sessions, visited the student union, and eaten in the university cafeteria without incident, on Thursday night a crowd of about 500 persons (including several adults from off campus) gathered near Hill Dormitory, where the three Tougaloo males were housed, and began chanting segregationist slogans. As reported by the campus newspaper, *The Mississippian,* the following day, the late-night demonstration lasted for more than an hour, during which time the vehicle belonging to one of the Tougaloo delegates had its windows smashed, its tires deflated, and its gas tank filled with sugar. The word "nigger" was

2495 Redding Road, Fairfield, Connecticut, May 27, 1964

Minister Malcolm X,
Suite 128,
Theresa Hotel,
2090 7th Avenue,
New York City

Dear Sir:

    I shall, to confirm our conversation by telephone this morning, call you Sunday evening to arrange an appointment. Meanwhile, I shall hold Monday entirely free. After checking trains again, I find that I was wrong about the time when I could get to New York. There is an early train and I could be at your hotel by a little after 9:00 AM, if that would help matters.

    I am enclosing a carbon of my earlier letter to you giving more detail about the kind of interview involved.

    Thank you.

    Very sincerely yours,

Robert Penn Warren

Letter Warren sent Malcolm X to arrange an interview when he was working on Who Speaks for the Negro?
(Robert Penn Warren Papers, Beinecke Library, Yale University)

painted in orange lettering on the side of the auto. Not until the Dean of Students, Franklin Moak; the Chief of Campus Police, Burnes Tatum; and the Director of Campus Security, Whitney Stuart, arrived and started taking the names of the protesters did the mob disband.

Many students, myself included, did not know about the disturbance until the following morning, when the campus and the city of Oxford were buzzing with accounts and rumors of the incident. Warren also learned about the occurrence the next day: on his way to Ole Miss he had stopped off in Memphis the previous evening to do a poetry reading for a standing-room-only audience of about 400 persons at Southwestern University, where he had once taught. Throughout the day Friday, however, Warren followed the aftermath of the racial disturbance with concerned interest and even alarm. Raymond Rohrbaugh, the professor with the Tougaloo delegation, announced that, "for our own personal safety," his group had decided to walk out of the festival and return to Tougaloo. Rohrbaugh told newspaper reporters that Ole Miss officials had informed him following the demonstration that "they would do the best they could to protect us, but they couldn't guarantee us anything."

Before leaving Ole Miss, however, Rohrbaugh lodged an "informal protest" and called upon festival officials to cancel the remainder of the program. "We felt the festival should not go on when a member organization could not be fully protected," he told newsmen. George Owens, the black president of Tougaloo College, drove to Ole Miss to accompany his professor and students back home. "The decision [to leave] already was made," he said later. "I just went up to bring them back." Shortly after midday on Friday Ole Miss campus police escorted the Tougaloo contingent off the campus, and a Mississippi Highway Patrol unit accompanied the group along the entire 150-mile route to Tougaloo.

On the two or three occasions that I was with Warren on Friday morning and afternoon he was noticeably agitated about the developments. He questioned me, and others, about the events of the night before, about the university's handling of the situation, and about Rohrbaugh's demand that the festival program be terminated. More than once he wondered aloud whether it would be appropriate for him to stay to complete his role in the program in view of what had transpired. My distinct impression was that Warren was not so much seeking advice as he was thinking out loud, weighing the pros and cons of the matter. It was obvious that he was genuinely concerned about the physical welfare and the civil rights of the Tougaloo delegation. "Shameful!" was his response to one reporter who asked him his opinion of the Thursday

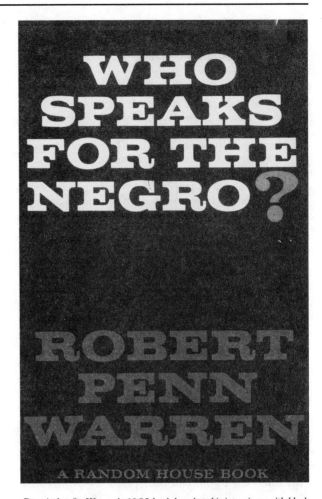

Dust jacket for Warren's 1965 book based on his interviews with black Americans in the South (Special Collections, Western Kentucky University Libraries)

night demonstration. But it was equally clear that Warren also felt strongly (maybe even more strongly now because of the circumstances) about the lecture he was scheduled to deliver in Ole Miss's Fulton Chapel that evening. That lecture, entitled "Faulkner, The South, the Negro, and Time," would not only serve to illuminate Faulkner's handling of race relations but would express Warren's deepfelt personal convictions as well.

The questions that Warren, along with university officials, reporters, and other observers, kept coming back to throughout the day were whether the incident on Thursday night had presented any real threat to the Tougaloo delegation and, consequently, whether the walkout represented a legitimate response to actual danger or was merely a publicity stunt designed to gain national attention for the civil rights movement. University apologists pointed out that no disturbance had been held outside the dormitories in which the three black coeds from Tougaloo or the two black Ole Miss students were housed, and that, further, the demonstrators had dispersed fairly quickly after the authorities arrived. The general view was that expressed by Paul Flowers the following Monday in his "Greenhouse" column in the Memphis *Commercial Appeal*:

> . . . a molehill aspired to become a mountain at the already battered University of Mississippi, where students and faculty members from some 27 colleges and universities, from South Carolina to Texas, gathered to pay tribute to the late William Faulkner. The same social issue–race–which many of us believe has been magnified all out of proportion to its real importance was the cause celebre to touch off a minor incident which fogged the atmosphere for a few hours.
>
> The incident was quickly and emphatically put into its proper context by sober students, officials of Ole Miss, law enforcement officers, and delegates to the festival.

I readily confess that Flowers' summary accurately reflects what was then (though it is not now) my own assessment of the situation–and this was the viewpoint that I conveyed to Warren when he inquired about my opinion on the matter.

But Warren, whose view of the situation was considerably more detached (and, I see now, infinitely wiser) than my admittedly parochial and defensive position, was truly caught on the horns of a moral dilemma. Unlike others of us, he was not willing to excuse a serious racial incident as being little more than a mischievous prank by unruly and ill-mannered university students. Moreover, he understood, as some of us had not yet learned, that psychological and emotional violence can be just as demeaning and damaging as physical attack. There was also, I think, a personal dimension to Warren's agony. As a born and bred Southerner who had three decades earlier (in *I'll Take My Stand*) endorsed a "separate but equal" approach to race relations, but as one who had subsequently been converted into an integrationist, Warren, I am convinced, was concerned that his decision at Ole Miss might compromise his current position as a leading Southern spokesman for racial equality and justice. Of all of the festival speakers who were asked to join the Tougaloo group in the walkout, it seems to me that Warren had the most to lose in terms of credibility, integrity, and status.

I can only guess as to how close Warren actually came to walking away from the festival. My belief was, and is, that he came very, very close–that a big part of him (perhaps the new Warren calling the old Warren to heel) wanted to leave. I do know that he wrestled with the problem long and hard.

And what finally kept him there was not the rationalizations offered by Ole Miss defenders like myself, but rather the speech that he carried in his briefcase. "Abandoning, or canceling, the literary festival is not the way to accomplish any desirable end," he told Paul Flowers. What he said to me Friday afternoon was a bit more succinct: "Dammit, I came here to deliver a speech, and I intend to deliver it."

And deliver it he did. On Friday evening at 8:00 Warren spoke in Fulton Chapel to a near-capacity crowd of 1200 persons. The audience included festival participants, Ole Miss faculty and students, citizens of Oxford, and quite a few people who had driven down from Memphis. Everyone present was white. We listened to Warren read, in a quiet voice that could barely be heard in the back of the auditorium, a paper that outlined Faulkner's views on history, humanity, and race. Warren spoke of the "curse" and "doom" of Southern history, with "its record of man's failure to realize his fine ideals, of the perversion of his ideals, of the cynical use of ideals as masks for brutal and self-aggrandizing action." He traced the tragedy that occurs when a society abdicates "the things which affirm human worth and express human brotherhood." In Faulkner's treatment of the abuses that Southern whites had heaped upon blacks, Warren found "the rejection of the brother, the kinsman, as a symbolic representation of the crime that is the final crime against both nature and the human community."

For Faulkner, Warren asserted, piety is not respect "for institutions and social arrangements, which are necessarily subject to the revisions of historical process," but instead "the reverence for the human capacity to struggle and endure, ultimately . . . reverence for the human effort for justice." Faulkner's heroes, therefore, are not characters like Gail Hightower, Quentin Compson, and even Ike McCaslin, who are "maimed by a perverted reverence for the past"; or Thomas Sutpen, Jason Compson, and Flem Snopes, whose present actions and future dreams are characterized by "abstract, loveless exploitation"; but rather the Dilseys and Nancys and Lenas and Chicks and Gavins and Ratliffs, who view time and history as constructive and redemptive. Indeed, Warren noted, Faulkner's life as well as his work reflected this struggle for redemption. And this redemption, for Faulkner and his characters, often turned on the fulcrum of race. Warren concluded his remarks with a poignant analogy that not only characterized Faulkner's life and career but

also, for some of us in the audience, reflected Warren's actions at the Southern Literary Festival:
"James Joyce went forth from Ireland to forge . . .
the conscience of his race. Faulkner did a more difficult thing. To forge the conscience of his race, he
stayed in his native spot and, in his soul, in vice and
virtue, re-enacted the history of that race." Warren,
it seemed to me, had engaged in just such a struggle,
and with a similar resolution, on this very day.

After Warren's presentation I waited offstage
to drive him back to the Alumni House, where he
was staying. He was surrounded by members of the
audience who had stayed to speak with him personally, shake his hand, ask for an autograph. Several
people thanked him for coming, and for having the
courage to say the things he had just said. During
his presentation I had observed the audience closely,
and it was obvious that his ideas were being carefully followed, and well received. Now, as I listened
to individual after individual tell him how grateful
they were for his remarks, I could sense that the lecture had produced a cathartic effect upon the listeners, as though the honesty and truth of Warren's
(and Faulkner's) words had served as a kind of confession, releasing the anguish and regret of the days,
months, and years of racial strife and tension and
positing the hope of a better time to come. And I
knew then why Warren had felt compelled to stay to
deliver his address.

During the short drive back to the Alumni
House I added my congratulations and thanks to
Warren for a job well done. He was clearly pleased
that the evening had gone so well, and he was especially gratified at the number of university students,
not only from Ole Miss but also from the many
other schools represented at the festival, who had
stopped by to talk with him. Though I did not have
the boldness to press him on the matter, I could tell
that, if earlier in the day he had questioned whether
he should stay or leave, he now knew that he had
made the right decision.

It has been almost a quarter century since
these events transpired, and I did not see Warren
again after that time, though I have continued to follow his career with interest and to read and teach his
novels, stories, poems, and essays. I still treasure
that Modern Library copy of *All the King's Men* that I
first read in Baltimore years ago. I am looking at it
now, with its inscription: "To / Bob Hamblin / grate-
fully /Robert Penn Warren / Oxford / April 23,
1965." I also have a gift copy of *Who Speaks for the*

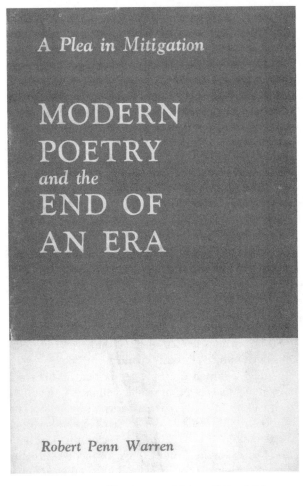

*Cover for a lecture Warren gave at Wesleyan College in Macon,
Georgia, in February 1966 (Special Collections,
Thomas Cooper Library, University of
South Carolina)*

Negro? that I received in the mail, compliments of
Warren, a few weeks after the conclusion of the
Southern Literary Festival. But the greatest treasure
I retain from my brief association with Warren is an
intangible one, though no less real than the inscription and the gift volume: it is the memory and example of an heroic Southerner who had the vision and
the courage to grow with the times and who demonstrated that April day in Oxford something that
many of us almost forgot in the 1960s—that it is just
as noble and brave to stay and fight as it is to walk
away in protest.

–Robert W. Hamblin, "Robert Penn Warren at
the 1965 Southern Literary Festival: A Personal
Recollection," *Southern Literary Journal*,
22 (Spring 1990): 53–62

* * *

This review was written by Warren's Yale colleague C. Vann Woodward.

Warren's Challenge to Race Dogma
Review of *Who Speaks for the Negro?*

Conventional wisdom on race relations has it that communications between white and Negro Americans have broken down. One corollary to this proposition is that the white man can never really understand the Negro mind, and two others turn upside down the ancient clichés that only a Southerner really understands the Negro, and that the Negro only tells the white man what he wants to hear. Robert Penn Warren's book is a challenge to all these tenets and dogmas. Warren is not only a white man but a Southerner, and he undertakes by personal interviews to understand what is going on in the minds of the leaders, spokesmen, and active participants of the Negro Revolution. The result is the most searching exploration of the thought and emotion, the tensions and conflicts of the greatest American social upheaval of this century.

The historian can only regret that he does not have on his shelves a comparable volume by an author of equal stature on the First American Revolution, the Antislavery Movement, the Radical Reconstruction, or the Populist Revolt. Such a book on the abolitionists, for example, would have provided insights beyond recapture on Garrison, Phillips, Birney, Theodore Weld, the Grimke sisters, Elijah Lovejoy, Harriet Tubman, John Brown, Fred Douglass, Gerrit Smith and scores of their collaborators.

And a book on the Reconstruction would have put to the men themselves the questions we are still asking about Summer, Stevens, Stanton, Ben Wade, and Ben Butler, the carpetbaggers and scalawags, and the young teachers and Freedmen's Bureau workers that were the shock troops of that abortive revolution.

In the heat of battle, long before the monuments are raised and the biographies written, it is harder to pick the names that will survive in history. Warren makes no such attempt. He gives scrupulous attention to obscure figures, young and old, because of the role they have played and the experience they have had—country parsons, college students, working men. His is no systematic or sociological survey, but he has worked in the North as well as in the South, among the rank and file as well as among the junior officers and the big brass. Among the latter he has managed to record full interviews with the leaders of all the major organizations, including Martin Luther King, Roy Wilkins, Whitney Young, James Farmer, James Forman, Malcolm X, Adam Clayton Powell, Bayard Rustin, and Aaron Henry, as well as briefer accounts of some of their lieutenants. As a writer himself he has a special interest in the novelists Ralph Ellison and James Baldwin and is able to draw from them many fresh revelations about their attitudes to their work and the movement. There is a spirited exchange with Professor Kenneth Clark on John Brown and a philosophical dialogue with Judge William Hastie. Warren is at his best with the young people like Robert Moses, Gilbert Moses, Ruth Turner, Izell Blair, and Stokely Carmichael.

The main body of the book consists of transcripts of tape-recorded conversations, but the skill and subtlety with which they are conducted and the running commentary on them lift the interviews out of the level of documentary and literal reporting. By a patterned recurrence of basic questions and comparison of responses Warren turns the interviews into a symposium among the many he questions. The novelist is at work as well as the reporter. "I want to make my reader see, hear, and feel as immediately as possible what I saw, heard, and felt." His characterizations are more than descriptions:

> "James Forman is a combat officer. His inner peace comes only, perhaps, in the immediate outer clash. He is bitter, or at least impatient, about those who do not have his special kind of total commitment. . . . He lives with the ulcers that have nearly killed him, with the threat of violence in his daily life, with the mixture of pessimism and grim humor. He lives intensely, I should guess, and painfully, in a strange drama of compulsion, bitterness and hope. This is what makes him demanding to the imagination. He is engaged in a struggle for reality. For his own reality."

And this on Martin Luther King:

> "Compactness and control—that is the first impression, even in the natural outgoing cordiality at the moment of greeting when the eyes brighten. At the handshake you notice that the hand is unusually large for a man of his stature, a strong hand. He has the tight-packed skin of a man who will be fat some day if he doesn't watch it, a skin with a slight sheen to his brownness . . . the physical compactness, the sense of completeness."

And Roy Wilkins:

> "He is, clearly, a thoughtful man with something detached and professorial in his tone, and his smile has a certain trace of sadness in it, a faintly ironical sadness. You feel that he knows a good deal about human nature, including his own—and yours. . . . He is prepared to deal with things as they are. He tries, apparently, to keep his mind firmly fixed on the thing, not the word; on the situation, not the shibboleth."

The Negro and his tragic plight and the white man in all the complexity of his relations with the Negro—especially in the Southern context—are not new or strange themes to Warren. They are woven into nearly all his fiction and much of his poetry. They are the central theme in *Band of Angels* and in his long poem, *Brothers to Dragons* and the subject of his short book *Segregation*. The present book is an extension of a long search for reality and truth. When he was asked, "What makes you think that Negroes will tell you the truth?" He replied, "Even a lie is a kind of truth." And he comments: "But that is not the only kind that we have here."

There is, in fact, a surprising amount of candor in the responses he evokes to the awkward questions, the kind often evaded: the growing class cleavage among the Negroes, the feuds among factions, the alienating effects of "success," the use of race as an alibi, the "snobbery of being black," the exploitation of white masochism ("Beat me, Daddy, I feel guilty."), the white myth of Negro sexuality and the Negro's ambivalence toward it. "I am sure you know Negroes are bastards, too," remarks a SNCC worker. And Judge Hastie quietly observes, "You know all Negroes spend at least a little time hating white people."

In his chapter of summation Warren is merciless in his exposure of white sentimentalities, masochistic self-indulgence, and upside-down Phariseeism. There is, for example, the "notion that the Negro—*qua* Negro—is intrinsically 'better,'" whether as Jack Kerouac's Noble Savage or the wise and witty milkmaid Kitten of *One Hundred Dollar Misunderstanding*. Or the notion that the Negro is going to redeem our spiritually bankrupt civilization, or the other side of the coin, that the white man is going to redeem the Negro.

Among the Negro leaders Warren finds no consensus and arrives at no pat generalizations. Instead he finds "an enormous variety of personality and talent," as well as "an enormous variety of attitudes and policies." No one leader is able to speak for the Negro. The numerous individuals who play roles of leadership display marked disagreement over fundamental issues of the movement. These include the nature of integration and race policy after achieving it; the efficacy of nonviolence and the need for adhering to it; the objectives of demonstrations and the dangers of "overreach"; the guilt of the white man and his capacity to "understand" the Negro; whether the Negro's future is brighter in the South or the North; the relation of the Negro problem to the poor-white problem; basic policies of preferential treatment, civil rights versus economic emphasis, and political strategy in the immediate future and the long run.

The alternatives are not drift and confusion on the one hand or ironbound, rock-ribbed orthodoxy on the

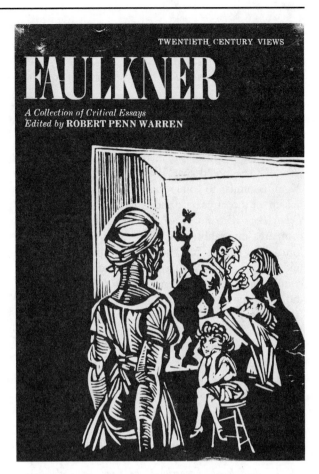

Dust jacket for a 1966 book on the contemporary writer Warren most admired. Faulkner, Warren asserts, "writes of two Souths: he reports one South and he creates another. On one hand he is a perfectly straight realistic writer, and on the other he is a symbolist" (Richland County Public Library).

other. "Fortunately," writes Warren, "a number of Negroes in key, or influential positions are men of intellectual power and depth of purpose, and these men have put their minds on these problems." The drive is not toward orthodoxy, but rather toward the imaginative and pragmatic exploration of possibilities. "In general," he concludes, "the Negro leadership has given the public little reason to be appalled, for in a situation as complicated as this it [would not be easy to imagine a higher] level of idealism, dedication and realistic intelligence. If leadership of that quality is supplanted by other, less savory types that are already lurking in the wings, and that certainly do not have any vision of a reconciled society, the white man has only himself to blame."

—C. Vann Woodward, *New Republic,*
152 (22 May 1965): 21–23

* * *

In this excerpt James A. Perkins examines Warren's treatment of his interviews with James Farmer, the first national director of the Congress of Racial Equality (CORE). He argues that Warren should be considered one of the founders of the New Journalism.

Who Speaks for the Negro? and the New Journalism

James H. Justus, in his *The Achievement of Robert Penn Warren,* noted that Warren's *Who Speaks for the Negro?* is similar to "other examples of 'the higher journalism' of recent years"; and Hugh Ruppersburg, in his *Robert Penn Warren and the American Imagination,* said "it compares favorably with other examples of the New Journalism which had begun to appear during the mid-1960s." These two scholars made an important connection, but they did not follow the implication of the connection to its logical and surprising conclusion. In this essay, I will use Warren's interview with James Farmer, in "The Big Brass" section, as well as Warren's treatment of events in which Farmer was an important participant to show that Robert Penn Warren was, at the very least, a co-creator of the techniques of the "New Journalism" in his 1965 work *Who Speaks for the Negro?*

The New Journalism was born in the 1960s, more precisely, it was born in 1965 with the publication of Truman Capote's *In Cold Blood* and Tom Wolfe, Jr.'s *The Kandy-Kolored, Tangerine-Flake Streamline Baby.* Since Robert Penn Warren's *Who Speaks for the Negro?* was also published that year (in fact it was published before either of the other two books) and since *Who Speaks for the Negro?* uses many of the techniques of the New Journalism, Warren should be considered as one of the founders of the New Journalism.

In fact when Tom Wolfe's cultural essays appeared in *Esquire,* Warren was already publishing sections of the manuscript that would become *Who Speaks for the Negro?* Truman Capote's *In Cold Blood* would be serialized later in *The New Yorker.* It is clear that Warren could have read them both; however, he never mentioned either the authors or their works in his interviews, and he had already written the better part of his work before either author's work began to appear. This seems to be one of those moments that occur in cultural history when the time is ripe for a breakthrough and a number of people move in the same direction toward the same innovation at the same time.

In a footnote, Hugh Ruppersburg says, "Warren's 'journalism' often resembles the work of John Hersey, author of *Hiroshima* and *The Algiers Hotel Incident* [*sic*], to whom Warren dedicated his poem 'New Dawn,' about the bombing of Hiroshima." Despite the parallel activity of Wolfe and Capote toward the creation of the new

Journalism, and despite the critical furor over the "death of the novel" which followed the publication of a *Life* profile on Capote, I believe Warren, using the strong, clear work of John Hersey as a guide to journalistic writing, was striking out on his own to create a blend of fictional technique and non-fictional content in *Who Speaks for the Negro?*

Warren himself was aware of the innovative nature of the work he was doing as he collected material for *Who Speaks for the Negro?* In a May 4, 1964, letter to James Farmer, he wrote: "What I am trying to do is somewhat different from the ordinary Newspaper interview. What I hope to get is a sort of portrait of the person interviewed, a sense of his personality and the workings of his mind. We touch on a number of topics, some of them having only a remote connection, if any, with Civil Rights, but the course of the interview is determined by the range of interests of the person interviewed." Of course it was Warren, not the person being interviewed, who was in control of the taping sessions. It is he who posed the questions, he who reminded the subjects of previous statements, and he who asked their opinions about the statements of others on the matters at hand. Finally, it was Warren who edited the work. In discussing the creative process which led to *Who Speaks for the Negro?,* Warren wrote in the book's "Foreword":

> The interviews were recorded on tape. In almost all instances the person interviewed checked the transcript for errors. [Farmer did not.] Many of the interviews were long, sometimes several hours, and in a few cases there was more than one conversation. [Farmer had two interviews.] It would have been impossible, and undesirable, to publish all the transcripts. I have chosen the sections which seem to me most significant and exciting, and within these sections have sometimes omitted repetitions and irrelevancies. I have not indicated such omissions. But except for a rare conjunction, transition, or explanatory phrase, I have made no verbal changes.

About this process, James H. Justus has said, "*Who Speaks for the Negro?* is very much Warren's document, which is to say that it is not merely edited." Hugh Ruppersburg disagrees with this assessment. He says "In 'The Big Brass,' the chapter devoted to the leaders of the movement, interviews are transcribed word for word, with an apparent minimum of editing."

Warren was aware of the obvious need for editing in the transcripts of the interviews. In a letter to James Farmer on July 7, 1964, which accompanied a copy of their conversation, Warren wrote: "Here is a copy of the transcript of our conversation. It is rather ragged in part, as you see, but it will be very valuable to me."

If we compare the transcript of the two interviews with James Farmer to the text about Farmer in "The Big Brass" chapter, we can see that Warren did considerable editing, and we can see what the shaping eye and ear of a fiction writer brought to this foray into extended journalism. The most important change from the transcripts to the book is in length. The following passage covers five lines in the book: "We find increasing tension. A number of new leaders are springing up from the Negro working class. Many have not had much education—they have developed some facility in the use of the techniques of nonviolent direct action" (195).

This passage is a pastiche composed of material taken from three pages of the June 11, 1964, transcript which covered 69 lines. This cutting creates focus and clarity. It is the sort of thing novelists do all the time when they cut the dull parts out of drafts and focus on the action or the development of character.

Perhaps the most interesting changes Warren made in this section of the work were those that masked the nature of the interviewer. On page 194, Warren asks: "What about the liberal who puts his views on record but who will not march?" In the transcript, that question is much longer and (if we read it through the "Doctor I have this friend who" ploy) much more revealing:

> You find situations like this—a white man that I know, who is quite a distinguished writer, has had some pressure for him to become an activist, at least associate himself outside. He has written eloquently and is planning on something that is very important, which would be on this subject, and he will be totally committed to; yet he has come in [for] some very harsh words because he won't go march.

A major problem for Warren in dealing with the Farmer material is that Warren interviewed Farmer on June 11, 1964, and did not interview him again until the last week in September when the book was about to go to the publisher. On July 7, 1964, Warren sent Farmer a copy of the transcript of the tape along with a letter that said in part, "Can you make any corrections, and return to me in the enclosed envelope? I'll be very grateful, for I know how pressed you are." That summer, James Farmer was very busy with other problems. On June 19, 1964, ten days after the interview, the United States Senate, after 83 days of debate (the longest debate in Senate history) passed the Civil Rights Bill 73 to 27. On June 20, 1964, three civil rights workers disappeared near the town of Philadelphia, Mississippi. Farmer did not learn about the disappearance of the COFO volunteer Andrew Goodman, along with Michael Schwerner and James Chaney, his two paid

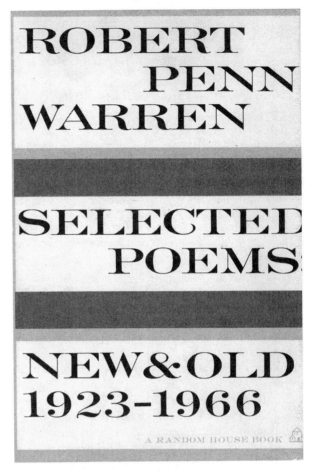

Dust jacket for the second of four volumes Warren titled "Selected Poems," this one published in 1966. He continued to revise the older poems he included in these volumes (Special Collections, Thomas Cooper Library, University of South Carolina).

CORE field representatives, in Mississippi until the morning of June 21, 1964, ten days after Warren interviewed him for the first time. If this mystery were not enough of a problem for Farmer, on July 18, 1964, the Harlem riots broke out, and the rise of more militant young black leadership threatened the historic multi-racial nature of CORE.

Although the bodies of the three civil rights workers were found in an earthen dam on August 4, no arrests were made in the case until October 3, 1964, just after Warren's second interview with Farmer at the end of September. Warren, in his chapter, "A Mississippi Journal," had to deal with the crime against the civil rights workers, and James Farmer, a source for much of the information about the crime, either knew nothing or was in no position to reveal what he knew at the times Warren interviewed him. Warren solved the problem by using the fictional technique of point-of-view rather than the nonfictional technique of documented sources. While this is a perfectly acceptable method in the New Journalism, it raises eyebrows in academic settings and among more traditional journalists.

My comparison of the transcripts of the two Farmer interviews with the text of *Who Speaks for the Negro?* suggests that Warren had a method for keeping his sources straight in his own mind. The material on James Farmer from page 189 to page 202 comes from the transcripts of the June 11, 1964, and the late September interviews. Warren repeats some of this material elsewhere in the book when he wishes to compare Farmer's answers to those of others. He generally introduces this material with a verbal clue that the reader has seen before: "James Farmer, as we may remember, said . . . " (264). On the other hand, Warren uses quotations by Farmer from other sources in his discussion of the disappearance of the three civil rights workers. When these quotations occur, Warren generally introduces them with a formulaic structure: "Mr. Farmer says" (115) or "James Farmer says" (126). By suppressing the source of the quotation or statement and by directing the statement through the narrative point of view of the book, Warren creates a fairly seamless web of information that reads with the smoothness of a novel. About the disappearance of the three civil rights workers, Warren writes: ". . . two of the victims at Philadelphia, Schwerner and Chaney, were paid field workers of CORE; and it was Negro workers of CORE who disappeared into the Negro community of Philadelphia, won the confidence of the local people, and gradually assembled evidence, including, Mr. Farmer says, an eyewitness account of the death of Chaney, which it

turned over to the FBI" (115). This is a story that James Farmer has been telling for thirty years. He told it in the press at the time; he wrote it out in his book *Lay Bare the Heart: An Autobiography of the Civil Rights Movement;* he spoke at Westminster College on February 15, 1994, and told the story once again as a corrective to the film *Mississippi Burning,* the latest misrepresentation of the events in the case. In the film, Willem Dafoe and Gene Hackman portray doggedly determined FBI agents who overcome all odds to break the code of silence and get the rednecks who violated the civil rights of the three men. Commenting at Westminster College on these events from the film, Farmer said: "The FBI was there all right, but we had to drag them in kicking and screaming all the way."

On two occasions Warren uses a different formulation to introduce material from James Farmer. On page 73 Warren writes:

> Some months later, an anecdote told me by James Farmer, of CORE, happened to make clear to me why the Snick boy would not stay slowed down. Medgar Evers had been driving Farmer up this same road, on the same errand I now had, to make a night call on Dr. Aaron Henry, the president of the NAACP up at Clarksdale, in the Delta, and Farmer had shown some apprehension at the speed. Medgar had said that if you are a black man in Mississippi, you never let anybody pass you at night, you never let anybody have a chance to stop you or ditch you. Too many people have been stopped or ditched.

The passage, of course, reminds the reader of the death of Medgar Evers, which Warren dealt with earlier in the chapter, but it also presages the deaths of the three civil rights workers who were stopped in a car at night on a Mississippi back road. It is a powerful passage. On page 120, Warren, commenting on the results of the Mississippi Summer Project writes:

> James Farmer, on this point, tells me: "A result of the Summer Project —and this was somewhat unfortunate, I think—was that the local people who had been involved in the Movement pulled out when they saw these skilled youngsters from the North. Now we find that after the students left, some of the local people are coming around and saying, 'Well, maybe you need me again.'"

Both of these passages appear outside the material centered on James Farmer in "The Big Brass" section of *Who Speaks for the Negro?* The first is a paraphrase of material from the June 11, 1964, interview; the second, which assesses the Mississippi Summer Voter Registration Project, is a quote from the late September interview. It is clear that Warren is stating that Farmer relayed this information directly to him. In the first case he says, "an anecdote told me by James Farmer of CORE" (73), and in the other he says, "James Farmer, on this point, tells me . . . " (120).

It is clear to me that, above all, whether he quoted his interview source directly or paraphrased, Warren was dedicated to accuracy in the writing of *Who Speaks for the Negro?* This is one of the characteristics Norman Sims identified in his work *The Literary Journalists.* Sims observed a variety of characteristics in the writings of the New Journalists: 1. Historic Sweep; 2. Attention to Language; 3. Participation and Immersion; 4. Symbolic Realities; 5. Accuracy; 6. Sense of Time and Place; 7. Grounded Observations; 8. Context; and 9. Voice. While Warren exhibited all of these characteristics to one degree or another, he avoided the common dangers of mixing journalism with fictional techniques. He did not create composite characters. He did not recreate events for which he had no source or to which he was not himself a witness. When he had questions of fact or was faced with conflicting information, he wrote letters to attempt to resolve the problems. While *Who Speaks for the Negro?* is concerned with a particular moment in American history and creates a sense of a time and a place, the civil rights movement in the American south of 1964–65, it fixes that moment in the context of an historic sweep that includes the first slave ship in Jamestown in 1619, *The Declaration of Independence,* and the Civil War. Warren came to his subject in this work through participation and immersion. He had written about race before, many times, but as he said of his book *Segregation,* in an interview with Tom Vitale (15 April 1985), reprinted in *Talking with Robert Penn Warren:*

> . . . it wasn't big enough because I got too interested in the question. So I went, or my agent went, to Look and made a contract with them. They would pay all of my expenses for two years or so of travel, if I would devote my time to it and mix in some poems, and I was in Mississippi and all over the place and talked to everybody.

Through participation and immersion, Warren was able to make grounded observations about his subject. Employing the poet's attention to language, he turned apparently simple objects like blood, a cleft stick, and the colors black and white into complex symbolic realities that both depicted and advanced his subject. Finally Warren created a voice in *Who Speaks for the Negro?* that was as clear and identifiable as the voice in any one of his novels. William Bedford Clark, in his *The American Vision of Robert Penn Warren,* observed: "As in *Segregation,* it is Warren who is the unspoken protagonist of *Who Speaks for the Negro?*" And James H. Justus has written: "Superfi-

cially, it is his most objective book, coming as close to being discursive as anything in his canon; but in its structure, its internal patterns, and its textual 'voice,' *Who Speaks for the Negro?* speaks for Robert Penn Warren."

And Robert Penn Warren speaks for American blacks. As Ruppersburg points out, "It is clear from the beginning (as in *Segregation*) that his sympathies lie with the civil rights movement." Warren used a number of the techniques associated with the New Journalism to answer the ironic question of the book's title. By faithfully recording a variety of voices, Warren showed that blacks are as unique and individual as whites and that no single black voice can fairly represent that diversity. In doing so, Warren answered the question in the book's title and became the only white author of his time to study seriously the civil rights movement. He also created in *Who Speaks for the Negro?* a volume that must be considered seminal in the history of the creation of the New Journalism.

If it is true that Robert Penn Warren in writing *Who Speaks for the Negro?* was employing the techniques of the New Journalists, the same devices introduced later in 1965 by Truman Capote and Tom Wolfe, Jr., why is it that Warren is not recognized as a founder of the New Journalism? The answer may be found in the content and tone of Warren's work. While Capote's work is an in-depth account of a particularly bloody and violent mass murder (the sort of thing for which the American public seems to have an endless fascination) and Wolfe's book exposes arcane facts surrounding a variety of American subcultures (the sort of thing that appears in the tabloids at the supermarket checkout counters), Warren's work calls on us to face squarely a major flaw in the American Dream, Racism. We can read either Capote or Wolfe and be comforted by the fact that no matter how interesting their subjects may be, they have little or nothing to do with our lives. Racism, however, remains unresolved and central to the American experience, and we still do not want to look at it. Although it was largely overlooked when it was published and is now out of print, *Who Speaks for the Negro?* speaks to and about America as clearly and as forcefully now as it did in 1965.

–James A. Perkins, "Robert Penn Warren and James Farmer: Notes on the Creation of New Journalism," *RWP,* 1 (2001): 163–171

* * *

The first leaf, recto and verso, from the manuscript of an unpublished novel, circa 1966. Warren eventually turned from this work to write his tenth and last novel, A Place to Come To *(Yale Collection of American Literature, Beinecke Rare Book and Manuscript Library).*

① Her head leaned down + her breath tickled
in your hair

② My mother smelled. But that was
a *different* smell. He felt awful.
But it was an awful on the
other side of very icy

In the 1960s Warren was devoting more time and energy to his poetry, his first love in writing. In the latter half of the decade, he published three volumes of poetry. Warren's Selected Poems: New and Old, 1923–1966 *(1966) includes the new poems in the section* Can I See Arcturus from Where I Stand?*, while the previously published poems often show some minor revisions. In this feature article Warren, who had given a reading at Union College from* Selected Poems*, discusses the volume and his career. The "in-progress novel" mentioned is* Meet Me in the Green Glen. *The reporter, William Kennedy, two years later published his first novel,* The Ink Truck *(1969); he is also the author of* Iron Weed *(1983).*

How a Poet Works

"How does a poem happen?" Robert Penn Warren was asking for the benefit of a gathering of students.

"I don't think themes for poems or novels are set up in a programmatic way. On a plane coming back from the West, moving over Pittsburgh at 2 o'clock in the morning, I happened to have some Emerson on my lap. This situation, this rather absurd, innocent man, Emerson, in this modern America with New York 40 minutes away—I had the thought that over Peoria we lost the sun. I was struck by the rhythm of it. Over Peoria we lost the sun. That's not bad . . . Emerson, me, America, and over Peoria we lost the sun. There were two views of man in there, two views of man's nature."

This inspiration has now come to fruition in Mr. Warren's *Selected Poems: New and Old, 1923–1966.* One of the new poems is called "Homage to Emerson, on Night Flight to New York." It is in seven parts, each part individualistically styled, a piling on of layers to illustrate a complex theme of contrasts: Passivity and struggle, violets and warts, the sublime night full of stars and the "black cement which so resembles the arctic ice of our recollections."

Mr. Warren passed lightly over the moment of inspiration and went on to other poetic matters, telling these undergraduates at Union College here of his attitude toward the creation of his 23rd published book. "Many of the poems . . . have been revised," he says in a preface. "But in revising old poems, I have tried not to tamper with meanings, only to sharpen old meanings."

Eject the Old Chestnuts

To the students he was saying: "You can't revise totally. You can strike out what is singularly bad, make cuts for wordiness. But you have to eject rather than revise. You can't pull some of those old chestnuts out of the fire.

"Everybody has certain concerns and themes, issues that involve you—a basic line of interest about the world. Almost any writer is bound to make false starts and get away from his central concern. Even though it might be good and people might like it, you can tell yourself eventually, 'It doesn't represent me. It's a trick I've done.' These are merely performances, the poems that went astray. It's like the child that went bad. You've got to guard against that."

Robert Penn Warren, eminent literary critic, two-time Pulitzer Prize winner (for *All the King's Men,* a novel, and *Promises,* a poetry collection that also won the National Book Award), teacher (Yale, but now on a year's leave), and journalist (*Who Speaks for the Negro?*), had been scheduled to speak at the college on the U.S. racial situation. He chose not to, feeling that the era he had written of in *Who Speaks for the Negro?* had passed, that he was no longer expert. He canceled the speaking engagement, but the college asked him to please come and speak on poetry.

So he mounted the stage of Union Memorial Chapel dressed in a tweed suit, brown tie, and dark blue shirt, peering over his half-spectacles at the audience of 1,000 or more. His listeners strained to understand his rapid speech, his swallowed words, the remnants of his Kentucky twang, and he said of poetry:

"All babies like it. La-la-la, as they like their thumbs and toes, they like making sounds. And the next step is writing a sonnet."

The poet, he said, cannot lie or fake it. "Lying doesn't come naturally to the poet. You're uncomfortable about it. And usually someone will tell you when you're faking it."

Metaphysics 'Not for Me'

After the speech, he discussed poetry further over a cup of tea in a dining room on campus. He equated his own poetic tradition with Ezra Pound, T. S. Eliot, Thomas Hardy, and the Elizabethans. "But the metaphysical strain, I began to feel, was not for me at a technical level."

He spoke of the difference between admiring the work of other poets and having a "hot relation" with their work. He profusely praised Randall Jarrell, for example, and then added: "But nothing in his writing has personal resonance for me. Nothing in it makes me angry because I didn't do it first, or makes me want to say, 'Dammit, why didn't I get that line?'"

His new book of poems came as an interruption of an interruption. He was at work on a novel, got halfway through it, and then laid it aside to write the Negro book, which he published in 1965. "Then," he said, "the poems began to come. And I rode with them as long as they came. When they run dry I stop and go back to prose."

The in-progress novel deals with a tinhorn Cleveland gangster, paroled from jail after turning state's evidence on a pal; he hides from vengeance in backcountry Tennessee. It is akin to *Flood* and *The Cave* and other of his novels, he says, because "it has the element of the outside in a closed world"—a consistent image in his prose.

"Most writers," he concluded, "are trying to find what they think or feel. They are not simply working from the given, but working toward the given, saying the unsayable, and steadily asking: 'What do I really feel about this?'"

—William Kennedy, *The National Observer,*
6 February 1967, p. 31

* * *

Incarnations: Poems, 1966–1968 *was published in October 1968, and* Audubon: A Vision *appeared in November 1969. This review is by Stanley Plumly, a poet at the beginning of his career.*

Robert Penn Warren's Vision
Reviews of *Incarnations: Poems, 1966–1968* and *Audubon: A Vision*

Little more than a year separates the publication of these two most recent volumes of Robert Penn Warren's poetry. Their significance, however, lies less in their relative proximity than in their relationship to his whole poetic *oeuvre*. Since *Promises, Poems 1954–56,* the volume in which Warren (like so many of his contemporaries) loosened up his line and the total texture of his poem—in which he, in effect, broke out of the confining rhetorical neatness (the well-measured meters and rhymes) of the Fugitives—he has moved progressively toward greater openness of form and, most important, a more total and deeply felt tragic sense of life. In the poems since the mid-fifties—amounting to three collections prior to the present volumes—he has especially plied the romantic's trade of confronting the corruptible, and corrupting, human element in an otherwise richly alive, innocent, even pristine natural world of cycle and change. Indeed, it has been his passionate emphatic contract with the alien humanity of that world, a whole lineage of characters and personae caught in their own claustrophobic sense of time and history, that has defined the focus of his attention. *Suffering, guilt,* and *redemption* have been the popular critical descriptions of this concern. In *Incarnations, Poems 1966–68,* Warren extends these preoccupations in perhaps the most "metaphysical" of his work to date; while in *Audubon: A Vision,* he achieves a synthesis, a sublimity of vision in which the violence and tragic pattern that have been accumulating from his very beginning as a

poet reach a kind of stillpoint. If *Incarnations* ends in the spiritual aridity and silence of "the cold incandescence of snow" in whose light "the eye / Sees the substance of the body dissolving," then *Audubon,* both figure and configuration—a man *and* his life—becomes Warren's difficult way out of "this whiteness."

Incarnations is patterned much like the three volumes which precede it. The book is conceived in three parts, those parts in titled sequences of poems, those poems (as in "The Leaf") often in sections. Such hierarchical arranging is significant because Warren never seems quite "finished" with an individual poem; instead he allows the full context of a particular sequence to absorb the silences, the open-ends. This poems-within-a-poem method has been—notably since *Promises*—an effective device for him; in this case it is even more so, as the poems seem freer in the variations of line length (from four or five accents to a more massive sweep across the page), in the acceleration of pace (through a typically prosy sort of enjambment), and, of course, in the spacing and repetition of images. In none of his poetry before has he allowed so much *time* for the poem to happen; nor has he worked so much before in terms of juxtaposition—image against image, image against statement—rather than coordination, in order to create those abrasive silences that are the chief tension-producing means in the open-ended poem. Again and again the poems in *Incarnations* close with a single line having been placed there by a process of stanzaic building and counter-building. Sometimes a final image is enough, as when the "rinsed" eyeballs "go gray as dead moons"; sometimes he must finish with a flat philosophical statement—"The world means only itself"; and sometimes a fragment is played off a statement—"The terror is, all promises are kept. // Even happiness."

The formal freedom of *Incarnations* only reinforces the inconclusiveness, the reaching out, the search the poems themselves are compelled to make. The title of the volume is ironically poised, for it is precisely the lack and/or denial of *spirit incarnate* that motivates this book. The *incarnations* represent manifestations of the flesh as flesh only, of the body as self-contained embodiment. The Word, therefore, becomes the poet's word made into the tentative flesh of the poem. Certainly the tonal *angst* that pervades the volume results from the poet's realization of the ironical depth of his title. Naturally the poems appear to stand in uneasy witness to their own "right" of passage. The initial two parts—"Island of Summer" and "Internal Injuries"—divide Warren's attention into a clear separation of subjects, if not concern. The first part is largely personal in impact, the "I" being situated in the mediating/meditating center of the experience. "Internal Injuries"—the poet's injuries as much as his catalysts'—involves two characters:

68 BR 1055

copy

IN SENATE

REGULAR SESSION, 1968

SENATE RESOLUTION NO. 50

WEDNESDAY, FEBRUARY 21, 1968

Senators William L. Sullivan and Carl T. Hadden, Sr., introduced the following resolution, which was ordered to be printed.

A RESOLUTION recognizing one of America's most brilliant literary artists.

WHEREAS, one of America's most brilliant literary artists was born in Todd County Kentucky and lived his formative years on the red clay soil of Southwest Kentucky; and

WHEREAS, he has written so often and so movingly about this state in his books and poems; and

WHEREAS, he has been a distinguished teacher at many universities, served as consultant in Poetry at the Library of Congress, founded and edited *The Southern Review*, received a number of coveted awards for his works; and

WHEREAS, he is the only writer to have been twice honored with the Pulitzer Prize, for fiction and poetry; and

WHEREAS, he has explored the dark caverns of the human spirit and, with compassion, revealed them in the stunning light of his intellect;

NOW, THEREFORE,

A Kentucky state resolution honoring Warren (Special Collections, Western Kentucky University Libraries)

2   S. R. 50

Be it resolved by the Senate of the General Assembly of the

Commonwealth of Kentucky:

1   That with this tribute the Senate of the Commonwealth of

2   Kentucky, severally and individually, posts recognizance, in the

3   sum of our admiration and respect, for ROBERT PENN

4   WARREN.

—————————oo—————————

Written by Boynton Merrill Jr

Jake, a cancer-eaten, incarcerated black, whose suffering is at once mitigated and sustained by morphine; and a Negro maid killed in a New York traffic accident. Both parts move by narrative extension. "Internal Injuries" is the more apparently ordered of the two because of the simple story line that carries us from the life to the death to the significance of each of the victims. We are made to follow Jake's pathetic muttering about his one elixir for the cancerous pain ("Jest keep that morphine moving, Cap.") through to "The Next Morning," the death and night, the "funeral" and finally the "I's" meditation on the meaning of the loss, in the midst of a renewed and renewing dawn ("Forgive us, this day, our joy"). With the Negro maid we begin with "The Event" (the accident), move to its relational and indifferent urban confine ("The jet prowls the sky and Penn Station looks bombed-out."), and then conclude with its larger human value placed in "The World as Parable." This sequence of poems ends, like Jake's, with a little denouement in which the speaker, and witness, tells his taxi driver that "I / Must change the address, I want to go to // A place where nothing is the same." The first part of *Incarnations,* "Island of Summer," being more centripetally based on the perceiving "I," is alogically and analogically arranged, as the separate poems, like their separate moments, build and relax intensity. The fifteen poems here do not so much lead into one another as they "talk" back and forth, advancing by argument rather than by plot, though the thematic problem posed initially in "What Day Is" is augmented as opposed to being solved by the enlarged metaphysical context of the final poem in the sequence, "The Leaf."

But whether by story or debate, parts I and II both share the same *incarnate* concerns.

> Where the slow fig's purple sloth
> Swells, I sit and meditate the
> Nature of the soul, the fig exposes,
> To the blaze of afternoon, one haunch
> As purple-black as Africa. . . .

The "Nature of the soul," however, is organically tied to and conditioned by its embodiment, which condition is, of course, "the hot sweet- / ness of flesh" in "its most / suicidal yearnings." And the flesh "wants," says the poet in the same "Riddle in the Garden," "to suffer extremely."

>   —oh, do
> be careful not to break that soft
>
> Gray bulge of fruit-skin of blister, for
> exposing that inwardness will
> increase your pain, for you
> are part of the world.

In *Incarnations* being "part of the world" is being of one flesh with it ("The world means only itself."), one bruised, ripe flesh with it. Throughout these two parts Warren is obsessed with images of fecundity, the "juice-dark hug" of life being only itself. This acute sense of fullness and fertility is matched by the hyperbolic quality of the imagery:

the dominant image of fruit has "Flesh like flame, purer / Than blood"; a gull wheels "white in the flame of / Air[']"; a ripe old lady on a Mediterranean beach becomes "an old hunchback in bikini," heaving "alone beneath the hump." Even "nothing" is fecund, "for there are voices, not / emptiness, for there is / a great fullness, it is / populated with nothingness." Like all embodiments of these incarnations, Jake and the black maid also achieve their destined richnesses.

As mediating consciousness the poet must, in all this self-consummation, confront the reality of his own past, his own heritage of flesh as final arbiter of spirit, his own death.

> The world
>
> Is fruitful, and I, too,
> In that I am the father
> Of my father's father's father. I,
> Of my father, have set my teeth on edge.

And with "teeth on edge," a Warren-like Paul Valéry stands "On the Cliff and Confront[s] The Furious Energies of Nature." In this metaphysical pose (and in this the finest poem in *Incarnations*), "in the bright intricacies / Of wind, his mind, like a leaf, / Turns. In the sun, it glitters." It glitters, yes, but like the bit of body it is, in the sun it too will ripen. So stands the *incarnate* condition of spirit contained and consumed by flesh that provides "Enclaves," the third and last part of this volume, with its power of acceptance, perhaps resignation. Only two small sections, with two poems each, make up this darkest of Warren's "pursuits." Neither heart ("contextless") nor soul (without "locus") can find a center of gravity because "in the sweet desolution of distance" there is only space. *Enclaves* implies definition and order, and therefore apparent meaning. But here, in these enclaves, only a crow calls "on the hem of silence"; or light rises from "the cold incandescence of snow." What we hear and see on this metaphysical landscape are the mind's abstractions.

> How may I know the true nature of Time, if
> Deep now in darkness that glittering enclave
> I dream, hangs?

For all its muscle and visceral power, and almost in spite of Warren's considerable ability to render an idea in the sheer terms of its necessary body ("Beauty / Is the fume-track of necessity."), the language in *Incarnations* occasionally becomes clogged or trite. With or without possible redeeming context, "the kiss of fate" is sophomoric, while "Long since the moon sank and the English / Finished fornicating in their ketches" is funny in the worst way. Nor can the forcing of a word such as "indifferency" be justified, especially when it is calcu-

---

Travel in Service to Work

In this excerpt, Warren's son Gabriel remembers his parents' attitude toward traveling.

. . . My parents had a great appetite for different places as a way of continuing to see the world through fresh eyes, and as a result I saw a fair bit of Europe as a child, even though we had a very stable home and school life in New England. Their pattern was never to move for movement's sake, but to settle down in one spot for a summer or longer periods of time, where they would quickly establish a work routine. The attitude was that travel was never a "vacation"—whatever that is—but was always somehow in service to the work, the work that really defined who they were. I inherited this sentiment, and live accordingly.

Two among many examples from my childhood: In 1961, we spent the summer in Brittany. It was magical, of course, for us kids, living in new surroundings, learning words in a new language, exploring things we never could at home. The beaches were still dotted with enormous concrete pillboxes from the war— I'm sure they are gone now—which naturally stimulated a child's imagination, and I learned to ride a "two wheeler" on a stony driveway that extracted its bits of flesh from my six-year-old knees in the process. That was also the summer my mother became besotted with the local oyster fishery, and the result was one of her best books, *The Oysters of Locmariaquer*.

In 1966–67 we spent two summers and the school year between them in the South of France. Both of the summers were spent on an island eight or ten miles off the coast, Isle de Port-Cros. It was a magical setting for all of us, adults and children alike. One incident is illustrative of the points mentioned above: I was ten years old, and on one of my long solitary ramblings deep in the forest, I stumbled upon an object of such power that I have it to this day: a Nazi helmet, with an entrance on one side and the exit on the other marking the passage of a rifle round. As a child will, my first reaction was to show this remarkable find to my parents. My father worked those summers at an outdoor table under a huge, spreading fig tree, focusing mainly on poetry. At the moment I came to him with my find, he had been struggling, stuck in the middle of a poem, seeking its resolution. In the finished version, there is an abrupt shift in the piece's middle from historical reference to a small boy and the extraordinary object he has found. It is called "Natural History" and is in *Incarnations*.

—Gabriel Warren, "A Son Remembers,"
RWP, 5 (2005): 14–15

Dust jacket for Warren's eighth volume of poetry (Special Collections, Thomas Cooper Library, University of South Carolina)

lated in a rhyming couplet with "sea." These instances are obviously rare in Warren, but they do help illustrate, however meagerly, one of the differences between a poem one writes and a poem one is compelled to write. In *Audubon: A Vision,* the language is as pure and as rich and finely textured as any of its namesake's infinitely detailed bird paintings. Who else but Robert Penn Warren could have fashioned this little long poem, albeit in parts and sequences, about a man who, like Adam, saw the New World new daily—so new, in fact, that he had to give its creatures *names.* And who else but this poet could see his poem as a vision—a view at once human, as in the dream, and transcendental, as in the tragic myth. *Audubon* is a paean to the romantic spirit; it is, at the same time, a dark hymn to the necessity for human suffering. In its very size lies its significance: its thirty slim pages seem to have been created out of the silence and intensity of a lifetime.

The poem works in a series of seven "parts," with individual "poems" developed within those parts. The open-endedness and sure use of white space hold here

as they did in *Incarnations.* But the violence and sweat of the image are now sublimated to the larger issue of reconciliation. Moreover, any semblance of plot is submerged in the vision of the poet, for although Warren follows the blatant chronology of John James Audubon's birth, life, and death, his real search, of course, is through the vertical dimension of Audubon as mythic figure. Hence the first part opens with the question: "What / Is man but his passion?" A response, if not an answer, is offered in the guise of the beautifully sensual great white heron. For Audubon it is at once a passionate and innocent sighting:

> Saw,
> Eastward and over the cypress swamp, the dawn,
> Redder than meat, break;
> And the large bird,
> Long neck outthrust, wings crooked to scull air, moved
> In a slow calligraphy. . . .

Warren, however, has launched his Audubon on an ontological journey, hardly on a painter's viewing of the gallery of nature in a Garden wilderness. So enter the chief antagonists and the poet's sacrificial characters: a Kentucky Hill woman ("her face / Is sweet in an outrage of sweetness") and her two brutalized sons. Part II, "The Dream He Never Knew the End Of," occupies the longest and central position in the total poem, and provides the romantic/Christian vision of the source of all corruption, man himself. Audubon seeks refuge with the woman and her sons only to be nearly murdered for his gold watch. Luckily the plot fails and woman and sons are summarily hanged together.

> The affair was not quick; both sons long jerking
>   and farting, but she,
> From the first, without motion, frozen
> In a rage of will, an ecstasy of iron, as though
> This was the dream that, lifelong, she had dreamed
>   toward.

What Audubon sees this time is no vision in nature but the obscenity of man as the victim of himself. The woman's "dream," this grotesque of destiny, becomes Audubon's guilt and his means of redemption. He sees "The face / Eyes-aglare, jaws clenched" in "a new dimension of beauty." With this knowledge, this new depth, he "continued to walk in the world." For the remainder of the poem Warren escorts his hero through the remainder of his life—a life, now that it is complete with suffering, of losses ("He tries to remember his childhood. / He tries to remember his wife. / He can remember nothing."); of tragic insight ("Knew the lust of the eye."); and of the tormented wisdom of the full, resonant, lived life ("'. . . in my sleep I continually

Warren in the late 1960s (Yale Collection of American Literature, Beinecke Rare Book and Manuscript Library)

dream of birds.'"). He dies in bed, his "last joy" being "the lullaby, they sang him, in Spanish, at sunset."

In the final two sections of the poem, Warren speaks directly through the "I," speaks of "the dream / Of a season past all seasons." Having made the journey along with his artist parallel, he can now conclude his "story" in an attitude beyond mere acceptance. It was a man, both total and incomplete, who painted the birds, and in the loveliest piece in *Audubon,* Warren creates a song to the "beautiful liability of their nature."

> They fly
> In air that glitters like fluent crystal
> And is hard as perfectly transparent iron, they cleave it
> With no effort.

If Audubon has slain them, he has also "put them where they are, and there we see them: / In our imagination." Asks the poet, implying Audubon the hunter as much as the painter, "What is love?" The answer is the answer being made through the whole poem: "One name for it is knowledge." *Audubon* ends with a kind of coda. Warren, now hero of his own tale as well as teller, is a boy again in his native Kentucky. He stands alone "in first dark," listening to the "great geese hoot northward." The hearing and the sighting are not unlike Audubon's own of the heron in the beginning

passage of the poem. The poet says, "I did not know what was happening in my heart," only that a "sound was passing northward." The name of the sound, of course, is "Time," but "you must not pronounce its name." Instead, tell me a story, in this century, and moment, of mania, a story of great distances and starlight, a story of deep delight. The name of the story will be Time.

–Stanley Plumly, "Robert Penn Warren's Vision,"
Southern Review, new series 6 (Autumn 1970):
1201–1208

* * *

In this excerpt from his 1984 study In the Heart's Last Kingdom: Robert Penn Warren's Major Poetry, *critic Calvin Bedient argues that Warren's "greatness as a writer began with his determination to concentrate on poetry as the extreme resource of language-knowledge, language-being–began with* Audubon: A Vision *(1969), forty-six years after he started publishing poems."*

On *Audubon: A Vision*

Audubon rose above his previous volumes like a curiously abrupt, grand escarpment, a repudiation of the scrub country of uncertain poetic purpose. Two proud differences announced themselves: an assured voice (at last his own, and major) and a personal and passionate knowledge of values. Warren may have been writing about a nineteenth-century Frenchman who became the very type of the "natural," wood-wholesome American, and he may have shown an equally unfashionable longing for majestic beauty and glory, but he invented a convincing contemporary manner (and structure), and there was no dismissing his grand sensibility: like the Rockies, it was there.

Casting off the regal diction with which he had earlier tried to warm himself, he began to blaze inwardly with a direct and passionate pursuit of the real. What he lived for was what he could not live without, and his words, at their best, seemed resonant with actual life. The joy he was after–namely, "knowledge based on the empathic imagination"–may have been jettisoned by "the world of science, technology, big organization–and of course the business culture"; but he would have it, singlehandedly he would replant it in America, if passion could do it, if anyone could do it. Both retreating and advancing to nature, like some latter-day Thoreau, Ishmael, or Whitman, he sought to reconcile, in Rilke's words, "the Individual and the All"– sought "the moment of exaltation, the artistically important Moment, . . . in which the two scales of the balance counterpoise one another."

Warren had always manifested, if at first murkily, a tragic hunger for "Truth," one that made him formidable, set him apart. That passion grew until it could scarcely be slaked. With *Audubon* it became clarified, beautiful, essential. If this Sisyphus of certain questions—What is Truth? What joy? Where lies glory?—even now only rolls them near to the summit of perfect understanding before they crash down again, still his evocations of the labor can seem blessed as well as sinewy; the effort itself is happiness and appears touched by a rare and difficult light. Warren is that very unusual thing, a poet of tragic joy—indeed the first such among American poets.

. . . .

*Bedient discusses other volumes—*Promises: Poems 1954–1956 *and* Incarnations: Poems 1966–1968—*that critics have praised as breakthrough books for Warren but argues that "in all the earlier volumes, without exception, the calibration of the style is repeatedly off, now too golden throated, now too gritty. A line, even a whole stanza, might dazzle, or simply serve, but in any given poem something (and often a great deal) will be amiss."*

But suddenly, in *Audubon,* you hear, in Dave Smith's fine phrase, "the human need to prevail by witness," indeed by "celebration." The language, as Smith adds, becomes "what it had been in fits and starts, a voice-instrument calibrated to final experience." The tone lets itself go out to adventure like the seeding cottonwood. His pride relenting, his heart submitting, Warren here writes lines that are experience-honoring, experience-blessed. Your eye has but to alight on

Dawn: his heart shook in the tension of the world.

Dawn: and what is your passion?

to feel the thrill of a direct and deep vitality. The colons themselves seem aquiver, marks of confrontation and expectation, two fingers taking a pulse.

Warren has a romantic and heroic idea of Audubon that exalts and chastens his own way of seeing and writing. Even as he all but alters Audubon out of recognition (sweetening and deepening him, and tightening him like a bow), so he is simplified and tautened in turn, in a reciprocal refashioning. Something of frontier sturdiness, of frontier plainness, independence, curiosity, and a love of living on the edge, comes into his poetry to stay. "He embodies one of the deepest American traits, the courage to plunge into the unknown . . . seeking the new"—these words, a mere ironic tink in Warren's novel *The Cave* (1959), resound when his recent poems are made the clapper. With *Audubon* he

Dust jacket for Warren's narrative poem inspired by the life of the ornithologist John James Audubon (Special Collections, Western Kentucky University Libraries)

became heroic and large-scaled without straining, without wondering how he dared. Simply, he set out to repioneer the sort of "love knowledge" he associated with Audubon and the wilderness, its pristine invitations, its diverse creatures and intimate interiors. Philosophically, too, he has put on seven-league boots; has "starward . . . stared / To the unnamed void where Space and God / Flinch to come."

Warren began to confront the great undomestic things—time, nature, truth, fate, glory, the "all"—in a way that made his earlier relation to them seem like viewing a distant river; now he was in the river. His words entered experience, or appeared to, fully and tragically and happily, impatient of defenses and eager for unambiguous truth (however rashly eager). No longer anxious to exude authority, Warren gained it at once, held it by the good faith of his relation to, his demands on, experience. His voice became as flecked as a forest floor with inimitable personal lights, his idiosyncrasies almost as marked as before, but more fragrant, more assuredly his, tried now and true, knowing their purpose. There was nothing dressy in the manner now, nothing wild, temperamental, and skittish; it was broken in, like a good mount, and fit for travel.

If before *Audubon* Warren seemed incapable of writing a masterpiece, he has since to write anything to equal it. Indeed, he has continued to publish some jarringly bad poems, if with a different badness than before, an aping of his worst fears about the draining of life into memory, banal or nightmarish Truth, and the like. Portentousness and pretentiousness still abound. But he has written several superb poems as well, poems that anyone ought to revere, and numerous poems with a tone so passionately and gravely serious, a manner so plunging and plangent, that the poetry is like the rumor of a still unseen waterfall: poetry whose strength feels elemental, makes you attend, whatever its chance limitations.

–Calvin Bedient, *In the Heart's Last Kingdom: Robert Penn Warren's Major Poetry* (Cambridge, Mass. & London: Harvard University Press, 1984), pp. 3–4, 10–12

* * *

In 1971 three books by Warren were published: his penultimate novel, Meet Me in the Green Glen; *his critical study* Homage to Theodore Dreiser, August 27, 1871–December 28, 1945, on the Centennial of His Birth; *and a volume he edited and introduced,* John Greenleaf Whittier's Poetry.

Acute, Critical Eye Trained on 'Wild Man' of American Letters
Review of *Homage to Theodore Dreiser*

Dreiser is the wild man of American letters and critics have never been quite sure what to do with him. Even his admirers, and he has never lacked for them, have freely admitted that he writes atrociously, that he has a deficient sense of art, and that his books are often ill-proportioned.

In spite of all this, his novels have a power and vitality which seem to place him among the major novelists, and one of them, "An American Tragedy," has a cumulative effect similar, if not identical, to that produced only by the greatest literary works. The task of the critic is to account for the undeniable power of Dreiser's best works.

Robert Penn Warren's acute critical study, "Homage to Theodore Dreiser: August 27, 1871 – December 28, 1945, On the Centennial of His Birth," uses biographical facts primarily as a means of interpreting Dreiser's novels. The method is about as far from traditional "new criticism" as it is possible to get. It is

more akin to those essays of Edmund Wilson in which he presents a psychological portrayal of the man as he is revealed in his works than it is to any other recent works of literary criticism that I know of. The attempt is to see a man's work as a product of his personality, his education, and his times.

Dreiser, it is said, was the first American novelist from the wrong side of the tracks, and he was destined to express, perhaps better than anyone else, the inarticulate yearnings for money, social prestige, and the emblems of the American way, expensive women and the paraphernalia of success.

The two extremes of the Dreiserian dream are represented by Frank Cowperwood, the superman hero of Dreiser's financial trilogy, and by Clyde Griffiths, the protagonist of "An American Tragedy." The financier is pure will. His desires are the same as Clyde's, but he has the ability to obtain them. Clyde, lacking everything except the superficial trappings of personality, is at the mercy of forces he can neither understand or control.

Warren says that illusion is the key word for Dreiser; certainly, all of his novels are concerned with it in one way or another. The universe, says Dreiser, goes on its blind way. Man lives by illusions. He erects them as barriers against the darkness, but night closes in. All is vanity.

Warren has prefixed to his critical study of Dreiser a poem in three parts entitled "Portrait." The portrait, of course, is that of Dreiser, and the poem restates in poetic form many of the insights of the short but valuable and important piece of criticism. In another writer, the introduction of a poem into such a work might seem a bit of effrontery, but here it merely adds a finishing touch in the form of a poetic tribute from one writer to another.

–William Parrill, *Nashville Tennessean,* 5 September 1971, p. 12C

* * *

This review is by John W. Aldridge, a critic of contemporary literature. He is the author of Time to Murder and Create: The Contemporary Novel in Crisis *(1966).*

The Enormous Spider Web of Warren's World
Review of *Meet Me in the Green Glen*

Robert Penn Warren's *Meet Me in the Green Glen* seems certain to be recognized as one of his most distinguished novels since *All the King's Men*. The new work is far more tightly structured than its immediate predecessors, *Wilderness* and *Flood;* the rhetorical fattiness that has always been characteristic of Warren's fiction has

Robert Penn Warren

HOMAGE TO THEODORE DREISER

ON THE CENTENARY OF HIS BIRTH

Whatever flames upon the night
Man's own resinous heart has fed.
                                    W. B. Yeats

Theodore Dreiser raises in a peculiarly poignant form the question of
the relation of life and art. The fiction Dreiser wrote is so much like the
life he led that sometimes we are hard put to say exactly what Dreiser -- the
artist -- added to what Dreiser -- the man -- had observed and experienced. It
is tempting to think of him as a kind of uninspired recorder blundering along
in a dreary effort to transcribe actuality. But the next temptation is to
think that what is good is good by the accident of the actuality that he
happened to live into -- not by any power that he, as artist, might have achieve.

What is wrong with this way of thinking is, of course, that it does not
account for the fact that, in one sense, art is the artist's way of understanding -- of creating even -- the actuality that he lives. In some artists
this process is so complex and indirect and the result as far from being a
document that the creative aspect is beyond dispute. But with some, as with
Dreiser, it is so direct, and the factual correspondences so precise, that we
may feel that to try to see the art as a creation of actuality is stupid, even
tautological. And to compound the problem, Dreiser did write volumnously about
himself and his work in the form of straight autobiography; and often these autobiographical writings are scarcely distinguishable from the fiction.

*****

Dreiser was, as F. O. Matthissen, one of his biographers, once remarked
in conversation, the first American writer from "across the tracks." That is,
he was the first writer not of the old American tradition.

Page from a draft for Warren's Homage to Theodore Dreiser, *published in 1971. Although apparently marked for deletion,
the first two paragraphs are only slightly revised in the book* (Southern Review *Records,
Louisiana State University Archives, LSU Libraries, Baton Rouge*).

HOMAGE TO

Theodore Dreiser

August 27, 1871 — December 28, 1945
ON THE CENTENNIAL OF HIS BIRTH
++
R O B E R T

P E N N

W A R R E N

RANDOM HOUSE
New York

Frontispiece and title page for Warren's tribute to the naturalistic novelist whose works include Sister Carrie *and* An American Tragedy
(Special Collections, Western Kentucky University Libraries)

been replaced by a hard texture of language very like his poetry. Yet the book is complex enough to sustain the illusion that there are several kinds of narrative form through which the action is simultaneously developed, each providing a view of the action both complete in itself and indispensable to the completion of the whole. As in most of Warren's novels, the central dramatic situation is that of the murder mystery, although this work can also be seen as a romantic parable existing with perfect rightness on the levels of melodrama and moral philosophy; a love story that, contrary to current fashions, is finally neither sentimental nor narcissistic; a prose poem remarkable for its lyric intensity; a Southern novel in which the characters are both realistically depicted cultural types and personifications of forces so violent and destructive that they seem almost more Elizabethan than contemporary.

The literary qualities of the book are considerable enough to assure it an important place among serious novels of the last several years. But of perhaps equal interest to admirers of Warren is the fact that he offers here a distillation of themes and materials which have preoccupied him throughout his career but have never

before been made visible in quite this concentrated a form. As a result, this novel may help to clarify Warren's position at a time when, in spite of his years of sustained achievement, the size of his critical reputation, and his wide popularity with the reading public, he still projects a rather anomalous image, is still somehow more admired as a writer than accepted as a shaper of consciousness.

Since 1939, in addition to many books of nonfiction and poetry, Warren has published eight novels, nearly all of them vital and original works which have been respectfully received and, in some cases, commercially very successful. Yet only *All the King's Men* can be said to have made a real impact upon the imagination of our time, and to have appealed equally to literary intellectuals and to the general public. A possible explanation is that *All the King's Men* was the sole instance in Warren's fiction when he dealt with contemporary life in terms that were familiar and fashionable to both classes of readers. Although the setting and many of the central materials of the book were specifically Southern, it was as a whole less regional than generally American.

% Pivot,
Furonniere- Stendhal,
38 CLAIX, France,
September 27, 1971.

Sorry about this
haste + messy
letter.

Dear Don and Lewis:

I have asked my agent, Owen Laster of the William
Morris outfit, to send you a manuscript. But let md
give you some background.

Years ago, while writing a poem-sequence called
"Ballad of a Sweet Dream of Peace" (which appears
in Promises), I was thinking of it as a sort of
dramatic poem or charade or something of the sort.
It came that way. The following winter, in Rome, I
talked about it with Alexei Haief, a conposer
friend of mine, who thought he might like to
do the music for some sort of version. It lay that
way a time. But I began to work toward some
dramatic projection of it, bit by bit. Then -- to
touch once more on the confused picture -- the National Council of Churches people commissioned Alexei
to do choruses for it (by this time I had a
draft). He did them, and the thing was produced at
the Loeb Theater at Harvard, directed by Robert Chapman. It worked. I was wanting to go on with it,
but things like new poems fell across it/ Finally,
I have done the rewriting. Last year ARC (Foundation
for Arts, Religion, and Culture) in the person of
Amos Wilder, asked to do it for their annual
get together, but either chorus probeems or
stage proboems blew it up. Anyway, they are publishing it in a book of their stuff sometimes before
too long. I have done more rewriting and am ready
to let it go. One delay was finding the music of
Haief. He had left it stored in America (he being off
kn Rome for most of the time now) and I had
mislaid my copies. But it has been traced down and
recopied properly. By, the thing is in shape.

I am anxious for it to get publication before the
ARC book, which, I thhink, is with Braziller, (I
expect to pubbish it later in a little separate
volume.) I am hoping that you can use it
with the music, which is now set up to follow
the text, coded in with the text. For one thing,
the SR is a place I'd like to be. For another, the
page size would accomodate the dramatic text and the
musical section. And I want it to be together with
the hope of getting effects that might be used for
productions in what few misguided churches might
want to do it. Anyway, I'd like to have it with you,
and have whatever extra cost of doing the music deduct-
ed from whatever payment there might be. If you have
to chose between tnis and my Twain piece, I'd rather
see this with you. Same rather thin continuing this.
Of course, if you wanted both, OK and fine. But I
can't think you would. I rush this to you in the
hope you might want to use it for Spring: Easter.

A letter from Warren to Donald E. Stanford and Lewis P. Simpson, editors of the new series of the Southern Review. *The work discussed here was eventually published in 1980 as* Ballad of a Sweet Dream of Peace: A Charade for Easter *(Donald E. Stanford Papers, Louisiana and Lower Mississippi Valley Collections; Louisiana State University Libraries, Baton Rouge).*

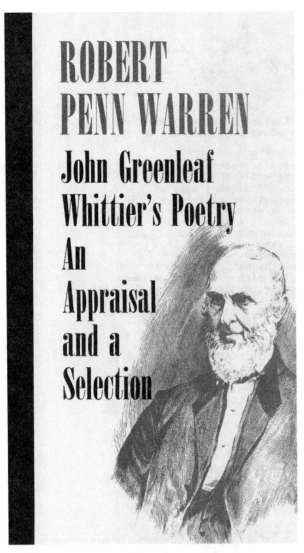

Cover for a collection Warren edited for a violently antisouthern poet.
Monroe Spears in his assessment of Warren's critical writing argues
that this book "demonstrates the primacy of nonliterary motives"
in Warren's criticism (Special Collections,
Thomas Cooper Library, University of
South Carolina).

The work also dramatized the dilemma of the narrator-protagonist, Jack Burden, within a philosophical framework that, on the face of it, seemed modishly existential—the tough-talking young cynic confronting the meaninglessness of his life, the empty relativism of his moral attitudes, at a moment when he is forced to define his responsibility for a series of tragedies that overtake almost all the people he has admired and loved. Jack Burden was the quintessential anti-hero of the Age of Anxiety, a textbook case of contemporary alienation with whom intellectuals could easily identify. The popular audience, on the other hand, undoubtedly responded almost altogether to the thriller aspects of the novel, and as usual their instincts for separating the glitter from the gold were infallible. There were murders and suicides by the dozen, just enough sex to titillate without really arousing, and the whole story was beautifully cast in the Hollywood mold. Not only were most of the characters stock movie types, but the seemingly effortless and quite successful translation of the novel into film made it clear that the meretricious values of that medium were highly compatible with certain, but by no means all, of the values implicit in Warren's materials.

His other novels have, for the most part, lacked these qualities of box office theatrics combined with high philosophical chic, and they have suffered from the additional difficulty of depending for their significance much more directly upon the Southern experience. This in itself would scarcely seem crippling when one considers that for a great many people the Southern experience is no less valid and real—and may even be considerably more dramatically complex—than the experience of New York or the Midwest, that it has enjoyed for a good many years the distinction of being a chief source of literary materials for the American novel, and that Warren's treatment of the South is imaginative enough to endow it with a dynamic life and a generality of meaning far larger than that of a merely regional subject-matter. But two factors have operated to cause the Southerness of his novels to be construed as a limitation. The first is that during the period of Warren's greatest productivity as a novelist, Faulkner had already established himself so securely as the official literary imagination of the South that it soon became almost impossible to think of the South except as a mythical Yoknapatawpha County or to believe that any other writer could possibly have anything new or important to say about it.

Also, over the same period, as a result partly of Faulkner's apparent exhaustion of the Southern material and partly of a radical shift of cultural interests, we began to take it for granted that the really central experience of our time is that of the Northern urban intellectual, of characters like Augie March, Herzog, and Portnoy, who personify the experience not of Wasp intellectuals of the Thirties and Forties—many of whom, significantly, have been both native Southerners and Faulkner's and Warren's most vigorous supporters—but of the New York literary establishment. Since urban intellectuals are now the principal shapers of literary opinion in this country, it is only natural that they would promote into celebrity such writers as Bellow, Mailer, and Roth with whom they can identify most closely, and that Warren, writing out of a background they find alien, would seem to them a peripheral and

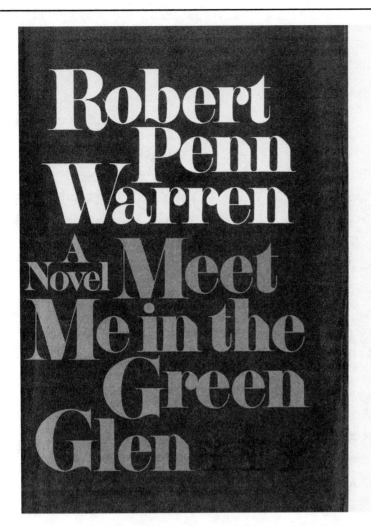

Mr. Warren's strength and skill as a storyteller have never been more evident than in this powerful new novel. The setting is a rural area of West Tennessee, and the action takes place in roughly the middle of this century.

The central character is Cassie Spottwood, who at forty-two has for nearly twenty years lived a life of isolation, frustration and despair as the wife of an invalid. When Angelo Passetto, young, exotic and competent, arrives by chance in her remote valley and agrees to stay, he brings to her an impossible dream of love which seems for a time to be coming true. When reality awakens her, she takes the desperate steps which lead to one climax after another in her tragic story. Four men are involved in Cassie's history, and each in his own way is, like her, the victim of a willingness, even eagerness, to cling to illusions as if they were truth and to act in terms of them.

It is a strange and complex story of love, betrayal, revenge, murder. The plot is tightly constructed and full of suspense; it moves inexorably toward events that culminate in murder; there is a dramatic trial, followed by the heroic efforts of a determined lawyer to reverse the judgment of the court. And, as always in Mr. Warren's fiction and poetry, it is a story full of sharp insights into the human predicament, of deep moral and philosophical significance.

Dust jacket and front flap for Warren's 1971 novel (Richland County Public Library)

rather parochial figure. This attitude is itself of course extremely parochial, but because it is also extremely influential, it has created the impression that only certain forms of American experience are suitable for literature, only certain writers are qualified to tell the real truth about American life.

Yet the problem is not merely that one kind of regional experience has been accepted as more authoritative than another kind. It is also that, perhaps as a result of this development, we have grown accustomed to a particular metaphysical approach to experience in fiction. We now seem to believe that the only really tenable view for the novelist is the nihilistic view, in which events without meaning are seen to occur in a world without standards, and neither author nor characters presume to suggest what standards there may once have been or ought to be. The fictional situation we tend to find most artistically serious and relevant to life is one involving the

continuous search for identity among people who have no realization of either the presence of the past or the possibility of the future, and so exist in a state of paralysis or dreary preoccupation with the merely sensational, with violence enacted without motive, sex enacted without passion or love–hence, from which all human meaning has disappeared. The fictional characters who speak to us most convincingly are usually those who become deranged by the anarchy of life to the point where they perhaps retreat, like Portnoy, into compulsive masturbation or, like Augie March, seek in the provisional structures of belief fabricated by others some means of understanding and controlling the anarchy in themselves. The experience depicted in our most respected novels again and again poses the problem described so well by Gide's Michel in *The Immoralist:* "To know how to free oneself is nothing; the arduous thing is to know what to do with one's freedom."

⑨ 1

Faulkner's use of time and other characteristics
in the section that we mean to use from Light in August

One of the most virtuoso displays ~~in fiction is~~ Faulkner's use *of narrative technique is to be found* ~~of time~~ in *Light in August.* ~~But~~ Of this rich and highly complicated novel, we shall print only some 20,000 words, a ~~brief section~~ *very small part of* from that a novel ~~which~~ has over 300,000 *words.*

The portion that ~~is include here~~ *in question* has to do with ~~x~~ the character Joe Christmas ~~and~~ *through* the section ~~to be~~ printed *here represents only a fraction* ~~is only a portion of~~ ~~of~~ the ~~space~~ *space* that Faulkner *devotes* ~~gives~~ to him. ~~Yet~~ *Nevertheless from the reader learns a great deal about Christmas* the passage ~~in question~~ *We print* ~~not only has its own interest and its own kind of suspense, but~~ *and even more about how Faulkner present character in action.* ~~constitutes a kind of showcase for some of F's most brilliant techniques.~~

~~Thus~~ We first meet with Joe Christmas in Chapter 2. He comes *to the town of Jefferson and gets a job at* ~~to~~ the sawmill ~~to work~~ but ~~is~~ *his fellow worker* ~~committed~~ *never get to know him,* wears a certain air ~~if mystery, and remains x unknown and a stranger to the other~~ ~~workers at the sawmill and to the village of Jefferson in which it~~ is ~~located.~~ Faulkner says of Joe that he *arrives in* ~~wears~~ "soiled city clothes," that his face is "dark" and "insufferable," and that his whole air is one of "cold and quiet contempt." *In the mill workers even his name seems.* ~~He even has that what the~~ ~~mill workers regard as an~~ outlandish ~~name.~~ ¶ In Chapter 4 ~~we learn~~ *reports* from one of the characters ~~in~~ the novel, that a Miss Joanna Burden, *middle-aged* a spinster who ~~lives~~ *lives close* in a big house on the edge of town, has been murdered and her house set on fire, presumably in an ~~x~~ attempt to destroy the evidence of how she died. *It is also reported* ~~We also learn~~ that *Joe Christmas has disappeared and that his* Christmas's companion, Joe Brown, has accused ~~Christmas of having~~ *him* ~~committed~~ the murder and *furthermore has announced* ~~has said~~ that Christmas is not a white man *everyone* as ~~the people of the community~~ had taken for granted, but is a Negro. *Miss Burden's murder has occurred nearly three years after Joe's arrival in Jefferson.* In Chapter 5 immediately after these revelations, made on

Page from an early draft of Warren's introduction to the excerpt from William Faulkner's Light in August *included in* American Literature: The Makers and the Making *(1973). The two-volume anthology was the result of his ten-year collaboration with Cleanth Brooks and R. W. B. Lewis (Yale Collection of American Literature, Beinecke Rare Book and Manuscript Library).*

Self-Discovery in American Literature:
The Makers and the Making

In 1963, Warren, Brooks, and R. W. B. Lewis began collaborating on an American literature anthology. That collaboration lasted for ten years, and their results were published by St. Martin's Press as American Literature: The Makers and the Making. *Lewis recalls the years of collaboration in this excerpt.*

. . . for a decade, from 1963 to 1973, the chief topic of textbook conversation was the American venture. This had begun when an editor from St. Martin's Press in New York approached Brooks and Warren with the idea of a textbook to be called *Understanding American Literature*. After thinking about it for a while, the two veteran textbook designers decided that they needed a bona fide Americanist to take part; and since I was on hand, a Yale colleague and friend, they invited me to join the team. At a later moment, and after considering alternatives, we changed the title to *American Literature: The Makers and the Making* (the phrases were Warren's).

. . . .

. . . the procedure was a "social" one. Cleanth Brooks made the point in the Letter to the Reader, which he drew up and which Warren and I endorsed: "Our method was inductive," Brooks said, "and our mode of working was social; that is, we read and we talked." We met and talked for an afternoon or for two and three days at a time—at the Brookses' home in Northford, at the Warrens' home in Vermont, at Calhoun College at Yale (where I was then the Master in residence). Usually, all three of us convened; but occasionally, if either Brooks or Warren was out of the country (Brooks, for example, was in London as the cultural attaché in 1965–1966), only two of us could come together. These latter sessions, and their findings, are carefully summarized by Brooks and Warren in their letters to one another.

We divided the authors and introductions among us as we moved ahead from period to period; and over the ensuing years, the letters speak of some of the individual undertakings—Brooks on poetry and southern writing, Warren on Cooper and Hawthorne, me on Emerson and Henry James. For Warren, it seems to have been an exhilarating voyage of discovery and rediscovery; and, as could later be realized, of self-discovery.

On May 20, 1965, as an example, Warren said he had "been on Hawthorne, have reread him almost entire, and a lot of stuff about him. Now I shall do that section as a trial balloon." Seven months later, Brooks wrote from the American Embassy in London: "I have used this Christmas lull to go back to your Hawthorne, re-read it, and I am much impressed. It seems to me the best thing that has ever been written on Hawthorne—the best that I know of, at any rate." Thirty-odd years later, I would second that judgment. What Brooks admired was the way the essay wove together biography and criticism—"discussing some text rather fully . . . and bringing in the relevant parts of [Hawthorne's] life as a man and an artist." That is exactly right; but my own enjoyment comes also from the sense that in the essay Warren is, so to say, standing shoulder to shoulder with Hawthorne, appraising him not as an academic critic but as a fellow practitioner of the art of fiction. In sizing up Hawthorne, Warren is indeed defining himself:

> He lived in the right ratio—right for the fueling of his genius—between an attachment to his region and a detached assessment of it; between attraction to the past and its repudiation; between attraction to the world and contempt for its gifts; . . . between a fascinated attentiveness to the realistic texture, forms, and characteristics of nature and human nature, and a compulsive flight from that welter of life toward abstract ideas.

There, in perfectly chosen wording, the southern-born resident of New England identifies the supreme New England creative temperament, and in the same wording expresses himself—in his own ambiguous relation to his own region, to the past of that region, to the world of nature and to abstract ideas.

—R. W. B. Lewis, "Afterword," in *Cleanth Brooks and Robert Penn Warren: A Literary Correspondence,* edited by James A. Grimshaw Jr., pp. 417–424

As his novels make clear and *All the King's Men* demonstrates in perhaps too programmatic a form, Warren is fully aware of this problem in its connection with contemporary nihilism. But he differs from most of our novelists in realizing that the question of what to do with one's freedom is unanswerable unless and until the limits of our freedom are defined by the beginnings of our responsibility. This is to suggest that Warren brings a morally conservative—albeit politically liberal—vision to the problems of nihilism and reveals a clear understanding of just how men should behave, how they may find, or search for and never find, their salvation through self-knowledge, what standards should be used to measure our fall from standards, in exactly what way we should relate to our history and confront what he calls "the awful responsibility of Time."

If such a view is unfashionable at this time, it probably is so because the urban liberal mind is unfamiliar with, or finds politically reprehensible, the premises on which it is based. Yet in a nihilistic and

Warren at a party in New York City to launch I. A. Richards: Essays in His Honor, *November 1973. Richards's critical works, including* Practical Criticism: A Study of Literary Judgement *(1929), influenced Warren's approach to teaching literature (Robert Penn Warren Birthplace Museum, Guthrie, Kentucky).*

dehumanizing society there is a massive, if seldom articulated need, of the kind confessed to by Nick Carraway in *The Great Gatsby* for "the world to be in uniform and at a sort of moral attention forever," and Warren gives concrete dramatic expression to this need. For him no contradiction exists between liberal politics and moral conservatism. Both are implicit in his broadly humanistic philosophy, and both are inextricably joined to his subject matter, which is always derived from the Southern experience. It is most unlikely that he would be able to dramatize the philosophy without the subject matter, for the South is uniquely a region in which the issues that most profoundly engage his imagination have a living and dynamic basis in social fact.

Warren once wrote that in Faulkner's view "the old order [of the South] . . . allowed the traditional man to define himself as human by setting up codes, concepts of virtue, obligations, and by accepting the risks of his humanity. Within the traditional order was a notion of truth, even if man in the flow of things did not succeed in realizing that truth." The same view might, with minor alterations, be attributed to Warren himself. For him as for Faulkner, the literary value of the South is that it provides cultural and mythic structures against which, since they rest upon an idealistic "notion of truth," human character and conduct can be morally—therefore, dramatically—evaluated amid conditions that are the exact opposite of those prevailing in the urban North. In fact, one of the central themes of the Southern novel is the conflict between an established humanistic tradition, with its inherited "concepts of virtue," and the forces of materialism, relativism, and opportunism that typify the modern South and the modern world. This is the sort of conflict which is exemplified in Faulkner by the opposition between his Compson-Sartoris and Sutpen-Snopes families. Historically, if not at the present time, the South has existed, or sought to exist, as the metaphysical antithesis of scientific rationalism. Warren has spoken of the tendency of science to create a division between intellect and emotion, between head and heart knowledge, which he calls "the terrible division of the age." Jack Burden's problem is that he cannot reconcile the teachings of his head and heart. By temperament a romantic and an idealist, he wants to love, have faith in, and give his assent to life. But his cynical intelligence causes him to see people as stereotypes—The Boss, The Brass-Bound Idealist, The Scholarly Attorney—and the process of existence as simply biological function, "the dark heave of the blood," "The Great Twitch." This divided view results in Burden's nearly fatal separation from those he loves and from himself. Only through discovering and affirming his identity with the past and accepting responsibility for having helped to shape it can he bring together the disparate sides of his nature.

The Southern mind has traditionally aspired to this kind of autonomy and relationship, this state of being harmonious with nature, history, and the flow of life, and it has attempted to exist by concepts of fidelity and responsibility intended to preserve both individual and communal order. The cavalier code of manly honor and feminine virtue is one such concept. As an ideal, it has had forces at work against it in Southern society that have always been of the strongest potential violence, self-destructiveness, and racial and sexual guilt. Unlike New England and the Midwest, where a long puritan history has led to the repression of so much of the demonic in human nature, the

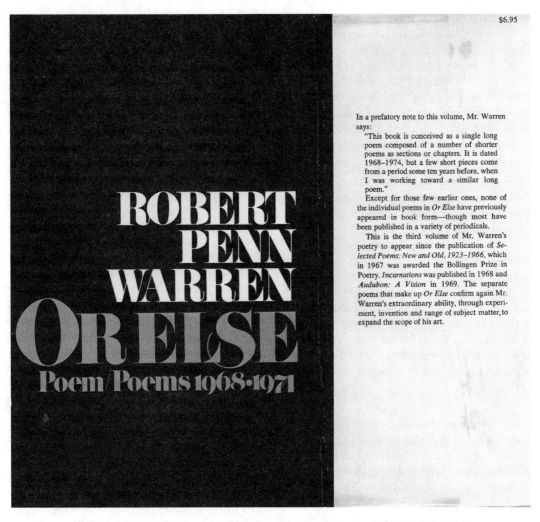

$6.95

In a prefatory note to this volume, Mr. Warren says:

"This book is conceived as a single long poem composed of a number of shorter poems as sections or chapters. It is dated 1968–1974, but a few short pieces come from a period some ten years before, when I was working toward a similar long poem."

Except for those few earlier ones, none of the individual poems in *Or Else* have previously appeared in book form—though most have been published in a variety of periodicals.

This is the third volume of Mr. Warren's poetry to appear since the publication of *Selected Poems: New and Old, 1923–1966*, which in 1967 was awarded the Bollingen Prize in Poetry. *Incarnations* was published in 1968 and *Audubon: A Vision* in 1969. The separate poems that make up *Or Else* confirm again Mr. Warren's extraordinary ability, through experiment, invention and range of subject matter, to expand the scope of his art.

Dust jacket and front flap for Warren's 1974 book, which was mainly written before he left Yale University
(Richland County Public Library)

South has existed in a state of constant dialectical tension between a romantic urge for absolute purity and the most sensuous appetite for corruption. Hence, it provides a moral situation in which the issue of guilt and responsibility can be dramatized because both the decorums of virtue and the potential for their violent overthrow are concretely present in the social scene.

In addition, the South has provided and continues in many areas to provide factual verification of the idea that past and present are closely interrelated, that there is an observable connection between past actions and present conditions. It is still quite common in the South for people to be born and spend their whole lives in the same community, to know the histories of their own and one another's families in intimate detail, and to live every day with the results of the deeds and misdeeds of their ancestors. Thus, experience confirms the truth of Warren's belief that "the world is like an enormous spider web,"

and, as Amantha Starr says in *Band of Angels,* "You live through time, that little piece of time . . . is yours, but that piece of time is not only your own life, it is the summing-up of all the other lives . . . It is, in other words, History, and what you are is an expression of History, and you do not live your life, but somehow your life lives you, and you are, therefore, only what History does to you."

The need to confront one's true nature within history, to live by an ideal of responsibility while learning to accept the facts of human existence, both past and present, these are ideas that can be used in fiction only when the writer has available social materials that embody them. As the examples of Warren and Faulkner make clear, the materials of the Southern experience do embody them in great abundance. Hence, it is not surprising that their novels represent the most vital alternative we have to the urban novel of anarchy. Warren's Southern contemporary, Allen

Tate, once observed that "in ages which suffer the decay of manners, religion, morals, codes, our indestructible vitality demands expression in violence and chaos . . . men who have lost both the higher myth of religion and the lower myth of historical dramatization have lost the forms of human action . . . they capitulate from their human role to a series of pragmatic conquests which, taken alone, are true only in some other world than that inhabited by men." That other world is the one most commonly reflected in novels of our time.

"A man that is born," said Joseph Conrad, "falls into a dream," and he may remain in a dream for the rest of his life unless some physical or psychic accident, some signal of destiny, forces him awake. The knowledge that he is in fact alive may come with overwhelming force and be destructive. But an acceptance of that knowledge is the only chance he has to confront himself and recognize his fate. For as Warren believes—and the idea is very Conradian—"The end of man is to know." Jack Burden's awakening to life occurs when he hears his mother's scream of anguish over the suicide of Judge Irwin, his real father, and discovers in that scream not only the identity of his father but a mother he can for the first time honor and love.

Nearly all of the characters in *Meet Me in the Green Glen* have fallen into a dream, find life unreal and themselves unreal in life, and there are those who exist permanently in the dream state. Others are awakened, some brutally, some with a great and exhilarating sense of liberation. But each is changed and given significance by the manner of his awakening and the truth or lie he awakens to. The catalyzing agent for them all is a young Sicilian, Angelo Passetto, who comes out of nowhere down a road one day in the Tennessee hill country, enters by chance the life of a woman named Cassie Spottwood, who can never be quite sure he is real but falls in love with him and, like Faulkner's Joanna Burden after becoming the lover of Joe Christmas, is awakened into sexuality and self- recognition. Angelo, however, remains locked in his narcissistic dream. Cassie is unreal to him. He sleepwalks through her life, taking from her, even in his way loving her, but is untransformed. Finally, he leaves her, and she, understanding his need, helps him to leave. Then, realizing for the first time her own need, Cassie murders her husband who has been paralyzed and in a coma for many years. Angelo is inevitably accused of the crime and although he is convicted, Cassie rises in the courtroom and proclaims her guilt. But she is taken in charge by her husband's old friend, Murray Guilfort, who manages to convince the authorities that she is insane.

In a sense the novel is really about Guilfort, the familiar figure in Warren's fiction of the man who has never found release from the prison of himself and so has lived his whole life in envy and fear of those who, like Cassie's husband, are or once were in vital possession of themselves and their freedom. Guilfort's recognition of his failure compels him in the end to suicide but not before he realizes that: "*The dream* [of life] *is a lie, but the dreaming is truth* . . . not knowing what it meant, but thinking that, if so many people moved across the world as though they knew what it meant, it must mean something."

Taken in terms of the events themselves nothing could conceivably be more melodramatic and sentimental. Cassie's last-minute courtroom confession is pure Perry Mason, while the story of her affair with Angelo, his conviction for a murder she committed and the closing image of her huddled semiconscious against the stone wall of the prison after he is electrocuted might have come straight from the tear-stained pages of a nineteenth-century ladies' magazine. Yet Warren contrives by some magic to make these bathetic materials not only acceptable but entirely convincing. The melodrama is given appropriateness by the fact that the characters belong to a pastoral milieu in which emotions are felt with an almost aboriginal nakedness and intensity, and as Warren has repeatedly demonstrated in his novels, it is in the extremities of violence and passion that the moral issues of human conduct may be most sharply defined. But he is also vindicated by his choice of form, the parabolic romance, where the characters are meant to be less true to life than crystallizations of elemental and extravagant attitudes.

In this respect, *Meet Me in the Green Glen* is, as I have said, a remarkably pure poetic distillation of Warren's typical themes and materials. As such, the novel possesses a coherence at the levels of idea and action which makes it impossible to separate one from the other. There is no conflict here between head and heart knowledge, between philosophical truth and feeling. Warren, if not his characters, has been able to transcend "the terrible division of the age" and to achieve an autonomy that is at once metaphysical and esthetic. He has done so undoubtedly because he is committed to a holistic vision of human experience and to a kind of literary material peculiarly suited to its dramatic expression. There is reassurance at just this time in seeing him affirm with continued power his belief that a possibility exists for us beyond the prevailing anarchy. But Warren finally offers no program for the rehabilitation of the moral environment. He is fully aware of the fact that life is a dialectical process and that, as he says, "in so far as [man] is to achieve redemption he must do so through an awareness of his condition that identifies him with the general human communion . . . The victory is never won, the redemption must be continually re-earned." He might have added what his novels seem always to suggest: that the victory is not in the redemption, but in the process of earning and re-earning. That is the process which creates such meaning as we have in history.

–John W. Aldridge, *Saturday Review,*
54 (9 October 1971): 31–32, 35–37

Last Walk of Season: 1974–1989

Warren's life remained full after his retirement from Yale. In 1974 he taught as a distinguished professor at Hunter College for a term, oversaw the publication of a volume of poems, Or Else: Poem/Poems 1968-1974, and delivered the third Jefferson Lecture in the Humanities address. He continued to travel, including trips to Greece in 1977, North Africa in 1981, and the Orkney Islands in 1986. Among the many tributes he received during his last fifteen years were honorary degrees from Harvard University, Johns Hopkins University, and Oxford University; his second Pulitzer Prize in poetry for Now and Then: Poems, 1976-1978 in 1979; a MacArthur Foundation Fellowship in 1981; and an appointment as the first United States Poet Laureate in 1986.

Warren published his tenth novel, A Place to Come To, in 1977, but thereafter he devoted most of his energy to poetry. Indeed, the most remarkable aspect of Warren's late career was his productivity as a poet. After he turned seventy he published seven major volumes of poetry: Selected Poems, 1923-1975 (1976); Now and Then: Poems, 1976-1978 (1978); Brother to Dragons: A Tale in Verse and Voices (A New Version) (1979); Being Here: Poetry, 1977-1980 (1980); Rumor Verified: Poems, 1979-1980 (1981); Chief Joseph of the Nez Perce (1982); and New and Selected Poems: 1923-1985 (1985). Harold Bloom, the author of The Anxiety of Influence (1973) and an admirer of Warren's poetry, believed that Warren had entered a new phase of his career with Incarnations: Poems 1966-1968 (1968). In his foreword to The Collected Poems of Robert Penn Warren (1998), Bloom asserted that Warren from 1966 to 1989 "wrote much the best poetry composed during those two decades in the United States. . . . between the ages of sixty-one and eighty-one, he had enjoyed a poetic renascence fully comparable to the great final phases of Thomas Hardy, William Butler Yeats, and Wallace Stevens." Cleanth Brooks, however, was one critic who disagreed with Bloom's assessment, in particular the idea that Warren was too much influenced by T. S. Eliot for much of his career. In the Summer 1993 issue of Southern Review, Brooks wrote that "even in his earliest poetry he [Warren] had found his own recognizably distinct voice. He never suffered from any anxiety of influence. From the first he knew who he was. Not even his older and much venerated poet friends, like John Crowe Ransom or Allen Tate, ever really pulled Warren into their orbit. In view of this continuity, what is actually striking is the power, and vitality and variety of Warren's work through the century into the 1980s."

Warren in his office at his home in Fairfield, Connecticut, in 1987 (photograph by Nancy Crampton; Special Collections, Western Kentucky University Libraries)

For the last time, for this or perhaps
Any year to come in unpredictable life, we climb,
In the westward hour, up the mountain trail
To see the last light.

–"Last Walk of Season,"
New and Selected Poems: 1932–1985

JOHN CROWE RANSOM

When, ~~back~~ in September 1921, I timidly entered one of the ~~sections~~ sections of English ~~Composition~~ at Vanderbilt University, I first laid eyes on John Crowe Ransom He was ~~perhaps~~ a trifle under average height, but erect and strongly built, with a handsome head, brown hair, and a penetrating blue gaze. His voice , though not particularly loud, was remarkably clear , the rsult I then surmised from his scarcely ended career aa a Captain of Artillery, but later ~~to~~ ascribed to his years at Oxford, where he had been a Rhodes Scholar. ~~distinguishing himself in classics and especially interested in philosophy .~~ . As I grew to know him a little better I obseved a constant and undefinable courtesy, cool in a strange way but friendly. And always, I was to observe, the close attention he gave to even the most stupid question a stupid freshman could dream up, and his carefully considered answer.

He was the first poet I had ever seen -- for he already had a book published by a real publisher in New York City , a book called Poems About God -- the first book I ever bought in a real bookstore. The title did not surprise me: I knew that his father was a learned preacher, had been a missionary to Brazil, and was a translator. But the role played by God in book puzzled me for a long time. I understood well enough the setting of the poems - the Southern backcountry, and knw that the author did, / for long back, the preachers-father had had a charge in a remote part of ~~Texas.~~ But what about "Grecian troughts" in that world? IA any case the poems her were not exactly the same kind that my own father in the evening might read to the children, "Horatius at the Bridge" or Tennyson.

In any case my teach ~~must be a poet. He~~ was sometimes absent-minded as a poet is supposed to be. For on at least ~~a couple of~~ occasions he came to class ~~at 8 A.M.~~ wit a freshly damp tooth brush sticking out above the handkerchief in the breat pocket of ~~his~~ coat. .

His section of English 1 was supposed to sharpen literacy two days a week, but he couldn't help sneaking in some comment on the origin of a word, ~~mentioning~~ some surprisingly precise phrase from a paper , or reading for the rgyt mic build ~~a paragraph from~~ some true artist. The "literature part" of English 1 was taught by the head of the department.

Page of a draft for Warren's tribute to John Crowe Ransom for the American Academy of Arts and Letters (Yale Collection of American Literature, Beinecke Rare Book and Manuscript Library)

Tribute to John Crowe Ransom

Warren delivered this tribute to his mentor and friend John Crowe Ransom at the meeting of the American Academy of Arts and Letters on 6 December 1974.

John Crowe Ransom was born in 1888 in the little town of Pulaski, Tennessee. His father was a scholarly Methodist minister who had translated the Bible into Portuguese. At Vanderbilt University, the son devoted himself to Latin and Greek, but interrupted his studies by a stint of teaching in Sullivan Hollow, Mississippi, a region reputed to be the last refuge for men whom the law, but nobody else, wanted and there, as not a few Americans before him, Ransom read his Plato in the wilderness. Later, at Oxford, he proceeded to an Honor's Degree in classics, with concentration in Greek Philosophy.

Upon his return to America, Ransom, after a year of teaching in New England, moved to a small southern university, with minimal salary and little chance for advancement, with that choice repudiating the sort of career that his powers of mind must have persuasively proposed to him. I do not suggest that this repudiation was to devote himself to poetry. Poetry had not yet entered the picture. It was, rather, to seek a certain kind of life for which he had a pious attachment. I have heard him say, "Life must come first"– and anyone who ever entered his house would have known it to be the habitat of a deep joy in life–a place where work was play and play was work, because of an abounding energy and the intensity of the life-sense.

Poetry did, however, eventually enter the picture, and more than once Ransom said that he wanted to be a "domestic poet." In a letter to Allen Tate he developed this notion, saying that he wanted to find, in his poetry, "the experience that is in the common actuals"; that he wanted "this experience to carry (by association of course) the dearest possible values to which we can attach ourselves"; and that he wanted "to face the disintegration or multiplication of those values as religiously and calmly as possible." Most of his poems are, on the surface at least, small, common,

domestic. A little girl finds her pet hen dead. A man, waking, loses his bright morning dream, and his wife Jane becomes "only Jane." A lover mourns the absence of his beloved.

Ransom is, then, no poet of modern alienation. Rather, one of reconciliation. But the poet is hard-minded and knows the inescapable biological, historical, and philosophical contexts which dictate that all reconciliation is doomed to be imperfect and fleeting, and that tenderness must ultimately exist in the long perspective of irony. If he is a poet of sentiment, he is a critic of rigorous mind, with an astute sense–in his own poetry as in his poetic theory–of the technical aspects of the literary art. And I should emphasize that for him the polarity of rigor of mind and warmth of heart, though generating an inevitable irony, represent inevitable dimensions of man's fully realized life. But rigor and tenderness, hardheadedness and love–these, in man and work, were united, beyond irony, in a sense of grave joy. I remember a letter in which the poet said that he rather liked getting old, for age made even more precious to him "all small, furry things, like kittens and children."

John Crowe Ransom died calmly in his sleep, on July 3 of last year, at the age of eighty-six. He once said that in writing a poem what he always wanted to do was to make "a beautiful thing." He made many beautiful things, in which a classic purity of outline and modern intensities and tensions find a unique fusion. And these things, speaking to the heart in their special accent, bear all the marks of being a permanent treasure–at least as long as the heart prizes the "common actuals" of life. And, it should be added, as long as the mind values even painful veracity more than self-indulgence and philosophic vision more than delusion.

John Crowe Ransom died with many honors, and this Academy honored itself by his election, in 1966, to Chair number 46 as the fifth occupant.

–Warren, "John Crowe Ransom (1888–1974),"
Southern Review, 11 (Spring 1975): 243–244

America and Poetry

In April 1974 at the Library of Congress, Warren gave the Jefferson Lecture in the Humanities, delivered in what his biographer Joseph Blotner describes as "his habitually rapid, rasping style." The lecture was published the following year as Democracy and Poetry.

In his essay on Warren as a critic, Monroe K. Spears writes that Warren "always shows a deep conviction of the importance of literature and of criticism, and he is always reasonable, humane, and moral. . . . He is not detached, remote, balanced, judicial; instead he is involved, often a passionate advocate, convinced of the worth of his subject and its value to society. The role grows out of teaching, as Warren conceives of it, and like a good teacher he advocates the writers and principles he believes in." Spears suggests that Warren's "most unusual quality is that he is openly patriotic and openly concerned with American politics, society, and history, though never confusing his categories." In this excerpt Spears places Warren's Democracy and Poetry *in the context of his career and summarizes its argument.*

A Defense of Poetry for Our Time

Democracy and Poetry (1975) may be taken as a critical last testament and valediction, for Warren said in 1977 that he had sworn never to write another line of criticism of any kind. More significantly, however, it may be taken as a credo, reaffirming Warren's lifelong and passionate commitment to both democracy and poetry and undertaking the tricky and perilous task of defining and reconciling the two. (The analogy that comes to mind is the task in Christian theology of explaining how the persons of the Trinity are both three and one.) Warren is committed absolutely to both poetry and democracy in its American manifestation: he remains an unashamed patriot, while being fully aware of the worst that can be said about the present state of the Republic and its history (for example he comments devastatingly on Nixon's taped remark "The Arts you know—they're Jews, they're left wing—in other words, stay away"). He knows how much nonsense has been written on the subject (from MacLeish's attacks on the Irresponsibles to Hillyer's attacks on the Bollingen award to Pound, not to mention innumerable Marxist and other sermons); and yet he confronts this most treacherous of all questions about poetry and is determined to make his beliefs explicit without sacrificing honesty or realism. If his position is sometimes more passionate profession of faith than impartial argument, it is an utterly serious redefinition and rededication. One is tempted to say, against the facile propagandists, that there is no connection between art and society (or, specifically, poetry and democracy). Certainly such a response is much easier than to say precisely what the connection is. Auden put this denial in its most extreme form ("if not a poem had been written, not a picture painted, not a bar of music composed, the history of man would be materially unchanged"), but most modern critics have been ironic, oblique, or skeptical about the relation of art and society.

In attempting to write a Defense of Poetry for our time, Warren argues that poetry is "a nourishment of the soul, and indeed of society, in that it keeps alive the sense of self and the correlated sense of a community." Poetry, he continues, "helps one to grasp reality and to grasp one's own life." He is not willing to distort or simplify reality, to "demote science, the purest expression of the love of intellectual beauty, to the role of a scullery maid or to deny the special, and in an economic sense primary, role of technology"; and he flinches "from those who, like Henry James, would assume art to be the justification of all life." (On the other hand one is obliged to note that Warren's solution seems to be primarily for the artist; it is for the reader only insofar as he participates in the experience [and discipline and labor] of the artist, just as his notion of democracy is based on the willingness of the common man to change, to strive to realize his potentialities and work to redeem himself.) "I am not suggesting that in an ideal use of free time a man would take to finger painting or raffia work. What I do suggest is that art obviously provides the most perfect example of self-fulfilling activity, the kind of activity of which gratuitous joy in the way of the doing is the mark, and in which the doer pursues the doing as a projection of his own nature upon objective nature, thereby discovering both the law of the medium . . . and his own nature. A man need not create art in order to participate, with varying degrees of consciousness, in the order of experience from which art flows." Warning very effectively of the trends toward passive consumerism and isolation in our society, Warren argues that poetry is "a sovereign antidote for passivity. For the basic fact about poetry is that it demands participation." Hence it is a model for and an agent in the creation of the self, which is possible only in a community. Poetry can achieve this because it embodies a total and unifying experience: its form "embodies the experience of a self vis-à-vis the world, not merely as a subject matter, but as translated into the experience of form. The form represents uniqueness made available to others, but the strange fact is that the uniqueness is not to be exhausted: the 'made thing' does not become a Euclidian theorem any more than love is exhausted by the sexual act." Hence it can heal our psychic divisions and impoverishments: "The self has been maimed in our society because, for one reason, we lose contact with the world's body, lose any holistic sense of our relation to the world, not merely in that there is a split between emotion and idea but also because perception and sensation are at a discount." Rhythm, Warren argues, "–not mere meter, but all the pulse of movement, density, and shadings of intensity of feeling–is the most intimate and compelling factor revealing to us the nature of the 'made thing.'" In all the arts "we can envisage a structure out of time as well as experience the sequential rhythms in time. And when we experience the contrast and interplay of rhythms of time and movement with those of non-time and stasis–that is, when we grasp a work in relation to the two orders of rhythm and both in terms of felt meaning–what a glorious *klang* of being awakens to unify mind and body, to repair, if even for a moment, what Martin Buber has called 'the injured wholeness of man.'" This seems to me a memorable statement of the function of art because it includes both poles, the formal-aesthetic and the emotional-psychological, and unifies them in an implied religious conception. But why should I try to embellish what Warren has said so well?

Warren proceeds to argue that "historically a strong and high art is to be associated only with societies of challenging vigor." On the other hand such societies have often been antidemocratic. Warren points out that democracy is a recent development, historically, since in earlier societies the laborers were not regarded as persons at all; but the poetry of such an elite order did develop the conception of self-hood, and he cites the examples of Greek epic and tragedy. To debate this much-vexed question of the relation of high art to the success and vigor of a society is tempting; but Warren's central point seems all too plausible: a society that, like ours, seems to be losing both its vigor and its concept of the self is likely to lose its capacity to produce great art as well. Or, to put it more positively, art can help to prevent this from happening and can thus be valuable to the society as well as to individuals. Though inevitably incomplete and vulnerable, Warren's is an honest and serious attempt to confront such questions, and it is worthy to stand in the great line of defenses of poetry with Sidney's and Shelley's.

–Monroe K. Spears, "The Critics Who Made Us,"
Sewanee Review, 94 (January-March, 1986):
108–110

* * *

This review, which appeared in the British publication TLS: The Times Literary Supplement, *was written by Henry Nash Smith, the author of* The Virgin Land: The American West as Symbol and Myth *(1950) and* Mark Twain: The Development of a Writer *(1962). Two years after writing this review Smith published* Democracy and the Novel: Popular Resistence to Classic American Writers *(1978). Warren had worked with the Texas-born Smith, then the chief editor of the* Southwest Review, *in 1934–1935.*

State of the Nation
Review of *Democracy and Poetry*

On July 4, 1876, the 100th anniversary of the Declaration of Independence was commemorated by a ceremony in Independence Square, Philadelphia, before the building in which the Declaration had been signed. The principal speaker on this occasion was William M. Evarts, a power in the Republican Party, who would

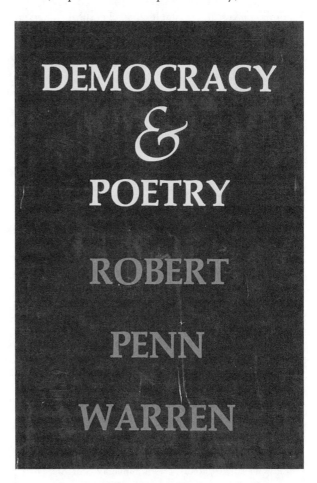

Dust jacket for the Jefferson Lecture in the Humanities published in 1975. The lecture is divided into two parts: "America and the Diminished Self" and "Poetry and Selfhood" (Special Collections, Thomas Cooper Library, University of South Carolina).

soon become Secretary of State under Rutherford B. Hayes. Evarts said, in part:

> Unity, liberty, power, prosperity—these are our possessions today. . . . The spirit of the nation is at the highest—its triumph over the inborn, inbred perils of its Constitution has chased away all fears, justified all hopes, and with universal joy we greet this day. We have not proved unworthy of a great ancestry; we have had the virtue to uphold what they so wisely, so firmly, established. With these proud possessions of the past, with powers matured, with principles settled, with habits formed, the nation passes as it were from preparatory growth to responsible development of character and the steady performance of duty.

The annual Thomas Jefferson Lectureship in the Humanities, established in 1972 by the National Endowment for the Humanities, is of course not the exact counterpart of the ceremony staged in Philadelphia in 1876, but the approach of the bicentennial celebrations makes it inevitable that the third Jefferson Lecture, by Robert Penn Warren, should call to mind that first centennial. *Democracy and Poetry* (which actually contains two discourses delivered on successive evenings in April 1974, the second considerably enlarged for publication) is predictably unpretentious where Evarts's address was still more predictably pompous. But even allowing for contrasting period styles, the collocation reveals a dramatic shift in mood. Indeed, Mr. Warren might almost be supposed to be engaged in a

---

"A Nothing Which Is Everything"

In the course of an interview in which he and Eleanor Clark participated, Warren commented further on a point he raised in Democracy and Poetry, *that the individual's achievement of selfhood may be overwhelmed by "the overarching, interlocking, and mutually supportive structures of science, technology, and big organization."*

My point was that there was a real danger that the "public" could become a great Black Hole, a Nothing which is Everything, the individual dying out. What I would like to see, what I hope for, is enough resistance in the human spirit to maintain the world of personality and the world of art: I equate these two things. But that doesn't mean that I advocate an art of pure self-involvement, any more than I advocate fixity of place or subject matter. You have to try to remain human—that's all—and try to carry your humanity with you. No place has a mystical virtue.

"Interview with Eleanor Clark and Robert Penn Warren," *New England Review,* 1 (Fall 1978)

---

sardonic commentary on Evarts. Americans, he declares,

> long back, developed their secular millennialism, which gave our citizens the conviction of being on the Great Gravy Train, with a first-class ticket. It is easy to see how we arrived at this notion. Our forefathers did have wonderful confidence and energy; as Thomas Jefferson remarked, Americans felt that any difficulty could be surmounted by "resolution" and "contrivance". . . . But the success that rewarded our resolution and contrivance led us, bit by bit, to believe that solutions would be almost automatic: pass a law, take a poll, draw up a budget, make a body count, hire an expert or a PR man, believe only optimistic reports. There is no use in rehearsing the long list of consequences of this attitude, but we may name a few: sick cities, blighted landscapes, an irrational economy, a farcical educational system, and a galloping inflation, not to mention the fact that, after spending astronomical sums, committing massive technical equipment, and suffering heavy casualties, we got the be-Jesus kicked out of us in the jungles of Asia. But we are still the City set on a Hill—or think we are—and the Chosen People with a hotline to the Most High.

The relation between these two passages is more complex than it might appear to be at first glance. Things were not going so well in 1876 as Evarts asserted and (just possibly) believed: he spoke in the eighth year of the administration of Ulysses S. Grant, at a time when corruption in the federal government had reached a level that would be reached again only in the administration of Richard M. Nixon. On the other hand, the very energy of Mr. Warren's indictment of American society reveals an underlying self-confidence. Nevertheless, his report on the state of the Union, impressive in its comprehensiveness as well as in its candour, is anything but reassuring. His quick but penetrating comments in the first lecture on major American writers from Fenimore Cooper onward are, as he says, "diagnostic". He notes how the nation's literature has "analysed and recorded a crucial ailment of our democracy: the progressive decay of the notion of the self". The second, longer lecture is "therapeutic", an effort "to indicate how, in the end, in the face of the increasingly disintegrative forces in our society, poetry may affirm and reinforce the notion of the self".

The problem of the self, of identity, may well seem less urgent to British readers than it does to Americans, who have been preoccupied with it since long before Crèvecoeur, in the decade of the federal constitution, asked his celebrated question: "What then *is* the American, this new man?" But Mr. Warren maintains that the weakening of the ordinary individual's sense of identity is now also a European problem. His second lecture ("Poetry and Selfhood") argues that democracy must always have a basis in fully developed, solid selves. And the principal threat to the achievement of selfhood he conceives to be "the overarching, interlocking, and mutually supportive structures of science, technology, and big organization".

This contention has been familiar at least from the time of Blake. But it leads up to the most original thesis advanced in Warren's lectures: namely, that the selfhood indispensable to democracy is best exemplified in poetry, the work of art, the "made thing", which "embodies the experience of a self vis-à-vis the world, not merely as subject matter, but as translated into the experience of form". Even though the poet himself may be highly disorganized, Mr. Warren continues, the poem he produces

> brings to focus and embodies issues and conflicts that permeate the circumambient society, with the result that the poem . . . evokes mysterious echoes in the selves of those who are drawn into it, thus providing a dialectic in the social process. The "made thing" becomes, then, a vital emblem of the struggle toward the achieving of the self, and that mark of struggle, the human signature, is what gives the aesthetic organization its numinousness. It is what makes us feel that the "made thing" nods mysteriously at us, at the deepest personal inward self.

The emphasis on the poem as an organization of forces recalls I. A. Richards's *Principles of Literary Criticism* and Warren's collaboration with Cleanth Brooks in the composition of *Understanding Poetry,* that bible of the New Criticism. But the reference to social process reveals how far the current of literary theory has flowed during the past two or three decades.

It is nevertheless true that the social process in the United States seems to proceed with little reference to the noumenon. One is more likely to hear that "poetry–at least 'high' poetry–is antidemocratic and encourages elitism". Mr. Warren does not have a formula capable of bridging the gap between serious art and the demand of the mass audience for easy satisfactions.

Instead, he throws out several observations about the problem that bear the imprint of his own experience as an artist addressing the faceless audience of the national market-place. First, he says, "there is a special fluidity in the world of art", so that the values of elitism there "run against the grain of the dominant business-managerial-technological culture", undercutting other elitisms and working "against all established patterns of prestige". In the second place, he believes we shall come ultimately to the time when man will be "released from the realm of necessity" by the development of technology. Although he recognizes that this vocabulary is Marxist, he points out

that the notion is not special to Marx; it is "a dream that yet timidly haunts our democratic aspirations and some of the more old-fashioned notions of education". And Mr. Warren believes that increased free time may lead the populace in general to recognize that art "provides the most perfect kind of self-fulfilling activity". Poetry is, finally, the "sovereign antidote" for the passivity that is the debilitating vice of the consumer society:

> For the basic fact about poetry is that it demands participation, from the secret physical echo in muscle and nerve that identifies us with the medium, to the imaginative enactment that stirs the deepest recesses where life-will and values reside.

It must be acknowledged that these are hopes rather than predictions. At the end Mr. Warren balances the vision of universal darkness at the end of the *Dunciad* against Saint Augustine's assertion of "a dim glimmering of light unput-out in man". Although he believes that "the technological and humanistic orders" may somehow achieve "interpenetration" or "unpredictable osmosis", he comes no nearer than Arnold to suggesting a practical programme. His position is in fact remarkably close to that set forth by the late Lionel Trilling, the first Jefferson lecturer, in his 1972 discourse on *Mind in the Modern World.* The dark view of the future shared by these two eminent men, so different in background and in temperament but alike in their moral and intellectual authority, is profoundly disturbing.

–Henry Nash Smith, "State of the Nation,"
TLS: The Times Literary Supplement,
20 February 1976, p. 199

* * *

This interview is from a forum in which Warren and six others responded to questions about the future of America as a prelude to the Bicentennial celebration.

"There Is Real Danger Of Dictatorial Power"

Q. Mr. Warren, your novel *All the King's Men* was based on the career of a potential dictator. In years ahead, could this country be taken over by a dictator?

A. Yes, *All the King's Men* did get its suggestion–suggestion, mind you–from Huey Long's career. [Huey Pierce Long, a U.S. Senator from Louisiana, was assassinated in 1935.] And yes, I do think that there is real and increasing danger of dictatorial power in the future. But my guess is that in the future such concentrations of power are less apt to come in America in the form of a Mussolini, Hitler or Stalin.

One idea that seems painfully persuasive is that in a world of massive population and exfoliating technology—in the technetronic age, as they call it—the boys who handle the postcomputer mechanisms, or who find themselves in charge of "conditioning" programs, will inevitably be in control—perhaps very high-minded control—with a vast, functionless, pampered and ultimately powerless population of nonexperts living on free time, unemployed and unemployable.

Can we beat that game? There are forces that now want participatory democracy, a democracy based on both individual need and individual responsibility—a community of mutual respect instead of a mechanistic society. Will they resist or co-operate with the forces that push, sometimes quite high-mindedly, toward the dehumanization of society and the centralization of control?

I am inclined to agree—and how modestly I use that word—with the philosopher Martin Buber when he says that something new is "slowly evolving in the human soul," which he describes as "the most intimate of all resistances—resistance to mass or collective loneliness." We see around us some evidence of the desire to find a humane order for ourselves—to find a democratic order based on a sense of real community. What are the chances? I don't know.

Q. Will Americans forget how to read, and will they get all their information and entertainment on television?

A. I cling to the notion that some significant number of Americans will, in spite of TV and other forces, cling to reading—because only in language can one dimension of the human imagination and self-understanding come into play.

What I mean is something like this: At one end of the scale of literature—reading—we have the muscular and neural experience of utterance, actual or suggested. Beyond this there is the whole complex of associations and specificities in language, and the complex interrelated play of image and idea with all other factors. All of this amounts to a special kind of intensification, enactment and fulfillment of the human being—the human self.

What really seems at stake is the death of the human pleasure—and fulfillment—in activity. Reading means activity. Watching TV, in general, does

not. It is, by and large, passivity. It tends to be a form of the compulsive-consumption characteristic of our society—and it is quite naturally associated with the advertising business. The non-participating viewer—and most programs make no demand beyond this—is a mere consumer. Everything is brought to him. Even "news" is, paradoxically, for his "benefit." Mere novelty takes precedence over significance all too often. World events are presented for his godlike diversion. All events tend to wind up as mere spectacle—so that cynical detachment and political and social alienation become a logical danger.

This leads to another aspect: The death of reading is associated with the death of the past. In reading we have the major connection with the past. Now we Americans—for both good and bad—have a contempt for the past. We set out to make a radically new kind of nation, in all ways, and our successes, beyond all expectation, have encouraged us to agree with Henry Ford that "history is bunk."

The next step—we can see this happening—is to discard the study of the past in favor of social science. And more and more the practical bias of such studies is oriented toward the manipulation of men. Now, I'm not saying that social sciences should not be studied. I'm saying that they should be studied in a humanistic context, and should not replace the sense of the past—the story of human action as human.

Your question asks if Americans will be "getting all their information and entertainment" from TV. Isn't there more to expect from TV—as well as from stage, screen and newsprint *and* books—than "information and entertainment"? What about the general life of the mind, the ethical sense, the constructive imagination—and, to be very old-fashioned, nobility and beauty?

Q. Are good books read more now than, say, 100 years ago?

A. Here we must take questions of population and the percentage of literacy into consideration, too. In America in the Civil War—America being the New England States and the spotty civilization of the Middle West—Tennyson sold books by the carload, and in 1866, "Snow-Bound" made Whittier rich. From 1871 on, Mark Twain was sold door-to-door in quantities to make the Fuller Brush man frantic with envy, and Henry James made an honest living.

In the last generation or so, really beginning in the 1920s, a more sophisticated public has been created, small but real. But is the real question a matter of recognition, critical awareness and sales? No–the real question is what gets written. So, looking back, we may ask how many Coopers, Hawthornes, Emersons, Melvilles, Mark Twains, Eliots, Pounds, Frosts, Faulkners and Dreisers we have lined up for the Bicentennial. That's where the rub comes.

I've been talking only about literature. Books are transportable. Pictures, for instance, are not. Early Americans could read Shakespeare and Milton, but they could not see Raphael. I never saw but one decent painting until I was 20–and there were no good reproductions, even that late. There are obviously great gains in the availability of painting and the creation of painting.

There's one other point of gain–even in literature. Dreiser was the first American writer–writer of significant scale–not of the old WASP [white Anglo-Saxon Protestant] stock and tradition, and his *Sister Carrie* didn't appear until 1899.

The range of American literature has definitely been broadened, if not necessarily deepened. We can only trust that depth will come.

–"What Kind of Future for America," *U.S. News & World Report,* 79 (7 July 1975): 48–49

* * *

The American Attitude Toward the Past

. . . Americans, by and large, have had little use for the past except for purposes of interior decorating (early American pine is expensive), personal vanity (it is nice to have the *Mayflower* or the Declaration of Independence in the family), or pietistic and self-congratulatory celebrations, such as our recent well-bred little hubbub about the Civil War. Henry Ford, sage and philosopher, spoke for many of us when he said, "History is bunk," and there is the force of parable in the fact that the house at Seventh and Market streets in Philadelphia, where Jefferson wrote the Declaration of Independence, was torn down, in 1883, to make space for a bank, and when the bank was torn down, in 1932, a hot-dog stand, more appropriate to the period, replaced it. Now, for a more cheerful if somewhat retarded note, in 1963 Congress approved the purchase of the site, and at last a more-or-less accurate replica of the Graff house will be visible to patriots on tour.

–Warren, "The Use of the Past," in *A Time to Hear and Answer: Essays for the Bicentennial Season* (University: University of Alabama Press, 1977), p. 5

"My subject tonight is the use of the past," Warren began his speech for the Franklin Lectures in the Sciences and Humanities at Auburn University in 1975. "I see the subject in the immediate context of the particular crises of the past two decades–political and cultural–for it seems to me that associated with those crises, sometimes as cause and sometimes as consequence, is a contempt for the past. But also, and more broadly, I see this subject in the context of impending celebration of our second centennial of nationhood." In this excerpt, William Bedford Clark discusses Warren's argument in the essay he titled "The Use of the Past."

On Warren's "Use of the Past"

Warren was too realistic, and too fair, a man to suggest that our nation's ahistorical impulse to free itself from the burden of time has bred nothing but unmitigated disaster. Indeed, much of America's greatness must be credited to its collective faith in the efficacy of new beginnings, as Warren freely admits:

The sense of being freed from the past, of being reborn, of being forever innocent, did give America an abounding energy, an undauntable self-reliance, and an unquenchable optimism, and we should be lacking in gratitude to Providence to deny these obvious benefits. But sometimes virtues have their defects, and sometimes, even, the defects tend to run away with the virtues. If, in America, the past was wiped out and Americans felt themselves to be–to adapt a phrase from Emerson–the "party of the Future," they also felt themselves to be a Chosen People, who, unlike the Jews, could never sin in God's sight. Furthermore, they came to feel that even their whims, appetites, and passing fancies were an index of God's will. ["Use of the Past" 6–7]

In short, Warren is suggesting that America's strengths carry within themselves the seeds of tragic failure; unchecked optimism, oblivious to the hard lessons of the past, may easily grow into hubris, the pride that precipitates the fall. The "party of the Future's" attendant millennialism and the corresponding conviction that Americans possess a "Hot Line to the Most High" may well manifest themselves as a ruthlessness in the national character, albeit a ruthlessness in the guise of a disinterested pursuit of the greater good. In this connection, Warren's subsequent allusion in his address to the crushing of Filipino resistence at the turn of the century bore an unmistakable, if unstated, relevance to the United States' late debacle in Southeast Asia, for, following Warren's line of reasoning (in which the insights of Reinhold Niebuhr play an acknowledged and formative role), Americans' often uncritical faith in the rightness of their cause belongs among the more dangerous "illusions of our national infancy" ("Use of the Past" 10).

In Love with America

On 4 April 1976, the public television program Bill Moyers' Journal *aired an interview with Warren from Yale University. In his biographical introduction, Moyers noted that Warren was "increasingly intrigued by the fate of democracy in a world of technology." These excerpts are from the transcript of the broadcast.*

ROBERT PENN WARREN: I'm in love with America, the funny part of it is, I really am. I've been in every state in the Union except one, and I'm going there within a month.

BILL MOYERS: Which state is that?

WARREN: That's Oregon. And I've traveled in the depression in a fifty dollar car, broken-down, old, green Studebaker. I wandered all over the West. I spent time on ranches here and ranches there and been in all sorts of places. And I've had change given back to me for gas in the Depression. Some guys say oh, keep the change buddy, you look worse than I do. I really fell in love with this country.

. . . .

MOYERS: I know you once wrote that Americans felt liberated from time, and that it gave them a sense of being, gave us a sense of being on a great gravy-train with a first class ticket.

WARREN: Well, we had the country of the future, the party of the future . . . we had the future ahead of us, and we had this vast space behind us on this continent. We had time and space. We could change the limitations of the European world. Such a simple thing as a man's hands becoming valuable. A man on the American continent in the 18th century was valuable, neighbors were valuable, hands were valuable, there were things for hands to do. And so the whole sense of the human value changed . . . right . . . beginning with the value of hands, what they could do. Or the value of a neighbor down the road a mile away instead of twenty miles away. These things made a whole difference in the sense of life. And it's a fundamental stimulus to our sense of our own destiny.

MOYERS: They also were a power incentive, were they not, to human dignity?

WARREN: To human dignity because the hands mean something. They're not just things owned by somebody else. They belong to that man. And then all of the rest of the factors that enter into the creation of American . . . the American spirit. All of those things are involved.

MOYERS: You said once . . .

WARREN: We could always move and the sense of time being time-bound and space-bound disappeared, but mitigated anyway. A whole psychology was born, it'd never been in the world before.

MOYERS: A very optimistic philosophy of progress.

WARREN: That's right. As Jefferson said, in writing to his daughter, Martha, he said, Americans–I think it was his daughter Martha, anyway–Americans fear nothing, you see, cannot be overcome by earnest application, you see, and what's the other word? Ingenuity.

MOYERS: Ingenuity.

WARREN: Americans assume that there are no insoluble problems.

MOYERS: We've really been, we've really been trapped, in a sense, by Thomas Jefferson's definitions of America in those terms, haven't we?

WARREN: That's right, we assume that we can solve anything rather easily. And we're always right. We think we're usually right about it. Since we can solve things, we're the ones who are right.

. . . .

MOYERS: What are the values that are most important to you now?

WARREN: Well, I can tell you what my pleasures are.

MOYERS: What are your pleasures?

WARREN: Put it this way. Because I'm selfish and want to fill my days in a way that pleases me. Well, it so happens that my chief interest in life, aside from my friendly affections and family affections which is another thing . . . though they're related . . . is the fact I like novels and poems, as I want to read them and I want to write them . . . as I have an occupation which to me, I can go beyond that, now why that occupation? It's the only way that I can try to make sense to myself of my own experience . . . is this way. Otherwise I feel rather lost . . . in the ruck of my experience and the experience I observe around me. If you write a poem or read the poem–somebody else has written one that suits you, that pleases you, this is the way of making your own life make sense to you. It's your way of trying to give shape to experience. And the satisfaction of living is feeling that you're living significantly.

MOYERS: Does it . . .

WARREN: That doesn't mean grandly, that means it has a meaning, it has a shape, that your life is not being wasted, it isn't just being from this to that.

–Bill Moyers' Journal, Educational Broadcasting Corporation, 4 April 1976, pp. 1, 3, 4–5

Warren ends his "preamble" with a series of sobering questions: "Are we ready to take our second centennial as an occasion that may, possibly, teach us something? Are we ready to face the idea that we may not, after all, be the Chosen People? Are we ready even to consider the possibility that we are moral narcissists of great talent and are, as a consequence, somewhat unlovely and sometimes unlovable? Are we ready to learn from our past that moral definition is difficult and that there is such a thing as what Niebuhr calls the 'irony of history'?" The necessity of asking ourselves such questions is imperative given the ironies of a historical predicament that means in effect that "what was once our future is now our past," but Warren notes that this cyclical paradox is itself "the deepest irony of all" and one that only a mature national consciousness is prepared to wrestle with ("Use of the Past" 11).

In Warren's view, as he proceeds to articulate it in his Franklin Lecture, a sense of history is of paramount importance, though he discounts the notion that the study of history in and of itself can provide us with tidy solutions to the dynamic problems of the present or insulate us from the risks of making mistakes in the future: "For the future is always full of booby traps, and there is no indication that historians make the best prime ministers, secretaries of state, or even advisors to presidents, kings, and emperors" ("Use of the Past" 16). Rather, the value of history lies in the fact that it provides us with images of humanity in action in the past in a way analogous to the working of literature upon our consciousnesses, and, by internalizing these images, we can come to assimilate the full burden of our humanity. If the past is sometimes a rebuke to the present, it is also the source of a solid foundation upon which to erect the vision of a future, since "the dynamic understanding of the past gives us the possibility of a future" ("Use of the Past" 29).

Underlying Warren's discussion are two premises that are central to his worldview: that the self isolated in time and alienated from the context of community is ultimately non-self and that a genuinely viable selfhood can come only by way of "earned" self-definition. We are called to participation in the world and must subject ourselves to a process of action and interaction with others. What Quentin Anderson has identified as the "imperial self," a dominant mode of the American imagination, was for Warren anathema, potentially destructive of both the individual who suffers from it and of the society that projects it on a more general level. So it is that the proper sense of the past, while not an absolute cure for the diseases of the self, diseases Warren viewed as especially rampant in our age of scientism and quantitative reductionism, is nonetheless a potent tonic, and it is hardly surprising that Warren sees in the creative act, specifically as embodied in literature, the fullest paradigm for the vital dialectic between the past and the self for which he calls. Like history, literature "gives us an image of the human soul confronting its fate," but that is only half the matter. It also provides an auxiliary "image of how the writer confronts the image of fate that is the work's content" ("Use of the Past" 25). This "doubleness" enables the reader to confront, albeit vicariously, his own fate and confront himself in the very act of such confrontation: "Literature, as Henri Bergson suggests, returns us to ourselves" ("Use of the Past" 26). Or, as Warren puts it a little later, "The truth we want to come to is the truth of ourselves, of our common humanity, available in the projected self of art. We discover a numinous consciousness and for the first time may see both ourselves in the world and the world in us" ("Use of the Past" 28).

–William Bedford Clark, *The American Vision of Robert Penn Warren* (Lexington: University Press of Kentucky, 1991), pp. 11–14

A Last Novel

A Place to Come To, Warren's last novel, traces the life of Jed Tewksbury, a southerner who becomes a respected scholar. It received mixed reviews.

Robert Penn Warren's Latest Celebration of the Years
Review of *A Place to Come To*

When one learns that *All The King's Men* was published in 1946 (and surely it must have been several years in the writing), there is generated the sense of generations that Robert Penn Warren's creative life has spanned. To speak, then, of a new novel by this man of letters is a very heartening thing, especially for those of us who feel, oppressively, the weight of those generations. *A Place to Come To* is the title of Warren's latest celebration of the years, and it has about it a sweep and ebullience that testifies to an unquenchable spirit, particularly in these limiting times.

Jed Tewksbury is an updated picaresque hero, with academia rather than the slammer for his *pied-a-terre*. Buck Tewksbury, his father, an Alabaman with colorful endowments, comes to a Rabelaisian end, the details of which become young Jed's cross for a time, and then his cachet. It is soon evident that Jed is a scholar, and when he goes on from Blackwell College in Alabama to the University of Chicago graduate school, his gritsy rendition of his father's flamboyant

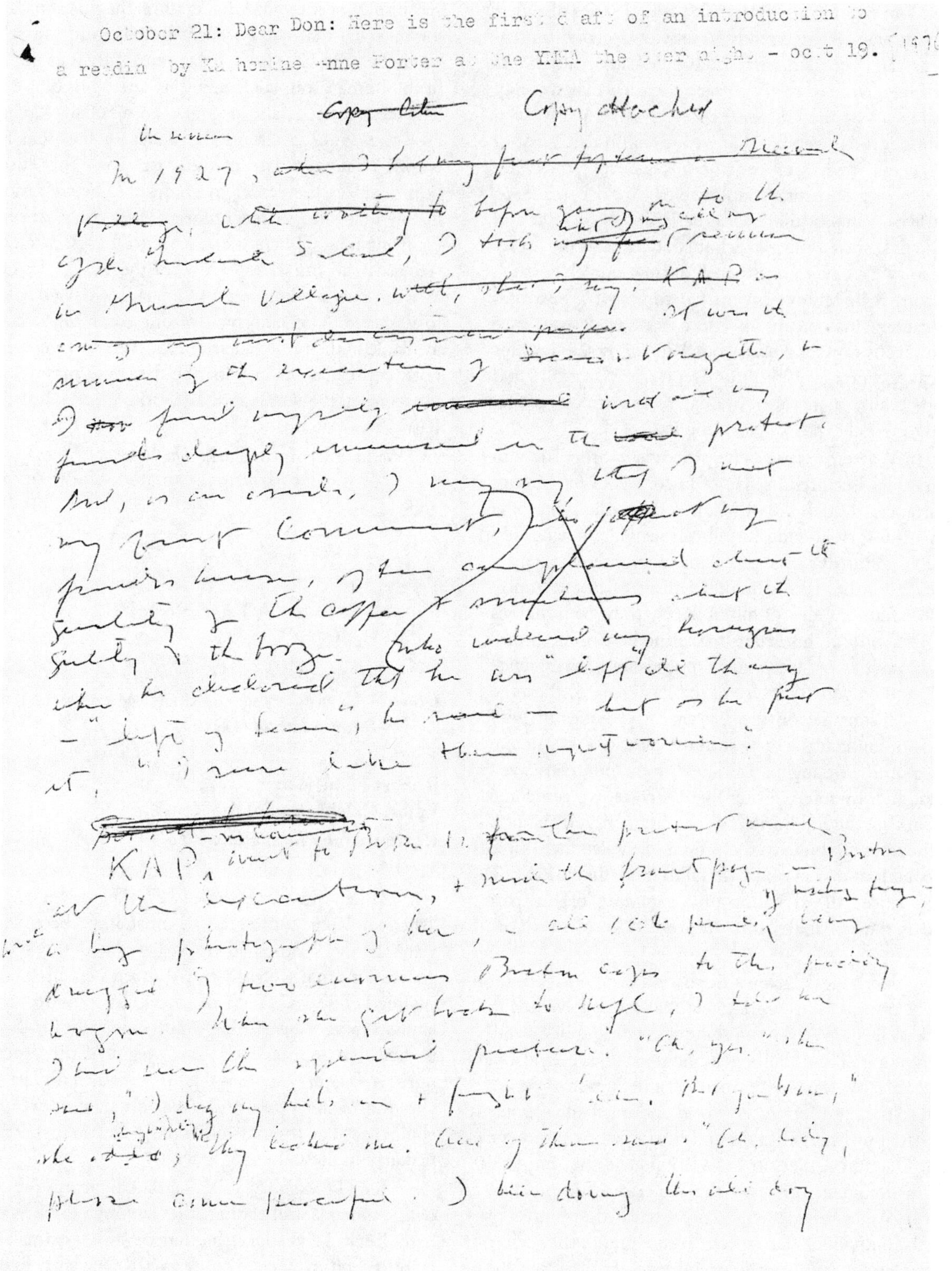
October 21: Dear Don: Here is the first draft of an introduction to a reading by Katherine Anne Porter at the YMHA the other night - oct. 19.

Copy attached

In 1927,

Pages from drafts of Warren's introduction for Katherine Anne Porter, who was the featured speaker at the Poetry Center of the YM-YWHA, the Jewish community center, in New York City on 18 October 1976 (Yale Collection of American Literature, Beinecke Rare Book and Manuscript Library)

Katherine Anne Porter -- Introduction

YMHA YMHA   October 18, 1976

In the summer of 1927 , before going on to the Yale Graduate School I took what I may call my seminar in Greenwich Village ~~to register up~~. It was the summer of the execution of Sacco and Vanzetti, and I found myself being educated by friends deep in the protest. And, as an aside , I broadened my horizons by getting acquainted with my first Communist -- whom explaining himself to me, declared that he "was left all the way" -- was "left of Lenin," he said -- ~~and But~~ wound up by remarking, even more emphatically, that he "sure liked them right women."

Well, to push on to the business of the evening: Katherine Anne Porter -- no Communist -- went to Boston to march in the protest against the execution, and made the front page , ~~in~~ a big photograph of her -- all 106 pounds of resisting fury -- being dragged by two enormous Boston cops to the paddy wagon, ~~in the background~~. When she got back to New York, I told her I had seen the splendid picture. "Oh, yes, " she said, " I dug my heels in and fought 'em. But you know," she added, "they licked me. One of them said: 'Aw, lady, please come peaceful. I been doing this all day and my feet hurt.' So I went peaceful, thinking of his poor feet."

This is not a rambling anecdote. It points to something, at the very heart of Katherine Anne Porter's fiction. On the one hand, a hard conviction, a love of truth, the toughness of intellect, and on the other, the human sympathy, even for the poor cop's feet.

To extend the contrast, I should say that on the one hand we find -- not "pretty writing," God forbid -- but what Edmund Wilson once called an "English of purity and precision almost unique in contemporary

The Germ of *A Place to Come To*

At the beginning of his 1981 interview with Saturday Review *Warren talked about his compulsion to write: "I know a thousand stories, everybody knows a thousand stories. But only one cockleburr catches in your fur and that subject is your question. You live with that question. You may not even know what that question is." Later Warren talked about an incident that had stuck in his mind for more than twenty years before he wrote* A Place to Come To.

SR: Do you see much of a connection between you and your protagonists?

WARREN: No, I don't. I can see certain similarities. But they are all different. Quite a few reviewers said my last novel [*A Place to Come To*] was an autobiographical novel. Well, it certainly was not. I didn't leave the South because I hated it at all. I lost my job [*laughs*]. I was fired twice down there. And my mother didn't write English like that. And my father didn't get killed by a mule's kicking him either. He died at 86 of a cancer he didn't tell anybody he had—an iron man. I tell you, that book's not even in any kind of a strange, twisted way autobiographical. Except one thing I've noticed about many Southerners who've left the south—people I knew, my generation or just a little bit earlier, a little bit later. They felt some kind of awful degradation about being a Southerner. Some of those people came north—some of them made terrific successes in business or elsewhere.

One I knew came to see me. I hadn't seen him since he and I were freshmen. But there wasn't enough action for him at Vanderbilt, so he went to Chicago. I never heard of him again until years later I was a professor at the University of Minnesota, living in a hotel. And the hotel called up and said there's a man here named so-and-so would like to speak to you. And he got on the phone and said, "May I come see you?" I said, "Sure" because I remembered him. And he came in, he was a gigantic wreck of a man—handsome and falling to pieces—he smelled of money in a way which is hard to believe. You know, he had really made it. And he came and he opened his briefcase and he showed me his house in Chicago, a great mansion, you see. And he showed me his summer place and a dock and a yacht and motorboats. Then he showed me a debutante party picture of his two daughters, and so forth. And he's showing me all these trophies. After years and years I hadn't seen him or heard his name. . . .

SR: Trying to justify himself to himself.

WARREN: Yes, and then, after showing me everything and taking congratulations and all that, suddenly he threw his head up—we'd had two or three drinks together—and he put his head in his hands and said, "Jesus, I'm lonelier than God." And that was the germ of my novel, this man who had made his kind of success and had no return.

–Carll Tucker, "Creators on Creating: Robert Penn Warren," *Saturday Review*, 8 (July 1981): 41

---

death becomes the sought-for high point of social evenings among the literati.

A few people have lasting influences in Jed's life. One, of course, is his father, who—despite each of his accomplishments—willy-nilly provides Jed with the ribald myth that seasons his life with a flavor that more and more comes to suit Jed's taste. Then there is his mother, a peasant woman, really, with the toughness, wit, and survival cunning that often goes with the class. These qualities also become part of Jed's inheritance.

Dr. Heinrich Stahlmann, an eminence at the U. of C., further fertilizes the young man's cultural soil by spading into it the riches of antiquity. Rozelle Hardcastle, every young man's dream of beauty and sexual apotheosis, appears and reappears in and out of Jed's life and bed, as such dreams will, if the lucky man is Jed Tewksbury. Rozelle's roots are in Dugton, Ala., as are Jed's, and although their careers are mainly separate, their hunger for each other remains lustily constant.

There is Dauphine Finkel, the intriguing Jewish woman, full of party-line paradoxes, whom Jed eventually marries. And Agnes Andersen, the tragic grind, whom he also marries, and whose fatal illness becomes for Jed a deal with death. The trade-off, in Jed's haunted mind, is his wife's life for his very successful dissertation on "Dante and the Metaphysics of Death."

It seems clear that Warren's intention was to make Jed an exemplary child of the century. War, upward mobility, and the dissolution of values are the currencies of Jed's years. Because of his mastery of languages, he finds himself behind enemy lines with Italian partisans during World War II. He is quite capable of executing prisoners, but not cold-bloodedly, because the Nazi he blasts is a specimen he loathes, and counts the world well rid of such virulent scum. Of dirt-farmer stock, he is eventually summoned to the land of Dante to receive honors for his scholarly work. When he learns that his dream-girl, Rozelle Hardcastle, is married to a clever black man who has been hoodwinking the upper crust of Nashville with his role of Indian swami, Jed is more amused than dismayed.

Page from Albert Erskine's editorial notes on A Place to Come To
(Yale Collection of American Literature, Beinecke Rare Book and Manuscript Library)

Things do not come full circle; rather they veer off the circumference of custom and ride outward to that unpredictable future in store for all of us.

The high kinetic charge of *A Place to Come To* is its recommendation. One wishes that its other qualities could be equally recommended, but unfortunately, despite Warren's many gifts, there's a tendency on his part to sacrifice credibility and cohesiveness for the sake of that kinesis.

Some things remain not only unexplained but also inexplicable: Jed's strange relationship with his mother, for example. Quite simply, they never see each other. Mrs. Tewksbury says she'd rather not, but her reasons, and Jed's accession to those reasons, remain largely unconvincing. Dauphine Finkel (the name may be symptomatic) has at best only a nominal existence. Although at one point Jed is supposed to be married to her for five years, during which time they produce a much-loved son, Ephraim, there persists an incorporeal unreality about the woman and about the connection. Dauphine simply isn't there, and one wonders why the author, knowledgeable as he is, didn't choose to avoid this ghost.

Rozelle Hardcastle, although very much present, also eludes definition. She is married to a very rich man named Butler, and then to another very rich man named J. Lawford Carrington, and then to the swami, but all this variety doesn't conduce to an understanding of what makes Rozelle run. She *seems* to be a woman with an eye for the main chance, and for some reason Jed never looks like the main chance. That would be understandable in an ambitious woman, but one isn't sure that Rozelle is that. She acts out a farrago of roles, none consistent with the other, and in the end this reader was left with the feeling of having been in contact with a lively program rather than a living woman.

But on balance, *A Place to Come To* is very much a book to read. Despite its faults, there is a solid accumulation of substance in Warren's story. Actually, history emerges the hero, and Jed Tewksbury proves to be a versatile, manly, charming guide for this tour through familiar time.

–Seymour Epstein, "Robert Penn Warren's Latest Celebration of the Years," *Chicago Tribune*, 6 March 1977, sec. 7, p. 1

* * *

This review is by Richard Howard, a poet and English professor at Johns Hopkins University.

A Technician's Romance
Review of *A Place to Come To*

Near the end of Robert Penn Warren's tenth novel, the narrator and central figure explains his boredom yet again: "But now my research and writing, like women, became valuable to me as a way to fill up time, and as I had more time to fill I had more fame. I tried to be kind to my students, but to bear

Grand Intentions

In this excerpt reviewer Julian Symons looks back at Warren's career as a novelist. An English critic, biographer, and mystery writer, Symons concludes that Warren "has never produced anything fully worthy of his major talent. The grandeur of his intentions is unmistakable, and the first four novels are memorable and splendid achievements, but they seemed to promise much more than he has given us in the past quarter of a century."

"Author of *All the King's Men*" the front of the dust-wrapper says by way of identifying Robert Penn Warren, and of expressing the hard truth that this is his mark of recognition for British readers. That this should be so is wrong but comprehensible, *All the King's Men* became a celebrated novel in part because the central character had some of the attributes of the Louisiana Kingfish Huey Long, the most successful political demagogue America has known in this century, in part because it was made into a brilliantly directed (by Robert Rossen) and finely acted (by Brod Crawford and others) film. This is not to deny the book's quality as a study in power and corruption, but to explain why it is so much more firmly fixed in public memory than Mr. Warren's other early novels, *Night Rider, At Heaven's Gate* and *World Enough and Time*. These studies of Southern mores have certainly never been appreciated in Britain at anything like their full worth.

Night Rider appeared in 1940, and the last of these four novels was published a quarter of a century ago. Since then Mr. Warren's work as a novelist has shown a steep decline. A style always luxuriant has fairly run riot to cover every narrative with a heavy gloss of rhetoric; a natural tendency towards melodrama has also spread unchecked; and a particularly American verbal coarseness has been encouraged by the Revolution of the Sexual Word. The heart sinks when one reads in the first paragraph of *A Place to Come To* how the narrator's father was killed when, "standing up in the front of his wagon to piss on the hindquarters of one of a span of mules and, being drunk, pitching forward on his head, still hanging on to his dong", his neck was broken by both the front and rear wheels. "Throughout, he was still hanging on to his dong."

The comedy of the hand-held dong gets a good deal of attention, but this opening passage is happily not characteristic of the book, which is a great deal better than any of Mr. Warren's recent novels, although much inferior to his best work. It is the story of Jed Tewksbury's search for personal identity. He is pushed out of the hick town of Dugton, Claxford County, Alabama, by a mother determined that he shall not be like his idle hard-drinking father, becomes an internationally known scholar, marries twice and when he returns to Nashville from Chicago has a violent love affair with a girl known at school, and ends up feeling some sort of accomplishment in the life of his son.

The opportunities for melodrama are obvious, and although less grossly indulged than in some of Mr. Warren's other books they are not denied. When Jed's first wife Agnes is dying of cancer he produces his first notable piece of work, "Dante and the Metaphysics of Death." On the night of her death he sits at his desk and "in the end, the pen began to move." Yet Agnes's death produces some of the best writing in the book as the deadly progress of her illness is charted in a sort of mathematical analysis. Even the writing of the essay is made more acceptable by Jed's viewing the whole thing analytically, as a contrast between theory and laboratory practice: "In the laboratory I gathered what data I could on the process by which death was defining the relation, past and present, between Agnes Andresen and Jediah Tewksbury. In my studies in theory I undertook to analyse the idea that for Dante death defines the meaning of life." Nothing can cancel the melodrama of the idea, but the coolness and irony of the writing leaven it.

Mr. Warren's books have a distinct individual flavour, but his personality is never obtruded into his work. His strengths as a novelist are an intense, lyrical awareness of the past, and a capacity for driving on and controlling a narrative in a way beyond the reach of more than two or three other novelists writing in English. Both are apparent here, in the skill with which he shifts from past to present and back again, and in the thickening texture of the narrative as Jed is forced to come to terms with his own nature. In the end, however, the book must be said to lack a subject important enough to justify the care spent on it. The implications of Willie Stark's career in *All the King's Men* are profound, and so are those of Percy Munn's steady movement towards violence in *Night Rider*. For characters to catch Mr. Warren's imagination fully they have to be of symbolic social importance, and Jed Tewksbury's search for a meaning to his career does not really involve anything but himself. If there is no figure who offers an adequate social standpoint in the later books, this is probably the result of a developing political scepticism in a man who was formerly a New Dealer, anxious for social change.

–Julian Symons, "In the Southern Style," *TLS: The Times Literary Supplement,* 29 April 1977, p. 506

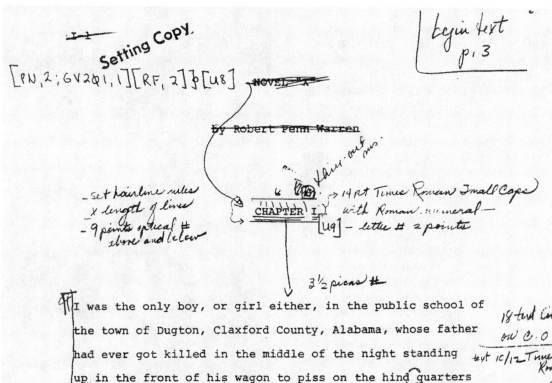

I was the only boy, or girl either, in the public school of
the town of Dugton, Claxford County, Alabama, whose father
had ever got killed in the middle of the night standing
up in the front of his wagon to piss on the hind quarters
of one of a span of mules and, being drunk, ~~had~~ pitching
forward on his head, still hanging on to his dong, and hitting
the pike in such a position and condition that both the left
front and the left rear wheels of the wagon rolled, with
perfect precision, over his unconscious neck, his having
passed out being, no doubt, the reason he took the fatal
plunge in the first place. Throughout, he was still holding
on to his dong.

I know this to be true, for when, on Sunday, well
before church time, they brought the body to our house,
Mr. Tutwayler, who, coming down the pike in his new Model T
that morning, had found the body, explained to the neighbors,
now ritually assembled, the original state of affairs, as
he had observed them. I, then nine years old, had, with a

*First page of the setting copy for Warren's last novel (Yale Collection of American Literature,
Beinecke Rare Book and Manuscript Library)*

down on them. I still had one belief, held with some passion, that good technicians–and you notice my choice of the term, for what it is worth–are better than bad ones."

It is difficult not to believe the novelist (and difficult not to believe he is speaking for himself, the obsessed professional) when he turns to us this way, addressing his readers directly from the center of his story. Here is a narrative of one man's self-recovery, believed in by its narrator and made believable to us only insofar as it is the product of a good technician. Of course, a good technician, in matters of fiction, is not necessarily a writer who avoids mistakes. Rather, I think he is a writer who can turn his mistakes, his crudities, and even his fatigue to his own advantage. He can perceive in a sentence about love-making–"I am sure that, in the occasion at my house, we both had expected to recapture something of the old magic"–both the corny shorthand that is unacceptable even to his hero *and* the necessary refinement of it, nearly a hundred pages later on: "I have never had the slightest notion of what happiness is–what I thought of all my life as happiness was only excitement." A good technician, then, is the storyteller who trusts his talent, if not his tale; his words, if not the world.

And it is hard for the reader to trust the tale told in *A Place to Come To*. So extreme are the terms of it, so sensational the world whose ways are grinningly recounted here, that we need a lot of slow convincing if we are to be brought round. We do get what we need, and Robert Penn Warren's novel is a success, but you would never believe it in any words but his.

Jediah Tewksbury, age nine, begins the telling of his story with the death of his father, at the end of World War I, in an accident that spreads a pall of penis envy over the boy's entire life. Not even in Hemingway has the central male figure been such a successful (and determined) lover as this affectless Alabama outsider, spurred by his iron-maiden mother to escape the South. With the assistance of the kind of old-maid Latin teacher that one assumes had been patented by Faulkner, Jed does escape the South, even though–once the University of Chicago, marriage, widowerhood, and even fighting with Italian partisans behind Nazi lines have intervened–the South is not to escape Jed. For the native returns–to Tennessee, and to a sybaritic set of high-living profligates, including, of course, the Pretty Girl from back home in Alabama, who is now up in the world and down on her luck. Jed makes terrible depredations, as an earlier generation of southern novelists used to say, among the ladies, and must again escape–to

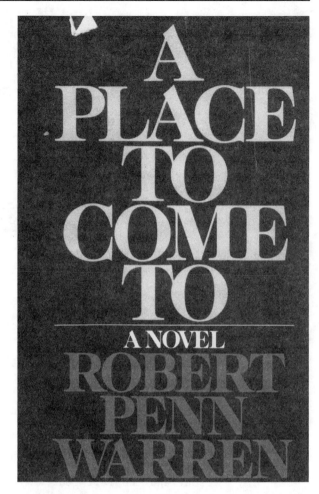

Dust jacket for Warren's tenth and last novel, in which the protagonist, Jed Tewksbury, shares Warren's interest in the work of Dante (Special Collections, Western Kentucky University Libraries)

Paris, Chicago, another marriage, fatherhood, fame, and fortune. "Hating the South I had fled it," he says, "and ever afterwards blamed my solitude on that fact. I had fled but had found nowhere to flee to. I told how I had tried to buy my way out of solitude by supporting the causes of virtue, but I felt isolated even from that virtue, an interloper, one might say, into Yankee virtue."

In that passage, surely, the difference between my graceless summary and Warren's "good technique" is apparent. Whenever one is tempted to put aside this romance–for that is what it is, this account of spiritual withdrawal–Warren is there at one's elbow, murmuring slyly that yes, the characters, even if they are only effigies, are incredible; and that yes, the plot is manipulated entirely by the appearance, at seasonable intervals, of letters, phone calls, and behind-the-scenes shenanigans; but that there is

From Percy Munn to Jed Tewksbury

Percy Munn, the protagonist of Warren's first published novel, *Night Rider,* was a character born for the role of the traditional Southern hero who through his own inner blankness, a blankness that matches the great blackness of the world, destroys himself by ever more desperate attempts to identify himself extrinsically. Warren's final novel takes as its subject the moral achievement of a poor white Southern American moving through and beyond the usual signifiers of accomplishment to learn to live with himself without "passing"–a triumph in history. The stories told in the two novels suggest Warren's movement from a high modern theme of the hollow and cultureless man to a more personal and Romantic vision of history and the possibilities of a fulfilled life–the author's own triumph.

The exile figure in Warren's fiction, nonfiction, and poetry places his work directly in the tradition of the self-making theme in American literature. Its significance in relation to that tradition, however, lies in the particular irony of inwardness with which Warren questions the tradition and reasserts it. As an image of the fluidity of selves, the wanderer signifies a postmodern freedom from the past and from a culturally imposed identity, yet such freedom is the same sort of unshackling necessary for both the traditional American success story and the story that only appears to be its antithesis–the common American-drifter theme. Despite this assertion of freedom, Warren's exile, like Southern literary exiles generally, is haunted by a regional past that asserts its reality in his consciousness as a psychological and philosophical problem, treated often as a textual problem, a problem of reading.

–Randy Hendricks, *Lonelier than God: Robert Penn Warren and the Southern Exile* (Athens: University of Georgia Press, 2000), p. 223

more to this romance of the Recovered Comrade than that. There are words here in which all things are said to happen, even made to happen, and these words are worth hearing out: "With the willing suspension of disbelief, life is thus the richer, even if you are fed, and know it, on a meat of shadows."

Of course, the Pretty Girl from back home turns up again–in Italy, where Jed is being given yet another honorary degree (he hates the things). She has married again (a false swami but a real Negro, as she insists), has learned Italian, French, and "Do you want me to tell you about Lévi-Strauss and structuralism?" Jed lets us off that last one, but treats us to others. Returning from the fool's gold of the Euro-

pean educational establishment, Jed takes Ephraim, his son by that odd, offstage second marriage of his, on a canoe trip, where we hear "Ephraim's voice by the fire while we drank whisky and he quoted Baudelaire, Rimbaud, Vigny, Valéry and Villon (which seemed to stuff infinitely his head, tucked away among his formulae)." Such an excursion would, I maintain, destroy any other novel by any other novelist. But Robert Penn Warren can permit himself these sensational effects of bathos, which seem to stuff infinitely his head, tucked away among his formulae: "The woman had thrust a being forth from her body into the blaze and strangeness of the world, and now, half a century later and half a hemisphere away, a heavy, swarthy man, running to belly and getting a little bald on the top of his head, lay naked in a strange room in a strange country, and the voices rising from the street below, as the afternoon shadow lengthened, were in a tongue that, all at once, was strange to him." That is Jed, on hearing in Italy of his mother's death back in Alabama.

These are the lapses, though, which the good technician so warily, so wickedly, takes up like dropped stitches. If we do not believe the Pretty Girl from back home could really tell us about structuralism, and if we do not for a moment credit the catalog of French poets recited over the campfire by the unimaginable son, we discover that the novelist, too, has had his little joke, and that if we submit to Jed and his sentimentalities ("Anything can become a way of life. Even death. Even the question why death should become a way of life could itself become a way of life. That question was there continuously and inevitably . . . but in its inevitability it had long since ceased to demand an answer. It had become . . . purely rhetorical"), we can gain something else.

What we gain is precisely the product of the good technician, the man upon whom nothing in the visible, tangible world is lost. This man is present in *A Place to Come To* (the "place" is the grave), as is the fabulous artificer of effigies obliged to articulate so shadowily the narrator's preposterous quest for authenticity. It is why I should like to call the book not a failed novel but a successful romance, for its theme is the gallantry of human experience, the high heroism of an effort–in this case, Jed Tewksbury's– to give the realia of life a shape and a texture that risk just the sort of solecisms I have instanced. The mistake would be to assume that Jed Tewksbury is Robert Penn Warren. And of course sometimes Jed speaks so wittily, so eloquently, and so idiosyncratically that one could easily make that mistake, as when he learns Latin: "If you found a new name for

A Movie and an Opera

In a 26 November 1977 letter to Donald Stanford, co-editor with Lewis P. Simpson of the new series of the Southern Review, *Warren gave an update on his current activities after* A Place to Come To. *No movie was made from* A Place to Come To, *and Warren did not complete another novel; however, Carlyle Floyd's opera* Willie Stark *was completed. It premiered in Houston on 24 April 1981 and then ran for three weeks at the Kennedy Center in Washington, D.C.*

Warren to Donald Stanford, 26 November 1977

I'm trying to get a novel off the ground, but may never succeed. Meanwhile, I'm spending most of my time with script-writer, director, and leading man (Robert Redford) getting my last novel (*Place*) turned into a movie (Universal). These guys are really bright and hard working, and I am enjoying the business. The director is just back from Tennessee, where he found his locations. So things do move. What's left of my time goes to the criticism of the libretto of the opera Kennedy Center commissioned from AKM. I'm totally unmusical, but the [m]an doing the job always does his own libretto, too. He has had several good successes and I hope he'll have another one. Carlyle Floyd by name. I have no idea when he'll get through—within the next year, I gather.

–Special Collections, Louisiana State
University Libraries

a thing, it became real. That was the magic of the name. And if you found the names for all the things of a world, you could create a world that was real and different. The crazy word on the page was like a little hole in a great wall. You could peek through the hole and see a world where everything was different and bright. That world, I realized with a strange numbness of awe, was not far away. It was just on the other side of a wall."

But by the end of the book we know better. We know that the fabulous artificer and the good technician have concocted an uneasy alliance, not a coincidence, and that the novel they have made together is a splendid hoax. Or as the technician says: "Until you can understand that these things are different but are the same, you know nothing about the nature of life. I proclaim this."

–Richard Howard, "A Technician's Romance,"
Saturday Review (19 March 1977): 30, 34

Late Poetry

This section mainly includes selected reviews and excerpts of critical essays about the last ten years of Warren's poetic career, which began with "Can I See Arcturus from Where I Stand?," the section of new poems in his third volume of selected poems in 1976, and concluded with "Altitudes and Extensions," the section for new work in his fourth and last selected poems volume in 1985.

This first review is by J. D. McClatchy, a poet and critic at the beginning of his career.

Rare Prosperities
Review of *Selected Poems, 1923–1975*

Robert Penn Warren last made a selection of his poetry just over a decade ago. Thirteen small poems have been further trimmed from that previous collection; the three books he has written since then, plus ten additional poems, have been added. Such a gathering would be valuable in any case, as a comprehensive survey of Warren's character and achievement as a poet. Certainly it is his poetry on which rests his claim to greatness, though a decade ago few would have predicted that with real confidence. After all, so much else about this artist was distracting. During the half-century of his career, his contributions to nearly every aspect of the literary art have been recognized, but his novels now seem more sturdy than significant, and his essays more feisty than definitive. But the poetry he has produced in the past ten years has altered our sense of his career and its consequence, so that this *Selected Poems* is not merely a useful book but a truly important one. Given Warren's odd habit of arranging his work in reverse chronological order, his new work allows us to see his earlier verse as both an anticipation and an echo, the effect of which is to throw his recent poetry into an even higher relief and so to dramatize a remarkable event in the literature of our time by suddenly revealing to us a poet of unexpected and extraordinary power. Instances are rare of poets discovering such absolute strength so late in life, but a phrase from John Ashbery's *Three Poems* almost describes the phenomenon: "The great careers are like that: a slow burst that narrows to a final release." That is not exactly the right term for Warren, since his grand late release is not a narrowing but an expansion—of language into a heightened virtuosity and intensity, and of theme into his special version of the visionary mode. Still, one is eager to say, the great careers are like that. In fact, Warren's most recent and distinctive advocate, Harold Bloom, is now arguing in print that alone among living writers Warren deserves to be counted with the best American

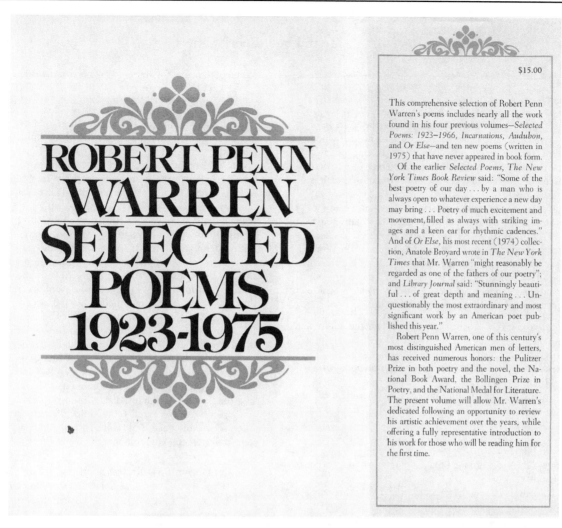

Dust jacket for Warren's third volume of selected poems, the first since Selected Poems, New and Old: 1923–1966
(Richland County Public Library)

poets of our century. The risks of both hyperbole and prophecy are well known, and I am less interested here in ranking Warren than in responding to the obvious excellence of his work.

There are three conspicuous phases to Warren's poetic career, and I often ask myself why I cannot read the first of those phases—the poems written before 1954—with much excitement or pleasure. Clearly "Bearded Oaks" or "Picnic Remembered" have long ago earned a place on the short-list of permanent poems. But I suspect that is less because they are worthy in themselves than because they are good poems of a certain kind. The kind of poem, that is, written by the group of Fugitives who were Warren's first peers and in whose company his work has since been discussed, compared, equated. John Crowe Ransom's wry (and overrated) elegies, and Allen Tate's severe odes and

indictments are the products of true neo-classical sensibilities. But the rough-hewn narratives and abstracted metaphysics of Warren's work from this period seem awkwardly restrained by the stiffness of their dry formalism and uncertain diction, as if to check the indulgence of his essentially American-Romantic imagination. The effect is like a bust carved in burl oak. Like so many other poets of that era, he was under the spell of Eliot, though less the lure of Eliot's techniques (which were superior) than of his tastes and attitudes. And so, in doctrine disguised as paradox, Warren lamented over "the inherited defect", and brooded on unredeemed human nature, on the violence and despair of a time "born to no adequate definition of terror." I am left unconvinced by such poses.

Once he abandoned cultural mythologies and confronted history more immediately, his verse

"Zestful but Minor"

In this excerpt from his review essay, Symons considered War-ren's Selected Poems 1923–1975 *and concluded that as a poet Warren "is interesting and zestful but minor."*

Mr. Warren's poems show qualities similar to those of his novels. He is splendid at telling stories, needs a good deal of space in which to achieve his effects, and produces often an oddly impersonal impression. There can be few collections in which the first person singular is used less than in *Selected Poems 1923–1975*. The early "Ballad of Billie Potts", about a couple of Kentucky villains who fail to rec-ognize their son when he returns to them after many years, and kill him as they have killed other travellers, has been much and rightly praised. "School Lesson Based on Word of Tragic Death of Entire Gillum Family" (their father killed them all with an ice-pick) shows the same narrative strength and deadpan manner. So does "Founding Fathers", which characteristically blends irony and admiration:

Some were given to study, read Greek in the forest and
    these
Longed for an epic to do their own deeds right honor:
Were Nestor by pigpen, in some tavern brawl played
    Achilles.
In the ring of Sam Houston they found, when he died, one
    word engraved: *Honor.*

Their children were broadcast, like millet seed flung in a
    wind-flare.
Wives died, were dropped like old shirts in some corner of
    country.
Said "Mister", in bed, the childbride; hadn't known what to
    find there;

Wept all morning for shame; took pleasure in silk; wore
    the keys to the pantry.

It is easy to underestimate this direct casual poetry, difficult to show its quality by quotation, because it is narrative force rather than the strength or subtlety of particular images that produces the effects. These are poems that really do need to be read aloud.

The ballads and narratives are only one side of Mr. Warren's poetic achievement. These selected poems have been ruthlessly pruned, with little left from his early collections, but they show the philo-sophical base, a kind of spoiled idealism, from which both poems and novels have been written. They show also the rhetorician who takes over too often in the novels, in phrases like "Time is always the new place / And no-place". Poems of philosophical reflec-tion, not primarily concerned with telling a story, tend to go off into abstractions about the nature of life, time, history. We can hear "history / Drip in darkness like a leaking pipe in the cellar", history has a "savvy insanity and wit", history "held to your breath clouds like a mirror", history "is what you can't / Resign from", etc. The comment is ungracious, in a time when so much tedious confessional verse is written, but Mr. Warren's avoidance of the personal often seems an evasion of reality, a way of saying not very much at considerable length.

–Julian Symons, "In the Southern Style," *TLS: The Times Literary Supplement,* 29 April 1977, p. 506

strengthens measurably, and the volumes from *Promises* (1957) through *Incarnations* (1968) give ample evidence of that. There are four long central poems that anchor this second period of his career, two celebrations and two elegies: *To a Little Girl, One Year Old, In a Ruined For-tress,* for his daughter; *Promises,* for his son; *Mortmain,* for his father; and *Tale of Time,* for his mother. Each of these moving familial poems is a part of Warren's effort during this time to explore "how cause flows backward from effect"–effects of either gain or loss, birth or death. His emphasis shifts now from guilt to grace; and even as grace, the reverse of guilt which gives form to experience, gives freedom, so too Warren's verse grows more supple and expressive, favoring sprawling forms whose dimensions and dynamics were determined by the life they record. It was during this period, too, that several characteristics of his work emerged more dis-tinctly–among them his juxtaposition or conflation of the narrative and the meditational, modes that most nearly parallel his instincts and notions. As a South-erner raised in a tradition of tale-telling and as a gifted

novelist, narratives seem a natural choice for Warren's poems, but behind the method is his deeper conviction that experience transpires in time and that an historical imagination is a prerequisite for an authentic poetry. This idea extends even to Warren's obsession with book-titles that include the dates of composition, and with arranging his poems into sequences that stress dra-matic interplay and cumulative force. And on the other hand, there is his penchant for discursive meditation, always inflected by his personal accent. As if experience and history were not finally self-sufficient, Warren often epitomizes them into conceptual dialectics. "To have truth", he says in one poem, "Something must be believed, / And repetition and congruence, / To say the least, are necessary." Truth, then, lies somewhere between the instance and eternity, the fact and the form. Poem by poem, Warren explores both sides of that border.

Incarnations was a transitional book, and an uneven one; indeed, all along Warren seems to have had trouble recognizing his own most successful work–

a question of taste, not talent. But I remember being astonished by several poems when that volume first appeared. They are still superb: "Natural History," "Myth on Mediterranean Beach: Aphrodite as Logos," "Masts at Dawn." The poet here begins to unfold the world's parable with the bold intellectual and sensuous command that has marked his poetry since that time. What might seem a surrender–"The world means only itself", concludes "Riddle in the Garden"–is actually his more complex project to find beauty in "the fume-track of necessity." "Masts at Dawn" offers the injunction another way: "We must try // To love so well the world that we may believe, in the end, in God." This necessity is urged in tones increasingly sharp, spare, eccentric, and often oracular. All of the work in this current phase of his career is spoken by this new voice. What before has struck the ear as stiff now sounds nearly scriptural. (In fact, I suspect that the Old Testament cadences are the strongest influence on Warren's new line.) The verse is now often free, the voice more formal. Some readers might consider it fustian or old-fashioned, but they would miss the strange, at times unsettling impact his use of inversion and stark enjambments produces. And there is always a marvelous lyrical counterpointing, such as this interlude from *Audubon:*

October: and the bear,
Daft in the honey-light, yawns.

The bear's tongue, pink as a baby's, out-crisps to the
   curled tip,
It bleeds the black blood of the blueberry.

The teeth are more importantly white
Than has ever been imagined.

The bear feels his own fat
Sweeten, like a drowse, deep to the bone.

Bemused, above the fume of ruined blueberries,
The last bee hums.

The wings, like mica, glint
In the sunlight.

He leans on his gun. Thinks
How thin is the membrane between himself and the world.

That quiet moment is one of the many superimposed images that make up *Audubon* and its cumulative definition of man, identified now with his passion, now with his fate. It is easy to see why the figure of Audubon–in his own words, "the Man Naked from his hand and yet free from acquired Sorrow"–must have been compelling to Warren, for he is at once artist and adventurer, always on the edge of things, wilderness or legend. The details War-

ren evokes from Audubon's history center on how "the world declares itself" to such a man, and portray how truth cannot be spoken or even embodied but "can only be enacted, and that in dream." What cannot be understood can be known. "What is love? / One name for it is knowledge." Poised between engagement and comprehension, between violence and awe, Audubon is Warren's most eloquent characterization, and his story has been shaped into one of the best long poems ever written by an American. One of the manifest advantages of this *Selected Poems* is that it makes *Audubon* easily available again.

Such a poem might have capped the career of any poet less unusual than Warren. Instead, he has gone on to extend and amplify his mastery in the collection titled *Or Else* (1974) and in the poems new to this volume. At first glance, *Or Else* seems a sort of anthology of Warren's tried and true: the down-home ballad, the political prayer, homages to dead writers, the rural narratives and metaphysical lyrics. He returns to all the familiar forms, but with a new emphasis and artistry. Throughout, he is driven by the "compulsion to try to convert what now is *was* / Back into what *is*." The book's blunt title, which implies both ultimatum and alternatives, is echoed in the staccato delivery of these overlapping attempts to sift lost evidence–his father's death, himself as a boy, a remembered chair or saw–for some sense of the continuity of a life's experiences. It is the noble Wordsworthian ambition to recapture redemptive spots of time: to wake, as Warren says, from "that darkness of sleep which / Is the past, and is / The self," with a question: "Have I learned how to live?" Warren often sounds such a moral note, but it can be deceptive since his concern is more existential–the necessarily defeated effort to restore the logic of the original dream, to resolve the innocence since fulfilled in "the realm of contingency."

Since "Time / Is the mirror into which you stare," the discovery of its history is always a self-definition–mirrored in a few controlling images: "Man lives by images. They / Lean at us from the world's wall, and Time's." Like the conjuring process of staring, there are certain images that are obsessive for Warren, that recur continually in his work and are at once its source and surface. The poem "Rattlesnake Country," for instance, ends among the dark roots of his "Indecipherable passion and compulsion":

I remember
The need to enter the night-lake and swim out toward
The distant moonset. Remember
The blue-tattered flick of white flame at the rock-hole
In the instant before I lifted up
My eyes to the high sky that shivered in its hot whiteness.

And sometimes–usually at dawn–I remember the cry on
   the mountain.

All I can do is to offer my testimony.

That mountain cry is sometimes a bird hung high in the sky, or a star, as in "Birth of Love," one of the very best poems Warren has ever written. On another of these night-swims, a man watches a woman climb ashore ahead of him to dry herself off with what light remains. It is a moment "nonsequential and absolute," a spot between times,

> . . . and in his heart he cries out that, if only
> He had such strength, he would put his hand forth
> And maintain it over her to guard, in all
> Her out-goings and in-comings, from whatever
> Inclemency of sky or slur of the world's weather
> Might ever be. In his heart
> He cries out. Above
>
> Height of the spruce-night and heave of the far mountain,
> he sees
> The first star pulse into being. It gleams there.
>
> I do not know what promise it makes to him.

An example of how obsessive these images are for the poet is the fact that this poem flashes back to a scene from a book now over thirty years old, *All the King's Men.* Jack Burden is remembering a storm-struck picnic with Anne and Adam Stanton when the three of them were teenagers. Jack and Anne are swimming under a dark sky: a gull crosses high over them. He watches her floating profile sharpened against "the far-off black trees."

> That was a picnic I never forgot.
> I suppose that that day I first saw Anne and Adam as separate, individual people, whose ways of acting were special, mysterious, and important. And perhaps, too, that day I first saw myself as a person. But that is not what I am talking about. What happened was this: I got an image in my head that never got out. We see a great many things and can remember a great many things, but that is different. We get very few of the true images in our heads of the kind I am talking about, the kind which become more and more vivid for us as if the passage of the years did not obscure their reality but, year by year, drew off another veil to expose a meaning which we had only dimly surmised at first. Very probably the last veil will not be removed, for there are not enough years, but the brightness of the image increases and our conviction increases that the brightness is meaning, or the legend of meaning, and without the image our lives would be nothing except an old piece of film rolled on a spool and thrown into a desk drawer among the unanswered letters.
> The image I got in my head that day was the image of her face lying in the water, very smooth, with the eyes closed, under the dark greenish-purple sky, with the white gull passing over.

That is a crucial gloss on the method and meaning of Warren's poetry. The brightening image which he has been unveiling for as long as his career is the deliberate mystery of identity, of the legends that alone define and sustain identity. His primary scene's most impressive aspect is the bird above—which in his poetry can be a hawk or star or sun, the symbol of power with which Warren has identified his ambitions from the very beginning, in a high Romantic gesture. One of the new poems here, the glorious "Evening Hawk," is its fullest testament:

> His wing
> Scythes down another day, his motion
> Is that of the honed steel-edge, we hear
> The crashless fall of stalks of Time.
>
> The head of each stalk is heavy with the gold of our error.
> Look! look! he is climbing the last light
> Who knows neither Time nor error, and under
> Whose eye, unforgiving, the world, unforgiven, swings
> Into shadow.
>
> Long now,
> The last thrush is still, the last bat
> Now cruises in his sharp hieroglyphics. His wisdom
> Is ancient, too, and immense. The star
> Is steady, like Plato, over the mountain.
>
> If there were no wind we might, we think, hear
> The earth grind on its axis, or history
> Drip in darkness like a leaking pipe in the cellar.

The rather anti-climactic mention of history at the end of this poem is meant to inhibit Warren's total giving of himself over to his ecstatic vision. But that is a measure of this poet's wisdom: to be able to encounter the sublime directly, and yet to temper his visionary impulse with a self-consciousness that includes both conscience and an eye for the incongruent detail. That hawk is, of course, the transcendental poet, but also a terrible divine presence, not unlike the "God" of Warren's late poetry who is an indifferent, unknowable, immanent principle of reality both feared and desired. Among the new poems, I would single out "A Way to Love God," "Loss, of Perhaps Love, in Our World of Contingency," and "Brotherhood in Pain" as especially powerful wrestlings with these themes of his "perfected pain of conscience."

In his *Democracy in America,* de Tocqueville predicted that the poetry of the future here would have as its subject not the senses but the inner soul and destinies of mankind, "man himself, taken aloof from his age and his country, and standing in the presence of Nature and of God, with his passions, his doubts, his rare prosperities, and inconceivable wretchedness." I can think of no better description of Robert Penn Warren. Among his contemporaries he is our most truly American poet, working in a large-scale imaginative tradition that continues to be vital source for poetry.

–J. D. McClatchy, "Rare Prosperities," *Poetry,* 131 (December 1977): 169–175

* * *

Harold Bloom on "Evening Hawk"

The hawk's motion is that of a scythe reaping time, but Warren has learned more than his distance from the hawk's state of being. I know no single line in him grander than the beautifully oxymoronic "The head of each stalk is heavy with the gold of our error." What is being harvested is our fault, and yet that mistake appears as golden grain. When the poet sublimely cries "Look! look!" to us, I do not hear a Yeatsian exultation, but rather an acceptance of a vision that will forgive us nothing, and yet does not rejoice in that stance. Emerson, Warren once snapped in a now notorious poem, "had forgiven God everything," which is true enough, since Emerson sensibly had forgiven himself everything, and God was identical with what was oldest in Emerson himself. Warren goes on forgiving God, and himself, nothing, and implies this is the only way to love God or the self. One does not imagine Ralph Waldo Emerson invoking the flight of a hawk as an image of the truth, but the poets of his tradition–notably Whitman, Stevens, and Hart Crane–have their own way of coming to terms with such an image. But, to Emersonians, the hawk is firmly part of Nature, of the Not-Me. Warren's trespasses upon a near-identity with the hawk clearly are no part of *that* American tradition.

–Harold Bloom, ed., *Robert Penn Warren*
(New York: Chelsea House, 1986),
p. 204

Intimations of Immortality
Review of *Now and Then*

If it were possible for William Wordsworth to review *Now and Then,* Robert Penn Warren's 12th collection of poems, he might find much to praise about the volume. Warren, he might point out, is a poet speaking to men in their own language, using rustic settings of the American South and images culled from nature. Any opacity, he might argue, stems not from "poetic diction" but from Warren's use of symbol, the heart of Romantic utterance, and from his thoughts "that do often lie too deep for tears." In many poems, Wordsworth would discern the pattern of *Tintern Abbey* and the *Immortality Ode:* A place from the past is fondly recollected, an emotion savored and relived–but with a fundamental difference.

Unlike Wordsworth, Warren does not yearn to bring back the splendor in the grass, the glory in the flower. Glory, Warren repeatedly tells us, is "the only thing that matters"; it lies, however, not behind us but before us. While Wordsworth and other Romantics eventually traded glory for despair or philosophy, Warren alights on glory at every turn in past, present, and future through what the Romantic poets called the shaping power of the imagination.

Imagination, the Romantics theorized, dissolves, diffuses, and dissipates experience to recreate it. Warren's definition seems mined from the Kentucky hills, his birthplace: Imagination is "only / The lie we must learn to live by, if ever / We mean to live at all." More homespun, less polished and abstruse, Warren's wry country wisdom succinctly sums up imagination's role in these poems.

By likening imagination to a "lie," Warren underlines its ability to transform utterly: the way a snake is reborn after sloughing off its dry, translucent skin; the way winter moonlight flooding a room bleaches its mundane objects into lustrous trophies.

Everywhere imagination bestows largess, life, and grace, converting mere memory into a glorious vision set in plaster by Piero della Francesca:

> *Well, what I remember most*
> *In a world long Time-pale and powdered . . .*
> *Is how K, through lane-dust or meadow,*
> *Seemed never to walk, but float*
> *With a singular joy and silence*
> *In his cloud of bird dogs, like angels*
> *With their eyes on his eyes like God . . . .*

In "Red-Tail Hawk and Pyre of Youth," the most successful poem in the collection, imagination transforms a boyhood experience into a rapturous encounter with the supernatural. Atop a ridge crest, on an afternoon "flooded in silver," a young hunter, like a youthful mariner armed with a 30-30, shoots a red-tailed hawk and is sent reeling by the consequences of his act. Wedded forever to the sky by this action, the boy feels his "heart leaping in joy past definition." Retrieved, stuffed, and mounted, the hawk, prominently placed in the young boy's room, gazes all the while at the growing boy with intense, glittering eyes. Years later, as a man, the speaker returns home to burn the hawk in a sacrificial pyre. He envisions another such union, praying for a second miraculous vision, at death, to bring him "the truth in blood-marriage of earth and air."

A Wordsworth or a Coleridge would movingly have recalled the hawk's slaughter and spiraling fall, but the intent would doubtless have been to recover the freshness of the first dream, to grieve its loss, to glean a lesson of life from the experience. Warren's expectations of past events are not so unrealistic. "Some dreams come true, some no," he muses, and, recalling how his heart leapt up, he nonetheless anticipates another dazzling theophany.

Unraveling the possibility of limitless bliss from the "world's tangled and hieroglyphic beauty" is Warren's poetic mission. In poem after poem, Warren's persona sets out on the quintessential Romantic quest: He yearns to name the world, to fathom its mystery:

Do you
Remember that Jacob Boehme saw
Sunlight flash on a pewter platter on
The table, and his life was totally changed?

Is the name of God nothing more than
The accidental flash on a platter? But what is accident?

On hawk wing, in heat lightning, on moonlit stream, or in star-filled sky, Warren repeatedly mirrors a visionary gleam akin to ecstasy. Yet he knows full well that he can catch only a glimmer, that his poems are nets that miss the essence. His young men grow sage and mellow, not bitter and disillusioned, and they realize that glory's consummation can be achieved only through death:

Again the owl calls, and with some sadness
*   you wonder*
If at last, when the air-scything shadow
*   descends*
And needles claw-clamp through gut, heart
*   and brain*
Will ecstasy melting with terror create the last
*   little cry?*
Is God's love but the last and most mysterious
*   word for death?*

The persona of "Ah, Anima!," having run forth screaming until "nameless," discards the husk of mortality to leap "into the blind and antiseptic anger of air." Warren portrays death as the dramatic event when:

Without warning, by day or night,
*   the appalling*
White blaze of God's Great Eye sweeps
*   the sky, History*
Turns tail and scuttles back
*   to its burrow*
Like a groundhog caught in a speeding
*   sportscar's headlight.*

Even the past—which Warren says elsewhere is essential to literature—is reduced to irrelevance in the face of Apocalyptic glory.

Readers of Warren's poems will rediscover many familiar nature images in this collection—hawks, buzzards, stars, snakes, stones, owls, skulls, moonlight, hills—but here they are changed into a new creation. This line, which appears in "The Mad Druggist" (1966)–". . . and the hawk, like philosophy, hung without motion, high, / where the sun-blaze of wind ran"–is alchemized into a mystical experience in "Red-Tail Hawk and Pyre of Youth." Skulls and jawbones, which everywhere dot Warren's earlier poems, become in "American Portrait: Old Style" this menacing image:

How the teeth in Time's jaw all snag
*   backward*
And whatever enters therein
Has less hope of remission than shark meat

Wordsworth, who vigorously maintained that a part of poetry's pleasure depends upon the meter, would find Warren's poetic line a marvel of versatility. Those few poems that rhyme do so with astonishing and apt felicity. The rhyme scheme in "Old Flame," for example, strikes just the proper note of droll recall. The enjambments of "Love Recognized" personify love's whimsical excitement. Jaggedness is the key to the surprise in these lines:

When the tooth cracks–zing!–it
Is like falling in love, or like
Remembering your mother's face when she–
*   and you only*
A child–smiled, or like
Falling into Truth.

After his own easy fashion, Warren, forever circling like one of his archetypal hawks, soars higher and higher toward–what? Religious experience? Mystical union? Ecstatic death? At 73, Warren is too shrewd to say outright. But he leaves us with an image that graphically intimates his vision of immortality. His persona, an older man, now looking forward and upward, marvels at the wild geese flying in perfect V upon V. He does not yet know who he is, but these geese, which he calls sky- and star-striders, rise and "know / The path of pathlessness, with all the joy / Of destiny fulfilling its own name." Face uplifted, arms outstretched, the speaker gazes heavenward, himself suddenly transformed, and his heart ". . . impacted with a fierce impulse / To unwordable utterance– / Toward sunset, at a great height."

And so the book ends. We wonder what will follow for Warren, great "sky-strider, star-strider." We wonder, grateful that "God / Has allowed man the grandeur of certain utterances."

–Paul Piazza, "Intimations of Immortality,"
The Chronicle Review, 30 October 1978, R–11

* * *

This review is by Peter Stitt, who later examined Warren's poetry, along with the work of Richard Wilbur, William Stafford, Louis Simpson, and James Wright, in The World's Hieroglyphic Beauty: Five American Poets *(1985).*

The Grandeur of Certain Utterances
Review of *Now and Then*

John Berryman, like many poets at transitional points in their careers, once expressed a longing for

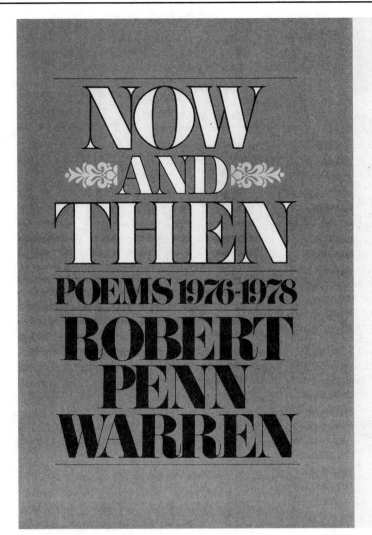

$8.95

"Warren . . . alone among living writers ranks with the foremost American poets of the century: Frost, Stevens, Hart Crane, Williams, Pound, Eliot. Reading through this collection, arranged in reverse chronology, one discovers Warren is that rarest kind of major poet: he has never stopped developing from his origins up to his work-in-progress."

These words are from Harold Bloom's review in *The New Leader* of Mr. Warren's most recent book of poetry, *Selected Poems: 1923–1975*. Of the same book Hilton Kramer, in *The New York Times Book Review*, wrote: ". . . among the finest poets of our time, and one who speaks to us with a moral intensity few others have even attempted." In the Philadelphia *Sunday* and *Evening Bulletin*, the poet Daniel Hoffman said: ". . . his work stands unparalleled among his contemporaries." And in *Poetry*, J. D. McClatchy: "Among his contemporaries he is our most truly American poet, working in a large-scale imaginative tradition that continues to be the vital source for poetry."

Now and Then provides strong confirmation of these opinions. All of these poems were written after *Selected Poems* had been prepared for the printer, and though most of them have appeared in a great variety of magazines, none has had previous book publication.

Dust jacket for the volume that earned Warren his second Pulitzer Prize in poetry (Richland County Public Library)

a late blossoming into poetic greatness–similar to that of the man he called an "opsimath": W. B. Yeats. Whatever the quality of his earlier work, Berryman never quite achieved this goal; instead of blossoming, his poetry seems to have withered at the end. The pattern he desired is, surely, a rare one, given only to a fortunate few. As the evidence continues to accumulate, book after book, year after year, it becomes increasingly obvious that Robert Penn Warren is a notable example of the breed. The pattern of his career is an interesting one. Early, in college and for many years after, he thought of himself primarily as a poet. The work he produced then–technically accomplished and with many admirers–looks, in retrospect and by comparison to his more recent efforts, relatively wooden. Then for ten years, beginning in about 1944, he wrote almost entirely fiction–novels and short stories. He began

many poems then, he has said, but was unable to complete them because they were competing with his stories: "Many times the germ of a short story could also be the germ of a poem, and I was wasting mine on short stories." In the middle fifties he gave up writing stories, and the poems have been flowing ever since. Beyond its historical and personal relevance, this anecdote points up an important artistic truth–Warren's poems almost always have a narrative basis; he achieves his lyricism and conveys his human and philosophical insights by telling stories in verse.

The dominating characteristic of this latest volume, *Now and Then: Poems 1976–1978*–that which sets it apart from earlier books–is a heightened sense of lyricism. Of course Warren has never been an entirely unmusical or antimusical poet. His work has simply reflected the dominant trend of twenti-

Warren on Porter

In his evaluation of Warren's career as a critic, Monroe K. Spears provides this précis of his essay on Katherine Anne Porter.

Warren's introduction to *Katherine Anne Porter: A Collection of Critical Essays* (1979) is one of his finest essays—perhaps second only to that on *Nostromo* and, like it, revealing much about Warren's own aims and ideals as writer. There is an apt comparison to Faulkner: "Both regarded the present as a product of the past, to be understood in that perspective, and both, though repudiating the romance of the past, saw in it certain human values now in jeopardy, most of all in jeopardy the sense of the responsible individual, and at the same time man's loss of his sense of community and sense of basic relation to nature." This is part of Porter's deeper theme, "the conviction that reality, the 'truth,' is never two-dimensional, is found in process not in stasis. All this gives the peculiar vibrance and the peculiar sense of a complex but severely balanced form to all the stories." She reveals inner tensions and complexity of motives, but "never confounds the shadowy and flickering shapes of the psychological situation with vagueness of structure in the fiction itself." She has the gift of "touching the key of feeling," but never exploits it: "Certainly, she never indulges in random emotionality; she knows that the gift must never be abused or it will vanish like fairy gold." "And always feeling appears against a backdrop of two other factors, the strain of irony that infuses the work (even though the writer knows that the exploitation of irony is as dangerous as that of feeling) and the rigor of form. The writer has some austerity of imagination that gives her a secret access to the spot whence feeling springs. She can deny herself, and her own feelings, and patiently repudiate the temptation to exploit the feeling of the reader, and therefore can, when the moment comes, truly enter into the heart of a character. One hesitates to think what price may have been paid for this priceless gift." "One feels that for her the act of composition is an act of knowing, and that, for her, knowledge, imaginatively achieved, is, in the end, life." "If a deep stoicism is the underlying attitude of this fiction, it is a stoicism without grimness or arrogance, and though shot through with irony and aware of a merciless evil in the world, yet capable of gaiety, tenderness, and sympathy, and its ethical center is found in those characters who . . . have the toughness to survive, but who survive by a loving sense of obligation to others, this sense being in the end, only a full affirmation of the life-sense, a joy in strength. . . . Like all strong art, this work is, paradoxically, both a question asked of life and a celebration of life; and the author knows in her bones that the more corrosive the question asked, the more powerful may be the celebration."

—Monroe K. Spears, "The Critics Who Made Us,"
Sewanee Review, 94 (January–March, 1986):
106–107

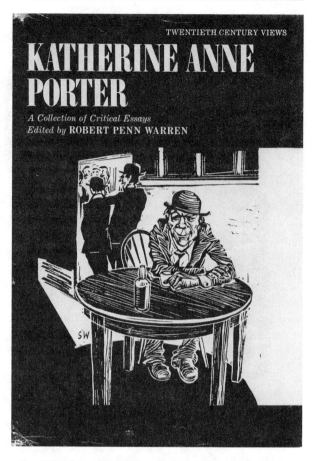

Dust jacket for a 1977 collection that includes Warren's introduction and his essay titled "Irony with a Center" (Richland County Public Library)

eth- century verse away from the mellifluent. Nor, on the other hand, has he ever practiced the plain style; a Southerner born and bred, he has a deeply-ingrained sense of rhetorical elevation; he knows how to make his poems sound as if they matter. What this has meant for Warren in recent volumes is something we might call the interrupted style. The rhythms present in a book like *Or Else* tend not to flow, feel clotted, largely because—perhaps in an effort to be absolutely accurate—the poet continually interrupts himself. His statements are qualified, clarified, encrusted with logical precision—as in these lines, among the best in the book: "But let us note, too, how glory, like gasoline spilled / On the cement in a garage, may flare, of a sudden, up // In a blinding blaze, from the filth of the world's floor."

Syntactically, the present volume shows a small step in the direction of simplification. But this is made up for by a greater rhythmical complexity. In an effort to achieve strong lines, a muscular verse, Warren has placed unusual reliance upon spondaics, upon jammed stresses. Important words are set together, uninterrupted by articles, conjunctions, prepositions: "To some wild white peak dreamed westward." Everywhere there is a heavy use of hyphenated words—which also jam stresses together: "past the last rock-slide at ridge-top and stubborn, / Raw tangle of cedar, I clambered, breath short and spit white // From lung depth." Such density is present everywhere in the volume, and gives an impressive weight to the poems.

Lyricism is everywhere here—from two-word phrases—Warren describes the grave at one point as the "grievous chasm"—through passages of various lengths, up to entire poems. I want to quote some lines of great beauty before going on to other things. Here is how the coming of day is described in "First Dawn Light":

> . . . Then, sudden, the glory, heart-full and ear-full,
>
> For triggered now is the mysterious mechanism
> Of the forest's joy, by temperature or by beam,
> And until a sludge-thumb smears the sunset's prism,
> You must wait to resume, in night's black hood, the reality
>   of dream.

In "Heart of Autumn," there comes a moment when geese spontaneously take off and turn to the South:

> . . . they know
> When the hour comes for the great wing-beat. Sky-strider,
> Star-strider—they rise, and the imperial utterance,
> Which cries out for distance, quivers in the wheeling sky.

"Heart of the Backlog" is a disturbing poem which envisions an escape into the emptiness of snowscape; Frostian in concept, perhaps, but not in cadence:

> Has the thought ever struck you to rise and go forth—yes,
>   lost
> In the whiteness—to never look upward, or back, only on,
> And no sound but the snow-crunch, and breath
> Gone crisp like the crumpling of paper? Listen!
> Could that be the creak of a wing-joint gigantic in
>   distance?

We could spend a good deal of time tracing the intricate sound patterns which interlock the words in these passages and make them poetry—chiefly, assonance and consonance reinforced by rhythm. We know writers who've retired at thirty, tired old men—while Robert Penn Warren, past the age of seventy, boldly strides forth, wearing new clothes.

The book is less surprising in its thematic concerns. As he did in *Or Else,* Warren here looks in two directions—to the past and to the future. In the first section, "Nostalgic," he recounts episodes from his earlier life, while in the longer second section, "Speculative," he turns philosophical. Because of this imbalance in favor of thought, the volume on the whole is more abstract than is usual in Warren's work. And yet he remains an unequivocal lover of the world's body, and even in the more theoretical poems there is generally still a concrete, narrative base. The chillingly impressive "Last Laugh," for example, is based on the life of Mark Twain—indeed, it captures his tortured personality better in a small scope than anything I have ever seen. The steering idea of the poem is Twain's conviction that "God was dead." The laugh comes at the end:

> And married rich, too, with an extra spin to the ball;
>
> For Livy loved God, and he'd show her the joke, how they
>   lied.
> Quite a tussle it was, but hot deck or cold, he was sly
> And won every hand but the last. Then at her bedside
> He watched dying eyes stare up at a comfortless sky,
>
> And was left alone with his joke, God dead, till he died.

The story is strikingly, shockingly, strong—and Warren's writing is at least its equal—indeed, the power of the verse may be said to create, in a sense, the power of the theme.

Not all the poems are up to this high standard—even Randall Jarrell never found a poet who was struck by lightning on every page of his book. And some of the things which have bothered critics of Warren before are found again here. But everytime the reader lapses into a comfortable lull for three or four pages, Warren can be counted on to slap him awake with an outstanding poem. Among the best are "Orphanage Boy," "Red-Tail Hawk and Pyre of Youth" (which almost leadens to prose in its middle then flares into gold at the end), "Dream," "Heat Lightning," "Rather Like a Dream," and more. My favorite, and one I would place among the very best poems Warren has written, is "Waiting." I will quote the entire poem, knowing this won't strain your patience—far from it; it is a poem which deserves, demands, the widest possible circulation:

> You will have to wait. Until it. Until
> The last owl hoot has quivered to a
>
> Vibrant silence and you realize that there is no breathing
> Beside you, and dark curdles toward dawn of no dawn.
>   Until
>
> Drouth breaks, too late to save the corn,
> But not too late for flood, and the hobbled cow, stranded

29.

Trodden by angels, triumphed on by saints.
But still he screamed.

But then to Nîmes I came, and that Square House --

R.P.W.: I've been to Nîmes -- long back, how many years?
There's good wine there, black,
Black as ink -- you know, for you once had it there.
Three sous the bottle, you wrote you paid for it.
It costs a lot more now, but worth it still.
I drank the wine, slept in a decent bed,
And the next morning stood in the sun-gilt place,
Indeed, And stared at your "Maison Quarrée."

JEFFERSON: I stood in the place. There is no way
For words to put that authoritative reserve and glorious frugality.
I saw the law of Rome and the light
Of just proportion and the heart's harmony.
And I said: "Here is a shape that shines, set
On a grundel of Nature's law, a rooftree
So innocent of imprecision
That a man may enter in to find his freedom
Like air breathed, and all his mind
Would glow like a coal under bellows -- this
Is a precinct where the correctness of human aspiration
Bespeaks the charmed space."

R.P.W.: So you find evidence for aspiration
In such a heap of organized rubble
(I call it cold and too obviously mathematical)
Thrown up by a parcel of those square-jawed looters
From the peninsula, stuck in a foreign land?

*

Page from a draft of Brother to Dragons (A New Version) *(Yale Collection of American Literature, Beinecke Rare Book and Manuscript Library)*

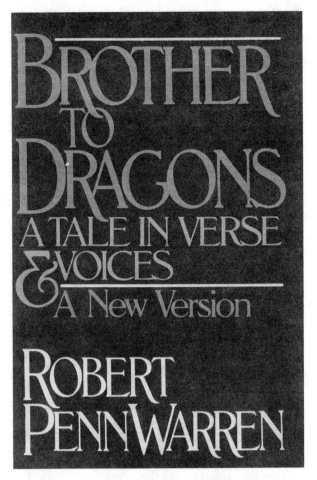

Cover for the book about the savage murder of a slave by two of Thomas Jefferson's nephews. This version was published in 1979, twenty-six years after the original (Special Collections, Western Kentucky University Libraries).

On a sudden islet, gargles in grief in the alder-brake. Until
The doctor enters the waiting room, and

His expression betrays all, and you wish
He'd take his goddam hand off your shoulder. Until

The woman you have lived with all the years
Says, without rancor, that life is the way life is, and she
   cannot
Remember when last she loved you, and had lived the lie
   only
For the children's sake. Until you become uncertain of
   French

Irregular verbs, and by a strange coincidence begin to take
   Catholic
Instruction from Monsignor O'Malley, who chews a hang-
   nail. Until

You realize, to your surprise, that our Savior died for us all,
And as tears gather in your eyes, you burst out laughing,

For the joke is certainly on Him, considering
What we are. Until

You pick the last alibi off, like a scab, and
Admire the inwardness, as beautiful as inflamed

Flesh, or summer sunrise. Until
You remember that, remarkably, common men have done
   noble deeds. Until

It grows on you that, at least, God
Has allowed man the grandeur of certain utterances.

True or not. But sometimes true.

"The grandeur of certain utterances"—such as these poems, which, in their lyrical and human wisdom, ring consistently true. Don't ask me how Warren does it after all these years—patience for sure, genius no doubt. But at least we can be certain of what he is, after all the novels, the stories, the essays, biographies, social and critical commentaries—he is the poet, an authentic singer whose every utterance makes melody. He has earned this highest praise.
   —Peter Stitt, "The Grandeur of Certain Utterances,"
      Georgia Review (Spring 1979): 214–217

* * *

Warren often sent drafts of his poems to his friend William Meredith, whose books include the Pulitzer Prize–winning Practical Accounts: New and Selected Poems *(1987). Meredith provided this critique of Warren's manuscript of* Being Here: Poetry 1977–1980. *Warren made handwritten notes on Meredith's typed letter, often writing "yes" beside his friend's criticisms.*

William Meredith to Warren, 2 July 1979

Dear Red,
   Not foreseeing immediately the hoped-for visit to W. Wardsboro; and having had this luminous typescript (with additions arriving at irregular intervals) for some seven weeks; and feeling, besides, that it is more useful to have written comments, I essay some remarks about the book.
   It is organized so that the poems distinguish themselves in the reader's mind, it moves and changes pace. The two poems which frame it—"October Picnic" and "Passersby" are as lovely as anything you've written, and hold the book in shape. (If one can assume anything of a reader, it is that the opening and closing are given double significance, as poems which bow to each other and enclose what they enclose). The dedication fixes another pair of poems at beginning and end: "When Life Begins" and "Safe in Shade," the latter a

Comparing the Versions of *Brother to Dragons*

In September 1979 Random House published Brother to Dragons (A New Version). *In this excerpt from his interpretation of the new work, Lewis P. Simpson notes some of the changes Warren made when he returned to the 1953 version.*

Of the many changes Robert Penn Warren has made in the new version of *Brother to Dragons,* I think the substantial change in the introductory speech by Jefferson at the very beginning may be the most significant. This new-version speech is in two "sections" (Warren's term). In the first Jefferson speaks in the first person:

My name is Thomas Jefferson. Thomas. I
Lived. Died. But
Dead, cannot lie down in the
Dark. Cannot, though dead, set
My mouth to the dark stream that I may unknow
All my knowing. Cannot, for if,
Kneeling in that final thirst, I thrust
Down my face, I see come glimmering upward,
White, white out of the absolute dark of depth,
My face. And it is only human.

In the second section of his initial speech, Jefferson speaks in the second person, presumably to the reader:

Have you ever tried to kiss that face in the mirror?
Or—ha, ha—has it ever tried to kiss you? Well,
You are only human. Is that a boast?

(1979, p. 5)

In the old version of *Brother to Dragons,* Jefferson says simply:

My name is Thomas Jefferson. I am he
Whose body is yet under the triple boast,
On my green mountain—

He gets no further before R. P. W. interrupts:

Yes, I've read your boast
Cut in the stone where your body still waits
On your green mountain, off in Virginia, awaiting
I suppose, whatever fulfillment of the boast
May yet be.

(1953, p. 5)

In the new version R. P. W.'s response after the rather long and uninterrupted first speech by Jefferson is more succinct:

Well, I've read your boast
Cut in stone, on the mountain, off in Virginia.

(1979, p. 5)

The abbreviated response is, I take it, decreed by the rather dire implications of the beginning for the tone and movement of the whole poem. By leaving out "whatever fulfillment of the boast/ May yet be," the poet foreshadows a subtle reduction (as contrasted with the old version) in his allowance for (perhaps we say in his tolerance of) "hope"—hope, that is, for its amelioration as, if one may put it so, a valid response to the human condition. This severe attitude toward such a fundamental spiritual trait of human kind—a trait that has often been considered to be the very essence of human kind in America—evidently results from Warren's intensified attention in the new poem to his lifelong search for the meaning of the self. Basically, I think, in the new-version *Brother to Dragons* Warren's search culminates in the compelling realization that the meaning of the self is to be discovered in the self's isolation in history; or, to put it in a contrary yet complementary way, in the isolation of history in the self.

. . . .

Although *Brother to Dragons* does not present a resolution of the meaning of the self in America—and is indeed primarily a struggle for the meaning of the American self, in which the polarities of thought and action, dream and reality are pronounced—the tendency of the argument is toward a revelation of the self as an entity. A complex of warring forces, the self is yet an entity in that it will do anything to survive. There is a glory in the definition of the American self in Warren's vision, but it is not a comfortable glory.

—Lewis P. Simpson, "The Concept of the Historical Self in *Brother to Dragons," Robert Penn Warren's* Brother to Dragons: *A Discussion,* edited by James A. Grimshaw Jr. (Baton Rouge: Louisiana State University Press, 1983), pp. 244–245, 249

recent one, I gather, and one of the fine poems in the book. The dedicatory dialogue between grandson and grandfather, and these two poems, reinforce and gloss the title you have given the book. Though the long questions the book asks go beyond the relationship established there, the character of the speaker refers to that boy and that dedicatee.

In my latest reading I marked the poems that I feel are the strongest. They are numerous, but more

interesting is the way they fall irregularly throughout the Contents, but never far enough apart to suggest a dead place. I'll list them at the end, as well as the poems which I think are less strong, conspicuously, or weak. You and I have talked about poems, yours and mine and others', long enough so that you know where my sensibility is always going to be blind to some of the things you do. I tell you what I don't like because I think I may still be right, not just to shame the devil. If not right, anyhow representative of a response which you may want to administer more effectively.

For example, two words, in two poems far apart in the book, strike me as having the effect of self-parody. unassuagable grief, in "Boyhood in Tobacco Country" seems to me wrong in the same way that ineluctable shift (60 pages later) is wrong, to wit, in context. They are both extravagant words, in context, and used (to my understated ear) for rhetoric, to make a bright Robert Penn Warren noise in a small verbal crisis, where it would be very hard to find a better word. You will notice that I don't suggest either word can simply be omitted: I'd like to see them replaced by the right words. When you use such words precisely, they shine ineluctably, otherwise I wouldn't quarrel with these two uses.

"Platonic Drowse," because it's recent, is probably dear to you. It's strong, god knows. I'm not sure it's exactly your poem. There's some Lawrentian fall-out in the air these days, and some readers will take the content for the poem, as they take violence for force. This is only by way of saying that whether or not it's your poem, it's not mine.

In "Grackles, Goodbye!" I'd omit the exclamation point in the title. It's earned in the last stanza, but seems a little shrill in the title. I feel the title of "Why?" undercuts the poem a little, where you need the word each of the six times it occurs. My suggestion would be to call the poem "Why have I wandered the asphalt of midnight," if another title doesn't suggest itself. (You know that I know that you know what you're doing, and what you want. I don't expect you to do what I suggest, but only to consider it. Sometimes my tone sounds as though we were in an (ugh) writers' workshop. We're really just sitting around the table at Shaktu, after luncheon.)

I don't care what Howard Moss says, I'd like to revise the last line of that splendid poem called "August Moon" to read

And to speak not a word.

"Empty White Blotch" puzzles me, and I gather that it puzzles you, because of the trouble you had deciding where to put it in the book. I like the sound of it (it would be a good Rorschak [sic] test to see how many of the poems a reader chooses as favorites are rhymed poems), but I find it a little melodramatic, the use of blasphemy more sensational than convincing. Here again, you should remember who's talking. And let me jump ahead to

"Lord Jesus." (My copy of this has "to be revised" written on it.) This seems to me the weakest poem in the book and has the same dread humorlessness that Hemingway's "Today is Friday" has, which is hell of a mean thing to say about anything. I think both of these poems grab at their central emotion through a ready-made symbol, one which you are not sufficiently flexible with (as some of our good Catholic friends would be) to make your own. (There's a very funny Alan Dugan poem, where the speaker drives the first nail in, nailing the left hand to the cross, and then says, I can't do everything by myself.) Well, like I say, I'm down on these two poems, probably for different reasons than your parish priest but not necessarily any more intelligent ones.

Never one to hesitate, I have a suggestion for a considerable revision of the Old Norwalk Dump poems, which in their present state are very fine. It occurred to me, reading them the first time, that there is a mild anti-climax in their order. I would reverse them, but in order to make that sequence lucid and consequential I would change the personal pronoun (which would entail changing the title) to the third person:

He finishes the Times. Shuts eyes. His head,
Inside, flickers like TV in a dark hospital room.

This is the world. Or is it? He hears
The morning curdle of traffic on their pleasant etc etc

If the suggestion would strengthen the poem, it would not strengthen it a lot. I think it would strengthen it enough to be worth the trouble. A title could make it clear that the he of the poem is not RPW.

"Cocktail Party" strikes me as a brittle insight, one of the poems I'd be happy to see omitted. Coming directly after such a powerful poem as "Vision," whose theme it is probably intended to play again and reinforce, it has for me the effect of undercutting. I think it is a poem where you let the tone carry away the possible complexity of the theme.

"Part of a Short Story" is the last poem that I'm going to throw rocks at. Because I sometimes write poems, and sometimes write short stories, I believe the title. I believe you have simply tried to make an urgent scene, originally rendered in prose, into a brief narrative poem. It's an ok narrative poem—the content is, in fact, so ok that a less careful reader than me might pass over the flawed prosody. But the effect on a careful reader is liable to be that he has struck some pages of very low-metabolism

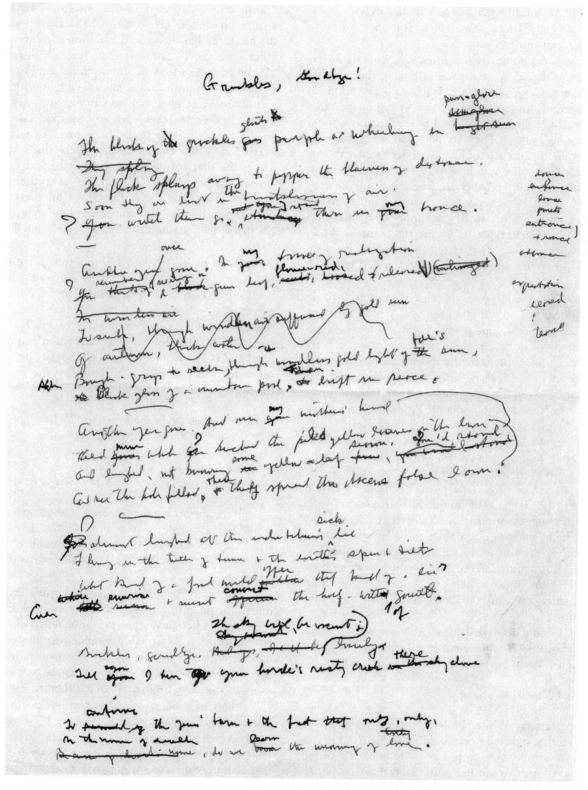

Draft of a poem that was included in Being Here *(Yale Collection of American Literature, Beinecke Rare Book and Manuscript Library)*

poetry. It does not read as well as any page of Brother to Dragons, to my ear.

"The Cross" is a tremendous poem. "Truth"—the brevity is of the essence of its considerable success. I marvel at how right you are (mostly, mostly) about sensing the scale of your poems.

In line 6 of "Weather Report" I would omit only.

I like "No Bird Does Call" when you read it to me, or gave it to me, last fall when Eudora was here. I like it now.

In "Timeless, Twinned" Line 12, I hear: or the nag of history, and for two reasons, colloquialism but also sense.

"Synonyms" is well-placed, between two strong short poems, itself a strong long poem.

I think I like "Ballad of your Puzzlement." The echo of "Preparations" (I think that's a later title put on the anonymous 17th C. poem: And if his sovereign (gracious?) majesty our lord, etc) at start and finish, framing the ballad-like imagery of the film—this works well.

"Aging Man in Woodland . . ." is a real tour de force, the B-rhymes.

"Better than Counting Sheep" is maybe my favorite in the book.

If I had to say why "A Few Axioms . . ." isn't one of my favorites, you could probably say it for me better. The character who speaks the poem adopts a looseness of tone which I feel is untrustworthy for achieving the precision of lyric poetry. The fact is the poem by and large does achieve that accuracy, and certainly belongs in the book, and where it is. I am simply not at ease with the good old boy tone of parts 2, 3 and 4, a tone I had trouble with in several sections of the Ode a couple of years ago. This is a place where I disqualify myself because it seems simply a matter of taste and not a critical point I'm making.

"Prairie Harvest" is a marvelous poem. "Can you devise an adequate definition of self, whatever you are?"—one of the themes of the book, of your books, earned as the last line of a wonderfully coiled poem.

"Acquaintance with Time in Autumn." I like "Antimony" better, for what it does. The texture or density of this poem is occasionally a little slack, to my ear. That is not a useful criticism, I know, unless you can hear it the way I hear it and tighten up a line or two. Doubtless you read it differently and better than I do.

"Passersby on a Snowy Night." What can I say? It has begun to memorize itself already. I'll stick my neck out and say I think you're a pretty good poet.

I don't know where to place "Auto Da Fé," which came after everything else. I could probably figure out where you'll put it, but I'd rather not play games like that. (Between "Lessons of History" and "Eagle Descending," is what I guessed). It's a fine, lucid flesh poem, a world away from "Platonic Drowse", which you probably are still more enamored of. Tell me where you're putting it in the book.

A niggle or two: In "When Life Begins" I can't read the second line of stanza 6. In "Why?", stanza three, the great bear needs an apostrophe. In "Deeper": Webster says cotton-mouth or cottonmouth, and Yankees will appreciate a hyphen. The first line of "Weather Report" should end with a comma, not a period.

I had a lovely time with the book, when I finally found time to read it as it deserves, and I wouldn't read it before that.

I've got a poem or two of my own now, and will send them along when they're ready. And you never have said diddlysquat about the poem I sent you with the long epigraph from "Recollection in Upper Ontario." Lost it, I'll bet.

Have you heard from Dan Boorstin about coming to the do for Archie MacLeish in October?

Richard has started work in pediatrics at St. John's Hospital in Brooklyn. It's a relief, after three years of medical studies, to have almost a 9 to 5 job, and I hope he'll be up here most weekends. At his graduation he read Whitman and Dr. Williams and said that Walt was the first P.A. (physicians assistant) from Brooklyn.

When I see a chance, I'll call and come visit you.

If the xerox place is open, I'll make a copy of these sassy pages, so you can respond by mail, if there's something you want me to amplify. (Or eat.)

Love to yourself and Eleanor and anybody like that who's with you,

as always,

Bill.

ps The poems I marked as strongest: October Picnic, When Life Begins, Recollection . . . , The Only Poem, August Moon, Sila, Vision, The Cross, Antimony . . . , Aging Man . . . , Better than Counting Sheep, Prairie Harvest, Passersby on a Snowy Night, Auto da Fé. Lots of others got A, but those got A+

–Beinecke Rare Book and Manuscript Library

* * *

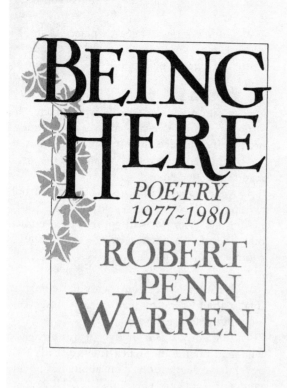

$8.95

The fifty poems in *Being Here*, Robert Penn Warren's largest new volume to date, were written in the two years following the completion of *Now and Then: Poems 1976–1978*, which was awarded the Pulitzer Prize for Poetry for 1978 and reinforced his position as this country's preeminent poet. It is a remarkable fact that in his seventies he has become more productive, and that his recent poems are not only more widely read than his early work but generally acclaimed as being even better:

"In the midst of his long careers as a university professor and prolific writer of superb novels, stories and essays, that he should have found the time and creative energy to write *so many* varied and wonderful poems is astonishing enough. But that now . . . he is writing in a more expansive vein, and with more youthful immediacy and deeper feeling than perhaps ever before, is nothing less than a joy."—*Book World*

"Good poets are rare. And good poets who manage to prolong their period of highest creativity for more than a few incandescent years are rarer still. But poets who continue to produce excellent verse well into old age are perhaps rarest of all. Membership in the last category is sparse: Thomas Hardy, William Butler Yeats, and a very few others. But it is becoming increasingly obvious that Robert Penn Warren deserves inclusion here, for at an age when the creative sap has dried up in most poets, Warren . . . seems to be reveling in a broadening and deepening of his powers."
—Richmond *News Leader*

Dust jacket for the first of two volumes of poems Warren published in 1980 (Richland County Public Library)

This review is by the poet and novelist James Dickey, author of Deliverance *(1970). Dickey later wrote that Warren's "friendship and example" were crucial and "never endingly fruitful" for him. Warren dedicated* Chief Joseph of the Nez Perce *(1982) to Dickey.*

Robert Penn Warren's Courage
Review of *Being Here*

In the excitement of young men coming together to form a new group of poets–later to be known as the Nashville Fugitives–Allen Tate wrote to Donald Davidson in 1924 of the latest and youngest Fugitive, Robert Penn Warren, "That boy's a wonder–has more sheer genius than any of us; watch him: His work from now on will have what none of us can achieve–power." That estimate was accurate then, and it has, as they say in the South, "proved out" several hundred times over in poetry as well as in remarkable fiction.

The source of Warren's stunning power is *angst,* a kind of radiant metaphysical terror, projected outward into the natural world, particularly into its waiting waste expanses; open field, ocean, desert, mountain range, or the constellations as they feed into the eye a misshapen, baffling, and yearning mythology bred on nothingness. He is direct, scathingly honest, and totally serious about what he feels, and in approach is as far as can be imagined from, say, Mallarmé, who urged poets to "give the initiative to *words.*" Warren gives the initiative to the experience, and renders himself wide open to it. He is not someone who "puts a pineapple together," as Wallace Stevens does, constructing its existence by multiple perceptions, by possibility and caprice rather than by felt necessity; he is not interested in the "ephemeras of the

Jefferson Davis Gets His Citizenship Back

ROBERT PENN WARREN

Dust jacket for a book that Warren wrote after attending a 1979 ceremony honoring the president of the Confederate States of America (Special Collections, Thomas Cooper Library, University of South Carolina)

with a highly individual intelligence; he is fully aware of the Longinian pit that yawns for those who strive for Sublimity and fail to attain it. Precariously in balance, he walks straight out over the sink-hole of Bombast; his native element is risk, and his chief attribute, daring.

The odd tone—utterly Warren's—is compounded of southern dialect, Elizabethanisms overstaying into country speech ("set foot") and always present in rural areas where mountains have gathered and preserved them, and a sometimes rather quaintly old-fangled scholastic vocabulary. The life-beat of the lines is predominantly Anglo-Saxon, as one can see—no; hear—as soon as the first hard stresses fall into place beside each other, and continue, as in "Recollection in Upper Ontario, From Long Before":

> Zack's up, foot's out! Or is it? A second she's standing.
> Then down—now over both rails—
> Down for good, and the last
> Thing I see is his hands out. To grab her, I reckoned.
>
> Time stops like no-Time. . . .

I like to imagine Warren's reading, and approving, Phelps Putnam's request that the god Chance "make us tough and mystical." Warren is very tough, with the farmer's hard, work-cramped hand everywhere over the field of the page, and he is also very mystical, particularly when he turns toward the great, contemplative expanses: broad fields, the sea hazing with curvature, deserts that do the same, or rise and dissolve into mountains, themselves half-in half-out of reality, stars—blinding vistas of snow and ice, as Warren is "Snowshoeing Back to Camp in Gloaming":

> So I stood on that knife-edge frontier
> Of Timelessness, knowing that yonder
> Ahead was the life I might live
> Could I but move
> Into the terror of unmarred whiteness under
> The be-nimbed and frozen sun.

Warren is a speaker who "alone has returned": a voice out of primitive starkness, with his only defenses—and these only occasionally usable—a gallows wit, scatological irony. He is above all a man who looks, and refuses to look away.

The best time to read Warren is at night. That is when the heart's sheer physicality is most deeply felt, most inescapable, most inexplicable. Night is the time when great distances can live for the beholder, and be lived by him; when the blood and the stars have relevance to each other. Despite three hundred-odd years of "progress," things may yet turn out to be as the physician William Harvey had them, when he said: "There is a spirit, a certain force, inherent in the blood, acting

tangent," but in the unanswered sound of his heart, under the awesome winter presence of the hunter Orion.

He plunges as though compulsively into the largest of subjects: those that seem to cry out for capitalization and afflatus and, more often than not in the work of many poets, achieve only the former. To state things in this fashion may make it seem almost necessary to charge Warren with being rhetorical in some kind of wrong way, and indeed in his on-going intensity he does not escape some of the implications of the charge. Balzac said to a friend bent on Art that the truth is emphatically *not* in the nuance, but what matters in a piece of writing is that it "possess a force that carries everything before it." This Warren certainly has. He is a poet of enormous courage,

superiorly to the powers of the elements . . . and the nature, yea, the soul in this spirit and blood is identical with the nature of the stars." The Warren of this book is starry-blooded, a night-walker, a night-watcher, a searcher lying motionless. And perhaps this is the best Warren of all, remembering other nights, darknesses, a cave from his childhood, in his "Speleology":

Years later, past dreams I have lain
In darkness and heard the depth of interminable song.
And hand laid to heart, have once again
thought: *This is me.*
And thought: *Who am I?* And hand on heart, wondered
What it would be like to be, in the end, part of all.

And in the darkness have even asked: *Is this all? What is all?*

It is his ability to state psychic dilemmas of this kind, and in this way—the grim, exalting light of self-education shining through the thick, correct, and sanctioned Other books onto the actual world—in a home-crafted idiom as sinewy as it is unforeseeable, that makes Warren the passionate and memorable artist that he is, and the greatest of our "impure" poets. If Wallace Stevens—to take Warren's most notable and obvious opposite—is "pure," Warren is impure; if Stevens changes reality by changing the angle of his eye, Warren fixes himself into it in wonder, horror, loathing, joy, but above all with unflinching involvement; if Stevens plays with it, tames it, and "understands" it, Warren encounters it nakedly, and without pretense, dallying, or skillful frivolity.

Once, in connection with a movie I was engaged in making, I met with the film director Sam Peckinpah in London to talk over possibilities. Although, as it turned out, he did not direct my story, I remember that as we parted he said to me, "Don't worry; everything'll be all right. No matter what happens, we're both trying to do the same thing. I do it with the pictures I put up on the screen, you do it with your words, but it's all the same: We're trying to give them images they can't forget." I have come to think of this, now, not in relation to movies, but as a characteristic of Robert Penn Warren's poems; they have given many such images to me. John Berryman asks of Stevens, "Why does he not wound?" No one would ever pose such a question in Warren's case. He wounds deeply, and he connects deeply; he strikes in at blood-level and gut-level, with all the force and authority of time, darkness, and distance themselves, and of the Nothingness beyond nothingness, which may even be God: Pascal's "infinite spaces" laid—or laid open—on the farmer's page.

–James Dickey, "Robert Penn Warren's Courage,"
Saturday Review, 7 (August 1980): 56–57

* * *

In this essay on his friend of more than fifty years, critic Malcolm Cowley contends that Warren's character is most clearly revealed in his poetry, especially his later books.

Robert Penn Warren, *aet.* 75

Red Warren tells me that we first met in 1927, "when I was a student," he says, "and you were a big man." A big man? I was twenty-nine and was determined to keep my independence by not becoming a well-known author; precariously I supported myself by writing book reviews and an occasional poem for *The Dial.* Red was twenty-two and had just earned his M.A. at Berkeley; it was before his postgraduate year at Yale and his Rhodes scholarship. Already–if I remember correctly–he had published two poems in *The New Republic,* one of which was "Kentucky Mountain Farm." I admired the poems and had heard about Red as the youngest member of what was already known as the Fugitive group. Here he was at last, in person: tall, long-necked, angular, with a lot of curly dark-red hair. He made abrupt gestures and seemed self-conscious except when telling a story in his low Kentucky voice.

That's all I remember of our meeting, which must have been in Allen Tate's basement flat in the Village. More clearly I remember an evening in the summer of 1930, when Red was back from Oxford. We got drunk on Wall Street cocktails at the Dizzy Club–"One drink and we give you a seat on the Curb"–and talked poetry for hours among all those gangsters. Later I would recognize some impressions of that evening in Red's second novel, *At Heaven's Gate* (1943).

"That was the decade," he said in a recent letter, "when from poverty I was mostly South-bound, & knew little of the N.Y. complications of life," especially the political complications; Red has always been a deliberate innocent in politics. "Your book," he continued, referring to *The Dream of the Golden Mountains,* "is an eye-opener in many ways. I don't mean to say that I think N.Y. is the center of the U.S.A. (it may now be dying–and for whose woe or weal I don't know), but then (1930–40) I knew the South, West & Middle West very well & the East was a foreign country–wise and ignorant." Writers in the East were then preoccupied with political struggles as reflected in literature. Red took no part in the struggles, even after he went to Huey Long's university in 1934 and founded (with Cleanth Brooks) a distinguished quarterly, *The Southern Review.* The quarterly adopted no political position, though its contributors were permitted to adopt a variety of these, so long as they expressed their notions clearly. It was only when Red went to the University of Iowa as a visiting lecturer, in 1941, that he was exposed unwillingly to the New York City type of political arguments.

He has a story about them, as about everything else; most of his world is reduced to stories. "At Univ. of Iowa," he says, "there was a stalwart graduate student

Celebrating Warren's 75th Birthday

Warren turned seventy-five on 24 April 1980. On 29 October of that year–four weeks after he had undergone prostate surgery–the University of Kentucky hosted the Robert Penn Warren 75th Birthday Symposium. Warren's biographer provides a description of the reception preceding the symposium.

Governor and Mrs. John Young Brown, Jr., were among their hosts. The old friends came from different parts of his life–Andrew Lytle, Cleanth Brooks, and Robert Heilman; Vann Woodward, R.W.B. Lewis, and Peter Davison. When it came Warren's turn after the evening's accolades, he said, "It's very easy in the rapture of assuaged vanity, as this occasion is for me, to feel that somehow you're worthy of it, in some small way at least. But I'm enough of a scholar, or at least a reader of literature and literary history, to know that fashions change." The thing to remember, he said, reciting and then paraphrasing a poem by Yeats, was that "the joy is in the doing, and not the end of the doing." Although he looked drawn at departure time, it had been a welcome change and rather "a jolly time, especially when Eleanor was officially made a 'Kentucky Colonel' with scroll to prove same."

–Joseph Blotner, *Robert Penn Warren: A Biography*
(New York: Random House, 1997),
p. 458

Cover for the program of the 1980 celebration of Warren's life and career (Special Collections, Western Kentucky University Libraries)

TELL ME A STORY

Long ago, in Kentucky, I, a boy, stood
By a dirt road, in first dark, and heard
The great geese hoot northward.

I could not see them, there being no moon
And the stars sparse. I heard them.

I did not know what was happening in my heart.

It was the season before the elderberry blooms,
Therefore they were going north.

The sound was passing northward.

Tell me a story.

In this century, and moment, of mania,
Tell me a story.

Make it a story of great distances, and starlight.

The name of the story will be Time,
But you must not pronounce its name.

Tell me a story of deep delight.

From SELECTED POEMS 1923-1975
by Robert Penn Warren

Souvenir of October 28, 1980 reception honoring Mr. and Mrs. Robert Penn Warren and hosted by Governor John Y. Brown Jr., Phyllis George Brown and President and Mrs. Otis Singletary on the occasion of the University of Kentucky's Robert Penn Warren 75th Birthday Symposium.

Keepsake from the celebration of Warren's seventy-fifth birthday (Special Collections, Western Kentucky University Libraries)

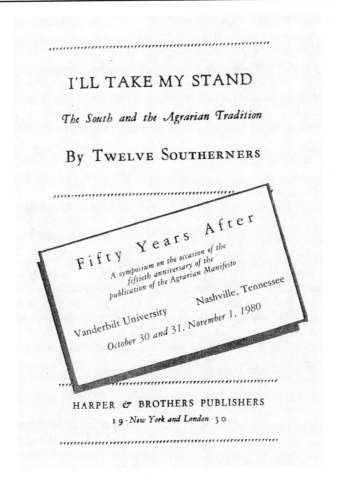

I'LL TAKE MY STAND

The South and the Agrarian Tradition

By TWELVE SOUTHERNERS

Fifty Years After

A symposium on the occasion of the fiftieth anniversary of the publication of the Agrarian Manifesto

Vanderbilt University

Nashville, Tennessee

October 30 and 31, November 1, 1980

HARPER & BROTHERS PUBLISHERS

19 · *New York and London* · 30

Cover for the fiftieth-anniversary symposium that was attended by Warren, Lyle Lanier, Andrew Lytle, and Cleanth Brooks (Special Collections, Western Kentucky University Libraries)

(female) from N.Y.C. who used to lecture me on American agriculture & how to save it. And driving in the country, we passed a flock of sheep. 'What,' she demanded in profound puzzlement, 'are those things?' 'Sheep,' says I, 'and I don't want to hear another word from you about Stalin unless he's got wool like that.' Long silence (for her a real feat) followed."

Red came through the political wars of the 1930's and 1940's without being wounded or inflicting wounds. He was never a politician, as I said, but rather a moralist, and this during a period when morality was going out of fashion. For him the confrontations at the heart of a drama are not between opposing doctrines, or social classes; they are between the individual and his own conscience, or consciousness. In his most famous book, *All the King's Men* (1946), he achieved the feat of writing a novel about Huey Long that is profoundly nonpolitical; nobody could use it in a campaign for votes. The one public issue on which he has taken a stand—in this case liberal—is race relations, and there he could do so because he approached the issue as essentially moral.

Although I have known Red Warren for more than fifty years, I never learned much about him directly. Largely that is the result of faulty communication: I have grown increasingly deaf and Red speaks rapidly, in a low voice, so that I have missed the point of his most illuminating stories. Once he took me into his father's store in Guthrie, Kentucky. It was in 1933 and Guthrie was then a singularly drab and impoverished railroad town. The post office displayed the names of everyone in the county who had paid a federal income tax for 1932; there were only two names. Red himself was a miserably paid instructor at Vanderbilt, out of favor with the administration because of his approach to literature. He told me that his father's boyhood ambition was to become a classical scholar, but that there hadn't been money enough for his education. His grandfather—but he didn't learn that until later—had been a major in Nathan Bedford Forrest's cavalry.

Little facts gleaned here and there. . . . One Sunday afternoon in that spring of 1933, the Fugitive group held a picnic on a houseboat moored in the Cumberland River upstream from Nashville. The river was in flood and the current swept past us at a rate to frighten timid swimmers. Red dived from the houseboat, swam arrow-straight across the river, and then swam back again as if the Cumberland in flood were a millpond. One of his friends told me that he liked to swim a mile before breakfast every morning. At twenty-eight he was already becoming a somewhat legendary character.

But what was he really like? The answer to that question was not to be found in conversation or in picnics on the river. The best place to look for it now is in his twelve published volumes of verse.

It occurred to me not long ago that, as a simple matter of statistics, Warren has published more lines of verse than any other major American poet of our century (exception being made for Conrad Aiken). He has produced a vast *oeuvre,* and that in itself is a considerable achievement, especially in an age marked until recently (fashions are changing) by the number of niggardly talents, men and women held back from writing by a dream of perfection and the fear of being caught out in errors of taste. Warren is generous, open, bold. He seems to be saying, "Why bother about possible errors of taste? The important matter is to get the thing said, accurately if possible, but at worst approximately, so long as the language shows a strict regard for truth."

The twelve volumes contain a great variety of subjects and moods and measures. Some of the verse is regular, rhymed in formal patterns, and some of it is so loosely hung together as to be almost invertebrate. One can't always be sure why a given line should end with a given word instead of rambling on through half a dozen others. But the poet knows—one gives him credit for that sure instinct—and the vast body of work is unified by being spoken in his unmistakable voice. Every poem is clearly by Robert Penn Warren; every line is distinctly signed.

This does not mean that every poem is of equal value. Some of them are rather too philosophical for my taste and not sufficiently relieved by Warren's matchless stories. Sometimes, having found what he thinks is the right pitch, he carries it too long—as if he didn't know how to break off except by making an inconsequential remark or by asking a vast question: "What is Love?" "What is History?" "What, ah, is Time?" That habit of asking questions tempts me to ask another in turn: whether it isn't the poet's task to answer those questions by giving examples, pictures, remembered moments that are truer than our philosophies? Warren does just that at his frequent best. He tells us what love is by picturing his wife naked on the seashore, his son raising both arms in the moonlight, his father speechless on his deathbed; those epiphanies are love in a poet's concrete terms. He tells us something about the nature of time by creating moments so absolute in themselves that time is momently abolished.

"What is it you cannot remember that is so true?" he asks at one point in his next-to-last book, *Now and Then* (1978). During recent years Warren has embarked, or has let himself be embarked, on a search for those half-forgotten truths. He is making what seems to me the most fruitful of all the efforts that are open to a poet in his eighth decade, namely, to remember and reconstitute his life, to reveal its essential form. The effort begins with his childhood in the Kentucky countryside and carries him through an extreme diversity of moods, landscapes, and—most important for him—persons; no other living poet has seen and felt so much of the world. His remembered life becomes a mixture of fact and fiction, "played against, or with," he says, "a shadowy narrative, a shadowy autobiography, if you will. . . . It may be said"—and he says it—"that our lives are our supreme fiction."

That is why the "real" Red Warren is to be found in his poetry, especially in his later books. What shall I say of him? He is a man who loves people but spends much of his time alone. He is extremely loyal to his friends, true to his lived background, but at the same time brutally realistic, with a fondness for depicting deeds of heartlessness or violence: murders, lynchings, suicides. He has bad dreams and remembers them. He is a countryman, a solitary walker, a swimmer (but not a hunter or a plowman), who seldom writes on urban themes; the best of those exceptions is a poem that pictures the South Bronx covered with snow and transformed into an untouched wilderness. He prays, but he doesn't know for what. Kind as he is to others, he is ruthless in protecting his working hours (and I hear that the floor of his study is covered with unanswered letters).

After he sent me his last book (1980), I wrote a letter to Red that didn't have to be answered. Here is part of it:

> *Being Here:* I read the poems twice, and had the feeling that many of them were written especially for me. That effort to recover in age the memories of boyhood and to puzzle out their meaning. That country background, west of the mountains. Those questions about the dead who crowd around you asking only to be named ("Better Than Counting Sheep"). That undischarged debt to your mother. That burden of guilt (and why should you have it, you of all people?). Often you add to my ownburden of guilt when I think, "I should have written that, I should have found the words." And to my sense of not having lived enough, felt enough, when I come across one of the scenes that you bring vividly to life—just as you bring the animals to life again: the six kittens beheaded with a corn knife, the other kitten with a broken leg saved from the garbage grinder, the deer in rut, the mountain lion, the drowned monkey on a Mediterranean beach. And yourself as a boy venturing deep into a cave and thinking, "This is me. . . . Who am I?" Or dreaming: how many dreams! till you think that yourself is only a dream of the moonlight. I read and envy you, being one who can seldom remember his dreams.

After mailing the letter I had some further reflections on one question it raised. Why did Red Warren—"of all people," I said once again—suffer often from a sense of guilt? Why should it afflict this upright man who has always worked hard and has never taken part in the vendettas of the literary life? Perhaps, I thought, there is one answer in a memory of childhood that he mentions several times: "How once I had lied to my mother and hid / In a closet and said, in darkness, aloud: 'I hate you.'" "But his mother, long before she died, had absolved him of that sin. Perhaps it is a feeling of having neglected his duties to dead friends whose names he has forgotten. Perhaps it is connected with something vividly remembered: "how once, in total fascination, I watched a black boy / Take a corn knife and decapitate six kittens? Did I dream / That again last night? . . . Did I wake / with guilt? . . . / Sometime we must probe more deeply the issue of complicity." The issue remains, but we cannot live with the burden of being accomplices in all the sins of our culture. Perhaps the poet's real torment is the Protestant conscience that keeps urging him to be better than any human soul can be.

As a cure of conscience, I should recommend to Red Warren an exercise about him in which I indulged the other night. Only half dreaming I pictured the two pans of a balance that was weighing out his life. In the one pan were heaped all the gifts that he has received from the world: the three Pulitzer Prizes (one for fiction, two for poetry), the National Book Award, the honorary degrees (fourteen by the last tally), the consultancy in poetry at the Library of Congress, the National Medal for Literature, the Presidential Medal of Freedom, the Bollingen Prize, the Common Wealth Award for Distinguished Service in Literature. . . . In the other pan were all the gifts he has bestowed on the world: the thirty-odd books (including, besides the poems, ten novels, a poetic drama in two versions, a prose drama, a collection of stories, a book of essays), the recreated boyhood in a Kentucky railroad town, the realization of his father's lost dream of scholarship, the years of devoted teaching, the inspiration of students—and of writers who have chosen his career as a model—all this and much more. It is a picture I recommend to Red Warren at seventy-five. "Heap up the gifts from the world," I said to myself (or to the court attendant who busied himself with medals and parchments). "There cannot be too many of them. They will never outweigh the gifts bestowed on the world that overflow the other pan."

—Malcolm Cowley, *Georgia Review*, 35, (Spring 1981): 7–12

* * *

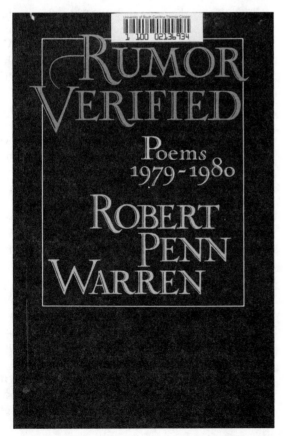

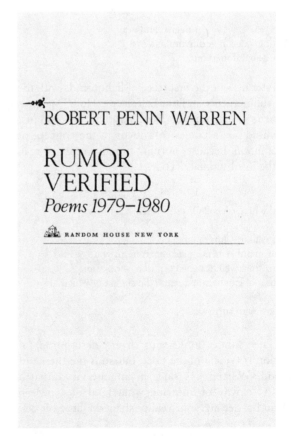

Cover and title page for Warren's fourth collection published after his retirement from Yale University in 1973
(Thomas Cooper Library, University of South Carolina)

Warren's working title for Rumor Verified *was "Have You Ever Eaten Stars?," but he changed it on the suggestion of his wife. This review is by Irvin Ehrenpreis, a distinguished scholar of eighteenth-century literature, known especially for his three-volume biography of Jonathan Swift. He also had a strong interest in American poetry and edited* Wallace Stevens: A Critical Anthology *(1972).*

Continuity and Change
Review of *Rumor Verified*

Staying power is rarely a feature of genius. American poets, especially, tend to fade when they age. But Robert Penn Warren, as his new book testifies, has gained strength with years.

Even the casual turner of pages will be struck by Warren's descriptions of landscape and the effects of light. He has the art of bestowing special significance on things seen, heard, or touched, without falsifying the simple act of perception. In his work, it is rare for a country scene, however minutely observed, to lack symbolic implications.

A favorite motif is dawn. The poet, wakeful and uneasy during the night, watches the dawn "seep in"—

> sluggish and gray
> As tidewater fingering timbers in a
> long-abandoned hulk.

The wateriness of the first trace of light blends with the poet's submergence in fluid half-sleep. "Hulk" suggests the poet's body, cut off from daytime perceptions. The whole poem comes to a focus in the concept of self-definition, because morning brings a sense of reality to the insubstantial sleeper:

> Are you
> Real when asleep? Or only when,
>
> Feet walking, lips talking, or
> Your member making its penetration, you
> Enact, in a well-designed set, that ectoplasmic
> Drama of laughter and tears, the climax of which always
>
> Strikes with surprise. . . .

The subtle movement from description to reflection is typical of the poet, but so is the theme of selfhood. Warren has said, in an interview, that a poem is "a way of knowing what kind of a person you can be, getting your reality shaped a little bit better."

Like most memorable poems composed by Americans, those by Warren keep returning us to the nature of personality—the relation between character and memory—or between immediate experience and analytical consciousness. In short lyrics, no more than two or three pages long, Warren powerfully confronts the gap between feeling and thought. Again and again the poet yields pleasurably to a moment of strong perceptions or deep emotion. But then he draws back and ponders it, unwilling to let the self dissolve in sensation. Literature, Warren said to another interviewer, starts from "the attempt to inspect one's own soul."

Certain images persist in Warren's work. In a new poem, "Minneapolis Story," a gold maple leaf drops from its bough, signifying the autumnal passage from experience to reflection; and in another new poem, "Millpond Lost," a leaf "golden, luxurious," falls on a millpond. As it touches the water, the poet stops imagining his own return to a scene from boyhood and confesses that he never went back. The same leaf appeared half a century ago in "The Return," where it fell slowly, "Uncertain as a casual memory," to meet its reflection rising from the depths of the water below. Even then, it was an emblem of memory trying and failing to recover the past.

Not only themes and images but also the forms of the poems connect the new work with the old. A wholly charming poem, "What Voice at Moth-Hour," in *Rumor Verified,* deals irresistibly with the poet's recollection of a childhood misdemeanor. On a spring evening in Kentucky, young Robert hid after dark among the trees and refused to come home even though he heard his anxious parents calling. The same incident was the subject of a poem published in 1957, "What Was the Promise That Smiled from the Maples at Evening?" But besides reworking an old theme, the poem has a familiar form—pentameter quatrains with lines rhyming alternately. The five-beat line and regular, four-line stanzas that appear several times in *Rumor Verified* are found as early as "To a Face in the Crowd," published when the poet was twenty.

Such devices might reflect the example of John Crowe Ransom and Allen Tate. Both these men were Warren's seniors in the remarkable group known as "the Fugitives," who met in Nashville, Tennessee, during the years 1915–1928, to read and criticize their own writing.

Warren's poems deal repeatedly with the mystery of success and failure—the danger of supposing that either is unavoidable or that one cannot become the other. Growing up in a region afflicted with fatalism, he had to educate himself to moral action and responsibility. "What poetry most significantly cele-

Eleanor Clark, circa 1981 (photograph by Bill Ferris; Special Collections,
Western Kentucky University Libraries)

brates," Warren declared in *Democracy and Poetry* (1975), "is the capacity of man to face the deep, dark inwardness of his nature and his fate."

Men long to perform a great deed because the experience itself is joyful. Once they possess fame, however, they discover how little it redeems the terrible disappointments inherent in any life. Yet the experience remains joyful. On the other hand, the exhilaration wears off, the burden of hopelessness descends, and it must be tolerated, even though one knows the burden will keep returning, for one also learns that it dissolves in the reality of love. As Warren says in a new poem, "Fear and Trembling,"

> Only at death of ambition does the deep
> Energy crack crust, spurt forth, and leap
>
> From grottoes, dark—and from the caverned enchainment?

While we can trace themes, images, and forms that endure through all of Warren's long career, change is fundamental to his talent. During the decade following World War II, Warren produced hardly any short poems. But then he gave up writing short stories and altered his conception of a lyric.

When he composed such verse again, it was, as he said, "more tied up with an event, an anecdote, an observation." The new poems were closer to the felt life of their author.

Meanwhile, that life was transformed. Warren's first marriage had terminated in divorce. He was married again, to Eleanor Clark (in 1952), and the couple soon had a daughter and a son. In 1955, Warren's father died. These large changes inevitably altered the poet's view of his world. He obviously delighted in fatherhood; and he began experimenting with what might be called the poetry of happiness. It strikes one that in Warren's narrative poem based on the life of *Audubon* (1969), the act of violence is frustrated. Although Warren dwells, in *Audubon,* on the paradoxes of love and destructiveness, sexuality and death, he also dwells on the interconnectedness of all living things. Audubon shoots the birds he loves (in order to study them), but he also gives them new life in his art.

During the past twelve years, Warren has opened himself up engagingly. *Rumor Verified* continues the development toward a direct use of personal experience. The title of the book refers to the axiom

Warren in North Africa in 1981 (photograph by Gabriel Penn Warren; courtesy of Gabriel Penn Warren)

that no man can escape the limitations of the human condition. An opening poem suggests the relation between love and wisdom, by presenting an ideal experience of sexual passion. Another poem dramatizes the strength of the human instinct for meaningful existence. The closing poems of the book are centered on the need to accept one's character with all its deficiencies and to work through it—not against it—toward an insight that may never be completely possessed. In the body of the book, Warren ponders the mysterious relation between time (or history) and the self that rises from it and yet persists against it.

Typically, the poems move from a memory or a startling experience to a meditation, sometimes in the shape of a question. Along with large generalizations they exhibit brilliantly concrete detail. Warren once said to an interviewer that what he would hunt for in a poem is "a vital and evaluating image."

In form, the new poems are surprisingly regular. Only a third are in quite free verse. Another third are in quatrains, usually rhymed. The rest are in various other forms, mainly irregular distichs or tercets. In the skillful "Sunset Scrupulously Observed," the flight of a jet is exquisitely contrasted with that of five swifts. The poet treats the plane as a splendid living creature and the birds as machines. The poem, in free verse, is a triumph of design; the main contrast is handsomely framed by the sun going down in the background and a flycatcher perched on a poplar in the foreground, opening and closing the poem with its presence and absence.

But the surprise of the book is "Moth-Hour," a poem in neat quatrains with expressively soft line endings, gentle, undulating rhythms, and subtle patterns of sound (particularly the use of "i" vowels). All these elements support the nostalgia of the speaker as he remembers how innocence gave way to experience when he made a boyish gesture toward separating himself from his parents: it was precisely their love that he had to resist if he was ever to grow into a deeply loving selfhood:

What voice at moth-hour did I hear calling
As I stood in the orchard while the white
Petals of apple blossoms were falling,
Whiter than moth-wing in that twilight?

What voice did I hear as I stood by the stream,
Bemused in the murmurous wisdom there uttered,
While ripples at stone, in their steely gleam,
Caught last light before it was shuttered?

What voice did I hear as I wandered alone
In a premature night of cedar, beech, oak,
Each foot set soft, then still as stone
Standing to wait while the first owl spoke?

The voice that I heard once at dewfall, I now
Can hear by a simple trick. If I close
My eyes, in that dusk I again know
The feel of damp grass between bare toes,

Can see the last zigzag, sky-skittering, high,
Of a bullbat, and even hear, far off, from
Swamp-cover, the whip-o-will, and as I
Once heard, hear the voice: *It's late! Come home.*

—Irvin Ehrenpreis, "Continuity and Change,"
Atlantic Monthly, 248 (December 1981):
88–91

* * *

James Dickey and Warren, February 1982 (Matthew J. Bruccoli Collection of James Dickey, Thomas Cooper Library)

This review article for TLS *is by Jay Parini, then a young writer who had published three books, including his first collection of poetry,* Singing in Time *(1972), and his first biography,* Theodore Roethke: An American Romantic *(1979).*

The Vatic Mantle
Review of *Now and Then, Being Here,* and *Rumor Verified*

Robert Penn Warren has stepped out boldly as a major poet, publishing four strong books of new verse in seven years. *Now and Then* (1978) established his position by astonishing readers with its ferocity and grandeur, and that memorable volume has not been surpassed by *Being Here* (1980) or his latest collection *Rumor Verified*. Nevertheless, these last three collections are of a piece, and Warren has emerged at the front of a field noticeably lacking in major figures since the death of Robert Lowell.

At the age of seventy-six, Warren seems literally pressed by time. This pressure has led to what some critics regard as over-production, and some of these poems do read like rough drafts. In a sense, we have been given entry to Warren's workshop; the poet tries out the same poem many different ways, narrowing in on the final version, which is usually stunning. A fair number of these works take the form of the descriptive poem in which a (presumably) older man climbs a hill in Vermont or stands overlooking a seascape, having come to a specific point and place in nature, whereupon he is overwhelmed by questions of time and identity.

Even Warren's worst poems are interesting for the way they grope towards the better work, struggling for clarification. In the best of them, such as "Heart of Autumn" in *Now and Then*, "Acquaintance with Time in Early Autumn" in *Being Here,* or "Mountain Mystery" in *Rumor Verified,* Warren makes us vividly aware of ourselves as creatures caught in the thresh of time. He sees the need to ask the right questions even while he dangles before us the insufficiency of any answers we might obtain. "If this is the way it is", he writes in a new poem called "If", then "we must live through it".

Warren began his career as the youngest member of the Fugitives, a disciple of John Crowe Ransom and Allen Tate. His early work was well-wrought, intellectually acute, witty and balanced. The technical virtuosity of such work was beyond reproach, although in retrospect it appears somewhat static and imitative. The best poetry of Warren's middle period was the verse play called *Brother to Dragons* (1953), which he has recently seen fit to revise. Here Warren's liking for narrative, previously confined to the novel, had the effect of releasing raw energy like adrenalin into the blood-stream of his poetry. However, it was not until Warren virtually abandoned novel-writing in the early 1970s that he was able to tap the same energy again. The poems that followed, though hardly unpolished or lacking in technical brilliance, possess a rawboned, jagged quality. Power is the word that comes to mind when reading these poems, which have something in common with the work of the great poets of vitality– Whitman, Hopkins, and Lawrence. Here, for example, is the opening of "Glimpses of Seasons":

> Gasp-glory of gold light of dawn on gold maple–
> Now forgotten green bough-loop, fat leaf-droop, and even
> The first reddening rondure of August or, slow,
> The birth of the grape's yearning bulge, as summer,
> Bemused in the dream of the sweetness of swelling,
> Forgets to define
> The mathematics of Time.

In his later work, Warren has rescued many of the virtues found in his early poems: wit, a muscular intellect, and a longing to get rapidly to the heart of things. He has added a clamorous urgency, an intensity occasioned by age, and a turn to what might be called autobiographical verse. The road was opened for him by Lowell, Snodgrass, and others, who made confessional poems respectable. Yet Warren has gone beyond confession, reaching through mere personal fact to impersonal truth; he has taken on the mantle of the vatic poet and turned his own life into an exemplar. The lyric "I" in these poems is simply man at his best: simple, learned, loving, and completely human. This man, faced with "the terror / Of knowledge" in the title poem, asks: "But what can you do?" Warren answers: "Perhaps pray to God for strength to face the verification / That you are simply a man, with a man's dead reckoning, nothing more."

A genuine humility informs these poems and saves them from pretentiousness. And Warren's predilection for grand philosophical speculation is held in check by the autobiographical mode, which insists that each poem be founded on an incident or place. Thus, having evoked his climb up a seawall beside the Mediterranean, the poet can get away with talk about "the agony of Time". We can absorb his question–"What lies in the turn of the season to fear?" in a poem called "Vermont Ballad: Change of Season" because he has rendered so concretely the transformations of autumn, the "fitful rain", which has "wrought new traceries, / New quirks, new love-knots, down the pane". Indeed, the title poem, "Rumor Verified", is an ode to humility, a poignant confession of moral inadequacy.

In an exact and haunting lyric "What Voice at Moth-Hour", Warren asks:

> What voice did I hear as I wandered alone
> In a premature night of cedar, beech, oak,
> Each foot set soft, then still as stone
> Standing to wait while the first owl spoke?

Stricken with knowledge and the burden of history, Warren is besieged by voices that demand his attention and ours as well.

–Jay Parini, "The Vatic Mantle," *TLS: The Times Literary Supplement,* 29 January 1982, p. 113

* * *

Chief Joseph, 1903 (photograph by Edward S. Curtis; Peabody Essex Museum)

A One-Shot Kill: Waiting for *Chief Joseph*

When Warren was asked by an interviewer about "the difference between the poetic and the novelistic impulse," he answered: "The novel is a documentary of a kind; a poem is not. The novel is an account of a long trailing. A poem is aiming for the one-shot kill." He went on to describe how he lived for years with the idea of writing about Chief Joseph.

. . . Years ago, 1935, I was visiting a friend of mine in Montana and he told me all about Chief Joseph and showed me where he'd fought. So I began to read Chief Joseph. I guess I've read everything there is about him except one book that's always checked out of the library. And I've seen dozens of pictures of him. And I found out a lot about the Northwest Indians, and so forth. Well, this was hanging around: I didn't know whether it was a novel or a poem or what the hell it was, all these years now since '35. Then, about three years ago I made some false starts–not any more than just thinking about it, notes. But it was all wrong. I just couldn't write an Indian novel, you know. But the poem suddenly came.

–Carll Tucker, "Creators on Creating: Robert Penn Warren," *Saturday Review,* 8 (July 1981): 40

February 1, 1982

Dear Albert:

Here is the last version. I have given it a close
reading and made a few obvious corrections. Before you
mark out spacing, etc., I imagine that you and I should
go over the MS to try to save a little space.

But most of all I want to have your critical remarks
and suggestions. Let me know when you are ready and have the
time for a careful session.

I pray for your favor.

Love to the beautiful ladies!

Ever yours - and all thanks.

Red

PS. We have just learned that Public TV is using poems from
Rosanna's little book . Don't kbow date yet.

Cover letter about Warren's Chief Joseph of the Nez Perce *and a page from the "Fourth Version" of the long poem that Warren sent Albert Erskine*
(Yale Collection of American Literature, Beinecke Rare Book and Manuscript Library)

Warren's Meditation on Time

James Dickey's commentary and reading of Warren's poetry took place in February 1982 as "Robert Penn Warren: A Public Program," which was part of the Southern Studies Program at the University of South Carolina.

Going back through Red Warren's work, I find that it is all a long, lyric, and dramatic meditation on time, which includes mortality, disease, terror, exultation, death, definition, and meaning or lack of meaning. All writers are obsessed with time, but Warren's preoccupation with it is unique, and takes many forms. It is fascinating to go through his poems and see how many forms he has used and experimented with, and how the preoccupations and the personality remain the same. The personality, as I once said in a review, is tough and mystical. The source of his stunning power is *angst,* a kind of radiant metaphysical terror, projected outward onto the natural world; in his later work particularly into its waiting waste expanses: open field, ocean, desert, mountain range, or the constellations as they feed into the eye a misshapen, baffling, and yearning mythology bred on nothingness.

So I stood on that knife-edge frontier
Of Timelessness, knowing that yonder
Ahead was the life I might live
Could I but move
Into the terror of unmarred whiteness under
The be-nimbed and frozen sun.

As intelligent as he is, Warren's idiom has the feeling usually of something home-crafted. He is a no-nonsense, gut-level kind of poet, and was such even from the beginning when he took part of his idiom from the metaphysical poets, particularly Andrew Marvell.

–James Dickey, "Warren's Poetry: A Reading and Commentary," in *A Southern Renascence Man: Views of Robert Penn Warren,* edited by Walter B. Edgar (Baton Rouge: Louisiana State University Press, 1982), pp. 81–82

CHIEF JOSEPH

I.

The Land of the Winding Waters, Wallowa,
The Land of the In-an-toin-mi,
Their Land , the land in the ages given,
By the Chief-in-the-Sky. Their ponies, crossed
With the strong blood of horses, well-bred, graze
Richly the green blade. Boys, bare-back, ride naked,
Leap on, shout "Ai-yah!" Shout, "Ai-yee" --
In unbridled glory, Eaglewing catches sun.
Gleams white. Boys plunge into water, gay as
The otter at gambol, with flat hands slap water,
Like beaver-tails slapping in warning, then dive,
Beaverlike, to depth, toes leaving the shimmer,
Uncoiling upwards, of bubbles. On sandbars
Boys lie , and sun dries the skin.
It glints golden, red, bronze. Each year
They go where from seaward surge salmon, infatuate,
Unfailing, leap falls, leap stones, leap the foaming
Rigor of current -- seeking, seeking,
In blind compulsion, like fate, the spawn-
Pool that blood remembers. What does our blood,
In arteries deep, heaving with pulse-thrust, -
In its eternal midnight, remember?
We stir in sleep. We, too, belong
To the world, and it is spread for our eyes.

SPACE

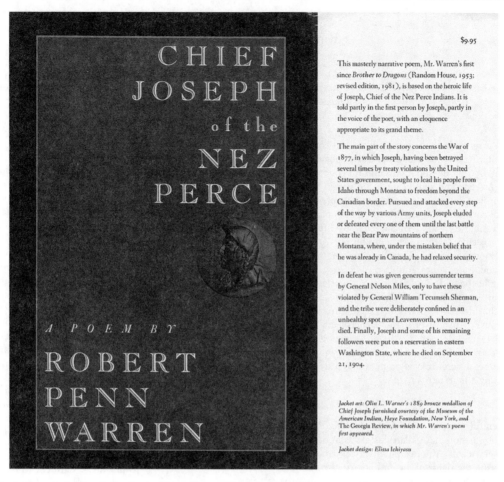

This masterly narrative poem, Mr. Warren's first since *Brother to Dragons* (Random House, 1953; revised edition, 1981), is based on the heroic life of Joseph, Chief of the Nez Perce Indians. It is told partly in the first person by Joseph, partly in the voice of the poet, with an eloquence appropriate to its grand theme.

The main part of the story concerns the War of 1877, in which Joseph, having been betrayed several times by treaty violations by the United States government, sought to lead his people from Idaho through Montana to freedom beyond the Canadian border. Pursued and attacked every step of the way by various Army units, Joseph eluded or defeated every one of them until the last battle near the Bear Paw mountains of northern Montana, where, under the mistaken belief that he was already in Canada, he had relaxed security.

In defeat he was given generous surrender terms by General Nelson Miles, only to have these violated by General William Tecumseh Sherman, and the tribe were deliberately confined in an unhealthy spot near Leavenworth, where many died. Finally, Joseph and some of his remaining followers were put on a reservation in eastern Washington State, where he died on September 21, 1904.

Jacket art: Olin L. Warner's 1889 bronze medallion of Chief Joseph furnished courtesy of the Museum of the American Indian, Heye Foundation, New York, and The Georgia Review, in which Mr. Warren's poem first appeared.

Jacket design: Elissa Ichiyasu

Dust jacket for the 1983 edition published by Random House; it was first published by Palaemon Press in 1982 (Richland County Public Library)

Warren's last volume of poetry published during his life was New and Selected Poems, 1923–1985. *This long review is by Sister Bernetta Quinn, whose books include* The Metamorphic Tradition in Modern Poetry *(1965).*

A Kind of Unconscious Autobiography
Review of *New and Selected Poems, 1923–1985*

"For what is a poem but a hazardous attempt at self-understanding?" says Robert Penn Warren in a *New York Times Book Review* article (May 10, 1985), written on the occasion of his latest "winnowing," the publication of *Poems New and Selected 1923–1985,* lyrics wonderful to have in a single volume even if their author has left out such favorites as "Gold Glade," "Time as Hypnosis," and three still available in Miller Williams' *Contemporary Poetry in America:* "Pursuit," "The Owl," "The Jet Must Be Looking for Something." In Warren's hands the "hazardous attempt" becomes a "self-interview," a tool for acquiring knowledge similar to the medieval *débat* (cf. "Debate: Question, Quarry,

Dream") in which one side of the artist questions a deeper level of his psyche to ascertain the meaning of experiences, of hopes and fears, of the nature of reality both transcendent and perceived.

"Blow, West Wind," an achievement comparable to the exquisitely crafted "Bearded Oaks," opens with "I know, I know–" but the poet, as a matter of fact, does not know. Over and over he interrogates himself on immensely important issues as he builds his artifacts out of language and memories, reverie and observations, dream and desire. All serious writers realize that only through the creative process do they find out what they think, but the intensity with which Warren perseveres in self-inquiry through poetry is unique. Hardly a lyric goes by without questions, usually abstract but sometimes concrete, like "Can iron bleed?" about a bear seen on Sunday morning at the Roman zoo, slugging at a door in the cage, its "great paws like iron on iron" ("Three Darknesses"). Strangely, Warren's entire book vibrates with the animal's action, impregnated with a mystery beyond the literal pounding, a mystery

Revising a Man into a Hero:
Warren's Chief Joseph

In this excerpt from his study of Warren's biographical narratives, Jonathan Cullick discusses the poet's treatment of men whom historians have treated as heroes.

. . . Warren creates a sense of historical connection by surrendering all pretense of neutral or objective narration, and by revising the myths and misconceptions of the past. A basic and significant tactic within this revisionary project is his questioning of the process that transforms men into heroes. Warren makes past heroes more accessible to a modern audience by humanizing them, an objective that is apparent in his poetry, particularly his long poems on Thomas Jefferson, *Brother to Dragons,* and John James Audubon, *Audubon: A Vision.* Appearing at the end of a long line of prose and poetic texts about American heroes, *Chief Joseph of the Nez Perce* is a text that defends a man's heroic stature. Warren's final narrative is an answer to the "deheroizing" of "The World of Daniel Boone," *Brother to Dragons,* and *Audubon: A Vision.* In *Chief Joseph of the Nez Perce* Warren acknowledges a hero, revising a man into a hero rather than revising a hero into a man.

. . . .

The central theme in *Chief Joseph of the Nez Perce* is the paradox of a nation that violates its ideals in the pursuit of those very ideals. America putatively expanded westward to bring the rights of life and liberty, the values of individualism, family, community, and economic prosperity to every corner of the continent. Yet in this process they denied the life, liberty, and individuality of the lands' aboriginal peoples, whose families, communities, and economies they displaced. The march toward the Pacific was the Manifest Destiny of one nation and the destruction of many others. *Chief Joseph of the Nez Perce* resurrects the voice of a Native American who believed in the same ideals championed by those who destroyed his people. At the same time, Chief Joseph's reverence for the land and his people's history become correctives to the American sense of detachment and abstraction from place and past. Thus, the poem proposes Chief Joseph as an ideal image for modern America, a true American hero.

Both *Brother to Dragons* and *Chief Joseph of the Nez Perce* reconcile traditional heroic records with a modern critical agenda. By exposing neglected information to the present, these poems destabilize fundamental misconceptions about American history. On the one hand, *Brother to Dragons* forces some acknowledgment that a horrible crime spots the mythically spotless image of the man who defined America's ideals and aspirations. *Chief Joseph of the Nez Perce,* on the other hand, argues for accepting a hero into American history. The poems are two sides of the same revisionary coin.

This distinction is what makes *Chief Joseph of the Nez Perce* a significant work in Warren's canon. *John Brown: The Making of a Martyr, Brother to Dragons, Audubon,* and other texts inform us who the hero is not. The Chief Joseph narrative poem nominates a hero. . . .

–Jonathan S. Cullick, *Making History*
(Baton Rouge: Louisiana State
University Press, 2000),
pp. 155, 158–159

---

recalling Faulkner's bear in the half-imaginary realm of Yoknapatawpha County. The creature seems to be demanding entrance "into the darkness of wisdom" just as Warren himself has demanded, even before he began writing, during his undergraduate days at Vanderbilt. In the initial poem of this most recent gathering he confides to the reader: ". . . the world has been / Trying to tell me something. There is something / Hidden in the dark." The bear symbolizes his longing to discover what the dark hides. Either as noun or adjective, dark (here equated with wisdom though the latter is ordinarily connected with light rather than darkness) is omnipresent in the Warren corpus. Even in scenes of contentment typical of the late pieces, which are illuminated by a rare domestic happiness that centers in his wife, Eleanor Clark, and their two children, Rosanna and Gabriel–poems such as "After the Dinner Party," which the *New York Times* reviewer William Pritchard prefers over all the rest of the poetry–dark stands for mortality, the death of the season of winter, the death of friends, introduced through the jest of someone long dead quoted at the dinner, the anticipated "weight of darkness" as sleep comes to end a pleasant day. These three encounters with darkness constitute an interior scrutiny aimed at the admission of clarity into landscapes of the soul otherwise frightening or at least depressing. Sometimes *dark* resonates with the clanging of grief, premonition, guilt–a triad in which the first and the last are linked–like the repeated cry of Milton's Samson, "O dark, dark, dark . . . "; the poem is quoted in "Folly on Royal Street before the Raw Face of God" ("amid the blaze of noon").

The technique by which the poet seeks truth (or Truth–truth nowhere more enigmatic than in Warren, not even in Montaigne's "'What is truth?' asked jesting Pilate, but would not wait for an answer") is a variation of the Socratic method. Since the probing is an "I" affair, or *you* with a first-person-singular meaning, it comes under "Poetry is a kind of unconscious autobiography." Though not so avowedly as Coleridge's "The

Rime of the Ancient Mariner," all poems arise in the subconscious, and more fundamentally in the unconscious.

In the *New York Times* article Robert Penn Warren turned aesthetician, looking back upon the sources of his lyrics, writes: "The eyes, or the mind, might fix on something. In general, it might be said that the vision (that is, object, event, or recollection) and voice might sometimes seem scarcely associated. But after a time— sometimes a long period–association might grow." What is meant in this passage by vision is not the supernaturally fabricated, "absurd" experience of "I Am Dreaming of a White Christmas: the Natural History of a Vision," but rather the source of insight in such a poem as "Vision" from *Being Here,* which begins, "The vision will come–the Truth be revealed." There is the horrifying chance that it may come and go without being known: "Can it be that the vision has, long back,

Illustration by Ansis Berzins drawn for Robert Penn Warren's Brother to Dragons: A Discussion *(1983). The illustration was not included in the volume because of the printing expense (Special Collections, Western Kentucky University Libraries).*

already come– / And you didn't recognize it?" Disturbed, the poet speculates as to whether the supreme moment of Truth might have been Ruth Warren's death, remembering how an orderly prepared his mother for surgery in 1931.

Certain configurations (a bird in a flaming sky over a mountain-scape, a completely motionless green or golden glen, the "lone and level" sands of a desert stretching out under a not-always-beneficent moon, the glittering expanse of snowy peaks or fields) repeat themselves throughout the fifty years of Warren poetry. Though discrete, the segments enjoy what his essay on the Ancient Mariner calls "the sacramental unity of the universe." This concept, now a commonplace of literary criticism as applied far beyond this narrative, is related to E. M. Forster's "connections," as well as to Tennyson's "flower in the crannied wall."

Roughly a third of the poems in this collection involve sunset, some of them also a hawk or an eagle, figures analyzed in my "Gull against the Crimson Sky: Bird Imagery in Warren's Later Poetry" *(The Southern Literary Journal).* An example is the fine sonnet "Mortal Limit," which like "Grackles, Goodbye" serves as his "The Wild Swans at Coole." In "Poetry Is a Kind of Unconscious Autobiography" he speaks of this incident, also used in "Blow, West Wind": "Or the vision of a hawk at sunset, years back, above the Tetons." The "I" in this recent lyric lifts his eyes to the kestrel riding "updraft in the sunset over Wyoming," far above the "coniferous darkness" (again the insistence on the dark). Like Yeats he asks himself: "Beyond what height /Hangs now the black speck? / Beyond what range will gold eyes see / New ranges to mark a last scrawl of light?" What he longs to learn about is not only this bird but also his own death, what chapters are still left, and (though "Mortal Limit" does not concern itself with the problem) what name he will at the end discover he has borne through all the routes he has taken. Under what name will he enter eternity?

Another such pattern of images has cactus replacing the hawk at its heart. It belongs to the "twilight" (or better, moonlit) world located deep within, constructed of elements from an Arizona desertscape, twin to that Southwest setting chosen for her old age by Georgia O'Keeffe, that painter of cow skulls, surrealistic blossoms, other emblems of the unconscious. Cacti are suitable flora for what Carl Jung calls "the shadow," that submerged part of the human mind needing to be brought forth into the sunlight and integrated for a healthy personality. Such examples of the *doppelgänger* novel as Kafka's *Metamorphosis,* Robert Louis Stevenson's *Dr. Jekyll and Mr. Hyde,* Conrad's *The Secret Sharer* have exploited "the shadow" with remarkable success. Sterile as these cacti seem with their defensive spikes

Drafts of "Old-Time Childhood in Kentucky," a poem first published in New and Selected Poems: 1923–1985
(Yale Collection of American Literature, Beinecke Rare Book and Manuscript Library)

Where Poems Come From

In a 1981 interview with Saturday Review, *Warren talked about how he wrote poems: "... I still do a lot of composing outdoors. Walking or swimming. I used to run a lot ... on gymnasium tracks. Ideas come to me when I'm relaxed. Poems in particular. I compose them in my head, memorize them, then I write them down." In a later interview Warren gave a fuller answer.*

Every time I'm asked where my ideas for poems come from, I try to think it through again. I don't come up with the same answer every time, either.

Sometimes you see some actual event that somehow starts a line. I drove my mother once to a funeral. I've got that scene in my mind; it was so strange to me that she would go miles into the country for the service of a woman whom she scarcely knew. But years later the event was a poem–the answer to that question.

Another time I saw a cock pheasant booming past my shoulder when I was passing on a snowy path. I looked back and saw the bird explode into the sunset. That became a poem, just right on the spot. I outlined it then and worked on it for some weeks afterward.

Sometimes, you just pick a certain phrase. You don't know what it means. For instance, "A great boulder in a stream by a house in Vermont." No poem: just an object. I'd seen it a thousand times, but

one day the boulder gave me a first line as I was lying on it drying off after swimming. It could be as accidental as that.

I get many ideas while on long swims. I sort of half-dream. It's a numbing, bemusing experience. And a thousand ideas drift into the head. There's rhythm and blankness, and you feel detached from yourself. It opens the head to suggestion.

Almost all poems are fragmentary autobiography. Sometimes I can trace an idea back to some fragment of memory. But I couldn't start making sense out of the events that gave rise to the fragment. It has to make its own sense, years later. A line or two may exist in your head and suddenly it goes somewhere. Something makes it click again.

Every poem is in one sense a symbol. Its meaning is always more than it says to you–the writer–and more than it specifies directly to a reader. Otherwise, it doesn't exist as a poem. It's just a statement of some kind which provokes the reader into his own poem.

–Alvin P. Sanoff, "'Pretty, Hell! Poetry Is Life': A Conversation with America's First Poet Laureate," *U.S. News & World Report,* 100 (23 June 1986): 74

intermediate version   *later version*

OLD-TIME CHILDHOOD IN KENTUCKY

When I was a boy I saw the world I was in.
I saw it for what it was. Canebrakes with
Track beaten down by bear paw. Tobacco,
In endless rows, the pink inner flesh of black fingers
Crushing to green juice tobacco worms plucked
From a leaf. The great trout,
Motionless, poised in the shadow of his
Enormous creek-boulder.
But the past and the future broke on me when I got older.

Strange, into the past I just grew. I handled the old bullet-mold.
I drew out a saber, touched an old bayonet, I dreamed
Of the death-scream. The old spurs I tried on.
The first great General Jackson had ridden just north
To our state to make a duel legal -- or avoid the law.
It was all for honor. He said: "I would have killed him,
Even with his hot lead in my brain." This for honor. I said longed
The magic word. I longed to understand. In darkness *and the magic word*
I named it, like a prayer. I longed to say it aloud, to be heard.
I saw with strategie of Bryan's Campaigns, saw
I saw the dispositions of troops at Austerlitz, but knew
It was far away, long ago. I saw
The marks of the old man's stick in the dust, heard
The old voice explaining. His eyes weren't too good,
And I read him the books he wanted. Read him
Breasted's History of Egypt, saw years uncoil like a snake.
I built a pyramid with great care. There interred
Pharoah's splendor and might.
Excavation next summer, exposed that glory to man's sight.

skeleton of
At a cave mouth my uncle showed me some crinoid stems,
And in limestone the delicate fishy form of a creature.
"All once under water," he said," no saying the millions
Of years. He walked off, the old man with me. "Oh, Grandpa,"
I said, "what can you do, things being like this?" "All you can,"
He said, looking off through tree tops, skyward. "Love
Your wife, love your get, keep your word, and
If need arises die for it, or what men die for. There aren't
Many choices. There but came to how -- some in peace, some in war.

He hobbled away. The woods seemed darker. I stood
In the encroachment of shadow, no suddenly old. but in time
I shut my eyes, head thrown back, eyelids black.
I stretched out both arms to the side, and , waterlike,
Wavered from hips and knees, feet yet firm on earth as though
You grew there in deep
Marine depth and increasing lightlessness, to discover
What you would be, might be, after ages --how many? -- rolled over.

Wavering from hips and knees, yet yet firm fixed
In earth, in mud, in sand, in stone, as though
that into
In arms back you grew there in deep marine
Depth & lightlessness, waiting to discover (but

and weird shapes, they admirably represent guilt. In a *New Yorker* lyric of the 1980s, "Three Darknesses," which takes place in a hospital room occupied by the poet, they rise out of memory to haunt a patient's sleepless night after he carelessly flips on a television Western: "Black / Stalks of cacti, like remnants of forgotten nightmares, loom / Near at hand"; granted the stereotypes of "cowboy operas," this "you" has no fear of virtue's defeat, unlike his feelings in the Arizona prototype out of his youth.

Bizarre decorations of the desert, cacti stand off from the beholder spookily, remote even if near (in "Afterward," this effect is expressed as "other cacti, near and as far as distance"). Their thorny black arms above the sands are drenched in the white light of the moon which affects the spirit of man just as it does the black tides of midnight. In their relation to remorse they resemble Ivan Albright's painted door with its funeral wreath in the Chicago Art Institute. Cacti belong to the furniture of ominous dreams, like the skull with which the poet tries to establish communication in "Afterward": "Oh, see // How a nameless skull, by weather uncovered or / The dateless winds // In the moonlit desert, smiles"—a smile he tries to return, hoping they can start a conversation of mutual comfort. "Unless" (named with one of those odd adverbs Warren likes to pick for titles) also evokes a sinister, cactus-haunted environment:

As when

The rattlesnake, among desert rocks
And Freudian cactus tall in moonlight,

Scrapes off the old integument, and flows away,
Clean and lethal and gleaming like water over moon-
bright sand. . . .

After its flat circular world "under the storm of the / Geometry of stars," with mountains "black and black-toothed" defining an "enormous circle / Of desert," one does not expect the last three words of the poem: "This is happiness." But then nothing is so surprising as happiness, nor often so unannounced in arrival.

As a metaphor for time the snake of the complex of desert images here is almost a cliché, like the river, which "The Distance Between: Picnic of Old Friends" calls "all the shadowy / Uncoil of Time." Snake and river are joined in "Doubleness in Time," reminiscent of the poetic Warren anecdote where bull-snakes impaled on pitchforks writhe into death as the farm day ends; the same writhing motion informs the late lyric piece as "Now" and "Then" (past and present) interweave with all the fluidity of a reptile.

Sometimes situations or events that Warren senses have unusual import are treated like parables. A notable illustration is "Boy Wandering Simms' Valley": amidst the debris of the bedroom in the deserted farm, the "remembered child" (cf. Quinn, "Warren and Jarrell: The Remembered Child," *The Southern Literary Journal*) stands in a brown "study," pondering ghastly relics of the widower's suicide—sheets rotted to spider-web flimsiness, leaf-strewn blankets sodden from a broken window. His eye falls upon a bedpan, symbol of the lonely husband's care of his sick wife, after whose death he has no more wish to live. The reality the object introduces opens up vistas as wide as later will be opened by the sight of his own wife, dripping silver as she dries herself after a night swim in "Birth of Love," modeled on Botticelli's *La Nascita de Venere*. As a boy he can only wonder "what life is, and love, and what they may be"; later he will know more, but far from all; the self-interviewing will go on, in poem after poem.

Parables, as Jesus, their New Testament constructor, tells the apostles, convey to auditors chosen out of the multitude—the prodigal son, the man lying beaten beside the road, the farmer who went out to sow his field—the hidden *why* beneath what happens. In art they represent the artist's blessed gift of power to dispel involuntary blindness (as in the followers of Jesus) though not voluntary (as in his enemies). Other lyrics in *Poems New and Selected 1923–1985* which recount an event containing a truth attainable by introspection include "Red-Tail Hawk and Pyre of Youth," "Minnesota Winter," "True Love," "Far West Once," each possessing a theme susceptible, like that of "Blackberry Winter," to fictional development.

Perhaps the parable most imbedded in Warren's emotions on the lower-than-consciousness level is "The Return: An Elegy" and its "echo" thirty years later, "Tale of Time." The first, done in 1931, is both an embodiment of and a turning away from the tenets of the New Criticism, a movement which Robert Penn Warren, Cleanth Brooks, R. P. Blackmur, John Crowe Ransom, Allen Tate, and others made so powerful that even yet *Understanding Poetry* is the most influential textbook of literary criticism in Japan. "The Return: An Elegy" relies on invented rather than actual situations and impersonality to correct that state of criticism before its advent known as "adventures among masterpieces," thriving on large doses of irony, wit, allusions, figures of speech, ambiguity, personae. Nothing could be further from what is now called "confessional." Arranged chronologically (from 1985 backward), the present volume ends in polished, metrically sophisticated poems ideal for a New Critic's explication.

Although "The Return: An Elegy" has often been erroneously considered conscious autobiography, the journey by train on a rainy night of a son to the bedside of his dying mother was intended as completely fictional, as Warren relates in *The Thirtieth Year to Heaven,* put out in 1980 by Emily Wilson's The Jackpine Press in Winston-Salem, North Carolina. But *was* it autobiography? The anthology presents the work of some younger American poets: Doug Abrams, Barbara Friend, Maria Ingram, Kate Jennings, Robert Schulte; these selected five older poets, each of whom was to select a lyric pivotal in his or her development, following it with a commentary. Robert Penn Warren seems glad of the chance to study the part that "The Return: An Elegy" played in his own career.

After his time as a Rhodes Scholar at Oxford, Warren came back to California, where in 1927 he had earned an M.A. at Berkeley. While he was spending the summer there working on his writing, he received a letter from his father reporting that his mother was ill but assuring him that there was no cause for apprehension nor for coming home. The opening of classes at Vanderbilt, where he expected to teach that fall, was not far away, and Nashville only fifty miles from Guthrie, Kentucky; he stayed on, as a second letter that August counseled. The

third, in October, brought the news that his mother was now critical. Starting immediately, he arrived at his hometown to learn from an acquaintance met on the street that Mrs. Warren was in the Hopkinstown hospital twenty miles away. In *The Thirtieth Year to Heaven* Warren writes: "I drove on—it was night now—to the hospital, in a state of great agitation, but certainly in no state resembling that of the fictional 'I' in 'The Return.'"

The poem moves from East to West as the protagonist, fantasizing during the train trip as to what he will find upon arrival, speeds through the dark rain. Here, as in more poignant and realistic passages elsewhere in Warren, the fox is identified with the mother, as are the cedar and whip-o-will ("What Voice at Moth-Hour"). The anxious interior monologue is drawn, at least partly, from Jacobean drama and T. S. Eliot:

I have only said what the wind said
wind shakes a bell the hollow head
By dawn, the wind, the blown rain
Will cease their antique concitation.
It is the hour when old ladies cough and wake,
The chair, the table, take their form again
And earth begins the matinal exhalation . . .

the old fox is dead
what have I said.

In the conclusion, worry about his mother as he worked away on his poetry that California summer (in all probability) pushes him into unconscious autobiography:

Could I stretch forth like God the hand and gather
For you my mother [the pronoun *my,* unexpected here, makes of the address a genuine lament]
If I could pluck
Against the dry essential of tomorrow
To lay upon the breast that gave me suck
Out of the dark the dark and swollen orchid of this sorrow.

As he writes the commentary for the 1980 volume, Warren sees "The Return: An Elegy" as prophecy, if not in the sense of a foretelling of the future, at least a vertical exploration of the present, as *prophet* is used of Flannery O'Connor. Even while he enjoyed the realization that his experiment was a movement towards greater freedom, openness, away from the Metaphysicals and pointing towards more memorable speech (as Auden defines poetry), he found himself battling through a tangle of dark emotions generated by the subject: vague feelings of "nameless complicity and guilt" so painful that they were to keep him away from this type of poetry for a long period.

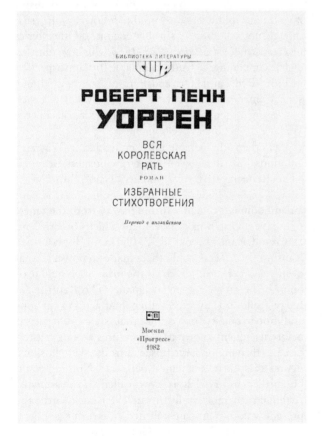

БИБЛИОТЕКА ЛИТЕРАТУРЫ

РОБЕРТ ПЕНН УОРРЕН

ВСЯ КОРОЛЕВСКАЯ РАТЬ
РОМАН

ИЗБРАННЫЕ СТИХОТВОРЕНИЯ

Перевод с английского

Москва
«Прогресс»
1982

Title page for a Russian translation of All the King's Men *(Special Collections, Western Kentucky University Libraries)*

The true version of that October 5, 1931, death of Ruth Warren appears in "Tale of Time," the titlepiece from a book three decades later. As her son says in the *New York Times* essay, the lyric is not fiction. In six parts, it begins with the funeral in Guthrie, Red's tearless sorrow expressed by the last leaf of an oak stung by autumn to gold. Inevitably the young university teacher must have reflected–who would not?–on his folly in not returning, on the talks they could have had, now forbidden eternally, the gold leaf far above him standing for the love he can no longer put into a conversation. The interval between the lowering of the coffin and the *chunk* of earth is too brief for any comprehension of grief, an aim which the rest of the sequence seeks to realize in dramatic episodes or reveries put together in random order.

The second section shows the poet in a return to Guthrie later, his desire to make real the faces the mother had been accustomed to see every day, faces like that of the druggist who kept a list of persons he wanted to get rid of, though even he (unlike the doctor and God) knew that Miss Ruth was too precious to die. "'What is death?'" "Answer Yes or No," is again in the self-interview manner, with three cynical possibilities as to the nature of death forthcoming in the dialogue between "you and me" (the two Warrens). The fourth flashes back to Squiggtown, where the whole family goes at night to bring comfort and financial help (his father's twenty-dollar bill) to an aged nurse dying there in a foul-smelling shanty, but also to receive comfort from someone who had loved the mother as they did. Although it would take a lifetime for the grief to be understood, the mission was not wholly unsatisfactory, as the poem says; it will take "eating the dead," as impossible as eating stars, but one way of putting the truth.

The rest of "Tale of Time" is first of all a communion with the mother, but also a journey into the poet's own heart at the end and a philosophical widening of addressée as the series closes: a reaching out as in Whitman's "Song of Myself" to whatever readers in the future will come upon his lines. The crisis of October 5, 1931, the loss of his mother, is not confined to this poem. "Natural History" returns to this smile in fantasy as, escaped from the grave, she counts "her golden memories of love": "Her breath is sweet as bruised violets" (the image associated with her in "The Return: An Elegy" if indeed the elegiac invention has autobiographical roots), "and her smile sways like daffodils reflected in a brook."

In her agony, Ruth Warren summoned up strength to leave each mourner around her bed a smile, a legacy which her son Robert Penn does not forget. In a recent poem, "Rumor at Twilight," after a good dinner, standing alone amidst the expensive shrubbery of his home, he asks the "you": "Can you really reconstruct your mother's smile?" Such is the attempt Hart Crane makes in "The Bridge" as he recalls the smile his mother almost brought him from church one Sunday morning in his boyhood. "Doubleness in Time," another of the present decade, is evidence of how the Hopkinstown, Kentucky, deathbed farewell continues to live within Warren's imagination:

> Her eyes,
>
> From one to another of those who
> Stand by, move. You hear,
> Almost, the grind in the socket.
> The face fixes on each face, and for
> Each face constructs
> A smile. . . .

Turned into a New Englander almost by accident, Warren is a man whose allegiance to place remains that of a southerner despite the glories of West Wardsboro, Vermont, where he spends vacation seasons, or the peace of Fairfield, Connecticut, or the romance of a Mediterranean villa and remoter settings such as Egypt. Most cherished among southern landscapes are those enshrining "timeless moments" suggestive of Joyce's "epiphanies" or Eliot's "still point" and "the lotus rose quietly, quietly" of "Burnt Norton." Prototype of all these instants of sudden illumination is the Marvellian "Bearded Oaks," though its stress on evolution disguises the suddenness. In this lyric, Louisiana becomes a lost Atlantis: the oaks seem seaweed on the bottom of an ocean of layered light, seaweed elevated into mythic persons treading back and forth on the couple on the grass, two lovers no more important than coral formations. These human "atolls" are independent of happiness, inappropriate to their suspended state, threatened by the tentacles of "Passion and slaughter, ruth, decay," in which the pain belongs, as does the golden nightingale in "Sailing to Byzantium," to "the artifice of eternity," to Being, not Becoming.

In "Bearded Oaks" the Louisiana pair, with no more breath than flies in amber, experience a stasis of togetherness which finds its foil in the loneliness of another southern poem, "The Owl," wherein the solitary poet enjoys like them a temporary though not wholly felicitous peace. These are only a few of the Warren explorations into a Promised Land occupied by Timelessness and Peace. As a mature man, Robert Penn Warren loved to come back to the site in Kentucky with hidden water falling musically over stone, the flaming milkweed flower, and all the rest of a beauty possible "Where time is not," a beauty threatened by the owl, the same predator as in "The Bird of Night," that close analogy by his friend Jarrell:

Later he would remember this, and start,
And once or twice again his tough old heart
Knew sickness that the rabbit's heart must know,
When star by star the great wings float,
And down the moonlit track below
Their mortal silken shadow sweeps the snow.
O scaled bent claw, infatuate deep throat!

("The Owl")

These moments—if the noun is not a contradiction in terms—continue to occur in New England, as witnessed in "First Moment of Autumn Recognized," separated from the Louisiana/Kentucky scenes by a lifetime. Its evocation of a Vermont afternoon swims in the air of what seems glittering champagne, bubbling, "delicious / On tongue of spirit":

We know
This to be no mere moment, however brief,
However blessed, for
Moment means time, and this is no time,
Only the dream, untimed, between
Season and season.

(An extensive critical essay could be written on the dream in Robert Penn Warren.) "Platonic Lassitude," which opens "Not one leaf stirs," is one more example of this annihilation of motion; "even the past dissolves like a dream of mist," until a crow calls from the black cliff, renewing the owl's threat.

"If we can think of timelessness, does it exist?" asks "Old Dog Dead" (the argument of Saint Anselm); in Part 3 Warren inquires in quaintly archaic terms: "Tell me, / Is there a garden where / The petal, dew-kissed, withereth not?" His youthful Muse had already in "The Garden" answered the second in the negative. Both queries are really only one: does an absolute exist, or should the poet disregard spiritual stirrings and reconcile himself to the skull, smiling or grim, of the Arizona desert? Is the broken statue of Ozymandias a better symbol of man's future than the single beech in the gold glade?

Warren ends his *New York Times* discussion of poetics by quoting from memory an American philosopher: "Isn't it William James who once said that any man who creates a philosophical system is really writing an autobiography?" Basic to any such system are "Who am I?" and "What is the world?" Pope John Paul II in his doctoral dissertation, *The Human Person,* searches patiently for a solution: is the self an abiding presence, responsible for choices? "Covered Bridge" speaks of:

Another land, another age, another self
Before all had happened that has happened since
And is now arranged on the shelf
Of memory in a sequence that I call Myself.

Family and Community Poems

In his 1982 study of Warren's poetry, Floyd Watkins noted that in his later work the poet has written more about family and community than he had in the past.

. . . Warren has created a complex and extensive world. No American author seems to have started out with a design for the creation of his own literary community in several works, but many there are who have persistently developed works about their cultures and their places. Warren's people—even in this imaginary Kentucky community without a name—derive from and represent a world as recognizably Warren's as Yoknapatawpha is Faulkner's or Winesburg, Ohio, is Anderson's. The community exists in Warren's poetic works, although neither poet nor critic can pinpoint the time when he came to recognize its existence.

The poetic chronicle of Warren's family has a scope of more than a hundred years, not less than the time span of the Gant (or Webber) and Sartoris and Compson families or of the political and literary sagas of the Lowells and the Adamses. The joys and sorrows of the Penns and the Warrens are created with lyrical intensity and with national and historical implications. What Faulkner was perhaps groping for when he wrote *Flags in the Dust* is reflected in a different form in Warren's poems of the personal and community past.

The community past and the family past give the poems a texture different from that usually found in the fiction. The poems about the past reveal that the deep feelings almost always concealed beneath the hard exteriors of the narrators in Warren's best novels are indeed related to the personal and lyrical feelings of the poet.

In the diverse poems, the dominant theme seems to be the desire to know. The effectiveness of this motif is due in part to its final failure. There are moments of joy and even of reconcilement, but one cannot achieve ultimate joy in the labor of the frontier, the relationships of the family, the completeness of knowledge, and the beauties of art, or in the knowledge of the amazing grace of personal or religious salvation.

—Floyd C. Watkins, *Then & Now: The Personal Past in the Poetry of Robert Penn Warren* (Lexington: University Press of Kentucky, 1982), pp. 169–170

Against this phenomenological position comes the dénouement of "Why You Climbed Up": "Then all begins again. And you are you." Since life is process, change, another key topic in philosophy, is crucial. "The Place" adds to this metaphysical self-interview, "Self is the cancellation of self, and now is the hour / Self is the mutilation of official meanings, and this is the place." *Now* and *this* change as does the actor. "What year will you know the fruit that is yourself?" ("Snowfall"). Warren is convinced that only upon finale of pilgrimage will truth break forth in apocalyptic vision or in a more subdued but incontrovertible form:

> The dire hour
> Is the time when you must speak
> To your naked self–never
> Before seen, nor known.
>   ("Sunset")

Through all the "four ages" he has struggled, as the Yeatsian "Whatever You Now Are" records, to tell singer from song, dancer from dance, self from self: about the self, when dawn breaks, "Will a more strange one yet inhabit the precinct of day?"

To know the world, the person needs above all to know the first person singular, or (as in most of the later Warren) the second person singular, as *you,* perceiver. In "Why Boy Came to Lonely Place" (note how the article is missing to lend universality), Warren at thirteen stands under "the ragged shadow of cedar" wondering what difference his absence years hence will make to the universe, repeating his name, unexpectedly terrified by the realization that that is all he is. He projects himself into the far dizzy tense when he will be no more than a fossil, such as those his uncle discloses to him in "Old-Time Childhood in Kentucky." He moves his hand reassuringly over his face; yet, if the poetry is taken as a whole (and his *"Or Else Poem/Poems 1968–1978"* urges that the lyrics *be* taken just this way) Robert Penn Warren intuits in the depth of his being that there is more to identity than matter. The hope is no easy hope but it is steady: "The vision will come–the Truth be revealed–but / Not even its vaguest nature you know–ah, truth // About what?" ("Vision").

In order to understand the world (and like Jarrell, Warren constantly regards the world as "alive," capable of understanding itself, speaking, even, and being understood), a dictionary of its language must be either located or devised. Many of the entries in such a lexicon will turn out to be synonyms or at least

The Warrens on a ferry crossing the Minch, which separates the Inner and Outer Hebrides, in 1983
(photograph by Gabriel Penn Warren; courtesy of Gabriel Penn Warren)

WEST WARDSBORO, VERMONT 05360

September 16, 1983.

Dear Cleanth:

I hear that you all have be n retured to us
in safety and, I trust, in happines . We lo k
forward to seeing you all next week -- if we can
ever do the mop-up here.

I want to thank you devoutly for the pains you
took with the poetry manuscript. It was very useful
to me, and surprising in a few instances. You upgrad
ed poems I was not at all sure about. I only
fear that you were too easy on the book -- which
is like you. But this leads to a broader thought,
which I have thought for a long time. You must --
you plural -- must have known of the dimension of
our attachment to Brookses and admiration.I can
look back longer than Eleanor, but with no more
feeling.But I want to say something more special
now. You can't imagine how much I owe you about
poetry-- on two counts. Our long collaborations
always brought something new and eye-opening to me,
seminal notions, for me, often couched in some
seemingly incidental or casual remark. One of the
happiest recolledtions I have, is that of the
long sessions of work on UP -- not to mention
all earlier and later conversations. The other co nt
has to do with the confidence you gaveme about my
own efforts. I'm sure that you were often over-
generous, but even allowing for that, it still
meant something fundamental to me. I have often wanted
say something like this to you, but I know
how you'd give an embarrassed shrug and disclaimer.
Anyway now I can say it without your interxuption.

The present MS has grown some sinxe you saw it,
In number of ossihle poems, clearly not all. But
I won't come at you about that. That much mercy in
me.

Give our love to Tinkie. we'll see you -- and
soon.

As ever,

No answer, please.

[handwritten in left margin: I have been not even a copy of the indifference]

Letter that Warren sent Cleanth Brooks while he was working on New and Selected Poems: 1923–1985 *(Yale Collection of American Literature, Beinecke Rare Book and Manuscript Library)*

analogates. Driven by the Gospel injunction to regard the kingdom of God as being within, Warren over and over begs a mysterious listener that he may learn the meaning of time, love, the past, life, history, joy, forgiveness, delight, truth, the soul, with or without capitals (assuming that each can be reduced to a definition or even a word: "Is *was* but a word for wisdom, its price?" in "Rattlesnake Country"), e.g., "Time is the dimension in which God strives to define His own Being," which prefaces *Being Here Poetry 1977–1980*. Abstract as his diction often becomes (happiness, logic, guilt, immortality, rumor, paradigm, antinomy, knowledge) he can rise in his best artifacts to "incarnation," a noun used in the plural for the title of his 1966–1968 volume. This gift for celebrating the concrete is fortunate, even if he is able to animate abstractions through metaphor and dramatic situations when operating within its antithesis. "Beauty is momentary in the mind," Stevens rightly says in "Peter Quince at the Clavier," and concludes his apothegm, "But in the flesh it is immortal."

One last reference to "Poetry Is a Kind of Unconscious Autobiography." Interviewing himself as his art progresses, Robert Penn Warren has become more and more aware of that part in poetry's sense played by sound, a part not fully realized by the maker: "The physical body, in tightening, tension, release, or flow becomes a participation in the groping toward a dramatic meaning." Admittedly poetry is speech (for Auden "memorable speech" and in Hopkins "speech for contemplation"), speech which at least mentally goes from potency to act. "The Return: An Elegy" shows how Warren was a master even in his twenties at marrying sound and meaning: "*Rain in the pine wind shaking the stiff pine* / Beneath the wind the hollow gorges whine" is clearly elegiac preparatory for the metaphor of mourner as stiff pine. It is to be expected that this extraordinary writer will go on asking his poems questions and coming ever closer to those answers which art is capable of giving.

–Bernetta Quinn, "A Kind of Unconscious Autobiography," *Southern Review*, 21 (April 1985): 416–427

Cover for Warren's last volume of poetry, which included new poems in the section titled "Altitudes and Extensions (1980–1984)"
(Special Collections, Western Kentucky University Libraries)

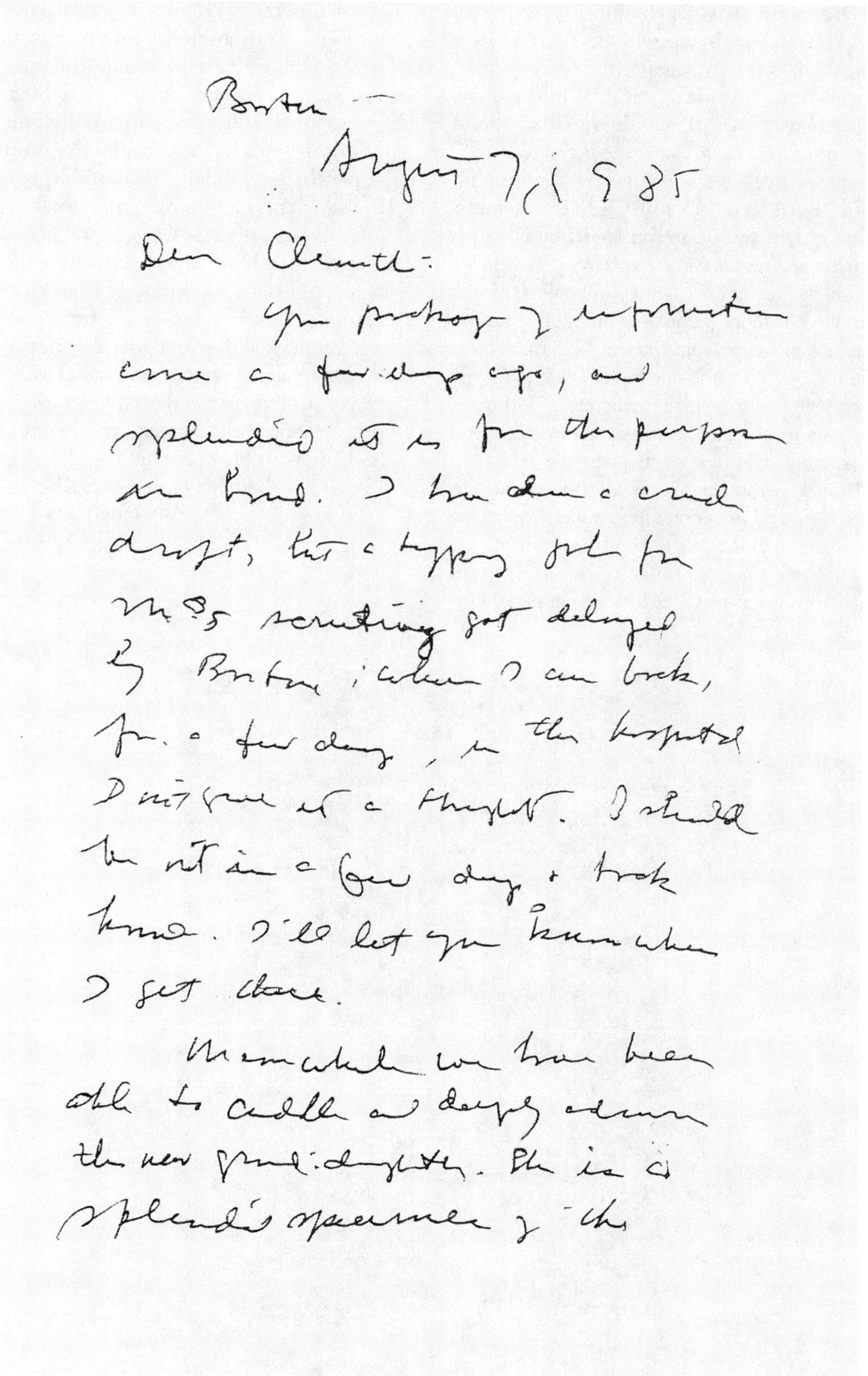
Boston —

August 7, 1985

Dear Cleanth:

Your package of information came a few days ago, and splendid it is for the purpose at hand. I have done a crude draft, but a typing job for MS scrutiny got delayed by Boston; when I am back, for a few days, in the hospital I will give it a thought. I should be out in a few days & back home. I'll let you know when I get there.

Meanwhile we have been able to cuddle and deeply admire the new grand-daughter. She is a splendid specimen of the

Letter written to Brooks the day before Warren underwent surgery for cancer (Yale Collection of American Literature, Beinecke Rare Book and Manuscript Library)

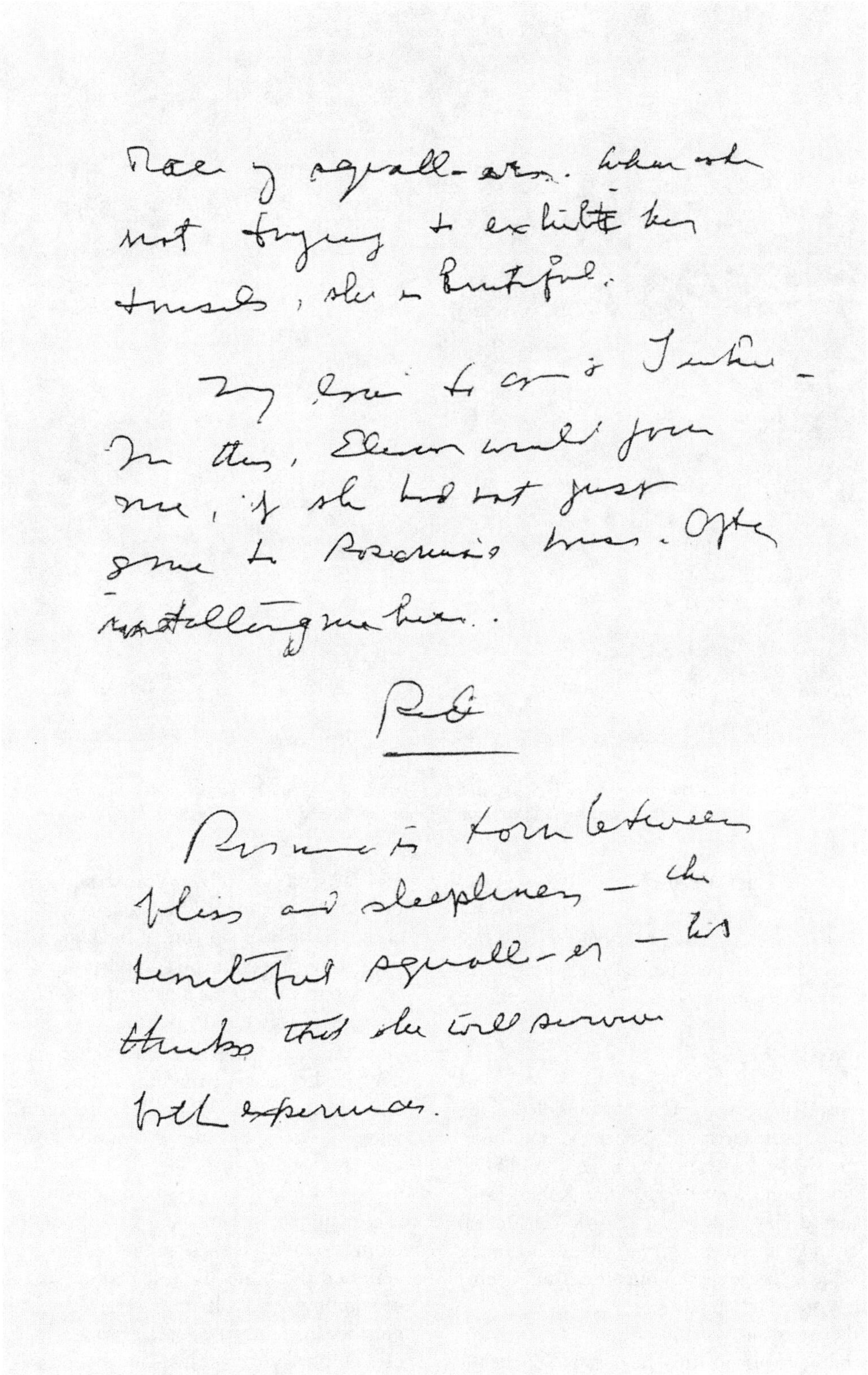

Race of squall-arm. When she
not trying to exhibit her
tricks, she is beautiful.

My love to you & Turkin —
For this, Eleanor would have
me, if she had not just
gone to Roseann's house. After
installing me here...

Rob

Roseann is torn between
bliss and sleepiness — the
beautiful squall-er — but
thinks that she will survive
both experiences.

Warren and Virginia Ferris at the Warrens' home in West Wardsboro, Vermont (photograph by William Ferris; Southern Historical Collection, William Ferris Collection, Wilson Library, University of North Carolina at Chapel Hill)

Last Years

This story of Warren's appointment in 1986 as the first U.S. Poet Laureate was carried in Time. *Because of his failing health, Warren served only the first year of his two-year appointment.*

All the Nation's Poet

For almost 210 years, the U.S. has muddled along without an official poet laureate. This lack did not noticeably hinder the work of such natives as Poe, Whitman, Dickinson, Eliot, Pound, Stevens, Frost and Robert Lowell. But it bothered Hawaiian Senator Spark Matsunaga, an avid reader and sometimes writer of poems, including one called *Ode to a Traffic Light* ("Impartial traffic cop / That blushingly speeding cars do stop . . . ")

From the moment Matsunaga entered Congress, as a member of the House in 1963, he began a lonely but determined campaign to create a national poetic license. Last year he finally succeeded. Librarian of Congress Daniel J. Boorstin agreed that each new consultant in poetry to the Library, a post that has existed for 50 years

and carries a one- or two-year term, would also bear the title of poet laureate. Matsunaga was understandably elated: "The poet laureate of the U.S. will raise the prestige and respect of the poet to the point where youngsters will aspire to become poets, just as politically minded youngsters aspire to the presidency."

At least one poet was inclined to disagree. "When I was growing up, a title would not have affected me at all," says Robert Penn Warren, 80, who last week became the nation's first poet laureate. "I started writing because it was what I wanted to do. I didn't need encouragement." In fact, Warren (who was poetry consultant to the Library of Congress in 1944–45) suggested he would not have accepted the honorific if it had carried the same sort of trappings as in Britain, where in 1668 John Dryden became the first poet laureate. "The idea of an official poet goes against our system," says Warren. "We aren't English. Over there, the laureate becomes a member of the government. Over here, I will just be an employee of the Library of Congress."

Warren going for a swim at his summer house in West Wardsboro, Vermont (photograph by William Ferris; Southern Historical Collection, William Ferris Collection, Wilson Library, University of North Carolina at Chapel Hill)

Cover for the 1985 New Directions edition of Warren's second novel (Yale Collection of American Literature, Beinecke Rare Book and Manuscript Library)

FIRST DRAFT of statement by Brooks and Warren fir Southern Revuew (winter 1985-86) to settle various false stories current about the founding, etc. Inclufing one of having been called in by H.P. Long.

FOUNDIMG OF SOUTHERN REVIEW

first draft

Man is the king of beasts because he is the master maker. Birds build nests, bees make coombs, etc. But man makes paintings, constitutions, interstellar flying machines , and nuclar bombs.   He also makes fictions, some pieces of which are called history -- history being made not only of established facts but of attitudes, that is, of interpretations. The truth is not in him, except sometimes on oath and only if xhjxxxixxxxfxxxxixxxxtxxxinkxxx objectively established fact is at stake.   In general, man cannot report a fact withovt being a little bit of an artist, a maker.

The so-called history of the <u>Southern Review</u> is a case in point. <u>History</u> is the wrong word here. It shouddbe <u>histories</u> -- plural -- because in the fok imagination, as embalmed even in accounts in print, In fact, there are various contradictory tales.   Even on certain xxxxxxfxxk sacresanct pages of the <u>Southern Review</u>. With perhaps some minor slip, but on oath if requored.

Ixxxnyxexxxexxxexexxixxxxxxxxxxxxxxxxxxxxxxxxxxxxxxxxxxxxxxx

Adter the arruval of R.P. Warren at LSU, in the fall of 1934 [*] ChailewsW. Pipkin, Cleanth Brooks , and Warren went to Shreveoort, Louisiana, to meet John (?) McGinnis and Henry Nash Smith , editors of the <u>Southe</u> <u>west Review</u> publishe by the Southwest Methodist University of Dallas , Texas, regarding the possibility of LSU joining with SMU in editing the <u>Southwest Review</u> and financing it. Undoubtesly,

---

[*] Italics here because in pages of the <u>SR</u>. the date is given as 1933.

been discussing

Pipkin, Dean of the Graduate School, had xxxxxxxxx the matter with xhxx President Smith of LSU, even though Brooks and Warren had had no conversation with the President or other oficial.(B ??) In any case, after the meeting at Shreveport, Brooks and Warren had

Page from a draft of an essay about the founding of the Southern Review *(Yale Collection of American Literature, Beinecke Rare Book and Manuscript Library)*

Warren will be receiving a bit more than the annual stipend of £100 and a case of wine that goes to his English counterpart (currently Poet Ted Hughes). The U.S. job pays $36,000, and an additional $10,000 has been appropriated for a poetry conference at which the poet laureate may read, if he wants to. He will not hold the title for life, but only until his term as consultant to the Library is over. And he will not be expected to produce occasional verse or commemorative odes at anyone's behest. "I would not think of doing such a thing," says Warren.

The poet laureateship may be a title in name only, but certainly no one is begrudging Warren's selection. He is a familiar name to the general public, probably best known for his novel *All the King's Men* (1946). He is the only person ever to win Pulitzer prizes for both poetry and fiction. His distinguished career seems to have made the introduction of a regal tradition into a democratic society easy for everyone involved. "I think he is such an obvious choice," says Librarian Boorstin, who made the appointment. "We were fortunate to have Robert Penn Warren with us, willing to take on this responsibility."

What may happen when Warren must relinquish the honor is already a vexing question. The prospect of regular spats over who will be the next laureate does not seem terribly poetic. Fairly soon the U.S. will have accumulated more laureates than the 18 that England has amassed in almost 300 years. In a calendar sent to friends and constituents, Matsunaga has written, "If the lessons of human experience were all written in verse, we might better learn and remember them." One metrical piece of advice: "Abandon what's foreign / After Penn Warren."

—*Time* (10 March 1986): 48

* * *

Warren and Brooks at LSU for the fiftieth-anniversary celebration of the founding of the Southern Review *(Charles East Papers, Louisiana and Lower Mississippi Valley Collections, Louisiana State University Libraries, Baton Rouge)*

This article was written by James Shannon, who had Warren as his master's thesis adviser when he attended the University of Minnesota.

Remembering Warren at the University of Minnesota

The opening of the school year turns my thoughts to the debt I owe some great teachers who, in different ways, took me in hand years ago and helped me discover the difference between learning and doing homework. In my youth the term "men-

tor" had not acquired the currency it has today. Looking back I realize now that six, maybe eight, of my teachers over the years were also models and mentors for me.

On occasion I have been able to tell some of them how much richer my life has been because of their influence on it. One such mentor I have never thanked explicitly. Today I would like to make amends for this omission.

Thirty-eight years ago this month I began my first class in graduate school at the University of Minnesota. The course was "The Technique of the Novel." The

---

Friday, October 11, 1985 THE DAILY REVEILLE Page 3

Campus

Warren admired by audience

By T. BRADLEY KEITH
Staff Writer

Robert Penn Warren returned to LSU Thursday night to speak at a national literary conference marking the anniversary of the Southern Review, which he co-founded fifty years ago.

Though he was plagued with technical problems throughout the evening which at times made him inaudible, Warren's mere presence moved the capacity crowd in the University Union Theater to three arousing standing ovations.

The winner of two Pulitzer Prizes and author of the universally renowned novel "All The King's Men", looked distinguished, but somewhat frail as he took the stage with the aid of his silver cane.

Warren was presented to the audience by Thomas A. Kirby, an emeritus professor of English at LSU, who introduced Warren as "America's most eminent poultry consultant."

Kirby's introduction called attention to one of the most humorous billings of Warren's career. In 1944, Warren was appointed to the position of poetry consultant for the Library of Congress. But in one of the great faux pas of the year, the Baton Rouge Morning Advocate reported that Warren had been appointed as "poultry consultant".

Warren made his way from a table at which he was sitting, to a podium across the stage amid a tumultuous standing ovation which lasted a full two minutes.

A hushed silence and stillness overcame the audience in anticipation of Warren's recital of what he considered some of his best poems. But the whining of the microphone and Warren's own naturally weak

voice made it all but impossible to understand what was being said.

The audience was not bothered by the incomprehensible reading, but rather seemed mesmerized by Warren's rising and falling intonations and the gentle lulling of his voice. The readings drew appropriate chuckles and pauses, however, from many in the audience who were initimately familiar with Warren's work.

Warren was not at first comfortable standing at the podium, and problems with the lighting and audio forced him to move back to the table, and to start his reading over again on five separate occasions. The look in Warren's eyes seemed to portray his discomfort and longing for a more intimate and personable environment in which to read.

The audience, however, was understanding and patient throughout the reading. They were here to see the man — the legend — and they couldn't have been happier.

After reading six of his own poems, Warren turned the mike over in a pre-arranged move to James Olney, currently the co-editor of The Southern Review.

"It is a great honor for me to be reading your poems aloud in your presence," Olney said to Warren.

"But I'm going to turn so I can't see the pain run across your face when I screw something up," Olney quipped.

Olney recited poems handpicked by Warren which mean the most to him now. Olney's recital was strong and captivating.

It was Warren's turn to be enthralled. You could **(See WARREN, page 5)**

Reveille photo by Darryl Collioux
ROBERT PENN WARREN — visiting LSU during the 50th anniversary of the Southern Review. Warren is the author of "All The King's Men" and is well-known as one of the literary voices of the south in the 1930s.

Warren

(From page 3)

see in Warren's eyes that hearing his own poems was taking him back. each poem summoning images of his life and passions in years past.

The loudest applause came at the end of Olney's reading of a Warren poem which ended with the line, "Only in the name of death, do we learn the true meaning of love".

Warren seemed genuinely moved by the final ovation, and moved to the right of stage to make his exit. He got no further than twenty feet before he was mobbed by a pack of autograph seekers.

Warren signed books spanning his entire career, from his first novel, "John Brown — The Making of a Martyr", to his most recently published book of

poems. Warren signed dozens of copies of his most famous novel, "All The King's Men".

Warren was very warm and animated while autographing, and chatted with each person fortunate enough to have their book signed. In each case, Warren checked out the publishing company and version of the book he was signing, and marvelled at the time that had gone by.

One man who had met Warren twenty years earlier at Yale, requested that he resign a prized possession — a signed copy of Warren's "Who Speaks for the Negro?".

Warren was finally rescued by his wife of 34 years, who was afraid they may never have a chance to leave. Warren left the theater with a stride which was somewhat frail and feeble, but with a vision which has remained clear and sure.

Report in the LSU campus newspaper on Warren's talk to a standing-room-only crowd at the University Auditorium as part of the celebration of the Southern Review *(Charles East Papers, Louisiana and Lower Mississippi Valley Collections, Louisiana State University Libraries, Baton Rouge)*

Bumper sticker celebrating Warren after he was appointed the Poet Laureate in 1986 (Collection of James A. Grimshaw Jr.)

Reading and Teaching Poetry

In this excerpt from an interview after he became Poet Laureate, Warren argues that memorization and recitation are critical to learning about poetry.

A poem you don't feel to your toes is not a very good one. But it also takes a person who knows how to feel to his toes to read a poem. Take a rhyme from Alexander Pope. He said the accused get convicted and hanged because the jurymen won't sit through another afternoon of dullness; they want to eat lunch. The line goes: "And wretches hang that jurymen may dine." That line has a spitting motion. The physical feeling in the line is the meaning of the line. There are other kinds of experiences that go into poetry, images and so forth. But it's the basic physicality that you have to become aware of. A lot of people don't understand that; they think poetry is just something pretty. Pretty, hell! It's life; it's a vital experience.

The trick in understanding poetry is to read a poem to yourself so that you hear it while you read it. You don't necessarily say the words; the muscles make the total movement of the words. I want to see how it tastes, how the muscular play is right to the toes. The language is not supposed to be simply signs on a paper. It's supposed to be heard–but heard as sound that's physically realized–and visualized. That's why it's important to memorize and recite poems.

When I was in school we were graded on memorization and on whether we had gotten the feel of a poem. At Vanderbilt in the freshman English course, I had to memorize at least 500 lines a term. Today, young people aren't asked to do that. When I taught at Yale I used to ask students in a seminar which of them could quote a poem all the way through. Only once did I ever get a person who could do so. Modern youngsters never have a chance to learn anything about poetry. It's the practicality of a world in which education no longer teaches you how to live, just how to learn to make a living. A whole side of the self is gone.

–Alvin P. Sanoff, "'Pretty, Hell! Poetry Is Life':
A Conversation with America's First Poet
Laureate," *U.S. News & World Report*
(23 June 1986): 74

SIX POEMS

BY ROBERT PENN WARREN

1987

TAMAZUNCHALE PRESS, NEWTON, IOWA

Title page for a volume measuring 4.0 x 6.5 centimeters that was published in a limited edition of 250 copies (Special Collections, Western Kentucky University Libraries)

teacher was Robert Penn Warren—novelist, poet, scholar, gentleman and teacher par excellence.

I can still recall many details of that first day in a third-floor room in Folwell Hall. Two modest red and white wall signs proclaimed "No Smoking." There were about a dozen of us in the class. Warren entered, carrying one sheet of paper and a pack of cigarettes. He lit up and started to talk as he paced back and forth in front of the blackboard.

From this single sheet he read off the titles of 10 novels we were to read, one a week for 10 weeks. For two hours each week we were to discuss the style and technique of a different author. We were all to buy paperback copies of the same edition of each text, so that we could mark them up and so that we could all cite the same words on the same page in analyzing a given passage.

Lighting a fresh cigarette from a spent one, Warren, moving all the time, asked us to do him a favor. He knew that the title of the course was "The Technique of the Novel." But he admitted that he could not define a novel. He had read several. He had written some. But he would have to ask us all to proceed on the premise that we knew in some vague way what this term signified, even though none of us could define it.

Without notes or text he spoke easily and rapidly about the myriad elements a novelist must somehow balance and fuse. Even in such introductory remarks his evident passion for his subject conveyed intellectual excitement to me. I was charmed. My earlier sense of apprehension on Day One of graduate school melted away.

In later classes Warren never told us we ought to like something we read. By framing his comments as queries he drew us steadily into dialogue. Here was a widely published, successful author (he had just sold the movie rights to *All The King's Men*) talking to us about writing, from the inside out.

His was an inductive method of close textual analysis, with dozens of questions about what works best in writing and why—the reverse of many pedants I had known who waxed eloquent about the beauty of a literary passage but with nary a clue as to why it was good writing. Warren pressed us for specific reasons whenever he sensed our agreement that a given passage did what its author intended.

In his class there was no such thing as a dumb question. Deeply courteous Southern gentleman that he is, Warren would take a poor question, fashion it into a good question, and give it an excellent answer. He taught me as much about courtesy between teacher and student as he did about rapport between a writer and a reader.

One day in his office I was present while he was being interviewed by a reporter from the New York Herald Tribune. In a classically inept question the reporter asked, "Dr. Warren, how does one go about writing a great novel?" Warren slowly looked out the window, at the floor, at the ceiling and then said, "I cannot tell you how any writer goes about writing a great novel. But I will tell you this. In order to write a very bad novel a writer must have a vast lack of interest in a host of other worthwhile topics." The wisdom in that one statement has been a guideline ever since for me about how to focus my energy and my time.

At the heart of my admiration of Robert Penn Warren is the fact that he is an accomplished and disciplined artist who made a decision early on to divide his time between the art of writing and the art of teaching. The Herald Tribune reporter also asked him why he continued to teach when his novels were best sellers. His simple reply was: "I could not write those novels unless I had regular contact with those irreverent students who have the audacity to question my judgments daily. They charge my batteries."

Warren is now Poet Laureate of the United States, the first person to hold this distinguished title. True to his own demanding principles, he has promised never to write testimonial verses for state occasions.

As one of his aging but grateful students I thank him from the heart for the tough-minded, graceful and generous guidance he gave many of us nearly 40 years ago, and for his fidelity to this day to the standards of personal and artistic integrity he exemplified then.

–James Shannon, "Overdue Tribute to a Teacher Who Made a Lifelong Difference," *Minneapolis Star and Tribune,* 7 September 1986, p. 25A

ROBERT PENN WARREN

A SOVIET - AMERICAN PERSPECTIVE

A Symposium Sponsored by

The Beinecke Rare Book and Manuscript Library
Yale University

Center for the Study of Southern Culture
The University of Mississippi

A.M. Gorky Institute of World Literature

August 8-9, 1987

Cover and page from the schedule for a program honoring Warren held in the Beinecke Rare Book and Manuscript Library on the Yale campus
(James Gee Library Archives, Texas A&M University–Commerce)

Saturday, August 8, 1987

9:00	William Ferris: Welcoming Remarks
9:15	Robert Penn Warren Interview with Robert MacNeil. Courtesy MACNEIL-LEHRER REPORT
9:30	Tatiana Morozova: "Robert Penn Warren and the Russian Literary Tradition"
10:30	Coffee
11:00	C. Vann Woodward: "Robert Penn Warren and Southern History"
12:00	Lunch
1:30	James H. Justus: "The Grandfather and the Stranger in the Work of Robert Penn Warren"
2:30	Nicolai Anastasiev: "Robert Penn Warren in the Soviet Union"
3:30	Coffee
4:00	James A. Grimshaw, Jr.: "Warren Studies: Trends of the 80's"
5:00	Reception (wine and cheese)

Sunday, August 9, 1987

9:30	Maya M. Koreneva: "Time in the Narrative Structure of Robert Penn Warren's Novel"
10:30	Coffee
11:00	Cleanth Brooks: "Robert Penn Warren: His Wrestle with Time and History"
12:00	Lunch
1:30	Sergei Chakovsky: "Robert Penn Warren—The Critic of William Faulkner's Work"
2:30	Lewis P. Simpson: "Robert Penn Warren and Thomas Jefferson"
3:30	Coffee
4:00	Cleanth Brooks and Sergei Chakovsky: Closing Remarks

This project is an activity of the American Council of Learned Societies-Soviet Academy of Sciences Commission on the Humanities and Social Sciences, administered in the United States by the International Research and Exchanges Board (IREX).

FPT $22.50

This collection represents the rich variety
of the work of over half a century in
fiction, nonfiction, and poetry by one
of our most distinguished men of letters.

The seven fiction selections, which
cover a span of forty-six years, begin with
"Prime Leaf" (1931), the author's first
published story, and end with the closing
section of his most recent novel, *A Place
to Come To* (1977).

There are six characteristic examples of
Warren's nonfiction writing: three literary
essays; his introduction to The Modern
Library edition of *All the King's Men*;
and, in their entirety, two short books,
*Segregation: The Inner Conflict in the
South* and *The Legacy of the Civil War:
Meditations on the Centennial*.

In the last fifty years Warren has published sixteen volumes of poetry. That ten
of these have appeared in the last two decades is indicative of the surge of creativity
that took place when he reached his sixties
and seventies with no diminution of his
imaginative power. Except for the addition
of four earlier poems, two excerpts from
Brother to Dragons: A New Version, and a
section of *Chief Joseph of the Nez Perce*, all
of the poems are from *New and Selected
Poems: 1923–1985*.

*Dust jacket for a 1987 collection of Warren's writings assembled by Albert Erskine. In his "Editor's Note" Erskine wrote that he made
his selections without Warren's advice but with his consent (Richland County Public Library).*

A Note of Thanks

Samuel Hynes, author of The Edwardian Turn of
Mind *(1968) and other scholarly works, published his memoir*
Flights of Passage: Reflections of a World War II Avia-
tor *in 1988.*

Samuel Hynes to Warren, 25 March 1988

You won't remember a conversation we had
thirty years ago, but I do. I was at Swarthmore
then, and just off—reluctantly—to a second hitch of
Marine Corps duty for the Korean War. I said that
at least I'd be able to write a war-book; and you
said that you'd have to settle for the Civil War (I
think you were writing *Wilderness* then, though I

didn't know it). Well, I've written my war-book at
last, and I would like you to have a copy. Not to
read, but as a very inadequate expression of my
great debt to you. It was your support, over many
years, that got me started and moved me along the
way. No doubt you've forgotten all about it (there
must be dozens of us out here, who have been
helped by you). But I haven't. So thanks: you were
a model and a friend and an encouragement when I
needed all of those.

—Yale Collection of American Literature, Beinecke
Rare Book and Manuscript Library

Robert Penn Warren   31

Why had my father never even mentioned the fact to me? Or why

never taken me on at least one pious pilgrimage to see the stone

of my other grandfather?

     Later on, to add to oddness, I learned that my father had

first come to the house of Anna Ruth as a friend of her older

brother, who was ~~of~~ the age of the suitor-to-be. By this time

my father must have been living in Clarksville, and perhaps had

come back to Cerulean only for the illness or death of his

father.

     The Penns had only become Kentuckians ~~we~~ by accident. With

his company, back in the early days of the Civil War, Captain

Penn had hanged some "bushwhackers," as guerrillas -- outlaws

using some military excuse for outlawry -- were commonly called.

After the War when Grandpa Penn came home to Tennessee and got

married and had a son, the heirs of local bushwhackers, now all

good unionists as circumstances naturally dictated, went to [GO TO PAGE 31-A]

law as well as to violence for revenge. So ~~the~~ Penn fled to

Kentucky and settled, ~~taking~~ with him his old nurse, Aunt Cat,

whom I ~~was actually to know when Grandpa Penn, born in 1836, was~~

~~approaching eighty.~~

     For a time Gabriel Thomas Penn apparently prospered, not

only as a tobacco grower but as a "buyer" -- an agent who would

~~buy up lots from farmers and market tobacco after it had been~~

graded. But Grandpa Penn was, as his daughters never forgot

to say, "visionary," and missed a payment on an insurance

Page from a draft for Warren's memoir Portrait of a Father *(Southern Review Records,*
Louisiana State University Archives, LSU Libraries, Baton Rouge)

Legacy

Warren died on 15 September 1989. This obituary appeared in The Washington Post.

Robert Penn Warren: A Voyage to the Heart

By the time Robert Penn Warren came to Washington as the nation's first Poet Laureate three years ago, he was an old man, frail, the hair that gave "Red" Warren his nickname faded to the color of ground ginger. But he was still fierce and courteous and absolutely unwilling to play the prescribed role of comfortably inspirational icon.

He gave a peppery press conference, easily scattering reporters' flaccid questions, sat stolid on stage while a friend read his poems.

When it came time the following year for him to visit Washington again for a gathering of poets, he was too sick to travel. Early Friday morning in Vermont, Warren died, 84 years old, his wife and daughter with him.

That day three years ago at the Library of Congress was the only time I met him. But, like thousands of readers over the last 50 years, I lived with his poetry and novels, felt them to be an essential part of my life and my country. When I heard of his death, I remembered a college English professor saying that over the last 25 years, Warren's poetry had become something transcendent. "He is," said the professor, "writing his way into heaven."

> *The masts go white slow, as light, like dew, from darkness*
> *Condensed on them, on oiled wood, on metal. Dew whitens in*
>   *darkness.*
> *I lie in my bed and think how, in darkness, the masts go white.*
> *The sound of the engine of the first fishing dory dies seaward.*
>   *Soon*
> *In the inland glen wakes the dawn-dove. We must try*
> *To love so well the world that we may believe, in the end, in*
>   *God.*
>
> —from "Masts at Dawn"

Warren wrote more than 50 books—novels and poetry, essays and children's stories and, with critic Cleanth Brooks, two influential textbooks called *Understanding Poetry* and *Understanding Fiction*. If the game of naming the Great American Novel is still being played anywhere, Warren's *All the King's Men* would easily make the final rounds.

A state marker near Guthrie, Kentucky (courtesy of Mrs. Robert D. Frey)

An exploration of what Warren called "the myth" of populist politician Huey Long, the novel is the story of Willie Stark, an idealistic Louisiana lawyer who lives through disillusionment to become a passionate, charismatic leader. It is also, and perhaps more importantly, the story of the book's narrator, Jack Burden, the press aide, who, through a tumultuous relationship with Stark, comes to terms with his own failures and those of the patrician class from which he fell.

"If you could not accept the past and its burden," Warren wrote, "there was no future, for without one there cannot be the other. . . . if you could accept the past you might hope for the future, for only out of the past can you make the future."

For that book Warren won the 1947 Pulitzer Prize, and won it twice more for poetry as well.

He was a student of time and power, responsibility and dreams, an explorer who treasured the will to question more than anything else. But his search for knowledge was never purely abstract, and that is one reason his poetry is so readable, so easily made a part of one's existence. He lived very much in the real world and wrote of it, whether Louisiana in the Depression or the 18th-century frontier or his own life as a man searching for meaning.

Warren was born in Guthrie, Ky., and although he lived much of his life far from the South in such surroundings as Yale, Oxford University, Vermont and Fairfield, Conn., he was a creature of his native region. His passion for history, he said, began early, fed by grandfathers' tales of the Civil War and a childhood of reading. All that he read and lived melts together in his writing: The lyricism and drama of his beloved Elizabethan poets, the accents and phrases of poor men and women met in Louisiana.

His manner was courteous, gracious in a way that clearly had little to do with New England. But there was also an astringent quality, and that's what a friend of mine saw when Warren gave a reading at Drew University some years ago.

During the question session, one of the solemn admirers in the audience asked Warren why he thought it was so hard for good young poets to be published. The poet responded he didn't think it was hard at all. The next question was so obtuse Warren could not answer it, and eventually the questioner gave up. Hoping to salvage the situation, a professor asked that old reliable "What are you reading these days?"

"Around our house," Warren intoned slowly, "we are reading Milton."

That was part of what you looked for in Warren: something unyielding, something challenging. And in his poetry you found it, along with a loving respect for nature, an eye that saw traces of the past in every landscape, a questioning voice that hoped the act of exploring everyday life was the path to faith.

It is to that questioning, human voice that my friends and I turn to mark the events of our lives. One writer who interviewed the author at home included a Warren poem in his son's christening. An *All the King's Men* passage about the transforming power of love was read at my wedding.

One of the obvious advantages of being a journalist is the brazen notion that it gives you the right to meet people you've always admired. For an hour at least, you can sit beside the author, visit the actress in her dressing room, follow the activist through the streets. Robert Penn Warren was not one to encourage such instant coziness. He chafed at safe and obvious questions, offered no easy epiphanies, reminded you that your love for his work had damn well better be accompanied with the same energy and hunger he demanded of himself.

So at his press conference three years ago, I asked nothing large. Better not to seek revelation, not to pretend that this encounter was anything more than a press conference before a jostling crowd in a too-small room. Better to watch him, then leave and read his written words with the deep and sweeping rhythm of his spoken voice still in my ears.

Over the next few weeks, people who knew Warren, who met him for more than a couple of hours, will reminisce, tell anecdotes in which they figure as more than a member of an audience. His wife, Eleanor Clark, the writer and fellow lover of Milton, will return to Connecticut. There will be a funeral and probably a memorial service stuffed with gleaming literary names.

They are his friends, or at least acquaintances. I was an observer—just a reader. But perhaps I should not say "just" a reader, because this is how readers will mourn Robert Penn Warren's passing: We will go home and, today or tomorrow, pick up a book.

Long ago, in Kentucky, I, a boy, stood
By a dirt road, in first dark, and heard
The great geese hoot northward.
I could not see them, there being no moon
And the stars sparse. I heard them.
I did not know what was happening in my heart.
It was the season before the elderberry blooms,
Therefore they were going north.
The sound was passing northward.

–from "Tell Me a Story"

–Elizabeth Kastor, "Robert Penn Warren: A Voyage to the Heart," *Washington Post,* 16 September 1989, pp. C1, C3

* * *

Inviting the Future

In the concluding chapter of her book Sleeping with the Boss: Female Subjectivity and Narrative Pattern in Robert Penn Warren *(1997), Lucy Ferriss cites a Warren quotation as an epigraph:*

We, too, even in our flicker of time, can earn a place in
    the story.
How?
By creating the future. That is the promise the past
    makes to us.
    –Robert Penn Warren, *New and Selected Essays*

While Ferriss acknowledges that "the risk any critic takes in reassessing the work of a writer from an earlier era is that the heart of the text will be twisted to prove a contemporary point so far from the writer's original intent as to cancel out the unity of the work as a whole," she contends that Warren's "awareness of history was profound enough" to anticipate a paradigm shift "that could weave his stories into its new cloth":

. . . To earn a place in the past, we need to create the future–neither more nor less. The fact that we cannot, indeed would not want to, envisage that new paradigm or future is exactly part of what Warren calls the "heartening promise" of history. And if Warren's remarks on literature and history fail to persuade us that he invites the future, loaded with all its theory, to weave him into the continuing past, we have his words on Coleridge–"Even if the poet himself should rise to contradict us, we could reply that the words of the poem speak louder than his actions"–to fortify our right to interpret.

    –Lucy Ferriss, *Sleeping with the Boss: Female
    Subjectivity and Narrative Pattern in
    Robert Penn Warren* (Baton Rouge:
    Louisiana State University
    Press, 1997), p. 138–139

This account of Warren's funeral and burial was written by the poet Peter Davison, whom Warren had befriended when Davison was a child in 1935.

Deep in the Blackness of Woods: A Farewell to Robert Penn Warren

The town center of Stratton, Vermont, consists of four frame structures set in a high saddle among mountains, not one building dedicated to commerce: a town hall, a town office, a school, and an old, unsteepled, seldom-used church, all white, with no houses close by. Mourners were conducting last rites there for a great American writer last Columbus Day weekend, while the highways lower down were jammed with motorists gawking at the flaming forests by way of celebrating the discovery of America.

The man his friends and family were burying was known as Red to everyone present, though his children and grandchildren called him Poppy. He had been born eighty-four years earlier, on April 24, 1905, just north of the Tennessee border in Guthrie, Kentucky, a town of about one thousand people, given over to tobacco farming, chickens, kinfolk, and storytelling. His father, a bank officer, was a Warren; his mother, a Penn. Both grandfathers had fought in the Civil War. The family evenings in his Guthrie childhood could not have differed very much from those in Stratton in his old age: low-lit rooms, dogs at the feet, a good fire, a glass of whiskey and a hearty dinner, woodland noises outdoors, and inside the sound of live voices telling stories or reading them aloud, more often than not in a high, nasal, slurred Kentucky accent.

The stories the husband in Vermont read to his wife, who could not see well enough to read, might be from the Bible, or *Odyssey* or *Aeneid*. In Guthrie the Bible had also been read, and the other stories had been told of slavery and its discontents, of scandal and conflict, of ribaldry and war, very much like those Warren would give his writing life to, in a body of work spanning forty volumes and six decades. The stories, recounted or invented, would involve a group of central themes: trust betrayed, the surprising darknesses of the human spirit, the discovery of love through death, the softening of fate by affection, the hardening of love by fatality (*John Brown: The Making of a Martyr, The Ballad of Billie Potts, All the King's Men, Promises, The Legacy of the Civil War, A Place to Come To, New and Selected Poems, 1923–1985*).

Robert Penn Warren began as a poet, a student of John Crowe Ransom at Vanderbilt University in Nashville, and in his twenties was already identified with the "fugitive" poets who included Ransom, Donald Davidson, Merrill Moore, Allen Tate, and John Peale Bishop. Starting at about age thirty with *Night Rider,* concerning the Kentucky tobacco wars of the nineteenth century, he gave himself over to fiction, and at forty-one, even before publication of *All the King's Men* (1946), the portrait of a southern demagogue, he moved to the North, never to live in the South again for any length of time. With his second marriage and the birth of his children in the 1950s, he began increasingly to revert to poetry, as Thomas Hardy in England had left novels in favor of poetry a half century earlier, marking the change with a huge epic poem. Hardy's was called *The Dynasts* (1903–1908); Warren's was called *Brother to Dragons* (1953), and it was the most ambitious attempt he ever made to get at the dark heart of the American dream. As he wrote in a 1979 preface: "Historical sense and poetic sense should not, in the end, be contradictory, for if poetry is the little myth we make, history is the big myth we live, and in our living, constantly remake."

From this time forward, as Warren's life took its shape from New England during the years he taught at

The church in Stratton, Vermont, where a private burial service was held for Robert Penn Warren on 8 October 1989 (courtesy of Mrs. Robert D. Frey)

Yale, lived in Connecticut, and summered in Vermont, his written work moved still deeper into poetry. In the last book he published in his lifetime, *A Robert Penn Warren Reader,* he listed thirty-eight books: seventeen books of poetry; eleven books of fiction; ten of criticism, biography, history, and so on, not including his collaborative textbooks, such as *Understanding Poetry,* which educated an entire generation. Warren moved gradually out of narrative poetry (though he never abandoned it) to lyrics and meditations, which filled the five volumes he published after his seventieth year.

These late poems combined his narrative instinct, his sense of the past, and his feeling for landscape with his remembrances of youth, in such lyrics as those with which he ended *Audubon: A Vision.*

Tell me a story.

In this century, and moment, of mania,
Tell me a story.

Make it a story of great distances, and starlight.

The name of the story will be Time,
But you must not pronounce its name.

Tell me a story of deep delight.

Over and over Warren's later poems would emanate from a speaker stunned with love for the mountainous landscape:

Season late, day late, sun just down, and the sky
Cold gunmetal but with a wash of live rose, and she,
From water the color of sky except where
Her motion has fractured it to shivering splinters of silver,
Rises. . . . ("Birth of Love")

Deep in the blackness of woods, the tendons
Of a massive oak bough snap with the sound of a
Pistol-shot. ("Reading Late at Night,
                    Thermometer Falling")

Out of the peak's black angularity of shadow, riding
The last tumultuous avalanche of
Light above pines and the guttural gorge,
The hawk comes. ("Evening Hawk")

338

```
                    SERVICE for RPW
                       October 8
                    Stratton Church
                        1 p.m.

    "Master of ceremonies:" Gabriel
    Reader for liturgy: Joe Blottner

              Music for entrance

    Music: Bill Crofut and Carver Blanchard

    Liturgy:
```

WE brought nothing into this world, and it is certain we can carry nothing out. The LORD gave, and the LORD hath taken away ; blessed be the name of the LORD. 1 *Tim.* vi. 7. *Job* i. 21.

LORD, thou hast been our refuge : from one generation to another.
Before the mountains were brought forth, or ever the earth and the world were made : thou art God from everlasting, and world without end.
Thou turnest man to destruction : again thou sayest, Come again, ye children of men.
For a thousand years in thy sight are but as yesterday : seeing that is past as a watch in the night.
As soon as thou scatterest them they are even as a sleep : and fade away suddenly like the grass.
In the morning it is green, and groweth up : but in the evening it is cut down, dried up, and withered.

```
    Reminiscences:    3 minutes each

              Cleanth Brooks
              Vann Woodward
              Albert Erskine
              Ralph Ellison
              Saul Bellow
              Tommy Lou Frey

    MUSIC

    Poems:
              "Channel Firing" (Thomas Hardy): John Coleman
              "The Oxen" (Thomas Hardy): Peter Davison
              "Grackles, Goodbye." (RPW): Dick Lewis
              "What Voice at Moth Hour" (RPW): Arnold Stein
    MUSIC
    Liturgy:
```
Behold, I shew you a mystery; We shall not all sleep, but we shall all be changed, in a moment, in the twinkling of an eye, at the last trump: for the trumpet shall sound, and the dead shall be raised incorruptible, and we shall be changed.

to pass the saying that is written, Death is swallowed up in victory.   Then shall be brought

Revised text of the program for Warren's funeral service (courtesy of Mrs. Robert D. Frey)

(Service   pg. 2)

~~"Abide with Me"~~ "The Ivy", from Incarnations
Exit from Church

At the grave:

Liturgy for the Burial of the Dead: Cleanth Brooks
"Bearded Oaks" (RPW): John Hollander
"Abide with me".

Vermont was the place where Robert Penn Warren, poet, freed himself to fly like a hawk.

The mourners had come to the white church in Stratton less to marvel at the Himalayas of Warren's career (such celebrations would take place later on, in New York and Nashville and New Haven) than to say goodbye to a friend in the place he had loved. They had come to recall a lean, muscular man, redheaded in his youth, a man of marvelous courtesy, broad wit, and snorting laughter, congenial and hospitable, enormously yet inconspicuously erudite, athletic afoot and in the water, craggy in both body and features, who till the end of his days told stories in a thick Kentucky accent that few found easy to take in. (He used five syllables and more than the prescribed number of consonants to pronounce the word *literature*.)

Those who loved Warren knew him not to be a religious man in the ordinary sense, but they also knew that a burial ceremony, even for a master writer, could not leap naked into newly invented language, as though death had never happened before. They resorted to one of the great literary texts in English, transplanted from a mother country, the Book of Common Prayer, its text unstained by postbellum adulterations. No minister would be necessary, for no sacrament was being administered.

One after another his friends and relatives arose, introduced by Warren's son, Gabriel, and made their way, some haltingly, to the front of the church. Warren's biographer, Joseph Blotner, read the comfortable words; the music of Bach was played, exquisitely, by Carver Blanchard with a guitar and lute and Bill Crofut with a banjo; his oldest companions, some faint of voice in advancing age, testified to their friend's virtues and lamented his loss. Cleanth Brooks, Warren's literary colleague of over fifty years, spoke of their scholarly and critical collaboration and praised his novels; Albert Erskine, his editor for forty years, described their chess competitions and how, as young men, they read together, as young men will, the gloomiest poetry they could find; C. Vann Woodward, like Warren a profound student of the American South, bore true witness to Warren's dauntlessness as a swimmer; Saul Bellow spoke of his friend's candor, generosity, lack of pretense; a niece from Kentucky spoke of the glowing presence in her family of "Uncle Robert Penn." Between these reminiscences other friends read poems by Thomas Hardy (nearer of kin to Warren's achievements in poetry and prose than any other writer in our language) and read or sang poems by Warren himself.

When the ceremony reached its end, the company made its way in caravan through a darkening afternoon along narrow back roads to a clearing in the woods a mile or two from the village center and, leaving their cars near the wall, walked up a knoll to an old graveyard, surrounded by oaks and maples, where the gravestones leaned, roughened with moss and lichen. The poet's four-year-old granddaughter, Chiara, was heard asking excitedly where Poppy's ashes were going to be buried. His wife, the writer Eleanor Clark, full of certitude and lean as the trees, stood with her handsome children, the sculptor Gabriel and the poet Rosanna, their spouses, and the three grandchildren (one newly born) at the heightened swell of the graveyard, and when all were finally gathered around the small excavation, Cleanth Brooks began reciting, in firm tones of resignation, the graveside words, "Man, that is born of woman, hath but a short time to live, and is full of misery. He cometh up and is cut down, like a flower; he fleeth as it were a shadow, and never continueth in one stay." The poet John Hollander read one of Warren's early poems, "Bearded Oaks." Carver Blanchard stepped forward with his guitar and sang, softly on the chilly air, "Abide with Me," which had never sounded more beautiful than at this wooded graveside. When there was nothing left but silence, an attendant brought forward a pearl-gray marble urn of ashes to Eleanor Clark, who placed it in the cleft that had been prepared for it, and she and her children and grandchildren stepped forward in turn and took up handfuls of the cool moist earth to lay atop the urn. It was as though time were slowing down: one after another the mourners stepped forward, stooped, added a handful of earth to the vacancy, and walked slowly off across the coarse grass toward the road where their cars waited to take them out of the forest, while the day grew darker with the coming on of the clouds, and a few flakes of snow began to fall. Few could help stopping to look back at the place where their friend lay, a place they might never see again, as other mourners filed past the grave, stooped, let their handfuls of earth drop, and moved on, while beneath their hands the urn disappeared.

This was ski country, logging country, maple country. What was a boy from Guthrie, Kentucky, trained at Vanderbilt, the University of California, Yale, and a Rhodes Scholar at Oxford; a professor who had taught at Vanderbilt, Louisiana State University, the University of Minnesota, and finally at Yale; a writer who had worked for nearly half his life in Connecticut but also in Mussolini's Sicily, in postwar Liguria, in Brittany and Grenoble, in Grasse in the south of France, who had traveled in Crete and Egypt, who had canoed in Canada, and who in his late seventies viewed the terrain of the Nez Percé rebellion in Montana–what was this man doing seeking his eternal rest in Vermont? It was not the first time, after all, nor no doubt the last, that an American writer, deeply identified with another region of the continent, had sought rest in New England. Willa Cather, born in Winchester, Virginia, and raised in Nebraska, is buried next to a classic white church in Jaffrey, New Hampshire. Robert Lee Frost, born and raised in San Francisco but schooled in New Hampshire and Massachusetts, lies near Bennington, Vermont. Henry James, who was born in New York and died in London, reposes with his family in Cambridge, Massachusetts, overlooking the Charles River.

There may be something about this landscape that restores to us our notions of what America was, what it might become. Out of the decades that Robert Penn Warren and Eleanor Clark had been summering near Stratton came a desire to lie there after death. The plainness of the central tradition in American writing takes us back always, as Emerson (whom Warren cordially disliked) told us in *Nature,* to nature, to the thing itself, the stone, the leaf, the tree. When in his old age Warren poured forth a torrent of poetry out of a lifetime's weathering, his memory looked upstream to the limestone hills of Kentucky, yet he found himself speaking of the past from a veritable place in the present, in the words of the title of his last novel, speaking from "a place to come to." Just as the poems of Thomas Hardy's old age are embedded in the turn of a road, the shape of a hill, the street of a village, the echo of the choir in a church in Wessex, so the poems of Warren's last, and perhaps finest, period characteristically speak themselves in the tongue of a man standing on a ridge of the Green Mountains while the sun sets and a hawk soars overhead, a hawk like the one a boy shot at in the first story Warren ever published, in 1931.

In the final years of Robert Penn Warren's rich life he had come to rest here, in the land of white clapboards and maple syrup and covered bridges, in the midst of green mountains, which the psalmist so hopefully adored as the source of help, and which spoke to Warren in his age more eloquently than the hills of his youth. He saw the transition as the darkness of a covered bridge, in a poem written near the end of his life:

> Another land, another age, another self
> Before all had happened that has happened since
> And is now arranged on the shelf
> Of memory in a sequence that I call Myself.

And he concludes,

> What pike, highway, or path has led you from land to
>   land,
> From year to year, to lie in what strange room,
> Where to prove identity you now lift up
> Your own hand–scarcely visible in that gloom.

Even in this rumination, written as he neared eighty, on the dark connections between youth and age, Red Warren could not help imagining his covered bridge as embodying a story, a "sequence that I call Myself." Why not accept burial where the darkness began to lighten, where the story ended rather than where it began?

–Peter Davison,
New England Monthly (March 1990): 37–39

* * *

In January 1990 the Southern Review *published four tributes to Warren, one of the original founders of that journal. All four men who contributed were current or former co-editors of the* Southern Review.

This tribute is by Donald E. Stanford, one of the co-editors when the new series of the Southern Review *began.*

Robert Penn Warren and the *Southern Review*

All of us seriously interested in contemporary literature are grateful to Robert Penn Warren for his remarkable accomplishments that won him three Pulitzer prizes in poetry and fiction, and also for his critical essays, for his book *Understanding Poetry* (written in collaboration with Cleanth Brooks) which changed the methods of teaching American and English poetry in this country, and for his founding and editing of the *Southern Review*–again in collaboration with Cleanth Brooks. As a former editor of the new *Southern Review* I am personally grateful to him for his encouragement of our efforts to reestablish (after a silence of over twenty years) his and Cleanth's distinguished periodical.

It was in conversation with Howard Baker and Yvor Winters at Stanford University in 1932 that I first heard about the talented Rhodes Scholar Red Warren who had been a graduate student at nearby University of California, Berkeley, where Baker knew him, but I had to wait thirty years to meet him. In the meantime I read every issue of his and Brooks' *Southern Review* which ran from 1935 to 1942, and I was invited to contribute a review essay to their magazine in 1941.

In the fall of 1963, after I had been appointed an editor of the new *Review*, I made arrangements to fly to Yale University to seek Warren's and Brooks' advice on how best to proceed with the difficult task of gaining an immediate readership for the new *Southern Review*. The new *Review*, like the original, was founded in a time of troubles. The first issue of Brooks' and Warren's magazine came out in the depths of the depression. The intellectual milieu of the thirties was dominated by angry and hungry young men disillusioned with capitalist democracy. The prevailing notion was that if you wanted to get anywhere in the literary world you had better be Marxist or quasi-Marxist. Brooks and Warren did not share this view, and they succeeded in establishing a quarterly that was primarily literary and not biased by political and economic concerns.

When I arrived on my visit to Yale in the last days of November 1963 President Kennedy had just been assassinated in a southern city. The place of the murder was accidental and the South had nothing to do with it, but there was, nevertheless, considerable

---

Truthful Knowledge

This excerpt is from a tribute by Cleanth Brooks; it was delivered at the memorial service held at the Cathedral Church of St. John the Divine, New York City, 14 November 1989.

I learned, too, about Warren's love of truth. He wanted knowledge but it must be proper knowledge, accurate knowledge, truthful knowledge. "The other side" had to be dealt with fairly and given its proper expression. This concern for truthful knowledge was to come out in many, many ways in his own writings as well as in his lectures. Most of all it comes out in his great poetry where, in more than one poem, he comes to say that real knowledge and real love are almost the same thing, or at least that one leads to the other. One cannot truly love something unless he truly knows it, including its defects; and to know something thoroughly, completely, becomes a form of love. This wisdom, which few of us attain to, is the strength of the great literature that Warren has shaped for us. He is dead, but his writings will live on to all of us who have the good sense to open our ears and eyes to them. The great writers as human beings die like the rest of us, but they have a voice which continues to speak to our deepest selves.

–Cleanth Brooks, *Southern Review,*
26 (January 1990): 2–4

---

irrational hostility towards the South throughout the nation and especially in New England. My morale therefore wasn't very high, but after lunch with Warren and Brooks my mood changed. They were enthusiastic about the new *Review,* they gave me much practical advice, and (when I insisted I wanted to establish continuity with the original *Review*) they suggested a thirtieth anniversary issue for the summer of 1965 to be made up entirely of work by contributors to the original *Review* and to which they would contribute. Warren also promised contributions to later issues and said that he would come to Baton Rouge in 1964 for a lecture. His lecture was a great success–over thirteen hundred people attended–the anniversary issue went well as did our other 1965 issues, and we were on our way.

Our main problem in the later sixties and early seventies was the Vietnam War. As in the thirties, the literary world was again in danger of domination by angry young men, this time understandably opposed to the war and insisting that there was little or no place for a conservative magazine devoted principally to literature and uninvolved with current politics. We remained uninvolved and pulled through. Warren's significant contributions, mostly literary or on literary subjects, helped us maintain our position. He kept up

The Robert Penn Warren Birthplace Museum, dedicated on 21 April 1990 (Robert Penn Warren Birthplace Museum, Guthrie, Kentucky)

a lively connection with the new *Review* and with his southern followers and friends for the rest of his life, publishing with us eight essays and twenty-two poems. Twenty-six articles and reviews (including interviews) about his work appeared in our pages. Of his essays I am especially impressed with his treatment of Melville's poetry in our fall 1967 issue. He was a chief participant in our 1985 fiftieth anniversary celebration in Baton Rouge where he and his wife, Eleanor Clark, were guests of honor. This was the last time I saw him.

Red Warren became one of the most influential and best-known literary figures of his day. He got his start on the faculty of Louisiana State University. His contributions to the culture of our state, as well as to the nation, will not be forgotten.

–Donald E. Stanford, *Southern Review*,
26 (January 1990): 5–6

* * *

This tribute is by Lewis P. Simpson, the other co-editor of the new series of the Southern Review. *His tribute was originally presented at the Salute to Southern Authors Dinner, Southern Festival of Books, in Nashville, Tennessee, 15 October 1989. Simpson's book,* The Fable of the Southern Writer, *which won the first Warren-Brooks Award for Outstanding Literary Criticism, contains a chapter on Warren, "The Loneliness Artist."*

Robert Penn Warren and the South

Any tribute to Robert Penn Warren must recognize the ironic but essential polar aspects of his relationship with the South: one, at the beginning of the most productive phase of his career he left his native world and, save for short visits, never returned; two, he never ceased to be fundamentally engaged with this world. Indeed as James Joyce was a self-declared exile from Ireland, who was always preoccupied with Ireland, Red Warren was a self-conscious exile from the South, who, if not so obsessively or quite so exclusively as Joyce with Ireland, was all his life preoccupied with the South.

I had never quite grasped the complex irony of this preoccupation until one day about a year ago I fulfilled a long-standing intention and in the company of my near neighbor and friend, the writer and editor Charles East, made a little journey to the places where Warren had lived from 1934 to 1942, when he was associated with the Department of English and the *Southern Review* at Louisiana State University.

In our image of Warren's career we tend to think of his arrival on the campus of LSU in 1934 as another event in a connection with the South that had been integral and continuous since his birth in Guthrie, Kentucky, in 1905. On the contrary, according to the implication of his own testimony in interviews and elsewhere, Warren's coming to Baton Rouge marked the beginning of the final phase of a struggle to return to the South that he had carried on since 1930, when, following what he would later refer to as "years of wandering," he had come back to Tennessee. Here he was for one year at Southwestern College in Memphis, and then for three more years on the campus of his undergraduate years, Vanderbilt.

Possibly Warren's reference to his "years of wandering" may be considered somewhat overly dramatic in view of the fact that these years, about six in all, were spent not in bohemian jaunting here and there over the world but mostly in graduate study at Berkeley, Yale, and Oxford (where Warren had the distinction of being a Rhodes Scholar). But nonetheless these were years that had removed Warren well beyond the South he had known as a boy and youth in rural Kentucky, where a significant part of his education had consisted in listening to stories about the War for Southern Independence, particularly as told by his

favorite grandfather, Gabriel Thomas Penn, a dedicated soldier of the Confederacy. These were also years that had distanced Warren from the South he had known as a precocious undergraduate at Vanderbilt, where he had been a member of the Fugitive Group and had formed an attachment to John Crowe Ransom, Allen Tate, Andrew Lytle, and Donald Davidson that brought him into the Agrarian Group in the later 1920s. Even as he had participated in the making of the Agrarian manifesto *I'll Take My Stand* (1930) Warren had questioned some of the Agrarian motives–as is evidenced in his contribution to the manifesto, a rationalization of segregation so halfhearted that Donald Davidson did not want to include it, and which Warren later quite explicitly and positively repudiated. Yet at the same time his years away from the South had been a period that had intensified Warren's attachment to other motives of the Agrarians, most profoundly a subtle but pervasive fear on their part of their personal displacement in the South, of their becoming rootless, or placeless, in short, exiles in their own land. When he came back to the South in

Cleanth Brooks (standing) and Eleanor Clark (center) at a luncheon in the Robert Penn Warren Birthplace Museum, held during the annual symposium in April (Robert Penn Warren Birthplace Museum, Guthrie, Kentucky)

the year in which *I'll Take My Stand* was published, Warren, to be sure, had been out into a world–the world after World War I–whose poets, novelists, and historians were dominated by a sensibility of deracination and exile that, anticipated even at the very beginning of the modern age in Dante, had by the time of Melville and Flaubert become general in Western literary life and in the century of Conrad, Yeats, Joyce, of Thomas Mann, Stein, Pound, Eliot, Hemingway, and Faulkner had become endemic. In this, our century–which has been not less the century of Ransom, Tate, Lytle, Davidson, and Warren–all writers, whether knowing actual exile or not, have been affected by emotions associated with *depaysement,* or the yearning for a lost homeland; and many have qualified to bear the generic name the Alsatian poet Iwan Goll conferred on the modern author, Jean Sans Terre, John the Landless, or, as we might put it in a very free translation, John the Placeless.

When he came back to Tennessee in 1930, Warren was pursuing what turned out to be only a yearning dream for a place that would allay the fear of placelessness he had experienced in his six years of itinerant existence. "The place I wanted to live," Warren reminisced in the later 1970s, "the place I thought was heaven to me, after my years of wandering, was Middle Tennessee. . . . But I couldn't make it work. . . . I was let out of Vanderbilt University, and had to go elsewhere for a job."

The elsewhere, LSU and the country around Baton Rouge, proved to be, as it turned out, the scene of the last effort Warren made to fulfill his yearning quest–a quest he could not effectively disassociate from the South–for a place of permanence, or, to employ the title of his last novel (1977), "a place to come to." I had not quite realized the pathos of Warren's search for this place until–in the knowledgeable company of Charles East–I followed the tangible trail of its final frustration in Baton Rouge and the surrounding countryside. The trail begins with the cottage of a former dairykeeper–located in the suburban outskirts of South Baton Rouge when Warren rented it in 1934–and proceeds to a tiny cabin with a tin roof and an attractive brick chimney in a beautiful forest of red oaks and water oaks–a cabin Warren himself, with the assistance of an "out-of-work carpenter," constructed on a six-acre tract that was well beyond the city limits when he purchased it in 1938 in a liquidation sale. The cabin is still on its original site, preserved on the estate of a Baton Rouge family. From thence the trail of Warren's quest leads down the Jefferson Highway, the old highway to New Orleans, to Prairieville. In this loosely-defined rural community, located some eighteen miles below Baton Rouge in Ascension Parish, Warren discovered a twelve-acre stretch of woods and

pasture with a substantial story-and-a-half bungalow located on it. Known when he purchased it in 1942 as the Frank Opedenmeyer Home Place, this rather handsome property remains today in more or less the same state it was in 1942. The fact that the house is not antebellum–it was in fact built in 1903–is somewhat offset by its placement in a grove of moss-shrouded live oaks growing along a steep bank, below which lies a typical South Louisiana bayou. The gray moss droops over the sluggish dark waters. Standing beneath the trees one cannot fail to remember Warren's poem, one of his favorites, "Bearded Oaks": "The oaks, how subtle and marine, / Bearded, and all the layered light / Above them swims." In Prairieville Warren had found the place he had been seeking, his place to come to, the place, as he said later, he "looked forward to enjoying . . . for keeps."

But he had only begun to convert the Opedenmeyer Home Place into the Warren Home Place when, ten months after he had purchased the Prairieville property–embittered by the failure of the LSU administration to continue its support of the *Southern Review* and even more by its unwillingness to meet a salary offer from the University of Minnesota, the sum involved being a mere two hundred dollars–Warren left the place he had thought to come to, this at the very moment when, having begun to establish himself as a novelist as well as a poet and critic, he was obviously on the way to becoming a major figure in the Southern Renascence. In recollection Warren said he felt himself "somehow squeezed out of the South" and so "fled to Yankee land."

It is a little difficult to understand now the depth of the crisis Warren experienced when he abandoned his quest for a place to come to in the South, for we–I refer to white southerners with an antebellum ancestry–have lost, or very nearly lost, the sense of an indissoluble bond between the mystery of one's identity as a person and one's identity as a southerner. I think of an exchange that took place about 1977 between William Styron and Warren on the question of why they are both living in New England instead of the South. Styron said it is simply because he has chosen to do so; but the explanation of simple choice would not, as I have suggested, do at all for Warren. Insisting that he "felt pressured" to leave the South, that it was not a matter of "choice," Warren made an important distinction between the rationale of his departure from the South and Styron's: "Perhaps," he said, "it is 'a generational matter.'" Perhaps in other words, it is a matter of whether or not one has experienced a tangible, living relationship with the mystery of the historical identity of the South of the Confederacy, the defeat, and the Reconstruction as embodied in the mystery of the identity of flesh-and-blood grandfathers and grand-mothers, aunts and uncles and cousins. By the time Styron's generation of writers came along the experience of this relationship had either disappeared or had become too attenuated to be fully meaningful. That is, meaningful in the sense of being incarnated in the mystery of the writer and in the art of his or her work. But Warren came along in time to reexperience–to reembody–in the power of his imagination and the skill of his art a distillation of the yet-living experience of memory and history available to a gifted grandchild of the Civil War.

The cost of Warren's art was a self-conscious and painful estrangement from the South, but Warren's estrangement was paradoxically his greatest resource, for it was informed by (to call on the famous phrase from Tate's "Ode to the Confederate Dead") a "knowledge carried to the heart." Under the terms of their history as citizens of a nation invented by history, this is a knowledge that is the heritage of all Americans; but it has never been more plainly manifest than in the experience of the old southerners. I mean the knowledge of the isolation of the individual in history as the irrevocable consequence of the vanquishment of the old society of myth and tradition by the society of science and history. This is the knowledge Jed Tewksbury discovers in *A Place to Come To*. A poor white boy from Alabama who becomes a famous Dante scholar and teaches for a time at Vanderbilt, Jed, who is, along with Jack Burden in *All the King's Men* and Brad Tolliver in *Flood,* one of three novelistic personae of Warren, knows the peculiarly intense quality the American sense of isolation has assumed in the South–a loneliness that is "a bleeding inward of the self, away from all the world around, into an internal infinitude, like a pit." Having been "bred up" to this kind of loneliness, Jed says, he took "full advantage of the opportunities it offered." "I was," he declares, "the original, gold-plated, thirty-third degree loneliness artist, the champion of Alabama."

The smart-assed cynicism of Jed Tewksbury imposes a comic mask on a tragic mask of the persona who, as Warren himself recognized increasingly in his later years, haunts his work: a singularly remarkable body of writings–poetical, fictional, historical, biographical, and critical–that essentially constitutes the "shadowy autobiography" of a man, a southerner, who for all his love of his family and for his legion of friends was at his essential core a "loneliness artist."

The last evocative moment in the story of this artist took place on Sunday, October 8, 1989, when an urn containing the ashes of Robert Penn Warren was buried in a lonely country cemetery not far from his beloved summer home at West Wardsboro, Vermont. I had some account of the last rites for Warren in a telephone conversation with my friend and former student, and Warren's friend and bibliographer, James A. Grimshaw. When, in accordance with his wish, the New England earth was opened for Warren, it was the first time in one hundred years that this old burying ground had been disturbed. We may fancy that this act expressed the last vision of a place to come to by a poet for whom the mystery of his identity was deeply fused with the mystery of place; for a poet who was an unmovable nonbeliever but who said repeatedly that he yet yearned to believe; for a poet who was southern to the bone–knew that he could never be at home save in the South–and yet knew as deeply that, because of his very nature as a southerner, he was an exile who could never come home again. After listening to Jim Grimshaw's quietly eloquent description of the remembrance for Warren in October–including a graphic detail at the graveside: the poet John Hollander's reading of Warren's Louisiana poem "Bearded Oaks" amid the burgeoning color of the New England autumn–I thought about how I have argued at times that between New England and the South there has been a fateful symbiotic relationship, this subsisting in the mystical truth that all southerners are spiritual New Englanders. This is an argument fraught with dark implications but perhaps also some happy ones. I cannot of course return to my argument here. But recalling to mind that a favorite phrase with Warren was "for the record," let me put on the record that at this time I take some consolation in my argument.

–Lewis P. Simpson, *Southern Review,*
26 (January 1990): 7–12

* * *

James Olney, one of the third-generation Southern Review *co-editors, wrote this tribute.*

On the Death and Life of Robert Penn Warren

Writing to Ethel Mannin in a letter of October 1938, only a few months before his death, W. B. Yeats spoke of "an essay on 'the idea of death' in the poetry of Rilke" in which he had found, he said, remarkable consonances with the thought of what he termed his "private philosophy" (as opposed to the "public philosophy" of *A Vision*). "According to Rilke," Yeats explained, "a man's death is born with him and if his life is successful and he escapes mere 'mass death' his nature is completed by his final union with it." In another letter, written within the month of his death, Yeats told Lady Elizabeth Pelham, "I am happy, and I think full of an energy, of an energy I had despised of. It seems to me that I have found what I wanted. When I try to put all into a phrase I say, 'Man can embody truth but he cannot know it.' I must embody it in the completion of my life." It seems to me peculiarly fitting that these late thoughts that Yeats had about death as the completion of a successful life and the embodiment of the idea of that life should come to mind on the occasion of Robert Penn Warren's death, for in his poetry Warren, like Yeats (and like few other poets besides Yeats), went on improving with age as if his nature were gradually and triumphantly being completed in his last years, as if he were fully embodying his truth, and writing it out in verse, in the completion of his life.

There have been a number of memorial services for Robert Penn Warren around the country these past two or three months, all testifying to this same sense of an almost unbelievably full and productive life, a successful life appropriately concluded—one in a small, disused church in rural Vermont, another in a corner of the vast Cathedral Church of St. John the Divine in New York City, others still at Yale University, Vanderbilt University, and Louisiana State University. In each instance one has the clear impression that the presiding spirit has been much more a spirit of celebration than of mourning, and properly so. This is not, of course, to deny the loss that Warren's death represents: the *Southern Review,* in particular, has lost a great and generous friend with Warren's death; indeed, were it not for Warren and his founding and presiding genius, there would never have been a *Southern Review* at Louisiana State University. The *Southern Review,* however, is but one of many legacies he has left behind, legacies that stand as his achievements in poetry, fiction, and drama, and in critical commentary of every sort, literary, social, cultural, historical.

What we have lost also, and this perhaps most of all, though his example remains as encouragement to live the moral life, is the presence among us of a good and generous man (to put it in unabashedly old-fashioned terms). In a recent telephone conversation, Daniel Hoffman referred to Warren's generosity to other poets, and certainly there are many around the country who could testify to this. Like so many others, I had the occasional opportunity—not as often as I should have liked but often enough to feel that I understood something of his personality—to observe this warm, ready openness and responsiveness in Red Warren's character. It was evident throughout the three or four days he spent at LSU in 1985 when we

celebrated the fiftieth anniversary of the founding of the Original Series of the *Southern Review;* it was there again at his inauguration as the first Poet Laureate of the United States (after a luncheon at the Library of Congress as various dignitaries offered up their encomia of Warren's work, he became visibly more restive and finally responded, "I feel like I've been listening to a bunch of hired mourners"—which, due to his accent, I heard at first as "hard mourners," but that seemed alright too); and finally I saw it most clearly when, with my then eleven-year-old son, I visited the Warrens in Fairfield, Connecticut, early in 1987. Never have I known anyone who more perfectly embodied the ideal of the host than Red Warren (though I must say parenthetically that even he could not have been so grand a host had he not had at his side Eleanor Clark). He was unfailingly, exquisitely considerate and thoughtful towards his guests in a way that, in our time, seemed almost anachronistic, as if he had adopted the ideal from the ancient Greeks for whom the gracious reception of guests represented the highest, most solemn obligation. Not that Red was solemn about it, not at all (as was humorously evident when, apropos of some supposed breach of hostly decorum, he feigned horror and ironically echoed Lady Macbeth's exclamation after the murder of Duncan: "Woe alas! / What, in our house?") but he refused to neglect his duties as host even in the tiniest of details: for example, although it was clearly very painful for him to do it because of his physical frailty at the time, he insisted on pulling the corks from wine bottles since, for him, it was unthinkable that he should require a guest to perform this duty of the host.

I think it was this same characteristic—this same generosity of spirit and quick, sensitive responsiveness to the needs of others—that made Red Warren the loving husband and father that he was, for it was not only in his public life as man of letters nor only in his semi-public/private life as host that his life was so perfectly rounded out and beautifully fulfilled; it was also, and especially, in his private existence as husband, as father and grandfather, that we can think of his as a pre-eminently good life. In such a great poem as "After the Dinner Party" (which, not insignificantly, is a very late poem) we can gain a sense of Red Warren in all his public and private roles and in the fullness of his humanity; and while, with that and other achievements in our mind, we must, in one sense, mourn his death, we must, in another sense, celebrate even more his life.

–James Olney, *Southern Review,*
26 (January 1990): 13–15

* * *

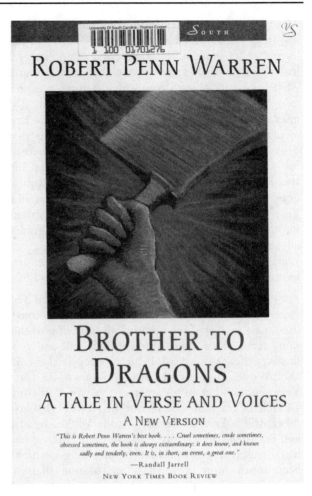

Covers for paperback editions of two of Warren's works, reprinted in 1994 and 1996 by the Louisiana State University Press
(Thomas Cooper Library, University of South Carolina)

Warren's legacy lives. And with the planned events to celebrate the centennial of his birth in 2005, scholars, teachers, students, and other readers of Warren's work have used the opportunity to reread and reexamine it. This essay is by Warren's daughter, Rosanna.

Places: A Memoir

I am writing in my father's study in Vermont, the little wooden cabin–perhaps "coop" would be the more accurate word for the single room and screen porch–perched on a wooded knoll over the stream and swimming pond. He had this study built in 1961 by our woodsman-carpenter-first selectman neighbor, Stubb Sampson, a man we revered for his forest lore and bedrock decency. It seems right that it should have been Stubb's rightly-judging eyes and steady hands that set this study in place. My father worked here almost every summer for a quarter of a century, hearing the same brook from which I now take dictation, smelling

the balsam, watching beech leaves tremble and clouds write ephemeral script across the dark surface of the pond. I have set myself the task of evoking a number of my father's work places and some of the poems he wrote there. And why not start here, where I have worked since his death in 1989?

My parents bought a small cabin on this property in 1959 for winter holidays and summers of writing. But the household, effervescent with my brother and me and our childhood pranks, with visiting cousins and friends, along with dogs, cats and canaries, threatened to spill out of that first cabin which was lit by kerosene lamps and for which we drew water by toiling away at a hand pump in summer and in winter by flailing along a snow path to plonk buckets into a mysterious well. In 1963 my brother and I watched the construction of the larger house, "Shack Two," across the sloping orchard, a crazy rhomboid eyrie designed by the young architect Bob Nevins to honor my mother's desire to reproduce what she loved in the cabin: a view of the mountain

Poster for a production of the Cass Mastern story, which Warren adapted from chapter four of All the King's Men
(Department of Mass Media, Communication, and Theater, Texas A&M University–Commerce)

from the veranda, a screened eating porch over the brook, and "moonlight in the potty." My father's study was in the woods beyond the new house, protected from its racket by a stand of balsam, beech, and spruce. My mother worked in an old hunter's cabin in the woods across the dirt road. And we children roamed free, wading the brook, hiking miles into the woods to explore beaver dams, building elf pavilions among the knotted pine roots and moss banks, writing our own plays and a family newspaper (my department) and building model boats and war machines (my brother's). From my father's study came the rat-a-tat-tat of his typewriter. Sometimes an enterprising woodpecker engaged in a duet with him, hammering away on the study roof joists in synchronized rapid-fire percussion.

We children knew that the hours from nine until two were sacrosanct work time for our parents, and we rarely disturbed them. We knew from observation that it was hard work writing books. But it also seemed as natural as the equally hard work of our mother chopping a trail through dense woods with a machete, or hanging out laundry on the line, or making vats of soup, or as our father's lugging large, flat stones from the brook and setting them in place to make paths, or digging and crowbarring old railway ties into the earth to make steps down to the pond. When I did, rarely, knock on his study door during work hours, I had the feeling of having drawn him up from a well of concentration much deeper than the spring from which we drew water for the cabin. What did I want, he would ask, with his quicksilver, affectionate and disheveled courtesy. His study floor was a sea of discarded paper. His big old Hermes typewriter, pea-soup green, stood on a small table in the far corner of the screen porch. If he was working on a novel or a textbook, typewritten sheets lay wildly about. But poems were a different matter. For them, he had a low-slung, canvas deck chair in which he sat, day-dreamily, with a yellow legal pad on his lap. No rat-a-tat-tat for poems. He sat and listened to the brook and the varying breezes and the scurrying of squirrels and chipmunks. What did he hear?

"All voice is but echo caught from a soundless voice."

Sitting in that chair of reverie, he heard voices of poems from many centuries he carried always within him. And he heard the voices of his Kentucky childhood. But also, over the years, he translated the sounds and sights of Vermont into a metaphysical drama, a quest for personal truth he kept renewing and recording until his last days. I look at these Vermont poems for traces of my father's voice and vision in a landscape we shared. For instance, "Hope," among his last poems in *Altitudes and Extensions*. I look here to see how care-

fully he watched and named the colors of sunset, and how he found in those shifting hues an inner landscape, a meditative process by which to transform private mood to some larger acceptance. The pacing of these free verse lines gives a measure not only for transitional light, but for transitional feeling. The poem does what most readers ask poems to do: to move us. That is, to move us from one state of mind and heart to another. In this case, we are moved from a curdling of soul to forgiveness. Every nuance of changing light in the poem, every line break, contributes to that process, but the movement is most dramatized in the enjambment between stanzas, "Let your soul // Be still."

Hope

In the orchidaceous light of evening
Watch how, from the lowest hedge-leaf, creeps,
Grass blade to blade, the purpling shadow. It spreads
Its spectral ash beneath the leveling, last
Gold rays that, westward, have found apertures
From the magnificent disaster of day.
Against gold light, beneath the maple leaf,
A pale blue gathers, accumulates, sifts
Downward to modulate the flowery softness
Of gold intrusive through the blackening spruce boughs.
Spruces heighten the last glory beyond their stubbornness.
They seem rigid in blackened bronze.
Wait, wait—as though a finger were placed to lips.
The first star petals timidly in what
Is not yet darkness. That audacity
Will be rewarded soon. In this transitional light,
While cinders in the west die, the world
Has its last blooming. Let your soul
Be still. All day it has curdled in your bosom
Denatured by intrusion of truth or lie, or both.
Lay both aside, nor debate their nature. Soon,
While not even a last bird twitters, the last bat goes.
Even the last motor fades into distance. The promise
Of moonrise will dawn, and slowly, in all fullness, the
    moon
Will dominate the sky, the world, the heart,
In white forgiveness.

"Hope" is one of my father's lonely poems. But he wrote, also, many poems of companionship. In "Last Walk of Season," composed only a few years before his death, he commemorates the beauty of a long marriage in the beauty of the late season and a worn and ancient landscape. Time and its erosions are felt here as a gift, not as destruction.

. . . We came where we had meant to come. And not
Too late. In the mountain's cup, moraine-dammed, the
    lake
Lies left by a glacier older than God. Beyond it, the sun,
Ghostly, dips, flame-huddled in mist. We undertake
Not to exist, except as part of that one

Sheet of stamps commemorating the centennial of Warren's birth (Bruccoli Clark Layman Archives)

Existence. We are thinking of happiness. In such case,
We must not count years. For happiness has no measur-
    able pace.
Scarcely in consciousness, a hand finds, on stone, a hand.
They are in contact. Past lake, over mountain, last light
Probes for contact with the soft-shadowed land.

Still, many of these Vermont poems risk solitari-
ness. *Pace* some critics, I would not call these poems self-
centered. The self encountered here, out on its errands
in the woods and mountains, is looking beyond solip-
sism to ask where it stands *vis-à-vis* death, love, and the
idea of God. In such poems, the idea of place becomes a
metaphysical laboratory, as it is in "The Place," set at
twilight near a mountaintop:

. . . Self is the cancellation of self, and now is the hour.
Self is the mutilation of official meanings, and this is the
    place.
You hear water of minor musical utterance
On stone, but from what direction?
You hear, distantly, a bird-call you cannot identify.
Is the shadow of the cliff creeping upon you?
You are afraid to look at your watch.

You think of the possibility of lying on stone
Among fern-fronds, and waiting
For the shadow to find you.
The stars would not be astonished
To catch a glimpse of the form through interstices
Of leaves now black as enameled tin. Nothing astounds
    the stars.
They have long lived. And you are not the first
To come to such a place seeking the most difficult knowl-
    edge.

The first place I remember my father working is
in the ruined fortress called La Rocca in the village of
Porto Ercole, a little north of Rome, where we lived
the first five summers of my life. La Rocca, which my
mother had discovered just after the war ("the war,"
for my parents' generation, was of course World War
II), had been built for Philip II of Spain in the 16th century. My father described it in the poem he dedicated to
me, "To a Little Girl, One Year Old, in a Ruined Fortress": "*Rocca:* fortress, hawk-heel, lion-paw, clamped on
a hill." I remember La Rocca. We lived in what had been
the stables for the garrison, an immense, cavernous

space with oak ceiling beams and a flagstone floor where Ernesta, wrinkled and smiling, prepared our meals on a charcoal fire in a stone fireplace at the far end of the room, and where we ate at a long oak table and played records on a gramophone with a curving brass horn. My baby brother and I played out in the wide, walled-in courtyard, now wild with thistles and agitated with chickens clucking and scattering, where the Spanish must have gone through their cavalry manoeuvres. Beyond a massive wall, in the interior of the fortress, Ernesta drew our water from the well with its creaking wheel for the bucket rope, and we peeked through an iron grate into the dark and urine-scented hole that led to the dungeons, where, it was rumored, vipers now lived. Across the inner courtyard, in a honeycomb of habitation massed against the outer wall, lived La Signorina, our ancient landlady. She was so miserly, I remember my mother saying, she ate moldy spaghetti. She looked to me as old as the fortress. We were protected, in this inner world, by the gigantic outer walls which dominated the whole spur of the peninsula, and by a wide and serious moat you could be killed falling into, and by an honest-to-God drawbridge. All this, to my brother and me, seemed perfectly natural. And it must have cost my parents almost nothing to rent. I add this financial note with a touch of indignation; I once heard someone sneer at my father for living in a "castle," as if he had betrayed his country and his class by going to Italy. Is it a crime, I ask, to live imaginatively, to move from one's origins–in this case, a small town in Kentucky–and to roam the world physically and mentally? How else but by distance can one know one's origins? And is not the greatest poverty, not lack of money, but lack of curiosity?

In the case of La Rocca, ruin taught my parents to ruminate, and they ruminated in their tiny guardhouses capped with conical roofs, built into the outer wall. Each guardhouse had three vertical slit windows–to shoot from, I suppose, or perhaps to pour boiling oil from–and just enough room for a portable Olivetti typewriter on the windowsill and a camp stool. There, commanding a view of the Mediterranean and visited by the occasional scorpion, my parents mused and wrote for five summers.

I was the little girl, one-year old, in the ruined fortress, and all my life I have held the poem at arm's length. At an affectionate, quizzical arm's length. Because, though I recognize and remember the place, that little girl is not me. She lives in the poem, where she will never grow older. I visit her occasionally. Not so much for her, but for the fact that my father's soul lives there too. His essential poetry; you can feel it as much in what the creative writing cadets will call over-writing–all those repetitions, blaze, and gold–as in the

prosaic and ironic matter-of-factness: "*Philipus me fecit:* he of Spain, the black-browed, the anguished, / For whom nothing prospered, though he loved God." The poem's energy jolts up from the collision between idealizing, gold-struck vision and the brute realities of war, poverty, and physical deformity. My father, a new father, contemplating his own first child, was discovering something in this poem, some new risk and vulnerability of feeling, casting out long lines far beyond the pentameter, and deferring verbs until the end of sentences: "And on the exposed approaches the last gold of gorse bloom, in the sirocco, shakes." The human sympathy in this poem was not new to him, but it found here a particularly acute shape in the scenes of the saintlike, triptych sister and the monstrous, damaged child. Unlike the Vermont poems, which tend toward solitude in the contemplation of nature, this poem and others from the Italian setting allow themselves to be hurt by history, by human nature, and they look steadfastly into that hurt: "I think of your goldness, of joy, but how empires grind, stars are hurled. / I smile stiff, saying *ciao,* saying *ciao,* and think: *This is the world.*"

The gesture of Italian greeting, *ciao,* so simple, so fundamental, stands in for the many ways in which my father's poems imagine connectedness in the recognition of suffering. He was not a religious man, but he had grown up in a religious culture with a heavy dose of old hellfire Presbyterian Calvinism. He had inherited various Christian promises and threats; he had knocked about the world long enough to see what hell people create for themselves and others, and to understand the need to find some ground for blessing. The greeting, *ciao,* turns up again in one of his most sympathetic poems, one which evokes but resists doctrinal consolation. Also set in the coastal landscape of La Rocca, "The Cross" describes the speaker walking the beach after a storm and finding, among other seasmashed debris, a drowned monkey. I cherish this poem for its clear language, its clearsightedness, and its ironic and large-hearted humanism. For it is humanism to reach out in brotherly fashion to a monkey:

> . . . And most desperately hunched by volcanic stone
> As though trying to cling in some final hope,
> But drowned hours back you could be damned sure,
> The monkey, wide-eyed, bewildered yet
> By the terrible screechings and jerks and bangs,
> And no friend to come and just say *ciao.*
> I took him up, looked in his eyes,
> As orbed as dark aggies, as bright as tears,
> With a glaucous glint in deep sightlessness,
> Yet still seeming human with all they had seen–
> Like yours or mine, if luck had run out.
> So, like a fool, I said *ciao* to him.
> Under wet fur I felt how skin slid loose

Production still from the 2005 movie version of All the King's Men, *with Sean Penn as Willie Stark (courtesy of Columbia Pictures Corporation)*

On the poor little bones, and the delicate
Fingers yet grasped, at God knew what.
So I sat with him there, watching wind abate.
No funnel on the horizon showed.
And of course, no sail. And the cliff's shadow
Had found the cove. Well, time to go.
I took time, yes, to bury him,
In a scraped-out hole, little cairn on top.
And I fool enough to improvise
A cross—
Two sticks tied together to prop in the sand.
But what use that? The sea comes back.

The summers of 1966 and 1967 we lived on a rough, forested island off the coast of the Côte d'Azur in the French Mediterranean. Port Cros was a nature reserve, protected from development, so it had no screaming discothèques, grand hotels or condominiums, and none of the frenzy of the beaches two hours away from us on the mainland at Cannes and St. Tropez. There was one tiny fishing village with a small hotel, and Le Manoir, where we stayed, an austere, stone and stucco hotel up the path from the port, nestled among eucalyptus and pines. The guests tended to be cranky French intellectuals and artists, and pensive *bourgeois* in retreat from TV, movies, and urban life. I remember Monsieur l'Astronome, a pompous *savant* who thrust math problems at the hotel guests at dinner (my ten-year-old brother infuriated him by solving the problem rapidly). The actor Jean-Louis Barrault could be seen, tanned very bronze, hiking alone on the steep trails, looking somber and not a little ferocious. Except for days of high wind, the *mistral,* we ate breakfast and dinner on a terrace overlooking the harbor, where sailboats bobbed at their moorings under the protection of the 17th-century fort at the far end of the port. Here, again, our parents worked from nine until two, my mother in a donkey shed and my father under a fig tree in the sheltered garden. At two in the afternoon we children joined them for a picnic lunch and then set off on the half-hour walk to the beach. This is the landscape that turns up in *Promises.*

The fig, the mullet, the sun, the sea: in these poems, I find my father testing the elemental, finding a new, dangerous balance in his lines and in his rhetoric. A heady test; he takes crazy, sensuous, Elizabethan-Biblical plunges. He extends one's sense of life; he plays nothing safe; if we follow him, we are taken out of our depths. I, for one, am grateful for these rather mad, prophetic encounters with the gods of fig and mullet. These poems thrust body and soul together: "Where the slow fig's purple sloth / Swells, I sit and meditate the / Nature of the soul . . ." ("Where the Slow Fig's Purple Sloth"). Snorkeling, my father had met the mullet, one of his totems, to be added to hawks and to Audubon's birds as a principle of reality:

The Red Mullet

The fig flames inward on the bough, and I,
Deep where the great mullet, red, lounges in
Black shadow of the shoal, have come. Where no light may
Come, he the great one, like flame, burns, and I
Have met him, eye to eye, the lower jaw horn,
Outthrust, arched down at the corners, merciless as

Genghis, motionless and mogul, and the eye of
The mullet is round, bulging, ringed like a target
In gold, vision is armor, he sees and does not

Forgive. The mullet has looked me in the eye, and forgiven
Nothing. At night I fear suffocation, is there
Enough air in the world for us all, therefore I

Swim much, dive deep to develop my lung-case. I am
Familiar with the agony of will in the deep place. Blood
Thickens as oxygen fails. Oh, mullet, thy flame

Burns in the shadow of the black shoal.

The Hebrew Bible, more than Christian Scripture, haunts these Port Cros poems. So there was my father, as ever agnostic, as ever God-tortured, having another go at his age-old question: ". . . We must try // To love so well the world that we may believe, in the end, in God" ("Masts at Dawn"). The ambiguous placement of the words acts out the tension of unbelief and yearning. The sentence proposes, not "to love the world so well," which would be the easy solution, but "to love so well the world"; and it asks us to consider "that we may believe in the end" as much as it tempts us to "believe . . . in God."

I will conclude these reflections by invoking a poem of my father's which has helped me to live. "The Leaf" is one of the Port Cros poems from *Promises*. I find myself going back to it, in quandaries of my own, as I try to discern my own truths, the limits and damages of my nature. I take it that that is one of the responsibilities of art, to help us in our struggle toward truthfulness—that private clarity upon which justice and compassion and the recognition of others must stand. "The Leaf" opens under my father's fig tree, his Eden, an Eden already guilt-struck:

Here the fig lets down the leaf, the leaf
Of the fig five fingers has, the fingers
Are broad, spatulate, stupid,
Ill-formed, and innocent—but of a hand, and the hand,

To hide me from the blaze of the wide world, drops,
Shamefast, down . . .

The lines I return to again and again open the second section:

We have undergone ourselves, therefore
What more is to be done for Truth's sake? I

Have watched the deployment of ants, I
Have conferred with the flaming mullet in a deep place . . .

To place the first person singular pronoun out so vulnerably at the ends of two consecutive lines may risk a terrible self-dramatization. I take it differently. For me, this poem puts the self in danger in order to sound its reaches and depths. And what is the worth of a life that has not taken such soundings? When the "I" has been tested, it can stand generously in relation to a "you." "The Leaf" is a father poem, in which my father hears his own paternal voices calling to him from a grave in Guthrie, Kentucky, and from Adam. I will borrow, or steal, or inherit, these lines, and use them in gratitude to evoke my hearing of my own father's voice in his poems, which have become common property to all who might need them:

From a further garden, from the shade of another tree,
My father's voice, in the moment when the cicada ceases,
    has called to me.

—Rosanna Warren, *RWP: An Annual of Robert Penn Warren Studies*, 5 (2005): 1–11

For Further Reading

Interviews

Cronin, Gloria L., and Ben Siegel, eds. *Conversations with Robert Penn Warren.* Jackson: University Press of Mississippi, 2005.

Ferris, William. "A Conversation with Robert Penn Warren." Video. University, Miss.: Center for the Study of Southern Culture, 1987.

Kennedy, William. "Robert Penn Warren: Willie Stark, Politics, and the Novel," in *Riding the Yellow Trolley Car.* New York: Viking, 1993, pp. 165–173.

Watkins, Floyd C., and John T. Hiers, eds. *Robert Penn Warren Talking: Interviews 1950–1978.* New York: Random House, 1980.

Watkins, Hiers, and Mary Louise Weaks, eds. *Talking with Robert Penn Warren.* Athens & London: University of Georgia Press, 1990.

Bibliographies

Eller, Jonathan, and C. Jason Smith. "Robert Penn Warren: A Bibliographical Survey, 1986–1993." *Mississippi Quarterly,* 48 (Winter 1994–1995): 169–194.

Grimshaw, James A., Jr. "Bibliographical Trends in Warren Criticism: The 1980s." *Southern Quarterly,* 31 (Summer 1993): 51–56.

Grimshaw. *Robert Penn Warren: A Descriptive Bibliography, 1922–1979.* Charlottesville: University Press of Virginia, 1981.

Huff, Mary Nance. *Robert Penn Warren: A Bibliography.* New York: David Lewis, 1968.

Nakadate, Neil. *Robert Penn Warren: A Reference Guide.* Boston: G. K. Hall, 1977.

Biographies

Blotner, Joseph. *Robert Penn Warren: A Biography.* New York: Random House, 1997.

Stone, Martha Jane. *The Warren Family of Trigg County, Kentucky.* Lexington: Poole Press, 1996.

Books about Warren

Bedient, Calvin. *"In the Heart's Last Kingdom": Robert Penn Warren's Major Poetry.* Cambridge, Mass.: Harvard University Press, 1984.

Beebe, Maurice, and Leslie A. Field, eds. *Robert Penn Warren's "All the King's Men": A Critical Handbook*. Belmont, Cal.: Wadsworth, 1966.

Bloom, Harold. *Robert Penn Warren's* All the King's Men. Modern Critical Interpretations. New York: Chelsea House, 1987.

Bloom, ed. *Robert Penn Warren*. Modern Critical Views. New York: Chelsea House, 1986.

Bohner, Charles. *Robert Penn Warren,* revised edition. Boston: Twayne, 1981.

Bradley, Patricia L. *Robert Penn Warren's Circus Aesthetic and the Southern Renaissance*. Knoxville: University of Tennessee Press, 2004.

Burt, John. *Robert Penn Warren and American Idealism*. New Haven: Yale University Press, 1988.

Casper, Leonard. *The Blood-Marriage of Earth and Sky: Robert Penn Warren's Later Novels*. Baton Rouge: Louisiana State University Press, 1997.

Casper. *Robert Penn Warren: The Dark and Bloody Ground*. Seattle: University of Washington Press, 1960.

Chambers, Robert H., ed. All the King's Men: *A Collection of Critical Essays*. Twentieth Century Interpretations. Englewood Cliffs, N.J.: Prentice-Hall, 1977.

Clark, William Bedford. *The American Vision of Robert Penn Warren*. Lexington: University Press of Kentucky, 1991.

Clark, ed. *Critical Essays on Robert Penn Warren*. Boston: G. K. Hall, 1981.

Cleopatra, Sr. *The Novels of Robert Penn Warren*. New Delhi [India]: Associated Publishing House, 1985.

Corrigan, Lesa Carnes. *Poems of Pure Imagination*. Baton Rouge: Louisiana State University Press, 1999.

Cullick, Jonathan S. *Making History: The Biographical Narratives of Robert Penn Warren*. Baton Rouge: Louisiana State University Press, 2000.

Edgar, Walter B., ed. *A Southern Renascence Man: Views of Robert Penn Warren*. Baton Rouge: Louisiana State University Press, 1984.

Ferriss, Lucy. *Sleeping with the Boss: Female Subjectivity and Narrative Pattern in Robert Penn Warren*. Baton Rouge: Louisiana State University Press, 1997.

Gray, Richard, ed. *Robert Penn Warren: A Collection of Critical Essays*. Twentieth Century Views. Englewood Cliffs, N.J.: Prentice-Hall, 1980.

Graziano, Frank, ed. *Homage to Robert Penn Warren: A Collection of Critical Essays*. Durango, Colo.: Logbridge-Rhodes, 1981.

Grimshaw, James A., Jr. *Understanding Robert Penn Warren*. Columbia: University of South Carolina Press, 2001.

Grimshaw, ed. *Robert Penn Warren's* Brother to Dragons: *A Discussion*. Baton Rouge: Louisiana State University Press, 1983.

Grimshaw, ed. *"Time's Glory": Original Essays on Robert Penn Warren*. Conway: University of Central Arkansas Press, 1986.

Guttenberg, Barnett. *Web of Being: The Novels of Robert Penn Warren*. Nashville: Vanderbilt University Press, 1975.

Hart, John A., ed. All the King's Men: *A Symposium.* Carnegie Series in English, no. 3. Pittsburgh: Carnegie Institute of Technology, 1957.

Hendricks, Randy. *Lonelier Than God: Robert Penn Warren and the Southern Exile.* Athens: University of Georgia Press, 2000.

Justus, James H. *The Achievement of Robert Penn Warren.* Baton Rouge: Louisiana State University Press, 1981.

Koppelman, Robert S. *Robert Penn Warren's Modernist Spirituality.* Columbia: University of Missouri Press, 1995.

Light, James F., ed. *Studies in* All the King's Men. Columbus, Ohio: Merrill, 1971.

Longley, John L., Jr., ed. *Robert Penn Warren: A Collection of Critical Essays.* New York: New York University Press, 1965.

Madden, David, ed. *The Legacy of Robert Penn Warren.* Baton Rouge: Louisiana State University Press, 2000.

Millichap, Joseph R., ed. *Robert Penn Warren: A Study of the Short Fiction.* New York: Twayne, 1992.

Moore, L. Hugh, Jr. *Robert Penn Warren and History.* The Hague: Mouton, 1970.

Nakadate, Neil, ed. *Robert Penn Warren: Critical Perspectives.* Lexington: University Press of Kentucky, 1981.

Runyon, Randolph Paul. *The Braided Dream: Robert Penn Warren's Late Poetry.* Lexington: University Press of Kentucky, 1990.

Runyon. *The Taciturn Text: The Fiction of Robert Penn Warren.* Columbus: Ohio State University Press, 1990.

Ruppersburg, Hugh. *Robert Penn Warren and the American Imagination.* Athens: University of Georgia Press, 1990.

Snipes, Katherine. *Robert Penn Warren.* New York: Ungar, 1983.

Strandberg, Victor H. *A Colder Fire: The Poetry of Robert Penn Warren.* Lexington: University of Kentucky Press, 1965.

Strandberg. *The Poetic Vision of Robert Penn Warren.* Lexington: University Press of Kentucky, 1977.

Szczesiul, Anthony. *Racial Politics and Robert Penn Warren's Poetry.* Gainesville: University Press of Florida, 2002.

Walker, Marshall. *Robert Penn Warren: A Vision Earned.* Edinburgh: Paul Harris, 1979.

Watkins, Floyd C. *Then & Now: The Personal Past in the Poetry of Robert Penn Warren.* Lexington: University Press of Kentucky, 1982.

Weeks, Dennis L., ed. *"To Love So Well the World": A Festschrift in Honor of Robert Penn Warren.* New York: Peter Lang, 1992.

Selected Essays about Warren

Brooks, Cleanth. "Afterword," *Southern Quarterly,* 31 (Summer 1993): 106–112.

Brooks. "Brooks on Warren," *Four Quarters,* 21 (May 1972): 19–22.

Brooks. "Episode and Anecdote in the Poetry of Robert Penn Warren," *Yale Review,* 70 (Summer 1981): 551–567.

Brooks. "A Tribute to Robert Penn Warren," *Southern Review,* 26 (Winter 1990): 2–4.

Burt, John. "Idealism and Rage in Proud Flesh," *RWP: An Annual of Robert Penn Warren Studies,* 1 (2001): 45–61.

Clark, William Bedford. "Letters from Home: Filial Guilt in Robert Penn Warren," *Sewanee Review,* 110 (Summer 2002): 385–405.

Clements, A. L. "A Meditation on Folk-History: The Dramatic Structure of Robert Penn Warren's *The Ballad of Billie Potts,*" *American Literature,* 49 (January 1978): 635–645.

Clements. "Sacramental Vision: The Poetry of Robert Penn Warren," *South Atlantic Bulletin,* 43, no. 4 (1978): 47–65.

Cowley, Malcolm. "Robert Penn Warren, aet. 75," *Georgia Review,* 35 (Spring 1981): 7–12.

Davison, Peter. "Deep in the Blackness of Woods: A Farewell to Robert Penn Warren," *New England Monthly* (March 1990): 37–39.

Drake, Robert. "Robert Penn Warren's Enormous Spider Web," *Mississippi Quarterly,* 48 (Winter 1994–1995): 11–16.

Ealy, Steven D. "An Early Glimpse of Robert Penn Warren's 'Last Wisdom,'" *RWP: An Annual of Robert Penn Warren Studies,* 4 (2004): 41–50.

Ealy. "'An Exciting Spiral': Robert Penn Warren on Race and Community," *RWP: An Annual of Robert Penn Warren Studies,* 2 (2002): 101–122.

Empson, William. "'The Ancient Mariner': An Answer to Warren," *Kenyon Review,* 15 (Winter 1993): 155–177.

Ferriss, Lucy. "The Aesthetics of Robert Penn Warren," *Style,* 36 (Spring 2002): 200–202.

Frankle, Aaron. "Working in the Theater with Robert Penn Warren," *RWP: An Annual of Robert Penn Warren Studies,* 2 (2002): 1–16.

Fridy, Will. "The Author and the Ballplayer: An Imprint of Memory in the Writings of Robert Penn Warren," *Mississippi Quarterly,* 44 (Spring 1991): 159–166.

Garrett, George. "Warren's Poetry: Some Things We Ought to Be Thinking About," *South Carolina Review,* 23 (1990): 49–57.

Girault, Norton R. "Recollections of Robert Penn Warren as Teacher in the 1930s," *Texas Writers Newsletter,* no. 31 (April 1982): 3–6.

Grimshaw, James A., Jr. "Robert Penn Warren: A Reminiscence," *Gettysburg Review,* 3 (Winter 1990): 210–211.

Grimshaw. "Strong to Stark: Deceiver, Demagogue, Dictator," *Texas College English,* 23 (Fall 1990): 17–22.

Hamblin, Robert W. "Robert Penn Warren at the 1965 Southern Literary Festival: A Personal Recollection," *Southern Literary Journal,* 22 (Spring 1990): 53–62.

Justus, James H. "The Power of Filiation in *All the King's Men,*" in *Modern American Fiction: Form and Function,* edited by Thomas Daniel Young. Baton Rouge: Louisiana State University Press, 1989, pp. 156–169.

Justus. "The Rival Texts of 'The Ballad of Billie Potts,'" *RWP: An Annual of Robert Penn Warren Studies,* 4 (2004): 51–59.

Justus. "Warren as Mentor: Pure and Impure Wisdom," in *The Legacy of Robert Penn Warren,* edited by David Madden. Baton Rouge: Louisiana State University Press, 2000, pp. 1–13.

Justus. "Warren's Later Poetry: Unverified Rumors of Wisdom," *Mississippi Quarterly*, 37 (Spring 1984): 161–167.

Justus. "Warren's *Terra*," *Mississippi Quarterly*, 48 (Winter 1994–1995): 133–146.

Koppelman, Robert S. "Warren and Oral Narrative: The Case for *Chief Joseph of the Nez Perce*," *RWP: An Annual of Robert Penn Warren Studies*, 4 (2004): 61–76.

Law, Richard G. "*At Heaven's Gate:* The Fires of Irony," *American Literature*, 53 (March 1981): 87–104.

Law. "Warren's *World Enough and Time*: 'Et in Arcadia Ego,'" in *"Time's Glory": Original Essays on Robert Penn Warren*, edited by James A. Grimshaw Jr. Conway: University of Central Arkansas Press, 1986, pp. 13–41.

Lewis, R. W. B. "The Great Dragon Country of Robert Penn Warren," *Southern Quarterly*, 31 (Summer 1993): 13–36.

McCarthy, Colman. "Robert Penn Warren at 75," *Washington Post*, 2 May 1980, p. A18.

Metress, Christopher. "Fighting Battles One by One: Robert Penn Warren's *Segregation*," *Southern Review*, 32 (Winter 1996): 166–171.

Miller, Victoria Thorpe. "Shared Lives and Separate Studies: The Literary Marriage of Eleanor Clark and Robert Penn Warren," *RWP: An Annual of Robert Penn Warren Studies*, 3 (2003): 135–159.

Millichap, Joseph R. "Robert Penn Warren's Divine Comedy," *Kentucky Philological Review*, 8 (1993): 34–39.

Nakadate, Neil. "Robert Penn Warren and the Confessional Novel," *Genre*, 2 (1969): 326–340.

Newton, Thomas A. "A Character Index of Robert Penn Warren's Long Works of Fiction," *Emporia State Research Studies*, 26 (Winter 1978): 3–104.

Olney, James. "On the Death and Life of Robert Penn Warren," *Southern Review*, 26 (Winter 1990): 13–15.

Olney. "Parents and Children in Robert Penn Warren's Autobiography," in *Home Ground: Southern Autobiography*, edited by J. Bill Berry. Columbia: University of Missouri Press, 1991, pp. 31–47.

Perkins, James A. "Notes on an Unpublished Robert Penn Warren Essay," *Southern Review*, 30 (Autumn 1994): 650–657.

Perkins. "Racism and the Personal Past in Robert Penn Warren," *Mississippi Quarterly*, 48 (Winter 1994–1995): 73–82.

Perkins. "Robert Penn Warren and James Farmer: Notes on the Creation of New Journalism," *RWP: An Annual of Robert Penn Warren Studies*, 1 (2001): 163–175.

Polk, Noel. "Editing *All the King's Men*," *Southern Review*, 38 (Autumn 2002): 849–860.

Polk. "The Text of the 'Restored' Edition of *All the King's Men*," *RWP: An Annual of Robert Penn Warren Studies*, 2 (2002): 17–64.

Quinn, Sister Bernetta. "Robert Penn Warren's Promised Land," *Southern Review*, 8 (Spring 1972): 329–358.

Rubin, Louis D., Jr. "R. P. W. 1905–1989," *Sewanee Review*, 98 (Spring 1990): 236–243.

Runyon, Randolph Paul. "Father, Son and Taciturn Text," in *"To Love So Well the World": A Festschrift in Honor of Robert Penn Warren*, edited by Dennis L. Weeks. New York: Peter Lang, 1992, pp. 113–121.

Ruoff, James E. "Robert Penn Warren's Pursuit of Justice: From Briar Patch to Cosmos," *Research Studies of the State College of Washington,* 27 (March 1959): 19–38.

Ryan, Alvin S. "Robert Penn Warren's *Night Rider:* The Nihilism of the Isolated Temperament," *Modern Fiction Studies,* 7 (Winter 1961–1963): 338–346.

Samway, Patrick H. "The Nobel Prize Deferred Again," *America,* 14 November 1987, pp. 359, 365.

Shepherd, Allen. "Chief Joseph, General Howard, Colonel Miles: The Context of Characterization in Warren's *Chief Joseph of the Nez Perce,*" *Mississippi Quarterly,* 39 (Winter 1985–1986): 21–30.

Shepherd. "The Craft of Salvage: Robert Penn Warren's 'God's Own Time' and Three Stories," *Kentucky Review,* 2, no. 1 (1980): 11–19.

Shepherd. "The Poles of Fiction: Warren's *At Heaven's Gate,*" *Texas Studies in Literature and Language,* 12 (Winter 1971): 709–718.

Simpson, Lewis P. "Robert Penn Warren: The Loneliness Artist," *Sewanee Review,* 99 (Summer 1991): 337–360.

Simpson. "Robert Penn Warren and the South," *Southern Review,* 26 (Winter 1990): 7–12.

Smith, Dave. "Robert Penn Warren: The Use of a Word Like Honor," *Yale Review,* 74 (Summer 1985): 574–580.

Spears, Monroe K. "The Critics Who Made Us: Robert Penn Warren," *Sewanee Review,* 94 (Winter 1986): 99–111.

Stanford, Donald E. "Robert Penn Warren and the *Southern Review,*" *Southern Review,* 26 (Winter 1990): 5–6.

Strandberg, Victor. "Warren's 'Worst' Book," *South Carolina Review,* 23 (1990): 74–83.

Strandberg. "Whatever Happened to 'You'?–A Poetic Odyssey," *RWP: An Annual of Robert Penn Warren Studies,* 1 (2001): 143–161.

Watkins, Floyd C. "Following the Tramp in Warren's 'Blackberry Winter,'" *Studies in Short Fiction,* 22 (Summer 1985): 343–345.

Watkins. "Robert Penn Warren's Roman Poems: You and the Emperors," *Essays in Literature,* 10 (Fall 1983): 255–262.

Watkins. "The Ungodly in Robert Penn Warren's Biblical Poems," *Southern Literary Journal,* 15 (Fall 1983): 34–46.

Weaks, Mary Louise. "The Search for a 'Terra' in *A Place to Come To,*" *Mississippi Quarterly,* 37 (Fall 1984): 455–468.

Wilcox, Earl. "Right On! *All the King's Men* in the Classroom," *Four Quarters,* 21 (May 1972): 69–78.

Winchell, Mark Royden. "A Place to Come From: The Nashville Agrarians and Robert Penn Warren," *Canadian Review of American Studies,* 15 (Summer 1984): 229–239.

Winchell. "Renaissance Men: Shakespeare's Influence on Robert Penn Warren," in *Shakespeare and Southern Writers: A Study in Influence,* edited by Philip C. Kolin. Jackson: University Press of Mississippi, 1985, pp. 137–158.

Woodward, C. Vann. "Exile at Yale," in *The Legacy of Robert Penn Warren,* edited by David Madden. Baton Rouge: Louisiana State University Press, 2000, pp. 23–31.

Young, Thomas Daniel. "*Brother to Dragons:* A Meditation on the Basic Nature of Man," *Mississippi Quarterly,* 37 (Spring 1984): 149–159.

Cumulative Index

Dictionary of Literary Biography, Volumes 1-320
Dictionary of Literary Biography Yearbook, 1980-2002
Dictionary of Literary Biography Documentary Series, Volumes 1-19
Concise Dictionary of American Literary Biography, Volumes 1-7
Concise Dictionary of British Literary Biography, Volumes 1-8
Concise Dictionary of World Literary Biography, Volumes 1-4

Cumulative Index

DLB before number: *Dictionary of Literary Biography,* Volumes 1-320
Y before number: *Dictionary of Literary Biography Yearbook,* 1980-2002
DS before number: *Dictionary of Literary Biography Documentary Series,* Volumes 1-19
CDALB before number: *Concise Dictionary of American Literary Biography,* Volumes 1-7
CDBLB before number: *Concise Dictionary of British Literary Biography,* Volumes 1-8
CDWLB before number: *Concise Dictionary of World Literary Biography,* Volumes 1-4

Channing, Edward Tyrrell
1790-1856. . . . . DLB-1, 59, 235

Channing, William Ellery
1780-1842. . . . . DLB-1, 59, 235

Channing, William Ellery, II
1817-1901. . . . . DLB-1, 223

Channing, William Henry
1810-1884. . . . . DLB-1, 59, 243

Chapelain, Jean 1595-1674 . . . . DLB-268

Chaplin, Charlie 1889-1977 . . . . DLB-44

Chapman, George
1559 or 1560-1634. . . . . DLB-62, 121

Chapman, Olive Murray 1892-1977. . . . . DLB-195

Chapman, R. W. 1881-1960. . . . . DLB-201

Chapman, William 1850-1917 . . . . DLB-99

John Chapman [publishing house] DLB-106

Chapman and Hall [publishing house] . . . DLB-106

Chappell, Fred 1936- DLB-6, 105

"A Detail in a Poem" DLB-105

Tribute to Peter Taylor Y-94

Chappell, William 1582-1649 . . . . DLB-236

Char, René 1907-1988 . . . . DLB-258

Charbonneau, Jean 1875-1960 . . . . DLB-92

Charbonneau, Robert 1911-1967 . . . . DLB-68

Charles, Gerda 1914-1996 . . . . DLB-14

William Charles [publishing house] DLB-49

Charles d'Orléans 1394-1465 . . . . DLB-208

Charley (see Mann, Charles)

Charrière, Isabelle de 1740-1805. . . . . . . DLB-313

Charskaia, Lidiia 1875-1937 . . . . DLB-295

Charteris, Leslie 1907-1993. . . . . DLB-77

Chartier, Alain circa 1385-1430 . . . . DLB-208

Charyn, Jerome 1937- Y-83

Chase, Borden 1900-1971 . . . . DLB-26

Chase, Edna Woolman 1877-1957 . . . . DLB-91

Chase, James Hadley (René Raymond)
1906-1985 .DLB-276

Chase, Mary Coyle 1907-1981 . . . . DLB-228

Chase-Riboud, Barbara 1936- DLB-33

Chateaubriand, François-René de
1768-1848. DLB-119

Châtelet, Gabrielle-Emilie Du
1706-1749 . . . . DLB-313

Chatterton, Thomas 1752-1770. . . . . DLB-109

Essay on Chatterton (1842), by
Robert Browning. DLB-32

Chatto and Windus DLB-106

Chatwin, Bruce 1940-1989. . . . . . . DLB-194, 204

Chaucer, Geoffrey
1340?-1400. . . . . DLB-146; CDBLB-1

New Chaucer Society. Y-00

Chaudhuri, Amit 1962- DLB-267

Chauncy, Charles 1705-1787 . . . . DLB-24

Chauveau, Pierre-Joseph-Olivier
1820-1890 . . . . DLB-99

Chávez, Denise 1948- DLB-122

Chávez, Fray Angélico 1910-1996 . . . . . . DLB-82

Chayefsky, Paddy 1923-1981. . . . .DLB-7, 44; Y-81

Cheesman, Evelyn 1881-1969 . . . . DLB-195

Cheever, Ezekiel 1615-1708 . . . . DLB-24

Cheever, George Barrell 1807-1890 . . . . . DLB-59

Cheever, John 1912-1982
. . . . . . .DLB-2, 102, 227; Y-80, 82; CDALB-1

Cheever, Susan 1943- Y-82

Cheke, Sir John 1514-1557 . . . . DLB-132

Chekhov, Anton Pavlovich 1860-1904. . . .DLB-277

Chelsea House DLB-46

Chênedollé, Charles de 1769-1833 . . . . . . DLB-217

Cheney, Brainard
Tribute to Caroline Gordon Y-81

Cheney, Ednah Dow 1824-1904 . . . . . DLB-1, 223

Cheney, Harriet Vaughan 1796-1889. . . . . DLB-99

Chénier, Marie-Joseph 1764-1811. . . . . . DLB-192

Cherny, Sasha 1880-1932. . . . . DLB-317

Chernyshevsky, Nikolai Gavrilovich
1828-1889 . . . . DLB-238

Cherry, Kelly 1940. . . . . Y-83

Cherryh, C. J. 1942- Y-80

Chesebro', Caroline 1825-1873 . . . . DLB-202

Chesney, Sir George Tomkyns
1830-1895 . . . . DLB-190

Chesnut, Mary Boykin 1823-1886 . . . . . . DLB-239

Chesnutt, Charles Waddell
1858-1932 . . . . .DLB-12, 50, 78

Chesson, Mrs. Nora (see Hopper, Nora)

Chester, Alfred 1928-1971 . . . . DLB-130

Chester, George Randolph 1869-1924 . . . DLB-78

The Chester Plays circa 1505-1532;
revisions until 1575 . . . . DLB-146

Chesterfield, Philip Dormer Stanhope,
Fourth Earl of 1694-1773 . . . . DLB-104

Chesterton, G. K. 1874-1936
. . .DLB-10, 19, 34, 70, 98, 149, 178; CDBLB-6

"The Ethics of Elfland" (1908). DLB-178

Chettle, Henry
circa 1560-circa 1607 . . . . DLB-136

Cheuse, Alan 1940- DLB-244

Chew, Ada Nield 1870-1945. . . . . DLB-135

Cheyney, Edward P. 1861-1947. . . . . DLB-47

Chiang Yee 1903-1977 . . . . DLB-312

Chiara, Piero 1913-1986. . . . . .DLB-177

Chicanos
Chicano History. DLB-82

Chicano Language. DLB-82

Chicano Literature: A Bibliography . . DLB-209

A Contemporary Flourescence of Chicano
Literature. Y-84

Literatura Chicanesca: The View From
Without. DLB-82

Child, Francis James 1825-1896 . . . DLB-1, 64, 235

Child, Lydia Maria 1802-1880 . . . . .DLB-1, 74, 243

Child, Philip 1898-1978 . . . . DLB-68

Childers, Erskine 1870-1922. . . . . DLB-70

Children's Literature
Afterword: Propaganda, Namby-Pamby,
and Some Books of Distinction . . . DLB-52

Children's Book Awards and Prizes. . . DLB-61

Children's Book Illustration in the
Twentieth Century DLB-61

Children's Illustrators, 1800-1880 . . . DLB-163

The Harry Potter Phenomenon. Y-99

Pony Stories, Omnibus
Essay on DLB-160

The Reality of One Woman's Dream:
The de Grummond Children's
Literature Collection Y-99

School Stories, 1914-1960 . . . . DLB-160

The Year in Children's
Books Y-92–96, 98–01

The Year in Children's Literature Y-97

Childress, Alice 1916-1994. . . . . . .DLB-7, 38, 249

Childress, Mark 1957- DLB-292

Childs, George W. 1829-1894 . . . . DLB-23

Chilton Book Company. DLB-46

Chin, Frank 1940- DLB-206, 312

Chin, Justin 1969- DLB-312

Chin, Marilyn 1955- DLB-312

Chinweizu 1943- DLB-157

Chinnov, Igor' 1909-1996 . . . . .DLB-317

Chitham, Edward 1932- DLB-155

Chittenden, Hiram Martin 1858-1917 . . . . DLB-47

Chivers, Thomas Holley 1809-1858 . . DLB-3, 248

Chkhartishvili, Grigorii Shalvovich
(see Akunin, Boris)

Chocano, José Santos 1875-1934 . . . . DLB-290

Cholmondeley, Mary 1859-1925 . . . . . . .DLB-197

Chomsky, Noam 1928- DLB-246

Chopin, Kate 1850-1904. . . DLB-12, 78; CDALB-3

Chopin, René 1885-1953 . . . . DLB-92

Choquette, Adrienne 1915-1973 . . . . DLB-68

Choquette, Robert 1905-1991 . . . . DLB-68

Choyce, Lesley 1951- DLB-251

Chrétien de Troyes
circa 1140-circa 1190 . . . . DLB-208

Christensen, Inger 1935- DLB-214

Christensen, Lars Saabye 1953- DLB-297

The Christian Examiner DLB-1

The Christian Publishing Company. DLB-49

Christie, Agatha
1890-1976. . . . . . .DLB-13, 77, 245; CDBLB-6

Christine de Pizan
circa 1365-circa 1431 . . . . DLB-208

Christopher, John (Sam Youd) 1922- . . DLB-255

Christus und die Samariterin circa 950. . . . . . DLB-148

Christy, Howard Chandler 1873-1952. . . DLB-188

Chu, Louis 1915-1970 . . . . DLB-312

Chukovskaia, Lidiia 1907-1996 . . . . DLB-302

Chulkov, Mikhail Dmitrievich
1743?-1792 . . . . DLB-150

Church, Benjamin 1734-1778 . . . . DLB-31

Church, Francis Pharcellus 1839-1906. . . . DLB-79

Church, Peggy Pond 1903-1986. . . . . . . DLB-212

Church, Richard 1893-1972 . . . . DLB-191

Church, William Conant 1836-1917 . . . . . DLB-79

H

I

K

Cumulative Index

N